JUST ENOUGH LIEBLING

BY A. J. LIEBLING

They All Sang (with Edward B. Marks)

Back Where I Came From

The Telephone Booth Indian

The Road Back to Paris

Republic of Silence

The Wayward Pressman

Mink and Red Herring

The Honest Rainmaker

Normandy Revisited

The Sweet Science

The Earl of Louisiana

The Press

The Most of A. J. Liebling

Between Meals

Mollie & Other War Pieces

Chicago: Second City

A Neutral Corner

Liebling at The New Yorker

A. J. LIEBLING

JUST ENOUGH LIEBLING

Classic Work by the Legendary

New Yorker Writer

INTRODUCTION BY DAVID REMNICK

NORTH POINT PRESS

A division of Farrar, Straus and Giroux

New York

North Point Press
A division of Farrar, Straus and Giroux
19 Union Square West, New York 10003

Compilation copyright © 2004 by the Estate of A. J. Liebling and the Monsell Estate
Introduction copyright © 2004 by David Remnick
All rights reserved
Distributed in Canada by Douglas & McIntyre Ltd.
Printed in the United States of America
Published in 2004 by North Point Press
First paperback edition, 2005

Most essays in this work originally appeared in
The New Yorker in slightly different form.

The Library of Congress has cataloged the hardcover edition as follows:
Liebling, A. J. (Abbott Joseph), 1904–1963.
Just enough Liebling / A. J. Liebling.— 1st ed.
p.   cm.
ISBN-13: 978-0-374-10443-6
ISBN-10: 0-374-10443-3 (hardcover : alk. paper)
I. Title.

PN4874.L44A25 2004
814'.52—dc22

2004050056

Paperback ISBN-13: 978-0-86547-727-8
Paperback ISBN-10: 0-86547-727-2

Designed by Jonathan D. Lippincott

www.fsgbooks.com

1   3   5   7   9   10   8   6   4   2

The publisher thanks James Barbour and Fred Warner,
who offered invaluable insights as the texts were chosen for this volume.

Contents

Introduction by David Remnick • ix

AT TABLE IN PARIS
A Good Appetite • 3
Paris the First • 21
Just Enough Money • 35

THE WAR AND AFTER
Letter from Paris, December 22, 1939 • 55
Letter from Paris, June 1, 1940 • 59
Westbound Tanker • 64
The Foamy Fields • 104
Quest for Mollie • 149
Days with the Daydaybay • 179
The Hounds with Sad Voices • 216

CITY LIFE
The Jollity Building • 231
from The Honest Rainmaker • 267

BOXIANA
Sugar Ray and the Milling Cove • 341
Ahab and Nemesis • 353
The University of Eighth Avenue • 369
Poet and Pedagogue • 398

THE PRESS
The World of Sport • 413
My Name in Big Letters • 423
Obits • 426
The Man Who Changed the Rules • 433
Death on the One Hand • 447
Harold Ross—The Impresario • 460

THE EARL OF LOUISIANA
"Joe Sims, Where the Hell?" • 471
Nothing but a Little Pissant • 493
Blam-Blam-Blam • 511

EPILOGUE
Paysage de Crépuscule • 521

Introduction:
Reporting It All

BY DAVID REMNICK

From the start of the American republic, the most tantalizing means of indulging a youthful desire for escape and recreation has been the sojourn in Paris. It's a long tradition, amply described. The literature begins with the decorous engagements in the letters of Benjamin Franklin and Abigail Adams and leads soon enough to the earthier liaisons in *Gentlemen Prefer Blondes* and *Tropic of Cancer*. Much is promised to the prospective traveler: if not a passage of enlightenment or erotic adventure, then at least a taste for boiled innards and string beans done right. As Mrs. Adams wrote home, pleasure is the "business of life" in Paris—there is another way to live, in other words—and this is the lasting gift, and illusion, that every visiting American brings home in his bags.

To this day, countless children of American privilege arrive in the Latin Quarter, bent double under their backpacks and concealing a money belt holding a Eurail pass and a freshly squeezed *carte orange*. One of the pleasures of such an indolent, never-to-be-repeated existence is the liberty it provides the student on leave from academy-drafted reading lists and deadlines that frog-march undergraduates up and down "The Magic Mountain" in the time it took Hans Castorp to catch cold. In the late seventies, while on a sojourn of my own, I bought or borrowed my books at Shakespeare & Company, the destination for English-speaking waywards on the Rue de la Bûcherie near Notre-Dame. One afternoon, while I was browsing in the "used" section, a friend pulled down a paperback by A. J. Liebling for me. I'd heard of Liebling but never read him. He was a hero to some of the "new journalists" of the sixties and seventies, who put him in a nonfiction lineage that begins with Defoe. But Liebling had died fifteen years earlier, in 1963, and almost all of his books were out of print. Sitting on the floor, I started *The Sweet Science*, with its introductory flourish:

> It is through Jack O'Brien, the *Arbiter Elegantiarum Philadelphiae*, that I trace my rapport with the historic past through the laying-on of hands. He hit me, for pedagogical example, and he had been hit by the great Bob Fitzsimmons, from whom he won the light-heavyweight title in 1906. Jack had a scar to show for it. Fitzsimmons had been hit by Corbett, Corbett by John L. Sullivan, he by Paddy Ryan, with the bare knuckles, and Ryan by Joe Goss, his predecessor, who as a young man had felt the fist of the great Jem Mace. It is a great thrill to feel that all that separates you from the early Victorians is a series of punches on the nose. I wonder if Professor Toynbee is as intimately attuned to his sources. The Sweet Science is joined onto the past like a man's arm to his shoulder.

I read half the book right there and the rest that night. The Rubens canvases at the Louvre were checked off in my guidebook, but for me Liebling was now the Baroque. His descriptions of the postwar boxing scene at Madison Square Garden, Yankee Stadium, the Polo Grounds, the country training camps, and the midtown gyms constitute a self-enclosed comic universe, and, in the construction and the telling, his pieces are superior even to William Hazlitt's famous account of the "Gasman" Hickman–Bill Neat bout in Hungerford, Berkshire, in 1821, and Liebling's own cherished model, *Boxiana*, the multivolume chronicles of the Regency-era fighters, by Pierce Egan. In a style of mock high diction undercut by the homeliness of the subject, of metaphorical flight and eccentric references—a style, in other words, that pays greater homage to the verbal dandyism of Egan (and Mencken and Runyon) than to the hard-boiled approach of the tabloids—Liebling made the art of bruising and its practitioners as vivid as any country fair in Dickens.

In *The Sweet Science*—in all his books—Liebling himself, the voice and the character, is immensely appealing: he is boundlessly curious, a listener, a boulevardier, a man of appetites and sympathy. He is erudite in an unsystematic, wised-up sort of way. His sentences are snaky and digressive, and thrive on the talk of the Times Square gyms and cigar stores. The boxing pieces are populated by the champions of his time—Ray Robinson, Joe Louis, Archie Moore, Rocky Marciano—but equally present are the artisans and satraps of the ring world, the sparring partners, the cut-and-bucket men and the professorial trainers, like Whitey Bimstein, who presided over Stillman's Gym, "the university of Eighth Avenue," as firmly as Robert Maynard Hutchins ran the University of Chicago. Bimstein was a prototypical Liebling cast member, New York to the bone. Asked about his experience outside the city, Bimstein allowed, "I like the country. It's a great spot."

Besotted with *The Sweet Science*, I went back to Shakespeare & Company and took the only other Liebling on the shelf, a copy of *The Road Back to Paris*, his first volume of dispatches from France during the Second World War. Combat journalism is prone to some of the same sins as sportswriting—the self-dramatizing narrative voice, the bogus pronouncements. Only the clichés, and the stakes, are different. Liebling, it was obvious, was incapable of cliché, and, if anything, he protested too adamantly his limitations as an observer of the world beyond home. He claimed innocence of high politics and the scale of evil he was about to engage: "Hitler had seemed to me revolting but unimportant, like old Gómez, the dictator of Venezuela." The only way he was prepared to imagine the German enemy was through homey, ahistorical analogy. "I did not think about Germany," he wrote. "When I was a small child I had had a succession of German governesses all indistinguishably known to me as Fräulein. They had been servile to my parents and domineering to me, stupid, whining, loud, and forever trying to frighten me with stories of children who had been burned to a crisp or eaten by an ogre because they had disobeyed other Fräuleins. . . . Anybody who had had a German governess could understand Poland."

Liebling's subjects in his maturity bloomed from the appetites and interests of his youth. As a reporter, he was both observer and memoirist, seeing and looking within. His love of New York became *Back Where I Came From*; an attention to battle and a passion for France led to *The Road to Paris*, *Mollie and Other War Pieces*, and *Normandy Revisited*; a romance with newspapers led to the criticism of *The Press* and *The Wayward Pressman*; his taste for rogues of all varieties became *The Telephone Booth Indian*, *The Honest Rainmaker*, and *The Earl of Louisiana*. The early passions are always present. His last book, *Between Meals*, is as much about the memory of exultant living as it is about the *gigot d'agneau* on his plate.

Abbott Joseph Liebling was not born to the demimonde. His father was a penniless Jewish immigrant from Austria who had become prosperous as a furrier. His mother was from a well-to-do Jewish family in San Francisco. By the time of Liebling's birth, on the Upper East Side of Manhattan, on October 18, 1904, there was no taste for religion in the house; any trace of the shtetl or the Lower East Side had been fairly expunged. The aspiration was toward comfort and a variety of Americanness. The Lieblings lived first in apartments in Manhattan and then in an oak-shaded house near the beaches of Far Rockaway. They were attended by a string of fräuleins, German maids, cooks, and family attendants, along with a "houseman" named Louis, "a Tyrolese from Meran." There were trips to Europe beginning when our hero was three, and, always, dinners at good restaurants in town.

Liebling, who started out "Abbott" and eventually insisted on "Joe," was the sort of brainy child who did not seem to mind that he was neither handsome nor athletic. He was plump and pigeon-toed, and had tiny, delicate hands, but he also had a certain confidence. (In middle age, he crowned his avoirdupois with thick-lensed, wire-rimmed spectacles and a bowler—gestures of the self-assured.) He did well in school in a happily random sort of way. With equal enthusiasm he memorized the names of Napoleon's marshals, the cast of *The Pickwick Papers*, and the characters in the

Sunday funnies. His guide to the greater world and to his own future was contained in the armload of papers his father brought
home from work every day: "It is impossible for me to estimate
how many of my early impressions of the world, correct and the
opposite, came to me through newspapers. Homicide, adultery,
no-hit pitching, and Balkanism were concepts that, left to my own
devices, I would have encountered much later in life."

Following a semi-successful run at Dartmouth (from which
he was booted for missing chapel once too often), Liebling attended Columbia's journalism school. Indifferent to the curric-
ulum and its modest expectations, he studied French and translated
the erotica of Restif de la Bretonne on the side. Otherwise, he
wrote later in *The Wayward Pressman*, the program had "all the intellectual status of a training school for future employees of the A &
P." Like many novice reporters, he had literary ambitions, which at
first he took to be the province of fiction. Over the years, he began
and abandoned many short stories and longer pieces, including a
novel called *The Girl with the Cauliflower Ear: A Romance*, about
a female boxer named Eula who, after plunging into an aquarium
tank in a moment of suicidal doubt, falls in love with an ichthyolo-
gist.

After finishing at Columbia, Liebling had a brief apprenticeship
on the *Evening World*, which opened up a gaudy landscape of police
shacks, curbside tragedies, and late-night card games. Liebling took
to it. A press pass for a child of the Rockaway bourgeoisie was a
ticket to experience, without experience's costs. "I liked to pound
up tenement stairs and burst in on families disarranged by sudden
misfortune," he wrote about his first assignments as a reporter. "It
gave me a chance to make contact with people I would never otherwise have met, and I learned almost immediately what every reporter knows, that most people are eager to talk about their
troubles and are rather flattered by the arrival of the *World* or the
Journal." He went on to a beginner's job in the *Times* sports department, where he was charged with writing up basketball box scores,
a chore that bored him to such a degree that he occasionally wrote
Ignoto—"Unknown," in Italian—in the space reserved for the name

of the referee. Some nights, according to Liebling, Ignoto officiated games throughout the city. Liebling claimed that when this crime was discovered his boss fired him for being irresponsible. He told the story repeatedly, and with relish, and it may even have been true. What is surely the case, his biographer Raymond Sokolov makes plain, is that Liebling was an indifferent stenographer. He had no future at the *Times*.

In 1926, Liebling's father came to the rescue by asking him if he might like to suspend his career (he was now starting work at the *Journal* in Providence) and take a year to "study" in Paris. Never has a son been in such ready agreement with his protector:

> I sensed my father's generous intention, and, fearing that he might change his mind, I told him that I didn't feel I should go, since I was indeed thinking of getting married. "The girl is ten years older than I am," I said, "and Mother might think she is kind of fast, because she is being kept by a cotton broker from Memphis, Tennessee, who only comes North once in a while. But you are a man of the world, and you understand that a woman can't always help herself. Basically . . ." Within the week, I had a letter of credit on the Irving Trust for two thousand dollars, and a reservation on the old *Caronia* for late in the summer, when the off-season rates would be in effect.

Thus began what surely must be recorded as the most salubrious year abroad since Flaubert left for Egypt. France was, for yet another American, a sentimental education. "I liked the sensation of immersion in a foreign element, as if floating in a summer sea, only my face out of water, and a pleasant buzzing in my ears," Liebling later wrote. "I was often alone, but seldom lonely." His monthly drawing account was sufficient to bankroll the young man's desire to study (lightly) at the Sorbonne and to dine (with relish) at the best of Paris's lower-priced restaurants. Liebling began to eat, and eat, as if his life, and his eventual livelihood, depended on it. It was soon his contention that, just as a fighter must put in his roadwork to extend his stamina for the later rounds, so, too, must a true eater (and fledgling food writer) consume enormously if he is to have a range of dietary experience worth sharing. What would he have to say, after all, on a diet of soda water and scrambled eggs? Proust's madeleine was a mere "tea biscuit" and a barrier to greater literary achievement: "In the light of what Proust wrote with so mild a stimulus, it is the world's loss that he did not have a heartier appetite. On a dozen Gardiners Island oysters, a bowl of clam chowder, a peck of steamers, some bay scallops, three sautéed soft-shelled crabs, a few ears of fresh-picked corn, a thin swordfish steak of generous area, a pair of lobsters, and a Long Island duck, he might have written a masterpiece."

It was under the instruction of Yves Mirande, a Parisian legend of both the stage and the plate, that Liebling learned to eat with ambition. In a typical meal, he followed the order of Darwinian evolution, beginning with the bivalves and halting only at the primates. As he writes in *Between Meals*, Mirande was for him a tutor of the heart and the body:

> In the restaurant on the Rue Saint-Augustin, M. Mirande would dazzle his juniors, French and American, by dispatching a lunch of raw Bayonne ham and fresh figs, a hot sausage in crust, spindles of filleted pike in a rich rose *sauce Nantua*, a leg of lamb larded with anchovies, artichokes on a pedestal of foie gras, and four or five kinds of cheese, with a good bottle of Bordeaux and one of champagne, after which he would call for the Armagnac and remind Madame to have ready for dinner the larks and ortolans she had promised him, with a few langoustes and a turbot—and, of course, a fine civet made from the *marcassin*, or young wild boar, that the lover of the leading lady in his current production had sent up from his estate in the Sologne. "And while I think of it," I once heard him say, "we haven't had any woodcock for days, or truffles baked in the ashes, and the cellar is becoming a disgrace—no more 'thirty-fours and hardly any 'thirty-sevens. Last week, I had to offer my publisher a bottle that was far

too good for him, simply because there was nothing between the insulting and the superlative."

When Liebling came home to New York, he proceeded to campaign for a job on Joseph Pulitzer's *World*, which carried the work of James M. Cain and Walter Lippmann and was known at the time as "the writer's paper." In order to attract the attention of the city editor, James W. Barrett, Liebling hired an out-of-work Norwegian seaman to walk for three days outside the Pulitzer Building, on Park Row, wearing sandwich boards that read, HIRE JOE LIEBLING. Barrett took no notice of the sandwich boards, but another editor hired Liebling as a freelance feature writer after reading one of his pieces. Now Liebling could begin hanging out at the saloons and night clubs, the racetracks and corner stores, where he met the harmless "parliament of monsters" who eventually appeared in *Back Where I Came From* and *The Honest Rainmaker*. The *World* was an all-access ticket for Liebling, then in his late twenties. He felt tickled to call it a job.

"The pattern of a newspaperman's life is like the plot of *Black Beauty*," he wrote. "Sometimes he finds a kind master who gives him a dry stall and an occasional bran mash in the form of a Christmas bonus, sometimes he falls into the hands of a mean owner who drives him in spite of spavins and expects him to live on potato peelings. The Sunday *World* was a dry-stall interlude in my wanderings."

Things turned chilly and damp after 1931, when the perfidious Roy Howard bought the *World* and merged it with his *Evening Telegram* to form the *World-Telegram*; but, in the meantime, Liebling, working alongside his new colleague and friend Joseph Mitchell, was set free to interview the likes of Casey Stengel and Louis-Ferdinand Céline, cover pinochle tournaments, and make heroes of the self-appointed "mayors" of various city neighborhoods. One of the commonplaces of feature writing at the time was a tendency to embroider. That is, there was a lot of making things up or, at the very least, helping things along. What is now a hanging of fense was then a risible misdemeanor. Details were embellished, colors heightened, dialogue faked. Liebling was a superior reporter and writer, but he also availed himself of the era's advantages. At this point, there is no telling precisely what his characters said and what Liebling supplied. Without making excuses for him, one can say that he did seem to make genre distinctions: his work on more serious matters—the war, the press—was factual. The rules have changed radically, and Liebling's gifts and reporting energies were such that he would surely have had little trouble adjusting to them, in a poolroom or on a battlefield.

Liebling joined Harold Ross's *New Yorker* in 1935, when he was thirty. He was informed that five stories were "reserved" for him, including "Africa, Big Game, Hunting In" and "Billiardists, Finger-Technique, Exploits." Nothing much came of that. But, after an awkward year in which he stuck too closely to the conventions of newspaper feature writing, Liebling had his first triumph at the magazine, doing all the reporting for a three-part profile of a preacher and mountebank named Father Divine. The piece, which was written mainly by St. Clair McKelway and was published under the title "Who Is This King of Glory?," helped Liebling get accustomed to the time and the space that no newspaper could afford him. He also perfected a singular interviewing style; according to Brendan Gill, he would "sit facing the person from whom he intended to elicit information; and then sit there and sit there, silently. . . . Liebling's method left the interviewee unnerved and at a loss as to what he was expected to defend himself against; by the time Liebling had put the first question to him, he was ready to babble almost any indiscretion."

Along with Mitchell, who fled the *World-Telegram* and joined the *New Yorker* staff in 1938, Liebling soon transformed the magazine. In voice and carriage, the two men complemented each other. They walked the city together and ate lunch together at the Red Devil and Villa Nova and drank at Bleeck's and Costello's, and, on weekends, they went to the Rockaway beaches together to wade in the ocean and listen to the crowds. Mitchell was a courtly North Carolinian; unlike Liebling, he came at the city from the outside in, though his sympathy for its characters was no less absolute. The temperaments of the two men, especially on the page, diverged. In person, Liebling could be unnervingly quiet, but in print he was an ebullient Falstaff to Mitchell's Feste, the melancholic clown in *Twelfth Night*. Liebling was ribaldly comic, prolific, a writer of big effects, while Mitchell could be as spare in his line as he was in his output. (Mitchell died in 1996, outliving Liebling by thirty-three years, but he stopped publishing after his masterpiece, "Joe Gould's Secret," ran in the magazine, in 1964—just eight months after Liebling's valedictory essay, "Paysage de Crépuscule.")

What Liebling and Mitchell shared most intensely was a love for the city and an unpretentious yet serious interest in the higher reaches of journalism. For his part, Liebling admired, and meant to emulate, the British writers of the eighteenth century who observed every corner of society, the Fancy who ruled things and the Poor who feigned to listen; he favored above all the ones who wrote least stingily both in volume and in metaphorical profusion—Defoe, Egan, and Hazlitt. Liebling also called on influences as varied as George Borrow, the British literary adventurer and Bible salesman, and Ibn Khaldun, the fourteenth-century Tunisian historian, and commonly quoted them for historical authority and ironic flavoring. Liebling's office contained just what his readers might have expected: stacks of newspapers, unfinished manuscripts, a three-volume edition of *Boxiana*, Harold Nicolson's *The Congress of Vienna*, the collected Camus, the latest Annual Report of the New-York Historical Society, Stendhal's *Journal*, and von Bernhardi's *Cavalry in War and Peace*.

Joy, pure and immediate, is a rare literary experience. Liebling provides it. And, from everything we know, joy is what he felt in the creating. No matter what else he may have been facing in his life—misery in marriage, persistent debt, the obesity and sickness that were the price of his appetites—he reveled in his work. Liebling so enjoyed himself at the offices of *The New Yorker*, where he worked for twenty-eight years, that he could be heard humming and snorting with laughter as he pulled the sheets from his type-writer and read them over. He knocked himself out, if he did say so himself. Reticence was not his way. Like Trollope polishing off several thousand words before leaving for his day job as surveyor general of Waltham Cross, Liebling wrote at a blinding rate, publishing hundreds of pieces, of all lengths, colors, and moods. He was occasionally seen in the magazine's bathroom stripped to the waist, washing up after a night's exertion at his Remington.

Despite Liebling's prodigious output at the magazine, and the collection of those pieces into books, he never ceased to see himself as a melancholy "wage slave," forever in debt. His letters, hundreds of them, are filled with the details of his shortfalls, tax problems, and dunning notices. His first wife, Ann McGinn, whom he married in 1934, had grown up in an orphanage and, as it soon became evident, was schizophrenic; she required long and expensive hospital stays. Even after their separation, Liebling continued to pay most of her bills. She suffered from hallucinations and "fugue states"; she would sometimes get up from a restaurant table, walk out the door, and disappear for days. Liebling's second wife, Lucille Spectorsky, was a spendthrift whom one friend, the *New Yorker* editor Gardner Botsford, recalls as "a big blonde from rural Kentucky, amiable if dumb." Liebling's only moments of conjugal peace came with the writer Jean Stafford, who had been married, unhappily, to Robert Lowell. Their union was hardly a picnic on the lawn—there was a great deal of drinking and decline, and Stafford stopped writing—but the four years they spent together were the least miserable either one had known.

And yet, professionally, Liebling was almost never blocked or unlucky. In 1939, when Harold Ross began to prepare for the coming war, he sent Liebling to Paris, a move that seems perfectly right now but occurred mostly because the magazine's correspondent in France, Janet Flanner, had to rush home to her ailing mother, and because, as Liebling recalled, "I had spent several man-hours of barroom time impressing St. Clair McKelway, then managing editor, with my profound knowledge of France." As Liebling readily admitted, he was not exactly Ernie Pyle but, rather, a New York reporter of a particular kind. "There is an old proverb that a girl may sleep with one man without being a trollop, but let a man cover one little war and he is a war correspondent," he wrote in *The Road Back to Paris*. "I belong to the one-war category. I have made no appearances for Mr. Colton Leigh, the lecture agent, either in a gas mask or out of one, and I have no fascinating reminiscences about Addis Ababa or the Cliveden set. Prior to October 1938 my only friends were prize fighters' seconds, Romance philologists, curators of tropical fish, kept women, promoters of spit-and-toilet-paper night clubs, bail bondsmen, press agents for wrestlers, horse clockers, newspaper reporters, and female psychiatrists." Ross was wary of this experience, and his advice to Liebling was "For God's sake keep away from low-life." Liebling was convinced that Ross was trying to "disinfect" the magazine and publish only pieces about "Supreme Court justices and the Persian Room of the Plaza." Nevertheless, he promised to keep his coverage "reasonably clean and high-class" and booked a ticket on a Pan American Clipper to Lisbon.

Reading Liebling's pieces from Paris (and, later, from London and the North African front), you don't get a coherent idea of the course of the war. There is little talk of high politics or the overall battlefield. But such coherence, the editors must have calculated, was the business of the *Times* in the short run and the historians in the long. What Liebling in his frequent dispatches provided was a richly textured sense of the day-to-day reality of occupation, invasion, and battle—a foxhole successor of *Homage to Catalonia*, a forerunner of *Dispatches*. In Paris, Liebling installed himself at the Hotel Louvois, looked up some old friends, and eventually followed the retreat of the government to Tours and then to Bordeaux.

Gardner Botsford, then an officer in the First Infantry Division, met him in Caumont, France, one afternoon. "One's first view of Liebling dressed for combat was a memorable one," Botsford writes in his memoir, *A Life of Privilege, Mostly*. He continues:

The only Army pants big enough to button around the magisterial paunch left him with a vast, drooping seat behind, a flapping void big enough to hold a beach umbrella. The legs of the pants were tucked into knee-high gaiters left over from the Spanish-American War, leading to a pair of thin-soled lounge-lizard civilian shoes. Other correspondents generally tried to look more military and more warlike than any soldier—parachutists' boots, aviators' scarves, tankers' jackets—but Liebling was not one to pretend. He was a correspondent, not a soldier, and he looked it.

As a correspondent, Liebling took history personally. The collapse of France, in June 1940, was a tragedy not only for the French. "France represented for me the historical continuity of intelligence and reasonable living," he wrote. "When this continuity is broken, nothing anywhere can have meaning until it is reestablished. After the Munich settlement I began to be anxious." At war, Liebling no longer employs the high-diction, low-reference voice of his city pieces. Though he was a writer of voluble digression and irony, he also knew something about control and modulation. His sentences are tighter, more direct, less jokey. In "Quest for Mollie," Liebling tells of traveling during one offensive on La Piste Forestière, a dirt road on the northern coast of Tunisia, where Allied forces had fought Italian and German troops, and coming across the refuse of fighting—"bits of the war . . . like beads on a string." He encountered a lone corpse, "a private known as Mollie." A month later, after the Allied victory in North Africa, Liebling heard more about "Mollie," evidently a colorful native of Hell's Kitchen, and so, back in New York, he moves around the city, from bar to union headquarters, reconstructing the often contradictory details of Mollie's life, and giving an ordinary young man a representative immortality. "When I walk through the West Side borderland between Times Square and the slums, where Mollie once lived, I often think of him and his big talk and his golf-suit grin. It cheers me to think there may be more like him all around me—a notion I would have dismissed as sheer romanticism before

World War II. Cynicism is often the shamefaced product of inexperience."

At all times, Liebling is self-mocking, close to the ground, reminding the reader that the correspondent has only a particular view of the war, that the best he can relay is what he actually sees in a given moment: the fear and the boredom and the discomfort. ("If there is any way you can get colder than you do when you sleep in a bedding roll on the ground in a tent in southern Tunisia two hours before dawn, I don't know about it.") Even in Normandy during the D Day invasion, there is no self-admiration or grandeur. His tone is clear and so is his gaze, even when he is swept up by what, for him, was surely the greatest triumph of the war, the liberation of Paris:

> For the first time in my life and probably the last, I have lived for a week in a great city where everybody is happy. Moreover, since this city is Paris, everybody makes this euphoria manifest. To drive along the boulevards in a jeep is like walking into some as yet unmade René Clair film, with hundreds of bicyclists coming toward you in a stream that divides before the jeep just when you feel sure that a collision is imminent. Among the bicyclists there are pretty girls, their hair dressed high on their heads in what seems to be the current mode here. These girls show legs of a length and slimness and firmness and brownness never associated with French womanhood. Food restrictions and the amount of bicycling that is necessary in getting around in a big city without any other means of transportation have endowed these girls with the best figures in the world, which they will doubtless be glad to trade in for three square meals, plentiful supplies of chocolate, and a seat in the family Citroën as soon as the situation becomes more normal. There are handsome young matrons with children mounted behind them on their bikes, and there are husky young workmen, stubby little *employés de bureau* in striped pants, and old professors in wing collars and chin whiskers, all of them smiling and all of them lifting

their right hands from the handlebars as they go past. The most frequently repeated phrase of the week is "*Enfin on respire.*" (At last, one breathes!)

Liebling's sense of civilization was finally righted, and, as ever, he sensed civilization through its pleasures, the anticipation of dessert, the bicyclists speeding through the streets, the careless exposure of a young woman's legs. Paris was free.

By the end of the war, Liebling's stature had begun to match his girth. He was a big voice in New York journalism, something new, and he needed a new subject at *The New Yorker*, beyond the recreations of the sweet science. He found it in the shenanigans and vanities of American newspapers. (Television had not begun in earnest, and radio seemed not to interest him.) Reviving the Wayward Press department, Liebling returned to the comic voice of his New York reporting pieces and retooled it for criticism. His politics leaned left, and he hardly concealed his disdain for most newspaper owners and for the conventions of right-wing journalism. In "Horsefeathers Swathed in Mink," he wrote, "There is no concept more generally cherished by publishers than that of the Undeserving Poor," and eviscerated even the *Times* for taking up the nonexistent case of a woman in a mink coat "with $60,000" in assets who was said to be receiving welfare checks from the city. He bashed the columnist Joseph Alsop, who "orbits the earth like a moon, descending for a day or two now and then to lecture an Arabian King or a Bessarabian prelate on his duties"; he did the same to Colonel Robert R. McCormick, the editor and publisher of the Chicago *Tribune*, who made preposterous around-the-world reporting trips in his private plane, putting Liebling in mind of "Tom Sawyer and his balloon." He was a critic but not a scold. After Stalin died, in March 1953, and the papers issued endless contradictory reports, all with boundless certainty, about the cause of his death, Liebling seemed a man in bliss as he sorted through the clippings spread across his desk. "Inconsiderate to the last, Josef Stalin, a man who never had to meet a deadline, had the bad taste to die in installments," he observed on March 28. In a later column, he wrote:

Within a week after Stalin's announced demise, the American public knew that he had died of natural causes or had been murdered subtly, either on the date named by Pravda or several weeks earlier; that the people of Moscow had demonstrated grief but (a *Journal-American* scoop) the demonstration had been a carefully organized fake; that his death portended either a hardening or a softening of policy toward the West, which, in turn, would lessen or increase the chances of open war; and that his death would either precipitate an immediate struggle for power among the surviving leaders or impel them to stand together until they got things running smoothly. It was freely predicted that in the event there was a struggle Malenkov would destroy his associates or his associates would destroy him. The subject permitted a rare blend of invective and speculation—both Hearst papers, as I recall, ran cartoons of Stalin being rebuffed at the gates of Heaven, where Hearst had no correspondents—and I have seldom enjoyed a week of newspaper reading more.

The names of those who came under Liebling's assault are now mainly forgotten, but their bigotry and jingoism and fakery all have resonant equivalents today. It is usually a tiresome exercise to imagine what some departed luminary would make of present-day follies: "What would Mencken have thought about George W. Bush?," and so on. With Liebling, however, the temptation is hard to resist, given the range and big-heartedness of his disapprovals. We miss the ferocity of his attack. What, indeed, would Liebling have made of Geraldo Rivera at war or Ann Coulter's best-selling charges of treason? What would he have written of the Tyson–Holyfield ear-biting fight or a Times Square in which Colonel Stingo and the porn palaces have been replaced by Madame Tussaud's and Toys R Us? Of the decline of French cooking or the rise of Rupert Murdoch? We imagine him laughing as he yanks a page from his typewriter.

Liebling finished his life and career with two masterpieces, *The Earl of Louisiana*, a book-length profile of Huey Long's half-mad brother Earl, and *Between Meals*, a memoir of Paris and pleasure it-self. At war and at home, Liebling had always feigned a certain in-difference to politics—or, rather, he approached the subject with the derision it usually deserves—and yet in his campaign travels through Louisiana with Earl Long he is hilarious and capable of glossing the racial dynamics and Mediterranean spirit of Louisiana, simply because he is a supreme observer. He writes:

> Uncle Earl wore a jacket, shirt, and tie, a pattern of states-manlike conventionality on a night when everybody off the platform was coatless and tieless. The tie itself was a quiet pattern of inkblots against an olive-and-pearl background, perhaps a souvenir Rorschach test from Galveston. The suit, a black job that dated from the days when he was fat and sassy, hung loosely about him as once it had upon a peg in the supermarket where the Governor liked to buy his clothes.
>
> He left the dude role to Morrison. And, in fact, before the night was over, he said:
>
> "I see Dellasoups has been elected one of the ten best-dressed men in America. He has fifty-dollar neckties and four-hundred-dollar suits. A four-hundred-dollar suit on old Uncle Earl would look like socks on a rooster."

As a voice in print, Liebling was almost invariably buoyant and alive. As a man, he tended toward diffidence, even periods of melancholy. The trait grew more pronounced as he aged. Money problems and health problems were wearing him down. What had been a torrent of words was, by 1963, a trickle. It took him months to work through a short piece on Camus's notebooks. Heart and kidney ailments, along with repeated bouts of the flu and the pain of chronic gout, made writing difficult. Soon he was no longer writing at all. "For the first time in his life, he developed a real block," Jean Stafford told Sokolov. "Depression was new to him." His head filled with Camus, Liebling made a reporting trip to

Algeria, but nothing came of it. He visited Paris and Normandy, knowing that it was likely for the last time. A kind of despair was overtaking him. One afternoon, Liebling and his friend and *New Yorker* colleague Philip Hamburger were returning to the office from lunch. "One of those New York grotesques appeared, half crippled, half spastic," Hamburger said later. "Joe took one look and began to cry. I could see something was wrong. He was on the edge." Liebling died on December 28. He was fifty-nine. His last words were in French.

At Table in Paris

A Good Appetite

The Proust madeleine phenomenon is now as firmly established in folklore as Newton's apple or Watt's steam kettle. The man ate a tea biscuit, the taste evoked memories, he wrote a book. This is capable of expression by the formula TMB, for Taste > Memory > Book. Some time ago, when I began to read a book called *The Food of France*, by Waverley Root, I had an inverse experience: BMT, for Book > Memory > Taste. Happily, the tastes that *The Food of France* re-created for me—small birds, stewed rabbit, stuffed tripe, Côte Rôtie, and Tavel—were more robust than that of the madeleine, which Larousse defines as "a light cake made with sugar, flour, lemon juice, brandy, and eggs." (The quantity of brandy in a madeleine would not furnish a gnat with an alcohol rub.) In the light of what Proust wrote with so mild a stimulus, it is the world's loss that he did not have a heartier appetite. On a dozen Gardiners Island oysters, a bowl of clam chowder, a peck of steamers, some bay scallops, three sautéed soft-shelled crabs, a few ears of fresh-picked corn, a thin swordfish steak of generous area, a pair of lobsters, and a Long Island duck, he might have written a masterpiece.

The primary requisite for writing well about food is a good appetite. Without this, it is impossible to accumulate, within the allotted span, enough experience of eating to have anything worth setting down. Each day brings only two opportunities for field work, and they are not to be wasted minimizing the intake of cholesterol. They are indispensable, like a prizefighter's hours on the road. (I have read that the late French professional gourmand Maurice Curnonsky ate but one meal a day—dinner. But that was late in his life, and I have always suspected his attainments anyway; so many mediocre witticisms are attributed to him that he could not have had much time for eating.) A good appetite gives an eater room to turn around in. For example, a nonprofessional eater I know went to the Restaurant Pierre, in the Place Gaillon, a couple of years ago, his mind set on a sensibly light meal: a dozen, or possibly eighteen, oysters, and a thick chunk of steak topped with beef marrow, which M. Pierre calls a *Délice de la Villette*—the equivalent of a "Stockyards' Delight." But as he arrived, he heard M. Pierre say to his headwaiter, "Here comes Monsieur L. Those two portions of cassoulet that are left—put them aside for him." A cassoulet is a substantial dish, of a complexity precluding its discussion here. (Mr. Root devotes three pages to the great controversy over what it should contain.) M. Pierre is the most amiable of restaurateurs, who prides himself on knowing in advance what his friends will like. A client of limited appetite would be obliged either to forgo his steak or to hurt M. Pierre's feelings. Monsieur L., however, was in no difficulty. He ate the two cassoulets, as was his normal practice; if he had consumed only one, his host would have feared that it wasn't up to standard. He then enjoyed his steak. The oysters offered no problem, since they present no bulk.

In the heroic age before the First World War, there were men and women who ate, in addition to a whacking lunch and a glorious dinner, a voluminous *souper* after the theater or the other amusements of the evening. I have known some of the survivors, octogenarians of unblemished appetite and unfailing good humor—spry, wry, and free of the ulcers that come from worrying about a balanced diet—but they have had no emulators in France since the doctors there discovered the existence of the human liver. From that time on, French life has been built to an increasing extent around that organ, and a niggling caution has replaced the old recklessness; the liver was the seat of the Maginot mentality. One of the last of the great around-the-clock gastronomes of France was

Yves Mirande, a small, merry author of farces and musical-comedy books. In 1955, Mirande celebrated his eightieth birthday with a speech before the curtain of the Théâtre Antoine, in the management of which he was associated with Mme B., a protégée of his, forty years younger than himself. But the theater was only half of his life. In addition, M. Mirande was an unofficial director of a restaurant on the Rue Saint-Augustin, which he had founded for another protégée, also forty years younger than himself; this was Mme G., a Gasconne and a magnificent cook. In the restaurant on the Rue Saint-Augustin, M. Mirande would dazzle his juniors, French and American, by dispatching a lunch of raw Bayonne ham and fresh figs, a hot sausage in crust, spindles of filleted pike in a rich rose *sauce Nantua*, a leg of lamb larded with anchovies, artichokes on a pedestal of foie gras, and four or five kinds of cheese, with a good bottle of Bordeaux and one of champagne, after which he would call for the Armagnac and remind Madame to have ready for dinner the larks and ortolans she had promised him, with a few langoustes and a turbot—and, of course, a fine civet made from the *marcassin*, or young wild boar, that the lover of the leading lady in his current production had sent up from his estate in the Sologne. "And while I think of it," I once heard him say, "we haven't had any woodcock for days, or truffles baked in the ashes, and the cellar is becoming a disgrace—no more 'thirty-fours and hardly any 'thirty-sevens. Last week, I had to offer my publisher a bottle that was far too good for him, simply because there was nothing between the insulting and the superlative."

M. Mirande had to his credit a hundred produced plays, including a number of great Paris hits, but he had just written his first book for print, so he said "my publisher" in a special mock-impressive tone. "An informal sketch for my definitive autobiography," he would say of this production. The informal sketch, which I cherish, begins with the most important decision in Mirande's life. He was almost seventeen and living in the small Breton port of Lannion—his offstage family name was Le Querrec—when his father, a retired naval officer, said to him, "It is time to decide your future career. Which will it be, the Navy or the Church?" No other choice was conceivable in Lannion. At dawn, Yves ran away to Paris.

There, he had read a thousand times, all the famous wits and co-cottes frequented the tables in front of the Café Napolitain, on the Boulevard des Capucines. He presented himself at the café at nine the next morning—late in the day for Lannion—and found that the place had not yet opened. Soon he became a newspaperman. It was a newspaper era as cynically animated as the corresponding period of the Bennett-Pulitzer-Hearst competition in New York, and in his second or third job he worked for a press lord who was as notional and niggardly as most press lords are; the publisher insisted that his reporters be well turned out, but did not pay them salaries that permitted cab fares when it rained. Mirande lived near the fashionable Montmartre cemetery and solved his rainy-day pants-crease problem by crashing funeral parties as they broke up and riding, gratis, in the carriages returning to the center of town. Early in his career, he became personal secretary to Clemenceau and then to Briand, but the gay theater attracted him more than politics, and he made the second great decision of his life after one of his political patrons had caused him to be appointed *sous-préfet* in a provincial city. A *sous-préfet* is the administrator of one of the districts into which each of the ninety *départements* of France is divided, and a young *sous-préfet* is often headed for a precocious rise to high positions of state. Mirande, attired in the magnificent uniform that was then de rigueur, went to his "capital," spent one night there, and then ran off to Paris again to direct a one-act farce. Nevertheless, his connections with the serious world remained cordial. In the restaurant on the Rue Saint-Augustin, he introduced me to Colette, by that time a national glory of letters.

The regimen fabricated by Mirande's culinary protégée, Mme. G., maintained him *en pleine forme*. When I first met him, in the restaurant, during the summer of the Liberation, he was a sprightly sixty-nine. In the spring of 1955, when we renewed a friendship that had begun in admiration of each other's appetite, he was as good as ever. On the occasion of our reunion, we began with a *truite au bleu*—a live trout simply done to death in hot water, like a Roman emperor in his bath. It was served up doused with enough melted butter to thrombose a regiment of Paul Dudley Whites, and accompanied, as was right, by an Alsatian wine—a Lacrimae Sanctae Odiliae, which once contributed slightly to my education. Long ago, when I was very young, I took out a woman in Strasbourg and, wishing to impress her with my knowledge of local customs, ordered a bottle of Ste. Odile. I was making the same mistake as if I had taken out a girl in Boston and offered her baked beans. "How quaint!" the woman in Strasbourg said. "I haven't drunk that for years." She excused herself to go to the telephone, and never came back.

After the trout, Mirande and I had two meat courses, since we could not decide in advance which we preferred. We had a magnificent *daube provençale*, because we were faithful to *la cuisine bourgeoise*, and then *pintadous*—young guinea hens, simply and tenderly roasted—with the first asparagus of the year, to show our fidelity to *la cuisine classique*. We had clarets with both courses—a Pétrus with the *daube*, a Cheval Blanc with the guineas. Mirande said that his doctor had discounseled Burgundies. It was the first time in our acquaintance that I had heard him admit he had a doctor, but I was reassured when he drank a bottle and a half of Krug after luncheon. We had three bottles between us—one to our loves, one to our countries, and one for symmetry, the last being on the house.

Mirande was a small, alert man with the face of a Celtic terrier—salient eyebrows and an upturned nose. He looked like an intelligent Lloyd George. That summer, in association with Mme B., his theatrical protégée, he planned to produce a new play of Sartre's. His mind kept young by the theater of Mme B., his metabolism protected by the restaurant of Mme G., Mirande seemed fortified against all eventualities for at least another twenty years. Then, perhaps, he would have to recruit new protégées. The Sunday following our reunion, I encountered him at Longchamp, a racecourse where the restaurant does not face the horses, and diners can keep first things first. There he sat, radiant, surrounded by celebrities and champagne buckets, sending out a relay team of commissionaires to bet for him on the successive tips that the proprietors of stables were ravished to furnish him between races. He was the embodiment of a happy man. (I myself had a nice thing at 27–1.)

The first alteration in Mirande's fortunes affected me so directly that I did not at once sense its gravity for him. Six weeks later, I was again in Paris. (That year, I was shuttling frequently between there and London.) I was alone on the evening I arrived, and looked forward to a pleasant dinner at Mme G.'s, which was within two hundred meters of the hotel, in the Square Louvois, where I always stop. Madame's was more than a place to eat, although one ate superbly there. Arriving, I would have a bit of talk with the proprietress, then with the waitresses—Germaine and Lucienne—who had composed the original staff. Waiters had been added as the house prospered, but they were of less marked personality. Madame was a bosomy woman—voluble, tawny, with a big nose and lank black hair—who made one think of a Saracen. (The Saracens reached Gascony in the eighth century.) Her conversation was a chronicle of letters and the theater—as good as a subscription to *Figaro Littéraire*, but more advanced. It was somewhere between the avant-garde and the main body, but within hailing distance of both and enriched with the names of the great people who had been in recently—M. Cocteau, Gene Kelly, la Comtesse de Vogüé. It was always well to give an appearance of listening, lest she someday fail to save for you the last order of larks *en brochette* and bestow them on a more attentive customer. With Germaine and Lucienne, whom I had known when we were all younger, in 1939, the year of the *drôle de guerre*, flirtation was now perfunctory, but the carte du jour was still the serious topic—for example, how the fat Belgian industrialist from Tournai had reacted to the *caille vendangeuse*, or quail potted with fresh grapes. "You know the man," Germaine would say. "If it isn't dazzling, he takes only two portions. But when he has three, then you can say to yourself . . ." She and Lucienne looked alike—compact little women, with high foreheads and cheekbones and solid, muscular legs, who walked like *chasseurs à pied*, 130 steps to the minute. In 1939, and again in 1944, Germaine had been a brunette and Lucienne a blonde, but in 1955 Germaine had become a blonde, too, and I found it hard to tell them apart.

Among my fellow customers at Mme G.'s I was always likely to see some friend out of the past. It is a risk to make an engagement for an entire evening with somebody you haven't seen for years. This is particularly true in France now. The almost embarrassingly pro-American acquaintance of the Liberation may be by now a Communist Party-line hack; the idealistic young Resistance journalist may have become an editorial writer for the reactionary newspaper of a textile magnate. The Vichy apologist you met in Washington in 1941, who called de Gaulle a traitor and the creation of the British Intelligence Service, may now tell you that the General is the best thing ever, while the fellow you knew as a de Gaulle aide in London may now compare him to Sulla destroying the Roman Republic. As for the women, who is to say which of them has resisted the years? But in a good restaurant that all have frequented, you are likely to meet any of them again, for good restaurants are not so many nowadays that a Frenchman will permanently desert one—unless, of course, he is broke, and in that case it would depress you to learn of his misfortunes. If you happen to encounter your old friends when they are already established at their tables, you have the opportunity to greet them cordially and to size them up. If you still like them, you can make a further engagement.

On the ghastly evening I speak of—a beautiful one in June—I perceived no change in the undistinguished exterior of Mme G.'s restaurant. The name—something like Prospéria—was the same, and since the plate-glass windows were backed with scrim, it was impossible to see inside. Nor, indeed, did I notice any difference when I first entered. The bar, the tables, the banquettes covered with leatherette, the simple décor of mirrors and pink marble slabs were the same. The premises had been a business employees' bar-and-café before Mme G., succeeding a long string of obscure proprietors, made it illustrious. She had changed the fare and the clientele but not the cadre. There are hundreds of identical fronts and interiors in Paris, turned out by some mass producer in the late twenties. I might have been warned by the fact that the room was empty, but it was only eight o'clock and still light outdoors. I had come unusually early because I was so hungry. A man whom I did not recognize came to meet me, rubbing his hands and hailing me as an old acquaintance. I thought he might be a waiter who had served me. (The waiters, as I have said, were not the marked personalities of the place.) He had me at a table before I sensed the trap.

"Madame goes well?" I asked politely.

"No, Madame is lightly ill," he said, with what I now realize was a guilty air.

He presented me with a carte du jour written in the familiar purple ink on the familiar wide sheet of paper with the name and telephone number of the restaurant at the top. The content of the menu, however, had become Italianized, the spelling had deteriorated, and the prices had diminished to a point where it would be a miracle if the food continued distinguished.

"Madame still conducts the restaurant?" I asked sharply.

I could now see that he was a Piedmontese of the most evasive description. From rubbing his hands he had switched to twisting them.

"Not exactly," he said, "but we make the same cuisine."

I could not descry anything in the smudged ink but misspelled noodles and unorthographical *"escaloppinis"*; Italians writing French by ear produce a regression to an unknown ancestor of both languages.

"Try us," my man pleaded, and, like a fool, I did. I was hungry. Forty minutes later, I stamped out into the street as purple as an aubergine with rage. The minestrone had been cabbage scraps in greasy water. I had chosen *côtes d'agneau* as the safest item in the mediocre catalog that the Prospéria's prospectus of bliss had turned into overnight. They had been cut from a tired Alpine billy goat and seared in machine oil, and the haricots verts with which they were served resembled decomposed whiskers from a theatrical-costume beard.

"The same cuisine?" I thundered as I flung my money on the falsified *addition* that I was too angry to verify. "You take me for a jackass!"

I am sure that as soon as I turned my back the scoundrel nodded. The restaurant has changed hands at least once since then.

In the morning, I telephoned Mirande. He confirmed the disaster. Mme G., ill, had closed the restaurant. Worse, she had sold the lease and the good will, and had definitely retired.

"What is the matter with her?" I asked in a tone appropriate to fatal disease.

"I think it was trying to read Simone de Beauvoir," he said. "A syncope."

Mme G. still lives, but Mirande is dead. When I met him in Paris the following November, his appearance gave no hint of decline. It was the season for his sable-lined overcoat *à l'impresario*, and a hat that was a furry cross between a porkpie and a homburg. Since the restaurant on the Rue Saint-Augustin no longer existed, I had invited him to lunch with me at a very small place called the Gratin Dauphinois, on the Rue Chabanais, directly across from the building that once housed the most celebrated sporting house in Paris. The Rue Chabanais is a short street that runs from the Square Louvois to the Rue des Petits Champs—perhaps a hundred yards—but before the reform wave stimulated by a Municipal Councilor named Marthe Richard at the end of the Second World War, the name Chabanais had a cachet all its own. Mme Richard will go down in history as the Carry Nation of sex. Now the house is closed, and the premises are devoted to some low commercial purpose. The walls of the midget Gratin Dauphinois are hung with cartoons that have a nostalgic reference to the past glories of the street.

Mirande, when he arrived, crackled with jokes about the locale. He taunted me with being a criminal who haunts the scene of his misdeeds. The fare at the Gratin is robust, as it is in Dauphiné, but it did not daunt Mirande. The wine card, similarly, is limited to the strong, rough wines of Arbois and the like, with a couple of Burgundies for clients who want to show off. There are no clarets; the proprietor hasn't heard of them. There are, of course, a few champagnes, for wedding parties or anniversaries, so Mirande, with Burgundies discounseled by his doctor, decided on champagne throughout the meal. This was a *drôle* combination with the mountain food, but I had forgotten about the lack of claret when I invited him.

We ordered a couple of dozen *escargots en pots de chambre* to begin with. These are snails baked and served, for the client's convenience, in individual earthenware crocks, instead of being forced back into shells. The snail, of course, has to be taken out of his shell to be prepared for cooking. The shell he is forced back into may not be his own. There is thus not even a sentimental justification for his reincarceration. The frankness of the service *en pot* does not improve the preparation of the snail, nor does it detract from it, but it does facilitate and accelerate his consumption. (The notion that the shell proves the snail's authenticity, like the head left on a woodcock, is invalid, as even a suburban housewife knows nowadays; you can buy a tin of snail shells in a supermarket and fill them with a mixture of nutted cream cheese and chopped olives.)

Mirande finished his dozen first, meticulously swabbing out the garlicky butter in each *pot* with a bit of bread that was fitted to the bore of the crock as precisely as a bullet to a rifle barrel. Tearing bread like that takes practice. We had emptied the first bottle of champagne when he placed his right hand delicately on the point of his waistcoat farthest removed from his spinal column.

"Liebling," he said, "I am not well."

It was like the moment when I first saw Joe Louis draped on the ropes. A great pity filled my heart. "*Maître*," I said, "I will take you home."

The dismayed *patronne* waved to her husband in the kitchen (he could see her through the opening he pushed the dishes through) to suspend the preparation of the *gendarme de Morteau*—the great smoked sausage in its tough skin—that we had proposed to follow the snails with. ("Short and broad in shape, it is made of pure pork and . . . is likely to be accompanied . . . by hot potato salad."—Root, page 217.) We had decided to substitute for the *pommes à l'huile* the *gratin dauphinois* itself. ("Thinly sliced potatoes are moistened with boiled milk and beaten egg, seasoned with salt, pepper, and nutmeg, and mixed with grated cheese, of the Gruyère type. The potatoes are then put into an earthenware dish which has been rubbed with garlic and then buttered, spotted with little dabs of butter, and sprinkled with more grated cheese. It is then cooked slowly in not too hot an oven."—Root, page 228.) After that, we were going to have a fowl in cream with *morilles*—wild black mushrooms of the mountains. We abandoned all.

I led Mirande into the street and hailed a taxi.

"I am not well, Liebling," he said. "I grow old."

He lived far from the restaurant, beyond the Place de l'Etoile, in the Paris of the successful. From time to time on our way, he would say, "It is nothing. You must excuse me. I am not well."

The apartment house in which he and Mme B. lived resembled one of the chic modern museums of the quarter, with entrance gained through a maze of garden patches sheathed in glass. Successive metal grilles swung open before us as I pushed buttons that Mirande indicated—in these modern palaces there are no visible flunkies—until we reached an elevator that smoothly shot us upward to his apartment, which was rather larger in area than the Square Louvois. The décor, with basalt columns and floors covered with the skin of jumbo Siberian tigers—a special strain force-fed to supply old-style movie stars—reminded me of the sets for *Belphégor*, a French serial of silent days that I enjoyed when I was a student at the Sorbonne in 1926. (It was, I think, about an ancient Egyptian high priest who came to life and set up bachelor quarters in Paris in the style of the Temple of Karnak.) Three or four maids rushed to relieve Mirande of his sable-lined coat, his hat, and his cane topped with the horn of an albino chamois. I helped him to a divan on which two Theda Baras could have defended their honor simultaneously against two villains of the silents without either couple's getting in the other's way. Most of the horizontal surfaces in the room were covered with sculpture and most of the vertical ones with large paintings. In pain though he was, Mirande called my attention to these works of art.

"All the sculptures are by Renoir," he said. "It was his hobby. And all the paintings are by Maillol. It was *his* hobby. If it were the other way around, I would be one of the richest chaps in France. Both men were my friends. But then, one doesn't give one's friends one's bread and butter. And, after all, it's less banal as it is."

After a minute, he asked me to help him to his bedroom, which was in a wing of the apartment all his own. When we got there, one of the maids came in and took his shoes off.

"I am in good hands now, Liebling," he said. "Farewell until next time. It is nothing."

I telephoned the next noon, and he said that his doctor, who was a fool, insisted that he was ill.

Again I left Paris, and when I returned, late the following January, I neglected Mirande. A Father William is a comforting companion for the middle-aged—he reminds you that the best is yet to be and that there's a dance in the old dame yet—but a sick old man is discouraging. My conscience stirred when I read in a gossip column in *France-Dimanche* that Toto Mirande was convalescing nicely and was devouring caviar at a great rate—with champagne, of course. (I had never thought of Mirande as Toto, which is baby slang for "little kid," but from then on I never referred to him in any other way; I didn't want anybody to think I wasn't in the know.) So the next day I sent him a pound of fresh caviar from Kaspia, in the Place de la Madeleine. It was the kind of medication I approved of.

I received a note from Mirande by tube next morning, reproaching me for spoiling him. He was going better, he wrote, and would telephone in a day or two to make an appointment for a return bout. When he called, he said that the idiotic doctor would not yet permit him to go out to a restaurant, and he invited me, instead, to a family dinner at Mme B.'s. "Only a few old friends, and not the cuisine I hope to give you at Maxim's next time," he said. "But one makes out."

On the appointed evening, I arrived early—or on time, which amounts to the same thing—chez Mme B.; you take taxis when you can get them in Paris at the rush hours. The handsome quarter overlooking the Seine above the Trocadéro is so dull that when my taxi deposited me before my host's door, I had no inclination to stroll to kill time. It is like Park Avenue or the near North Side of Chicago. So I was the first or second guest to arrive, and Mme B.'s fourteen-year-old daughter, by a past marriage, received me in the Belphégor room, apologizing because her mother was still with

Toto—she called him that. She need not have told me, for at that
moment I heard Madame, who is famous for her determined voice,
storming at an unmistakable someone: "You go too far, Toto. It's
disgusting. People all over Paris are kind enough to send you caviar,
and because you call it monotonous, you throw it at the maid! If
you think servants are easy to come by . . ."

When they entered the room a few minutes later, my old friend
was all smiles. "How did you know I adore caviar to such a point?"
he asked me. But I was worried because of what I had heard; the
Mirande I remembered would never have been irritated by the ob-
ligation to eat a few extra kilos of fresh caviar. The little girl, who
hoped I had not heard, embraced Toto. "Don't be angry with *Ma-
man*!" she implored him.

My fellow guests included the youngish new wife of an old former Premier, who was unavoidably detained in Lille at a congress
of the party he now headed; it mustered four deputies, of whom
two formed a Left Wing and two a Right Wing. ("If they had
elected a fifth at the last election, or if, by good luck, one had been
defeated, they could afford the luxury of a Center," Mirande told
me in identifying the lady. "*C'est malheureux*, a party without a Center. It limits the possibilities of maneuver.") There was also an
amiable couple in their advanced sixties or beginning seventies,
of whom the husband was the grand manitou of Veuve Clicquot
champagne. Mirande introduced them by their right name, which I
forget, and during the rest of the evening addressed them as M.
and Mme Clicquot. There was a forceful, black-haired man from
the Midi, in the youth of middle age—square-shouldered, stocky,
decisive, blatantly virile—who, I was told, managed Mme B.'s
vinicultural enterprises in Provence. There were two guests of less
decided individuality, whom I barely remember, and filling out
the party were the young girl—shy, carefully unsophisticated and
unadorned—Mme B., Mirande, and me. Mme B. had a strong triangular face on a strong triangular base—a strong chin, high
cheekbones, and a wide, strong jaw, but full of stormy good nature.
She was a woman who, if she had been a man, would have wanted
to be called Honest John. She had a high color and an iron hand-

grip, and repeatedly affirmed that there was no affectation about her, that she was *sans façon*, that she called her shots as she saw them. "I won't apologize," she said to me. "I know you're a great feeder, like Toto here, but I won't offer you the sort of menu he used to get in that restaurant you know of, where he ruined his plumbing. Oh, that woman! I used to be so jealous. I can offer only a simple home dinner." And she waved us toward a marble table about twenty-two feet long. Unfortunately for me, she meant it. The dinner began with a kidney-and-mushroom mince served in a giant popover—the kind of thing you might get at a literary hotel in New York. The inner side of the pastry had the feeling of a baby's palm, in the true tearoom tradition.

"It is savory but healthy," Madame said firmly, setting an example by taking a large second helping before starting the dish on its second round. Mirande regarded the untouched doughy fabric on his plate with diaphanously veiled horror, but he had an excuse in the state of his health. "It's still a little rich for me, darling," he murmured. The others, including me, delivered salvos of compliments. I do not squander my moral courage on minor crises. M. Clicquot said, "Impossible to obtain anything like this chez Lapérouse!" Mme Clicquot said, "Not even at the Tour d'Argent!"

"And what do you think of my little wine?" Mme B. asked M. Clicquot. "I'm so anxious for your professional opinion—as a rival producer, you know."

The wine was a thin *rosé* in an Art Nouveau bottle with a label that was a triumph of lithography; it had spires and monks and troubadours and blondes in wimples on it, and the name of the *cru* was spelled out in letters with Gothic curlicues and pennons. The name was something like Château Guillaume d'Aquitaine, *grand vin*.

"What a madly gay little wine, my dear!" M. Clicquot said, repressing, but not soon enough, a grimace of pain.

"One would say a Tavel of a good year," I cried, "if one were a complete bloody fool." I did not say the second clause aloud.

My old friend looked at me with new respect. He was discovering in me a capacity for hypocrisy that he had never credited me with before.

The main course was a shoulder of mutton with white beans—the poor relation of a gigot, and an excellent dish in its way, when not too dry. This was.

For the second wine, the man from the Midi proudly produced a red, in a bottle without a label, which he offered to M. Clicquot with the air of a tomcat bringing a field mouse to its master's feet. "Tell me what you think of this," he said as he filled the champagne man's glass.

M. Clicquot—a veteran of such challenges, I could well imagine—held the glass against the light, dramatically inhaled the bouquet, and then drank, after a slight stiffening of the features that indicated to me that he knew what he was in for. Having emptied half the glass, he deliberated.

"It has a lovely color," he said.

"But what is it? What is it?" the man from the Midi insisted.

"There are things about it that remind me of a Beaujolais," M. Clicquot said (he must have meant that it was wet), "but on the whole I should compare it to a Bordeaux" (without doubt unfavorably).

Mme B.'s agent was beside himself with triumph. "Not one or the other!" he crowed. "It's from the domaine—the Château Guillaume d'Aquitaine!"

The admirable M. Clicquot professed astonishment, and I, when I had emptied a glass, said that there would be a vast market for the wine in America if it could be properly presented. "Unfortunately," I said, "the cost of advertising . . ." and I rolled my eyes skyward.

"Ah, yes," Mme B. cried sadly. "The cost of advertising!"

I caught Mirande looking at me again, and thought of the Pétrus and the Cheval Blanc of our last meal together chez Mme G. He drank a glass of the red. After all, he wasn't going to die of thirst.

For dessert, we had a simple fruit tart with milk—just the thing for an invalid's stomach, although Mirande didn't eat it.

M. Clicquot retrieved the evening, oenologically, by producing two bottles of a wine "impossible to find in the cellars of any restaurant in France"—Veuve Clicquot '19. There is at present a great to-do among wine merchants in France and the United States about young wines, and an accompanying tendency to cry down the "legend" of the old. For that matter, hardware clerks, when you ask for a can opener with a wooden handle that is thick enough to give a grip and long enough for leverage, try to sell you complicated mechanical folderols. The motivation in both cases is the same—simple greed. To deal in wines of varied ages requires judgment, the sum of experience and flair. It involves the risk of money, because every lot of wine, like every human being, has a life span, and it is this that the good vintner must estimate. His object should be to sell his wine at its moment of maximum value—to the drinker as well as the merchant. The vintner who handles only young wines is like an insurance company that will write policies only on children; the unqualified dealer wants to risk nothing and at the same time to avoid tying up his money. The client misled by brochures warning him off clarets and champagnes that are over ten years old and assuring him that Beaujolais should be drunk green will miss the major pleasures of wine drinking. To deal wisely in wines and merely to sell them are things as different as being an expert in ancient coins and selling Indian-head pennies over a souvenir counter.

Despite these convictions of mine about wine, I should never have tried a thirty-seven-year-old champagne on the recommendation of a lesser authority than the blessed M. Clicquot. It is the oldest by far that I have ever drunk. (H. Warner Allen, in *The Wines of France*, published circa 1924, which is my personal wine bible, says, "In the matter of age, champagne is a capricious wine. As a general rule, it has passed its best between fifteen and twenty, yet a bottle thirty years old may prove excellent, though all its fellows may be quite undrinkable." He cites Saintsbury's note that "a Perrier Jouet of 1857 was still majestical in 1884," adding, "And all wine-drinkers know of such amazing discoveries." Mr. Root, whose book is not a foolish panegyric of everything French, is hard on champagne, in my opinion. He falls into a critical error more common among writers less intelligent: he attacks it for not being something else. Because its excellences are not those of Burgundy or Bordeaux, he underrates the peculiar qualities it does not share with them, as one who would chide Dickens for not being Stendhal, or Marciano for not being Benny Leonard.)

The Veuve Clicquot '19 was tart without brashness—a refined but effective understatement of younger champagnes, which run too much to rhetoric, at best. Even so, the force was all there, to judge from the two glasses that were a shade more than my share. The wine still had a discreet *cordon*—the ring of bubbles that forms inside the glass—and it had developed the color known as "partridge eye." I have never seen a partridge's eye, because the bird, unlike woodcock, is served without the head, but the color the term indicates is that of serous blood or a maple leaf on the turn.

"How nice it was, life in 1919, eh, M. Clicquot?" Mirande said as he sipped his second glass.

After we had finished M. Clicquot's offering, we played a game called lying poker for table stakes, each player being allowed a capital of five hundred francs, not to be replenished under any circumstances. When Mme B. had won everybody's five hundred francs, the party broke up. Mirande promised me that he would be up and about soon, and would show me how men reveled in the heroic days of *la belle époque*, but I had a feeling that the bell was cracked.

I left Paris and came back to it seven times during the next year, but never saw him. Once, being in his quarter in the company of a remarkably pretty woman, I called him up, simply because I knew he would like to look at her, but he was too tired. I forget when I last talked to him on the telephone. During the next winter, while I was away in Egypt or Jordan or someplace where French papers don't circulate, he died, and I did not learn of it until I returned to Europe.

When Mirande first faltered, in the Rue Chabanais, I had failed to correlate cause and effect. I had even felt a certain selfish alarm. If eating well was beginning to affect Mirande at eighty, I thought, I had better begin taking in sail. After all, I was only thirty years his junior. But after the dinner at Mme B.'s, and in the light of subsequent reflection, I saw that what had undermined his constitution was Mme G.'s defection from the restaurant business. For years, he

had been able to escape Mme B.'s solicitude for his health by lunch-
ing and dining in the restaurant of Mme G., the sight of whom
Mme B. could not support. Entranced by Mme G.'s magnificent
food, he had continued to live "like a cock in a pie"—eating as well,
and very nearly as much, as when he was thirty. The organs of the
interior—never very intelligent, in spite of what the psychosomatic
quacks say—received each day the amount of pleasure to which
they were accustomed, and never marked the passage of time; it
was the indispensable roadwork of the prizefighter. When Mme G.,
good soul, retired, moderation began its fatal inroads on his resistance. My old friend's appetite, insufficiently stimulated, started to
loaf—the insidious result, no doubt, of the advice of the doctor
whose existence he had revealed to me by that slip of the tongue
about why he no longer drank Burgundy. Mirande commenced,
perhaps, by omitting the fish course after the oysters, or the oysters
before the fish, then began neglecting his cheeses and skipping the
second bottle of wine on odd Wednesdays. What he called his pipes
(*"ma tuyauterie"*), being insufficiently exercised, lost their tone, like
the leg muscles of a retired champion. When, in his kindly effort to
please me, he challenged the *escargots en pots de chambre*, he was like
an old fighter who tries a comeback without training for it. That,
however, was only the revelation of the rot that had already taken
place. What always happens happened. The damage was done, but
it could so easily have been averted had he been warned against the
fatal trap of abstinence.

(1959)

Paris the First

My personal Paris is like Byblos in Lebanon, a pile of cities stacked in order of seniority, the oldest at the bottom. Byblos has its culinary associations, too, because the low strata are peppered with large casseroles containing skeletons of a people who boiled their dead and folded them. I know, because I have been told, that I was in Paris in 1907, when I was three, at a hotel on Cours-la-Reine, but I remember nothing about that earliest visit. The first Paris I remember was a colonnaded city, like a stage set of a street with one side perpetually cool shade and the other bright, hot sun. In the middle of the street there was a cuirassier, the nearest thing to a knight in armor I had seen outside a picture book, immense in his plastron and boots. He sat a horse with two tails, one in the usual place and one hanging from the back of the man's helmet. This was the Rue de Rivoli in the dog days of 1911, when my family paused there on the way home to New York from a holiday in Europe proper, or *odiosa*, a place where the inhabitants spoke German, as did my oppressors, the Frauleins. Fraulein, to me, had the strong specific meaning of nursegirl. It was to be years before I realized that it could be applied to an unmarried woman not in service. Many Frauleins *in* service must have been married, but I never thought of one as *Frau*. Frauleins were my immemorial enemies, interposed between my parents and me, like wicked bailiffs between kind barons and their serfs. They were the bad doorkeepers of a benign sultan. Without their officious intervention, I was sure, I could have been with my parents twenty-four hours a day, and they would have been charmed to have me. There were two incidents of the 1907 trip that I did remember in 1911, and remember still, but they happened in Germany.

In Wiesbaden in 1907 a Fraulein named Martha had dragged me at unforgettable speed, my feet touching the ground only occasionally, through what I remembered as a mile of streets, to see a tall man in a white uniform with a cape, sitting in a white automobile on some hideous *Platz*, surrounded by a cheering crowd. He was, she told me in hysteric shrieks, the Kaiser. Her tone would have been appropriate to announce the Second Coming. Martha ranked in the Frauleinian dynasty like Caligula among Roman emperors. She was one of the worst. In Nuremberg that same summer she had packed me off to the torture tower in the old keep to see the Iron Maiden, a hinged hollow figure lined with spikes. The guide-lecturer said that prisoners were put inside and then squashed and blinded simultaneously. I understand now that the Maiden was a fake, but it was a *German* fake. Then they showed me the mouth of the well down which the torturers used to drop the broken bodies. The guide held a lighted candle and Martha held me in her arms and let me look down. Then he chucked a stone in and we waited an impressively long time before we heard it hit the water.

"It happens to naughty children, too," Martha said.

She bought me a miniature Iron Maiden as a souvenir.

My wars against the Frauleins left me with a blurred recollection of injustice and struggle, like the collective memory of the Irish, for whom I have an anomalous sympathy at their most difficult. We are like the children of long, hard deliveries, incredulous of our freedom even when we reach the clear. The Fraulein, I have thought often since, was a remarkably effective device for siphoning off from the parents the hostility that analysts assure us is the parents' due. Careful bootleggers in Harlem during Prohibition used to pass suspect alcohol through an old felt hat, on the theory that the poison would remain there. The Fraulein had the function of the felt hat. As full of the discharged hostility as the hat was of fusel oil, she shifted to another job when the child outgrew her. She left it as harmless to its parents as a baby rattlesnake milked of venom. To the child who began conscious life under the rule of a Fraulein, even the least bearable mother appeared an angel.

The device seems to me, looking back, more sensible than that of the kind nanny described in English novels. The nannies siphon off not the hostility, but the affection, leaving the protagonists incapable of liking anybody else for the rest of their lives. (Anticipating that these notes will be utilized at some future date by biographers, some analytically oriented, I shall make their path clearer by expositions like the above from time to time.)

It never occurred to me to wonder why my parents paid the Frauleins who deprived them of the pleasure of my constant company. I was sure the witches, like those in the fairy tales with which they tried to terrify me, had imposed themselves on the kind king and queen by some cunning swindle. We had a Fraulein with us even in Paris, although, to defend my pride, I insisted she was there only to take care of my sister, who was two and change. I was nearly seven. In fact, though, Fraulein had authority over me, too, especially in my parents' absences. I was only fourth in the chain of command, and my sister, the only member of the party I outranked, was too dumb to take orders from me.

France was better than Europe proper, because it was on the way home from it. The language sounded better, although I couldn't understand what people said in it. We lived at the Hotel Regina, where the Place des Pyramides debouches into the Rue de Rivoli, and when we went out on foot we stayed under the colonnade because of the heat. We seldom got beyond the Place de la Concorde, because my sister, who in later years became as nimble as a roebuck, could not then walk worth a damn. For years afterward I thought of Paris as a city mostly roofed over, like a souk. I don't know why I think of the cuirassier as a permanent feature of the set. There may have been a fixed guard in front of one of the hotels because a visiting royal personage or head of state was in residence. But it is possible that I saw the soldier only once, and was so impressed that I never forgot him.

My parents abandoned the three of us often and went out into unroofed regions in a fiacre or a taxi. Hippomobile and automobile ages overlapped; it was no longer dashing to motor, nor yet quaint to prefer a carriage. My own prejudice in favor of horses was so strong that when I chanced to be with my parents they deferred to it.

All of us had stayed four weeks at Marienbad, a spa in Bohemia that is now known by some Slavic name, while Mother reduced her weight. Having reduced, she had an excuse to gather a wardrobe for her new figure before we went home. (She was sure to put the weight back on before the *Kaiserin Augusta Victoria* docked in Hoboken, nine days after leaving Cherbourg, but the dresses could always be let out.) Father had to accompany her to see how pretty she looked and to authorize expenditures that he would have rejected in horror if he had not been there to see her. He was not only proud of her looks—"A regular Lillian Russell," he would say—but sensitive to the good opinion of the mannequins and *vendeuses*. The sight of a pretty woman had an airborne chemical effect, like nerve gas. It relaxed the rubber band around his wallet. He was, moreover, helpless in Paris without Mother because he did not have French and thought she was fluent in it. It was an illusion she maintained as long as they traveled together.

"If you talk English to them they double the price," he used to say.

He did not suffer from this disadvantage in Europa Odiosa, since he spoke German, but it gave him little pleasure. What I principally remember him talking about in Marienbad was how a waiter captain had tried to swindle us by putting twenty-three rolls on our breakfast bill when we had taken only twenty-one. Mother, when on a diet, limited herself to three rolls.

Once that summer they took me, unforgettably, to Napoleon's tomb, where the gold light, the marble, and the massed battle flags made an image of Napoleonic glory that has always helped me understand the side of Stendhal that is least rational. If brief exposure to the glories of the Empire, a hundred years later, could so dazzle me, I find it easy to pardon the effect upon a lieutenant of dragoons eighteen years old, riding in the midst of the Sixth Light Dragoons, uniform bottle-green, red waistcoat, white breeches, helmet with crest, horsetail, and red cockade.

Napoleon's name and general repute were already known to me. He was a deity of the small personal Olympus I was putting together for myself, like a collection of the pictures of baseball players that then came in packages of cigarettes. The captain of the team was George Washington, and there were also Miss Russell (Aphrodite) and Enrico Caruso (Pan). Washington was Zeus, or boss god. His stern virtue—"I cannot tell a lie"—put him above me and everybody else I knew, because we all lied frequently. His hatchet inspired a terror I could not then explain to myself. I can see now that his craggy *old* face under the white hair—I had no notion then that he wore a powdered wig—equated him with the Old Man of the Tribe, or father-persona, vested with power symbolized by the ax. He looked mean enough to use it. The cherry tree, of course, is a son-substitute—Isaac is to Abraham as cherry tree to Washington—and even the merest fool can see what the candied cherries are, symbolically speaking. (The show windows of the Platt-Deutsch and Greek confectionery stores in New York were full of candied cherries, cardboard or chocolate hatchets, and cardboard cherry trees, bearing edible cherries, for a week before Washington's birthday. Here we have the personae and materia of a cult, with a built-in miracle play.) I knew Miss Russell, like Washington, only by hearsay. In my cosmogony she was already a figure of the past, associated with my prehistory and my parents' salad days, because they talked about her that way. I was astonished, on checking her dates when I wrote this, to read that she retired from the stage only in 1912, at the age of fifty-one. In 1911, although no longer in perihelion, she was an undefeated champion still, about to retire into wealthy marriage with a Pittsburgh publisher. Miss Russell had been the reigning American Beauty, on and off stage, since about 1885. She was a butterscotch sundae of a woman, as beautiful as a tulip of beer with a high white collar. If a Western millionaire, one of the Hearst or Mackay kind, could have given an architect carte blanche to design him a woman, she would have looked like Lillian. She was San Simeon in corsets.

Mother, who was seventeen years younger, had bloomed in an age when all blond little girls with blue eyes wanted to grow up to be Lillian Russells. At puberty, if the girls were still pretty, their relatives began to compare them to their model.

Miss Russell embodied a style. Her hats were famously enormous and beplumed, even in an era of big, feathered hats. In photographs she seems to be wearing a forest of ostrich plumes above a mesa with an underbrush of satin bows. Her contours did not encourage fasting among her imitators. In building up to a similar opulence, I suppose, a younger woman developed eating habits that were hard to curb after she reached the target figure. That may have been Mother's difficulty.

A popular dessert named for the star, the Lillian Russell, was a half cantaloupe holding about a pint and three quarters of ice cream. If an actress had a dish named after her now, the recipe would be four phenobarbital tablets and a jigger of Metrecal. The consecrated silhouette was an hourglass. Hence, I imagine, rose a dietary dilemma. A woman had to eat to stay plump above and below the pinch and slender in between.

Corsets afforded only partial and painful aid. I remember, as a small child, that in the bathing pavilion at Far Rockaway, the women, before going out on the beach, would summon the locker man, a leathery old drunk, to pull the strings of their corsets tight. In cinching them up, he would sometimes place his bare foot in the small of a whaleboned back. They tipped him for doing them this violence. People then were willing to go to more pains than now in order to look nice. The women were not alone in this. Marshall Mannerheim in his *Memoirs* recalls that officers of the Russian Imperial Guard used to put on their doeskin trousers, sit in a bath, and then let them dry tight to the skin.

Miss Russell and her imitators held their beautiful chins high, to arch the neck and prevent wrinkles. It was no time for an undecided profile. Throats, arms, and backs counted more points than they do today because women wore low-necked gowns more often. People dressed for the dress circle in the Metropolitan Opera House then, for example, where now they wear street clothes in the boxes. Merely well-off couples, like my parents, with no social pretensions, often dressed just to go to friends' houses for dinner. I can remember Mother pausing in my bedroom to show herself off on some of these occasions in a white gown with gold sequins or a lilac with silver. I agreed with Father that she was a regular Lillian Russell.

Miss Russell, as reflected in my mother, furnished my basic pattern of feminine beauty. But the type already trembled on the brink of the archaic in 1911, like silent films the year before sound came in. Irene Castle lurked just around the corner of history, light of foot, long-legged, and sparse, and by the early twenties, when I began to look purposefully at females, I would not find a Russellinear woman anywhere. (To this sharp bend in the river of womanly morphology I sometimes attribute my insatiable nostalgia for the past: I have a fixation on a form of animal life that no longer exists.)

Caruso, the fourth in my pantheon, was a Disembodied Voice, which is an essential feature of the history of any religion. His, with which I was familiar, came out of the horn, shaped like a morning-glory, of our Victrola. I could not understand what he said, which made it more awesome. Mostly, it seems to me now, he sang "E Lucevan le Stelle." I can identify it, at fifty years' distance, by the place where Cavaradossi sobs. Caruso sobbed louder than any other tenor, and when he did, my father always said, "That's art. You can tell a real artist by touches like that."

Tosca, Father used to say, was the touchstone for sopranos, too. "When she lays Scarpia out and puts the candles by the corpse, you can tell whether she can act," he would say. "She's just stabbed him, you know, and then she gets superstitious."

The only reason I would have liked to go to the Metropolitan in person was to see the stabbing; I wondered how they managed the blood. The music, I judged from the phonograph records, was something one could easily have too much of. The description "a regular Caruso" was as valid praise as "a regular Lillian Russell," but neither meant that the person so qualified was literally a deity—just that the amateur could sing well, or that the girl was a peach. There had been a third god on the same level, but his foot had slipped.

"A regular Jim Jeffries" no longer meant, in 1911, what it had before 1910, when that Caucasian Colossus had lost to Jack Johnson. You couldn't very well say that a white boy was a regular Jack Johnson.

Caruso was also a Pan-god, or satyr. Everybody knew that he had once followed a woman into the monkey house at the Central Park Zoo and pinched her in the rear. The woman had had him arrested. The incident had filled headlines; it had become legend. Thirty years later I was to learn that it was a press agent's trick, put up to attract attention to the tenor's appearance in a new role, Rodolfo in *La Bohème*. But then it was a myth that I accepted as fully as the story of George Washington and the cherry tree. Caruso, again like Miss Russell, was a deity often made manifest to my parents, more worthy than myself. Home from the Opera, they talked about his tonsils as if they were my Uncle Mike's.

In those days the people of New York saw its gods in the flesh, on the stage of the Met or the Colonial Theatre, or strutting in front of Kid McCoy's saloon, according to the departments over which they presided. They were not a reconstituted mess of dots on a screen.

Culture impinged on daily life. My father, when shaving, sang the Toreador's air from *Carmen* every morning while stropping his razor. I associated this habit of his with the Caruso cult, too, but erroneously. Father, like Escamillo, was a baritone. There was only one word in his version of the song, and that deformed by a feminine ending that he dragged in for euphony:

"To-reea-Dora" . . .

He sang the rest of the music to a devocabularized lyric—"Ta, ra, ta, ra, *tah*."

He could shave with a straight blade on a transatlantic liner in a storm. The electric razor fosters no comparable talents.

I do not denigrate my pantheon of fifty years ago. An aesthetic taste founded on the gold light in the tomb and Lillian Russell's figure and Caruso singing Cavaradossi—and Sousa's Band and the Buffalo Bill show—is bound to be big and rich. It can be pruned down afterward.

In the Paris evenings, Father and Mother dined *en ville*, leaving the three of us to take supper in our room. Fraulein and I would share some uninspiring dish like cold cuts or an omelet, and my sister would have consommé and a soft-boiled egg, which made her unhappy. This particular Fraulein was rather nice, the only one I remember without distaste. I had, in any case, attained an age that forbade the worst personal indignities. (The most annoying was when they got the wash rag into your ear, meanwhile pulling the lobe with their other hand, but the most publicly humbling was when they spit on a handkerchief and wiped a smudge off your nose.) This Fraulein was Volks-Deutsch, from northern Hungary, and looked more Hungarian than German, with a good figure, ruddy complexion, and heavy black eyebrows. The room waiter was an Alsatian and won her confidence by speaking German. On the first night we were there, though, when he came back for the dishes after my sister and I were in our beds, he showed he was just like all the other Frenchmen, Fraulein told my mother the next day. He got fresh. Thereafter, she told him to leave the dishes for the maid to collect next morning, and she barricaded the door with chairs.

"But what could he do to you, Fraulein?" I asked her.

We nagged the poor girl so, during those hot days, that Mother advised her to take us to Rumpelmayer's *confiserie* under the colonnade, near the Hotel Continental, for what we had seen advertised on a window card as an American ice-cream soda. Fraulein could build a whole day of peace around the excursion, keeping us in line during the morning by threatening not to take us if we weren't good, then making us have a nap after lunch as preparation for the treat. Afterward we might, if she was lucky, be sick, and she could put us to bed again.

The day came, and we went. Fraulein and I had the sodas, but they were not, in my opinion, up to the standard of the West Side of New York. Trying, at this long distance in time, to appraise the trouble, I do not think Rumpelmayer's had a genuine soda-fountain pump to gas them up with. I suspect that famous *salon de thé* of slopping a bottle of Perrier over a parfait. Boys liked their sodas very gassy then, with a sharp, metallic bite that reminded me of the smell of a bicycle-repair shop. My sister was allowed, I suppose, to have some of the ice cream out of my soda. Then the waitress brought the bill. Fraulein, who had expected they would cost ten cents, like the ones at home, did not have enough French money with her to pay it.

There was a conference, made more memorable because

Fraulein spoke no French, and they trusted nobody who spoke German. The allegorical statue of Strasbourg among the cities of France in the Place de la Concorde was draped permanently in black; it was knee-high in funeral wreaths. We had once walked that far. *La revanche* was in the air, like humidity. Finally, Fraulein and the management reached a *Konkordat*: she was to go back to the hotel and change some Austrian kronen—Rumpelmayer's wouldn't. She was to take Norma, who was already howling, with her. I was to be left as collateral.

She explained the deal to me before she left. I did not like it; I proposed we leave Norma. She said patiently that the reason Rumpelmayer's was releasing her even temporarily was to get Norma out of there. I demanded a supplement of pastry on the principle of extra danger pay, but Fraulein said that the management would advance no further credit.

So there I sat, for what seemed the second seven years of my life, my apprehension steadily growing, while she walked the couple of hundred yards back to the Regina and took Norma to the bathroom and came back. Before she made it I decided a dozen times that she wouldn't. When at last she reappeared, she asked me not to tell my parents what had happened, and I blackmailed her out of an éclair.

It was a prophetic trauma. I have spent a large aggregate portion of my life since in situations that repeated the quarter hour at Rumpelmayer's, waiting for a loan to bail me out. No matter how sure I am that the money will arrive, I have the same anxiety. My first stay in hock should have infected me with a horror of Paris forever, but it didn't, although I did not know how deeply I was in love. There would come a time when, if I had compared my life to a cake, the sojourns in Paris would have represented the chocolate filling. The intervening layers were plain sponge. But my infatuations do not begin at first taste. I nibble, reflect, come back for more, and find myself forever addicted.

I remember, from that first Paris, the gold light in the Tomb, the cuirassier, and the *vespasiennes* where no Fraulein could pursue me. Finally, there were two toys that I bore off with me to the *Kaiserin*

Augusta Victoria. One was a chef *legumier* who hacked away at a carrot with a big knife—another version, had I but recognized it, of the George Washington myth. The other was a scale fire engine with hose no thicker than vermicelli through which I could pump real water.

The chef symbolized in my unconscious Paris, *ville gastronomique*, and the engine with its squirt Paris, *ville d'art*. The graphic arts had their origin in the free patterns made in the snow by Ice Age man with warm water. This accounts for the fact that there have been few good women painters. Lot's wife, who looked behind her, may have been a pioneer, but we had a head start of several million years.

The years from 1911 to 1924 were plain sponge, yet that dull stratum clinched my allegiance. Nineteen fourteen was the year of transition to Francophile from mere Germanophobe. On August 1, Fraulein Germania's armies crossed the frontier, and the "Marseillaise" became my favorite tune. I was by that time already a compulsive newspaper reader instead of a tentative one, as I had been in 1911. I counted on Papa Joffre and the cuirassier to avenge my early indignities. Joffre's face reminded me of Santa Claus, a pleasant association, although I had long ceased to believe. (When I saw Santa Clauses on street corners, I knew I would soon get a lot of presents, and it set up a pleasant mood. When I see them now, I know I will have to give a lot, and I am filled with bile.) All through August, though, the French retreated. The Germans—I forget when they became Huns—advanced toward Rumpelmayer's and the Hotel Regina. It was a personal humiliation, because in America I was surrounded by German rooters.

We were quartered at a hotel called Schaefer's in Lake Hopatcong, a hot summer resort in New Jersey. Schaefer's was a German-American kind of place, as much roadhouse as hotel, built on the side of a hill, with a dark, cool bar on the lowest level. There was a fruit machine in this crypt, and I would play it every day, until I had lost the last nickel I could wheedle or extort from my mother. Then I would drink sarsaparilla and eat Swiss cheese sandwiches on rye while I read the Waverly Novels. The sarsaparilla and sandwiches went on the bill. The novels came from a mission-oak bookcase in the hall outside the dining room. When Fraulein—the Paris one was still with us—would drive me into the distasteful fresh air, I would walk down to a pier, sit down again, and fish for perch. I never caught one big enough to eat.

The bar, aromatic of stale beer, presented an aspect of Teutonic culture I could appreciate, and my antipathy might have shaded into indifference if the war hadn't started. When it did, though, Otto, the bartender, and Fred and Karl, the waiters, began to crow offensively about their national superiority to everybody else. The French, they said, bewrayed themselves from fear, and the English were fairies. As I was a great reader of G. A. Henty, this involved me on a second front.

Victory followed victory, and as the help's chests swelled, Fraulein's bosom heaved with them. She was an Austro-Hungarian subject, and an ally. Karl was cockeyed and he pinched lady guests' bottoms when he thought he could get away with it. He had long hinted he was a remittance man, and he now professed to have been an officer on a U-boat. Fraulein looked at him otherwise than she had upon the Alsatian waiter in Paris. My attitude toward her was now ambivalent, for I had begun to take a sneaking interest in women and half regretted that I no longer shared a room with her and Norma; I would have welcomed the opportunities for observation. I therefore resented Fraulein Fasching's interest in Karl. Patriotism, I sensed, could be employed for ulterior purposes. I told her that if he was so brave he should go home and join the navy. She explained that since the cowardly English held the sea he couldn't—he was breaking his heart over it. But it was hardly worth regretting, because even if there were boats going, the Germans and Austrians would win the war before Karl could get there. He was having his *Schnecke* and eating it. I longed for Joffre to turn the tables, but he looked to be two out and ten runs behind in the last half of the ninth inning. The Marne determined my second nationality forever. I became a Frenchman at one remove.

By that time, I think, we were back in our house at Far Rockaway, a boundary province of Greater New York on Long Island.

Like all frontier dwellers I was chauvinistic, and I thought of people who lived across the street in Nassau County as hicks. It was a tall, gaunt house, painted dark green and darkened by oaks that stood too close. (Thirty years later I saw it again and it had been divided into flats.) There Fraulein, reeling under the shock of Joffre's and my combined attack, received fresh support from Louis, our house-man, a Tyrolese from Meran. He had been working as a waiter in another summer hotel while we were away.

Louis was as Pan-German as Fraulein. He predicted that the Marne was only a temporary setback. The French were merely a kind of Wops—I would see. He had his own kind of frontier chauvin-ism—anti-Italian. He had an impressive trick of jumping out of a third-floor window, grabbing a limb of an oak tree, and swinging his way down by changing handholds, like a pre-Weissmuller Tarzan.

I was then in 5B. The war enlisted me and filled my proxy life for four years. When it ended I was a sophomore in high school. I grew up in it, transferring in fantasy from the cuirassiers, when I saw cav-alry wouldn't do, to the heroic poilus, defenders of Verdun. I served a brief period as an officer of heroic Senegalese, and a short bit with the heroic Escadrille Lafayette. I also did a turn as liaison with our gallant allies, the heroic Brusiloff's heroic Cossacks. It is more vivid to me, even now, than the following World War; that is because I saw it through the eyes of correspondents who knew how to use their imaginations. Each fall, when the offensive that had begun so optimistically bogged down, I would say to Fraulein and Louis, like a Dodger fan, "Wait till next year." It was no longer fun for Fraulein—her brother was a surgeon with the Austrian army in Galicia, and after the sinking of the *Lusitania* it was clear which side was out of favor here.

Then in the Verdun spring—1916—while I walked along the parapet of my trench to show my fellows the Huns couldn't shoot, I began to feel queer and got sent home from school. Mother put me to bed, and it shortly transpired that I had typhoid fever. I had caught it by eating oysters from polluted waters—they had not been sold as such, of course—and I soon drifted into delirium, where I stayed for weeks of combat service on several fronts I had not yet visited. I had a particularly arduous indefinite period as a Serbian army horse, being ferried across a river as one in a bunch of bananas. On arriving at the other side of the river I was presented at a formal review of cuirassiers, where General Nivelle, the heroic commander of Verdun's heroic defenders, decorated me with the Médaille Militaire, which he attached to my right horse-ear by a safety pin. I put the medal under my pillow.

I had two trained nurses who lived in the house and worked around the clock—my parents didn't think well of the local hospital. As I achieved a patchy lucidity, I became aware of Miss Galt and Miss McCarthy as nurses in a military hospital. (I had stopped being a horse, but still had the medal, safe under the pillow.) They were kind, but I was peevish, and they sometimes said the conventional things.

Once, then, when the fever had departed and they thought I was quite all right in the head again, I gagged or whimpered at some measure of therapy, and Miss McCarthy said, "Don't be a crybaby."

It roused the *grand decoré* in me, and I yelped, "Crybaby? How do you think I got that medal under my pillow?"

"Medal under what pillow?" she asked.

I lifted myself on an elbow and turned the pillow over, but my decoration wasn't there.

I was never so disappointed in my heroic life.*

(1959)

---

* Thirty-six years later, in 1952, I got a French decoration for the most disappointing of reasons: being a writer—I sometimes take it surreptitiously from its case and stare at it, pretending that I won it by jumping a horse over the bayonets of a British square at Waterloo and, once in, decapitating a Colonel the Honorable Something-or-Other, a Tory back-bencher in the House of Commons.

Just Enough Money

If, as I was saying before I digressed, the first requisite for writing well about food is a good appetite, the second is to put in your apprenticeship as a feeder when you have enough money to pay the check but not enough to produce indifference to the size of the total. (I also meant to say, previously, that Waverley Root has a good appetite, but I never got around to it.) The optimum financial position for a serious apprentice feeder is to have funds in hand for three more days, with a reasonable, but not certain, prospect of reinforcements thereafter. The student at the Sorbonne waiting for his remittance, the newspaperman waiting for his salary, the freelance writer waiting for a check that he has cause to believe is in the mail—all are favorably situated to learn. (It goes without saying that it is essential to be in France.) The man of appetite who will stint himself when he can see three days ahead has no vocation, and I dismiss from consideration, as manic, the fellow who will spend the lot on one great feast and then live on fried potatoes until his next increment; Tuaregs eat that way, but only because they never know when they are going to come by their next sheep. The clearheaded voracious man learns because he tries to compose his meals to obtain an appreciable quantity of pleasure from each. It is from this weighing of delights against their cost that the student eater (particularly if he is a student at the University of Paris) erects the scale of values that will serve him until he dies or has to reside in the Middle West for a long period. The scale is different for each eater, as it is for each writer.

Eating is highly subjective, and the man who accepts say-so in youth will wind up in bad and overtouted restaurants in middle age, ordering what the maître d'hôtel suggests. He will have been guided to them by food-snob publications, and he will fall into the habit of drinking too much before dinner to kill the taste of what he has been told he should like but doesn't. An illustration: For about six years, I kept hearing of a restaurant in the richest shire of Connecticut whose proprietor, a Frenchman, had been an assistant of a disciple of the great Escoffier. Report had it that in these wilds— inhabited only by executives of the highest grade, walking the woods like the King of Nemi until somebody came on from Winnetka to cut their throats—the restaurateur gave full vent to the creative flame. His clients took what he chose to give them. If they declined, they had to go down the pike to some joint where a steak cost only twelve dollars, and word would get around that they felt their crowns in danger—they had been detected economizing. I finally arranged to be smuggled out to the place disguised as a Time-Life Executive Vice-Publisher in Charge of Hosannas with the mission of entertaining the advertising manager of the Hebrew National Delicatessen Corporation. When we arrived, we found the Yale-blue vicuña rope up and the bar full of couples in the hundred-thousand-dollar bracket, dead drunk as they waited for tables; knowing that this would be no back-yard cookout, they had taken prophylactic anesthesia. But when I tasted the food, I perceived that they had been needlessly alarmed. The Frenchman, discouraged because for four years no customers had tasted what they were eating, had taken to bourbon-on-the-rocks. In a morose way, he had resigned himself to becoming dishonestly rich. The food was no better than Howard Johnson's, and the customers, had they not been paralyzed by the time they got to it, would have liked it as well. The *spécialité de la maison*, the unhappy *patron* said when I interrogated him, was jellied oysters dyed red, white, and blue. "At least they are aware of that," he said. "The colors attract their attention." There was an on-the-hour service of Brink's armored cars between his door and the night-deposit vault of a bank in New York, conveying the money that rolled into the *caisse*. The wheels, like a

juggernaut's, rolled over his secret heart. His intention in the beginning had been noble, but he was a victim of the system.

The reference room where I pursued my own first earnest researches as a feeder without the crippling handicap of affluence was
the Restaurant des Beaux-Arts, on the Rue Bonaparte, in 1926–27. I
was a student, in a highly generalized way, at the Sorbonne, taking
targets of opportunity for study. Eating soon developed into one of
my major subjects. The franc was at twenty-six to the dollar, and the
researcher, if he had only a certain sum—say, six francs—to spend,
soon established for himself whether, for example, a half bottle of
Tavel *supérieur*, at three and a half francs, and braised beef heart and
yellow turnips, at two and a half, gave him more or less pleasure
than a *contre-filet* of beef, at five francs, and a half bottle of *ordinaire*,
at one franc. He might find that he liked the heart, with its strong,
rich flavor and odd texture, nearly as well as the beef, and that since
the Tavel was overwhelmingly better than the cheap wine, he had
done well to order the first pair. Or he might find that he so much
preferred the generous, sanguine *contre-filet* that he could accept the
undistinguished *picrate* instead of the Tavel. As in a bridge tournament, the learner played duplicate hands, making the opposite
choice of fare the next time the problem presented itself. (It was seldom as simple as my example, of course, because a meal usually
included at least an hors d'oeuvre and a cheese, and there was a
complexity of each to choose from. The arrival, in season, of fresh
asparagus or venison further complicated matters. In the first case,
the investigator had to decide what course to omit in order to fit
the asparagus in, and, in the second, whether to forgo all else in
order to afford venison.)

A rich man, faced with this simple sumptuary dilemma, would
have ordered both the Tavel *and* the *contre-filet*. He would then
never know whether he liked beef heart, or whether an *ordinaire*
wouldn't do him as well as something better. (There are people to
whom wine is merely an alcoholized sauce, although they may have
sensitive palates for meat or pastries.) When one considers the millions of permutations of foods and wines to test, it is easy to see
that life is too short for the formulation of dogma. Each eater can

but establish a few general principles that are true only for him. Our hypothetical rich *client* might even have ordered a Pommard, because it was listed at a higher price than the Tavel, and because he was more likely to be acquainted with it. He would then never have learned that a good Tavel is better than a fair-to-middling Pommard—better than a fair-to-middling almost anything, in my opinion. In student restaurants, renowned wines like Pommard were apt to be mediocre specimens of their kind, since the customers could never have afforded the going prices of the best growths and years. A man who is rich in his adolescence is almost doomed to be a dilettante at table. This is not because all millionaires are stupid but because they are not impelled to experiment. In learning to eat, as in psychoanalysis, the customer, in order to profit, must be sensible of the cost.

There is small likelihood that a rich man will frequent modest restaurants even at the beginning of his gustatory career; he will patronize restaurants, sometimes good, where the prices are high and the repertory is limited to dishes for which it is conventionally permissible to charge high prices. From this list, he will order the dishes that in his limited experience he has already found agreeable. Later, when his habits are formed, he will distrust the originality that he has never been constrained to develop. A diet based chiefly on game birds and oysters becomes a habit as easily as a diet of jelly doughnuts and hamburgers. It is a better habit, of course, but restrictive just the same. Even in Paris, one can dine in the costly restaurants for years without learning that there are fish other than sole, turbot, salmon (in season), trout, and the Mediterranean *rouget* and *loup de mer*. The fresh herring or sardine *sauce moutarde*; the *colin froid mayonnaise*; the conger eel *en matelote*; the small freshwater fish of the Seine and the Marne, fried crisp and served *en buisson*; the whiting *en colère* (his tail in his mouth, as if contorted with anger); and even the skate and the *dorade*—all these, except by special and infrequent invitation, are out of the swim. (It is a standing tourist joke to say that the fishermen on the quays of the Seine never catch anything, but in fact they often take home the makings of a nice fish fry, especially in winter. In my hotel on the Square

Louvois, I had a room waiter—a Czech naturalized in France—who used to catch hundreds of *goujons* and *ablettes* on his days off. He once brought a shoe box of them to my room to prove that Seine fishing was not pure whimsy.) All the fish I have mentioned have their habitats in humbler restaurants, the only places where the aspirant eater can become familiar with their honest fishy tastes and the decisive modes of accommodation that suit them. Personally, I like tastes that know their own minds. The reason that people who detest fish often tolerate sole is that sole doesn't taste very much like fish, and even this degree of resemblance disappears when it is submerged in the kind of sauce that patrons of Piedmontese restaurants in London and New York think characteristically French. People with the same apathy toward decided flavor relish "South African lobster" tails—frozen as long as the Siberian mammoth— because they don't taste lobstery. ("South African lobsters" are a kind of sea crayfish, or langouste, but that would be nothing against them if they were fresh.) They prefer processed cheese because it isn't cheesy, and synthetic vanilla extract because it isn't vanillary. They have made a triumph of the Delicious apple because it doesn't taste like an apple, and of the Golden Delicious because it doesn't taste like anything. In a related field, "dry" (non-beery) beer and "light" (non-Scotchlike) Scotch are more of the same. The standard of perfection for vodka (no color, no taste, no smell) was expounded to me long ago by the then Estonian consul-general in New York, and it accounts perfectly for the drink's rising popularity with those who like their alcohol in conjunction with the reassuring tastes of infancy—tomato juice, orange juice, chicken broth. It is the ideal intoxicant for the drinker who wants no reminder of how hurt Mother would be if she knew what he was doing.

The consistently rich man is also unlikely to make the acquaintance of meat dishes of robust taste—the hot andouille and andouillette, which are close-packed sausages of smoked tripe, and the boudin, or blood pudding, and all its relatives that figure in the pages of Rabelais and on the menus of the market restaurants. He will not meet the civets, or dark, winey stews of domestic rabbit and old turkey. A tough old turkey with plenty of character makes the best civet, and only in a civet is turkey good to eat. Young turkey, like young sheep, calf, spring chicken, and baby lobster, is a pale preliminary phase of its species. The pig, the pigeon, and the goat—as suckling, squab, and kid—are the only animals that are at their best to eat when immature. The first in later life becomes gross through indolence; the second and third grow muscular through overactivity. And the world of tripery is barred to the well-heeled, except for occasional exposure to an expurgated version of *tripes à la mode de Caen*. They have never seen *gras-double* (tripe cooked with vegetables, principally onions) or *pieds et paquets* (sheep's tripe and calves' feet with salt pork). In his book, Waverley Root dismisses tripe, but he is no plutocrat; his rejection is deliberate, after fair trial. Still, his insensibility to its charms seems to me odd in a New Englander, as he is by origin. Fried pickled honeycomb tripe used to be the most agreeable feature of a winter breakfast in New Hampshire, and Fall River, Root's home town, is in the same cultural circumscription.

Finally, to have done with our rich man, seldom does he see even the simple, well-pounded *bifteck* or the pot-au-feu itself—the foundation glory of French cooking. Alexandre Dumas the elder wrote in his *Dictionary Cuisine*: "French cooking, the first of all cuisines, owes its superiority to the excellence of French bouillon. This excellence derives from a sort of intuition with which I shall not say our cooks but our women of the people are endowed." This bouillon is one of the two end products of the pot. The other is the material that has produced it—beef, carrots, parsnips, white turnips, leeks, celery, onions, cloves, garlic, and cracked marrowbones, and, for the dress version, fowl. Served *in* some of the bouillon, this constitutes the dish known as pot-au-feu. Dumas is against poultry "unless it is old," but advises that "an old pigeon, a partridge, or a rabbit roasted in advance, a crow in November or December" works wonders. He postulates "seven hours of sustained simmering," with constant attention to the "scum" that forms on the surface and to the water level. ("Think twice before adding water, though if your meat actually rises above the level of the bouillon it is necessary to add boiling water to cover it.") This supervision demands the full-time presence of the cook in the kitchen through-out the day, and the maintenance of the temperature calls for a con-siderable outlay in fuel. It is one reason that the pot-au-feu has declined as a chief element of the working-class diet in France. Women go out to work, and gas costs too much. For a genuinely good pot-au-feu, Dumas says, one should take a fresh piece of beef—"a twelve-to-fifteen-pound rump"—and simmer it seven hours in the bouillon of the beef that you simmered seven hours the day before. He does not say what good housekeepers did with the first piece of beef—perhaps cut it into sandwiches for the children's lunch. He regrets that even when he wrote, in 1869, excessive haste was beginning to mar cookery; the demanding ritual of the pot it-self had been abandoned. This was "a receptacle that never left the fire, day or night," Dumas writes. "A chicken was put into it as a chicken was withdrawn, a piece of beef as a piece was taken out, and a glass of water whenever a cup of broth was removed. Every kind of meat that cooked in this bouillon gained, rather than lost, in flavor." Pot-au-feu is so hard to find in chic restaurants nowadays that every Saturday evening there is a mass pilgrimage from the fashionable quarters to Chez Benoit, near the Châtelet—a small but not cheap restaurant that serves it once a week. I have never found a crow in Benoit's pot, but all the rest is good.

A drastically poor man, naturally, has even less chance than a drastically rich one to educate himself gastronomically. For him eat-ing becomes merely a matter of subsistence; he can exercise no choice. The chief attraction of the cheapest student restaurants in my time was advertised on their largest placards: *"Pain à Discrétion"* ("All the Bread You Want"). They did not graduate discriminating eaters. During that invaluable year, I met a keen observer who gave me a tip: "If you run across a restaurant where you often see priests eating with priests, or sporting girls with sporting girls, you may be confident that it is good. Those are two classes of people who like to eat well and get their money's worth. If you see a priest eating with a layman, though, don't be too sure about the money's worth. The fellow *en civil* may be a rich parishioner, and the good Father won't worry about the price. And if the girl is with a man, you can't count on anything. It may be her kept man, in which case she won't care what she spends on him, or the man who is keeping her, in which case she won't care what he spends on her."

Failing the sure indications cited above, a good augury is the presence of French newspapermen.

The Restaurant des Beaux-Arts, where I did my early research, was across the street from the Ecole des Beaux-Arts, and not, in fact, precisely in my quarter, which was that of the university proper, a good half mile away, on the other side of the Boulevard Saint-Germain. It was a half mile that made as much difference as the border between France and Switzerland. The language was the same, but not the inhabitants. Along the Rue Bonaparte there were antiquarians, and in the streets leading off it there were practitioners of the ancillary arts—picture framers and bookbinders. The bookshops of the Rue Bonaparte, of which there were many, dealt in fine editions and rare books, instead of the used textbooks and works of erudition that predominated around the university. The students of the Beaux-Arts were only a small element of the population of the neighborhood, and they were a different breed from the students of the Boulevard Saint-Michel and its tributaries, such as the Rue de l'Ecole de Médecine, where I lived. They were older and seemingly in easier circumstances. I suspected them of commercial art and of helping Italians to forge antiques. Because there was more money about, and because the quarter had a larger proportion of adult, experienced eaters, it was better territory for restaurants than the immediate neighborhood of the Sorbonne. I had matriculated at the Faculté des Lettres and at the Ecole des Chartes, which forms medievalists, but since I had ceased attending classes after the first two weeks, I had no need to stick close to home. One of the chief joys of that academic year was that it was one long cut without fear of retribution.

I chanced upon the Restaurant des Beaux-Arts while strolling one noon and tried it because it looked neither chic nor sordid, and the prices on the menu were about right for me: *pâté maison*, 75 centimes; sardines, 1 franc; artichoke, 1.25; and so on. A legend over the door referred to the proprietor as a M. Teyssedre, but the heading

of the bill of fare called him Balazuc. Which name represented a former proprietor and which the current one I never learned. I had a
distaste for asking direct questions, a practice I considered ill-bred.
This had handicapped me during my brief career as a reporter in
Providence, Rhode Island, but not as much as you might think. Direct questions tighten a man up, and even if he answers, he will not
tell you anything you have not asked him. What you want is to get
him to tell you his story. After he has, you can ask clarifying questions, such as "How did you come to have the ax in your hand?" I
had interrupted this journalistic grind after one year, at the suggestion of my father, a wise man. "You used to talk about wanting to
go to Europe for a year of study," he said to me one spring day in
1926, when I was home in New York for a weekend. "You are getting so interested in what you are doing that if you don't go now
you never will. You might even get married."

I sensed my father's generous intention, and, fearing that he
might change his mind, I told him that I didn't feel I should go,
since I was indeed thinking of getting married. "The girl is ten years
older than I am," I said, "and Mother might think she is kind of
fast, because she is being kept by a cotton broker from Memphis,
Tennessee, who only comes North once in a while. But you are a
man of the world, and you understand that a woman can't always
help herself. Basically . . ." Within the week, I had a letter of credit
on the Irving Trust for two thousand dollars, and a reservation on
the old *Caronia* for late in the summer, when the off-season rates
would be in effect. It was characteristic of my father that even while
doing a remarkably generous thing he did not want to waste the
difference between a full-season and an off-season passage on a one-
class boat. (He never called a liner anything but a boat, and I always
found it hard to do otherwise myself, until I stopped trying. "Boat"
is an expression of affection, not disrespect; it is like calling a
woman a girl. What may be ships in proportion to Oxford, where
the dictionary is written, are boats in proportion to New York,
where they nuzzle up to the bank to feed, like the waterfowl in Central Park.)

While I continued to work on the Providence paper until the

rates changed, Father, with my mother and sister, embarked for Europe on a Holland America boat—full-season rate and first class—so that my sister might take advantage of her summer holiday from school. I was to join them for a few days at the end of the summer, after which they would return to the United States and I would apply myself to my studies. Fortunately, I discovered that the titulary of a letter of credit can draw on it at the issuing bank as easily as abroad. By the time I sailed, I was eight hundred dollars into the letter, and after a week in Paris at a hotel off the Champs-Elysées I found, without astonishment, that I had spent more than half of the paternal fellowship that was intended to last me all year. The academic year would not begin until November, and I realized that I would be lucky to have anything at all by then. At this juncture, the cotton broker's girl came to my rescue in a vision, as an angel came to Constantine's. I telegraphed to my parents, who were at Lake Como, that I was on my way to join them. From my attitude when I got there—reserved, dignified, preoccupied—my father sensed that I was in trouble. The morning after my arrival, I proposed that we take a walk, just the two of us, by the lake. Soon we felt thirst, and we entered the trellised arbor of a hotel more modest than ours and ordered a bottle of rustic wine that recalled the stuff that Big Tony, my barber in Providence, used to manufacture in his yard on Federal Hill. Warmed by this homelike glow, I told my father that I had dilapidated his generous gift; I had dissipated in riotous living 72 percent of the good man's unsolicited benefaction. Now there was only one honorable thing for me to do—go back to work, get married, and settle down. "She is so noble that she wouldn't tell me," I said, "but I'm afraid I left her in the lurch."

"God damn it," he said, "I knew I should never have given you that money in one piece. But I want you to continue your education. How much will you need every month?"

"Two hundred," I said, moderately. Later, I wished I had asked for fifty more; he might have gone for it. "You stay in Paris," he said—he knew I had chosen the Sorbonne—"and I'll have the Irving send you two hundred dollars every month. No more lump sums. When a young man gets tangled up with that kind of women, they can ruin his whole life."

That was how I came to be living in Paris that academic year in a financial situation that facilitated my researches. Looking back, I am sure my father knew that I wanted to stay on, and that there was no girl to worry about. But he also understood that I couldn't simply beg; for pride's sake, I had to offer a fake quid pro quo and pretend to myself that he believed me. He had a very good idea of the value of leisure, not having had any until it was too late to become accustomed to it, and a very good idea of the pleasure afforded by knowledge that has no commercial use, having never had time to acquire more than a few odd bits. His parents had brought him to America when he was eight years old; he went to work at ten, opened his own firm at twenty-one, started being rich at thirty, and died broke at sixty-five—a perfect Horatio Alger story, except that Alger never followed his heroes through. At the moment, though, he had the money, and he knew the best things it would buy.

The great day of each month, then, was the one when my draft arrived at the main office of the Crédit Lyonnais—the Irving's correspondent bank—on the Boulevard des Italiens. It was never even approximately certain what day the draft would get there; there was no air mail, and I could not be sure what ship it was on. The Crédit, on receiving the draft, would notify me, again by ordinary mail, and that would use up another day. After the second of the month, I would begin to be haunted by the notion that the funds might have arrived and that I could save a day by walking over and inquiring. Consequently, I walked a good many times across the river and the city from the Rue de l'Ecole de Médecine to the Boulevard des Italiens, via the Rue Bonaparte, where I would lunch at the Maison Teyssedre or Balazuc. There were long vertical black enamel plaques on either side of the restaurant door, bearing, in gold letters, such information as "Room for Parties," "Telephone," "Snails," "Specialty of Broils," and, most notably, "Renowned Cellar, Great Specialty of Wines of the Rhône." The Great Specialty dated back to the regime of a proprietor anteceding M. Teyssedre-Balazuc. This prehistoric *patron*, undoubtedly an immigrant from Languedoc or Provence, had set up a bridgehead in Paris for the wines of his region of origin.

The wines of the Rhône each have a decided individuality, viable even when taken in conjunction with *brandade de morue*—a delightful purée of salt codfish, olive oil, and crushed garlic—which is their compatriot. *Brandade*, according to Root, is "definitely not the sort of dish that is likely to be served at the Tour d'Argent." "Subtlety," that hackneyed wine word, is a cliché seldom employed in writing about Rhône wines; their appeal is totally unambiguous. The Maison Teyssedre-Balazuc had the whole gamut, beginning with a rough, faintly sour Côtes du Rhône—which means, I suppose, anything grown along that river as it runs its 380-mile course through France. It continued with a Tavel and then a Tavel *supérieur*. The proprietor got his wines in barrel and bottled them in the Renowned Cellar; the plain Tavel came to the table in a bottle with a blue wax seal over the cork, the *supérieur* in a bottle with a purple seal. It cost two cents more a pint. I do not pretend to remember every price on the card of the Restaurant des Beaux-Arts, but one figure has remained graven in my heart like "Constantinople" in the dying Czar's. A half bottle of Tavel *supérieur* was 3.50; I can still see the figure when I close my eyes, written in purple ink on the cheap, grayish paper of the carte. This is a mnemonic testimonial to how good the wine was, and to how many times I struggled with my profligate tendencies at that particular point in the menu, arguing that the unqualified Tavel, which was very good, was quite good enough; two cents a day multiplied by thirty, I frequently told myself, mounted up to fifteen francs a month. I don't think I ever won the argument; my spendthrift palate carried the day. Tavel has a rose-cerise *robe*, like a number of well-known racing silks, but its taste is not thin or acidulous, as that of most of its mimics is. The taste is warm but dry, like an enthusiasm held under restraint, and there is a tantalizing suspicion of bitterness when the wine hits the top of the palate. With the second glass, the enthusiasm gains; with the third, it is overpowering. The effect is generous and calorific, stimulative of cerebration and the social instincts. "An apparently light but treacherous *rosé*," Root calls it, with a nuance of resentment that hints at some old misadventure.

Tavel is from a place of that name in Languedoc, just west of the Rhône. In 1926, there were in all France only two well-known wines that were neither red nor white. One was Tavel, and the other

Arbois, from the Jura—and Arbois is not a rose-colored but an "onion-peel" wine, with russet and purple glints. In the late thirties, the *rosés* began to proliferate in wine regions where they had never been known before, as growers discovered how marketable they were, and to this day they continue to pop up like measles on the wine map. Most often *rosés* are made from red wine grapes, but the process is abbreviated by removing the liquid prematurely from contact with the grape skins. This saves time and trouble. The product is a semi-aborted red wine. Any normally white wine can be converted into a *rosé* simply by adding a dosage of red wine* or cochineal.

In 1926 and 1927, for example, I never heard of Anjou *rosé* wine, although I read wine cards every day and spent a week of purposeful drinking in Angers, a glorious white-wine city. Alsace is another famous white-wine country that now lends its name to countless cases of a pinkish cross between No-Cal and vinegar; if, in 1926, I had crossed the sacred threshold of Valentin Sorg's restaurant in Strasbourg and asked the sommelier for a *rosé d'Alsace*, he would have, quite properly, kicked me into Germany. The list is endless now; flipping the coated-paper pages of any dealer's brochure, you see *rosés* from Bordeaux, Burgundy, all the South of France, California, Chile, Algeria, and heaven knows where else. Pink champagne, colored by the same procedure, has existed for a century and was invented for the African and Anglo-Saxon trade. The "discovery" of the demand for pink wine approximately coincided with the repeal of Prohibition in the United States. (The American housewife is susceptible to eye and color appeal.) In England, too, in the same period, a new class of wine buyer was rising with the social revolution. Pink worked its miracle there, and also in France itself, where many families previously limited to the cheapest kind of bulk wine were beginning to graduate to "nice things."

Logically, there is no reason any good white- or red-wine region

* "Some [peasants] will give you a quick recipe for *rosé* which shall not pollute these pages."—The late Morton Shand's classic, *A Book of French Wines*, Jonathan Cape, Ltd., London, 1960 edition.

should not produce equally good *rosé*, but in practice the proprietors of the good vineyards have no cause to change the nature of their wines; they can sell every drop they make. It is impossible to imagine a proprietor at Montrachet, or Chablis, or Pouilly, for example, tinting his wine to make a Bourgogne *rosé*. It is almost as hard to imagine it of a producer of first-rate Alsatian or Angevin wines. The wines converted to *rosé* in the great-wine provinces are therefore, I suspect, the worst ones—a suspicion confirmed by almost every experience I have had of them. As for the *rosés* from the cheap-wine provinces, they are as bad as their coarse progenitors, but are presented in fancy bottles of untraditional form—a trick learned from the perfume industry. The bottles are generally decorated with art labels in the style of Robida's illustrations for Rabelais, and the wines are peddled at a price out of all proportion to their inconsiderable merits. There is also behind their gruesome spread the push of a report, put out by some French adman, that while white wine is to be served only with certain aliments, and red wine only with certain others, *rosé* "goes with everything," and so can be served without embarrassment by the inexperienced hostess. The truth is, of course, that if a wine isn't good it doesn't "go" with anything, and if it is it can go in any company.* Tavel though, is the good, the old, and, as far as I am concerned, still the only worthy *rosé*.†

At the Restaurant des Beaux-Arts, the Tavel *supérieur* was as high on the list as I would let my eyes ascend until I felt that the new money was on its way. When I had my first supersensory intimation

---

* Mr. Frank Schoonmaker, a writer on wine and a dealer in it who has done much to diffuse *rosé* in this country, wrote to me after the first appearance of this statement that I "surely wouldn't want to serve a good claret with sardine or a Montrachet with roast beef." To this I must answer that I wouldn't serve a Montrachet or any other good wine of *any* color with sardines, since they would make it taste like more sardines. Beer might be a better idea, or in its default, *rosé*, and I offer, without charge, the advertising slogan "*Rosé*, the perfect companion for fish oil."

† The eminent Shand, in 1960 (*A Book of French Wines*), wrote with more authority but no less bitterness of the Pink Plague: "Odd little *rosés* were belatedly exhumed from a more than provincial obscurity to set before clamorous foreign holiday parties; or if none such had ever existed steps were speedily taken to produce a native *rosé*."

of its approach, I began to think of the prizes higher on the card—Côte Rôtie, Châteauneuf-du-Pape, and white as well as red Hermitage, which cost from three to five francs more, by the half bottle, than my customary Purple Seal. Racing men like to say that a great horse usually has a great name—impressive and euphonious—and these three wines bear similar cachets. The Pope's new castle and the Hermitage evoke medieval pomp and piety, but the name Côte Rôtie—the hillside roasted in the sun—is the friendliest of the three, as is the wine, which has a cleaner taste than Châteauneuf and a warmer one than Hermitage. Châteauneuf often seems to be a wine that there is too much of to be true, and it varies damnably in all respects save alcoholic content, which is high. Red Hermitage is certainly distinguished; as its boosters like to say, of all Rhône wines it most resembles a great Burgundy, but perhaps for that reason it was hardest for a young man to understand. It was least like a *vin du Rhône*. As for the scarce white Hermitage, of which I haven't encountered a bottle in many years, it left a glorious but vague memory. Côte Rôtie was my darling. Drinking it, I fancied I could see that literally roasting but miraculously green hillside, popping with goodness, like the skin of a roasting duck, while little wine-colored devils chased little nymphs along its simmering rivulets of wine. (Thirty years later, I had a prolonged return match with Côte Rôtie, when I discovered it on the wine card of Prunier's, in London. I approached it with foreboding, as you return to a favorite author whom you haven't read for a long time, hoping that he will be as good as you remember. But I need have had no fear. Like Dickens, Côte Rôtie meets the test. It is no Rudyard Kipling in a bottle, making one suspect a defective memory or a defective cork.)

On days when I merely suspected money to be at the bank, I would continue from the Restaurant des Beaux-Arts to the Boulevard des Italiens by any variation of route that occurred to me, looking in the windows of the rare-book dealers for the sort of buy I could afford only once a month. Since on most of my trips I drew a blank at the Crédit Lyonnais, I had plenty of time for window-shopping and for inspection of the bookstalls on the quays. To this

I attribute my possession of some of the best books I own—the *Moyen de Parvenir*, for example, printed at Chinon in the early seventeenth century, with the note on its title page: "New edition, corrected of divers faults that weren't there, and augmented by many others entirely new."

On the *good* day, when I had actually received the notification, I had to walk over again to collect, but this time I had a different stride. Simply from the way I carried myself when I left my hotel on the Rue de l'Ecole de Médecine, my landlord, M. Perès, knew that I would pay my bill that night, together with the six or seven hundred francs I invariably owed him for personal bites. He would tap cheerfully on the glass of the window that divided his well-heated office and living quarters from the less well-heated entrance hall, and wave an arm with the gesture that he had probably used to pull his company out of the trenches for a charge at Verdun. He was a *grand blessé* and a Chevalier of the Legion of Honor, *à titre militaire*, with a silver plate in his head that lessened his resistance to liquor, as he frequently reminded Madame when she bawled him out for drinking too much. "One little glass, and you see how I am!" he would say mournfully. In fact, he and I had usually had six each at the Taverne Soufflet, and he convived with other lodgers as well—notably with an Irishman named O'Hea, who worked in a bank, and a spendthrift Korean, who kept a girl.

At the restaurant, I would drink Côte Rôtie, as I had premeditated, and would have one or two Armagnacs after lunch. After that, I was all business in my trajectory across Paris, pausing only nine or ten times to look at the water in the river, and two or three more to look at girls. At the Crédit, I would be received with scornful solemnity, like a suitor for the hand of a miser's daughter. I was made to sit on a bare wooden bench with other wretches come to claim money from the bank, all feeling more like culprits by the minute. A French bank, by the somber intensity of its addiction to money, establishes an emotional claim on funds in transit. The client feels in the moral position of a wayward mother who has left her babe on a doorstep and later comes back to claim it from the foster parents, who now consider it their own. I would be given a

metal check with a number on it, and just as I had begun to doze
off from the effects of a good lunch, the Côte Rôtie, the brisk walk,
and the poor ventilation, a *huissier* who had played Harpagon in
repertoire at Angers would shake me by the shoulder. I would advance toward a grille behind which another Harpagon, in an alpaca
coat, held the draft, confident that he could riddle my pretensions
to the identity I professed. Sometimes, by the ferocity of his distrust, he made me doubt who I was. I would stand fumbling in the
wrong pocket for my *carte d'identité*, which had a knack of passing
from one part of my apparel to another, like a prestidigitator's coin,
and then for my passport, which on such occasions was equally elu-
sive. The sneer on Harpagon's cuttlefish bone of a face would grow
triumphant, and I expected him to push a button behind his grille
that would summon a squad of detectives. At last, I would find my
fugitive credentials and present them, and he would hand over the
draft. Then he would send me back to the bench, a *huissier* would
present me with another number, and it all had to be done over
again—this time with my Kafka impersonation enacted before another Harpagon, at another grille, who would hand out the sub-
stantive money. Finally, with two hundred times twenty-six francs,
minus a few deductions for official stamps, I would step out onto
the Boulevard des Italiens—a once-a-month Monte Cristo. "Taxi!"
I would cry. There was no need to walk back.

(1959)

The War and After

Letter from Paris,
December 22, 1939

(BY CABLE)

Unless something unexpected happens within the next ten days, 1939 will be remembered in France as the year that began in uncertainty and ended in mild boredom. Many of the same people who three months ago were ready to pop into their cellars like prairie dogs at the first purring of an airplane motor, expecting Paris to be expunged between dark and dawn, are complaining now because the restaurants do not serve beefsteak on Mondays, Tuesdays, and Fridays, and because the season has produced no new plays worth seeing. Persons who in October 1938 predicted that the least opposition to Hitler would mean the end of Western civilization should logically feel an enormous admiration for General Gamelin, who has protected France completely with a loss of human life slightly less than the annual mortality from tuberculosis in New York City. Curiously enough, however, there is a certain disappointment among the less reflective elements of the population; the appetite for disaster in some human beings is so strong that they feel let down when nothing terrible happens. Cartoonists here have developed a number of wartime civilian characters on the order of Caspar Milquetoast. One of them, a petit bourgeois called Bajus, was shown in a recent comic strip listening to a radio address by Hitler. At each howl from the radio set ("I will destroy England before breakfast," "I will show the French what total war means"), little Bajus's hair stood on end, and at the close of the speech he turned to his radio, saying, "Oh, please, Adolf, don't stop; frighten me again."

Thousands of Bajuses feel deprived of the terror which had become the most interesting component of their daily lives. If the people who warned that a Hitler provoked might tear the world apart feel silly, the equally numerous Frenchmen who said that the West couldn't be saved without the aid of Russia feel even sillier, for the floundering of the Russian Army in Finland and the ineffectiveness of the Soviet's vintage-1911 battleships have convinced everybody here that the Russians would have been of no use against Germany. Silliest of all appear the Frenchmen who, like Colonel de La Rocque, insisted that what France needed was a totalitarian government, on the ground that dictatorships are more efficient than democracies because they make up their minds quicker. It is obvious that Hitler hasn't made up his mind for months.

In the absence of major disasters, small annoyances have reassumed peacetime proportions. A few weeks ago, for example, a shortage of lemons happened to coincide with the oyster season, a fact which Parisians found hard to bear, and thus the rigors of war were brought home to the metropolis. Now there is a scarcity of coffee in the grocery shops, although you can still get all you want in hotels and restaurants. Fauchon's great food shop by the Madeleine has a sign over one of its counters reading, "Fresh caviar, no coffee."

The recent speech by M. Reynaud, Minister of Finance, in which he hinted that the war might involve a long period of military inactivity and that it would be won by economy at home, pointed up his role as one of the strong members of the government. It is a sensible policy, but the strain upon French patience will increase as the Germans and Russians gobble neutrals. There will then be the danger that a miracle man will emerge, like General Nivelle in 1916, who will promise to break the Siegfried Line, capture Hitler, and send the boys home in six weeks—the classic etiology of catastrophe.

Nineteen thirty-nine will also be remembered as a bad year for crime and the French novel. There was a definite cause for the first phenomenon: on the first day of war the police here rounded up every criminal fit for military service and got him a good place in the army, not too far from the front. Criminals unfit for military service and aliens with police records were clapped into concentration camps. Then a decree made looting during *alertes* punishable by death. Finally, since people do not stay out late nights, the opportunities for housebreakers have been decreased. The result of all this, according to the police, has been a reduction in the number of crimes committed since the war to only 3 percent of what it was during the corresponding months last year.

The reason 1939 has been a bad year for novels is not so clear. All the novels which were entered for the Prix Goncourt were written before the war began and the winner, Phillippe Hériat's *Les Enfants Gâtés*, is said by reviewers to have deserved the award, but a comparison with, say, 1933, when André Malraux's *La Condition Humaine* won the prize, shows a lamentable falling off. In literature, as in champagnes, there are nonvintage years. *Les Enfants Gâtés* is in part the story of a French girl's exotic romance in America; when she wants to do something typically American, she breakfasts at the Rainbow Room on grapefruit and malted milk, which should give you the idea.

The Military Governor of Paris plans to let people stay in bars and restaurants until two o'clock Christmas morning—the latest closing hour since August. The Governor could not well insist on his usual eleven o'clock shutdown of subways and bus lines because the churches want to hold midnight Mass and the restaurant men said that if Catholics could stay out until all hours of the night without provoking an air raid, there was no reason nonbelievers shouldn't stay out for a little fun. The Catholics then said they would like an hour for refreshment and possible song after Mass, and the Governor finally set the two o'clock closing hour.

For the rest, it has so far been a nearly normal Paris Christmas season, with carillons and life-size mechanical figures in the windows of the Galeries Lafayette, postcard hucksters' stalls along the

Boulevards, and a special Christmas circus at the Médrano, with the three Fratellinis appearing as guest stars. The great clowns are not as limber as they used to be, and they take fewer falls, but they have some good mechanical gags and their marvelous faces. The oldest brother got one of the big laughs of the evening when he made his entrance carrying an ordinary gas mask—which shows how the atmosphere of the city has changed since September. The French like old favorites. They go to see them over and over again to observe how time is treating them, and if a performer appears to be in good health, they are delighted. "*Tiens*," a Parisian will say, "I went to see Mistinguett last night and she is as good as she was in 1936"—when, of course, she was already the oldest soubrette in the world. Mistinguett, as a matter of fact, has just opened in a revue and Cécile Sorel may be expected back from Belgium any minute now.

Letter from Paris, June 1, 1940

(BY WIRELESS)

These have been three strained weeks in Paris. Each Tuesday has brought a shock, and after each disappointment the French have rebounded and gone on more grimly than ever about the business of winning a war which, they say, has just begun. The Dutch surrendered Holland on Tuesday, May 14, freeing a part of the invading German Army for use in Belgium; on Tuesday, May 21, M. Reynaud made his famous "danger" speech, announcing the enemy's advance and the change in the High Command; on Tuesday, May 28, all France learned of the surrender of King Leopold.

The press is already preparing for what may be next Tuesday's blow by predicting that the speech Mussolini is scheduled to make then will announce Italy's entry into the war on Germany's side. It would seem that the editors are purposely appearing more pessimistic than they feel, for at the moment there is still no certainty that Il Duce has made up his mind. If his speech turns out to be anything less than a declaration of war, everybody will feel encouraged. Meanwhile, the army is strengthening itself.

The first reaction to Leopold's desertion was one of indignation; at last, it was clear, the war had developed a traitor of major stature capable, unlike such small fry as Quisling, of absorbing the quantity of ill will which the public had to bestow. Then, as the heroic fight by the betrayed French and British troops in Flanders continued, Paris, for the first time since the outbreak of the war, began to identify itself with an army in battle. The withdrawal of the Anglo-Franco-Belgian Army of the North toward the Channel ports, at first a purely strategic retreat, had been viewed, as was only natural, in a rather discouraged fashion. When the Belgians, constituting about half of the army, stepped aside, leaving their comrades almost surrounded by Germans, and that remnant of an army, instead of quitting, lashed out harder than ever, the public was galvanized.

Five days have passed since Leopold's surrender. The army of Flanders is still fighting, thousands of soldiers have been evacuated to England (despite the boast of the German radio that the Reich's aviators would sink every ship that tried to take men off), and each day of battle eliminates German troops and matériel from the next offensive.

From a military standpoint, the Belgian defection was a blow, for a large army solidly established on the coast between Zeebrugge and Calais would have been a lasting threat to German maneuvers, and a great counteroffensive could have been prepared while the men there held the attention of many German divisions. The battle in its present form, however, may have a greater influence on the result of the war: it is the battle of the breaking of the spell. The quick German invasion, after the long, indolent winter, had a hypnotic effect. People wondered at first whether the armies of the democracies had lost their fighting qualities and whether the enemy might not be just a trifle superhuman after all, but five days of battle by French and British troops against four times their number of Germans, days in which the trapped divisions have pierced enemy lines repeatedly, have restored national pride.

There has even been a minor break in "Hitler luck." For the past two days the Allied troops embarking at Dunkerque have been favored by cloudy skies, which have made accurate bombing of boats more difficult. Parisians who had relatives in the French Army of the North, and who for a few hours Tuesday had resigned themselves to the thought that those men would soon be dead or prisoners, are now in some cases smiling, for a great many "landed safe" messages are coming through from England.

————

Public opinion in the Allied countries, as a matter of fact, reacts miraculously to disaster. The regime of complacency in the first seven inactive months nearly destroyed civilian war spirit, as well as military efficiency, with tales of magnificent northern fortifications and of soaring airplane production and of how a war could be won without losing lives or spending money. The twenty-three days of the German offensive have got the French and English really fighting, as they have not been since 1918.

The Allied governments, realizing that gloomy frankness is a spur, have done a masterly job of anticipating the next German move. The English press proclaims with certainty that when the battle of Flanders is over, the Germans are going to attack England, and the French newspapers, with the same positive note, announce that the Germans will turn toward Paris. The effect is to get people on both sides of the Channel ready for anything that may happen.

There has been no mass evacuation of Paris, but during the last twenty-three days more and more people with children or without any definite reason for staying here have moved out—until things settle down, they say. A good many restaurants and small businesses that struggled along through the winter are closing for lack of patronage and their proprietors are joining the emigration. The blackout at night is complete, and cinemas and cafés close at ten-thirty. A few night clubs in Montmartre and one or two music halls gamely struggle on, finding their main difficulty not so much the early closing hour as the preoccupation of their normal public with other things. Luckily for the spirits of the moody, nights are extremely short, since, under daylight-saving time, twilight lasts until nearly ten.

The heart of the city doesn't appear deserted, and never in history have so many police been in evidence, all of them now carrying rifles for use against parachutists. Except in its very center, however, Paris at present suggests a quiet neighborhood in Washington. Practically all the Belgian refugees have now been moved south from Paris. Their last days here were not so filled with cordiality as the first. Most of them, of course, completely disapproved of the

King's surrender, but Parisians, while trying to be fair, couldn't help thinking of their friends in the Army of the North.

People who have arrived from the provinces lately report that the western and southwestern parts of France are so crowded with Belgians and northerners that it's hard to find a bed in towns formerly known only to commercial travelers. If Italy enters the war, there will be another great migration into the southwest from the southeast. "Up here," Parisians who remain reassure each other, with winks, "there is plenty of room. Perhaps we will run the Grand Prix this year after all—in the Métro."

The intervention of Italy, if it comes, will be embarrassing but not fatal. The Italian air force may raise hob with the south of France, because the French will be able to spare few planes from the northern front, but the Duce's army is not particularly feared and his fleet is clearly outmatched by what the Allies have in the Mediterranean. Even now, few Parisians are earnestly angry at Italy. The average Frenchman's conception of the average Italian may not be flattering to Fascist dignity, but it is not unfriendly, either. "I always think of an Italian," the night porter in a hotel here recently told a guest, "as a man who eats a lot of tomatoes and plays a mandolin."

The bravest Frenchmen are sometimes dismayed, though, when they think of Paris being bombed from the air, because, they say, there is no city in Germany worthy of reprisal. "Berlin, viewed from an architectural and historical standpoint, is a rolling dirtiness," a Parisian remarked the other day. The feeling about Italian cities is different. Nobody here wants to think of bombing Florence or Rome, whose lovely aspects French artists have studied for centuries.

The danger of Italy is less in the thoughts of people here than the shortage of Allied planes. If the Allies had a few thousand more on hand right now, they could win the war this summer, say the

French, or if they were assured that several thousand planes would be delivered to them over the period of the next few months, they could hang on and win later. This war is beginning to recall the old nursery lines about the kingdom that was lost because of the lack of a horseshoe nail. Only this isn't a nursery kingdom.

Westbound Tanker

(MARCH 21, 1942)

A tanker is a kind of ship that inspires small affection. It is an oilcan with a Diesel motor to push it through the water, and it looks painfully functional. Its silhouette suggests a monster submarine with two conning towers. A destroyer's clipper-ship ancestry is patent in the lines of its hull, but neither tankers nor submarines betray any origin. They seem to have been improvised simultaneously by some rudely practical person and then put in the water to fight each other. A tanker scores a point when it completes a voyage. When the oil reservoirs of the Allied bases are full, the tankers are beating the submarines. They have been doing that since the beginning of this war, but few people think of a tanker as a fighting ship. When a tanker gets sunk you read about it in the paper, but when it docks safely nobody hangs any flags in the streets.

The *Regnbue*, on which I came home from England to the United States, is a Norwegian tanker. It is not remarkable in any way. Norway had a tanker fleet second only to that of the United States, and Norwegian tankers in 1941 carried 50 percent of the oil that had gone to Britain since the war began. The *Regnbue*—the name means "Rainbow," as you may have surmised—was built at Gothenburg, Sweden, in 1930. She displaces nine thousand tons, a good, middling tanker size, and can do eleven knots loaded, a fair, medium speed. Her lead-gray hull was streaked with rust, and her masts and funnel and deckhouses showed only a trace of paint the first time I saw her. A grimy Norwegian flag, ragged at the edges, flapped from her mizzenmast, and there was a cowled four-inch gun on a platform raised above her poop. I was joining her as a passenger, but I didn't learn her name until I got close enough to read it on a small sign on the side of her bridge. This was because the Norwegian Trade Mission in London, through which I had booked my passage, believes in secrecy about ship movements. Since the German invasion of Norway, the Norwegian Government-in-exile has chartered most of the Norwegian ships in the world to the British Ministry of War Transport. The ships still fly Norway's flag, have predominantly Norwegian crews, and are, for the duration, in the custody of the Trade Mission.

An official at the Trade Mission, knowing I was ready to leave on short notice, had called me up at my hotel in London one Saturday morning and said that if I didn't mind sailing from London instead of a west-coast port, they had a ship for me. I said I didn't mind, although this would add several days to the voyage. Next morning I took a taxi to the Mission offices on Leadenhall Street and there handed over my passage money. The man who had telephoned me said that the ship was bound for New York in water ballast to take on cargo there. He gave me a sealed envelope addressed to one Captain W. Petersen and a slip of paper bearing written instructions for getting to the ship. I was to take a certain train at Fenchurch Street Station early Monday morning and travel to a small station near the Essex shore, a ride of an hour and a half. A taximan would meet me at the station and drive me to a pier, where I would find a boatman named Mace. Mace would put me aboard Captain Petersen's ship.

Shortly after eleven o'clock on Monday, December 1, I found myself in Mace's launch, moving through the water of the Thames Estuary toward the tanker, which lay about a mile offshore. The only other passenger in the launch was a Norwegian port engineer who was going out to examine the ship's motors. "Look at that paintwork!" the engineer said as we neared the *Regnbue*. "Tankers make such quick turn-arounds the crews have no chance to paint. Discharge in twenty-four hours or less, take bunker and water, and out to sea again. Oil docks are always in some place like *this*, too— miles from the center of the city. The men don't get a chance to see the town. I know. I was in tankers in the last war." Before he had time to tell me more about them, we were under the rope ladder leading to the *Regnbue*'s main deck. It was an extremely uninviting ladder, but the engineer went up it as if it were an escalator. A seaman dropped a line to Mace, who made a loop through the handles of my suitcase and portable typewriter, which then rose through the air like Little Eva going to heaven. I went up the ladder in my turn with neither grace nor relish. My style must have amused one of the several men who were leaning over the rail, because he looked down at me, then turned to the man next to him and said, "Commando."

This fellow, who was wearing a white jacket, was obviously a steward. He was of medium size but had long arms, so the jacket sleeves ended midway between elbow and wrist, baring the tattooing on his wide forearms. On the right arm he had a sailor and his lass above the legend, in English, "True Love." The design on the left arm was a full-rigged ship with the inscription "Hilse fra Yokohama," which means "Greetings from Yokohama." His head was large and bald except for two tufts of red hair at the temples, looking like a circus clown's wig. He had a bulging forehead and a flat face with small eyes, a turned-up nose, and a wide mouth. As soon as I got my breath, I said, "Passenger," and he took me in charge with a professional steward's manner, which, I afterward learned, he had acquired while working for a fleet of bauxite freighters that often carried tourists. The bauxite freighters had operated out of a port the steward called Noolians, and most of the tourists had been vacationing schoolteachers from the Middle West. Fearing emotional involvement with a schoolteacher, he had switched to tankers. "Tankers is safe," he said. "No schoolteachers." His name was Harry Larsen.

The steward led me along the rust-stained steel deck to the ship's forward deckhouse. The main deck of a tanker is simply the steel carapace over the tanks. In rough weather the seas break over this deck. The human activities of the ship are concentrated in two deckhouses, fore and aft. The forward one is like a four-story house rising from the main deck and contains the bridge and the captain's and deck officers' quarters. A long catwalk ten feet above the main deck serves as the highroad between the deckhouses, and even on the catwalk you are likely to get doused when there is a sea running. The engine room and the galley, the ship's one funnel, the cannon, the refrigerator, the crew's quarters, and the cat's sandbox are all jammed in and around the stern deckhouse. The steward showed me to my cabin, which was the one called the owner's, although the owner had never used it. It was next to the captain's office. His bedroom was on the other side of the office, and we were to share a bathroom. It was a fairly good cabin, with two portholes, a bed, a divan, and a desk. The steward said that the captain was still ashore, but I should make myself at home.

I went out on deck to look around and was pleased to see one of the British Navy's barrage-balloon boats alongside. A balloon boat is a lighter with a half-dozen or so bright, silvery balloons floating above it, each attached to a slender wire. The *Regnbue* dropped a wire cable aboard the lighter, and a couple of naval ratings rove the end of a balloon cable to ours. They let go the cable and the balloon rose above our foremast, securely attached, as we thought, to the *Regnbue*. It wasn't, though. It blew away two nights later, but it was a pretty embellishment as long as we had it. While I was watching the transfer, a little man in a blue uniform came over and stood next to me. I asked him when he thought we would get under way. He said that he was the pilot and was going to take the ship a short distance farther down the river that afternoon. The captain was coming aboard after we got down river. The pilot was a black-haired, red-faced Londoner with a habit of laughing nervously after practically everything he said. "Good thing about a tanker in water ballast," he said. "She's just a box of air, what? Tanks half full of sea water, all the rest air—wants a long time to sink if she's torpedoed. Much as forty minutes, perhaps, eh?" He laughed. I said that I thought this was very nice, and he said that now you take a loaded tanker, it was just the opposite—the very worst sort of ship to be torpedoed aboard. "Flaming oil all about. Rather depressing, what?" he said. I agreed.

The steward came along and told us that dinner was on the table in the saloon, so the pilot and I followed him down a flight of stairs into a large, rectangular room with paneled walls and a dark green carpet. The most impressive feature of the saloon was a portrait, nearly life-size, of an old gentleman with a face the color of a Killarney rose and a bifurcated beard that looked like two blobs of whipped cream. The artist had used plenty of paint of the best quality. I could imagine a jury of boatswains giving the picture grand prize at a *salon*. "The founder of the line that owned this ship," the pilot said.

"Capitalist!" the steward said, simply and with distaste.

"Rum thing on Norwegian ships," the pilot said, "the captain doesn't eat with the other officers. As a passenger you'll mess down here in the saloon with the captain, and there'll be just the two of you at every meal. But in every other respect they're more democratic than our ships. Odd, what?"

The pilot had been at Dunkirk, he told me a bit later on. "I was in command of seven motorboats," he said, with his laugh, "transferring troops from the beach to destroyers. I lost the boats one by one. A motorboat doesn't take much smashing, does it? When the last one foundered, my two ratings and I swam to a destroyer's boat. What I shan't forget," he said, after a pause, "is the motorbike races on Dunkirk beach. Chaps waiting to be taken off, you know. Never saw better sport. There were soldiers making book on the races. Couldn't leave the beach until all bets were settled or they'd be known as welshers."

The dinner of pea soup, corned beef, and baked beans, ending with a double-size can of California peaches for the pilot and me, was big by London standards. The portions were on a scale I had almost forgotten, and there was a lot of butter. The steward said the food had been loaded at Corpus Christi, Texas, in October. "We don't take any food in England," he said. "I hope we get to New York for Christmas. I got nothing to make Christmas at sea—no newts, no frewts, no yin for drinking."

"We ought to make it," I said, with the confidence of inexperience.

"It depends what kind commodore we get," the steward said. "If we get slow commodore, old man retire from Navy fifty year and only come back for the war, we lucky to get New York for New Year's. I don't care much for New York anyhow," he added loftily. "Too much noise, too many Norweeyans in Brooklyn, argue, argue, argue! I like better Camden, New Yersey, go with the Polish girls."

The ship moved slowly down the estuary during the afternoon. We dropped anchor again before dark at a point where the Thames had definitely ceased to seem like a river and where half a dozen other ships already rode at anchor. Our men looked at them curiously, as one surveys the other occupants of the lounge car at the beginning of a long railroad journey. There were a couple of British tankers with fancy Spanish names, a gray, medium-size Dutch freighter, and a big, boxlike Elder Dempster boat that had once been in the West African service. I have seen the Dutch freighter's name in a newspaper since. She had shot down a German plane. There was also a stubby, soot-black Norwegian steamer of not more than three thousand tons, which had a single funnel so narrow and long that it reminded me of an American riverboat. The third officer, a husky blond chap who wore an orange turtleneck sweater, pointed to the stubby ship and said to me, "That is the slowest ship in the world. Once she made one trip from Cape Town in four convooeys. They started two weeks apart, and she kept on losing one convooey and getting into the next. She was going full speed the whole time." All the ships were, like ourselves, light and bound for America to get a cargo.

The pilot came down from the bridge and joined me when the ship was at anchor. I asked him when he thought we should get to New York, and he said that with luck we ought to make it in about twenty days. It depended a lot on what connections we made at the assembly ports, he said. The *Regnbue* was going all the way around Scotland to get to the west coast of Britain. We would spend the first few days of our voyage in a small convoy sailing up the east coast of England to our first assembly port. From there, we would go to the west coast in a larger convoy, but we might have to wait a couple of days while this larger convoy was being assembled. Then we would proceed to the second assembly port and go through the same business there. We might be just in time to leave with a transatlantic convoy or we might have to wait a week. There was no way of telling. "The most ticklish bit in the trip begins about twelve hours above here," the pilot added consolingly. "If we get off tomorrow morning, you'll be in it by night."

Captain Petersen came aboard shortly before nightfall. He was a small, stoop-shouldered man. His brown shoregoing suit was carefully pressed. He had a long, curved nose and lank, sandy hair, and he spoke English slowly but accurately, using American idioms. He had lived in Philadelphia, where he worked in an oil refinery, during part of the last war, he told me, and then had moved to Hoboken, where he had roomed in the house of an Irish policeman. After the war he had gone back to Norway to enter navigation school with the money he had earned in America. All the reminiscences of the United States that he politely introduced into our conversation dated from before 1919. He gave detailed accounts of several Chaplin comedies, like *The Count* and *The Cure*, which he had seen then. We went down to supper with the pilot, and Captain Petersen, pointing to the whiskered portrait, said to me, "That is a man who once owned eighty sailing ships. Even when he was ninety-two he combed his beard for one hour every morning. I remember seeing him in my home town when I was a boy. The company owns only a couple of ships now. It belongs to an old lady, who lives in my town also."

His town is a sleepy little city in southern Norway which in the nineteenth century was a great port for sailing ships. The *Regnbue*, the captain explained to me, is emphatically a ship from his town. Not only is she owned there—although, as he explained, owners captive in Norway had no control over their ships for the duration of the war—but skipper, chief officer, and second officer all came from there and had known each other as schoolboys. Both the captain and the chief officer, a man named Gjertsen, had even been married aboard the *Regnbue*. Their brides had joined them on the ship at Antwerp and Constanta, Rumania, respectively. Petersen had been second officer and Gjertsen third officer then, and they had honeymooned in turn in the captain's suite. The wives were at home now. "The second and third officers have wives in Norway, too," he said, "and so has the chief engineer. I was lucky enough to have a vacation in December 1939, so I saw my wife and boy only a little while before the Germans came."

Petersen told me that when the Germans invaded Norway the Norwegian Government had commandeered Norwegian ships all over the world, ordering those at sea to put into neutral or Allied ports. A radio message had been sufficient to accomplish this. Only a small part of the merchant marine had been caught at home. Now the exiled government's income from ship hire not only supported it but provided a surplus, which is to be used for the nation's reconstruction after the Germans are driven out. He didn't show any doubt that they would be driven out, nor did anyone I talked to on the *Regnbue*. The boatswain, a weathered gnome of a man, once said to me, "I couldn't sleep at night if I didn't believe on it." The owners of the ships were nearly all caught in the invasion. The Government had promised that after the war they would receive compensation for the use of their ships, provided they paid allotments to the sailors' families in the meanwhile. So the captive families had been receiving small amounts of money, but even with money there isn't much food.

There was a door at each side of the saloon. One led to the pantry and steward's cabin, the other to the deck officers' quarters. The officers had their mess aft, in the other deckhouse. After supper on a normal evening aboard the *Regnbue*, I was to learn, the captain and the steward visited the deck officers. Then, at about eight o'clock, everybody visited the steward and drank coffee, made in a big electric percolator, which the steward brought in from the pantry. I suppose a torpedo would have disrupted this routine, but nothing less could have. This evening marked my initiation into the ship's social life. Since we were still in port, it was a *soirée de gala*; none of the officers had to stand watch, and it was all right to use the short-wave radio in Gjertsen's cabin. Such sets are sealed at sea because they cause a radiation which can betray a ship's position. For news of the outside world you depend on what the wireless operator picks up on long-wave.

Around seven o'clock the captain, the pilot, the steward, and I marched into Gjertsen's cabin, where the other officers already were gathered. Gjertsen, a tall, dark man who looked something like Lincoln, was stretched out on his berth halfway between floor and ceiling. His wedding picture hung just above the berth. Gjertsen had not been home since 1937. Haraldsen, the second officer, who was small and jolly, turned the dials of the radio, with occasional professional counsel from Grung, the wireless operator, a serious young fellow whom the others considered something of a dandy. He came from Bergen, which is almost a big city. Bull, the third officer, the big fellow in the orange sweater, sat on the divan looking at a picture of the backsides of thirty-two bathing girls in *Life*. He didn't turn the page all evening. Nilsen, the gunner, sat on the floor and said nothing. He hardly ever said anything to anybody. The captain explained to me later that it was because Nilsen was a whaler. Whalers talk themselves out on their first voyage, the captain said. They exhaust all possible topics of conversation, then fall silent for life. "It isn't like a lighthouse-keeper," Petersen said. "He hasn't had a chance to talk in months, so he is bursting with it. But a whaling man is talked out." Gjertsen hated the radio, but he insisted on keeping the set in his cabin because he liked company. No matter what kind of music Haraldsen got, Gjertsen said it was rotten and Haraldsen should turn to something else. Whenever they got a news program he just fell asleep. He said there was enough trouble on the ocean without dialing for it. They were all low that evening because of a broadcast by the Norwegian radio of the news that the Germans were planning to cut off the money for their families. "I wonder how long people in the old country will be able to keep from starving," Haraldsen said helplessly. "Why don't the British start the invasion?" Grung demanded, looking sternly at the English pilot. "All the fellows who escape from Norway say there are only a few thousand Germans there."

"Full moon tomorrow night," the pilot said pleasantly, by way of changing the subject.

"Yes, fine moon for dive bombers," the radioman said resentfully. "We'll be right in the middle of E-boat Alley then."

"Maybe there'll be fog," the pilot suggested helpfully. "Fog is no good for bombers."

"Fog is fine for E-boats," Grung said. "Can't see them coming." Grung, I was to learn, liked to have something to complain about; actually, he worried little about enemy action. Danger at sea is like having a jumpy appendix: men can live with it for years, knowing in an academic way that it may cause trouble, but forgetting about it most of the time. Haraldsen said that the *Regnbue* had always been a lucky ship—fourteen crossings since the war began and never a conning tower sighted. Everybody banged on wood. "The *Meddelfjord* always was a lucky ship, too, before the last time," Grung said, insisting on his right to grumble. "I lost a good pal on her, the second engineer. Burned to death in the sea. The oil was blazing on top of the water, and the fellows had to swim in it. That was a nice joke!"

"We didn't miss that by much ourselves," the captain said to me. "We were together with the *Meddelfjord* at Newcastle, both bound for London. We stayed to discharge some of our oil. The *Meddelfjord* and eight other ships went on. Three of them were sunk by planes and motor torpedo boats."

Bull put down his magazine and said in a matter-of-fact tone, "I like to catch a Yerman. Bile him in ile."

Unexpectedly, Nilsen, the silent, spoke up. "I have no respect for them," he said.

Before coming aboard I had calculated roughly that the chances are at least ninety to one against being torpedoed on any one crossing. Incidentally, the American marine-insurance companies then charged a premium of 1 percent to insure tanker cargo, which indicated that they thought the odds are considerably longer than a hundred to one. It is not a great risk to take, once. The men in the *Regnbue* lived continually with this risk, which is quite a different thing. They seldom talked of danger except when they were angry about something else, like no shore leave or the British failure to invade the Continent.

Bull started turning the dials of the radio set again and got a program of jazz music from Stockholm. A woman was singing something that sounded like "Klop, klop, klop! Sving, sving, sving!" Bull and Haraldsen laughed so hard they could barely stand it. "I can't explain it to you," Haraldsen said to me, "but to a Norwegian the Swedish language sounds always very funny." We had three or four cups of strong coffee apiece in the pantry and then went to our cabins. Norwegians use coffee as a sedative.

Long before I got up next morning I could hear the anchor chain coming in, and when I got out on deck we were moving along in a column of eight ships. The strings of signal flags looked like holiday bunting, and each ship had its own bright new balloon. Half a dozen sloops and corvettes in pink-and-green camouflage milled around our column. The convoy was probably not moving better than eight knots, so the corvettes looked lightning fast. Machine guns were being tested on all the ships, and the intermittent bursts of gunfire added to the gaiety. The tracer bullets from the machine guns are fun to watch as they skitter over the water; they seem a superior kind of flying fish, with electric light and central heating. We had a pair of Hotchkisses mounted, one on each side of the bridge. If we were attacked they would be manned by the two seamen on lookout. We also had two British machine gunners, who manned a small fort on the poop deck, where they had a couple of Lewis guns. There was not enough open space around for our gun crew to try out our four-inch gun, but an antiaircraft battery on shore was practicing. Its guns went off at one-minute intervals, and the shells made a straight line of white smoke puffs across the sky, like pearls on a string. A couple of mine sweepers dragging magnetized floats went ahead of us, in case the Luftwaffe had planted any magnetics during the night.

We dropped the pilot at noon. Life on the ship picked up its sea rhythm. The crew consisted of the usual three watches, each of which was on duty four hours and then rested eight. Haraldsen, the second officer, was on the bridge from twelve to four, Gjertsen, the chief, from four to eight, and Bull, the third officer, from eight to twelve, when Haraldsen relieved him. I had a chance to get to know some of the sailors, because they came forward to stand their watches on the bridge. However, the engineer officers and the rest of the crew, down at the other end of the ship, remained relative strangers.

When the men came forward they wore life jackets. The officers, when they went up to the bridge, carried their life jackets with them and tied them to a stanchion. I had bought a kapok-lined reefer from Gieves, the naval outfitter in Piccadilly, a swank garment that purported to double as an overcoat and life jacket. It was supposed to close with a zipper, and each clash with the zipper presented a completely new tactical problem. The zipper changed its defensive arrangements to meet my attacks; I could never throw it twice with the same hold. Sometimes I could close it in a couple of minutes, but on other occasions it beat me. I was sure that if a torpedo ever struck us, I would go down in a death grapple with my zipper. I had an ordinary life jacket in my cabin, of course, but I had paid good money for the reefer. I was also given a huge, one-piece rubber suit, so stiff that it stood up in a corner of my cabin like a suit of armor. It was a Norwegian invention, Captain Petersen said, and everybody on the ship had one. The idea was to climb into its legs and tie yourself into the rest of it, so only your face showed. The air in the folds of the suit would both hold you up and insulate you from the cold of the water. This consoled me until Grung, the radioman, told me that a crew had once demonstrated the invention for the Norwegian Minister of Shipping and that while all of them had floated for hours, a couple of fellows who went in head first had floated upside down. Grung was a man of few enthusiasms. For example, we had a large escort for such a small convoy, and this made him unhappy. "There must be trouble expected or there wouldn't be so many," he said.

Late in the afternoon we reached the bad spot about which the pilot had told me. This is a lane along the East Anglian coast that London newspapers have named E-boat Alley. The commodore of the convoy was in the ship ahead of us, a British tanker. Commodores are usually commanders in His Majesty's Navy; they carry a pair of aides and a squad of signalmen with them and communicate their orders by flag signal or flash lamp. This commodore would go with us only as far as the first assembly port; he was an east-coast specialist.

I was in the saloon just before suppertime, reading Hakluyt's

Principall Navigations, Voiages and Discoveries of the English Nation,
when I heard a noise that sounded exactly like a very emphatic blast
during the excavation of a building site. The ship quivered, as if she
had taken a big sea. Larsen, the steward, was the only other man
around; he was laying out a few plates of salami and ham and herring salad as table decorations. I took it for granted that the noise
was a depth charge and said "My, my!" to show how calm I was.
Larsen winked and said, "Mak raddy der bahding suit!" Both of us,
I imagine, wanted to run out on deck and see what had happened,
but since we had only recently met, we tried to impress each other.
Captain Petersen came down to supper ten minutes later and said
that a mine had gone off a hundred feet from the commodore's ship
and almost knocked her out of the water. "Gjertsen was on the
bridge and saw it," he said. "He says it threw a column of water
higher than the ship's masts. She was hidden completely. Then,
when the water settled, Gjertsen could see the ship was still there,
but she had only a little way on. Then she hoisted two red lights to
signal she was out of control. The blast must have damaged her
rudder. So she has to go back to port."

"Goodbye, Commodore," Larsen said unfeelingly.

"It must have been one of those acoustic mines," the captain
said, "but it didn't work well. It went off too soon." There was a
certain wonder in his tone, as if he felt that the Germans must be
overrated.

The explosion of the mine was the only evidence of enemy action we were to encounter during the whole trip.

Larsen, the steward, had it figured out that in order to get to
New York by Christmas we would have to leave the west coast of
England by December 7. "We get off with lucky seven and in seventeen days we come to New York," he said. "Get there Christmas
Eve, the immigration officers ain't working, and we stay on the ship
until December 26." This was a sample of what I got to know as
Scandinavian optimism. We didn't reach even the first of our two
assembly ports until December 5, so it looked certain that we would
spend Christmas at sea. We were seventy-two hours going up the
east coast from London, anchoring each night because of heavy fog.

The second time we anchored, Larsen began getting out and repairing the green-and-red paper Christmas decorations that formed part of the tanker's stores. He went about his work during the day muttering a sad little refrain that I sometimes caught myself repeating: "No newts, no frewts, no yin for drinking."

The crew looked forward to spending its shore leave in Brooklyn, even if we got to New York after Christmas. To a Norwegian the finest part of the United States is Brooklyn. For the duration of the war it is the Norwegian fatherland. When a Norwegian seaman meets an American, he usually begins the conversation with, "I got a cousin in Brooklyn." Haraldsen, the second officer, had two brothers there. Larsen pretended to be supercilious about Brooklyn, but he fooled nobody on the *Regnbue*. The *Regnbue* had been in the Thames for only a couple of days, and few of her men had gone into London. The ship had been anchored at such an awkward distance from the city that it had hardly seemed worth the journey. Some men had got drunk at a hotel not far from the oil dock. Others had not even set foot on land. Corpus Christi, Texas, the ship's last American port of call, had not been exactly a Brooklyn, either.

Olsen the carpenter, Grung the radioman, and I were visiting the steward and drinking coffee on one of the foggy nights, and Olsen said, "The last time I was in Brooklyn I didn't take my shoes off for three weeks. My feet was so swollen I had to cut my shoes off." Olsen was a man who liked to startle people. "It must have been good liquor you were drinking," I said. This was just the kind of opening Olsen wanted. He put his head on one side and looked at me fixedly for a full half-minute, as if I were a dangerous lunatic. "Good liquor!" he finally said, contemptuously. "A man is a fool to drink good liquor. I never drink liquor that tastes good." He stared at me again, as if expecting me to leap at his throat, and then said, "Because why? I get drinking it too fast. Then I get drunk too quick. The best thing is whisky that tastes bad. Then you stop between drinks about ten minutes, until you need another one. Then you can keep on drinking for a month." The carpenter was a solid, rectangular fellow of fifty, with blue eyes set wide apart in a boiled-ham face. He could with equal competence make a davit out of iron pipe or reseat a rattan chair. He was the ship's delegate of the Norwegian Seamen's Union, to which all the men belonged.

The steward lay in his berth at the summit of a stack of drawers. There was no other place for him, because the rest of us occupied all the chairs. He said, "In Brooklyn I live in Hotel St. Yorge. Yentlemen! I don't go on Court Street in Eyetalian saloons. I yust buy good old bottle aquavit and go to my room and drink like yentleman. Go to Norweeyan church Sunday and put five dollars in collection. Brooklyn women too smart. Better leave 'em alone."

The radioman said that once he and some shipmates had been in a taxi-dance hall near Borough Hall and had asked a couple of hostesses to sit down and have a drink. The hostesses had charged them four dollars apiece for their time. "You got more for your money in Constanta," he said. Constanta, in Rumania, used to be a great port for Norwegian tankers before the war. "We had a man on one ship going down to Constanta," the carpenter said, "and he wouldn't believe all we told him about it. He said he had been in every other port in the world, and he wouldn't lose his head in Constanta. So he went ashore one night, and two days later we seen a man walking down on the dock with nothing on but his socks, and it was him. Always lots of fun in Constanta."

The steward found this so amusing that he reared up on the back of his neck and kicked the ceiling. He had been a leading light of the gymnastic society in a small town in southern Norway, and he liked to use the edge of his berth as a gymnastic bar. He spent a good deal of time composing to English and American girls on a portable typewriter he had in his cabin, and when he was at a loss for an English phrase he would get up, face his berth, and jump high in the air, twisting in time to land in a sitting position. Usually three or four jumps would bring him the phrase he wanted, and he would return to his typewriter. The steward called his cabin Larsen's Club, and the atmosphere was congenially ribald except when Captain Petersen was there. The skipper came in every night for his three cups of coffee. Captain Petersen was a friendly man who did not stand on formality, but he was a Methodist and a teetotaler. He didn't try to deter anybody else from drinking or talking randy, but Larsen seldom kicked the ceiling when the skipper was around. All the men were cut off from their home country and lonely, and the captain was the loneliest of all. Once he said to me, "It isn't so bad for a man who drinks and—" He stopped suddenly, as if just understanding what he had said, and went off to his cabin looking miserable.

At meals with Captain Petersen I had plenty of time for eating, because there was not much conversation. Once he said, as he began on his first plate of cabbage soup, "I have an uncle in New York who has been fifty-two years with the Methodist Book Concern." Twenty minutes later, having finished his second helping of farina pudding, he said, "He came over in a windjammer." On another occasion he said, "We had a Chinaman on the ship once. When we came to Shanghai he couldn't talk to the other Chinamen." After an interlude during which he ate three plates of lobscouse, a stew made of leftover meats and vegetables, he explained, "He came from another part of China." And once, taking a long look at the shipowner's portrait, he said, "I went to see an art gallery near Bordeaux." After eating a large quantity of dried codfish cooked with raisins, cabbage, and onions, he added, "Some of the frames were that wide," indicating with his hands how impressively wide they were. Once, in an effort to make talk, I asked him, "How would you say, 'Please pass me the butter, Mr. Petersen,' in Norwegian?" He said, "We don't use 'please' or 'mister.' It sounds too polite. And you never have to say 'pass me' something in a Norwegian house, because the people *force* food on you, so if you said 'pass' they would think they forgot something and their feelings would be hurt. The word for butter is *smor*."

It was morning when we reached our first assembly port, and the captain went ashore to see the naval authorities. He returned with word that we would sail next evening. In the afternoon a boat came out from shore and a naval officer climbed aboard to tell the captain that our destination had been changed from New York to Port Arthur, Texas. Luckily, the *Regnbue* had enough fuel for the longer journey or we would have lost more time taking bunker. The captain told me of the change and said he was sorry I would be carried so far from New York, but things like that happened all the time. The changes weren't made for strategic reasons, because no one could tell three weeks or a month in advance how the U-boats would be distributed off the American coast. It was just that there probably weren't enough "dirty" tankers to handle all the heavy oils from the Gulf of Mexico. A "clean" tanker handles only gasoline. A "dirty" tanker has tanks equipped with heating coils to keep heavy oils liquid. The *Regnbue*, the captain said with pride, was a first-class dirty tanker.

News of the change of destination quickly got about among the crew. There isn't much point in secrecy aboard a ship if none of the men are allowed to go ashore. Port Arthur is a dismal place compared to Brooklyn, and the seamen were disappointed. There are no Norwegians in Port Arthur, and no taxi-dance halls. Mikkelsen, the electrician, said that you couldn't even buy whisky in a saloon in Port Arthur; you had to buy a bottle at a package store and take it into a soft-drink joint to get a setup. Perhaps the most disappointed men on the ship were the British machine gunners, Ramsay and Robinson. They had been out to India and Australia with other ships but never to America. "Where is Texas?" Robinson asked me. "Will I be able to get up to New York for a weekend?" Ramsay, who was a lance bombardier, laughed derisively. "You haven't got money enough to get that far," he said. "It's all of two hundred miles." Robinson earned three shillings and three-pence a day, of which the War Office sent one and three to his mother in Salford, slap up against Manchester. Ramsay drew nine-pence more for his single chevron, and he was always boasting to Robinson about his opulence.

The Britishers belonged to the Maritime Anti-Aircraft Regiment, generally called the Sea Soldiers at home. The Sea Soldiers ride on merchant ships in the manner of old-time American stage-coach guards. They have had more training with automatic arms than the seamen who man machine guns and are supposed to steady the seamen in a fight. Robinson and Ramsay had been partners on other ships and had been in a long-running battle with some Axis submarines off the west coast of Africa just before they joined the *Regnbue*. Convoys were nearly always attacked off the African coast, they said. There was a belief among seamen that the Germans had a submarine base at Dakar, no matter what Pétain said. Robinson was a quiet lad who said, "A odn't been sottisfied i' infantry, so thought A'd try summat else, and this was fair champion—nowt to do." Ramsay was a Glaswegian, a hyperenergetic type who was always shadow-boxing on deck and shouting "Pooh!" or "Cool!" for no apparent reason. He used to brag about how many German planes he had shot down, although it is hard to apportion credit for bringing down a plane when a whole convoy is blazing away at it. One day he said that if we captured a German submarine—not a likely prospect—he would personally kill all the prisoners. Gjertsen, the chief officer, said to him seriously, "You can't kill anybody on this ship without the captain say so." This made Ramsay sulk. There were three other Britishers on the ship—a man in the engine room, a seaman, and a messboy. English seamen like to get on Norwegian ships when there is an opportunity, because the pay is better than the British scale. Nearly all seafaring Norwegians speak English, so there is no trouble about understanding orders. The only fellows on the *Regnbue* who knew no English were five youths who recently, and separately, had escaped from Norway by crossing the North Sea in small boats. They were all studying a textbook on Basic English. They had received word that after they had escaped their parents had been put in prison. News from Norway reaches England quite regularly by boat. There are even motorboats that smuggle mail between the two coasts.

Most of the men grew thoughtful when we cleared the first assembly port. We were within three hundred miles of Norway now, and could not help thinking about it. Otherwise the tension, which had never been great, seemed to have completely vanished. There was no further danger from motor torpedo boats and not much from dive bombers. The big Focke-Wulf Kuriers and the submarine packs generally operated farther to the west, where the large convoys form, so we felt relatively safe. We had parted company with a couple of ships at the assembly port and picked up a couple of others. What bothered me was the weather. Captain Petersen advised me to chew on dry crackers and drink no water. The steward said, "Don't use nothing yuicy. Yust dry stuff."

The prescription of "a brisk walk around the deck," classic on passenger liners, is not much good on a tanker, because deck space is so limited. You can take a few steps on the bridge or make a circuit of the forward deckhouse, picking your way among ropes, slings, boats, and the entrances to two companionways. If you go aft you have a slightly longer promenade around the after deckhouse, although you have to crawl under the gun platform once on each lap to complete the circuit. The main deck, between the two deckhouses and forward of the bridge, is low and lashed by spray. There is a catwalk, an elevated pathway between the two deckhouses, but men with work to do are constantly passing back and forth on it, so there is no room for a *flâneur*.

At the beginning of the voyage I had decided to let my beard grow until I got home again. The boatswain, who came from a port in the far north of Norway, counseled me to shave my beard, on the ground that it would bring fine weather and then the ship wouldn't rock. The boatswain was a small man who looked as dry and tough as jerked meat. He had ice-blue eyes and a long, drooping, ginger-colored mustache, and he repeated his joke about the beard every morning. Then, later in the day, he would manage to ask me the time and say, "I had two gold watches but they're on the bottom now." His last ship had been bombed and sunk at her dock in Liverpool, and he had lost all his gear on board. Fortunately, he had been spending the night on shore with a respectable lady friend— the widow of an old shipmate, he was always careful to explain when he told the story. He had a French wife in Caen, but he had not seen her in seven years, because big ships seldom went there. I once tried to talk French with him, but he said with a sigh, "*Ya goobliay toute.*" The boatswain was aware that he said the same things every day, but he said them to be friendly. After all, nobody can think of something new to say when he sees the same shipmates daily for weeks on end. The quip about the beard contented the boatswain, and he laughed every time he said it. His laugh sounded like cakes of ice knocking together.

On December 7 we were in a gale. I turned in early and put my watch and fountain pen in the desk drawer, where they rattled like dice in a nervous crapshooter's hand. There is a difference of thirteen and a half hours between the time in Hawaii and Great Britain, and I was asleep before Grung, the radioman, picked up the first bulletin about the attack on Pearl Harbor. I heard the news when I went up on the bridge next morning. Bull, the third officer, pumped my hand and said, "We both allies now!" It felt more natural to be a belligerent on a belligerent ship than that anomalous creature, a neutral among belligerent friends. I tried to visualize New York. People at home must be frightfully angry, I imagined. I kept telling the Norwegians, "Americans aren't like the English. They get mad much quicker, and they stay mad." (I was to feel pretty silly about that after I got back to New York.) We all wondered why the fleet had been in Pearl Harbor and how the Japs had got there. The BBC bulletins received by the radioman were skimpy. We were actually near the base of the British Home Fleet, but suddenly we felt far from the war. The ship had sailed with two neutrals aboard, and now it had none. The other neutral had been an ordinary seaman named Sandor, who was a Rumanian. Great Britain had declared war on Rumania a few days after we cleared, so Sandor had become an enemy alien. He took the news calmly. "Can't send me back now," he said. He had stowed away on the *Regnbue* at Constanta in the early summer of 1939 and had stayed with her ever since. He had learned Norwegian and English on the ship.

We were glad to get to our second assembly port, where we were permitted to turn on the short-wave radio in the chief officer's cabin. We sat around it for hours, listening to the BBC, the Norwegian broadcasts from London and Boston, and even Radio Paris, the Quisling station in Oslo, and Lord Hawhaw. We got some of our best laughs from an Italian English-language announcer who used to sink Allied shipping in astronomical quantities twice a day. It was a Norwegian broadcast from Boston, I remember, that told us Lindbergh had endorsed the war and a Free French announcer in London who said Senator Wheeler had done the same thing. The steward was amused. "Next thing, Quisling against Yermans!" he shouted.

As soon as we arrived at the second assembly port, the captain went ashore. When he came back he said that we were starting for America early the next morning. The port was at the head of a deep and narrow bay. The *Regnbue* and nine other ships were to start just before dawn and go to sea to meet vessels that would simultaneously leave other assembly ports. There would be from fifty to a hundred in the combined convoy, which was to be a very slow one. It would make only eight knots, because it included a lot of ships like the Norwegian steamer that Bull, the third officer, had pointed out to me some days before as the slowest ship in the world. We had lost her in the gale on December 7, but she had steamed into the second assembly port twelve hours behind us. She was called the *Blaskjell*, which means "mussel." An eight-knot convoy takes a long time to get across the ocean, Captain Petersen said, but going that way was better than hanging about waiting for a ten-knotter. Fast ships go alone, on the theory that they can run away from any submarine they sight, but the *Regnbue* was not nearly that fast.

It was about seven o'clock when we hove anchor next morning, but the moon was still high in the sky. The other ships that were going out showed one light apiece, and a corvette was talking to us in Morse code squawked out on a whistle that sounded like Donald Duck. A westerly wind was howling, and I remembered that we had received a gale warning the evening before. The moon slipped into a cloud abruptly, like a watch going into a fat man's vest pocket, and didn't come out again. When it is as dark as it was that morning it is hard for a landsman to tell if a ship is moving, because he can't see her position in relation to anything else. But after a while I was sure. When it began to get light I went up on the bridge and looked at the ships in front of us and astern. They were already plunging about. When you look at other ships in a heavy sea the extravagance of their contortions surprises you. Your own ship is going through the same motions, but you wouldn't believe they were so extreme unless you saw the other ships. The farther we got down the bay, the worse the weather grew. The commodore's ship, about a mile ahead of us, sent up a string of flags; the ships between us repeated the signal. Bull, who was on the bridge, said,

"Commodore wants us slow down, says he can't hold his position." He threw the engine-room telegraph to "Half Speed." In heavy weather the *Regnbue* steered well only at full speed, and the men at the wheel had an unhappy time from then on. Now and then her bow came clear out of the water—from watching other tankers I could see exactly how it happened—and the sea gave her a ringing slap on the bottom. I felt that this was an impertinence, precisely the sort of thing a German would do if he were running the ocean.

By noon we were getting away from land. I went down to the saloon to have dinner with Captain Petersen and found him already ladling his third plate of milk soup out of the tureen. Milk soup is made of condensed milk and water, heavily sugared and full of rice, raisins, dried apricots, canned peaches, and anything else sweet the cook can find about the galley. It is served hot at the beginning of a meal, and only a Norwegian can see any sense in it. It appeared on the table regularly twice a week, and at each appearance the steward said, "Fawny soup today, Liebling." At the beginning of every meal, without exception, he would say to me, "*Vaer so god*" ("Be so good"), and bow. I would say the same thing to him and bow, and we would both laugh. It was like the boatswain's joke about the beard.

On the bridge that afternoon the captain was preoccupied. He said that unless we could go at full speed, he didn't see how we could get to the rendezvous before dark, but only about one other ship in our lot could keep up with us at full speed. Our entire escort was one eight-hundred-ton corvette, and if we left the convoy, we left the escort. Sometimes you have a big escort and sometimes you have a small one. It's like going into a shop in England: you get what they have in stock. Haraldsen, the second officer, who was also on the bridge, was as jolly as usual. "By and by Florida!" he would shout when water whipped across the front of the wheel-house and splashed in our faces. That was *his* standard joke. The corvette seemed to stand on its head every time it went into a wave, and Haraldsen got a lot of fun watching it. "The little feller is do-ing good," he would say. "I hope they got a good belly." By three o'clock we had lost the *Blaskjell* and two of the others, and a half-hour later we could see the commodore's ship turning. The commodore was signaling us to return to port. He had judged that there was no chance of reaching the rendezvous before nightfall, and he didn't want us to be out on the ocean alone when morning came. "We made about thirty miles in nine hours," Captain Petersen said. We turned, and on the way back to the assembly port we picked up the *Blaskjell* and passed her. At nine o'clock we were again at anchor in our old berth.

The boatswain was not the only one who looked suspiciously at my beard after the return. "This has always been a lucky ship," the carpenter said. "I think we got a Rasmus on board now." A Rasmus is the Norwegian equivalent of a Jonah. The next day the weather was fine. The carpenter said that this was just what you might expect now that we had missed the convoy. Captain Petersen put on his brown suit and went ashore. He came back with word that we were stuck for at least a week. We had already been at sea for a fortnight. It was not entirely bad news to the boatswain and the steward. The boatswain could now put the men to work painting the ship. When a ship's paint gets streaky, a boatswain becomes melancholy and embarrassed, like a housewife who has not had time to wash the curtains. Griffin, the English seaman on board, once said to me, "If the bos'n ain't a bastard, the ship's no good." He added that the *Regnbue* was quite a good ship. The steward saw a chance to get the supplies he needed for Christmas. About all that the captain and I had been hearing lately at our meals was a monologue by Larsen about the horrors of Christmas at sea without newts or frewts or yin. Once a ship has left the port of origin, navy people permit only the captain and the radioman to go ashore—the radioman for a single conference before a convoy leaves—so Larsen gave the captain a list to take to a ship chandler. The captain found no nuts or fruits, but in a couple of days a lighter brought out a case of gin and two cases of whisky, which the steward put away in the pantry closet. Ordinarily, I was told, no liquor was served on the ship except to pilots and immigration officers, but Christmas was always an exception.

The days at anchor were tranquil. Every morning the captain

went ashore and the rest of us painted and theorized about our false start for America. The officers worked alongside the men, and I daubed a bit for company. Some of the men argued that we should have started for our rendezvous at midnight instead of just before dawn, and others said that with a wind like that against us we shouldn't have started at all. Haraldsen said why complain, maybe the convoy we had missed would be attacked anyway. (A couple of days later we heard that all but fourteen ships out of seventy had had to turn back because of the weather.) Evenings, we listened to the radio and talked about the war. The men talked a lot about what they were going to do with Quislings in Norway after the war. They used Quisling as a generic term, just as we do. Some of the men wanted to put them on Bear Island, up north of Norway. Others just wanted to kill them. Even the messboys were angry at Knut Hamsun and Johan Bojer for having betrayed Norwegian culture. The ship had a library of four hundred volumes. None of the seamen would read Hamsun or Bojer now. Norwegians seem more interested in books than music, and the captain was the only one who mentioned Kirsten Flagstad to me. He said Wagner had gone to her head.

Often, when Captain Petersen sat down to a meal, he would look at the customary plates of cold meat on the table and say, "I wonder what they have to eat in the old country now," or "I wonder what my wife has to eat." When we had fish he would say, "My wife never liked fish. Her father was a butcher," or else "My father-in-law always said, 'Fish is fish, but meat is nourishment.' " Once he heard me humming that old barroom favorite, "M-O-T-H-E-R." He said, "I heard a fellow sing that in vaudeville in Philadelphia. He had his wife on the stage and their six children. When he sang it one kid held up a card with 'M' on it. The next kid held up 'O' and so on until the smallest one held up 'R.' It was the cleverest thing I ever saw on the stage." Often he showed me photographs of his wife and their little boy.

We put to sea again a few days before Christmas. Just before we left, a naval man came out to say that our destination was now Baton Rouge. Nobody even speculated about the reason for this second change. We took it for granted that there was some kind of a muddle. Despite my beard and the carpenter's forebodings, we had normal North Atlantic winter weather this time. Early in the afternoon we sighted a huge fleet of ships on the horizon. This was to be a ten-knot convoy, so we had left the *Blaskjell* and a couple of other tubs behind. "Now we'll have something to look at," Haraldsen, the second officer, said as the courses of the large group and our small one converged. Every ship in a convoy has a number. Number forty-four had been assigned to us at the assembly port, and as we joined the others we hoisted the four flag and the pennon that corresponds to a ditto mark. All we had to do was find the forty-three ship and fall in behind her.

The small convoys we had traveled in along the coasts had gone in either single file or a column of twos. This one was in a column of eights. We had ships to port and starboard as well as ahead but only an escorting corvette behind us, as we were a file-closer. This tickled Haraldsen, because we wouldn't have to repeat any of the commodore's signals. A signal is passed down a file of ships, each repeating it for the benefit of the one behind. All the file-closer has to do is run up the answering pennon to acknowledge the message. Grung, the radioman, came out of his shack to look at the escort. There were only four corvettes for fifty-six large ships. "It's a bad yoke," he said bitterly. "Those English lords are sitting with girls behind drawn curtains on large estates and we can go to hell." When we had had a large escort on the east coast, Grung had said that was a bad sign. Haraldsen said, "Oh boy, I wish I had one of them girls here! Some fun." He had worked as a carpenter in New York during the building boom from 1924 to 1929 and talked of this as the romantic period of his life. "I got fifteen dollars a day," he said. "Fellows would wait for you in front of your yob—Yews, you know—and say, 'Listen, come with me. I give you a dollar more.' I like Yews." He had been on sailing ships during the last war, but he did not recall them with the same affection as, for example, John Masefield or Lincoln Colcord. "A sailing ship is hell in cold weather," he once told me.

It takes a combination of keen eyes and accurate navigation to keep a ship in its proper position in a convoy during the night, and the fleet is usually rather jumbled in the morning. This situation helped to kill time aboard the *Regnbue*. In the morning everybody was eager to see how badly the convoy had broken ranks. Bull, the third officer, was always on watch at dawn, and every morning he would say, with a sort of pride, "Dis der vorst convooey I ever see. Every morning all over der Atlahntic." The *Regnbue* nearly always held its position in relation to the commodore; either we kept to our course accurately or there was a telepathy which made him and us commit the same errors. Some of the other ships, however, would be far off on the horizon. This would always amuse Bull and the lookouts. The forty-three ship, which was supposed to stay just ahead of us, was nearly always miles to starboard, and when she tried to get back into her place we would, for the fun of it, speed up so that she couldn't edge in. She was an old tanker and slower than the *Regnbue*. Her skipper must have been a rather fussy sort; she would break into an angry rash of signal flags, and her radioman would bring out his signal flash lamp and deliver a harangue in Morse. Finally we would let her ease into the column. It usually took an hour or so to get everybody aligned. The ships always reminded me of numbered liberty horses forming sequences in a circus.

After the convoy was re-formed we could kill another half-hour trying to count the ships. There were a few less every day. Ships drop out with engine trouble or get so far off the course during the night that they lose sight of the convoy. These run a bigger risk than the ones that keep pace, but most of them turn up in port eventually. Two ships carried catafighters; that is, Hurricane fighters that could be shot into the air from catapults if a Focke-Wulf appeared. In profile, the catapults looked like cocked pistols. We used to find comfort in looking at them, even though Grung said that the pilots were probably seasick and the planes would break away from their lashings in a storm just before we were attacked by an air fleet. Sometimes ships in convoy talk to each other out of boredom, like prisoners tapping on cell walls. One morning I found Bull, signal lamp in hand, carrying on a parley with a British tanker in the column to starboard. When at last he put the lamp down I asked what it was all about, and he said, "Oh, they invite us to come aboard for lunch."

"What did you tell them?" I asked.

"Oh," Bull replied, "I say, 'If you got a drop of yin, I wouldn't say no.'"

When you are in convoy it is sometimes impossible to remember whether a thing happened yesterday or the day before yesterday or the day before that. You watch the other ships and you read whatever there is to read and you play jokes on the ship's cat. You go to the pantry and slam the refrigerator door, and the cat runs in, thinking you are going to give him something to eat. Then you pretend to ignore him. Finally, when his whining becomes unbearable, you throw him a few bits of crabmeat. I had brought three books along with me on the *Regnbue*, but I had finished them in the three weeks we spent idling off the British coast. After that I read several ninepenny thrillers by Agatha Christie and Valentine Williams that happened to be aboard, and then a copy of *Pilgrim's Progress*, donated to the ship by the Glasgow Y.M.C.A. Eventually I was reduced to looking at September numbers of *Life*. Once I found an early 1939 issue of *Redbook*. I read every page of it gratefully, though it contained six stories about husbands who strayed but found that they liked their wives best after all. There was a strict blackout every evening, but I didn't mind it as much as I had in London, because on the ship there was no place to go anyhow. One of the lifeboats had a fashion of working loose from its fastenings in heavy weather, and then the boatswain would summon a gang to heave on the ropes until he could make it fast again. I used to look forward to the chance of pulling on one of the ropes. Whenever the crew had to make the boat fast while I was napping in my cabin, I felt slighted.

Some of the men were always speculating about our destination, Baton Rouge. It didn't show on any of the maps on the ship. If it had, they figured, the size of the print might have given them an idea of how big the town was. My own guess was that it was a city of a hundred thousand. Actually, the population is thirty-four thou-

sand. American cities weren't listed in *Hvem, Hvad, Hvor*, the Norwegian equivalent of the *World Almanac*, and the favorite reference
work on board. *Hvem, Hvad, Hvor* means "Who, What, Where."
The book contains street plans of every city in Norway, even places
of as few as five thousand inhabitants. The men used to mark the locations of their houses and show them to each other and to me.
Once, Gjertsen, the chief officer, showed me where he lived in his
home town. The next day he came into my cabin looking for me,
with *Hvem, Hvad, Hvor* in his hand. "I made a mistake," he said,
pointing to the plan of the place. "*Here* is where I live," and he
showed me a dot about a quarter of an inch from the one he had
made before.

As Christmas drew near, Larsen, the steward, was often missing
from his cabin during the evenings. He was aft in the galley with
the cook, constructing great quantities of "fat things" and "poor
men," the Norwegian terms for doughnuts and crullers, respectively. On his journeys aft he carried with him a thick, calf-bound
Norwegian cookbook. Larsen had formerly been a cook; he sometimes regretted his change-over from creative to executive catering.
The cook was a tall, thin young man who looked as if he were built
of candle wax. Together they elaborated on the plans for the Christmas Eve dinner. Rumors were spread by one of the British machine
gunners, who had talked to the third engineer, who had it straight
from a messboy, that there would be turkey. While the convoy
moved along at its steady ten knots, nobody aboard the *Regnbue*
talked of anything but the coming dinner.

On the great night the table was laid for a dozen persons in the
saloon, where ordinarily the captain and I dined alone. We were
lucky; the sea was reasonably calm. The steward and the boy who
helped him in the saloon, which was forward, would have had
a hard time in a gale, for the galley was in the after deckhouse
and they had to carry all the food over the long catwalk between.
Promptly at six o'clock the engineer officers came forward to dine
with us. Larsen, the chief engineer, who was not related to Larsen
the steward, was a girthy, middle-aged man who resembled Hen-
drik Willem van Loon. If I looked aft on a fair day I could generally

see him standing by a door of the engine room with his hands in his pockets. He was a fixture in the seascape, like Nilsen, the gunner and ex-whaler, who silently paced the deck near the four-inch gun. Equally immutable was the British machine gunner on duty, wearing a pointed hood and sitting inside a little concrete breastwork on the poop deck, looking like a jack-in-the-box. Chief Engineer Larsen and his officers seldom came forward to visit us. To mark the occasion on this night, they were wearing collars and neckties. They looked scrubbed and solemn, and so did Captain Petersen and the three deck officers and the gunner and the radioman, all of whom were at the table.

Steward Larsen had set three glasses at each place—one, he told me, for port, one for whisky, and a third for gin. He had no aquavit for the Christmas dinner, and gin was supposed to replace it. To get the meal started, the steward brought in some porridge called *jul grot*, which is traditional and practically tasteless. Engineer Larsen said "Skoal" and emptied a glass of gin. We all said "Skoal" and did likewise. Then Steward Larsen served a thick soup with canned shrimp and crabmeat and chicken in it. We all drank again. The steward next served fish pudding, and there was more drinking of skoals. Then he brought in the turkey with the pride of a Soviet explorer presenting a hunk of frozen mammoth excavated from a glacier. The turkey had been in the ship's cold room since the September equinox, and the ship chandler's turkeys are presumed to have been dead for quite a while before they come aboard. We had plenty of canned vegetables and, above all, plenty of gin. The teetotaler Methodist captain, who stuck to his principles and didn't drink, brought out a couple of songbooks that he had got from a Norwegian church and suggested we sing some Christmas hymns. His guests sang them, without much pleasure, it seemed to me, and we ate a lot of jello covered with vanilla sauce and drank some more gin. All the men's faces remained rigid and solemn. Engineer Larsen said, in English, "Merry Christmas to our American friend." The captain whispered to me, "You can tell he's from Oslo. He talks too much." The steward then brought in mounds of doughnuts and crullers, and some fancy drinks in tall glasses. He called the tall drinks Larsen's Spezials. They were triple portions of gin with lump sugar and canned cherries. Everyone said, "Thank you, Steward. Very good." The whisky was served straight, as a dessert liqueur. We all began drinking it out of jiggers and saying "Skoal" some more. The singing got fairly continuous and the choice of numbers gradually grew more secular. Most Norwegian songs, I noticed, have many verses, and the men who are not singing pay no attention to the one who is. They look as if they are trying to recall the innumerable verses they are going to sing in their turn. We all got together on one patriotic number, though. The last line, translated into English, was "If Norway goes under, I want to go, too." We clasped hands on that one.

The captain asked me to sing "My Old Kentucky Home," which I couldn't remember many words of, but fortunately three other fellows started to sing three other songs at the same time. The steward, considering his official duties over, drew up a chair to the table and received congratulations. The cook, looking taller and more solemn than ever, came in and was hailed as a great man. The drinkers still made intermittent efforts to remain grave. They yielded slowly, as if they were trying to protect their pleasure. Now the dignitaries of the crew, who had finished a dinner with exactly the same menu in their own quarters, began to appear in the saloon and take seats at the table—first the argumentative carpenter, then the boatswain with the cackle, and finally the pumpman, a tall fellow who looked like a Hapsburg and spent his life shooting compressed air into clogged oil tanks. The carpenter arose to sing a song. He had the same argumentative, deliberate delivery that he had in conversation, and he paused so long between verses that the chief officer, who had come down off the bridge and entered the saloon just after the carpenter had finished a verse, thought the all-clear had sounded and began a song of his own. The usually timid cook, buoyed up by one of Larsen's Spezials, thundered, "Shut up, Chief Officer! Let the carpenter sing!" As the chief officer and the fourth engineer joined the party, the third officer and another of the engineers left to stand their watches. The machine gunner from Glasgow arrived to wish the captain a merry Christmas and snitch a bottle of whisky. Two seamen, lads of about eighteen, came in to convey the respects of the crew. They had, I imagine, thought of this mission themselves. One, a small, neat boy with a straw-blond mustache, sang a long song with the refrain "*Farvel, farvel*" ("Farewell, farewell"). It appeared to make him very unhappy. Nearly all the seamen on the *Regnbue* were youngsters, which would have been true on a Norwegian ship even before the war. After three and a half years at sea they are eligible to take a course at a mates' school if they can save or borrow the price. Boys who don't like the sea quit before then.

Presently Steward Larsen pulled me by the arm and took me off with him to visit the rest of the crew. Before leaving the saloon, he had handed out a bottle of whisky to each four men, and on the whole they were doing all right with it. "I am a Commoonist," he kept saying to me on our way aft, "so I want you to love these fellers." Everybody on the ship had received as a Christmas greeting from the Norwegian Government a facsimile letter signed "Haakon, Rex." The letters, which had been put aboard at London for the captain to hand out, told Norwegian seamen that they were their country's mainstay. The "Commoonist" read this letter over and over again and cried every time. The Government had also sent the crew a set of phonograph records of patriotic songs. The favorite was called "*Du Gamle Mor*" ("Thou Old Mother"), which means Norway. The boys aft were all wearing blue stocking caps, which had come in a Christmas-gift bundle with a card saying they had been knitted by a Miss Georgie Gunn, of 1035 Park Avenue, New York City.

By the time Larsen and I staggered back over the catwalk to the saloon, everybody but Captain Petersen was unashamedly happy. It was very close in the blacked-out saloon with all the ports shut, and I went up to the bridge for air. Bull, the third officer, was on watch up there. He had been moderately dizzy when he had gone on watch at eight o'clock after eating his dinner, he told me, but now he felt only a sense of sober well-being. "I see ships all around," he said, "so ve must be in de meddel de convooey." Sandor, the Rumanian seaman who had stowed away on the ship in 1939 and remained aboard ever since, was on lookout duty. He said, "This makes three Christmas on ship since I left home. No good. On ship you see thirty, thirty-five peoples. On shore you see hoondreds peoples. I like to get one Christmas ashore." Sandor's chances were not bright. The British immigration officers at our second assembly port had told him that, since he was now an enemy alien, he would not be allowed on shore in Britain for the remainder of the war. They had added that the Americans would probably also refuse to let him land, so he might have to remain afloat indefinitely. Griffin, the English seaman, was at the wheel. When Sandor spelled him, Griffin came out of the wheelhouse and we wished each other Merry Christmas. I had heard so much talk about home towns and traditions that night that I asked Griffin where he was from. "Blowed if I know," he said cheerfully. "Sandor don't know where 'e's going and I don't know where I come from."

When I went down to my cabin, a row that would have done credit to an early convention of the American Legion was going on in the saloon. I looked in, but everybody was shouting in Norwegian and no one looked sufficiently detached to translate for me, so I didn't hear what it was all about until the next day, when I was told that someone had been trying to get subscriptions to the Norwegian Air Force Spitfire Fund and that Grung, the radioman, had protested that the Norwegian Government, even in exile, was giving $300,000 a year to missionaries in China and Africa. "Let them spend the missionary money for Spitfires before they bother workingmen," he had said. The steward had called Grung a bad name and Grung had pushed him over a case of empty whisky bottles. Later, when I happened to see Grung coming out of the radio shack, I asked him what Larsen had called him. "He called me a Commoonist," Grung said.

The party gave us something to talk about for a couple of days afterward. The carpenter went around repeating a line he had memorized from the label of an Old Angus whisky bottle: "Yentle as a lamb." He would say it and roll his eyes and then exclaim, "Yeezis!" On Christmas morning an English ship signaled to us, "Merry Christmas. Keep your chins and thumbs up." Grung and Bull had a consultation and then, not being able to think of anything witty, just ran up the answering flag meaning "Message noted."

One morning, when we were about halfway across the Atlantic, I found Bull in a particularly good humor. "Look around," he said, handing me a glass. "Vare is escort?" I had a good look around and there wasn't any. The corvettes had disappeared during the night. "Does that mean we've reached the safe part of the Atlantic?" I asked. "Safe yust so long ve see no submarine," Bull said. Captain Petersen, who came up a half-hour later to look around, said, "Maybe the escort from America was supposed to meet us here, and it didn't, and the British Corvettes had a date to meet an eastbound convoy off Iceland. We don't count as much as eastbound ships, because they're loaded." We went on all day without an escort. Grung came out of his shack and stared at three hundred and fifty thousand tons of valuable shipping moving placidly on, unprotected and unattacked. "Admiral Raeder must be lousy," he said at last.

Next morning a force of Canadian destroyers met us. No harm had been done. It wasn't the only time the *Regnbue* had traveled in an unconvoyed convoy, Bull said. Once she had left Halifax in a convoy escorted by a battleship that was returning from an American dockyard. A couple of hundred miles out, the battleship had been summoned to help hunt the *Bismarck*, so she had moved off at thirty knots and left the merchantmen to push on by themselves to England. There were never enough vessels for convoy duty, Bull said, but luckily there never seemed to be enough submarines, either. The Battle of the Atlantic sounded imposing, but it was rather like a football game with five men on a side.

A few days after we met the Canadians, the ships bound for Gulf ports split off from the convoy. We were one of them. Each ship was to proceed as an individual, the theory at that time being that waters within a few hundred miles of the American coast were fairly safe. We had always cherished a notion that we were one of the fastest ships in our convoy. When dispersal day came, however, most of the others bound for the south quickly left us behind. Twenty-four hours after the split we were alone in the ocean, without another ship in sight. We steered southwest within a couple of hundred miles of the coast for nearly two weeks and saw only two vessels, neither of them a warship. Nor did we sight a single patrol plane. We hoped that no hostile aircraft carrier would ever have the same luck. The *Regnbue*, now that she was alone, zigzagged in a constant series of tangents to her course. This lost a mile an hour, which still further delayed my homecoming.

The weather stayed seasonably rough. We never ran into the kind of storm that sends smashed ships to port to make pictures for the newspaper photographers, but for days on end we couldn't see the sun long enough to get a position, and on New Year's Eve, when we were thirty-one days out of London, we had a sixty-mile gale, which made a second holiday party impossible. The day before we left the convoy I had been standing at the wheelhouse window watching the extraordinary antics of the tankers around us. A tanker in water ballast is a good sea boat but not a comfortable one. It rides the waves like a canoe, but it has a tendency to twist from side to side as it comes down. As I have already noted, this is even more disconcerting to watch than to endure. I was thinking about this when Mikkelsen, the electrician, a big, snaggle-toothed West Norwegian, came up and stood next to me. He looked at the ships for a while, then said quietly, "Fine weather." According to his lights it probably was.

After you leave your convoy you may have no other ships to watch and discuss, but you have a chance to fire your gun. That is an event to look forward to for days. Admiralty regulations require a ship to fire at least two shots on each trip. The captain gave Nilsen, the gunner, the order to prepare to fire these ritual shots. A day was set for the performance—not too soon, because, on account of scarcity of ammunition, we couldn't afford such pleasures more than once and we wanted to prolong the period of anticipation. The ordinarily silent Nilsen became the embodiment of the busy-executive type. The other members of the gun crew were the Hapsburg pumpman, two Diesel motormen, the fourth engineer, and the little sailor who had sung "*Farvel.*" They assumed new dignity among their fellows during the days before the gun practice. Everybody on the *Regnbue* told jokes about the last time the gun had been fired. Some said that Larsen, the chief engineer, had been asleep in his cabin when the gun went off and had been knocked off his divan. Others told the same story about the cook, the steward, or the second officer. All of this was invention, because nobody on a merchant ship sleeps when the gun is to be fired. One might as well expect a small boy to sleep late on Christmas morning.

On the big day the raised gun platform served as an excellent stage for the gun crew and the protagonist, the gun. The boatswain had distributed pounds of cotton batting, and we had stuffed our ears with wads of the stuff. The little sailor, a romantic chap, had carefully smudged his forehead with black grease so that he would look like one of Admiral Tordenskjold's powder monkeys. An empty oil drum would serve as target. A couple of sailors threw it off the stern. Nilsen's crew loaded the gun. Then, after the ship had gone an estimated two thousand meters, they fired. There was a great spat of flame from the gun's muzzle, a satisfactory roar, and something splashed in the water a long distance away. I could not see the oil drum, but Haraldsen, the second officer, who had once been an ensign in the Norwegian Navy, said that the shell had not missed by much. We all shouted "Hurrah!" It was better than the Fourth of July. The gun was reloaded and fired again. After the second shot we all felt much safer, because we knew that the gun would not burst until the next trip.

The days continued alike as we went on, but they had a different feeling. After we had passed Hatteras even the carpenter and the radioman, the ship's leading grousers, began to admit it was probable we would make port. And all through the ship men made plans for whatever shore leave they might get. Larsen, the steward, who had once worked out of the port of "Noolians," proposed to the cook and a couple of others that they hire a taxi at Baton Rouge and drive straight to the French Quarter in New Orleans. "I always say I'm going to save money," he told me, "but when I get near land I can't keep my temper." Captain Petersen looked forward to renewing acquaintance with the pastor of the Norwegian church in New Orleans, where he planned to go by train. A few of the men owned electric flatirons, and these were in heavy demand by shipmates who wanted to press their pants. Grung, the radioman, was in charge of the pay list. All of the men had fairly large sums coming to them, and each signified to Grung the amount he wanted to draw at Baton Rouge. Usually a man changed his mind several times, raising the ante each time. The cook and the steward held long conferences about stores, occasionally asking me how to spell "bitterscots pewding" or "tomates cetseps." The steward said that he would send the list ashore to a ship chandler in "Noolians" when we went through customs and have the stuff trucked up to Baton Rouge.

The ship had not taken stores for more than three months now, and the eggs caused a daily argument between the steward and me. For several mornings he had served them hard-boiled, a sign he had no real confidence in them. Each morning I would open my first egg and say, "*Darlig*," which is Norwegian for "Bad."

The steward would protest, "*Naj, naj.*"

"But this one has green spots inside the shell," I would say.

"Ex like dot sometimes," he would maintain.

The captain always ate his eggs without any remark; his silence accused me of finicking. At last, one morning toward the end of the voyage, he opened an egg and looked at the steward. "*Darlig*," he said. The steward looked embarrassed. Then the captain ate the egg; a bad hard-boiled egg is probably as nourishing as a good one.

Next morning the steward brought me an amorphous yellow mass on a plate. It tasted mostly of sugar, but he offered me a jug of maple- and cane-sugar syrup to pour on it. I took a spoonful, fancying it some Norse confection, and said, "Not bad. What do you call it?" The steward said, "I call it ummelet. Same ex." Once the captain opened up a bit more than usual and talked about the Oxford Movement. The Movement had been strong in Norway, he said, and had frequently coincided with Quislingism. "A shipowner in my town," he once said to me, "got crazy about the Oxford Movement. He took his wife and children to a public meeting, and then he got up in the meeting and said that when he went to Antwerp on business he used to use bad women. His wife fainted. I don't call that a Christian." Several times the captain talked about his native town. "It has two fine hotels, and the harbor is full of beautiful little islands," he said once. "You can take your family in a boat fishing and then have a picnic on an island. In the winter we go skiing. My boy is three years old, and he has his second pair of skis. In the summer we used to have lobster parties, or dumpling-and-buttermilk parties. But it probably isn't like that now."

"By and by Florida" had been a gag line with Haraldsen, the second officer, throughout the voyage, but one day we really got there. It was the first land we had sighted since leaving Britain, and it looked exactly like the newsreels, with fine, white hotels and palm trees and scores of spic-and-span motorboats in the blue water offshore, fishing for whatever people fish for in Florida. The weather was clear but cold. When we got close to shore we were permitted to use the radio receiving set in the chief officer's cabin again, and one of the first things I heard was an announcer saying, "There is no frost in Florida. This morning's temperature was thirty-seven." I tried to get some war news and heard another announcer saying, "The slant-eyed specialists in treachery continue their advance toward Singapore." One, two, three, four, five seconds. "You could not employ them better than by making a lather of creamy Sweetheart soap." We sailed along the shore. There were plenty of airplanes overhead now. They swooped almost to our masthead and looked us over every five minutes. It made all the men happy just to see the coast. From the bridge we kept looking through our glasses for bathing girls, but the weather was too cold for them. We wondered what the people in the Palm Beach and Miami hotels thought of our rusty ship, with its wheelhouse fortified with concrete slabs and its ragged red flag with the blue cross. Fellows kept making attempts at jokes, like "There's the dog track; let's go" or "Grung, get out the flash lamp and signal women that want a date yust wait on the beach. I going to swim in."

That afternoon the steward came into my cabin and said that the captain and the officers were giving me a farewell supper that evening. As on Christmas Eve, it was formal dress—collars and neckties. The occasion itself was solemn; Norwegians are not effusive. My companions just sat there, talking Norwegian among themselves and ignoring me. Nobody made a speech, but at the end of the meal the cook carried in a cake about the size and shape of an Aztec calendar stone. It was encrusted with slightly damp sugar. He held it out to me, and I stood up and reached for it. It nearly pulled me forward on my face, and as I looked down on the top, I saw, written in icing, *"Farvel."*

A few nights later we were at the mouth of the Mississippi, waiting for a pilot. A northerly gale howled down at us straight from Lake Michigan. There were plenty of lights visible on the shore, more than I had seen at a comparable hour since leaving New York in the summer. Somehow I had expected our lights to go out when we entered the war. It seemed strange coming in our blacked-out ship to a country that was neither neutral *nor* dark. A boy in a rowboat brought out the pilot, a heavyset, shivering man in a leatherette jacket who announced as soon as he came aboard that it was the coldest damn winter he had ever known in Louisiana. He brought aboard a copy of the New Orleans *Times-Picayune*, containing a lot of basketball scores and society notes and a few stories about a war that seemed to be on some remote sphere. A naval party came aboard and sealed the radio shack. The pilot took us seventeen miles up the river and then was relieved by a second pilot, who was going to take us the eighty remaining miles to New Orleans. I turned in.

We dropped anchor off quarantine in New Orleans at about ten o'clock on the morning of the forty-second day out of London. It was Sunday. We had to pass the immigration and public-health officers' inspections before the *Regnbue* could continue up the river. I had my suitcase packed before the government officers arrived, hoping that I would be able to go back to shore with them. It was the sort of day we had had off Florida, chilly but bright, and the city looked good in the sunlight. The *Regnbue*'s men, lining the rails, talked about how fine it would be to be going ashore again. I had been at sea for only six weeks, but few of them had set foot ashore in four months. The immigration-and-health boat came out soon after ten with a party including a doctor and a rat inspector. The immigration men brought five armed guards to post about the

ship to see that none of our allies would try to land too soon. Soon
a customs officer came aboard and asked the captain if any man
on the ship had more than three hundred cigarettes. Seamen buy
their cigarettes in America, and our men had started to run short a
fortnight before. Captain Petersen did not seem astonished by the
question. He sent Grung to take a census of the cigarettes on
board. Grung came back after a half-hour with word that only
the second engineer had more than three hundred cigarettes. He
had three hundred and twenty-five. The customs man asked if the
twenty-five were loose, and Grung said that five of them were. The
customs man said he thought he could let the second engineer keep
the other twenty, although, he pointed out, he was making an exception. I pictured a large convoy missing a tide while the United
States Customs counted cigarettes. Then the customs man asked
about liquor, because he would have to seal up what we had on
board. Grung went on a search for liquor and reported back that
we had had two bottles of whisky and one of gin but that one of the
public-health men had drunk about half of one of the bottles of
whisky.

Next the immigration men came to the consideration of me.
They said that since I had a good passport and had apparently been
born in New York, I probably had a right to land in the United
States, but not until my baggage had been passed by a customs appraiser. Unfortunately, they said, no appraisers had come along.
"The last thing I expected to find on this ship was a passenger," the
head immigration man said, giving me a rat inspector's look. He
said that unless I wanted to stay on the ship for twenty-four hours
longer I would have to pay two days' wages for the appraiser myself. Double pay for Sunday work. I said that would be all right,
and they sent for an appraiser. It cost me $13.33. While waiting for
the appraiser, I went out on deck. Captain Petersen came out, too,
and we stood looking at the shore. He was quiet, as usual, but he
seemed to be struggling with an unusual emotion. At last he said,
"Say, is it true the Hippodrome has been torn down?"

I said, "Yes, and the Sixth Avenue El, too."

Again he looked troubled, and I thought he was going to say he would miss me, but he said, "*The Big Show* were a wonderful play." That was an extravaganza that had played at the Hipp in 1917, when the captain had lived in Hoboken.

I said, "Yes, with Joe Jackson."

"A very funny man," Captain Petersen said.

A shabby motorboat came toward us from the left bank of the river. Captain Petersen said, "It must be a ship chandler after our business." There was a man on the forward deck with a megaphone, and as the boat came under our bow he called up inquiringly, "Captain, Captain?" Petersen pointed to his peaked cap, his emblem of office. The fellow shouted, "We got orders to send you on to Curaçao! You got enough bunker?" Curaçao is nine days from New Orleans for a ten-knot boat. Petersen showed no sign of surprise or disappointment. "We need bunker," he shouted back, "but we can get out in twenty-four hours!"

An hour later, when I was in a boat going ashore, I could see most of the *Regnbue* fellows on deck, leaning over the rail. There was the carpenter, with his square head and his obstinate shoulders, and the tall pumpman, and the electrician, and the two British gunners in their khaki uniforms. I could make out the bearish form of Sandor, the Rumanian, who would not have to stay on board alone now, because the others would stay with him. And there was Larsen, the steward, in a belted, horizon-blue overcoat and a bright green hat, his shoregoing uniform. He wouldn't go ashore, after all.

The Foamy Fields

(MARCH 20, 1943–APRIL 17, 1943)

If there is any way you can get colder than you do when you sleep in a bedding roll on the ground in a tent in southern Tunisia two hours before dawn, I don't know about it. The particular tent I remember was at an airfield in a Tunisian valley. The surface of the terrain was mostly limestone. If you put all the blankets on top of you and just slept on the canvas cover of the roll, you ached all over, and if you divided the blankets and put some of them under you, you froze on top. The tent was a large, circular one with a French stencil on the outside saying it had been rented from a firm in Marseilles and not to fold it wet, but it belonged to the United States Army now. It had been set up over a pit four feet deep, so men sleeping in it were safe from flying bomb fragments. The tall tent pole, even if severed, would probably straddle the pit and not hit anybody. It was too wide a hole to be good during a strafing, but then strafings come in the daytime and in the daytime nobody lived in it. I had thrown my roll into the tent because I thought it was vacant and it seemed as good a spot as any other when I arrived at the field as a war correspondent. I later discovered that I was sharing it with two enlisted men.

I never saw my tentmates clearly, because they were always in the tent by the time I turned in at night, when we were not al-

---

"The Foamy Fields" was written and originally published during wartime. After the war, Liebling revealed in footnotes and postscript (included here) some identities, locations, and additions that had to remain secret or were unknown when the piece first appeared.

lowed to have lights on, and they got up a few minutes before I did in the morning, when it was still dark. I used to hear them moving around, however, and sometimes talk to them. One was from Mississippi and the other from North Carolina, and both were airplane mechanics. The first night I stumbled through the darkness into the tent, they heard me and one of them said, "I hope you don't mind, but the tent we were sleeping in got all tore to pieces with shrapnel last night, so we just moved our stuff in here." I had been hearing about the events of the previous evening from everybody I met on the field. "You can thank God you wasn't here last night," the other man said earnestly. The field is so skillfully hidden in the mountains that it is hard to find by night, and usually the Germans just wander around overhead, dropping their stuff on the wrong hillsides, but for once they had found the right place and some of the light anti-aircraft on the field had started shooting tracers. "It was these guns that gave away where we was," the first soldier said. "Only for that they would have gone away and never knowed the first bomb had hit the field. But after that they knew they was on the beam and they come back and the next bomb set some gasoline on fire and then they really did go to town. Ruined a P-thirty-eight that tore herself up in a belly landing a week ago and I had just got her about fixed up again, and now she's got shrapnel holes just about everywhere and she's hopeless. All that work wasted. Killed three fellows that was sleeping in a B-twenty-six on the field and woke up and thought that was no safe place, so they started to run across the field to a slit trench and a bomb got them. Never got the B-twenty-six at all. If they'd stayed there, they'd been alive today, but who the hell would have stayed there?"*

"That shrapnel has a lot of force behind it," the other voice in the tent said. "There was a three-quarter-ton truck down on the field and a jaggedy piece of shrapnel went right through one of the tires and spang through the chassis. You could see the holes both sides where she went in and come out. We was in our tent when the

---

* The B-26 was Lieutenant-General James Doolittle's personal plane. He was on a tour of inspection, and the three soldiers were members of his crew.

shooting started, but not for long. We run up into the hills so far in fifteen minutes it took us four hours to walk back next morning. When we got back we found we didn't have no tent." There was a pause, and then the first soldier said, "Good night, sir," and I fell asleep.

When the cold woke me up, I put my flashlight under the blankets so I could look at my watch. It was five o'clock. Some Arab dogs, or perhaps jackals, were barking in the hills, and I lay uncomfortably dozing until I heard one of the soldiers blowing his nose. He blew a few times and said, "It's funny that as cold as it gets up here nobody seems to get a real cold. My nose runs like a spring branch, but it don't never develop."

When the night turned gray in the entrance to the tent, I woke again, looked at my watch, and saw that it was seven. I got up and found that the soldiers had already gone. Like everyone else at the field, I had been sleeping in my clothes. The only water obtainable was so cold that I did not bother to wash my face. I got my mess kit and walked toward the place, next to the kitchen, where they were starting fires under two great caldrons to heat dish water. One contained soapy water and the other rinsing water. The fires shot up from a deep hole underneath them, and a group of soldiers had gathered around and were holding the palms of their hands toward the flames, trying to get warm. The men belonged to a maintenance detachment of mechanics picked from a number of service squadrons that had been sent to new advanced airdromes, where planes have to be repaired practically without equipment for the job. That morning most of the men seemed pretty cheerful because nothing had happened during the night, but one fellow with a lot of beard on his face was critical. "This location was all right as long as we had all the planes on one side of us, so we was sort of off the runway," he said, "but now that they moved in those planes on the other side of us, we're just like a piece of meat between two slices of bread. A fine ham sandwich for Jerry. If he misses either side, he hits us. I guess that is how you get to be an officer, thinking up a location for a camp like this. I never washed out of Yale so I could be an officer, but I got more sense than that."

"Cheer up, pal," another soldier said. "All you got to do is dig. I got my dugout down so deep already it reminds me of the Borough Hall station. Some night I'll give myself a shave and climb on board a Woodlawn express." Most of the men in camp, I had already noticed, were taking up excavation as a hobby and some of them had worked up elaborate private trench systems. "You couldn't get any guy in camp to dig three days ago," the Brooklyn soldier said, "and now you can't lay down a shovel for a minute without somebody sucks it up."

Another soldier, who wore a white silk scarf loosely knotted around his extremely dirty neck, a style generally affected by fliers, said, "What kills me is my girl's brother is in the horse cavalry, probably deep in the heart of Texas, and he used to razz me because I wasn't a combat soldier."

The Brooklyn man said to him, "Ah, here's Mac with a parachute tied around his neck just like a dashing pilot. Mac, you look like a page out of *Esquire.*"

When my hands began to feel warm, I joined the line which had formed in front of the mess tent. As we passed through, we got bacon, rice, apple butter, margarine, and hard biscuits in our mess tins and tea in our canteen cups. The outfit was on partly British rations, but it was a fairly good breakfast anyway, except for the tea, which came to the cooks with sugar and powdered milk already mixed in it. "I guess that's why they're rationing coffee at home, so we can have tea all the time," the soldier ahead of me said. I recognized the bacon as the fat kind the English get from America. By some miracle of lend-lease they had now succeeded in delivering it back to us; the background of bookkeeping staggered the imagination. After we had got our food, we collected a pile of empty gasoline cans to use for chairs and tables. The five-gallon can, known as a flimsy, is one of the two most protean articles in the Army. You can build houses out of it, use it as furniture, or, with slight structural alterations, make a stove or a locker. Its only rival for versatility is the metal shell of the Army helmet, which can be used as an entrenching tool, a shaving bowl, a wash basin, or a cooking utensil, at the discretion of the owner. The helmet may also serve on occasion as a bathtub. The bather fills it with water, removes one article of clothing at a time, rubs the water hastily over the surface thus exposed, and replaces the garment before taking off another one.*

There was no officers' mess. I had noticed Major George Lehmann, the commanding officer of the base, and First Lieutenant McCreedy, the chaplain, in the line not far behind me. Major Lehmann is a tall, fair, stolid man who told me that he had lived in Pittsfield, Massachusetts, where he had a job with the General Electric Company. When I had reported, on my arrival at the field, at his dugout the evening before, he had hospitably suggested that I stow my blanket roll wherever I could find a hole in the ground, eat at the general mess shack, and stay as long as I pleased. "There are fighter squadrons and some bombers and some engineers and anti-aircraft here, and you can wander around and talk to anybody that interests you," he had said.

Father McCreedy is a short, chubby priest who came from Bethlehem, Pennsylvania, and had been assigned to a parish in Philadelphia. He always referred to the pastor of this parish, a Father McGinley, as "my boss," and asked me several times if I knew George Jean Nathan, who he said was a friend of Father McGinley. Father McCreedy had been officiating at the interment of the fellows killed in the raid the evening before, and that was all he would talk about during breakfast. He had induced a mechanic to engrave the men's names on metal plates with an electric needle. These plates would serve as enduring grave markers. It is part of a chaplain's duty to see that the dead are buried and to dispose of their effects. Father McCreedy was also special-services officer of the camp, in charge of recreation and the issue of athletic equipment. "So what with one thing and another, they keep me busy here," he said. He told me he did not like New York. "Outside of Madison Square Garden and the Yankee Stadium, you can have it." He wore an outsize tin hat all the time. "I know a chaplain is not supposed to be a combatant," he said, "but if parachute troops came to my tent by

---

* This is known as a whore's bath. The impelling reason for exposing only one surface at a time was cold, not modesty.

night, they'd shoot at me because they wouldn't know I was a chaplain, and I want something solid on my head." He had had a deep hole dug in front of his tent and sometimes, toward dusk, when German planes were expected, he would stand in it waiting and smoking a cigar, with the glowing end of it just clearing the hole.

When I had finished breakfast and scrubbed up my mess kit, I strolled around the post to see what it was like. As the sun rose higher, the air grew warm and the great, reddish mountains looked friendly. Some of them had table tops, and the landscape reminded me of Western movies in Technicolor.* I got talking to a soldier named Bill Phelps, who came from the town of Twenty-nine Palms, California. He was working on a bomber that had something the matter with its insides. He confirmed my notion that the country looked like the American West. "This is exactly the way it is around home," he said, "only we got no Ayrabs." A French writer has described the valley bottoms in southern Tunisia as foamy seas of white sand and green alfa grass. They are good, natural airfields, wide and level and fast-drying, but there is always plenty of dust in the air. I walked to a part of the field where there were a lot of P-38s, those double-bodied planes that look so very futuristic, and started to talk to a couple of sergeants who were working on one. "This is Lieutenant Hoelle's plane," one of them said, "and we just finished putting a new wing on it. That counts as just a little repair job out here. Holy God, at home, if a plane was hurt like that, they would send it back to the factory or take it apart for salvage. All we do here is drive a two-and-a-half-ton truck up under the damaged wing and lift it off, and then we put the new wing on the truck and run it alongside the plane again and fix up that eighty-thousand-dollar airplane like we was sticking together a radio set. We think nothing of it. It's a great ship, the thirty-eight. Rugged. You know how this

---

* This use of the familiar false as touchstone of the unfamiliar real recurred often both in writing and conversation during World War II. "Just like a movie!" was a standard reaction. It assured the speaker of the authenticity of what he had just experienced.

one got hurt? Lieutenant Hoelle was strafing some trucks and he come in to attack so low he hit his right wing against a telephone pole. Any other plane, that wing would have come off right there. Hitting the pole that way flipped him over on his back, and he was flying upside down ten feet off the ground. He gripped that stick so hard the inside of his hand was black and blue for a week afterward, and she come right side up and he flew her home. Any one-engine plane would have slipped and crashed into the ground, but those two counterrotating props eliminate torque." I tried to look as though I understood. "Lieutenant Hoelle is a real man," the sergeant said.*

I asked him where Hoelle and the other P-38 pilots were, and he directed me to the P-38 squadron's operations room, a rectangular structure mostly below ground, with walls made out of the sides of gasoline cans and a canvas roof camouflaged with earth. A length of stovepipe stuck out through the roof, making it definitely the most ambitious structure on the field.

Hoelle was the nearest man to the door when I stepped down into the operations shack. He was a big, square-shouldered youngster with heavy eyebrows and a slightly aquiline nose. I explained who I was and asked him who was in charge, and he said, "I am. I'm the squadron C.O. My name's Hoelle." He pronounced it "Holly." There was a fire in a stove, and the shack was warm. Two tiny black puppies lay on a pilot's red scarf in a helmet in the middle of the dirt floor, and they seemed to be the center of attention. Six or eight lieutenants, in flying togs that ranged from overalls to British Army battle dress, were sitting on gasoline cans or sprawled on a couple of cots. They were all looking at the puppies and talking either to them or their mother, a small Irish setter over in one corner, whom they addressed as Red. "One of the boys brought Red along with him from England," Hoelle said. "We think that the dog that got

* These praises of the Lightning now look as old-fashioned as a cavalryman's praise of the Anglo-Arab charger, and the mechanic's talk about an eighty-thousand-dollar airplane sounds like a reference to the good nickel cigar.

her in trouble is a big, long-legged black one at the airport we were quartered at there."

"These are going to be real beautiful dogs, just like Irish setters, only with black hair," one of the pilots said in a defensive tone. He was obviously Red's master.

"This is a correspondent," Hoelle said to the group, and one of the boys on a cot moved over and made room for me. I sat down, and the fellow who had moved over said his name was Larry Adler but he wasn't the harmonica player and when he was home he lived on Ocean Parkway in Brooklyn. "I wouldn't mind being there right now," he added.

There was not much in the shack except the cots, the tin cans, a packing case, the stove, a phonograph, a portable typewriter, a telephone, and a sort of bulletin board that showed which pilots were on mission, which were due to go on patrol, and which were on alert call, but it was a cheerful place. It reminded me of one of those secret-society shacks that small boys are always building out of pickup materials in vacant lots. Adler got up and said he would have to go on patrol. "It's pretty monotonous," he said, "like driving a fast car thirty miles an hour along a big, smooth road where there's no traffic. We just stooge around near the field and at this time of day nothing ever happens."

Another lieutenant came over and said he was the intelligence officer of the squadron. Intelligence and armament officers, who do not fly, take a more aggressive pride in their squadron's accomplishments than the pilots, who don't like to be suspected of bragging. "We've been out here for a month," the intelligence officer said, "and we have been doing everything—escorting bombers over places like Sfax and Sousse, shooting up vehicles and puncturing tanks, going on fighter sweeps to scare up a fight, and flying high looking for a target and then plunging straight down on it and shooting hell out of it. We've got twenty-nine German planes, including bombers and transports with troops in them and fighters, and the boys have flown an average of forty combat missions apiece. That's more than one a day. Maybe you'd like to see some of the boys' own reports on what they have been doing."

I said that this sounded fine, and he handed me a sheaf of the simple statements pilots write out when they put in a claim for shooting down a German plane. I copied part of a report by a pilot named Earnhart, who I thought showed a sense of literary style. He had had, according to the intelligence officer, about the same kind of experience as everybody else in the squadron. Earnhart had shot down a Junkers 52, which is a troop-carrier, in the episode he was describing, and then he had been attacked by several enemy fighters. "As I was climbing away from them," he wrote, "a 20-millimeter explosive shell hit the windshield and deflected through the top of the canopy and down on the instrument panel. Three pieces of shell hit me, in the left chest, left arm, and left knee. I dropped my belly tank and, having the ship under control, headed for my home base. On the way I applied a tourniquet to my leg, administered a hypodermic, and took sulfanilamide tablets. I landed the ship at my own base one hour after I had been hit by the shell. The plane was repaired. Claim, one Ju 52 destroyed." The intelligence officer introduced Earnhart to me. He was a calm, slender, dark-haired boy and he persisted in addressing me as sir. He said he came from Lebanon, Ohio, and had gone to Ohio State.

Still another lieutenant I met was named Gustke. He came from Detroit. Gustke had been shot down behind the German lines and had made his way back to the field. He was a tall, gangling type, with a long nose and a prominent Adam's apple. "I crash-landed the plane and stepped out of it wearing my parachute," he told me, "and the first thing I met was some Arabs who looked hostile to me, and as luck would have it I had forgotten to bring along my forty-five, so I tripped my parachute and threw it to them, and you know how crazy Arabs are about cloth or anything like that. They all got fighting among themselves for the parachute, and while they were doing that I ran like hell and got away from them. I got to a place where there were some Frenchmen, and they hid me overnight and the next day put me on a horse and gave me a guide, who brought me back over some mountains to inside the French lines. I had a pretty sore ass from riding the horse."

A pilot from Texas named Ribb, who stood nearby as Gustke and I talked, broke in to tell me that they had a fine bunch of fellows and that when they were in the air they took care of each other and did not leave anybody alone at the end of the formation to be picked off by the enemy. "In this gang we have no ass-end Charlies," he said feelingly.

I asked Lieutenant Hoelle what was in the cards for the afternoon, and he said that eight of the boys, including himself, were going out to strafe some German tanks that had been reported working up into French territory. "We carry a cannon, which the P-forties don't, so we can really puncture a tank the size they use around here," he said. "We expect to meet some P-forties over the target, and they will stay up high and give us cover against any German fighters while we do a job on the tanks. Maybe I had better call the boys together and talk it over."

A couple of pilots had begun a game of blackjack on the top of the packing case, and he told them to quit, so he could spread a map on it. At that moment an enlisted man came in with a lot of mail and some Christmas packages that had been deposited by a courier plane. It was long after Christmas, but that made the things even more welcome, and all the pilots made a rush for their packages and started tearing them open. Earnhart, who was going on the strafe job, got some National Biscuit crackers and some butterscotch candy and a couple of tubes of shaving cream that he said he couldn't use because he had an electric razor, and the operations officer, a lieutenant named Lusk, got some very rich homemade cookies that an aunt and uncle had sent him from Denver. We were all gobbling butterscotch and cookies as we gathered round the map Hoelle had spread. It was about as formal an affair as looking at a road map to find your way to Washington, Connecticut, from New Milford. "We used to make more fuss over briefings in England," the intelligence officer said, "but when you're flying two or three times a day, what the hell?" He pointed out the place on the map where the tanks were supposed to be, and all the fellows said they knew where it was, having been there before. Hoelle said they would take off at noon. After a while he and the seven other boys went out onto the field to get ready, and I went with them. On the way there was more talk about P-38s and how some Italian prisoners had told their captors that the Italian Army could win the war easy if it wasn't for those fork-tailed airplanes coming over and shooting them up, a notion that seemed particularly to amuse the pilots. Then I went to the P-38 squadron mess with Adler, who had just returned from patrol duty and wasn't going out on the strafe job, and Gustke, who was also remaining behind. This mess was relatively luxurious. They had tables with plates and knives and forks on them, so they had no mess tins to wash after every meal. "We live well here," Adler said. "Everything high class."

"The place the planes are going is not very far away," Gustke said, "so they ought to be back around half past two."

When we had finished lunch, I took another stroll around the post. I was walking toward the P-38 squadron's operations shack when I saw the planes begin to return from the mission. The first that came in had only the nose wheel of its landing gear down. There was evidently something the matter with the two other wheels. The plane slid in on its belly and stopped in a cloud of dust. Another plane was hovering over the field. I noticed, just after I spotted this one, that a little ambulance was tearing out onto the field. Only one of the two propellers of this plane was turning, but it landed all right, and then I counted one, two, three others, which landed in good shape. Five out of eight. I broke into a jog toward the operations shack. Gustke was standing before the door looking across the field with binoculars. I asked him if he knew whose plane had belly-landed, and he said it was a Lieutenant Moffat's and that a big, rough Texas pilot the other fellows called Wolf had been in the plane that had come in with one engine out. "I see Earnhart and Keith and Carlton, too," he said, "but Hoelle and the other two are missing."

A jeep was coming from the field toward the operations shack, and when it got nearer we could see Wolf in it. He looked excited. He was holding his right forearm with his left hand, and when the jeep got up to the shack he jumped out, still holding his arm.

"Is it a bullet hole?" Gustke asked.

"You're a sonofabitch it's a bullet hole!" Wolf shouted. "The sonofabitching P-forty's sonofabitching around! As we came in, we saw four fighters coming in the opposite direction and Moffat and I went up to look at them and they were P-forties, coming away. The other fellows was on the deck and we started to get down nearer them, to about five thousand, and these sonofa-bitching one nineties came out of the sun and hit Moffat and me the first burst and then went down after the others. There was ground fire coming up at us, too, and the sonofabitches said we was going to be over friendly territory. I'm God-damn lucky not to be killed."*

"Did we get any of them?" Gustke asked.

"I know I didn't get any," Wolf said, "but I saw at least four planes burning on the ground. I don't know who the hell they were."

By that time another jeep had arrived with Earnhart, looking utterly calm, and one of the mechanics from the field. "My plane is all right," Earnhart told Gustke. "All gassed up and ready to go. They can use that for patrol."

The telephone inside the shack rang. It was the post first-aid station calling to say that Moffat was badly cut up by glass from his windshield but would be all right. The mechanic said that the cockpit of Moffat's plane was knee-deep in hydraulic fluid and oil and gas. "No wonder the hydraulic system wouldn't work when he tried to get the wheels down," the mechanic said. The phone rang again. This time it was group operations, calling for Earnhart, Keith, and Carlton, all three of them unwounded, to go over there and tell them what had happened. The three pilots went away, and a couple of the men got Wolf back into a jeep and took him off to the first-aid station. Hoelle and the two other pilots were still missing. That left only Gustke and me, and he said in a sad young voice, like a boy whose chum has moved to another city, "Now we have lost our buddies."

A couple of days later I learned that Hoelle had bailed out in disputed territory and made his way back to our lines, but the two other boys are either dead or prisoners.

* Normal confusion.

Not many Mondays ago I was standing in a chow line with my mess tins at an airfield* in southern Tunisia, waiting to get into a dugout where some mess attendants were ladling out a breakfast of stew and coffee. The field is enormous, a naturally flat airdrome of white sand and alfa grass that doesn't hold rainwater long enough to spoil the runways—terrain of the kind a French writer once said looked like foamy seas. All around the field there are bulky, reddish mountains. To the east, the sun was just coming up over one of them, and the air was very cold. The mess shack was covered on top and three sides by a mound of earth. It served officers and men of a squadron of P-40 fighters, and on that particular Monday morning I stood between a corporal named Jake Goldstein, who in civilian life had been a Broadway songwriter, and a private named John Smith, of New Hope, Pennsylvania, who used to help his father, a contractor, build houses. Goldstein told me about a lyric he had just written for a song to be called "Bombs." "The music that I think of when it goes through my head now," he said, "is kind of a little like the old tune called 'Smiles,' but maybe I can change it around later. The lyric goes:

> There are bombs that sound so snappy,
> There are bombs that leave folks sad,
> There are bombs that fell on dear old Dover,
> But those bombs are not so bad.

The idea is that the real bad bomb is when this girl quit me and blew up my heart."

"It sounds great," I told the Corporal.

"It will be even bigger than a number I wrote called 'What Do You Hear from Your Heart?'" Goldstein said. "Probably you remember it. Bing Crosby sang it once on the Kraft Cheese Hour. If you happen to give me a little writeup, remember that my name

---

* This time it was Thélepte, in Tunisia.

in the songwriting business is Jack Gould." Private Smith started to tell me that he had once installed some plumbing for a friend of mine, Sam Spewack, the writer, in New Hope. "His wife, Bella, couldn't make up her mind where she wanted the can," Smith said, "so I said—"

I never heard any more about Bella Spewack's plumbing, because Major Robert Christman, the commanding officer of the squadron, came up to me and said, "Well, it's a nice, quiet morning." He had his back to the east. I didn't get a chance to answer him, because I started to run like hell to get to the west side of the mound. A number of soldiers who had been scattered about eating their breakfast off the tops of empty gasoline cans had already started running and dropping their mess things. They always faced eastward while they ate in the morning so that they could see the Messerschmitts come over the mountains in the sunrise. This morning there were nine Messerschmitts. By the time I hit the ground on the lee side of the mound, slender airplanes were twisting above us in a sky crisscrossed by tracer bullets—a whole planetarium of angry worlds and meteors. Behind our shelter we watched and sweated it out. It is nearly impossible to tell Messerschmitts from P-40s when they are maneuvering in a fight, except when one plane breaks off action and leaves its opponent hopelessly behind. Then you know that the one which is distanced is a P-40. You can't help yelling encouragement as you watch a fight, even though no one can hear you and you cannot tell the combatants apart. The Messerschmitts, which were there to strafe us, flew right over the mess shack and began giving the runways and the planes on the field a going-over.

We had sent up four planes on patrol that morning and they tried to engage the strafing planes, but other Germans, flying high to protect the strafers, engaged the patrol. Some "alert" planes that we had in readiness on the perimeter of the field took off in the middle of the scrap, and that was a pretty thing to watch. I saw one of our patrol planes come in and belly-land on the field, smoking. Then I saw another plane twisting out of the sky in a spin that had the soldiers yelling. We all felt that the spinning plane was a Messerschmitt, and it looked like a sure thing to crash into one of the mountains north of us. When the plane pulled out and disappeared over the summit, the yell died like the howl at Ebbets Field when the ball looks as if it's going into the bleachers and then is snagged by a visiting outfielder. It was a Messerschmitt, all right. A couple of minutes later every one of the German planes had disappeared, with our ships after them like a squad of heavy-footed comedy cops chasing small boys.

The fellows who had ducked for cover hoisted themselves off the ground and looked around for the mess things they had dropped. They were excited and sheepish, as they always are after a strafe party. It is humiliating to have someone run you away, so you make a joke about it. One soldier yelled to another, "When you said 'Flop!' I was there already!" Another, who spoke with a Brooklyn accent, shouted, "Jeez, those tracers looked just like Luna Park!"*

We formed the chow line again and one fellow yelled to a friend, "What would you recommend as a good, safe place to eat?"

"Lindy's, at Fifty-first Street," the other soldier answered.

"The way the guys ran, it was like a Christmas rush at Macy's," somebody else said.

Everybody tried hard to be casual. Our appetites were even better than they had been before, the excitement having joggled up our internal secretions. There were arguments about whether the plane that had escaped over the mountain would crash before reaching the German lines. I was scraping the last bits of stew from my mess tin with a sliver of hard biscuit when a soldier came up and told me that Major ——,† whom I had never met, had been killed on the field, that five men had been wounded, and that one A-20 bomber had been ruined on the ground.

---

* See note on p. 109. Luna was an amusement park at Coney Island, so famous that it gave its name to imitations all over Europe. Fireworks were a nightly feature, but they were pretty pallid compared to any respectable antiaircraft barrage. Luna is no more.

† We were not allowed by the censor to mention names of casualties until they had appeared in the lists published at home. Now I cannot fill in this blank, because I forget the poor gentleman's name.

———

After I had washed up my tins, I walked over to the P-40 squadron operations shack, because I wanted to talk to a pilot familiarly known as Horse about a fight he had been in two days before. The day it had happened I had been visiting a P-38 squadron's head-quarters on the field. I had seen eight P-38s go out to attack some German tanks and only five come back, two of them badly dam-aged. A lot of Focke-Wulf 190s had attacked the P-38s over the tar-get, and Horse and three other P-40 pilots, who were protecting the 38s, had been up above the 190s. Horse was a big fellow with a square, tan face and a blond beard. He came from a town called Quanah, in Texas, and he was always showing his friends a tinted picture of his girl, who was in the Waves. Horse was twenty-five, which made him practically a patriarch in that squadron, and every-body knew that he was being groomed to command a squadron of his own when he got his captaincy. He was something of a wit. Once I heard one of the other boys say that now that the field had been in operation for six weeks, he thought it was time the men should build a sit-down latrine. "The next thing we know," Horse said, "you'll be wanting to send home for your wife."

I found Horse and asked him about the fight. He said he was sorry that the 38s had had such a bad knock. "I guess maybe it was partly our fault," he said. "Four of our ships had been sent out to be high cover for the thirty-eights. They didn't see any thirty-eights or Jerries either, so when their gas was beginning to run low they started for home.* Myself and three other fellows had started out to relieve them and we passed them as they came back. The thirty-eights must have arrived over the tanks just then, and the one nineties must have been hiding at the base of a cloud bank above the thirty-eights but far below us. When we got directly over the area, we could see tracers flying way down on the deck. The one nineties had dived from the cloud and bounced the thirty-eights, who never had a chance, and the thirty-eights were streaking for home. We

* See note p. 115 on confusion.

started down toward the one nineties, but it takes a P-forty a long time to get anywhere and we couldn't help. Then four more one nineties dived from way up top and bounced us. I looped up behind one of them as he dived. My two wing men were right with me. I put a good burst into the sonofabitch and he started to burn, and I followed him down. I must have fired a hundred and twenty-five rounds from each gun. It was more fun than a county fair. Gray, my fourth man, put a lot of lead into another one ninety, and I doubt if it ever got home. The other two Jerries just kept on going."

The P-40 operations shack was set deep in the ground and had a double tier of bunks along three of its walls. Sand and grass were heaped over the top of the shack, and the pilots said that even when they flew right over it, it was hard to see, which cheered them considerably. The pilots were flying at least two missions a day and spent most of the rest of the time lying in the bunks in their flying clothes, under as many coats and blankets as they could find. The atmosphere in the shack was a thick porridge of dust diluted by thin trickles of cold air. Major Christman, the squadron leader, once said in a pleased tone, "This joint always reminds me of a scene in *Journey's End*."* The pilots, most of whom were in their earliest twenties, took a certain perverse satisfaction in their surroundings. "Here we know we're at war," one of them said to me. "Not that I wouldn't change for a room and bath at a good hotel."

During most of my stay at the field I lived not in the Journey's End shack but in one known as the Hotel Léon because technically it belonged to a French lieutenant named Léon,† a liaison officer between the French forces and our fliers. It was the newest and finest dugout on the field, with wooden walls and a wooden floor and a partition dividing it down the middle, and the floor was sunk about

---

* See note p. 109 on citations of the fictitious as criteria of reality.
† I suppressed his last name, Caplan, because he might have had relatives in France, who, if my piece in *The New Yorker* had reached France (highly unlikely), might have been made to suffer. Léon, when I saw him long after the war, was the number two man in the French Shell Oil Company—a *potentat petrolier*.

five feet below ground level. When I arrived at the field, there were plans to cover the part of the shack that projected above ground with sand, in which Léon intended to plant alfa. I was traveling with an Associated Press correspondent named Norgaard, and soon after our arrival Léon, a slender man with a thin, intelligent face and round, brown eyes, welcomed us to his palace. We put our stuff into the shack and emerged to find Léon throwing a modest shovelful of sand against one of the walls. Norgaard offered to help him. "There is only one shovel," Léon said with relief, pressing it into Norgaard's hands. "It is highly interesting for our comfort and safety that the house be covered entirely with sand. I am very occupied." Then he walked rapidly away, and Norgaard and I took turns piling sand around the Hotel Léon for endless hours afterward. Léon always referred to a telephone switchboard as a switching board, oil paper as oily paper, a pup tent as a puppy tent, and a bedding roll as a rolling bed.

After my talk with Horse, I walked over to the Hotel Léon and found it crowded, as it usually was. Only Léon and Norgaard and I, together with Major Philip Cochran and Captain Robert Wylie, lived in the hotel, but during the day Cochran and Léon used it as an office, and that was why it was crowded. When I first came to the field, it had been operating for six weeks practically as an outpost, for there was just a unit of American infantry, fifty miles to the southeast, between it and the region occupied by Rommel's army. Cochran, though only a major, had run the field for almost the entire period, but by the time I arrived he had reverted to the status of operations officer. The shack had telephone lines to detachments of French troops scattered thinly through the hills to our east, and they called up at all hours to tell Léon where German tanks were moving or to ask our people to do some air reconnaissance or drop bags of food to a platoon somewhere on a mountain. The French had no trucks to transport food. Sometimes Cochran flew with American transport planes to tell them where to drop parachute troops and sometimes he flew with bombers to tell them where to drop bombs. Because of Cochran's and Léon's range of activities, they always had a lot of visitors.

Attached to the partition in the shack were two field telephones, one of which answered you in French and the other in English. Two soldier clerks, who were usually pounding typewriters, sat on a bench in front of a shelf along one wall. One of them was Corporal Goldstein, the songwriter. The other was a private first class named Otto, who wore metal-rimmed spectacles with round lenses and belonged to the Pentecostal brethren, an evangelical sect which is against fighting and profanity. Otto owned some barber tools, and he cut officers' hair during office hours and enlisted men's at night. That morning he was cutting the hair of Kostia Rozanoff,* the commandant of the Lafayette Escadrille, a French P-40 outfit that was stationed at the field. Rozanoff was a blond, round-headed Parisian whose great-grandfather was Russian. Otto, perhaps taking a cue from the shape of Rozanoff's skull, had clipped him until he looked like Erich von Stroheim, but there was no mirror, so Rozanoff was happy anyway. Cochran, dressed in a dirty old leather flying jacket, had just come back from a mission in the course of which he thought he had destroyed a 190, and was trying to tell about that while nearly everybody else in the shack was trying to tell him about the morning's strafing. Also in the shack was Colonel Edson D. Raff, the well-known parachutist, who had once unexpectedly found himself in command of all the American ground forces in southern Tunisia and for weeks had successfully bluffed enemy forces many times larger. He had flown in from his post in Gafsa in a small plane which he used as his personal transport. He was crowded in behind Otto's barbering elbow and was trying to talk to Cochran over Rozanoff's head. Raff is short and always wears a short carbine slung over his left shoulder, even indoors. He invariably flies very low in his plane to minimize the risk of being spotted by a Messerschmitt. "I have one foot trailing on the ground," he says.

Lieutenant Colonel William Momyer, the commanding officer of the field, was sitting between Rozanoff and Corporal Goldstein, telling about a mission he had been on himself that morning, es-

---

* Rozanoff survived to fly jets. He will recur.

corting a lot of A-20s over Kebili, a town where the Italians had begun to repair a dynamited causeway across the Chott Djerid. "I bet the wops will never get any workmen to go back to that place," Momyer said. "We scared hell out of them." Momyer had shot down a Junkers 88 and a Messerschmitt within a week. He was hot.

Among the others in the shack that morning were Norgaard, the Associated Press man, and a tall P-40 pilot named Harris, who kept asking Léon whether any French unit had telephoned to report finding the Messerschmitt he had been shooting at during the strafing episode, because he was sure it must have crashed. It was the Messerschmitt we had seen pull out of the spin over the mountain. The English-speaking telephone rang and Captain Wylie answered it. He has the kind of telephone voice that goes with a large, expensive office, which he probably had in civilian life. It was somebody up the line asking for Major ———, the officer who had just been machine-gunned in the strafing. "Major ——— has been killed," Wylie said. "Is there anything I can do for you?"

There was a variety of stuff on the field when I was there. In addition to Christman's P-40 squadron and the Lafayette Escadrille, there was a second American P-40 squadron commanded by a Major Hubbard, which had a full set of pilots but only five ships. This was because the powers that be had taken away the other ships and given them to the Lafayettes in the interest of international good will. Hubbard's pilots were not sore at the Lafayettes, but they didn't think much of the powers that be. There was also a bomber squadron. The people on our field were not by any means sitting targets. They constantly annoyed the Germans, and that is why the Germans were so keen on "neutralizing" the field. But they didn't come back that day, and neither lunch nor dinner was disturbed.

The guests of the Hotel Léon often didn't go to the mess shack for dinner, because Léon would prepare dinner for them on the premises. He was a talented cook who needed the stimulation of a public, which was, that Monday evening, us. He also needed Wylie to keep the fire in the stove going, Cochran to wash dishes, and me and Norgaard to perform assorted chores. He got eggs from the Arabs and wine from a nearby French engineer unit, and he had gathered a choice assortment of canned goods from the quartermaster's stores. He also bought sheep and pigs from farmers. Léon's idea of a campaign supper was a *soufflé de poisson*, a gigot, and an *omelette brûlée à l'armagnac*. He made the soufflé out of canned salmon. The only trouble with dining at Léon's was that dinner was seldom ready before half past eight and it took until nearly midnight to clean up afterward.

During that Monday dinner we speculated on what the enemy would do next day. Norgaard said it was hell to have to get up early to catch the Germans' morning performance, but Cochran, the airfield's official prophet, and a successful one, said, "They'll want to make this one a big one tomorrow, so you can sleep late. They won't be over until two-thirty in the afternoon." Momyer, who was having dinner at the hotel that night, agreed that there would be something doing, but he didn't predict the time of day. Léon said, "I think also that there is something cooking in." Momyer decided to maintain a patrol of eight planes over the field all day. "Of course, maybe that's just what they want us to do, use our planes defensively, so we will fly less missions," he said, "but I think this time we ought to do it."

I had such faith in Cochran that it never occurred to me that the Germans would attack us before the hour he had named, and they didn't. The only enemy over the field the following morning was Photo Freddie, a German reconnaissance pilot who had become a local character. He came every morning at about forty thousand feet, flying a special Junkers 86 job so lightened that it could outclimb any fighter. The antiaircraft guns would fire, putting a row of neat, white smoke puffs a couple of miles below the seat of Freddie's pants, the patrol planes would lift languidly in his direction, like the hand of a fat man waving away a fly, and Photo Freddie would scoot off toward Sicily, or wherever he came from, to develop his pictures, thus discovering where all the planes on the field were placed. The planes were always moved around after he left, and we used to wonder what the general of the Luftwaffe said to poor Freddie when the bombers failed to find the planes where he had photographed them. Now and then some pilot tried to catch Photo Freddie by getting an early start, climbing high above the field, and then stooging around until he appeared. Freddie, however, varied the hour of his matutinal visits, and since a P-40 cannot fly indefinitely, the pilot would get disgusted and come down. I do not think anybody really wanted to hurt Freddie anyway. He was part of the local fauna, like the pet hens that wandered about the field and popped into slit trenches when bombs began to fall.

At about twenty minutes past two that afternoon Norgaard and I returned to the Hotel Léon to do some writing. An Alsatian corporal in the French army was working in front of the shack, making a door for the entrance. The corporal had been assigned by the French command to build Léon's house, and he was a hard worker. He always kept his rifle by him while he was working. He had a long brown beard, which he said he was going to let grow until the Germans were driven out of Tunisia. Only Goldstein and Otto were inside the hut this time. I said to Goldstein, "Why don't you write a new number called 'One Ninety, I Love You'?" Otto, who had been reading the *Pentecostal Herald*, said, "I do not think that would be a good title. It would not be popular." At that precise moment all of us heard the deep woomp of heavy ack-ack. It came from one of the British batteries in the mountains around the field. We grabbed our tin hats and started for the doorway. By the time we got there, the usual antiaircraft show was on. In the din we could easily distinguish the sound of our Bofors guns, which were making their peculiar seasick noises—not so much a succession of reports as one continuous retch. The floor of the shack, as I have said, was five feet below ground level and the Alsatian had not yet got around to building steps down to the entrance, so we had a nice, rectangular hole just outside from which to watch developments. The Germans were bombing now, and every time a bomb exploded, some of the sand heaped against the wooden walls was driven into the shack through the knotholes. The only trouble was that whenever a bomb went off we pulled in our heads and stopped observing. Then we looked out again until the next thump. After several of these thumps there was a straight row of columns of black smoke a couple of hundred yards to our right. I poked my head above ground level and discovered the Alsatian corporal kneeling and firing his rifle, presumably at an airplane which I could not see. The smoke began to clear and we hoisted ourselves out of the hole to try and find out what had happened. "I do not think I touched," the Alsatian said. A number of dogfights were still going on over the mountains. Scattered about the field, men, dragging themselves out of slit trenches, were pointing to the side of a mountain to the north, where there was smoke above a downed plane.

Léon had a little and old Citroën car, which he said had become, through constant association with the United States Army, "one naturalized small jeeps." He had left it parked behind the shack, and as Norgaard and I stood gawping about, Léon came running and shouted that he was going out to the fallen plane. We climbed into the naturalized jeeps and started across the field toward the mountainside. At one of the runways, we met a group of P-40 pilots, including Horse, and I yelled to them, "Was it theirs or ours?" "Ours, I think," Horse said. We kept on going. When we reached the other side of the field, we cut across country, and Léon could not make much speed. A couple of soldiers with rifles thumbed a ride and jumped on the running boards. As we went out across plowed fields and up the mountain toward the plane, we passed dozens of soldiers hurrying in the same direction.

When we arrived where the plane had fallen, we found three trucks and at least fifty men already there. The plane had been a Messerschmitt 109 belonging to the bombers' fighter escort. Flames were roaring above the portion deepest in the earth, which I judged was the engine. Screws, bolts, rings, and unidentifiable bits of metal were scattered over an area at least seventy-five yards square. Intermingled with all this were widely scattered red threads, like the bits left in a butcher's grinder when he has finished preparing an order of chopped steak. "He never even tried to pull out," a soldier said. "He must have been shot through the brain. I seen the whole thing. The plane fell five thousand feet like a hunk of lead." There was a sour smell over everything—not intolerable, just sour. "Where is the pilot?" Norgaard asked. The soldier waved his hand with a gesture that included the whole area. Norgaard, apparently for the first time, noticed the red threads. Most of the soldiers were rummaging amid the wreckage, searching for souvenirs. Somebody said that the pilot's automatic pistol, always the keepsake most eagerly sought, had already been found and appropriated. Another soldier had picked up some French and Italian money. How these things had survived the pilot's disintegration I do not know. While the soldiers walked about, turning over bits of the plane with their feet, looking for some object which could serve as a memento, an American plane came over and everybody began to run before someone recognized it for what it was. Just as we came back, a soldier started kicking at something on the ground and screaming. He was one of the fellows who had ridden out on our running boards. He yelled, "There's the sonofabitch's God-damn guts! He wanted my guts! He nearly had my guts, God damn him!" Another soldier went up to him and bellowed, "Shut up! It ain't nice to talk that way!" A lot of other men began to gather around. For a minute or so the soldier who had screamed stood there silently, his shoulders pumping up and down, and then he began to blubber.

Léon picked up a large swatch of the Messerschmitt's tail fabric as a trophy, and as the soldiers walked away from the wreck most of them carried either similar fragments or pieces of metal. After a while Norgaard and I climbed into Léon's car and the three of us started back toward the field. When we arrived, we learned that a lieutenant named Walter Scholl, who had never been in a fight before, had shot down the Messerschmitt. He was the fellow who, in the Cornell-Dartmouth football game of 1940, threw the famous fifth-down touchdown pass for Cornell, the one that was completed for what was considered a Cornell victory until movies of the game showed that it shouldn't have been Cornell's ball at all and the decision had to be reversed. But this was one win that they couldn't take away from him. Two other pilots had shot down two Junkers 88 bombers. One of our planes on the ground had been destroyed, and a slit trench had caved in on two fellows, nearly frightening them to death before they could be dug out.

Norgaard often said that the country reminded him of New Mexico, and with plenty of reason. Both are desert countries of mountains and mesas, and in both there are sunsets that owe their beauty to the dust in the air. The white, rectangular Arab houses, with their blue doors, are like the houses certain Indians build in New Mexico, and the Arabs' saddle blankets and pottery and even the women's silver bracelets are like Navajo things. The horses, which look like famished mustangs, have the same lope and are similarly bridlewise; burros are all over the place, and so is cactus. These resemblances are something less than a coincidence, because the Moors carried their ways of house-building and their handicraft patterns and even their breed of horses and method of breaking them to Spain, and the Spaniards carried them to New Mexico eight hundred years later.* All these things go to make up a culture that belongs to a high plateau country where there are sheep to furnish wool for blankets and where people have too little cash to buy dishes in a store, where the soil is so poor that people have no use for heavy plow horses but want a breed that they can ride for long distances and that will live on nearly nothing.

"This horse is young," an Arab once said to Norgaard and me as he showed us a runty bay colt tied in front of a combined general store and barbershop in a village about a mile from the airfield. "If I had had a little barley to feed him, he would be bigger, but what barley we had we have ourselves eaten. It is a poor country."

We used to go down to this village to get eggs when we were too lazy to make the chow line for breakfast or when we felt hungry at any time of day. We'd take them back to the shack and cook

---

* The cactus, though, was imported *from* Latin America into North Africa, where it is considered a prime fodder plant, particularly appreciated by camels.

them. Solitary Arabs squat along the roadside all over North Africa, waiting for military vehicles. When one comes into sight, the Arab pulls an egg out from under his rags and holds it up between thumb and forefinger like a magician at a night club. The price of eggs—always high, of course—varies in inverse ratio to the distance from a military post. Near big towns that are a long way from any post the Arabs get only five francs (ten cents at the new rate of exchange) for an egg, but in villages close to garrisons eggs are sometimes hard to find at any price. Norgaard and I followed a standard protocol to get them. First we went into the general store and barbershop, which was just a couple of almost empty rooms that were part of a mud house, and shook hands with all the male members of the establishment. Naturally, we never saw any of the females. Then we presented a box of matches to the head of the house, an ex-soldier who spoke French, and he invited us to drink coffee. The Arabs have better coffee and more sugar than the Europeans in North Africa. While we drank the coffee, we sat with the patriarch of the family on a white iron bed of European manufacture. The patriarch had a white beard and was always knitting socks; he stopped only to scratch himself. Once, as we were drinking coffee, we watched our French-speaking friend shave a customer's head. He simply started each stroke at the top of the cranium and scraped downward. He used no lather; the customer moistened his own poll with spittle after each stroke of the razor. Once, when the customer made a particularly awful face, all the other Arabs sitting around the room laughed. During the coffee-drinking stage of the negotiations we presented the Arabs with a can of fifty English cigarettes. After that they presented us with ten to fifteen eggs. Soldiers who were not such good friends of theirs usually got twenty eggs for fifty cigarettes, but it always costs something to maintain one's social life. One day I asked the barber why the old man scratched himself, and he said, laughing, "Because of the black spots. We all have them, and they itch." With much hilarity the Arabs showed us the hard, black spots, apparently under their skins, from which they were suffering. I judged the trouble to be a degenerate form of the Black Death, tamed during the centuries by the rugged constitutions of our hosts. Norgaard thought that the spots were just chiggers.

The Germans had come over our airfield on a Monday morning and strafed it and they had come back on Tuesday afternoon and bombed the place. They were going to start an offensive in southern Tunisia, we later learned, so they wanted to knock out this, the most advanced American field. On Wednesday morning the Germans made no attack. That afternoon Norgaard and I decided that we needed some eggs, so we walked down to the Arab village. I carried the eggs home in my field hat, a visored cap which has long flaps to cover your neck and ears when it is cold and which makes a good egg bag. We got back to the Hotel Léon between five and six o'clock. Major Cochran was out flying, and Léon was out foraging. Jake and Otto had gone to chow. There was less than an hour of daylight left.

Cochran, with his fine instinct for divining what the Germans were likely to do, had been sure that they would come over for the third day in succession, and Lieutenant Colonel William Momyer, the commanding officer of the field, had maintained a patrol of P-40s over the field all day. Cochran was among those taking their turns on patrol duty now. In forty minutes more all the planes would have to come down, because the field had no landing lights. And nothing had happened yet.

The walk had made Norgaard and me hungry and we decided to have our eggs immediately. We threw some kindling wood in the stove to stir the fire up and I put some olive oil in the mess tin in which I was going to scramble the eggs. The olive oil belonged to Léon. I took the lid off the hole in the top of the stove, put the mess tin over the hole, and broke all the eggs into the oil. I think there were eleven of them. They floated around half submerged, and although I stirred them with a fork, they didn't scramble. We decided that I had used too much oil, so we added some cheese to act as a cement. Before the cheese had time to take effect, we heard a loud explosion outside—plainly a bomb—and felt the shack rock.

Norgaard grabbed his tin hat and ran out the door to look, and I was just going to follow him when I reflected that if I left this horrible brew on the stove hole a spark might ignite the oil and thus set fire to the shack. I carefully put the mess on a bench and replaced the lid on the stove. I put on my helmet and followed Norgaard out into a kind of foxhole outside our door. More bombs exploded and then all we could hear was the racket of the Bofors cannon and .50 caliber machine guns defending the field. I went back inside, removed the stove lid, and put the eggs on again. Just as some warmth began to return to the chill mess, another stick of bombs went off. In the course of the next minute or so, I repeated my entire routine. Before I finished cooking dinner, I had to repeat it three times more. Finally the eggs and the cheese stuck together after a fashion and I drained the oil off. Then, since no bombs had dropped for a couple of minutes, I poured half the concoction into Norgaard's canteen cup, I put what was left in my mess tin, and we ate.

After we had eaten, we left the shack and started toward the large, round pit, some fifty yards away, which served as a control room for the field. Night had closed in. There had been no firing now for ten minutes, but as we approached the pit, our antiaircraft opened up again, firing from all around the field simultaneously. The Bofors tracer shells, which look like roseate Roman candles, reminded me of the fireworks on the lagoon at the World's Fair in Flushing. The burst ended as abruptly as it had begun, except that one battery of .50s kept on for an extra second or two and then stopped in an embarrassed manner.

We saw a lot of our pilots clustered around the pit. A corporal named Dick usually stood in the pit talking to our planes in the air by radio telephone, but Major Robert Christman, the C.O. of one of the post's fighter squadrons, was in Dick's place. I recognized Christman's voice as he spoke into the telephone, asking, "Did you see the gunfire? Did you see the gunfire?" You wouldn't ask a Jerry that if you were shooting at him, so I knew they were firing the antiaircraft guns to light one or more of our planes home. Christman asked again, "Did you see the gunfire? Did you see the gunfire?" Then he said to somebody else in the pit, probably Dick, "Hold this a minute." He stuck his head up over the side of the pit and shouted in the direction of a nearby dugout, "They say they saw the fire! Cochran's going to lead in and land to show the other ship the way! Lord, how that Cochran swears when he's excited! Tell the ack-ack to hold everything!" The switchboard through which the control room communicated with all the ack-ack batteries was in the dugout. Nothing was convenient on that field. It sometimes seemed that one of the pilots had scratched the whole thing out of the ground with a broken propeller blade after a forced landing.

We could see a plane showing red and green lights slowly circling over the field, descending gradually in long, deliberate spirals, as if the pilot wanted somebody to follow him. Then there was a blast of machine-gun fire and a fountain of tracers sprayed up from a distant edge of the field. "God damn them!" Christman yelled. "Tell them to hold that fire! What do they want to do—shoot Phil down?" The plane coasted slowly, imperturbably lower. It was Cochran's firm belief, I knew, that the ack-ack on the field had never hit anything, so he probably wasn't worried. The plane skimmed over the surface of the field. There was one pitiful red light on the field for it to land by. "He'll never make it that way," a pilot near me said. "What the hell is he doing? He'll overshoot. No, there he goes up again."

In a minute Christman, back at the phone once more, said, "Cochran went up because the other fellow couldn't see him. The other ship says he saw the gunfire, though. Now he wants a burst on the southern edge of the field only." Somebody in the switchboard dugout yelled, "Come on now! Battery C only, Battery C only! Everybody else *hold* it!" All the guns on the field immediately fired together. I could hear Momyer's voice yelling in the dugout, "God damn it, I'll have them all court-martialed!" Christman shouted, "He says he saw it and now he can see Cochran! He's coming in!" Cochran was again circling in the blackness above the field. The pilot next to me said, "This is sure sweating it out." I recognized him, partly by his voice and partly by the height of his shoulders, as Horse, the big Texan who wore a square beard.

"Did we get any of theirs?" I asked Horse.

"Yes, sir," Horse said. "Bent got one for sure. He's in already. And a French post has telephoned that another one is down near there in flames and that pilot out there with Cochran had one smoking. He must have chased it so far he couldn't get back before dark. Must have forgot himself. I don't rightly know who he is."

The ack-ack batteries fired again. They apparently did what was wanted this time, because nobody cursed. Christman called up from the pit, "They want one more burst, all together, and then they're coming in!" The message was relayed and the ack-ack fired another salvo. Now there were two planes, both showing lights, moving in the sky above the field, one high and one low. "Cochran's coming in," Horse said. "Look at him. Just like it was day and he could see everything." The lower pair of lights drifted downward, straightened out and ran forward along the field, and stopped. The other lights slowly followed them down, seemed to hesitate a moment, then slanted toward the ground, and coasted into a horizontal. "Good landing," Horse said. "We sure sweated that one." The second pilot to land turned out to be a lieutenant named Thomas, who had become too absorbed in the pursuit of a Junkers 88 to turn back until he had shot it down. That made three Junkers for us, each carrying a crew of four men. I learned that the German bombs had spoiled, to use the airmen's term, two of our planes on the field. A couple of minutes later a jeep that had gone out to meet Cochran's plane brought him to where the rest of us were standing. He is a short, box-chested man, and the two or three flying jackets he was wearing made him look shorter and stockier than he really is. He was feeling good. "I'm sorry I cursed you out, Bob! I was excited!" he yelled down into the control pit to Christman. Momyer, who had come out of the dugout, made as if to grab Cochran and hug him, but stopped in astonishment when he heard Cochran being so polite. It seemed to remind him of something. Looking rather thoughtful, he went back into the dugout and called up the lieutenant colonel in command of the ack-ack, which he had been abusing. "Thank you very much, Colonel," I heard him say. "Your boys certainly saved the day."

That evening was a happy one. Léon's shack was crowded with pilots talking about the successful fight and scrambling eggs and eating them out of mess tins. Cochran felt so good that he decided to have his first haircut since he had left New York three months before, so he sent over to the enlisted men's quarters for Otto to do the job. Otto is a young man with reddish hair and white eyebrows and a long nose, and he had a habit of getting interested in a conversation between two senior officers and breaking into it. Once, hearing Colonel Edson D. Raff, the parachute-troop commander, telling Lieutenant Colonel Momyer that he could take Tunis with no more than 450 men, Otto blurted out, "How can you be so sure?" Aside from this failing he is a good soldier and when he gives a haircut he really cuts off hair, so nobody can say he is looking for a return engagement in the near future.

It was well after dark when Léon came in from his foraging, which had been a success too. "I have bought three small peegs," he announced triumphantly, "and when they are theek enough we shall eat them." He had left them in the care of a hotelier in a town a few miles away. They were subsequently taken, and presumably eaten, by the Germans. At the time, however, Léon thought it a safe *logement* for the pigs. "I have also talked with the aide of General Koeltz," Léon said to Cochran and Momyer, "and he says that in the case any pilot sees any trucks moving on the road of which we have spoken yesterday, he is allowed to shoot without permission." While Otto cut Cochran's hair, we added up the box score of the three-day German attack on the field. The home team felt that it had done pretty well. During the Monday strafing the Germans had spoiled one of our planes on the field and another in the air and had killed one officer, a major, with machine-gun bullets. We had merely damaged one of their fighters. On Tuesday, while they had spoiled two more of our planes on the ground with bombs, we had shot down a Messerschmitt 109 and two Junkers 88s. That meant that we had lost a total of three planes but only one life while they had lost three planes and nine lives. One of our missions had also destroyed a Focke-Wulf 190 on Monday morning and a Messerschmitt had been badly damaged in the dogfight that had accompanied the strafing of our field. Wednesday evening we had destroyed three more planes and twelve men, and the Germans had succeeded only in damaging two planes on the ground, which gave us an imposing lead. "They won't be over tomorrow morning," Cochran said. "Maybe not all day. They'll want to think things over and try something big to make up for their losses and get the lead back. They'll be like a guy doubling his bet in a crap game."

That field had been fought over many times before in the course of history and a corner of it had been the site of a Numidian city. Bent, a pilot who talked with a British accent and had once done some digging among old ruins in England, said that every time he flew over that corner he could plainly see the gridiron pattern of the ancient streets on the ground. Horse, the bearded pilot, was irreverent about Bent's claims. "Maybe a couple of thousand years from now," he said, "people will dig around this same field and find a lot of C-ration cans that we've left and attribute them to archaeology. They'll say, 'Those Americans must surely have been a pygmy race to wear such small helmets. It scarcely seems possible they had much brains. No wonder they rode around in such funny airplanes as the P-forty.' "*

Another officer who turned up in Léon's shack that evening was Major (afterward Lieutenant Colonel) Vincent Sheean, who always points out these days that he was once a correspondent himself. He said he had been driving in a jeep on a road near the field when the bombing started, so he had stopped and jumped into a ditch. Sheean had come down from the second highest headquarters of the African Air Forces to see that the French pilots of the Lafayette Escadrille, which had recently arrived at our field, received understanding and kind treatment from their American comrades. A

---

* I was back in 1956, but even the C-ration cans are gone. The natives of those parts are extremely poor, and may have thought even tin cans worth salvaging.

couple of the Lafayette pilots happened to be in the shack when he arrived; they had received so much kind treatment that they could hardly remember the words of "Auprès de Ma Blonde," which they were trying to teach to Momyer on a purely phonetic basis.

The next day, Thursday, was as quiet as Cochran had said it would be. The Germans left us completely alone. In the morning the Lafayette Escadrille fellows went on their first mission, covering a French local offensive in a mountain pass, and returned without meeting any enemy aircraft.

The exposed position of our mess shack had begun to worry Major Christman's men after the strafing we had received the Monday before, and he had ordered the chow line transferred to a place called the Ravine, a deep, winding gulch on the other side of the high road along one end of the field. Most of the men lived in the Ravine and felt safe there. They had scooped out caves in its sides and used their shelter halves to make doors. One stretch of the gully was marked by a sign that said "Park Avenue." Sheean and I stood in the chow line for lunch and then took an afternoon stroll along Park Avenue. Afterward I went back to Léon's shack to write a letter and found it crowded, as usual. An engineer officer who had been at the field a couple of days was asking Cochran how he could be expected to get on with the construction job he had been sent there to do if new bomb holes appeared on the field every day and his detachment had to fill them up. "We've been filling up bomb holes ever since we been here, and it looks like we won't get a chance to do anything else," the engineer said. "My colonel sent me down here to build revetments for airplanes and he's going to expect me back soon." Another visitor, a captain in the Royal Engineers, asked him if there were any unexploded bombs on the runways. Men on the field always referred to this British captain as the booby-trap man, the planting of fiendish traps for the enemy being his specialty, and added with respect, "Even the parachute troops say he's crazy." He had made several jumps with Colonel Raff's parachutists to install his humorous devices in places where he thought German soldiers would later get involved with them. The American officer told him that there were several unexploded bombs on the runways and that he had marked off their positions with empty oil drums.

"But haven't you removed the fuses?" the booby-trap man asked with obvious astonishment.

"To hell with that!" his American colleague said with feeling. "They won't do any harm if they do go off. It's a big field."

"Oh, but they'll make quite a lot of noise," the booby-trap man said, still vaguely unhappy.

The American officer looked at the booby-trap man and Cochran as if they were both lunatics and went out of the hut without saying anything more. "How *extraordinary!*" the booby-trap man said. "He didn't even seem interested." He sounded hurt, like a young mother who has just learned that a visitor does not care for babies.

The booby-trap man looked like a conventional sort of Englishman, with a fair, boyish face and a shy smile. He spoke with the careful accent of the north countryman who has been to a university and he did not himself use the term "booby trap." He preferred to call his darlings, variously, trip mechanisms, push mechanisms, pull mechanisms, and antipersonnel switches. Trip mechanisms, for instance, are the ones soldiers inadvertently set off by stumbling over a concealed wire, and pull mechanisms are those they explode by picking up some innocent-seeming object like a corned-beef tin. The captain was an amateur botanist and seldom went out without a couple of pocketfuls of small devices to set about the countryside in likely spots as he ambled along collecting specimens of Tunisian grasses. I asked him that afternoon how he had started on what was to become his military career, and he said with his shy smile, "I expect it was at public school, when I used to put hedgehogs in the other boys' beds. After a while the hedgehogs began to pall and I invented a system for detuning the school piano, so that when the music master sat down to play 'God Save the King' it sounded god-awful."

"I sometimes try to imagine what your married life will be like,

Captain," Cochran said. "Someday the baby will be in the crib and your wife will go to pick it up and the whole house will blow up because you've wired the baby to a booby trap."

"I trust I shall be able to restrain my professional instincts to fit the circumstances of domestic life," the booby-trap man said rather stiffly. He was a man who really took his branch of warfare seriously.

Sleep in the Hotel Léon was usually interrupted in the gray hour before dawn by the jangle of a field telephone that spoke French. Then Léon would sit up and pull the telephone from the holster in which it hung at the foot of his bed. He slept wearing all the clothes he possessed, which included several sweaters, a long military overcoat, and a muffler. When he grabbed the phone, he would say, "*Allo! Oui?*" (The rest of us sometimes would sing "Sweet Allo, Oui" to the tune of "Sweet Eloise.") The French voice at the other end of the phone was almost always audible, and, so that the half-awake American officers in the shack would get the idea of what was going on, Léon would reply in a hybrid jargon. He would say, for example, "One *ennemi appareil* flying sousewest over point 106? *Merci, mon capitaine.*" Then he would hang up and fall back into bed, muttering, "*Imbécile*, why he don't fly west? He will be losted."

A partition divided Léon's shack into a bedroom, in which four of us slept side by side, and an office, in which only two slept. In the bedroom were Léon, Major Cochran, Norgaard, and myself. Captain Robert Wylie and Vincent Sheean slept in the office. We would try to ignore Léon's first morning call, but before long there would be another; Cochran would be asking what was going on, and we would hear the roar of the motors down on the field being warmed up for the dawn patrol and the morning missions. Then we would hear Wylie clattering around our stove in his G.I. shoes and there would be a glow in the shack when he put the match to the paper with which he started the fire. Wylie, who wasn't a flying officer, always tried to have the shack warm by the time Cochran got up, and he wanted the Major to stay in bed until the last minute. He was as solicitous as a trainer with a favorite colt, and the rest of us benefited from the care he took of Cochran, because we didn't get up early, either. Wylie is a wiry man with a high forehead and a pepper-and-salt mustache. He wears glasses and looks like an advertising artist's conception of an executive who is in good humor because he has had an excellent night's sleep owing to Sanka. He is a highly adaptable man. After Wylie had puttered around for a while, we would sit up one by one and stretch and complain about being disturbed or about the cold and then go outside to wash. Morn-ings on which the antiaircraft opened up against early visitors, the tempo was accelerated. Cochran undressed at night by loosening the knot in his tie and drew it tight again in the morning as a sign that he was dressed. These were symbolic gestures he never omitted.

On the morning of the fifth and last day of our small private war, it was the antiaircraft that brought us out of bed. We scrambled for the door, lugging our tin hats, our toothbrushes, and our canteens. The Germans were already almost over our field, but they were quite high, since our patrol planes had engaged them on the way in and they could not break off the fight to strafe us. The German planes were single-engined fighters, which sometimes carry wing or belly bombs, but this time they were not bombing. Some of the defending planes were marked with the tricolor *cocarde* of the French army. It was, I suppose, a historic combat, because the pilots of the Lafayette Escadrille, which was stationed at the field, were making the first French air fight against the Germans since the armistice of 1940. The Escadrille, which had been equipped with a number of our Curtiss P-40s in Morocco, had been with us only a few days.

As we watched, a plane fell, apparently far on the other side of a ridge of mountains near the field, and we yelled happily, thinking it was a Messerschmitt. After the fight we were to learn that it had been a P-40 with a French sergeant pilot. Cochran kept up an expert running commentary on what all the pilots were trying to do, but he frequently didn't know which were French and which German. During the battle we simultaneously watched and brushed our teeth. A couple of the French planes landed on the field while the others were still fighting, so we knew that they must have been shot up. Finally, one group of planes above the field started away and the others chased them, but the first planes simply outclimbed their pursuers and left them behind; then there was no longer any doubt about which were Messerschmitts and which were Curtisses. One German plane remained over the field, at perhaps thirty thousand feet, even after the rest of the invaders had disappeared. "That's what kills me," Cochran said, pointing to the lone plane. "There's that sucker stooging around and casing the joint for a future job and he's so high nobody can bother him." Finally the stooge, evidently having found out all he wanted to know, took his leisurely departure.

A group of P-40s rose to relieve the Lafayettes, and the French planes came buzzing in like bees settling on a sugared stick. In a few minutes Kostia Rozanoff, commandant of the Escadrille, and his pilots had gathered in Léon's shack to discuss the fight. All of them had had combat experience in 1939 and 1940, but the engagement this morning had been the *rentrée*, and they were as excited as if they had never seen a Messerschmitt before. Despite the fact that they were old hands, Cochran said, they had fought recklessly, climbing up to meet the Messerschmitts instead of waiting until the Germans dived. "If they don't dive," Cochran had frequently warned his own pilots, "you just don't fight." The French pilots' ardor had got them a beating, for besides the pilot whom we had seen fall and who, Rozanoff said, had not bailed out and was quite certainly killed, the two planes that had landed during the combat were riddled and would be of no use except for salvage, and one of their pilots had been wounded. The Germans apparently had suffered no damage at all. Rozanoff, a chunky, blond man who gets his name, as well as his coloring and his high cheekbones, from his Russian ancestry, is thirty-seven and has a deep voice, like Chaliapin's. He said that the pilot who had been killed was his wing man and he could not understand how he had failed to see the Messerschmitt that had attacked him from the rear. "I cry him turn," Rozanoff kept saying. "I turn. He turns not. Poor little one."

It was extremely sad that the first Escadrille combat had not been a victory; it would have been such a fine story to bolster French morale all over the world. I remembered the sergeant pilot, who had been a likable fellow. An officer of the district gendarmerie brought the sergeant's wedding ring back to the field later in the morning.

My friend Norgaard and I had chosen that Friday for our departure from the field. We were going in to the big city, where the censors and the cable offices were, to write some stuff and get it off. There was air transportation between our field and the more settled places to the west, where staff officers and diplomats lived, but the service did not run on a formal schedule. Big Douglas transports skimmed in over the mountains once and sometimes twice a day, carrying mail and supplies, and they usually had room for passengers going back. They came at a different hour each day to make it as hard as possible for the Germans to waylay them. When they came, they stayed merely as long as was necessary, and the only way to be sure of a ride was to have your bedding roll made up and to stay near the landing field waiting for the transports to appear. When they did, an officer would drive you and your luggage out to them in a jeep and you would get your stuff aboard. Norgaard and I hung around in front of our shack that morning, waiting. As the day wore on, a strong wind came up and blew great clouds of sand. At about eleven o'clock two transports arrived, escorted by some Spitfires. Cochran had planned to drive us down to the transports, but he was called to the telephone, and Christman said that he would drive us instead.

When we arrived where the transports were standing on the runway, the transport captain, whose name, I noted from the leather strip on the breast of his flying jacket, was Lively, came over to the jeep and asked where his Spits could get gas. His ship was named the *Scarlett O'Hara*. He and Christman started discussing what was the quickest way to get the gas. Christman and Norgaard and I stayed in the jeep. Dust was blowing over the field a mile a minute. Suddenly Christman looked over his shoulder, called on

God, and vanished. Within a moment Lively was also gone. I turned around to speak to Norgaard, and discovered that he too had evaporated. I hate to sit in an empty jeep when I don't know why the other passengers have jumped. I do not remember actually getting out myself, but I know that I was already running when I heard somebody yell, "Hit the dirt!" Under the circumstances, this sounded so sensible that I bellyflopped to the ground, and I landed so hard that I skinned my knees and elbows. No surface in the world offers less cover than a runway. I regretted that my body, which is thick, was not thinner. I could guess what had happened: German strafers had ridden in on the dust storm and nobody had seen them until they opened fire. I knew that the very nasty noises above me were being made by airplane cannon and that the even nastier ones close to me came from the detonation of the small explosive shells they fire. The strafers, I figured, were heading for the transports—large, expensive, unarmored jobs that you could punch holes in with a beer-can opener. I was therefore in line with the target and was very sorry to be where I was.

As soon as there was a lull in the noises overhead, I got up and ran toward the edge of the runway to get away from the transports, but more noises came before I made it, so I flopped again. After they had passed, I got up and ran off the runway. I saw a soldier in a fine, large hole nearly six feet deep. He shouted, "Come right in, sir!" You can have Oscar of the Waldorf any time; I will always remember that soldier as my favorite host. I jumped in and squeezed up against him. Almost immediately the noises came a third time and two transport pilots jumped down on my back. I was astonished that I had been able to outrun such relatively young men. I was thirty-eight.

By this time all of our machine guns along the edges of the field were firing away, and there was a fourth pass, as the fliers say, and a loud crash, as if one of the Germans had dropped a bomb. A minute or two later the noise began to die down. Looking up from the bottom of the hole, we could see a man descending in a parachute. The big, white chute was swaying this way and that in the wind. The man had an awful time landing. We could see that even from a distance. The chute dragged him and bounced hell out of him after he landed. Afterward, word got around the field that he was an American. I didn't find out until a couple of days later, though, that the man with the chute had been Horse. In landing, he hit his head against the ground and suffered a concussion of the brain. They put him in an ambulance and started for the nearest hospital, which was forty miles by road, but he had bad luck. The Germans had been strafing that road, too, that morning, and when the ambulance got within five miles of the hospital, it was blocked by two burning ammunition trucks. The shells on the trucks were exploding. The squadron surgeon and the ambulance-driver put Horse on a stretcher and carried him around the trucks to a safe point on the other side, and an ambulance from the hospital came out to pick him up, but by the time it got there he was dead.*

When the shooting at the field was over, the pilots and the soldier and I got out of the hole and walked back toward the transports, which were still there. Norgaard climbed out of another hole not far away. He said that when he had jumped out of the jeep he had crawled under it, and there he had found a transport lieutenant who had the same idea. They had given up the jeep after the first pass and run for it, just as I had already done. We stared at the parallel furrows the Messerschmitt cannon had plowed down the runway, as if they had been the teeth of a rake, and ourselves the field mice between them. The transport boys borrowed our jeep to get gas for the Spits, which had been immobilized during the raid because their tanks were empty. When the boys came back, we climbed into one of the transports. The big planes took off almost immediately. "Leave them laughing," Norgaard said to me when he recovered sufficient breath to say anything.

We learned later that the strafing had been done by eight Messerschmitts flying in four loose pairs, and that was why there had been

* Horse's square name was Alton B. Watkins, but hardly anybody at Thélepte knew. Father McCreedy buried him under a metal plate marked "Horace."

four passes. Another Messerschmitt, making a run by itself, had dropped one bomb, ineffectually. There had also been a high cover of Messerschmitts; one of them had accounted for Horse. We were told that Cochran had said, with a hint of admiration in his voice, "It is getting so that the Germans patrol our field for us." A lot of Air Force generals who were on a tour of inspection visited the field shortly after we left, said that the situation was very grave, and left, too. This point in the war over the field may be compared to the one in a Western movie at which the villain has kicked hell out of the heroine and just about wrestled her to the brink of ruin in a locked room.*

At about two-thirty that same afternoon the Lafayette Escadrille was patrolling the field, in the company of two pilots from the American P-40 squadron commanded by Major Hubbard. This squadron had its full complement of pilots but only five planes. The pilots took turns flying the five ships, so they were not getting a great deal of practice. Nevertheless, Hubbard's squadron had already scored two victories that week. The two American pilots in the air were Hubbard and a man named Beggs. Two of their mates, Boone and Smith, were on the ground on alert call, sitting in their planes ready to reinforce the patrol if they were called.

This field didn't have one of those elaborate radio airplane-detectors that warn swank airdromes of the approach of enemy aircraft. It had to rely on its patrol system and on tips that watchers telephoned in. The tipsters were not infallible, as Norgaard and I had noticed that morning, and in the afternoon they slipped up again. Ten Junkers 88 bombers unexpectedly appeared, flying toward the field at three thousand feet. There was an escort of four fighters, unusually small for so many bombers, flying high above them and, as someone described it to me, acting oddly uninterested. The Frenchmen on patrol, also flying high, made one swipe at the escort and it disappeared, not to be seen again. Nine of the bombers were flying in three loose V's and one ship was trailing the third V. Hubbard took the bomber on the right of the first V and

* See note on p. 109.

shot it down. Beggs got the middle one and a Frenchman knocked down the one on the left. The other Junkers had begun to drop their bombs. Boone and Smith came up off the field through the falling bombs to join the battle. Hubbard shot down another plane, and Boone, who had never fired a shot at a man or a plane before, came up behind one Junkers and blasted it out of the sky; it caromed against another Junkers on the way down, which gave Boone two planes with one burst of fire. He went on to destroy two more. Smith, opening fire at extreme range for fear that he would be shut out, blew the rudder off another Junkers, which also crashed. The tenth Junkers headed for home, but it never got there; the French picked off that one. It was the jackpot, ten out of ten. It was also the end of the five-day war over our airfield. No producer of Westerns ever wound up a film more satisfactorily.* The Germans stayed away, in fact, for nineteen days and then came back only once, for a quick sneak raid.

Of the ten German bomber crews, only four men came out of the fight alive and two of these died in the hospital. The two others said that the ten bombers had been escorted by four Italian Macchi C. 202 fighters, which had deserted them. Why the Luftwaffe should have entrusted four Macchis with the protection of ten Junkers 88s is harder to explain than the result. The Germans, fortunately for our side, sometimes vary their extreme guile with extreme stupidity.

I didn't have a chance to return to the airfield for about ten days, and then I stopped in on my way down to Gafsa, where the Americans were supposed to be launching a ground offensive. Captain Wylie, who told me about the big day at the field, said that Boone had come into the operations shack looking rather incredulous himself. "Probably I'm crazy," he had said to Wylie, "but I think I just shot down four planes."† The Frenchmen thought up a gag.

---

* See note on p. 109. From here on, I will cease to call attention to this phenomenon.
† His luck did not last. He was killed a couple of weeks later.

They said it was a victory for three nations—"The Americans shot down seven planes, we shot down two, and the Italians shot down the tenth so the crew couldn't tell on them."

The Americans left the field undefeated, for the two P-40 squadrons were relieved not long afterward by other outfits and sent back from the fighting zone to rest. Christman's squadron had been fighting there steadily for two months. I met the fellows from Christman's bunch again while I was trying to get a ride into civilization from another airfield, a bit west of the one where they had been stationed. A lot of trucks drove up and deposited the officers and men of the squadron on the field, with their weapons, their barracks bags, and their bedding rolls. Christman was there, and Private Otto, the squadron barber, and Corporal Jake Goldstein, the reformed songwriter. I renewed my acquaintance with a pilot named Fackler, whom I remembered especially because he had once, finding himself flying formation with two Messerschmitts who thought he was another Messerschmitt, shot one of them down, and I again met Thomas, the Oklahoma boy who had been lost in the air one night and had been lighted home by the fire of the field's antiaircraft guns, and a nonflying lieutenant named Lamb, who used to practice law in New York, and a dozen others. I felt as if I had known them all for a long time.

Eleven transports came in to take the squadron west, and I arranged to travel in one of them. I was in the lead ship of the flight, and the transport major who commanded it told me that his orders were to drop the squadron at a field only about an hour's flight away. Then the transports would go on to their base, taking me along with them. It was pleasant to see the faces of the P-40 boys aboard my transport when it took off. They didn't know anything about the field they were going to, but they knew that they were going for a rest, so they expected that there would at least be huts and showers there. They looked somewhat astonished when the transports settled down in a vast field of stubble without a sign of a building anywhere around it. There were a few B-25 bombers on the field and in the distance some tents. A transport sergeant came out of the pilot's compartment forward in our plane and worked his way toward the tail of our ship, climbing over the barracks bags heaped in the space between the seats. "I guess this is where you get out," he told the P-40 fellows.

A couple of soldiers jumped out and the rest began passing out bags and rifles to them. Pretty soon all the stuff was piled outside the plane and the soldiers were standing on the field, turning their backs to a sharp wind and audibly wondering where the hell the barracks were. A jeep with an officer in it drove out from among the tents and made its way among the transports until it arrived at our ship. The transport major talked to the officer in the jeep, and then they both drove over to the transport Christman was traveling in and picked him up, and the three of them drove back to the tents. Some soldiers who had been near the jeep had heard the field's officer say that nobody there had been notified that they were coming. The transport major had replied that all he knew was that he had orders to leave them there. The soldiers who had heard the conversation communicated the news to the others by Army telegraphy. "Situation normal!"* one soldier called out, and everybody laughed. Soldiers are fatalistic about such situations.

Some time before a report had circulated among the men that the squadron was to go back to the United States. Now I heard one soldier say, "This don't look like no United States to me."

Another one said, "When we get back there, Freddie Bartholomew will be running for President." He didn't seem sore.

Somebody said, "I hear they're going to start us here and let us hack our way through to South Africa."

Somebody else began a descant on a favorite Army fantasy: what civilian life will be like after the war. "I bet if my wife gives me a piece of steak," he said, "I'll say to her, 'What the hell is this? Give me stew.' "

Another one said, "I bet she'll be surprised when you jump into bed with all your clothes on."

The delicacy of their speculations diminished from there on.

After a while the jeep came back. The transport major got out

* See note on confusion p. 115.

and said, "There seems to be some mistake. You'd better put your stuff back in the ship." We all got back into the planes, and the major told me that this obviously wasn't the place to leave the men but that he would have to wait until base operations could get headquarters on the telephone and find out their destination. We sat in the planes for an hour; then another officer came out in a jeep and said that nobody at headquarters knew anything about the squadron, so the major had better not take it any place else. The major told his sergeant to instruct the men to take their luggage off the planes. "We enjoy doing this. It's no trouble at all," one of the soldiers in my plane said. The transports took off and left them standing there. I learned later that they eventually got straightened out. After two or three days someone at headquarters remembered them; the pilots were sent to western Morocco and the ground echelon was moved to another field.

All this happened what seems now to be long ago, in the pioneer days of the American Army in Tunisia. The old field, from which I had watched the five-day war, was never knocked out from the air, but it was taken by German ground troops with tanks, and then the Americans took it back and went on. The Hotel Léon, if the Germans hadn't burned it, was certainly full of booby traps for the Americans when they got there. I shouldn't like to have slept in it. Léon is now in a large Algerian city, where he has been assigned to a calmer liaison job. Cochran was promoted and decorated and posted to a new command.*

* He is now back in Erie, Pennsylvania.

Quest for Mollie

(MAY 26, 1945; JUNE 2, 1945)

Mollie is a part of the history of La Piste Forestière, and La Piste Forestière is perhaps the most important part of the history of Mollie. La Piste Forestière, or the Foresters' Track, is a dirt road that connects Cap Serrat, on the northern coast of western Tunisia, with Sedjenane, a town twenty miles inland. The country it runs through is covered with small hills, and almost all the hills are coated with a ten-foot growth of tall bushes and short trees, so close together that once you leave the road you can't see fifty feet in front of you. From the top of any hill you can see the top of another hill, but, because of the growth, you can't tell whether there are men on it. This made the country hard to fight in. The hillsides that have no trees are bright with wild flowers in the spring, and when some other war correspondents and I traveled back and forth along the Foresters' Track in jeeps, we sometimes used to measure our slow progress by reference to the almost geometrical patterns of color on such slopes. There was, for example, the hill with a rough yellow triangle of buttercups against a reddish purple background of other blooms; it indicated that you were five miles from the road's junction with the main highway at Sedjenane. With luck you might reach the junction in two hours, but this was extremely unlikely, for the road was just wide enough for one truck—not for a truck and a jeep or even for a truck and a motorcycle. Only a man on foot or on a horse could progress along the margin of the road when there was a vehicle on it, and the horse would often have to scramble by with two feet off the road, like the sidehill bear of eastern Tennessee. When a jeep met a convoy, it sometimes had to back up for hundreds of yards to where there was room to get off the road and wait. Then, when all the heavy vehicles had passed, the jeep would resume its journey, perhaps to meet another convoy before it had recovered the lost yardage. Even when you got in behind trucks going your way, they were packed so closely together that they advanced at a crawl, so you did too. Bits of the war were threaded along the Foresters' Track like beads on a string, and the opportunity to become familiar with them was forced upon you. Mollie, for me, was the gaudiest bead.

The reason the Foresters' Track is such a miserable excuse for a road is that in normal times there is little need for it. There is a lighthouse at Cap Serrat and a forest warden's house about halfway between that and Sedjenane. The few Berbers in the district, who live in brush shelters in the bush, have no vehicles or need of a road. But in late April and early May of 1943, La Piste Forestière was an important military thoroughfare. The Allied armies, here facing east, lay in a great arc with their right flank at Sousse, on the Gulf of Tunis, and this little road was the only supply line for twenty miles of front; that is, the extreme left flank of the Allied line. The actual front line ran parallel to the road and only a few hundred yards east of it during the first days of the offensive that was to end the Allies' North African campaign, but because of the hills and the brush, people on the road couldn't see the fighting. However, American artillery placed just west of the road—it would have been an engineering feat to get it any considerable distance into the brush— constantly fired over our heads as our jeeps piddled along. The gunners hoped that some of their shells were falling on the Germans and Italians who were trying to halt our infantry's advance with fire from hidden mortars and machine guns. The Luftwaffe in Africa had predeceased the enemy ground forces; the budget of planes allotted it for the African adventure was exhausted, I suppose, and the German High Command sent no more. This was lucky for us, because one good strafing, at any hour, would have jammed the road with burned-out vehicles and Allied dead. By repeating the strafing once a day, the Germans could have kept the road permanently out of commission. The potential danger from the air did not worry us for long, however. You soon become accustomed to immunity, even when you cannot understand the reason for it.

Trucks left ammunition along the side of the road to be carried up to the fighting lines on the backs of requisitioned mules and horses and little Arab donkeys, a strangely assorted herd conducted by an equally scratch lot of soldiers. The Washington army had decided years before that the war was now 100 percent mechanized, so the field army, quite a different organization, had to improvise its animal transport as it went along. The wounded were carried down to the road by stretcher bearers. Ambulances, moving with the same disheartening slowness as everything else, picked up the casualties and took them out to a clearing station near the yellow-triangle hill I have mentioned, where some of the viable ones were patched up for the further slow haul out. Cruder surgical units, strung out along the road, took such cases as they were equipped to handle. These units were always right by the side of the road, since in that claustrophobe's nightmare of a country there was no other place for them to be. The advanced units were French and had women nurses with them. A French doctor I knew used to say that it helped the men bear pain if nurses were looking at them. "Since we have so little anesthesia," he said, "we rely upon vanity." Sometimes I would sit in my jeep and watch that doctor work. He had broken down a few saplings and bushes by the side of the road to clear a space for his ambulance, and next to the ambulance he had set up a camp stool and a folding table with some instruments on it. Once a traffic jam stopped my jeep near his post when he had a tanned giant perched on the camp stool, a second lieutenant in the Corps Franc d'Afrique. The man's breasts were hanging off his chest in a kind of bloody ruff. "A bit of courage now, my son, will save you a great deal of trouble later on," the doctor said as he prepared to do something or other. I assumed, perhaps pessimistically, that he was going to hack off the bits of flesh as you would trim the ragged edges of an ill-cut page. "Go easy, Doctor," the young man said. "I'm such a softie." Then the traffic started to move, so I don't know what the doctor did to him.

The Corps Franc d'Afrique was a unit that had a short and glorious history. Soon after the Allied landings in North Africa, in October 1942, the Corps Franc organized itself, literally, out of the elements the Darlanists in control of the North African government distrusted too much to incorporate into the regular French Army— Jews, anti-Nazis from concentration camps, de Gaullists, and other Allied sympathizers. A French general named Joseph de Goislard de Montsabert, who had helped plan the landings, had been thrown out by his collaborationist superiors, who, even after Darlan's agreement to play ball with the forces of democracy, had remained his superiors. De Montsabert, because he had a red face and snowy hair, was known to his troops as Strawberry in Cream. There had been, among the French in North Africa, a number of other professional officers and many reservists who, like the General, were apparently left out of the war because they were suspected of favoring de Gaulle or merely of being hostile to Germany. The Darlan regime had refused to mobilize the Jews because it clung to the Vichy thesis that they were not full citizens, and it did not want them to establish a claim to future consideration, and it was holding thousands of Spanish and German refugees and French Communists in concentration camps.

De Montsabert and a few of his officer friends, talking on the street in Algiers one rainy November day of that year, decided to start a "Free Corps" of men who wanted to fight but whom the government would not allow to. They took over a room in a schoolhouse on the Rue Mogador as headquarters and advertised in the *Echo d'Alger* for volunteers. The ad appeared once and then the Darlanist censorship, which was still operating under the Americans, like every other element of Vichy rule, suppressed it. But scores of volunteers had already appeared at the schoolhouse and de Montsabert sent them out with pieces of schoolroom chalk to write "Join the Corps Franc" on walls all over the city. Hundreds of new volunteers came in. General Giraud, who had arrived in Africa to command all the French but had subsequently accepted a role secondary to Darlan's, heard of the movement and interceded for it. Giraud, whatever his limitations, considered it natural that anybody in his right mind should want to fight the Germans. Darlan and his Fascist friends began to think of the Corps Franc as a means of getting undesirables out of the way, so the government recognized it but at the same time refused it any equipment. The Corps began life with a miscellany of matériel begged from the British and Americans. Its men wore British battle dress and French insignia of rank, lived on American C rations, and carried any sort of weapons they could lay their hands on. The most characteristic feature of their appearance was a long beard, but even this was not universal, because some of the soldiers were too young to grow one. After the Corps Franc's arrival in Tunisia, it added to its heterogeneous equipment a great deal more stuff it captured from the enemy. The Corps went into the line in February of 1943, in the zone north of Sedjenane, and it remained there into the spring.

Late April in Tunisia is like late June in New York, and heat and dust were great nuisances to our men when they were attacking. In February and March, however, coastal Tunisia is drenched with a cold and constant downpour. The Foresters' Track was two feet deep in water when the Corps Franc began to fight along it. There were two battalions to start with—about twelve hundred men—to cover a sector twenty miles long. A third and fourth battalion had been added by the time the Americans began their offensive. The Corps, in the beginning, had only two ambulances, converted farm trucks owned by a Belgian colonist in Morocco. The Belgian and his son had driven the trucks across North Africa to join the Corps. But the trucks were unable to negotiate the flooded Track, so the men of the Corps carried their wounded out to Sedjenane on their shoulders. I once asked my doctor friend why they had not used mules. "The mules rolled over in the water and crushed the wounded men," he said. "We know. We tried it with wounded prisoners."

Now that the great attack was on, there were other troops along the Track with the Corps—the Sixtieth Infantry of the American Ninth Division, part of the American Ninth Division's artillery, an American tank-destroyer battalion, some Moroccan units, and some American motortruck and medical outfits. The medics and the artillery made the French feel pampered and their morale got very high. One hot morning, I passed a lean, elderly soldier of the Corps Franc who was burying two of his comrades. He looked about sixty—there was no age limit in the Corps—and had a long, drooping mustache of a faded biscuit color. He had finished one grave and was sitting down to rest and cool off before beginning the other. The two dead men lay with their feet to the road. Blueflies had settled on their faces. I told my jeep driver to stop and asked the gravedigger what men these were. "One stiff was an Arab from Biskra," the old soldier said, "and the other a Spaniard, a nihilist from Oran." I asked him how his work was going. He wiped the sweat from his forehead and said happily, "Monsieur, like on roller skates."

A quarter of the men in the Corps Franc were Jews. A Jewish lieutenant named Rosenberg was its posthumous hero by the time I arrived in the Foresters' Track country. He had commanded a detachment of twenty men covering the retreat of his battalion during a German counterattack in early March. This was a sequel to the counterattack against the Americans at Kasserine Pass in late February, and both assaults were prototypes, on a small scale, of the counteroffensive the Germans were to launch in Belgium at the end of 1944—the last flurry of the hooked and dying fish. Rosenberg, holding one of the innumerable little hills with his men, had decided that it was not fitting for a Jew to retire, even when the Germans looked as though they had surrounded his position. He and his men held on until the rest of the battalion had made its escape. Then he rose, and, intoning the "Marseillaise," led his men in an attack with hand grenades. He and most of his men were, of course, killed.

Besides the Jews, the Corps had hundreds of political prisoners from labor camps in southern Algeria—Spanish Republicans who had fled to Africa in 1939, anti-Nazi Germans who had come even before that, and French "Communists and de Gaullists," to employ the usual Vichy designation for dissidents. The political prisoners had been released upon agreeing to enter the Corps Franc, which they did not consider an onerous condition. There were also hundreds of Frenchmen who had joined because they distrusted the Vichy officers in the regular Army, or because they were "hard heads" who detested any species of regularity, or because they were too old or ill for more conventional fighting units. In the Corps Franc, they were at liberty to march and fight until they dropped. There were also a fair number of Mohammedans, good soldiers who had joined to earn the princely wage of twenty-three francs a day, ten times what they would have got if they had waited to be mobilized in their regular units. Whenever I had a chance, I asked Corps Franc soldiers who they had been in civilian life and why they had enlisted. I remember a former carabinero who had fought in the Spanish Loyalist Army, and a baker of Italian parentage from Bône, in Algeria, who said, "I am a Communist. Rich people are poison to me."

Other members of the Corps who made a special impression on me were a former admiral in the Spanish Republican Navy, who was now a company commander and would not allow junior officers to shout at soldiers; a Hungarian poet who had been studying medicine at the University of Algiers; a sixteen-year-old Alsatian from Strasbourg who had run away from home to avoid having to become a German citizen; and a French captain, a shipping broker in civil life, who proclaimed himself a Royalist. The captain's sixteen-year-old son was also in the Corps; the boy was a motorcycle dispatch rider. I also remember two tough Parisians who had not seen each other since one had escaped from jail in Dakar, where they had both been imprisoned for trying to join the Free French in Brazzaville. The other had escaped later. "Say, it's you, old pimp!" one of the men shouted joyously. "And how did you get out of the jug, old rottenness?" the second man shouted back. Once I shared a luncheon of C-ration vegetable hash, scallions, and medlars with a little fifty-three-year-old second lieutenant, one of those Frenchmen with a face like a parakeet, who until 1942 had been vice-president of the Paris Municipal Council, in which he represented the *arrondissement* of the Opéra. He had got out a clandestine paper and had helped Jewish friends smuggle millions of francs out of France. Betrayed to the Gestapo, he had been arrested and put in Cherche-

Midi Prison; he had escaped with the aid of a jailer and come to Africa and the Corps Franc. The middle-aged soldier who waited on us spoke French with a farce-comedy Russian accent; he had been a waiter at the Scheherazade, a night club in Montmartre, and had often served the lieutenant when he was a civilian. A handsome young Viennese half-Jew, who had been on the Austrian track team in the last Olympic Games, once asked me for some sulfanilamide. He had been in a labor camp for six months without seeing a woman but had been allowed one night's leave in Oran before being sent on to the front. He wanted the sulfanilamide, he said, so that he could treat himself; he was afraid that a doctor might order him away from the firing line. And in a hospital tent at the clearing station I came across a man with a French flag wrapped around his waist; the medics discovered it when they cut his shirt away. He was a hard-looking, blondish chap with a mouthful of gold teeth and a face adorned by a cross-shaped knife scar—the *croix de vache* with which procurers sometimes mark business rivals. An interesting collection of obscene tattooing showed on the parts of him that the flag did not cover. Outwardly he was not a sentimental type.

"Where are you from?" I asked him.

"Belleville," he said. Belleville is a part of Paris not distinguished for its elegance.

"What did you do in civilian life?" I inquired.

That made him grin. "I lived on my income," he said.

"Why did you choose the Corps Franc?"

"Because I understood," he said.

The American soldiers interspersed with the men of the Corps Franc along the Foresters' Track found them a fantastic lot. Most of the men then in the Ninth Division came from New York, New Jersey, or New England, and their ideas of North Africa and Frenchmen had been acquired from films with Ronald Colman as Beau Geste or Charles Boyer as Charles Boyer. They thought the Frenchmen very reckless. The Ninth had had its first experience in battle on the road to Maknassy, in southern Tunisia, only a few weeks ear-

lier, and it was not yet a polished division. The men of the Ninth in
Germany later took risks as nonchalantly as any Corps Franc soldier
used to, but at the time I am speaking of they would sometimes call
the Frenchmen "those crazy headhunters." This term reflected a tendency to confuse the Corps Franc with the Moroccans in the same
zone; the Moroccans are not headhunters, either, but there is a popular American belief that they are paid according to how many enemy ears they bring in.

There were two tabors, or battalions, of Moroccans in the zone;
a tabor consists of several goums, or companies, and each soldier
who is a member of a company is called a goumier. For the sake of
simplicity and euphony, Americans called the Moroccan soldiers
themselves goums. The goums used to ride along the side of the
road on bay mules or gray horses—sure-footed, mountain-bred
animals—until they got near the place where they were going to
fight. Then they would dismount and go off into the brush on bare
feet, and return with their booty when they had finished their business. The goum's sole outer garment is the *djellabah*, which looks
like a long brown bathrobe with a hood. It is made of cotton,
wool, linen, goat's hair, or camel's hair and usually has vertical
black stripes. It sheds water, insulates against heat and cold, is a
substitute for a pup tent at night, and serves as a repository for
everything the goum gloms, like the capacious garment of a professional shoplifter. In their Moroccan homeland the goums live with
their wives and children in their own villages and are supposed to
pay themselves with the spoils of tribes that resist the French government. In Tunisia the spoils were pretty well confined to soldiers'
gear. As a goum killed or captured more and more enemies, he
would put on layer after layer of tunics and trousers, always wearing the *djellabah* over everything. The girth of the goums increased
as the campaign wore on. This swollen effect gave a goum an air of
prosperity and importance, in his opinion; his standing as a warrior,
he thought, was in direct ratio to his circumference. A goum who
was doing well often wore, between sorties, one German and one
Italian boot and carried a string of extra boots over his saddlebow.
The funny part of it was that a goum wearing six men's clothing

could slip noiselessly through a thicket that was impassable to a skinny American. The French officers commanding the goums assured me that their men were not paid by the ear; if a goum occasionally had a few dried ears concealed in a fold of his *djellabah*, one officer explained, it was because goums had discovered that such souvenirs had a trade value in G.I. cigarettes and chewing gum. "Far from paying for ears," this officer said, "we have recently been offering a small reward for live prisoners for interrogation. It is evident that a prisoner without ears is not a good subject for interrogation, because he does not hear the questions plainly." To hold the goums' respect, the officers had to be able to march, climb, and fight with them, and a goum is as inexhaustible as a mountain sheep and about as fastidious as a hyena. Most goums come from the Atlas Mountains and few of them speak Arabic, much less French, so the officers have to be fluent in the southern Berber dialects, which are all that the men know. The goums are trying companions in minefields, because, as one officer remarked, "They say, 'If it is the will of God, we go up,' and then they just push forward." Neither they nor the Corps Franc had mine detectors. An American captain named Yankauer, who was the surgeon at the clearing station near the yellow-triangle hill, was once digging scraps of steel out of a goum who had stepped on a mine. The man let out one short squeal—there was no anesthetic—and then began a steady chant. Yankauer asked a goum officer, who was waiting his turn on the table, what the goum was saying. The officer translated, "He chants, 'God forgive me, I am a woman. God forgive me, I am a woman,' because, you see, he has cried aloud, so he is ashamed." The goums' chief weapons were curved knives and long rifles of the vintage of 1871, and one of the supply problems of the campaign for the American G-4 was finding ammunition for these antediluvian small arms. Colonel Pierre Magnan, who had succeeded de Montsabert in command of the Corps Franc, was the senior French officer in the zone. I was with him one day when the commander of a newly arrived tabor presented himself for orders. "How are you fixed for automatic weapons, Major?" Magnan asked. "We have two old machine guns," the goum officer said. Then, when he saw

Magnan's glum look, he added cheerily, "But don't worry, my Colonel, we use them only on maneuvers."

Magnan was a trim, rather elegant officer who, before the Allied landings, had commanded a crack infantry regiment in Morocco. On the morning of the American landings, he had arrested General Noguès, the Governor General of Morocco, and then asked him to prevent any fighting between the French and Americans by welcoming the invading forces. Noguès had telephoned to a tank regiment to come and arrest Magnan. Magnan, unwilling to shed French blood, had surrendered to the tankmen and become a prisoner in his turn. The liberated Noguès had then ordered a resistance which cost hundreds of French and American lives. Magnan was kept in prison for several days after Noguès, who was backed by our State Department, had consented to be agreeable to the Allies. Magnan had then been released, but he was deprived of his command and consigned to the Corps Franc. He now commands a division in France, and de Montsabert has a *corps d'armée*, so the scheme to keep them down has not been precisely a success.

The Axis forces north of Sedjenane must have been as hard put to it for supply routes as we were. I don't remember the roads the Intelligence maps showed behind the enemy's lines, but they could not have been numerous or elaborate. The Germans did not seem to have a great deal of artillery, but they occasionally landed shells on our road. Once, I remember, they shot up a couple of tank destroyers shortly after the jeep I was in had pulled out to let them pass. Throughout, it was a stubborn, nasty sort of fighting in the brush, and casualties arrived in a steady trickle rather than any great spurt, because large-scale attacks were impossible. Our men fought their way a few hundred yards further east each day, toward Ferryville and Bizerte. Eventually, when Rommel's forces crumpled, men of the Corps Franc, in trucks driven by American soldiers, got to Bizerte before any other Allied troops.

On Easter Sunday, which came late in April, I was out along the Track all day, riding in a jeep with Hal Boyle, a correspondent for the Associated Press. At the end of the afternoon we headed home, hoping to get back to the press camp before night so that we wouldn't have to buck a stream of two-and-a-half-ton trucks and armored vehicles in the blackout. Traffic seemed, if anything, heavier than usual along the Foresters' Track, as it always did when you were in a hurry. The jeep stopped for minutes at a time, which gave Boyle the opportunity to climb out and get the names and home addresses of American soldiers for his stories. Sometimes he would stay behind, talking, and catch up with the jeep the next time it was snagged. We could have walked along the Track faster than we rode. Finally we came to a dip in the road. Fifty yards below and to our right there was a shallow stream, and there was almost no brush on the slope from the road down to the water. This, for the Foresters' Track country, was a considerable clearing, and it was being used for a number of activities. Some goums were watering their mounts in the stream, some French and American soldiers were heating rations over brush fires, a number of vehicles were parked there, and Colonel Magnan and some officers were holding a staff meeting. As we approached the clearing, we were stopped again for a moment by the traffic. A dismal American soldier came out of the brush on our left, tugging a gaunt, reluctant white horse. "Come along, Horrible," the soldier said in a tone of intensest loathing. "This God-damn horse got me lost three times today," he said to us, looking over his shoulder at the sneering, wall-eyed beast. He evidently thought the horse was supposed to guide him.

We moved downhill a bit and stopped again, this time behind an ambulance that was loading wounded. There was a group of soldiers around the ambulance. Boyle and I got out to look. There were four wounded men, all badly hit. They were breathing hard and probably didn't know what was going on. Shock and heavy doses of morphia were making their move easy, or at least quiet. The four men were all from the Sixtieth Infantry of the Ninth Division. A soldier by the road said that they had been on a patrol and had exchanged shots with a couple of Germans; the Germans had popped up waving white handkerchiefs, the Americans had stood up to take them prisoners, and another German, lying concealed, had opened on them with a machine gun. It was the sort of thing that had happened dozens of times to other units, and that un-doubtedly has happened hundreds of times since. Such casualties, a Polish officer once said to me, are an entry fee to battle. That doesn't make them easy to take, however. The soldiers had been told about this particular trick in their training courses, but they had probably thought it was a fable invented to make them hate the enemy. Now the men around the ambulance had really begun to hate the enemy.

While Boyle was getting the names and addresses of the men, I saw another American soldier by the side of the road. This one was dead. A soldier nearby said that the dead man had been a private known as Mollie. A blanket covered his face, so I surmised that it had been shattered, but there was no blood on the ground, so I judged that he had been killed in the brush and carried down to the road to await transport. A big, wild-looking sergeant was standing alongside him—a hawk-nosed, red-necked man with a couple of front teeth missing—and I asked him if the dead man had been in the patrol with the four wounded ones. "Jeez, no!" the sergeant said, looking at me as if I ought to know about the man with the blanket over his face. "That's Mollie. Comrade Molotov. The Mayor of Broadway. Didn't you ever hear of him? Jeez, Mac, he once captured six hundred Eyetalians by himself and brought them all back along with him. Sniper got him, I guess. I don't know, be-cause he went out with the French, and he was found dead up there in the hills. He always liked to do crazy things—go off by himself with a pair of big field glasses he had and watch the enemy put in minefields, or take off and be an artillery spotter for a while, or drive a tank. From the minute he seen those frogs, he was bound to go off with them."

"Was his name really Molotov?" I asked.

"No," said the sergeant, "he just called himself that. The boys mostly shortened it to Mollie. I don't even know what his real name was—Warren, I think. Carl Warren. He used to say he was a Broadway big shot. 'Just ask anybody around Forty-fourth Street,' he used to say. 'They all know me.' Me, I'm from White Plains—I never heard of him before he joined up."

"I had him with me on a patrol that was to contact the French when the regiment was moving into this zone last Thursday," a stocky blond corporal said. "The first French patrol we met, Mollie says to me, 'This is too far back for me. I'm going up in the hills with these frogs and get me some Lugers.' He was always collecting things he captured off Germans and Italians, but the one thing he didn't have yet was a Luger. I knew if I didn't let him go he would take off anyway and get into more trouble with the C.O. He was always in trouble. So I said, 'All right, but the frogs got to give me a receipt for you, so I can prove you didn't go A.W.O.L.' One of the soldiers with me could speak French, so he explained it and the frog noncom give me a receipt on a piece of toilet paper and Mollie went off with them." The corporal fished in one of the pockets of his field jacket and brought out a sheet of tissue. On it, the French noncom had written, in pencil, "*Pris avec moi le soldat américain Molotov, 23 avril, '43, Namin, caporal chef.*"

"Mollie couldn't speak French," the American corporal went on, "but he always got on good with the frogs. It's funny where those big field glasses went, though. He used to always have them around his neck, but somebody must have figured they were no more good to him after he was dead, so they sucked them up. He used to always say that he was a big-shot gambler and that he used to watch the horse races with those glasses."

By now the four wounded men had been loaded into the ambulance. It moved off. Obviously, there was a good story in Mollie, but he was not available for an interview. The driver of the truck behind our jeep was giving us the horn, so I pulled Boyle toward the jeep. He got in, still looking back at Mollie, who said nothing to keep him, and we drove away. When we had gone a little way, at our customary slow pace, a tall lieutenant signaled to us from the roadside that he wanted a hitch and we stopped and indicated that he should hop aboard. He told us his name was Carl Ruff. He was from New York. Ruff was dog-tired from scrambling through the bush. I said something about Mollie, and Ruff said that he had not known him alive but had been the first American to see his body, on Good Friday morning. The French had led him to it. "He was on the slope of a hill," Ruff said, "and slugs from an automatic rifle had hit him in the right eye and chest. He must have been working his way up the hill, crouching, when the German opened on him and hit him in the chest, and then as he fell, the other bullet probably got him in the eye. He couldn't have lived a minute."

It was a month later, aboard the United States War Shipping Administration steamer *Monterey*, a luxury liner that had been converted to war service without any needless suppression of comfort, that I next heard of Molotov, the Mayor of Broadway. The *Monterey* was on her way from Casablanca to New York. On the passenger list were four correspondents besides myself, a thousand German prisoners, five hundred wounded Americans, all of whom would need long hospitalization, and a couple of hundred officers and men who were being transferred or were on various errands. It was one of the advantages of being a correspondent that one could go to America without being a German or wounded, or without being phenomenally lucky, which the unwounded soldiers on our boat considered that they were. The crossing had almost a holiday atmosphere. We were homeward bound after a great victory in the North African campaign, the first the Allies had scored over Germany in a war nearly four years old. The weather was perfect and the *Monterey*, which was not overcrowded and had wide decks and comfortable lounges, had the aspect and feeling of a cruise ship. The wounded were glad, in their sad way, to be going home. The prisoners were in good spirits, too; they seemed to regard the journey as a Nazi Strength through Joy excursion. They organized vaudeville shows, boxing matches, and art exhibitions, with the energetic cooperation of the ship's chaplain, who found much to admire in the Christian cheerfulness with which they endured their increased rations. A couple of anti-Nazi prisoners had announced themselves on the first day out, but the German noncoms had knocked them about and set them to cleaning latrines, so order had soon been restored. "That's an army where they really have some discipline!" one of the American officers on board told me enviously. The prisoners had to put up with some hardships, of course.

They complained one evening when ice cream was served to the wounded but not to them, and another time they didn't think the transport surgeon, a Jew, was "sympathetic" enough to a German officer with a stomach ache.

The hospital orderlies would wheel the legless wounded out on the promenade deck in wheelchairs to see the German boxing bouts, and the other wounded would follow them, some swinging along on crutches or hopping on one foot, some with their arms in slings or casts, some with their broken necks held stiffly in casts and harnesses. They had mixed reactions to the bouts. An arm case named Sanderson, a private who wore the Ninth Division shoulder patch, told me one day that he wished he could be turned loose on the prisoners with a tommygun, because he didn't like to see them jumping about in front of his legless pals. Another arm case, named Shapiro, from the same division, always got a lot of amusement out of the show. Shapiro was a rugged-looking boy from the Brownsville part of Brooklyn. He explained how he felt one day after two Afrika Korps heavyweights had gone through a couple of rounds of grunting, posturing, and slapping. "Every time I see them box, I know we can't lose the war," he said. "The Master Race—phooey! Any kid off the street could of took the both of them."

Shapiro and Sanderson, I learned during one ringside conversation with them, had both been in the Sixtieth Infantry, Molotov's old regiment. They had been wounded in the fighting around Maknassy, in southern Tunisia, early in April, the first serious action the regiment had been in. Molotov had been killed late in April, during the drive on Bizerte, and until I told them, the boys hadn't heard he was dead. I asked them if they had known him.

"How could you help it?" Shapiro said. "There will never be anybody in the division as well-known as him. In the first place, you couldn't help noticing him on account of his clothes. He looked like a soldier out of some other army, always wearing them twenty-dollar green tailor-made officers' shirts and sometimes riding boots, with a French berrit with a long rooster feather that he got off an Italian prisoner's hat, and a long black-and-red cape that he got off another prisoner for a can of C ration."

"And the officers let him get away with it?" I asked.

"Not in the rear areas, they didn't," Shapiro said. "But in combat, Mollie was an asset. Major Kauffman, his battalion commander, knew it, so he would kind of go along with him. But he would never have him made even a pfc. Mollie couldn't of stood the responsibility. He was the greatest natural-born foul-up* in the Army," Shapiro added reverently. "He was court-martialed twenty or thirty times, but the Major always got him out of it. He had the biggest blanket roll in the Ninth Division, with a wall tent inside it and some Arabian carpets and bronze lamps and a folding washstand and about five changes of uniform, none of them regulation, and he would always manage to get it on a truck when we moved. When he pitched his tent, it looked like a concession at Coney Island. I was with him when he got his first issue of clothing at Camp Dix in 1941. 'I've threw better stuff than this away,' he said. He never liked to wear issue. He was up for court-martial for deserting his post when he was on guard duty at Fort Bragg, but the regiment sailed for Morocco before they could try him, and he did so good in the landing at Port Lyautey that they kind of forgave him. Then he went over the hill again when he was guarding a dock at Oran in the winter, but they moved us up into the combat zone before they could try him then, so he beat that rap, too. He was a very lucky fellow. I can hardly think of him being dead."

"Well, what was so good about him?" I asked.

Sanderson, who was a thin, sharp-faced boy from Michigan, answered me with the embarrassed frankness of a modern mother explaining the facts of life to her offspring. "Sir," he said, "it may not sound nice to say it, and I do not want to knock anyone, but in battle almost everybody is frightened, especially the first couple of times. Once in a while you find a fellow who isn't frightened at all. He goes forward and the other fellows go along with him. So he is very important. Probably he is a popoff, and he kids the other guys, and they all feel better. Mostly those quiet, determined fellows crack up before the popoffs. Mollie was the biggest popoff and the biggest screwball and the biggest foul-up I ever saw, and he wasn't afraid of nothing. Some fellows get brave with experience, I guess,

---

* A euphemism, of course.

but Mollie never had any fear to begin with. Like one time on the road to Maknassy, the battalion was trying to take some hills and we were getting no place. They were just Italians in front of us, but they had plenty of stuff and they were in cover and we were in the open. Mollie stands right up, wearing the cape and the berrit with the feather, and he says, 'I bet those Italians would surrender if somebody asked them to. What the hell do they want to fight for?' he says. So he walks across the minefield and up the hill to the Italians, waving his arms and making funny motions, and they shoot at him for a while and then stop, thinking he is crazy. He goes up there yelling *'Veni qua!'* which he says afterward is New York Italian for 'Come here!' and *'Feeneesh la guerre!'* which is French, and when he gets to the Italians he finds a soldier who was a barber in Astoria but went home on a visit and got drafted in the Italian Army, so the barber translates for him and the Italians say sure, they would like to surrender, and Mollie comes back to the lines with five hundred and sixty-eight prisoners. He had about ten Italian automatics strapped to his belt and fifteen field glasses hung over his shoulders. So instead of being stopped, we took the position and cleaned up on the enemy. That was good for the morale of the battalion. The next time we got in a fight, we said to ourselves, 'Those guys are just looking for an easy out,' so we got up and chased them the hell away from there. A disciplined soldier would never have did what Mollie done. He was a very unusual guy. He gave the battalion confidence and the battalion gave the regiment confidence, because the other battalions said, 'If the Second can take all those prisoners, we can, too.' And the Thirty-ninth and the Forty-seventh Regiments probably said to themselves, 'If the Sixtieth is winning all them fights, we can also.' So you might say that Mollie made the whole division." I found out afterward that Sanderson had oversimplified the story, but it was essentially true and the tradition endures in the Ninth Division.

"What kind of a looking fellow was Mollie?" I asked.

"He was a good-looking kid," Shapiro said. "Medium-sized, around a hundred and sixty pounds, with long, curly blond hair. They could almost never get him to have his hair cut. Once, when it got too bad, Major Kauffman took him by the hand and said,

'Come along with me. We'll get a haircut together.' So he sat him down and held on to him while the G.I. barber cut both their hair. And everything he wore had to be sharp. I remember that after the French surrendered to us at Port Lyautey, a lot of French officers gave a party and invited a couple of officers from the battalion to it, and when the officers got there they found Mollie was there, and the Frenchmen were all bowing to him and saluting him. He was dressed so sharp they thought he was an officer, too—maybe a colonel."

Another boy, a badly wounded one in a wheelchair, heard us talking about Mollie and rolled his chair over to us. "It was the field glasses I'll always remember," he said. "From the first day we landed on the beach in Morocco, Mollie had those glasses. He told some fellows once he captured them from a French general, but he told some others he brought them all the way from New York. He told them he used to watch horse races with the glasses; he was fit to be tied when he got to Morocco and found there was no scratch sheets. 'Ain't there no way to telegraph a bet on a race?' he said, and then he let out a howl. 'Vot a schvindle!' That was his favorite saying—'Vot a schvindle!' He was always bitching about something. He used to go out scouting with the glasses, all alone, and find the enemy and tip Major Kauffman off where they were. He had a lot of curiosity. He always had plenty of money, but he would never tell where he got it from. He just let people understand he was a big shot—maybe in some racket. When we was down at Fort Bragg, he and another fellow, a ser-geant, had a big Buick that he kept outside the camp, and they used to go riding all around the country. They used to get some swell stuff."

"He never shot crap for less than fifty dollars a roll when he had the dice," Shapiro said, "and he never slept with any woman under an actress." The way Shapiro said it, it was as if he had said, "He never saluted anybody under the rank of brigadier general."

During the rest of the voyage, I heard more about Mollie. I found nobody who was sure of his real name, but the majority opinion

was that it was something like Carl Warren. "But he wasn't American stock or Irish," Sanderson said one day in a group discussion.
"He seemed to me more German-American." Another boy in the
conversation said that Mollie had told him he was of Russian descent. Sanderson was sure that Molotov wasn't Russian. "Somebody just called him that because he was a radical, I guess," he said.
"He was always hollering he was framed." "He used to have a big
map of the eastern front in his tent in Morocco," another soldier
said, "and every time the Russians advanced he would mark it with
pins and holler, 'Hey, Comrade, howdya like that!' " One boy remembered that Mollie had won fifteen hundred dollars in a crap
game at Fort Bragg. "He had it for about three days," he said, "and
then lost it to a civilian. When he got cleaned in a game, he would
never borrow a buck to play on with. He would just leave. Then the
next time he played, he would have a new roll. Right after we
landed in Morocco, he was awful flush, even for him, and he told a
couple of guys he'd climbed over the wall of an old fort the French
had just surrendered and there, in some office, he found a briefcase
with fifty thousand francs in it. The next thing he done was hire
twelve Arabs to cook and clean and wash dishes for him."

"I was inducted the same time with him, at Grand Central
Palace," an armless youngster said, "and him and me and the bunch
was marched down to Penn Station to take the train. That was way
back in January 1941," he added, as if referring to a prehistoric
event. "He was wearing a blue double-breasted jacket and a dark-
blue sport shirt open at the neck and gray flannel trousers and a
camel's-hair overcoat. They took us into a restaurant on Thirty-
fourth Street to buy us a feed and Mollie started buying beers
for the whole crowd. 'Come on, Comrades,' he says. 'Plenty more
where this comes from.' Then he led the singing on the train all the
way down to Dix. But as soon as he got down there and they took
all his fancy clothes away from him, he was licked. 'Vot a schvindle!'
he says. He drew K.P. a lot at Dix, but he always paid some other
guy to do it for him. The only thing he could ever do good outside
of combat was D.R.O.—that's dining-room orderly at the officers'
mess. I've seen him carry three stacks of dishes on each arm."

When I told them how Mollie had been killed, Shapiro said that that was just what you'd have expected of Mollie. "He never liked to stay with his own unit," he said. "You could hardly even tell what battalion he was in."

I was not to see the Army's official version of what Mollie had done in the fight against the six hundred Italians until the next summer, when I caught up with the Second Battalion of the Sixtieth Infantry near Marigny, in Normandy. Mollie's protector, Major Michael S. Kauffman, by then a lieutenant colonel, was still commanding officer. "Mollie didn't capture the lot by himself," Kauffman said, "but he was instrumental in getting them, and there were about six hundred of them all right. The battalion S-two got out a mimeographed training pamphlet about that fight, because there were some points in it that we thought instructive. I'll get you a copy." The pamphlet he gave me bears the slightly ambitious title "The Battle of Sened, 23 March, '43, G Co. 60th Infantry Dawn Attack on Sened, Tunisia." The Sened of the title was the village of Sened, in the high *djebel* a couple of miles south of the Sened railroad station. It was country I remembered well: a bare plain with occasional bunch grass, with naked red-rock hills rising above it. The Americans had fought there several times; I had seen the taking of the railroad station by another regiment at the beginning of February 1943, and it had been lost and retaken between then and March 23.

On the first page of the pamphlet there was a map showing the Italian position, on two hills separated by a narrow gorge, and the jump-off position of the Americans, two much smaller hills a couple of miles to the north. Then there was a list of "combat lessons to be learned," some of which were: "A small aggressive force can knock out a large group by determined action," "Individuals, soldiers with initiative, aggressiveness, and courage, can influence a large battle," and "Confusion is normal in combat." I have often since thought that this last would make a fine title for a book on war. The pamphlet told how an Italian force estimated at from thirty men to three thousand, according to the various persons interviewed in advance of the fight by S-2 ("Question civilians," the pamphlet said. "Don't rely on one estimate of enemy strength. Weigh all information in the light of its source."), had taken refuge in the village of Sened. G Company, about 150 men, had been ordered to clean out the Italians. It had artillery support from some guns of the First Armored Division; in fact, a Lieutenant Colonel MacPherson, an artillery battalion commander, was actually the senior American officer in the action. This colonel, acting as his own forward observer, had looked over the situation and at four in the afternoon of March 22 had ordered the first platoon of the company to attack. It was soon apparent, judging by the defenders' fire, that the lowest estimate of the enemy's strength was very wrong and that there were at least several hundred Italians on the two hills. Then, in the words of the pamphlet, "Private Molotov"—even his officers had long since forgotten his civilian name—"crawls to enemy position with Pfc. De Marco (both are volunteers) and arranges surrender conference. C.O. refuses to surrender and fire fight continues. Individual enemy riflemen begin to throw down their arms. First platoon returns to Sened Station at dark with 147 prisoners, including 3 officers."

"De Marco was a friend of Molotov's," Colonel Kauffman told me. "It was Mollie's idea to go up to the enemy position, and De Marco did the talking. It must have been pretty effective, because all those Italians came back with them."

"G Company," the pamphlet continued, "attacks again at dawn, first and third platoons attacking. Entrance to town is deep narrow gorge between two long ridges. Town lies in continuation of gorge, surrounded on all sides by 1,000–2,000 foot *djebels* as shown in sketch. (Possible enemy escape route was used by Ancient Romans as park for wild animals used in gladiatorial matches.) Approach to gorge entrance is terraced and well concealed by a large olive-tree grove; five (5) or six (6) field pieces in grove have been knocked out by previous day's artillery fire."

Although the pamphlet didn't say so, the olive groves had once covered all the plain. That plain is now given over to bunch grass, but it was carefully irrigated in the days of the Roman Empire. The "wild animals used in gladiatorial matches" were for the arena at the splendid stone city of Capsa, now the sprawling, dried-mud Arab town of Gafsa, fifteen miles from Sened.

"Company attacks as shown on sketch," the pamphlet continued, "third platoon making steep rocky climb around right, first platoon (Molotov's) around left. Light machine guns and mortars follow close behind by bounds, grenadiers move well to front with mission of flushing enemy out of numerous caves where he has taken up defensive positions. Left platoon, commanded by Sergeant Vernon Mugerditchian, moves slowly over ground devoid of concealment, and finally comes to rest. Molotov goes out alone, keeping abreast of faster moving platoon on right, and assists Lt. Col. MacPherson in artillery direction by shouting."

The combined artillery and infantry fire made the Italians quit. The pamphlet says, in closing, "Italian captain leads column of prisoners out of hills, bringing total of 537 (including officers). Total booty includes 2 large trucks, 3 small trucks, several personnel carrier motorcycles, 200 pistols, machine guns, rifles, and ammunition."

"Mollie liked to go out ahead and feel he was running the show," Colonel Kauffman said. "We put him in for a D.S.C. for what he did, but it was turned down. Then we put in for a Silver Star, and that was granted, but he was killed before he ever heard about it. He was a terrible soldier. He and another fellow were to be tried by a general court-martial for quitting their guard posts on the docks at Oran, but we had to go into action before court could be held. The other fellow had his court after the end of the campaign and got five years."

The officers of the battalion, and those at division headquarters, knew that I was going to write a story about Mollie sometime. Whenever I would encounter one of them, in a country tavern or at a corps or Army headquarters, or on a dusty road behind the lines, during our final campaign before Germany's surrender, he would ask me when I was going to "do Mollie." I am doing him now.

Even after I had been back in the States for a while that summer of 1943, I had an intermittent interest in Mollie, although La Piste

Forestière assumed a curious unreality after I had been living on lower Fifth Avenue a couple of weeks. I asked a fellow I knew at the *Times* to check back through the casualty lists and see if the death of a soldier with a name like "Carl Warren" had been reported, since I knew the lists gave the addresses of the next of kin and I thought I might be able to find out more about Mollie. The *Times* man found out that there hadn't been any such name but that there was often a long interval between casualties and publication. I took to turning mechanically to the new lists as they came out and looking through the *W*s. One day I saw listed, among the Army dead, "Karl C. Warner, sister Mrs. Ulidjak, 230 E. Eightieth Street, Manhattan." The juxtaposition of "a name like Warren" with one that I took to be Russian or Ukrainian made me suspect that Warner was Molotov, and it turned out that I was right.

A couple of days later, I went uptown to look for Mrs. Ulidjak. Number 230 is between Second and Third Avenues, in a block overshadowed by the great, brute mass of the Manhattan Storage & Warehouse Company's building at the corner of Eightieth. Along the block there were a crumbling, red-brick elementary school of the type Fusion administrations like to keep going so that they can hold the tax rate down, a yellowish, old-fashioned Baptist church, some boys playing ball in the street, and a banner, bearing a number of service stars, hung on a line stretched across the street. As yet, it had no gold stars. Number 230 is what is still called a "new-law tenement," although the law governing this type of construction is fifty years old: a six-story walkup with the apartments built around air shafts. Ulidjak was one of the names on the mailboxes in the vestibule. I pushed the button beside it, and in a minute there was an answering buzz and I walked upstairs. A thin, pale woman with a long, bony face and straight blond hair pulled back into a bun came to the apartment door. She looked under thirty and wore silver-rimmed spectacles. This was Mrs. Ulidjak, Private Warner's sister. Her husband is in the Merchant Marine. She didn't seem startled when I said I was a correspondent; every American expects to be interviewed by a reporter sometime. Mrs. Ulidjak had been notified of her brother's death by the War Department over a week before, but she had no idea how it had happened or where. She said he had been in the Sixtieth Infantry, all right, so I was sure Warner had been Mollie. "Was he fighting the Japs?" she asked me. When I told her no, she seemed slightly disappointed. "And you were there?" she asked. I said I had been. Then, apparently trying to visualize me in the context of war, she asked, "Did you wear a helmet, like Ernie Pyle? Gee, they must be heavy to wear. Did it hurt your head much?" When I had reassured her on this point, she led me into a small sitting room with a window opening on a dark air shaft. A young man and a young woman, who Mrs. Ulidjak said were neighbors, were in the room, but they went into the adjoining kitchen, apparently so that they would not feel obliged to look solemn.

"Was your name Warner, too, before you were married?" I asked Mrs. Ulidjak.

"No," she said, "Karl and I were named Petuskia—that's Russian—but he changed to Warner when he came to New York because he thought it sounded sweller. We were from a little place called Cokesburg, in western Pennsylvania. He hardly ever came up here. He had his own friends."

"Did he go to high school in Cokesburg?" I asked.

The idea amused Mrs. Ulidjak. "No, just grammar school," she said. "He was a pit boy in the coal mines until we came to New York. But he always liked to dress nice. You can ask any of the cops around the Mall in Central Park about him. Curly, they used to call him, or Blondy. He was quite a lady's man."

Then I asked her the question that had puzzled Mollie's Army friends: "What did he do for a living before he went into the Army?"

"He was a bartender down to Jimmy Kelly's, the night club in the Village," Mrs. Ulidjak said.

She then told me that her brother's Christian name really was Karl and that he was twenty-six when he was killed, although he had looked several years younger. Both parents are dead. The parents had never told her, as far as she could remember, what part of Russia they came from. When I said that Mollie had been a hero, she was pleased, and said he had always had an awful crust. She called the young neighbors, who seemed to be of Italian descent, back into the sitting room and made me repeat the story of how Mollie captured the six hundred Italians (I hadn't seen the official version of his exploit yet and naturally I gave him full credit in mine). "Six hundred wops!" Mrs. Ulidjak exclaimed gaily. She got a lot of fun out of Mollie's "big-shot" stories, too. She showed me a large, expensive-looking photograph of him "addressing" a golf ball. He was wearing light-colored plus-fours, white stockings, and brogues with tassels, and there was a big, happy grin on his face that made it plain that he was not going to hit the ball but was just posing. He had a wide, plump face with high cheekbones and square white teeth, and the hair about which I had so often heard looked at least six inches long. "He had a room at 456 West Forty-fourth Street, and a little Jewish tailor down in that neighborhood made all those nice things for him special," she said admiringly. She had never heard him called Molotov.

I went over to West Forty-fourth Street a few days later. The 400 block, between Ninth and Tenth Avenues, looks more depressing than the one the Ulidjaks live on. It is mostly shops dealing in the cheap merchandise that is used as premiums, and stores that sell waiters' supplies, and lodging houses favored by waiters and cooks. It was evident from the look of the house at Number 456 that though Mollie had spent a disproportionate share of his income on clothes, he had wasted nothing on his living quarters. No one at Number 456 remembered Mollie. The tenants and the janitor had all come there since his time. I couldn't find the little tailor. But on the north side of Forty-fourth Street, near Ninth Avenue, there is a building occupied by the Warner Brothers' Eastern offices, and I was sure that this had given Mollie the idea of calling himself Warner.

That evening I went down to Jimmy Kelly's, on Sullivan Street. Kelly's is the kind of club that never changes much but that you seldom remember anything specific about unless you have had a fight there. I had been there a few times in the late thirties, but I couldn't remember the bartender's face. Kelly's has a dance floor a little bigger than two tablecloths, and there is always a show with young, sometimes pretty girls imitating the specialties that more famous and experienced performers are doing at clubs uptown, and a master of ceremonies making cracks so old that they have been used in Hollywood musicals. The man behind the bar the night I showed up said he had been there several years and had known his predecessor, whose name was not Molotov. He had never heard of a bartender named Molotov or Warner or Mollie or Karl at Kelly's. After I had had a couple of Scotches and had told him the story, he said he wondered if the fellow I meant hadn't been a busboy. The description seemed to fit one who had worked there. "We all used to call this kid Curly," he said, "but Ray, the waiter who is the union delegate, might remember his real name."

Ray was a scholarly-looking man with a high, narrow forehead and shell-rimmed spectacles. "Curly's name *was* Karl C. Warner," he said after he had been told what I wanted to know. "I remember it from his union card. He was a man who would always stand up for his fellow-worker. Waiters and Waitresses Local Number One sent him down here in the summer of 1940 and he worked until late the next fall. He was outspoken but a hard worker and strong—he could carry three stacks of dishes on each arm. A busboy has a lot to do in a place like this when there is a rush on—clearing away dishes, setting up for new parties, bringing the waiters their orders—and a stupid boy can spoil the waiters' lives for them. We had another boy here at the same time, an Irish boy, who kidded Curly about the fancy clothes he wore, so they went down in the basement and fought for a couple of hours one afternoon. Nobody won the fight. They just fought until they were tired and then stopped. Curly had wide interests for a busboy," Ray continued. "When there was no rush on, he would sometimes stop by a customer's table, particularly if it was some man who looked important, and talk to him for ten minutes or so. The customers didn't seem to mind. He had a nice way about him. He had a kind of curiosity."

The Army stories about Mollie's wealth made Ray and the bartender laugh. "He used to come back here now and then during the first year he was in the Army," Ray said, "and always he would borrow ten or twenty dollars from one of us waiters. We would lend it to him because we liked him, without expecting to get it back." A busboy at Kelly's is paid only nominal wages, Ray told me—just about enough to cover his laundry bill—but the waiters chip in a percentage of their tips for the boys. "I guess Curly averaged about forty a week here," he said. "If he was anxious to get extra money, he might have had a lunch job someplace else at the same time, but I never heard about it. A tailor like he had probably made those suits for about twenty-five per. What else did he have to spend money on? His night life was here. He used to tell us he had worked at El Morocco, but we used to say, 'What's the difference? Dirty dishes are the same all over.' "

At the union headquarters, which are on the twelfth floor of a loft building on West Fortieth Street, Mollie was also remembered. The serious, chunky young woman in the union secretary's office said, "Warner was always a dissident. He would speak up at every meeting and object to everything. But we all liked him. He stopped paying dues a few months before he went into the Army, but at Christmastime in 1941 he came back here and said he heard that union members in the services were getting a present from the local, so he wanted one, too. So we gave it to him, of course. The secretary will be interested to know he is dead."

The young woman called the secretary, a plump, olive-complexioned man, from his desk in an inner room and said to him, "You remember Karl Warner, the blond boy with curly hair? He has been killed in Africa. He was a hero."

"Is that so?" the secretary said. "Well, get a man to put up a gold paper star on the flag in the members' hall right away and draw up a notice to put on the bulletin board. He is the first member of Local Number One to die in this war."

I thought how pleased Mollie would have been to be restored to good standing in the union, without even having paid up his dues. Then I thought of how much fun he would have had on the Mall in Central Park, in the summertime, if he could only have gone up there with his Silver Star ribbon on, and a lot of enemy souvenirs. I also thought of how far La Piste Forestière was from the kitchen in Jimmy Kelly's.

When I walk through the West Side borderland between Times Square and the slums, where Mollie once lived, I often think of him and his big talk and his golf-suit grin. It cheers me to think there may be more like him all around me—a notion I would have dismissed as sheer romanticism before World War II. Cynicism is often the shamefaced product of inexperience.

He has become a posthumous pal, though I never knew him when he was alive. He was full of curiosity—he would have made a great explorer—and fond of high living, which is the only legitimate incentive for liking money. He had faith in the reason of his fellow-man, as when he sensed that the Italians at Sened were no more eager to fight than he was. The action that earned him his Silver Star cost no lives. It saved them. He bragged, but when challenged he would not back off. The brag was like the line a deckhand throws over a bollard—it pulled performance after it. I lived with him so long that I once half-convinced myself he was not dead. This was when I began to write a play about him, and was reminded by more experienced hands that it is customary for the protagonist of a work of that nature to remain alive until the last act.

Suppose, I said, that the corpse with the face shot away that I saw by La Piste was not Mollie at all, but that Mollie had put his uniform and dog-tags on a dead goumier and gone over the hill wearing a Moroccan *djellabah*, to wage a less restricted kind of war, accumulating swag as he went? And suppose he was living in Morocco now, with a harem, a racing stable, and a couple of Saharan oil wells? And suppose he returned to New York as a member of the Moroccan, or the Mauretanian, Delegation to the United Nations, or, better yet, a Delegate from the Tuareg state that is sure to be formed sooner or later? The last would afford him the advantage of a veil covering his face below the eyes, to conceal his grin.

Mollie would like the fancy togs, and if any old rival, perhaps the Irish busboy, recognized him in the last scene and twitted him with his defection, he could pull out from his flowing sleeves hundreds of dried Nazi ears to prove he had waged war effectually to the last. If Allah has so willed it, the thing is.

Or suppose he had switched uniforms with a dead German, and thereafter, as a secret agent, confounded all the Wehrmacht's plans? He liked to operate in disguise, as he proved when he fooled the French officers at Casablanca, and superior officers of foreign powers confided in him on sight. I like him better as a Tuareg, and I think he would have liked Tuaregs better as company. I dropped the play because that was all the plot I could think of.

Long after I abandoned thought of writing about Mollie again, I had a letter from a lady in Mechanicsburg, Pennsylvania, that cleared up the question of how Mollie transmuted his last name. It had nothing to do with Warner Bros.—a warning, this, against adopting mere plausibility in place of valid evidence. She wrote that her brother, a Mr. Karl Warner, had come to Cokesburg as boss of a construction job in about 1932, and had given the Petuskia boy a job as watchman, in defiance of all local counsel. Young Petuskia was considered a bad risk. The boy proved honest, and afterward wanted to pull up stakes and follow the construction gang when it left town. Warner told him he was too young. The Mechanicsburg lady was sure the boy had subsequently taken the Warner name in honor of her brother.

I am sure she is right, but it sounds like a detail out of an old-fashioned boys' book.

Days with the Daydaybay

(MAY 19, 1956)

Reading a French newspaper in a restaurant in Paris one winter, I came upon a heading of a kind that would not ordinarily interest me: "*Ventes de Charité*." I had time to spare, however, having asked for my check while the waiter was skinning a *truite au bleu* for another customer, so I read the first item in the column. (After all, the waiter was quite right: the *truite*, if abandoned, would get cold, and the check wouldn't.) The item stated:

> The sale for the benefit of the Veterans of the 2nd Armored Division will open today in the salons of the Sorbonne (entrance: Rue des Ecoles). Presiding will be Mme la Maréchale Leclerc de Hauteclocque, who will direct a booth devoted exclusively to souvenirs of the General. Numerous booths will be devoted to exotic products and artifacts. At the book booth authors such as André Maurois and Louise de Vilmorin will autograph their works.

I divined without trouble that Mme la Maréchale was the widow of General Leclerc, who had been made a Marshal of France after his death in an airplane accident in Algeria, in 1947. Leclerc's name in obscurity, before he escaped to England to join General de Gaulle in 1940, had been de Hauteclocque—Philippe-François-Marie de Hauteclocque, to give him his full due. De Hauteclocque was a name that had marked him from school days as an unreformed aristocrat. In England, taking a pseudonym to protect his family from reprisals, he had chosen a common French name, the exact equivalent of Clark. Changing from de Hauteclocque to Leclerc was like shucking tails for a sweatshirt. Once, in 1944, as a correspondent with the American First Army, I asked him what his real name was. It was an awkwardly worded question, because everybody knew by that time. All I really wanted was to verify the spelling; those two *c*'s are tricky.

"What does my name matter as long as I fight?" he asked. He had been affable up to that point, or as affable as he knew how to be, but the question about the name nettled him. I thought that he was like the countless little boys who have wished, and have gone on wishing all their lives, that they hadn't been named Elwyn or Abbott.

We were in a field near Fleuré, in the Département de L'Orne in Normandy, and all around us were vehicles that the Americans had supplied to the Deuxième Division Blindée, or D.D.B.—pronounced by the French as a single word, "Daydaybay." The Daydaybay was known to the American forces as the French Second Armored Division; there was an American Second Armored Division in western France, too. Fleuré, which is so small that if you are driving fast you are likely to miss it entirely, is near Argentan, which was then the southern jaw of the pincers that Bradley and Montgomery were trying to close on the escaping Visigoths of the Seventh Army and the Fifth Panzer Army. The Daydaybay, pushing out into the middle of the receding Germans, joyfully managed to get itself surrounded, and killed a great many of the enemy before being called back to the American side of the gap. Leclerc, a red-haired little man with a long nose and a bristling red mustache, reminded me of an interrupted terrier that sniffs more rats under a barn door.

Like so many quests for simplicity, Leclerc's, I noted with regret while still awaiting the check for my meal, had ended only in further complication. As a surname, Leclerc de Hauteclocque is even more of a mouthful than de Hauteclocque. Moreover, I reflected, there is by now hardly a town in what became the Daydaybay's path across France—from the Cotentin to the Rhine—that is without its Avenue du Général Leclerc, a name that is perpetuated because "Avenue du Maréchal Posthume Leclerc de Hauteclocque" just won't fit on a street sign.

Then, remembering a journey I had once made in attendance upon the Daydaybay, it occurred to me that I might as well go over to the Sorbonne and spend a few francs with my old fellow-travelers. I had nothing else in the world to do except go back to my hotel room and work, and I hate that. When I was at last allowed to pay for my simple repast—a dozen oysters followed by a pair of thrushes roasted with juniper berries—I decided to walk to the Sorbonne in order to prolong my respite. I find it hard to deter myself from walking in Paris, with or without a pretext. There was a time when I thought I might never walk in Paris again, for it had fallen under a spell that was supposed to last a thousand years, and now, I suppose, I walk its streets for reassurance.

From the restaurant, which is the Fontaine Gaillon, I walked up the Rue Saint-Augustin and turned down the Rue de Richelieu, a narrow gulch of one-way, hornless traffic these days, where, if you step off the meager sidewalk to let an old woman with a market basket pass, you risk silent obliteration by a motorized baby buggy magniloquently called an automobile. One of the unadvertised benefits of the law forbidding Parisians on wheels to sound their horns is the increased pleasure of the driver, who is now under mandate to sneak up without warning on his prey. This swells his *tableau de chasse*, or total bag. (The highest award of the Friendly League for the Ecrabouillement Piéton, or Squashing of Pedestrians, goes to the member who succeeds in killing a man with a motor scooter, which is considered comparable to getting an elephant with a bow and arrow.) I followed the street down past the discouraging baroque bulk of the Bibliothèque Nationale and the charming front of the Hôtel de Malte, which received its first guests in 1777. As I approached the Rue de Rivoli, I passed under the colonnade of the Comédie Française, with its wall medallions of Molière, Racine, and the rest, in a Hydrox Biscuit style of sculpture, and its yellow *affiches* announcing the casts of next week's *Cinnas* and *Athalies*. Coming out from under the colonnade, I paused in front of a bust of Alfred de Musset to read again on its socle one of my favorite cheer-up bits of literature:

Les plus désespérés sont les chants les plus beaux
Et j'en sais d'immortels, qui sont des purs sanglots—

which might be freely translated as

The most utterly lachrymose lyrics are frequently good jobs,
And I could cite some deathless instances that are
    unadulterated sobs.

I repeat the couplet to myself when I am feeling low, and it works
as well as three fingers of bourbon.

On reaching the Seine, I walked past the fishing-tackle shops
and the bird stores to the Pont au Change, at the Châtelet, and then
across the Ile de la Cité, past the Préfecture of Police, where the
Paris police barricaded themselves against the German garrison and
raised the tricolor on August 19, 1944, setting off the week of insur-
rection. When I got over on the Left Bank, I ascended the Boulevard Saint-Michel as far as the big, brassy Restaurant Dupont, at the
corner of the Rue des Ecoles. The Dupont never fails to enrage me,
because it occupies the disfigured former premises of the Taverne
Soufflet, an establishment of majesty and tranquillity, which in
1926, when I first stayed in the Latin Quarter as a casual student at
the Sorbonne, was still the exact image of the French cafés Maupassant had taught me to expect.

In the Soufflet, the long banquettes were upholstered in garnet
plush, with backs topped by a manger of brass rails, into which the
customers tossed their overcoats after crumpling them up into the
smallest possible bundles. The tables in front of the banquettes had
white marble tops and were placed end to end, with no space
between. There were vast mirrors, which permitted refracted flirtation. The waiters were individualists who improved on acquaintance; they had little use for a newcomer until he had been in the
Quarter long enough to achieve their own cultural standing. The
girls who frequented the Soufflet did not frequent the Café d'Harcourt or the Source, farther up the Boulevard, nor did the demoi-
selles of the d'Harcourt or the Source invade the Soufflet. Each

habitual customer at the Soufflet had his table, and each girl had hers. There she would arrive in mid-afternoon and begin to write on stationery furnished by the house. The girls were as prolific as a pack of Mme de Sévignés, but none of them was ever seen to affix a postage stamp to an envelope. Perhaps they were diarists. Any one of them could nurse an infusion of peppermint through a long afternoon; it was the *consommation* that she felt the least temptation to finish, and so the one that enabled her to hold the franchise longest. Male acquaintances would pause by the girls' tables to shake hands, to chat, and, rarely, to stand treat. The girls knew the limitations of the academic budget. They snubbed nobody because he bought seldom. They were young, averaging only a year or two older than the students, and not particularly pretty.

The students in the cafés were exclusively male. A number of co-eds attended lectures, but they used no makeup, wore cotton stockings, took masses of notes, and disappeared as soon as class was over. They went straight home, I imagine, or else to a room in some dark and hideous *pension de famille*, with a window giving on a court into which boys threw lynched cats. I used to suspect that in order to win their parents' consent to such unwomanly careers the coeds had to make a show of being completely uninterested in sex, like nuns, and that in default of a habit they utilized steel barrettes and straight hair to advertise this indifference. Nowadays there are almost as many *étudiantes* as *étudiants* in the cafés of the Quarter—a lot of them married and living with their husbands, and others still single but living *en ménage*. The *petites femmes* of the kind I remember, a species peculiar to the environs of the university, have been eliminated, like the Soufflet. Many of the women students today are prettier than the Soufflet girls, but they are more intimidating.

"Ce n'était pas vraiment du vice," a very old friend of mine who still inhabits the Quarter said recently, reminiscing. *"C'était une espèce d'artisanat."* From the point of view of the bashful foreigner, one advantage of the *petite* who could always be found in the same place was that he could observe her at leisure—for several evenings, if he chose. He might learn to like the way she looked up to greet fellows she knew, or the way her head sat on her neck or her neck on her

shoulders. That would achieve what Stendhal baptized the "crystal-lization." By the time the young man approached, he felt that he knew her as well as the girls in his high-school class, whom he had first observed in the same manner. He would find her receptive but not precipitate, practical but not rapacious. The greatest treat he could offer, within what the boys on the quarterlies would now call the Soufflet's frame of reference, was the prix-fixe dinner on the wide balcony that overhung the *grande salle*. (It was not reasonable to as-sume that a customer who could afford better would be at the Soufflet at all.) The prix fixe more than nourished the girl; it raised her standing with the management and with her other male acquain-tances. Best of all, it infuriated her colleagues who had not been in-vited anywhere and who bitterly watched her as they masticated the sandwiches that hunger had at length impelled them to order grudg-ingly for themselves. The prix fixe, at sixteen francs, comprised a choice of soup or a spectacular *hors d'oeuvre varié* and then fish, en-trée, vegetable, salad, and cheese and fruit or dessert. Wine was included, but coffee wasn't. The franc was twenty-five to the dollar.

I cannot truthfully say that I think of all these details specifically whenever I see the Restaurant Dupont on the site of the Taverne Soufflet, but I have thought about one or another of them so often on reaching that corner that the memory of the whole scene hits me ready-blended, like a smell. As for the Dupont, it is one of a chain of restaurants, all flaunting the disputable slogan "*Chez Dupont, Tout Est Bon*." It has fluorescent lighting overhead and elec-tric lamps, with candy-striped shades, on wall brackets. The walls are further decorated with posters displaying offensive colored photographs of fried eggs and blobs of pink ice cream and con-veying such inspirational messages from the management as "Eat Oysters—Good for Your Health" and "The Management in-sists upon impeccable courtesy and compliance on the part of its employees—Messieurs les Clients are urgently recommended to re-port with exactitude any infraction of servility." The Dupont wait-ers, naturally, pay no attention to the latter poster, but they tolerate it. Those of the old Soufflet would have ripped it from the wall and made Messieurs les Clients eat it.

In front of the Dupont I paused to look across the Boulevard Saint-Michel at the patisserie in the building that, shaped like a flat-iron, stands where the Rue Racine and the Rue de l'Ecole de Médecine converge. The patisserie, which used to be open all night, closes early now, but it is still there, and that is something. Above the bargain bookstore in the acute angle of the Rue Racine and the Boulevard is the Hôtel de la Faculté, where, in the fall of 1927, I last saw Angèle, one of the pleasantest girls at the Soufflet. Angèle was twenty years old and chunky, and she had a snub nose. On this occasion she complained of having a fever and said she was going to die. Three or four of us from the Soufflet, sitting on her bed, assured her that she would be up and around in a few days. Shortly thereafter she died, and since then I have wondered sometimes what a girl with a snub nose has to do to be taken seriously. In the Rue de l'Ecole de Médecine, from which the Medical School has departed, is a plaque marking the birthplace of Sarah Bernhardt, who made hundreds of thousands of people cry by merely pretending to die. She had the profile for it.

When I had had my look, I turned, entered the Rue des Ecoles, and walked on, past the entrance to the narrow Rue Champollion and past the Brasserie Balzar, another surviving landmark. Outside the Sorbonne I saw posters bearing the emblem of the Dayday-bay—a white silhouette map of France with the Cross of Lorraine on a blue field superimposed. A blue banner hung above the door, and on the wide steps in front of it there was a double stream of well-dressed people, some making for the entrance and the others leaving it. Those going in were empty-handed; those coming out carried amateurishly wrapped packages. Inside the door, I found myself in the high marble vestibule at the foot of the Grand Escalier of the Sorbonne, a place I hadn't been in for nearly thirty years. It looked just about the same.

In 1926, all an American needed in order to matriculate at the Sorbonne was a diploma from an American university. The old fellow who took your minuscule matriculation fee wouldn't even make you unroll the diploma. "Ahbay?" he would ask, signifying Bachelor of Arts, and if you said "Ahbay," he would nod knowingly and extend to you the privilege of listening to the big-league medievalists. (At least, that was the privilege I was interested in.) Ahbay was the only American degree the old boy had heard of, and it served no useful purpose to open your diploma and explain that it was Bay anything else.

M. Ferdinand Lot, the professor who in those days taught the Dawn of the Middle Ages, gave out a bibliography as long as my two arms. When I went to the library to get started on it, I saw a considerable number of my fellow-students—who, unlike me, were working for degrees—standing in line and waiting for books that other students were reading, several of them sitting on the floor, for lack of seats. This made me feel guilty, so I bought some of the books from dealers and took them to my room to read, and soon I stopped going to Professor Lot's lectures. I was afraid of being found out as a dilettante. Another of my lecturers was Professor Antoine Thomas, who taught Old Provençal. I remember that he had a spade-shaped white beard and that he accused Professor Anglade, of the University of Toulouse, his rival in their common field, of approaching the origin of a verb I have forgotten "*avec sa légèreté coutumière*" ("with his habitual frivolity"). What an epithet can be derived from that—"Frivolous philologist!" For thirty years I have been waiting for a chance to use it, but every time I get into an argument with a savant, he turns out to be of some other persuasion—a psychologist, perhaps, or a podiatrist. The neck my knife would fit has never presented itself.

When I had whiffed all these matters, in the same manner that I had my memories of the Soufflet, I climbed a flight of white marble stairs that leads off to the left of the Grand Escalier and takes one to the salons where the charity sale for the benefit of the Daydaybay was being held. The salons of the Sorbonne are a set of high-ceilinged rooms, each about forty feet by sixty, arranged en suite for exhibitions and academic receptions. Outside the entrance to the sale, I perused a panel listing the maids and matrons who were serving at various booths and counters. A high proportion of the names were *en courants d'air*—spread out in bits, with drafts through them—like Leclerc de Hauteclocque. I could see that Mme la Maréchale had built up a social cachet for the Daydaybay in the years following the General's death. I observed none of the Corsican, Mussulman, and Jewish names that had been so common in the ranks. Nearly every counter—toys, comestibles, books, perfumes, yard goods, flowers—was garrisoned by women with horse-cavalry surnames, usually a promise of a high standard of good looks.

Inside, I made a clockwise tour of the counters and bought a book, entitled *Leclerc et Ses Hommes* and illustrated in color, from its tall and distinguished-looking author, identified by a card on the table in front of him as Pierre Nord. I told M. Nord that I had accompanied the Daydaybay into Paris on August 25, 1944, the day of the Liberation. M. Nord informed me that he was a colonel in the Regular Army, and that Nord was a nom de plume. He is not the sort of author who dismisses customers with a mere signature, and after a moment of thought he wrote in my book, "In homage to a sincere fraternity of arms, to the American friend and war correspondent of our difficult years. Faithfully, Pierre Nord (Colonel Brouillard)." It made me inflate my chest, and I went and bought a flask of white pepper, a carton of matches, and a can of pineapple, each from a different pretty girl. The salons were crowded, and the warm air, heavy with the evaporation of samples at the perfume counter, made me sweat; I took off my hat, which happened to be what elegant Londoners call a titfer (tit fer tat, bowler hat) and the French a *melon*. Try, sometime, taking off a hard hat, holding it, and wiping your brow with a handkerchief while grasping a book and a flask of white pepper in one hand and a can of pineapple and a carton of matches in the other. Of course, the dicer fell to the floor, where it rolled between a woman's feet. In attempting to get to it, I bumped into her. "*Polisson!*" she said firmly.

The situation was saved by a one-legged chap on crutches, who swung down like a bird from a perch and retrieved my hat for me. He was selling copies of a publication entitled *L'Amicale Sportive des Mutilés de France*. I bought one and asked if he had been with the division at the Liberation. "No, Monsieur," he said apologetically. "I joined up after the division got here. I was wounded in front of Strasbourg." He was embarrassed by not having lost his leg soon enough.

I had somehow had an idea that the benefit would be like the reunion of an American division, with a lot of old noncoms lined up at a bar to exchange lies, and, as a possible French variant, a continuous raffle for ducks and geese. But the *vente* for the Daydaybay was exactly like a *vente* for any other charity with excellent social sponsorship. Except for a number of amputees selling *L'Amicale Sportive*, there was nobody present who looked to me like a former noncom or enlisted man. That is probably the way a charity sale should be in order to turn a profit for good works, but it did not correspond with my recollections of hot roads, dead Germans, and cheering crowds. I therefore descended the white marble stairs, carefully reenthroning my titfer when I got beyond jostling range, and walked over to a place called L'Alsace à Paris, a few blocks away, which has nothing in particular to recommend it except that the proprietor, Robert, used to be the *patron* of the Taverne Soufflet. The waiters, who are not Alsatians, wear red waistcoats, as in all Paris Alsaces; the prices are fairly stiff, and there are no little women. "This is a more serious affair than the old place," M. Robert says. He still has the same students among his clientele— students of the twenties, grown into bald dentists and sedate *avocats*. I ordered a *formidable*, which is a liter of beer in a stone mug, and, while rehydrating, reviewed the recollections that my late experience did not correspond with.

On Monday evening, August 21, 1944, I attended a press conference that was addressed by the then Lieutenant General Omar Nelson Bradley at Laval, a town in the Département de la Mayenne, in western France. Bradley, whose infrequent lectures I had been following with rapt attention ever since he took over II Corps in North Africa, in April 1943, had in sixteen months progressed from the command of a corps through that of an army (the First) to that of an army group (the Twelfth), but his manner—benevolent, pedagogical, and slightly apologetic—had not changed. A month before the Laval press conference, I had listened to him in a shed behind Mme Hamel's at Vouilly, as he outlined to correspondents the plan for the First Army's new offensive. Before that, I had heard

him at Béja, in Tunisia, explaining how he was going to try to take
Bizerte, and then in Bryanston Square, London, offering his opinion, take it for what it was worth, that we would get ashore in
France. At Laval, everybody knew that the most recent effort, like
the ones previously adumbrated by the General, had come off
nicely. It had been set back a couple of days by rain and had then
wheezed a bit when the most impressive assemblage of air power
ever up to then on view outside a Howard Hughes production flew
over from England and, getting mixed up, dropped a lot of its
bombs on the American Thirtieth Division instead of on the Germans, just beyond. But, once under way, the offensive had discom-
bobulated all the German defensive arrangements in the West and
had changed the war of position into one of pursuit, with the First,
now confided to Hodges, sweeping north behind the German Seventh Army and Fifth Panzer Army and joining the British, Canadians, and Poles in a grand *battue* of fugitives at the Argentan-Falaise
escape gap while Patton's newly activated Third dashed southwest
and then east.

As Group Commander, Bradley controlled both the First and
the Third, and he had selected Laval as the headquarters of the moment because it was approximately behind the point where the
zones of the two armies overlapped. Laval was a good long jeep
ride from First Army Headquarters and press camp, at Bagnoles-de-
l'Orne, in central Normandy. It was equally far, I suppose, from
Third Army Headquarters, although I have no idea where the
Third was. (To judge by the telling of it by Third Army correspondents, its advance elements were already on the outskirts of Vienna,
but you couldn't believe everything those fellows said.) As the conference wouldn't be over until after dark and none of us First Army
correspondents wanted to ride any farther than we had to on a road
full of blacked-out trucks and tanks, my colleagues had entrusted
me with the mission of reserving promising billets for them in hotels and inns along the way back to Bagnoles-de-l'Orne. I had done
that, saving for an officer friend—Lieutenant Roy Chitterling—and
myself accommodations in a small town called Ernée, whose hotel
looked too comfortable to tell the others about.

It was the most cheerful briefing I had yet attended. Tall, bespectacled, and Missouri-speaking, Bradley had the pleased look of a Sunday-school superintendent announcing that the cake sale had brought in $11.50 more than anticipated. The German Seventh Army was in a satisfactory state of disintegration, he said, although "annihilation" might be too rosy a term to use in describing it yet, since a number of its men, abandoning their equipment, had made their way out through the gap. A part of our First had crossed the Seine between Mantes and Vernon, northwest of Paris, and the Third was hooking around Melun, south of Paris. We all knew there had been an American landing in the south of France on August 15, and we assumed that up north Montgomery's Britons and Canadians were barreling along at last. They constituted the Twenty-first Army Group, and Bradley's briefing did not cover them.

The General said, with a smile, that he knew what we all wanted to find out was when did we get to Paris. Well, the important thing was to destroy the German armies, and the next after that was to secure Paris as nearly intact as possible. So we would just hook around Paris, north and south, he said, and the German garrison would probably pull out to avoid capture, since, with Americans across the Seine both above and below the city, it would have no military usefulness, as the Germans were sure to see. A Third Army correspondent said that General Patton had bet him five dollars the Third would be in Paris before the First, and General Bradley remarked that he might just take it into his head to tell General Patton to go someplace else. First Army people present regarded this as a good omen. One thing we could be sure of, Bradley said—we weren't going to make a rush for Paris.

Bradley has what psychiatrists call a therapeutic personality. We all shook hands with him after the briefing, like members of a congregation shaking hands with their minister, and one of the First Army correspondents said, "General, I'm always glad to see you, because you always make me feel good." Then Chitterling and I got on the road at the head of our motorcade, and started dropping jeeps off a couple at a time—each jeep containing three or four correspondents and a driver—as we came to the various auberges in which we had booked rooms. After we had dropped the last one, we pushed on to Ernée. Since General Bradley had assured us that there was no hurry about Paris, Chitterling and I played hooky the next day, pursuing some projects that failed to pan out, and did not get back to Bagnoles until Wednesday. There seemed to be no reason for haste; from a journalistic point of view, the war was marking time. You could drive in a jeep all day without finding any rational German resistance, although you might run into a band of vindictive fugitives and so get yourself shot. Or you might find isolated groups shooting away their stocks of ammunition because their commanding officers had listened to too much Wagner, like the drunken *Kommandant* of the fort at Saint-Malo who had made a senseless four-day stand against an all-out barrage and had then capitulated, contrary to the orders of the Führer. But such episodes were anodyne after the events of the breakthrough; the next big story coming up was the redemption of Paris, which the General had told us wouldn't occur immediately. It would be the biggest story of all for me, because I had left the city on June 10, 1940, when crowds of would-be refugees were overflowing into the streets around the railway stations. In my mind, the war would pretty well end with the road back to Paris. The rest would be epilogue.

I was bowled over, therefore, when, on returning to the press camp Wednesday afternoon, Chitterling and I found that it had been deserted by the other correspondents. Bagnoles-de-l'Orne is a summer resort of the most grisly vintage and variety, encumbered with great clapboard-and-stucco hotels of the early days of the Third Republic. The hotels are built around shallow lakes, which, while the press camp was there, at least, were so choked with the stems and leaves of water lilies that they were no good for swimming. I believe that when the place is operating normally, the guests at the hotels partake of purgative waters and talk about their insides, but by the time the First Army reached the town, in the summer of 1944, the hotels had been abandoned, and we roosted in them, doubly depressed by the lack of running water because the bathtubs reminded us of comforts we had almost forgotten.

Now only a few of the officers and enlisted men in the press-relations detachment were still around, and they were packing. In a few minutes, they informed Chitterling and me, they would be off for Paris, where they were to set up a new press headquarters in the Hôtel Scribe, near the Opéra. All my fellow-correspondents, they further related, were probably there already. What had happened, we gathered, was that the forces of the Resistance had unexpectedly risen in Paris and thrown the Germans out. They had then sent a messenger to Bradley asking him to come in fast and save them from the kind of revenge the Germans were currently visiting on Warsaw. The road to Paris was clear. The messenger had arrived in Laval after we left, and the General had revised all his thinking about Paris. I was consequently in a fair way to being scooped on the story I had been looking forward to for four years, two months, and thirteen days. As for Chitterling, my fellow-sybarite, he not only had missed the takeoff but was in Dutch with his superior officers.

I ran upstairs to the room I had shared with another correspondent, grabbed my sleeping bag off the floor, tied up all my junk in it, and came down demanding instant transportation to Paris. Chitterling would have been glad to take me, but, being in the doghouse, he had already been condemned to some menial task like checking the inventory of bales of carbon paper. There was, however, a young first lieutenant named Jack Roach, formerly a press-association reporter in Philadelphia, who controlled, on a provisional basis, a magnificent conveyance—a Chevrolet touring car built in Belgium before the war. It had been liberated from the Germans, and somehow or other Roach had got it. I can't for the life of me remember who was in command of the rear echelon of First Army Public Relations, which was rapidly dwindling as its officers, in order of seniority, provided themselves with missions to Paris. The command may have got down as far as Roach himself by that time.

At any rate, Roach and I took the Chevrolet and set out for La Ville Lumière, figuring we ought to hit it that evening if the roads ahead were as clear as had been rumored. That, I thought, would not be too late for the best of the celebration. We were intensely excited. How many times in his life does a man start out for what he is certain is going to be a phenomenally happy occasion? I don't think that Roach, who was in his middle twenties, had ever been in Paris, but that gave his anticipation a special quality. And for me, at forty, and with nearly half that many years of scattered memories of Paris behind me, it was like finding my Annabel Lee again. All the previous spring, in London, I had been reading clandestine newspapers smuggled out of France. I had cried over them. I do not regret my sentimentality; I wish I had something now that I could be as sentimental about.

When Roach and I had gone a fair piece of the way, we realized that we had brought no food along, either for ourselves or for hungry people we might meet. Living off the country was all very well in Normandy, Brittany, and Anjou—rich farming provinces unable to reach their customary markets and surcharged, like unmilked cows, with their own products. But Paris, we expected, would be short of food. We found the solution of our supply problem on the road ahead of us: a two-and-a-half-ton truck stacked high with cases of K rations, which were flat waxed-cardboard packages—thirty-six to a case—each containing the ready-to-eat components of a nourishing, harmless, and gastronomically despicable meal, calculated, I always supposed, to discourage overindulgence. (Among troops actively engaged, a K ration beat nothing to eat, but it was a photo finish.) These components were a round tin of alleged pork and egg, ground up together and worked to a consistency like the inside of a sick lobster's claw, and tasting like boardwalk cotton candy without any sugar in it; a few sourballs or other boiled sweets (I remember one particularly horrid variety that was flavored with root beer); four cigarettes; and a pinch of soluble coffee, dehydrated vegetarian bouillon, or lemonade powder. You sometimes had to open six packages to find one with coffee in it, and smokers had to open five to get the equivalent of a pack of cigarettes. The rest of a K ration so opened was then chucked away, except in Arab countries, where it could be traded for shell eggs, fowl, or little girls.

Atop the stacks of cases on the truck, at least ten feet above the road, stood a Negro soldier of the Quartermaster Corps. The crown of his helmet was a good sixteen feet above where he would land if he fell. His driver, I saw when we had overtaken the truck and were passing it, was another Q.M.C. soldier. But we did not overtake it until we had witnessed an extraordinary spectacle. There were a lot of jeeps on the road whose occupants had taken off, like us, à l'improviste, and as these vehicles passed the truck, the soldier up top would throw cases of K rations down into their rear seats. It was the way he did this that was remarkable. The truck was going about forty miles an hour, and a jeep would pull up on it, going about forty-five. As it did so, the soldier, standing up there, facing the rear—his feet spread wide apart to brace him on his gradually diminishing platform—would yell "How many?" and the jeep driver would hold up one, two, or three fingers, usually three. The soldier would have the first case already in the air, leading the driver, who would instinctively hunch forward over the wheel. But the case would fall harmlessly behind him every time. The second would land right on top of it. The third might land a couple of inches farther back, or even hit the stern end of the jeep and carom in, since by now the Q.M.C. bombardier would have to twist and throw it after the passing vehicle. These near misses must have pained him, for he was clearly a precisionist. He raised each successive case high above his head before he sent it crashing down, like an Old Black Jove hurling well-meant thunderbolts. I watched him until we had got our share, and then I turned my head and looked over my shoulder until we lost him from sight, some time afterward, and I never saw him conk anybody or throw any groceries out into the road. The driver was good, too; he held the same even course and pace, like a well-trained circus horse. It was, of course, a wholly unauthorized distribution of Army supplies, and maybe when that talented team reached the end of their run, some niggling quartermaster lieutenant chewed them out because they were a few hundred cases short, but I would have given them the Legion of Merit. Their gesture was so lordly that when I heard our cases crash behind me on the floor of the Chevrolet, I momentarily believed that they might contain fresh caviar, écrevisses à la nage, and a covey of smoked partridges.

I remember no other incident between Bagnoles-de-l'Orne and Chartres, a journey that, as the *Carte Michelin* reminds me now, is about 160 kilometers, or a hundred miles. All the way to Chartres, we accepted our hot tip at its face value and assumed that we were going straight through into Paris that night. I recall the excitement of seeing the first stone road markers that gave the distance not only to Alençon and Chartres but to Paris. The excitement increased as the number of kilometers decreased. When we reached Chartres, we were nearly two thirds of the way from Bagnoles to Paris and we had a couple of hours of daylight left, but there we were held up. Army was moving divisions from north to south and south to north, passing them through each other like a dealer giving cards a fast shuffle—the kind of *passe-passe* that is a good G-3's delight and that it sometimes seemed to me the boys did just for the hell of it. To Roach and me, it was like being caught on the wrong side of a St. Patrick's Day parade. Then, in the mixed crowd of soldiers and civilians that was packed around the principal carrefour of the city, half a dozen blocks from the Cathedral, I noticed a small private, first class, gesticulating and running toward us. As he approached, I saw he was Allan Morrison, a soldier-reporter for the *Stars & Stripes*, who has since become New York editor of the picture magazine *Ebony*, an ameliorated Amerafrican version of *Life*. He was the diagnostician who first divined the reason for the protracted resistance of the fort at Saint-Malo. "The C.O. is loaded," he said. "When he finishes his last bottle of sauce, they'll run up a white flag."

Morrison was hitchhiking, so I beckoned him aboard, and he climbed over the side and perched on our stack of K rations. A moment later, I recognized the lieutenant colonel who was out in the middle of the carrefour directing traffic, and I was able to surmise, correctly, that the shuffling of troops was not being run off in strict accordance with standard practice. The lieutenant colonel was a First Division fellow named Chuck Horner, and he was letting an endless column of his own people through; the only trucks that were moving were full of First Division soldiers. This was an old First Division trick. Army M.P.s were supposed to handle such matters, but those assigned to the task were usually enlisted men. If one of them showed up and tried to stop a First Division column to let the vehicles of some other outfit through for a while, a First Division lieutenant colonel, or even a higher officer in the outfit, would pull rank on him. I knew a First Division colonel who became a major general and got a division all his own. Once, when I was stuck for half an hour in a column halted at a road intersection, I got out of my jeep and walked up ahead to see what was happening. It was the major general personally passing his whole division through. I was glad he had not acquired a corps.

I had last seen Horner in North Africa hunting for enemy parachutists, who turned out to be soldiers of the Twelfth Air Force shooting tracers to celebrate Christmas Eve. ("It's the Air Force mentality," Horner said when he had finished his reconnaissance. He was very vexed.) I now reminded him of the occasion, and he agreed to let us through the First Division column. The First was not going into Paris, Horner told me; it would cross the Seine farther south, where there was still serious opposition. "Wouldn't you know it?" he said. "The bad divisions always get the soft jobs." The First pitied itself for being indispensable.

After we got on the Paris side of Chartres, traffic thinned out, and before long we were alone. "If everybody is going into Paris, I don't see why we're the only ones on the road," Roach said, with what made excellent sense. Morrison gave us the benefit of his inquiring reportorial mind by asking, "Who told you the way was clear all the way into Paris?" When we replied that everybody at Bagnoles-de-l'Orne had said so, Morrison asked, "Who told *them?* That's a long way back from here." Roach, who was not going to succumb to a climate of anxiety set up by an enlisted man, said, "Well, if the other correspondents didn't go into Paris, where are they? We haven't passed any on the road." This prompted Morrison to remark, "Maybe some prison-camp paper in Germany is going to have a hell of a staff." Twilight was coming on, and it suddenly seemed to me that my conversation with Lieutenant Colonel Horner had been a long while ago. There have been times in my life when I have missed the First Division more than anything else on earth.

When I was a boy member of the St. Agnes Branch of the New

York Public Library, I enjoyed reading about Jeb Stuart and imagining myself in his position, but by 1944 I no longer thought of myself as a man to lead a raid behind enemy lines, and our 1937-or-so Chevrolet was no armored division. As an assimilated captain (the grade bestowed on all war correspondents), I was the senior member of the expedition. Lieutenant Roach, the ranking active soldier, had received most of his battle training in the Philadelphia Bureau of the United Press, and his combat effectiveness was not enhanced by an oversize helmet that was likely to fall over his eyes if he moved suddenly. Private First Class Morrison's attitude was that of an objective observer, exactly as it is taught in schools of journalism. He was our whole enlisted strength.

"If we keep on going, we're bound to meet someone," I said decisively.

"That is exactly what I am afraid of," Morrison said.

To turn back was unthinkable, but we continued in a mood of modified rapture. I remember getting to a spot where a road branches north toward Rambouillet. That, we later learned, was the way most of the correspondents ahead of us had gone. But we held straight on. After a while, we came upon a couple of American soldiers in a jeep, which encouraged us. They said they were members of a troop of motorized cavalry belonging to the Seventh Armored Division and that their outfit was a couple of miles down a side road, preparing to spend the night there. Roach said their commanding officer ought to be able to give us some dope about what lay ahead. If the cavalry, which was made up of reconnaissance troops, was bedding down forty or fifty miles short of Paris, it hardly seemed likely that anybody had gone into the city by that route. We thought we might as well ask, though, so we turned down the side road and found the outfit, with its vehicles dispersed in a field.

"How much of our stuff is there out ahead of us, Lieutenant?" I asked the boy who was in command.

"Nothing," he replied. "Why should there be?"

I felt as mad as a man who is about to take a dip in a swimming pool and discovers that somebody has let all the water out of it. "Then why isn't there a sign on the road, or an M.P., or something?" I demanded. "After all, somebody might get captured this way."

"Ain't no Germans, either," the lieutenant replied reasonably. "We've had patrols up that road twenty miles. Can't find any."

"Well, it's a hell of a way to take Paris," I said. "Back at Bagnoles, they told us we were going right into Paris today."

"Bagnoles?" the lieutenant said. "Where's that? I'd like to go to Paris myself someday. Always heard it well spoken of."

"It's all right to go on, then?" Roach asked.

"You'll be safe enough along the main road," the lieutenant replied. "But don't go down any of the side roads, because there might be stray krauts along them, trying to escape. And don't try to drive after dark, because the country is full of F.F.I. [Forces Françaises de l'Intérieur], and they shoot at everything."

It was nearly dark by then. We could have slept out in the field, but there didn't seem much point to that when we could probably find beds at some hotel a little farther along the highway. Besides, I wanted to be as close up as possible in order to rush into the capital the next morning. So after we got back on the highway, we pushed on as far as the first crossroads agglomeration—I think the town was called Bonnelles—where there was a building that we thought might be a hotel. It was blacked out, of course, but light leaked defiantly from around every door and window. As soon as we got inside, we could see that we were in the provinces no longer but within the Sunday-outing belt of a big city. The name of the hotel was something like Au Retour de la Chasse et Rendez-Vous des Pêcheurs à la Ligne. There was a big, bare, partly dismantled dining room that was really just a boarded-in porch—obviously designed for use only in summer, the season of *boulistes* and lovers. There was also a bar, the full length of which would be required only on Sundays during the hunting (rabbit) and fishing (carp) seasons, when the sportsmen returned to discuss their evil luck over a pastis before reintegrating with their socially mediocre *arrondissements*. (The huntsmen and fishermen of the better neighborhoods miss bigger game with more expensive weapons at a greater distance from the city.) Since neither ammunition nor gasoline had been available for recreational purposes during the four years of the Occupation, business had been subnormal, and the place looked it. The barnlike ground floor was overrun with young men and women wearing the tricolor armbands of the Resistance. Each of the fellows had one or two weapons; German pistols (stolen) and tommyguns (parachuted) predominated. We got a big welcome.

Part of the difficulty of trying to reconstruct the days preceding the Liberation is that one now knows too much; I have since heard and read so often about what happened in Paris between August 15, when the police went on strike, and August 25, when the German garrison surrendered, that it is hard to recall the state of ignorance in which Roach and Morrison and I approached the city. It must have been there at the crossroads hotel, on the night of Wednesday, August 23, that we first heard any of the details. There were still some organized groups of Germans in the suburbs between where we were and Paris, the F.F.I. people told us, but there was no continuous line, and some of the kids we talked with had been in and out of the city several times during the past week, to help in the fighting and share in the excitement. News of the battle was on tap in the hotel twenty-four hours a day, the very shapely sweater-girl daughter of the proprietor informed me, since the telephone lines into Paris were still open; all you had to do was call and ask the *téléphonistes* what was happening. The German officers in control of the French telephone system either had skipped or, in the confusion, had lost track of which telephone centrals were now outside the rapidly shrinking Wehrmacht orbit. It must have been at the hotel, too, that we first heard how open fighting had begun in Paris on the previous Saturday, when the Germans gave the order to disarm the French police. The latter, refusing to be disarmed, had begun the defense of their headquarters, on the Ile de la Cité. Resistance groups had seized several other strong points, and the garrison had besieged them. On Monday, it seemed, there had been an abortive armistice. A distorted account of this development, trickling through to Bagnoles, had given rise to the report that the road was clear. But the fighting had continued, and now, as the Germans were pulling out, leaving only a rear guard, the Resistance, in turn, was besieging these hind-end Charlies.

"All these years, I have dreamed of seeing my first Allied soldier," the proprietor's daughter said. "This morning I saw him. He was alone in a jeep—a scout. He stopped in front of the door to ask directions. I rushed out, I precipitated myself on him, I threw my arms around him, I kissed him. I broke his glasses. He was furious."

That night, Roach, Morrison, and I slept in beds. The young F.F.I.s stayed up, because they were too excited to sleep, like children on the night before Christmas. They didn't even have a collaborator to shoot as a means of passing the time, an F.F.I. lieutenant told me shortly before I retired. "This is such a dreary little place," he said apologetically. "We had only a few *collabos* to start with, and now they've all skipped."

I shared the young F.F.I.s' excitement, although I realized how irrational it was, for, no matter how delighted, I was still capable of realizing that the liberation of Paris would not solve all the problems of the world, or even terminate the war. Nevertheless, before I fell asleep I saw American planes burning on the ghostly hills above the phosphate mine at Metlaoui, in Tunisia, and remembered the names of the pilots in them. Our side had come a long way around.

When I went downstairs next morning, a couple of jeeps bearing the emblem of the Daydaybay were parked in the garage with our Chevrolet. A French captain, a medic, was shaving painstakingly, a basin of hot water on the hood of a jeep in front of him, his field mirror hanging from a nail on a post. The captain said the Daydaybay was going to liberate Paris. When the Allied command advanced the date of the Liberation, the Daydaybay, officially attached to V Corps of the First Army, was resting after some hard fighting at the Argentan-Falaise gap, which it had helped to seal. The Daydaybay had been on the road all night long, the captain said, and by now its tanks were up ahead of us. The captain's report banished any misgivings I may still have had about those groups of Germans between us and Paris and also explained the paucity of American troops on the Paris side of Chartres. It was through the captain that

I got my first hint of the Allied command's decision to have the only French division in the north rescue the capital, instead of ordering an American division straight in. It was one of the wisest decisions of the war, helping to compensate for a thousand wounding stupidities in Anglo-American relations with the French. For all practical purposes, it constituted recognition of General de Gaulle's Provisional Government as the government of France, because Leclerc was more Gaullist than his chief. The presence of the Daydaybay in Paris would preclude any last-minute State Department–Foreign Office deal with collaborationists anxious to hedge their bets, like Darlan in Africa. We had nourished angry suspicions of such a deal by declining to recognize the Provisional Government officially.

The captain was making a careful toilette for his *rentrée* into Paris, which he expected to celebrate that evening. He was a specialist in colonial medicine, he told me, and at the time Paris fell, he was in Equatorial Africa, whence he had returned by stages—Lake Chad to Fezzan, Fezzan to Tunisia, Tunisia to Morocco (where the Daydaybay was put together and given its equipment), Morocco to England, and England to Bonnelles. All these steps had been made in the train of Leclerc, who had accumulated rank and firepower as he moved along, beginning as a thirty-eight-year-old major and winding up as a forty-one-year-old general of a division. Leclerc and the captain had left Chad in 1942 with the equivalent of one weak regiment—thirty-five hundred men in all, including three thousand Central African Negroes. Now they were on the outskirts of Paris surrounded by a magnificent division. It was a unique example of attrition in reverse. The captain's and my routes back to Paris had coincided once before. That was at Enfidaville, when the Allies were beginning their final drive to Tunis and Leclerc's troops were attached to the Fourth Indian Division of the British Eighth Army. At Enfidaville, I nearly had my first encounter with Leclerc, who was sleeping in a Ford sedan out beyond his front line—"*pour être tranquille*," his aide informed me—while mortar shells burst on all sides of his improvised dormitory. The aide said that if I wished to wait around until the General awoke, the General would be glad to talk to me. I replied that I had nothing important to discuss, and went back to have tea at Division.

Leclerc had brought his officers and noncoms along with him to stiffen the cadres of his new division, but he had left his black soldiers in North Africa. Although there were thus only a few hundred Chadians in the Daydaybay, it remained, in the popular imagination, "Leclerc's Army from Chad." I had seen the division on the road above Avranches on August 8, on its way to the front. The men were exuberant, sprawling over their tanks—all span-new Shermans—like kids on a hay ride. They had painted the sides of their vehicles with the names of French towns, regions, and rivers (Tarbes, Cévennes, Moselle, La Villette, and so on), and had topped their tankers' uniforms with the forage caps of their former branches of the service—red for the artillerists, blue for the chasseurs and marines. They were all volunteers, and, on the entire western front, they were the only soldiers in either the Allied or the Axis armies who were fighting on their home territory. They were also the only ground soldiers I remember during the war who were eager to fight. Ten days after I came across the division near Avranches, I had my talk with Leclerc in the field at Fleuré. In the meanwhile, the Daydaybay had flung itself in the path of the retreating German armies, got itself surrounded, cut its way out again, sunk its teeth in their hams, and kicked them in the ankle. It was the occasion when I asked the General about his name. I also asked him how his fellows compared with the blacks he had left in Africa. He replied that they fought as well but had less discipline.

When Roach and Morrison and I got out on the road that morning, we found ourselves in the midst of the armored infantry regiment of the Daydaybay, which was traveling in open half-tracks. Now that the tanks of the Daydaybay had gone through, the citizens of the populous countryside had no fear that the Germans would return, and so they turned out en masse to line the road as their men rode by. We were in the truck-gardening belt that surrounds Paris, and about all the inhabitants had to offer their liberators was tomatoes. While I know of few simple gastronomic pleasures comparable to a raw ripe tomato, I will concede that eight or ten such vegetables, coming at a soldier simultaneously from different directions, soon detract from his military appearance, and this the troops in the half-tracks, though appreciative of the generous spirit behind the gesture, were discovering.

Above Arpajon, where the long snake of vehicles from the west debouched into the north-south highway that connects Paris with Orléans, we passed a middling-pretentious villa, set back from the highway. A long-legged young woman in a bathing suit was lounging in a deck chair by the front door, her bare toes pointing at the oncoming column as she waved a promise—purely symbolic, of course—of what the young men in the half-tracks had been dreaming for four years of getting back to. Three small children clustered about her knees, discouraging a too personal reaction. The Daydaybay crawled by—fifteen thousand men on a moving belt of appetite.

I have read since that it rained during the night and early morning, while the Daydaybay was moving toward Paris. But mood and weather were in accord now, and the three of us in the Chevrolet tried to get along to the homecoming celebration quickly. Since we were attached to none of the division units, we were not obliged to stay in place in the line, so Roach began to weave his way forward, at first past half-tracks and then past tanks, scooting along the shoulders of the road when there were any and then ducking back to travel in the wake of the armor, until another opportunity presented itself. Our appearance helped. We were Americans, and Roach's First Army shoulder patch and my correspondent's green flash gave the impression that we were on an urgent mission. I encouraged this by asking French M.P.s along the way where General Leclerc found himself. Every time I asked, they waved us forward, which didn't surprise me, remembering my near encounter with him at Enfidaville.

The solidity and nonchalance of the column, now within twenty miles of Paris, convinced me that the Germans had simply skedaddled. I surmised that as we entered the Porte d'Orléans, they would be going out the Porte de la Villette, on the other side of town. I have always preferred to enter a beleaguered city in this fashion. Violence interferes with the enjoyment of the sentiments appropriate to such an occasion; shooting, if bilateral, spoils everything. As we skittered happily along in the Chevrolet, the only question in my mind was whether Leclerc would retain enough sense of noblesse oblige to share with those American allies who found themselves by chance in his immediate vicinity the *vin d'honneur* that was sure to be offered him as he entered the city.

We passed the tank that was leading the procession, and Morrison, from the rear seat, asked me if I didn't think I might have received another wrong steer. For some time, as we pushed along, the welcoming throng had been thinning out, and now it had dwindled to nothing. This, of course, is always an ominous sign. No one had thrown a tomato to us for a couple of miles when, suddenly, we spotted two jeeps ahead of us, one of them flying a general's fanion. "Don't get ahead of him," I told Roach. "He might be offended." Just as we began to pull up on the jeeps, they stopped. There was the sound of an *arrivée*—an incoming shell—and then a spout of dirt and smoke two hundred yards to the right of the highway; it had clearly crossed over the road between us and the jeeps. Leclerc got out of his jeep—we knew it was he because he carried a cane— and began to look about him with interest. He did not look long; within a few seconds we saw him wave his cane, like a pointer, in the direction he evidently thought the shell had come from. Then he hopped back into his jeep, and both vehicles turned around and started toward us, the General undoubtedly pleased as Polichinelle at having spotted an antitank gun before it could hurt one of his cherished armored vehicles. He was the only divisional commander I ever saw use himself as a decoy to draw fire. Roach asked if I thought Leclerc would be angry if we preceded him back down the road. I replied that in retreat the place of honor is in the rear, and we might as well leave it to the General.

We soon reached the main body of vehicles again, and saw that the parade had temporarily disbanded; deploying from the Paris-Orléans highway, the tanks were taking off along feeder roads and the half-tracks across fields, as if preparing to pinch in on the point of resistance. Leclerc, after a brief pause at the first tank he came to, headed down a tarred crossroad. "Maybe he's going to try another way through," Roach said. "Let's follow him." Not being able to read Morrison's mind, I couldn't tell whether Roach's proposal represented the inclination of the majority, and I was ashamed to suggest putting the matter to a vote. So we hustled along after the General.

I have no coherent recollection of the next few hours, which we spent running up and down crossroads, hoping they would lead us to a nice, clear, Franco-American-held path into Paris, or else following half-tracks loaded with infantrymen along minor lanes that ran parallel to the main highway. The men in the half-tracks were passing wine bottles from hand to hand, for the inhabitants of the region, having run out of tomatoes, had levied on their cellars to produce new offerings, and there was a festival atmosphere. Each time we attached ourselves to a company of vehicles, one of us would say, "Maybe this outfit will go all the way through," but each time, after a mile or two, there would be a barrage of antitank *arrivées* and the vehicles would stop and fan out from the road.

An armored division is a superior instrument for long sweeps across open country but ill-adapted to fighting in the suburbs of a great city. Between Arpajon and Paris the terrain is finely veined with roads and closely dotted with villages. Roads converge upon each village, and every village crossroads offers an ideal emplacement for a concealed antitank gun, which an approaching tank, hemmed in by buildings on either side, must face head on. In such circumstances, the safe, cautious procedure is to stop the tanks, call up the half-tracks, and deploy infantrymen around each strong point, but there were two persuasive arguments against such strategy on that August 24. One was that there were so many antitank emplacements and so few infantrymen—since the Daydaybay, as an armored division, carried with it only one infantry regiment—that the thrust would have slowed to a crawl, and the other was Leclerc's and the whole Daydaybay's overpowering haste to get into Paris. The Germans, rightly calculating that the Allies would never again bomb them in Paris, had dismantled all their antiaircraft defenses in the zone, and the weapons taken from those installations gave them an abundance of the deadliest kind of antitank artillery. Rommel, it is now known, had wanted to bring this stuff forward months earlier and use it on the battlefield, but he had been overruled. Antiaircraft belonged to the Luftwaffe, the Luftwaffe belonged to Goering, and Goering hated Rommel.

The Daydaybay's irregularly progressing advance elements were followed by a great wheeled throng, including us, that was always just far enough back not to be shot at, which meant not quite far enough forward to see what was going on, with the result that nobody could understand why the headway being made was so intermittent; it was like a huge crowd following a pack of coon hounds by their sound, unaware that the dogs have met up with a wildcat. In the throng, in addition to the supply and ammunition trains and all the other rear elements of the division, were many vehicles whose occupants, whether military or civilian, had no connection with the Daydaybay. There were, for example, increasing numbers of American trucks carrying provisions for Paris, because Group had envisaged the possibility that the city would be found on the verge of famine, and of civilian charcoal-fueled trucks, mounting odd revolving chimneys that belched stinking smoke, and jammed with delegations of F.F.I. from behind the Allied lines. The F.F.I., who were willing enough, could have been used as infantry if the division staff had had liaison with them, but it is hard to improvise such an arrangement on a battlefield. So they mostly just followed along with the rest of us, though occasionally some of them dismounted to hunt down a German in a haystack after the tanks had cleaned out a gun position. There were Army jeeps from all over the front, carrying officers who, like those at Bagnoles-de-l'Orne, had invented missions for themselves that would take them to Paris. And there were the correspondents, military and civilian, too. Morrison and I spotted jeeploads of our colleagues at every turning, giving me happy reassurance that I had made up the head start that so appalled me the day before.

The many tangential roads were a constant challenge, and

Roach, Morrison, and I kept trying new ones, always figuring that we might still come on one that was clear all the way into Paris. But whatever road we tried led us to fighting. We could tell that the advance units were moving nearer Paris all the time, though, because at each try we got farther from our line of departure, which was where the parade had come to a halt. After we explored all the accessible roads, we went back over those on which we had first run into fighting, and here the evidence of progress was all about us, in the form of burned-out vehicles (most of them, unfortunately, bearing the Daydaybay emblem), knocked-out antitank guns, and German dead and wounded, lying by the roadside with their feet toward the pavement, waiting to be picked up, sometime, by French ambulances. They had been laid out there in orderly fashion, as if they had dressed their lines, by German prisoners, working in pairs under the orders of F.F.I. boys with tommyguns. It must have been disquieting to a member of the Führer's master race to feel, as he walked along holding a leg of a wounded man in each hand, that there was within kicking distance of his rear a seventeen-year-old with a tommygun pointed at his kidneys and a wild desire to use it. We came across unwounded and unutilized prisoners, too, holding their hands high over their heads and doing a shoeless goose step in response to the orders of their F.F.I. guards. (Boots of real leather had become extremely scarce in France, and the F.F.I.s figured that since the collective Occupant was responsible for this state of affairs, it was fair enough to glom the individual Occupant's boots when he was taken prisoner.) The prisoners' faces had the same color as those of the dead Germans—greenish white under the dust from the road—as if, physiologically, the processes of death had already begun, a reaction to an anticipated situation. Yet I saw only one Frenchman justify such a reaction. A wounded German was lying, quite still, by the roadside, when two armed civilians approached him. One pulled at his boots and the other pointed an automatic—German—at his head and fired. There was no excuse for it.

The Daydaybay's infantrymen, in their half-tracks, followed the tanks at a distance of a little less than a mile. The commander of each combat group—four or five tanks and as many half-tracks—committed his infantry only when he had to, since to detruck and deploy them, move them up on foot, envelop a position, and then take it by small-arms fire might require anywhere from fifteen minutes to an hour. That accounted for the heavy losses of the tankers and for the boredom of the infantry, who, in their open vehicles under a baking August sun, began to sweat wine. I remember two troglodytic types—an Arab and a Frenchman from some part of the Mediterranean littoral—locked in unfraternal combat while their *compagnons de voiture* tried unsuccessfully to pry them apart. "*Tapette!*" each of the contestants shouted in one of the other's ears as they struggled. The insult, which is French slang for "homosexual," was never used with less apparent foundation. They looked like pithecanthropi with gold teeth. (I did not see either of them at Mme la Maréchale's recent party.)

On each road we tried, we met jeeploads of correspondents and of officers attempting to maintain liaison with Division, but the jeep we met most frequently was General Leclerc's. Leaning forward as he sat, tapping on the floor with his cane, he looked as if he were riding the jeep toward an obstacle on a steeplechase course. Leclerc was forty-one, a year younger than the Ulysses S. Grant of the Wilderness Campaign, and, like Grant, he was by training and predilection a horseman. Watching him in his jeep made me realize for the first time how valuable a horse must have been in the old days as an outlet for the emotional energy of a fretting commander. The constant conflict of wills, on a level slightly below that of thought, and the horse's reflexes, impossible to ignore even during great crises, must have offered a distraction from the pressures of the moment. Leclerc, I knew, had been a cavalryman, and I have since learned that when he first saw action, as a lieutenant in Morocco in 1926, he had two horses killed under him. And now he had only a jeep to sit, and a jeep is insensitive to the eager tremolo of the legs. Still, he was riding it as best he could. To be so near Paris and not yet have it made him strain the long nose and the bristling red mustache in close pursuit of the point of the visor of his three-star-general's kepi.

I had, it is true, been talking with Leclerc only a week or so earlier, but now, as we passed and repassed each other on the road, I never found what I deemed a suitable opportunity to remind him of our acquiantance, and the same diffidence restrained me even when, just beyond a railroad culvert, his vehicle and ours stopped close together in deference to a shelling by an unanticipated battery. During a pause in the shelling, he continued on his way, but we decided to turn back and try some other route, and presently we met a jeep carrying an American brigadier general from V Corps, the unit of which the Daydaybay was theoretically a part. The general waved to us to stop, and when we did, he got out in the road and asked us if we had seen Leclerc. He was a very precise-looking brigadier general, with rimless glasses and a neatly trimmed black mustache, and he carried a well-filled map case under his right arm. We pointed in the direction in which we assumed Leclerc was still riding, if his luck had held out, and the brigadier sighed. "I've been looking for him at what is supposed to be Division Headquarters, and they told me they hadn't heard from him for hours," he said. "The division isn't where it's supposed to be, and I can't find Leclerc to tell him so. God damn it," he added, with unexpected warmth, "this isn't an advance at all! It's the march of a gypsy band." The brigadier turned, the set of his shoulders a form of professional reproof, climbed back into his vehicle, and took off after the unhorsed cavalier, who, as a matter of principle, tried to stay out of touch with Corps as much as possible. He loathed receiving orders. "He was a commander who knew how to make himself adored without making a single concession to popularity," a man who served under him said to me once. "Whenever he did a kindness, he always covered it with a hard word."

Late in the afternoon, having worked all the subsidiary roads in vain, we went back to the Paris-Orléans highway and found it clear for at least ten miles beyond where we had left it that morning. There was almost the fine free feeling of our ride to Chartres the day before as we raced up past Montlhéry and into Longjumeau, an ancient town that chiefly consists of a single endless street, walled on both sides with houses. In the coaching days, Longjumeau was the last change of horses before Paris. On its interminable street, we came upon the tail end of a long string of motionless vehicles. The

Germans were making another stand up ahead, at Fresnes, where they were using a prison as an antitank fort. I acquired from a source that I believed authentic—and it turned out to be so—the information that the division would not go into Paris until the next morning. It is strange that I cannot remember now who told me, because it must have been somebody I trusted like my mother, or Roach, Morrison, and I would have waited in the street all night. The fighting at Fresnes, which we did not try to see, was savage.

Longjumeau, with its locked and tightly shuttered house fronts, offered small promise of an entertaining billet, so we turned back toward more open country and took the turnoff to the Tower of Montlhéry. A difference between the Paris suburbs and those of New York is that in the former, crabbed old medieval towns are interspersed with the latest jerry-built speculative developments. The town of Montlhéry, huddled on the slope of a hill a mile or so east of the highway, might as well be, from its appearance, in a remote corner of Burgundy as where it is, thirteen miles from the Porte d'Orléans. On the other side of the highway is the Montlhéry automobile race track, an incongruous annex to the ancient commune. We took the road that leads up through the steep, narrow streets of the town to the ancient Tower, on the top of the hill. (*Monument historique*, completed A.D. 1015, 137 meters above sea level at its base, 168 at its summit, it says in the guidebooks.)

Only the Tower remains of a castle that dominated the southern approach to Paris for six centuries, served as a fortress for insurrectionary French lords in a drawn battle against Louis XI in 1465, and was finally dismantled by Henry IV in 1591, so that it could never again be used as a center of rebellion. The four encircling walls have long since disappeared, the stones having been carted away by thrifty house-builders. Trees have grown up over most of the site. After passing through the town, the road skirts the outline of the vanished outermost wall. In peacetime, Sunday motorists park their cars along it and walk up to where the Tower stands solitary on the wooded hilltop. To cater to these visitors, a rustic restaurant and bar, called the Auberge de la Tour, has been built near the road, with a wide concrete terrace that affords a view in the direction of Melun and Fontainebleau, and it was here that we stopped.

The interior of the Auberge de la Tour (*"Terrasse—Jeux—Panorama Splendide"*), like that of our stopping place the night before, was in a state of ecstatic ebullition. M. Bertrand, the *patron*, by whom we were made welcome, is one of those Frenchmen who wear a cap and sweater in all seasons and invariably speak in a deep baritone. His eyes bulge in a friendly but disillusioned manner, advising the world that he is not a man to be taken in. His handclasp is strong and his conversation informed and libidinous, as an innkeeper's should be. His chalet is crowded with paintings in which he descries the hands of Old Masters. M. Bertrand is the *crieur aux ventes*, or auctioneer, of the district, which is in itself an assurance that he is a glib fellow. In selling the effects of the deceased, he told me over our first glass of wine, he was occasionally able to come by some good things; he was, after all, the only connoisseur between Melun and Saint-Michel. He bought not for resale, he said, but as an investment, with a view to creating an estate for his descendants.

"That Géricault there, for example," M. Bertrand said, pointing to a dark oil painting of a lean young thoroughbred in a stall. "There aren't many *guinguettes* where you'd find a Géricault. It's unfortunate he didn't sign it, but it's the real thing. I know his style." Mme Bertrand, a stout, red-faced woman with high cheekbones and narrow eyes, produced a bottle of a dreadful sweet aperitif wine called Cap Corse—the only prewar aperitif in the house, she said—which she had saved for this great day. We all felt obliged to smack our lips over it.

An F.F.I. boy asked me if Morrison was "an American colonial." I told him no, he was an American, just like Roach and me—we came all colors. So the boy said that if Morrison was that sort of American, he must be conversant with the latest *tendances du jazz hot*. As it happened, Morrison was, and the boy went to a cupboard and fetched a clarinet. Then Roach, Morrison, and I and the boy, and about five other F.F.I. youngsters in shirt sleeves went out on to the *terrasse* with the *panorama splendide* in the late twilight and pulled up chairs around a couple of tables. The clarinetist put his feet up on his table, tilted his chair back, and announced that he was going to play *"Dans l'Ambiance"*—or, as he translated it, "Een de Mud." Then he lifted the clarinet to his lips and played "In the Mood" while Morrison encouraged him with the whole sectarian gamut of facial appreciation and a few quiet, satisfied groans. "Een de Mud" sounded better than any other music I've ever heard. The clarinet gloated over the routed Ostrogoths. The thin sound, wriggling up toward the old Tower, woke birds that had turned in for the night. M. Bertrand's son, a slight youth of eighteen, said the Germans had disapproved of jazz, regarding an interest in it as evidence of Allied sympathies, and had forbidden it to be played in public places. The *zazous*, or hepcats, however, were not discouraged by this from playing at dances but, instead, amused themselves by working out musical arrangements that began as Viennese waltzes, then switched to jazz and back again before any Germans present could call the turn. The *zazous* also affected *le genre jazz* in their clothes, the Bertrand boy said; they wore what Americans call zoot suits. There was nothing much *l'Occupant* could do about that.

In time, the clarinetist finished his recital. It was full dark by then. I could tell by his voice when he spoke that it had done him good to get that dissident music out of him, blasting it forth into the night after the hour of the Occupation curfew. He told us he was not a professional musician—as we had all suggested he must be—but a typewriter repairman. There had been no new typewriters in Paris since the Occupation, he said, and the maintenance of the old ones had become a fine art. I asked him what my banged-about portable Underwood would bring on the black market, and he said, readily, 56,000 francs, which, at the going rate of 50 to the dollar, would have been $1,120.

The jazz connoisseurs of Montlhéry had not been completely cut off from the *potins* and *nouvelles tendances* of the American jazz world, the lads said. They had had not only the *émissions* of the London radio but reports on the situation from four American and two Canadian aviators and jazz fanciers who had lived in the village for several weeks after being shot down over France and who had departed only that afternoon, when an American detachment showed up there. The airmen had reached Montlhéry by a branch line of the underground railroad that was washed out a short while after their arrival in the village. "They were all *fanatiques du jazz*," young Bertrand said. "Unhappily, they spoke hardly any French, but by whistling, tapping with the foot, and now and then a word, we could make ourselves understood to one another."

Until D Day, Allied airmen shot down over France and retrieved by the Resistance were frequently taken to Paris and thence rerouted toward the Spanish frontier. Paris was the turntable. The Allied landings, however, had made communications between Paris and the rest of France uncertain, and from then on most of the Allied fliers who were shot down had to sit it out where they were until they were rescued. The *fanatiques du jazz* stranded in Montlhéry were in this position. All our airmen who flew over France carried photographs of themselves taken in civilian clothes and suitable for attaching to *cartes d'identité*. The Resistance supplied the *cartes*— forged, of course, and usually describing the bearer as a deaf-mute. The high incidence of deafness and mutism in Occupied territory might have astonished an Occupant with more intellectual curiosity. The airmen in Montlhéry had been dressed in French clothes and billeted with "relatives." It became easy to explain newcomers after the landings by saying they were fugitives from the war area.

"The Sunday afternoon before last, we gave a concert on the terrace here," young Bertrand said. "No jazz on the program, of course, but we had a very good crowd and had a lot of fun—all except for the best-known *collabos*. The *collabos* were feeling sick. We were very gay, because we knew by word of mouth and through the B.B.C. how fast the Americans were advancing. *Les Fritz* were furious, but they couldn't forbid innocent amusements without acknowledging that their position was becoming critical. Officially they were still saying the offensive was a local attack that would be contained. The airmen came to the concert and mingled with us young people—all pals of theirs. If a Gestapo man had asked them for their cards, he would have made the discovery that deaf men are crazy about music. Those aviators were nice boys. The town won't be the same without them. It is the only regrettable result of the Liberation."

The night was black and quiet. If there was sporadic shooting up ahead, as there must have been, the wind was wrong, for we heard none. We might have been sitting out under the trees on a New England lawn. There wasn't a uniform in the Auberge, except for Roach's, Morrison's, and mine, in which (I feel safe in speaking for my two companions) none of us had ever felt natural. We were as tired as if we had spent all day swimming, and tired in the same contented way.

I was up early next morning, and while waiting for the others to turn out, I climbed up the fifty yards or so to the Tower, traversing the remains of a causeway that crosses the remains of a moat. The top of the hill is the highest point between Montlhéry and Paris. A very informative booklet, which I did not have then but which I recently bought, for fifty francs, says that the Tower is 24.III kilometers from the Panthéon and dominates it by 31 meters. Because of its height, the booklet adds, it was a station on the semaphore-telegraph line that linked Paris with the Spanish border in the days before the electric telegraph made the service obsolete, and in 1874 scientists used the Tower to measure the speed of light. One could hardly imagine the Germans' passing up a bet like that, and, sure enough, they had built a brick observation-and-listening post on a flat stretch beside the Tower. I was staring up at the Tower, the first ruin I had seen in months that didn't look as if it could be blamed on the Allied Air Forces, when I heard an American voice say, "Good morning!" Turning, I saw that the voice emanated from a Signal Corps lieutenant, who, I suppose, had emanated from the brick building. Neither voice (Philadelphia, perhaps) nor lieutenant (five ten, pale under a black stubble, serious mouth) was distinctive, but he was a man I won't forget.

"I've been up here since yesterday morning, sir," he said. "Recon troop brought me up here with a couple of other men, so we could look around. I haven't been of any use, but I've been having a wonderful time looking at Paris through a good glass. I've never been to

Paris, but I've been reading about it all my life. I know it by heart, from the maps. Just where everything is. And there it is! God, I just can't take my eyes off it! Come over here and I'll show it to you." He handed me his binoculars, a magnificent Signal Corps pair, and led me over to the northern edge of a broken parapet. Paris was there, all right—there in the same place I had left it four years, two months, and fifteen days before.

"I got the map right here," the lieutenant said, and he unrolled it and laid it out on a flat stone. Then he straightened up and said, "But I don't need the map, because I've got all the landmarks cold. Now, over there," he went on, pointing to the dome of the Invalides, "is the Opera House. Once you get that clear, you have your orientation. And over there," he continued, pointing now to the Opéra, "is the City Hall—you know, the Chamber of Deputies. Isn't it beautiful?"

"It's beautiful," I said, and meant it.

The lieutenant got the Eiffel Tower right. "I suppose you know what that beautiful white church is up on the hill?" he next said, swiveling my elbow into line with Sacré-Coeur. I was going to name it, but something warned me not to, so I shook my head. "Why, it's Notre Dame, of course!" he said, and I was glad that I had kept my mouth shut.

"I can't wait to get down there," the lieutenant said. "It's the most beautiful city in the world."

I thanked him from the bottom of my heart. I hope he made it.

The Hounds with Sad Voices

(NOVEMBER 16, 1957)

I remembered another Norman house called a château, where the press lived for a week after the breakthrough, but the memory was like Le Grand Meaulnes' of the house he dreamed. I no longer knew precisely where it was, nor could I recall the surname of the proprietor, though I had one in my mind—de Fives. From Vouilly the press camp moved to a place called Canisy, of which I remember nothing except that the tents were in an apple orchard; and then in a few days to a house on the skirts of the Forest of St.-Sever. It was near a hamlet called Fontenermont, which is near the small ancient town of St.-Sever, which is not far from the small city of Vire.

This was a baroque house, although in rural Normandy, where the baroque lingered, it may have been of the late eighteenth century. It was tall in relation to its length, with a square tower that had a top like an *accent circonflexe* (∧). It was of gray granite, like most of the other buildings of the region of Vire, which is hilly and in many places wooded—the Bocage, or Bosky Land. Compared to the flat and rich Bessin, where Vouilly lay, the Bocage is romantic and energetic. The land is still good, but shading off toward the austerity of Brittany to the south. In the Bocage you begin to smell Brittany. It has a high incidence of small noblemen, of families that officered the Army, the Navy, and the Church before the Revolution.

This house might have been built by a retired frigate's captain or a colonel, a younger son of such a family, returned from the wars against the English in the East or West Indies, and content in middle age to follow the staghounds in the Forest of St.-Sever. They hunted the stag with dignity and clamor, the slow, deep-voiced hounds driving him in wide, then narrowing circles, he running from the sound and not the sight of them, working into the center of the deep but not sufficiently entangled woods. At last he would stand exhausted in a clearing, or in a pond, up to his neck in water. Then the hired huntsman would advance and cut his throat, and the bandsmen would play their taradiddles for wind instruments. The horses, never out of a canter all day, would be turned toward home and the waiting holocausts of venison and game birds and the old Calvados, the dice boxes, and the canopied curtained beds closed like confessionals and full of secrets.

This family had enjoyed another period of prosperity in a more recent era, to judge from the vestiges of the chic of the early Third Republic that cluttered the house, like props for the production of a dramatic version of *Bel-Ami*. There were trophies of African spears and Arab scimitars on the walls, which were papered with an imitation of brocade, and faded green plush portieres drooped crazily from valances askew. Notably there was a stuffed leopard, its lips pulled back in a savage snarl from teeth that were no longer present. Age affects the grip even of plaster gums. The background of the leopard's rosettes had faded to the color of bad California white wine. Most of the furniture was crank and perilous to sit upon.

It all reminded me, sadly, of the illustrations in the thirty-volume-or-so set of Maupassant, bound in three-quarter green imitation morocco with gold ornaments on the spine, that had been the chief advertisement of sophistication behind the glass of my parents' Globe-Wernicke sectional bookcases. In those volumes I sought my first clues to sex, and to this day I retain a prejudice that gentlemen with curved jet-black mustaches and long-tailed coats are wickeder than others, and that ladies with big behinds and small feet are the most irresistible. I had arrived, at last, in my chosen décor, but sixty years too late. Maupassant was a Norman, and my long liaison with Normandy began in the Globe-Wernicke mahogany sectional bookcases, and probably in a bad translation.

I thought the proprietor, when young, might have shared the

glories of the Normans-transplanted-to-Paris I remembered in the illustrations, slipping from behind portieres exactly like the ones that now hung in shreds, to put their arms about the hourglass waists of chambermaids in white lace caps. I was sure he had slain the leopard and had his photograph published, wearing *le casque tropical*, his feet and the stock of his rifle behind the prostrate victim's head: "*M. le Vicomte de Fives avec une belle pièce de gibier. Ce léopard faisait la terreur des noirs du Limpopo français avant que le sportsman normand l'arretait en pleine fureur avec une balle bien placée dans chaque narine.*" But by the time we arrived he had regressed into peasantism. A great, heavy figure of a man, he went about in shirt sleeves, with checked denim trousers held around his pendulous paunch by an old harness strap.

The only vestige of the old chic that I confidently attributed to him was a hard straw hat, a *canotier*, or boater, that he wore indoors and out. (He was probably bald.) The old man's face and wattles were suffused with blood, and his mustache, of the color and aspect of hempen rope, no longer curled upward, as I was sure it must have once, but hung limp under his forceful nose.

The house stood on a low ridge with a higher ridge behind it. Our tents were pitched out behind the house, and to get to it we had to walk across what had once been a garden with flower beds marked out with rocks, and gravel paths between them. These boundaries were wiped out now; the rose bushes had gone to briar, but there were still late-season blooms, falling to pieces on their stalks. Petunias ran as wild as morning glory on a beach, and there were dusty zinnias.

We spent our days upon the roads, now that the war was all of movement, but in the evening we returned, and after supper wrote our dispatches in the blacked-out house, using as typewriter tables Levantine taborets inlaid with mother-of-pearl stars like those that cluttered living rooms from Lodz to Laramie in 1900. They still manufacture them in Damascus, but they must export them to places like the Dominican Republic. The censors and the Press Wireless men were set up amid the shards of elegance as we were.

Between the edge of our camp and the beginning of the garden we had to walk along the outside of a run fenced in with chicken wire, which contained eight or ten gaunt, sad hounds, with long heads and short legs, whose sad voices had the quality, at first emission, of echoes that have bounced around a valley. They were bassets of some kind, I knew at once, but higher on the leg and of a less studiously abnormal appearance than the English sort. Their flanks, as corrugated with ribs as a hunger striker's, were white flecked with black, their long, wide, trailing ears solid black, and their faces black flecked with white. They were *bassets de Gascogne*, the old man told some one of us, the only pack of that strain in the northwest of France. I never talked to him myself; he did not invite conversation.

They were so thin, the old man was reported to have said, because under the conditions of the Occupation and rationing, it was hard to get meat to feed them on—even the meat of old horses brought high prices as *filet Longchamp*. (And because of the same phenomenon, I thought uncharitably, he would be sure not to feed them any of his own livestock when he killed.) Because the Germans had allowed the Normans to possess no ammunition for hunting, much less use any, the dogs were unexercised and unhappy. The old man said his hounds were of such an ancient and glorious breed that he could have sold them in couples, or one by one, at whopping prices, particularly to the Germans, but he had not wanted to disperse his breeding stock. I think he fed them on snared rabbits and other oddments as available.

The jeep drivers and cooks, some of whom came from hound-dog country, used to spend a lot of time in front of the chicken wire talking to the dogs, but the bassets were distant and surly. They scorned K rations. They might be down, but they were not so flat as all that.

If the soldiers had been horse cavalry, they might have found an unpopular officer's mount for the hounds to eat, but they had only jeeps. One night somebody stole one of the bassets, but I was away on an overnight trip to the Falaise pocket and so escaped suspicion. The abduction made a great stir. The old man protested to the lieutenant colonel in command of the press camp that it was not a question of the theft of a vulgar dog. His pack was a national historical monument, and Haro XVIII's disappearance reflected the blackness of the error committed by Louis XVI when he temporized with the mob. It was a delayed effect of the Revolution.

The lieutenant colonel made a serious try to find the historic animal, but he failed, as I expected he would. I have seen soldiers carry large dogs aboard a transport slung across their shoulders in barracks bags, and setters abducted from England leap from the cockpits of fighter planes landed on Tunisian airfields. The First Army moved ahead toward the Seine, and the press camp followed to Bagnoles-de-l'Orne, but the fate of Haro XVIII remained a mystery.

My fear of Michel's scorn kept me from trying to rediscover this house unaided. I could foresee his reactions if I asked him to begin inquiring after a house whose owner, of whose name I was uncertain, had once kept dogs with sad voices, or if I even let him know that such was the object of my search. When we arrived at l'Hôtel du Cheval Blanc in the city of Vire, however, I dismissed Michel and the Versailles, lunched, and then went on foot in search of M. Marcel Le Cornec, the publisher and editor of *La Voix du Bocage*— The Voice of the Bosky Country—a newspaper that I have received in New York every week since the conclusion of the war by M. Le Cornec's courtesy.

M. Le Cornec is a man of sensibility as well as intelligence. He respects the capricious forms nostalgia often takes, and when I related to him my desire to see for inconsequential reasons this Château of the Mournful Hounds, he volunteered to help me find it. St.-Sever and Fontenermont are fifteen miles or so from Vire, but well within the zone of circulation and influence of *La Voix du Bocage*, which is the most powerful organ of public opinion between St. Lô and Avranches. But, to begin with, he said, my recollection of the family name as de Fives and of the old man as a Vicomte must be erroneous.

M. Le Cornec is a tall and very handsome man who looks like George Washington *en littérateur*, Roman nose, blue eyes, high complexion, and mane of white hair long in back, over a string tie and corduroy jacket. He is, as his name shows, of Breton family origin, but began life in Paris. There he was a commercial artist during the twenties. He came to Vire to design packages and draw advertisements for a wholesale grocery firm.

Vire, like a number of other Norman towns at rail and road junctions, was destroyed by the Allied air bombardment of June 6 designed to stop the Germans from reinforcing their coastal troops. The city's printing plants disappeared in the ruins. When Vire was freed in August, M. Le Cornec founded its first postwar newspaper, printing at first in a less damaged city, until he could reestablish printing in Vire. I do not remember now, although M. Le Cornec told me, whether the publisher of the prewar paper was killed in the bombardment or disqualified for collaboration. At any rate, M. Le Cornec and his wife, a witty and spirited woman, made a paper with a decided personality.

Since M. Le Cornec is not a native, he takes an objective view of the remarkable world in which he lives. He keeps the paper's face straight, but his amusement sometimes filters through his long and circumstantial accounts of such affairs as the suit for defamation, for endless billions of francs, that a rich farmer brought against *La Voix du Bocage* ten years ago, for printing a speech of the mayor of the farmer's community. In the speech the mayor accused his *administré* of "moistening his milk" before selling it. To moisten milk is, in Norman, to add water to it.

When the farmer sued, *La Voix* recorded the news, along with a restatement of the grounds on which he was suing. He then sued them for a reiteration of libel. But the mayor's speech was an official statement, since he had made it at a meeting of the municipal council. *La Voix* contended that a newspaper must publish official statements. What had loosed the mayor's wrath against the rich farmer was that the rich farmer opposed the use of municipal funds to provide free milk for school children. Reading *La Voix* in New York, I was sure that was why the paper reprinted the story so many times, but they never said so.

Vire was the place where I stayed longest on my first exciting *prise de connaissance* with lower Normandy in 1926. I saw it for only a few minutes in 1944, so dreadfully demolished that I could not bear it for longer. Now a Vire had risen on the old site, solid, ugly, new without being modern. There was, in 1955, still a noise of drills and bulldozers. Construction was going on, but it was already irremediable. Each property owner had wrung as much money as he could from the State for reconstruction of what he said he had had, and then built a house containing the maximum number of cubic feet that could be roofed over, leaving the upper floors to be finished at his leisure in the years to come. One surviving monument was the Tour de l'Horloge, the old Clock Tower, that had once been a gate in the medieval city wall. The rest of the wall had been leveled by Henri IV, after the Wars of Religion.

The tower, with the gateway under it, stood astride the main street of the Vire I knew. Traffic passed between its legs. The bombs had cleared a space around it but left it crazily erect at the hub of the city. The traffic now passed around instead of through, and, indeed, the vibration set up by trucks might have brought La Tour down on the drivers' heads if they had persisted in the old way.

The sixteenth-century clock that banged out the time every quarter of an hour, night and day, was silent, knocked out of time when the bombs fell. The old Hôtel du Cheval Blanc stood next to the Clock Tower, and a guest unable to fall deeply asleep in fourteen minutes flat had a fat chance of getting to sleep at all. The new Cheval Blanc has been erected fifty yards from the old site, and when I slept there I was willing to forgive the municipal council for not having restored the historic chimes. There is a limit to my archaelogical purism. But I found it harder to forgive that the surrounding proprietors had been allowed to mass high, bloated new buildings all around the new traffic circle, and that the bit of space remaining in the center was used for parking automobiles, instead of for a plaza or small park. So the Tower stands like a stag at bay in a pond, the ugliness ringing it and closing in, awaiting the inevitable hour when some municipal engineer will declare it a menace and workmen will come to cut its throat. Vire will then be indistinguishable from St. Lô or Isigny or any of the other rebuilt towns of the same size. I spent an unhappy afternoon walking about.

I had M. and Mme Le Cornec to dinner that evening at the new Cheval Blanc. Michel had found himself a cheaper lodging in town. The pre–June 6 Cheval Blanc was a posting inn several hundred years old, but as gradually accumulated as the rest of pre-bombardment Vire. It had an archway leading from the street to the courtyard behind the house, and at the back of the courtyard was the old stable, remodeled into a garage, with a café and a billiard table on the floor above.

You reached the café by a narrow stairway, and once there you drank horrid-tasting French drinks like St. Raphael, Gentiane Suze, and Raspail, and talked to commercial travelers from Cherbourg and Le Havre, who voyaged by train and made a point of passing the night at Vire instead of Granville at the end of the line from Paris, because Granville was infested with large, expensive summer hotels. One ate better for less at Le Cheval Blanc or at its rival in Vire, the St. Pierre, they said, and then, one was more at home. On a drummer's earnings, one couldn't rivalize with the swells, "a?" they said, closing the sentence with a sound like the "a" in "at," which is customarily transcribed *hein*. (When I first read the green Maupassants, I thought this ever recurrent *hein* was pronounced like the first syllable in "Heinie." I was disillusioned because I never heard anybody say it.)

The commercial travelers sometimes talked about the miserable Norman character, which impelled their customers to demand goods in niggardly quantities at prices based on shipments in carloads, and even to demand rebates on single shoes because they had sold the other of the pair to a one-legged man who refused to pay for two. But mostly they spoke of hotels where the best and the most food was to be obtained at a fixed price: the Hôtel du Centre et de la Victoire at Caen is one I still remember. Others, widely traveled, would oppose to the best of these Norman bargains the meals, four times as marvelous and only half as dear, to be obtained in other provinces.

At l'Hôtel du Commerce in Vendôme, for example, a fellow told me, one had for lunch a magnificent hors d'oeuvre—*rillettes*, pâté, country ham, good things, what? and then *tripes à la mode de Caen* copiously served, a magnificent beefsteak with potatoes, and half a pheasant, followed by *fromage cendré*, the cheese of the country that is lightly coated with ashes, *pommes bonne femme*, and all you could drink of wine.

"It isn't great wine, but it's still better than the cider you get with the prix fixe in this region of misers."

"Don't you pay extra for the pheasant at Vendôme?" I asked.

"A small supplementary payment," he admitted.

In the following winter I lunched at the Hôtel du Commerce in Vendôme with a friend who was an instructor in a school for Armenian orphans in a château that a New York rug merchant had bought from the Duc de Dodon Rochefoucauld. The rug man had not thought fit to hire the Duc's chef for the orphans, and my *convive* brought a hearty appetite to the meal, which was served at the head of a long table, with a half dozen *commis-voyageurs* ranged around the other end of the board.

Paniguian, my friend, was twenty-four and I was twenty-three. We were both confirmed gluttons. We ate the precise menu that the *commis-voyageur* at Vire had described, with some amendment in the wine department. We had a bottle of the landlord's best local wine to begin with and then a Corton Clos du Roi with the pheasant. The gentlemen of commerce were patronizing when we sat down and placed our napkins in our laps. They tied theirs around their necks, so that they could forget caution in grappling with their grub. But when we cleaned the serving platters of *rillettes*, of *pâté de lièvre*, of *jambon cru du pays*, of *andouilles* (inferior to those of Vire, but acceptable), and even of salt herring and scraps of gigot left over from yesterday's Sunday dinner and freshened with onion, they were admirative. They still felt superior, though. One was sportsman enough to warn us, "Attention, there's more to come!"

It was presumption on his part to think we didn't know.

After we devastated the *tripes à la mode de Caen* a look of speculation broke water in their faces, as in a pool shark's when his intended victim runs fifteen from the break.

Our performance on the beefsteaks and soufflé potatoes was so apocalyptic that I saw one of them pause, his fork halfway to his mouth, to watch us—a pause so unusual, for a Frenchman eating, that I thought for a moment he had a stroke. When we had eaten five or six beefsteaks apiece while each of them was dispatching a humdrum three, the waitress cleared the table, and all of us regarded one another with satisfaction, like men who have rowed a creditable race in the same boat. The drummers' fear that we would eat all the beefsteaks was assuaged. They were full and could afford to be complimentary.

"Here you truly ring the bell!" one drummer said, and another corroborated, "What one sends oneself, it's something!"

The waitress placed a cheese tray and a couple of baskets of Saint-Jeans, which we call seckel pears, before the drummers, and went away.

One called down to us, "Why aren't you having any cheese? Are you full already?"

Then his paternal bonhomie changed to an expression of compound hate, a mixture of xenophobia (the franc was falling) and the Spirit of the Barricades. He saw the waitress bringing in the pheasant, just for us.

It was a remarkable pheasant, served skinned on a lightly toasted loaf of bread, in which a trough had been made and filled with a salmi of the bird's insides. I have never since believed the legend that all game must be hung, because I had seen the gunner bring in the pheasant early that morning. It remains the best bird in my memory.

Long before we had eaten all and crushed each bone in our teeth, the drummers had disappeared. They could not bear watching us and had elected to take their coffee and eau-de-vie in a café down the street. After we had done full justice to the goat cheese in ashes, the seckel pears, and the puckered baked apples with cores of jelly, we called for the *patron* and congratulated him on an unforgettable meal. We offered him a glass of his own best Armagnac, taking a gamble that, since we were not in Normandy, he might respond by buying us the next round.

The *patron* said modestly that it was the regular Monday lunch, all except that little bird that he had been fortunate enough to come by that morning, and it was too bad we hadn't come later in the week, when he made an effort.

"You know how it is on Monday," he said. "After the substantial repasts of Sunday, nobody has any appetite."

This has developed from a merely culinary into a geographical digression, but I can never approach the memory of that meal without wanting to go into it. It has the same attraction for me as Costello's saloon. I seldom encounter a pheasant nearly so good nowadays, and when I do, an hors d'oeuvre and possibly the tripe is all I can manage at one meal besides the bird. (I am writing this on a lunch exclusively of turtle soup, as I am trying to take off weight.)

Monsieur Secher, the *patron* of the old Cheval Blanc, was not so lavish with his meals *en pension* as his colleague at Vendôme, although he set what I thought was a remarkable table. Even the travelers admitted it wasn't bad. He stood, in relation to the meals at fixed price, in the position of a great couturier who has consented to sponsor a line of ready-to-wear. He was not truly *engagé* in this mass aspect of his art.

Monsieur Secher lived in his chef's toque as the old man at Fontenermont lived in his straw hat. It is conceivable he wore this toque to bed, to stimulate dreams about food. He was a tall, slender man, who had performed his military service at the school of cavalry at Saumur in the epoch made familiar to movie-goers by *Les Grandes Manoeuvres*, with Gérard Philipe and Danielle Darrieux, and he wore a waxed mustache and imperial. His primary interest in the hotel was the creation of *spécialités sur commande* for clients with plenty of money, who were rare in those days of relatively limited *automobilisme*. Vire is 150 miles from Paris. What happened upstairs—if the water closets ceased to function or the one electric-light bulb in a bedroom was extinct—was of little moment to him. Sleep was to him a fashion of passing time between meals and love an activity for people without imagination.

From my arrival he cultivated me as a prospective client for one of the *plats* he had presented at a gastronomic exposition in Paris, where he had put on a Day Consecrated to the Classic Cuisine of Vire. He had won a magnificent specimen of calligraphy on parchment attesting his glory. An American, even a young one, must be in at least easy circumstances, he believed. I was not flush, though, and wanted to be sure, before I gave him his head, that I would be able to finish the month out and return by rail to Paris.

When, near the end of the month, I was sure that I had a safe margin of twenty-five dollars, about 750 francs at the rate then, I commissioned a repast *de gala*.

On that evening, when I came to the dining room I was placed at a table by myself, sequestered from the vulgarians of the long table. They had to make do with Cistercian fare such as *potage mongole*, *merlan en colère*, and *canard aux navets*, followed by a salad. What the meal began with, I am ashamed to say I do not remember, nor how it ended. But the main dish was a partridge Olivier Basselin, cooked in cream and old Calvados, a dish named in honor of a fifteenth-century poet and drunkard reputed to have lived in Vire. The poems formerly ascribed to Basselin are now known to be the work of a hoaxing Virois named Le Houx who lived two centuries later, but Le Houx made use of a name and a tradition already extant. The peculiar glory of the partridge Basselin was that the cream smoothed the Calvados and both impregnated the bird without turning it into a mess like Stroganoff. It tasted like a partridge that had been fed all its life from a bottle of Calvados fifty years old.

Thirteen years later, in the first winter of the Second World War, I returned to Vire and stopped at the Cheval Blanc again, but I learned that M. Secher had sold the hotel and gone to Angers. There he had bought another of the same name, l'Auberge du Cheval Blanc. Two much younger people, a Monsieur and Madame Delaunay, had taken over the Vire Cheval Blanc, but had not changed it. Vire, too, was the same.

Early in 1940 I went from Paris to Angers to prepare a story on the Polish Government-in-Exile, which had set up its capital there, and naturally I went to the Angevin Auberge du Cheval Blanc. Monsieur Secher was himself an Angevin.

Angers is a great city compared to Vire. It had then perhaps 100,000 inhabitants—Vire had 5,000. It had a great cathedral, that of St. Maurice, a Château-Fort that is one of the marvels of France, a municipal theater, a night life centering around the Place du Ralliement, a diplomatic corps accredited to the Polish Government, two or three restaurants renowned throughout France, and a history that once encompassed that of England. (It was the Angevin Henry II who became King of England, not an Englishman who became Count of Anjou.) All this, I thought, must have produced some effect on M. Secher, who was on his native soil again.

The Auberge du Cheval Blanc at Angers was even older and more intricately accumulatively constructed than the one at Vire. Part of it dated from the thirteenth century. It had a courtyard, and in a small glassed-in office adjoining it sat M. Secher, still wearing a toque.

I went in and reintroduced myself. He professed to remember me, and we chatted awhile about Vire and the war. I asked him if he preferred Angers to Vire; I expected he would. He thought a moment and then said, "It is difficult to say. The chickens here are better, beyond discussion. They are more delicate and symmetrical. The vegetables are also better, and the fruit, there's no comparison. But the charcuterie of Vire is hard to beat. And the cream, the butter, the cheese! What a delight! Not a bad country for game, either, you know. Monsieur, your question is very hard to answer."

City Life

The Jollity Building

In the Jollity Building, which stands six stories high and covers half of a Broadway block in the high Forties, the term *promoter* means a man who mulcts another man of a dollar, or any fraction or multiple thereof. The verb *to promote* always takes a personal object, and the highest praise you can accord someone in the Jollity Building is to say, "He has promoted some very smart people." The Jollity Building—it actually has a somewhat different name, and the names of its inhabitants are not the ones which will appear below—is representative of perhaps a dozen or so buildings in the upper stories of which the small-scale amusement industry nests like a tramp pigeon. All of them draw a major part of their income from the rental of their stores at street level, and most of them contain on their lower floors a dance hall or a billiard parlor, or both. The Jollity Building has both. The dance hall, known as Jollity Danceland, occupies the second floor. The poolroom is in the basement. It is difficult in such a building to rent office space to any business house that wants to be taken very seriously, so the upper floors fill up with the petty nomads of Broadway—chiefly orchestra leaders, theatrical agents, bookmakers, and miscellaneous promoters.

Eight coin-box telephone booths in the lobby of the Jollity Building serve as offices for promoters and others who cannot raise the price of desk space on an upper floor. The phones are used mostly for incoming calls. It is a matter of perpetual regret to Morty, the renting agent of the building, that he cannot collect rent from the occupants of the booths. He always refers to them as the

Telephone Booth Indians, because in their lives the telephone booth furnishes sustenance as well as shelter, as the buffalo did for the Arapaho and Sioux. A Telephone Booth Indian on the hunt often tells a prospective investor to call him a certain hour in the afternoon, giving the victim the number of the phone in one of the booths. The Indian implies, of course, that it is a private line. Then the Indian has to hang in the booth until the fellow calls. *To hang*, in Indian language, means to loiter. "I used to hang in Forty-sixth Street, front of *Variety*," a small bookmaker may say, referring to a previous business location. Seeing the Indians hanging in the telephone booths is painful to Morty, but there is nothing he can do about it. The regular occupants of the booths recognize one another's rights. It may be understood among them, for instance, that a certain orchestra leader receives calls in a particular booth between three and four in the afternoon and that a competitor has the same booth from four to five. In these circumstances, ethical Indians take telephone messages for each other. There are always fewer vacancies in the telephone booths than in any other part of the Jollity Building.

While awaiting a call, an Indian may occasionally emerge for air, unless the lobby is so crowded that there is a chance he might lose his place to a transient who does not understand the house rules. Usually, however, the Indian hangs in the booth with the door open, leaning against the wall and reading a scratch sheet in order to conserve time. Then, if somebody rings up and agrees to lend him two dollars, he will already have picked a horse on which to lose that amount. When an impatient stranger shows signs of wanting to use a telephone, the man in the booth closes the door, takes the receiver off the hook, and makes motions with his lips, as if talking. To add verisimilitude to a long performance, he occasionally hangs up, takes the receiver down again, drops a nickel in the slot, whirls the dial three or four times, and hangs up again, after which the nickel comes back. Eventually the stranger goes away, and the man in the booth returns to the study of his scratch sheet. At mealtimes, the Telephone Booth Indians sometimes descend singly to the Jollity Building's lunch counter, which is at one end of the poolroom in the basement. The busiest lunch periods are the most favorable for a stunt the boys have worked out to get free nourishment. An Indian seats himself at the counter and eats two or three pastrami sandwiches. As he is finishing his lunch, one of his comrades appears at the head of the stairs and shouts that he is wanted on the telephone. The Indian rushes upstairs, absentmindedly omitting to pay for his meal. Barney, the lunch-counter proprietor, is too busy to go after him when he fails to return after a reasonable time. An Indian can rarely fool Barney more than once or twice. The maneuver requires nice timing and unlimited faith in one's accomplice. Should the accomplice fail to make his entrance, the Indian at the counter might be compelled to eat pastrami sandwiches indefinitely, acquiring frightful indigestion and piling up an appalling debt.

Morty, the renting agent, is a thin, sallow man of forty whose expression has been compared, a little unfairly, to that of a dead robin. He is not, however, a man without feeling; he takes a personal interest in the people who spend much of their lives in the Jollity Building. It is about the same sort of interest that Curator Raymond Ditmars takes in the Bronx Zoo's vampire bats. "I know more heels than any other man in the world," Morty sometimes says, not without pride. "Everywhere I go around Broadway, I get 'Hello, how are you?' Heels that haven't been with me for years, some of them." Morty usually reserves the appellation *heel* for the people who rent the forty-eight cubicles, each furnished with a desk and two chairs, on the third floor of the Jollity Building. These cubicles are formed by partitions of wood and frosted glass which do not quite reach the ceiling. Sufficient air to maintain human life is supposed to circulate over the partitions. The offices rent for $10.00 and $12.50 a month, payable in advance. "Twelve and a half dollars with air, ten dollars without air," Morty says facetiously. "Very often the heels who rent them take the air without telling me." Sometimes a Telephone Booth Indian acquires enough capital to rent a cubicle. He thus rises in the social scale and becomes a heel. A cubicle has three advantages over a telephone booth. One is that you cannot get a desk into a telephone booth. Another is that you can play pinochle in a cubicle. Another is that a heel gets his name on the directory in the lobby, and the white letters have a bold, legitimate look.

The vertical social structure of the Jollity Building is subject to continual shifts. Not only do Indians become heels, but a heel occasionally accumulates forty or fifty dollars with which to pay a month's rent on one of the larger offices, all of them unfurnished, on the fourth, fifth, or sixth floor. He then becomes a tenant. Morty always views such progress with suspicion, because it involves signing a lease, and once a heel has signed a lease, you cannot put him out without serving a dispossess notice and waiting ten days. A tenant, in Morty's opinion, is just a heel who is planning to get ten days' free rent. "Any time a heel acts prosperous enough to rent an office," Morty says, "you know he's getting ready to take you." A dispossessed tenant often reappears in the Jollity Building as an Indian. It is a life cycle. Morty has people in the building who have been Telephone Booth Indians, heels, and tenants several times each. He likes them best when they are in the heel stage. "You can't collect rent from a guy who hangs in the lobby," he says in explanation, "and with a regular tenant of an unfurnished office, you got too many headaches." He sometimes breaks off a conversation with a friendly heel by saying, "Excuse me, I got to go upstairs and insult a tenant."

As if to show his predilection for the heels, Morty has his own office on the third floor. It is a large corner room with windows on two sides. There is a flattering picture of the Jollity Building on one of the walls, and six framed plans, one of each floor, on another wall. Also in the office are an unattractive, respectable-looking secretary and, on Morty's desk, a rather depressing photograph of his wife. The conventionality of this décor makes Morty unhappy, and he spends as little time as possible in his office. Between nine o'clock in the morning, when he arrives and dejectedly looks through his mail for rent checks he does not expect to find, and six-thirty in the evening, when he goes home to Rockaway, he lives mostly amid the pulsating activity outside his office door.

The furnished cubicles on the third floor yield an income of about five hundred dollars a month, which, as Morty says, is not hay. Until a few years ago, the Jollity Building used to feel it should provide switchboard service for these offices. The outgoing telephone calls of the heels were supposed to be paid for at the end of every business day. This system necessitated the use of a cordon of elevator boys to prevent tenants from escaping. "Any heel who made several telephone calls toward the end of the month, you could kiss him goodbye," Morty says. "As soon as he made up his mind to go out of business he started thinking of people to telephone. It was cheaper for him to go out of business than settle for the calls, anyhow. The only way you can tell if a heel is still in business, most of the time, anyway, is to look in his office for his hat. If his hat is gone, he is out of business." A minor annoyance of the switchboard system was the tendency of heels to call the operator and ask for the time. "None of them were going anywhere, but they all wanted to know the time," Morty says resentfully. "None of them had watches. Nobody would be in this building unless he had already hocked his watch." There are lady heels, too, but if they are young Morty calls them "heads." (Morty meticulously refers to all youngish women as "heads," which has the same meaning as "broads" or "dolls" but is newer; he does not want his conversation to sound archaic.) Heads also abused the switchboard system. "One head that used to claim to sell stockings," says Morty, "called the board one day, and when the operator said, 'Five o'clock,' this head said, 'My God, I didn't eat yet!' If there had been no switchboard, she would never have known she was hungry. She would have saved a lot of money."

As a consequence of these abuses, the switchboard was abolished, and practically all the heels now make their telephone calls from three open coin-box telephones against the wall in a corridor that bisects the third floor. The wall for several feet on each side of the telephones is covered with numbers the heels have jotted down. The Jollity Building pays a young man named Angelo to sit at a table in a small niche near the telephones and answer incoming calls. He screams "Who?" into the mouthpiece and then shuffles off to find whatever heel is wanted. On days when Angelo is particularly weary, he just says, "He ain't in," and hangs up. He also receives and distributes the mail for the heels. Angelo is a pallid chap who has been at various periods a chorus boy, a taxi driver, and a drummer in one of the bands which maintain headquarters in the Jollity Building. "Every time a heel comes in," Angelo says, "he wants to know 'Are you sure there isn't a letter for me that feels like it had a check in it? . . . That's funny, the fellow swore he mailed it last night.' Then he tries to borrow a nickel from me so he can telephone."

Not having a nickel is a universal trait of people who rent the cubicles, and they spend a considerable portion of the business day hanging by the third-floor telephones, waiting for the arrival of somebody to borrow a nickel from. While waiting, they talk to Angelo, who makes it a rule not to believe anything they say. There are no booths in the corridor because Morty does not want any Telephone Booth Indians to develop on the third floor.

Morty himself often goes to visit with Angelo and terrifies the heels with his bilious stare. "They all say they got something big for next week," he tells Angelo in a loud, carrying voice, "but the rent is 'I'll see you tomorrow.'" Morty's friends sometimes drop in there to visit him. He likes to sit on Angelo's table with them and tell about the current collection of furnished-office inhabitants. "Who is that phony-looking heel who just passed, you want to know?" he may say during such a recapitulation. "Hey, this is funny. He happens to be legitimate—autos to hire. The heel in the next office publishes a horse magazine. If he gets a winner, he eats. Then there's one of them heels that hires girls to sell permanent waves for fifty cents down, door to door. The girl takes the fifty cents and gives the dame a ticket, but when the dame goes to look for the beauty parlor it says on the ticket, there is no such beauty parlor at that address.

"We got two heels writing plays. They figure they got nothing to do, so they might as well write a play, and if it clicks, they might also eat. Then we got a lady heel who represents Brazilian music publishers and also does a bit of booking; also a head who is running a school for hat-check girls, as it seems the hat-check profession is very complicated for some of the type of minds they got in it. Those heads who walk through the hall are going no place. They just stick their potato in every office and say, 'Anything for me today?' They do not even look to see if it is a theatrical office. If they expected to find anything, they would not be over here. What would anybody here have to offer? Once in a while a sap from the suburbs walks into one of the offices on this floor thinking he can get some talent cheap. 'Sure,' some heel says, 'I got just the thing you want.' They run down in the lobby looking for somebody. They ask some head they meet in the lobby, 'Are you a performer?' They try the other little agents that they know. The whole date is worth probably four dollars, and the forty cents' commission they split sometimes four ways."

Morty's favorite heel of the current lot is a tall Chesterfieldian old man named Dr. Titus Heatherington, who is the president of the Anti-Hitlerian League of the Western Hemisphere. Dr. Heatherington for many years lectured in vacant stores on sex topics and sold a manual of facts every young man should know. "The line became, in a manner of speaking, exhausted," Dr. Heatherington says, "because of the increasing sophistication of the contemporary adolescent, so I interested myself in this great crusade, in which I distribute at a nominal price a very fascinating book by Cornelius Vanderbilt, Jr., and everything in it must be exactly as stated, because otherwise Hitler could have sued Mr. Vanderbilt for libel. Incidentally, I sell a lot more books than I have for years. I do particularly well at Coney Island."

Heels are often, paradoxically, more affluent than the official lessees of larger offices. Many fellows who rent the big units take in subtenants, and if there are enough of them, each man's share of the rent may be less than the ten dollars a month minimum rent a heel has to pay. One two-desk office on the fourth, fifth, or sixth floor may serve as headquarters for four theatrical agents, a band leader, a music arranger, a manager of prizefighters, and a dealer in pawn tickets. They agree on a schedule by which each man has the exclusive use of a desk for a few hours every day, to impress people who call by appointment, and the office is used collectively, when no outsiders are present, for games of rummy. All the fellows in the office receive their telephone calls on a single coin-box machine affixed to the wall. Subtenants often make bets among themselves, the amount of the wager corresponding to each bettor's share of the rent. The loser is supposed to pay double rent, the winner nothing. This causes difficulties for Morty when he comes to collect the rent. The official lessee always protests that he would like to pay on the dot but the other boys haven't paid him. Subtenants who have won bets consider themselves absolved of any responsibility, and the fellows who are supposed to pay double are invariably broke. Morty makes an average of fifteen calls to collect a month's rent on an office, and thus acquires a much greater intimacy with the tenants than the agents of a place like Rockefeller Center or River House.

Desk room in a large office has the advantage of being much more dignified than a cubicle on the third floor, but there is one drawback: Morty's rule that not more than two firm names may be listed on the directory in the lobby for any one office. Callers therefore have to ask the elevator boys where to find some of the subtenants. If the elevator boys do not like the subtenant in question, they say they never heard of him. Nor will the implacable Morty permit more than two names to be painted on any office door. Junior subtenants get around the rule by having a sign painter put their names on strips of cardboard which they insert between the glass and the wooden frame of the door or affix to the glass by strips of tape. "You cannot let a tenant creep on you," Morty says in justification of his severity. "You let them get away with eight names on the door, and the next thing they will be asking you for eight keys to the men's room."

Morty's parents were named Goldberg, and he was born in the Bensonhurst region of Brooklyn. He almost finished a commercial course in high school before he got his first job, being an order clerk for a chain of dairy-and-herring stores. In the morning he would drive to each of these stores and find out from the store managers what supplies they needed from the company's warehouse. Since he had little to do in the afternoons, he began after a while to deliver packages for a bootlegger who had been a high-school classmate and by chance had an office in the Jollity Building.

The name on the door of the office was the Music Writers Mutual Publishing Company. About a quarter of the firms in the building at that time were fronts for bootleggers, Morty recalls. "Repeal was a terrible blow to property values in this district," he says. "Bootleggers were always the best pay." Seeing a greater future in bootlegging than in dairy goods and herring, Morty soon went to work for his old classmate on a full-time basis. The moment Morty decided that his future lay on Broadway, he translated his name from Goldberg into Ormont. " '*Or*' is French for gold," he sometimes explains, "and '*mont*' is the same as 'berg.' But the point is it's got more class than Goldberg."

By diligent application, Morty worked his way up to a partnership in the Music Writers Mutual Publishing Company. The partners made good use of their company's name. They advertised in pulp magazines, offering to write music for lyrics or lyrics for music, to guarantee publication, and to send back to the aspiring song writer a hundred free copies of his work, all for one hundred dollars. The Music Writers Mutual agreed to pay him the customary royalties on all copies sold. There never were any royalties, because Morty and his partner had only the author's hundred copies printed. They kept a piano in their office and hired a professional musician for thirty-five dollars a week to set music to lyrics. Morty himself occasionally wrote lyrics to the tunes clients sent in, and had a lot of fun doing it. At times the music business went so well that the partners were tempted to give up bootlegging. There were so many similar publishing firms, however, that there was not a steady living in it. "But you would be surprised," Morty says now, "how near it came to paying our overhead." The volume of mail made it look bona fide. They built up a prosperous semi-wholesale liquor business, specializing in furnishing whiskey to firms in the Garment Center, which used it for presents to out-of-town buyers. "The idea on that stuff was that it should be as reasonable as possible without killing anybody," Morty says. "It was a good, legitimate dollar." The Depression in the garment industry ruined the Music Writers Mutual Publishing Company's business even before repeal and left Morty broke.

The Jollity Building belongs to the estate of an old New York family, and in the twenties the trustees had installed as manager one of the least promising members of the family, a middle-aged, alcoholic Harvard man whom they wanted to keep out of harm's way. Morty had been such a good tenant and seemed so knowing a fellow that the Harvard man offered him a job at twenty-five dollars a week as his assistant. When the manager ran off with eleven thousand dollars in rents and a head he had met in the lobby, Morty took over his job. He has held it ever since. The trustees feel, as one of them has expressed it, that "Mr. Ormont understands the milieu." He now gets fifty dollars a week and 2 per-cent of the total rents, which adds about two thousand a year to his income.

The nostalgia Morty often feels for the opportunities of Prohibition days is shared by the senior tenant in the building, the propri-etor of the Quick Art Theatrical Sign Painting Company, on the sixth floor. The sign painter, a Mr. Hy Sky—a name made up of the first syllable of his first name, Hyman, and the last syllable of a sur-name which no one can remember—is a bulky, red-faced man who has rented space in the Jollity Building for twenty-five years. With his brother, a lean, sardonic man known as Si Sky, he paints signs and lobby displays for burlesque and movie houses and does odd jobs of lettering for people in all sorts of trades. He is an extremely fast letterer and he handles a large volume of steady business, but it lacks the exhilaration of Prohibition years. Then he was sometimes put to work at two o'clock in the morning redecorating a clip joint, so that it could not be identified by a man who had just been robbed of a bank roll and might return with cops the next day. "Was that fun!" Hy howls reminiscently. "And always cash in ad-vance! If the joint had green walls, we would make them pink. We would move the bar opposite to where it was, and if there was booths in the place, we would paint them a different color and change them around. Then the next day, when the cops came in with the sap, they would say, 'Is this the place? Try to remember the side of the door the bar was on as you come in.' The sap would hes-itate, and the cops would say, 'I guess he can't identify the premises,' and they would shove him along. It was a nice, comfortable dollar for me."

Hy has a clinical appreciation of meretricious types which he tries unsuccessfully to arouse in Morty. Sometimes, when Hy has a particularly preposterous liar in his place, he will telephone the renting agent's office and shout, "Morty, pop up and see the character I got here! He is the most phoniest character I seen in several years." The person referred to seldom resents such a description. People in the Jollity Building neighborhood like to be thought of as characters. "He is a real character," they say, with respect, of any fascinatingly repulsive acquaintance. Most promoters are characters. Hy Sky attributes the stability of his own business to the fact that he is willing to "earn a hard dollar." "The trouble with the characters," he says, "is they are always looking for a soft dollar. The result is they knock theirselves out trying too hard to have it easy. So what do they get after all? Only the miss-meal cramps." Nevertheless, it always gives Hy a genteel pleasure to collaborate, in a strictly legitimate way, with any of the promoters he knows. The promoter may engage him to paint a sign saying, "A new night club will open soon on these premises. Concessionaires interested telephone So-and-So at such-and-such a number." The name is the promoter's own, and the telephone given is, as Hy knows, in a booth in the Jollity lobby. The promoter, Hy also knows, will place this sign in front of a vacant night club with which he has absolutely no connection, in the hope that some small hat-check concessionaire with money to invest in a new club will read the sign before someone gets around to removing it and take it seriously. If the concessionaire telephones, the promoter will make an appointment to receive him in a Jollity cubicle borrowed from some other promoter for the occasion and will try to get a couple of hundred dollars as a deposit on the concession. If successful, he will lose the money on a horse in the sixth race at an obscure track in California. The chances of getting any money out of this promotional scheme are exceedingly slight, but the pleasure of the promoter when the device succeeds is comparable to that of a sportsman who catches a big fish on a light line. Contemplation of the ineffectual larceny in the promoter's heart causes Hy to laugh constantly while lettering such a sign. A contributory cause of his laughter is the knowledge that he will receive the only dollar that is likely to change hands in the transaction—the dollar he gets for painting the sign.

Musicians are not characters, in Hy's estimation, but merely a mild variety of phony. As such, they afford him a tempered amusement. When two impressive band leaders in large, fluffy overcoats call upon him for a communal cardboard door sign, toward the cost of which each contributes twenty-five cents, he innocently inquires, "How many of you are there in that office?" One of the band leaders will reply grandiosely, "Oh, we all have separate offices; the sign is for the door to quite a huge suite." Hy laughs so hard he bends double to relieve the strain on his diaphragm. His brother, Si, who lives in continual fear that Hy will die of apoplexy, abandons his work and slaps Hy's back until the crowing abates. "A suite," Hy repeats weakly at intervals for a half-hour afterward, "a huge suite they got, like on the subway at six o'clock you could get." Hy also paints, at an average price of twenty-five cents, cardboard backs for music racks. These pieces of cardboard, whose only function is to identify the band, bear in bright letters its name, which is usually something like Everett Winterbottom's Rhumba Raiders. When a Jollity Building band leader has acquired a sign for his door and a set of these lettered cardboards, he is equipped for business. If, by some unlikely chance, he gets an engagement, usually to play a week end in a cabaret in Queens or the Bronx, he hurries out to the curb on Seventh Avenue in front of Charlie's Bar & Grill, where there are always plenty of musicians, and picks up the number of fellows he requires, generally four. The men tapped go over to Eighth Avenue and get their instruments out of pawn. A musician who owns several instruments usually leaves them all in a pawnshop, ransoming one when he needs it to play a date and putting it back the next day. If, when he has a chance to work, he lacks the money to redeem an instrument, he borrows the money from a Jollity Building six-for-fiver, a fellow who will lend you five dollars if you promise to pay him six dollars within twenty-four hours. Meanwhile, the band leader looks up a fellow who rents out orchestra arrangements guaranteed to be exact, illegal copies of those one or another of the big bandsmen has exclusive use of. The band leader puts the arrangements and his cardboards under his arm and goes down to Charlie's to wait for the other musicians to come back from the hock shop. That night Everett Winterbottom's Rhumba Raiders ride again. The only worry in the world the Raiders have, at least for the moment, is that they will have to finish their engagement before a union delegate discovers them and takes away their cards. Each man is going to receive three dollars a night, which is seven dollars below union scale.

2. FROM HUNGER

It is likely that when the six-story Jollity Building, so called, is pulled down, it will be replaced by a one- or two-story taxpayer, because buildings along Broadway now derive their chief incomes from the stores at street level, and taxpayers, which earn just as much from their stores, are cheaper to operate. When the Jollity Building comes down, the small theatrical agents, the sleazy customers, the band leaders in worn camel's-hair overcoats, the aged professors of acrobatic dancing, and all the petty promoters who hang, as the phrase goes, in the Jollity Building's upper floors will spill out into the street and join the musicians who are waiting for jobs and the pitchmen who sell self-threading needles along the curb.

Meanwhile, day after day, small-time performers ride the elevators and wander through the grimy halls of the Jollity Building looking for work. Jack McGuire, who in the evening is a bouncer in Jollity Danceland, on the second floor, thoroughly understands the discouraged performers. "They're just like mice," he says, "they been pushed around so much." Jack is a heavyweight prizefighter who recently retired for the forty-eighth time in the last five years. He still looks impressively healthy, since few of his fights have lasted more than one round. "It was the greatest two-minute battle you ever seen," he said a while ago, describing his latest comeback, against a local boy in Plainfield, New Jersey. "For the first thirty seconds I was ahead on points." Jack's face is of a warm, soft pink induced by the prolonged application of hot towels in the Jollity Building barbershop, which is just off the lobby. Sprawled in the sixth barber chair from the door, he sleeps off hang-overs. His shoulders, naturally wide, are accentuated by the padding Broadway clothiers lavish on their customers. Among the putty-colored, sharp-nosed little men and the thin-legged women in the elevators, he looks like an animal of a different breed. His small eyes follow the performers constantly. During the day, Jack is a runner for a great number of agents. He learns from them where there are openings for various types of talent—ballroom-dancing teams, Irish tenors, singing hostesses, and so on—and then steers performers to the agents handling the jobs. He has strolled about the Jollity Building so long that he knows hundreds of them by sight. "Such-and-such an agent is looking for a ballroom team," he will tell a husband-and-wife pair he knows. "A week in a Chink joint in Yonkers." He gives them one of the agent's cards, on which he writes "Jack." If the team gets the week, at forty dollars, it must pay a commission of four dollars to the agent, and another of two dollars to Jack. The second commission is entirely extra-legal, since Jack is not a licensed agent, but Jack often steers performers to a job they wouldn't have had otherwise, so they don't kick. Agents are glad to have Jack work with them, because buyers of talent want instantaneous service and few acts can be reached by telephone during the day. Sometimes, when an act is held over for a second week and fails to pay the agent his additional commission, Jack is engaged to put the muscle on the unethical performer. When Jack encounters him, usually in Charlie's Bar & Grill or at the I. & Y. cigar store, which are both near the Jollity Building, he says, "Say, I hear your agent is looking for you." The hint is enough ordinarily. When it is not, Jack uses the muscle.

The proprietor of Jollity Danceland is the most solvent tenant in the building and he pays by far the largest rent. The dance hall has an entrance of its own on the street and is reached by stairway and elevators reserved for customers. Jack receives five dollars a night for bouncing there. At one time the proprietor planned to put the bouncers on a piecework basis, but he changed his mind, to Jack's lasting regret. "I would of bounced all the customers," he says. "I would of made my fortune sure." Between the hours of six and eight every evening, at a small gymnasium west of Tenth Avenue, Jack trains a few amateur boxers he manages. There is not much money in managing amateurs, who never earn more than sixteen dollars in a night, but Jack thinks that someday one of his protégés might show promise, and then he could sell the boy's contract to an established manager. With all these sources of income, McGuire would live in affluence, by Jollity Building standards, if it were not for his thirst, which is perpetual. When he drinks, he sometimes threatens to put the muscle on strangers who refuse to pay for his liquor. This detracts from his popularity at the neighborhood bars, and the bartenders resort to chemical expedients to get rid of him. Jack is proud of the immunity he has developed. "I got so I like those Mickey Finns as good as beer," he often tells acquaintances.

Although Jack has never paid any office rent, he is on familiar terms with Morty Ormont, the lugubrious renting agent of the Jollity Building, whom he encounters in the barbershop and at the lunch counter in the basement. He sometimes borrows a dollar from Morty, always giving him a hundred-dollar check on a bank in Lynchburg, Virginia, as security. Morty, of course, knows that Jack has no account in the bank. In the Jollity Building, checks are considered not as literal drafts on existent funds but as a particularly solemn form of promise to repay a loan, since it is believed that the holder of a bad check has it in his power to throw the check writer into jail for twenty-five years. When Jack repays the dollar, usually in four installments, Morty gives the check back to him. Practically everybody in the Jollity Building carries a checkbook. Fellows who cannot borrow from Morty even by giving him checks sometimes ask him to vouch for them so they can borrow from six-for-fivers, the chaps who lend five dollars one day and collect six dollars the next. "Will you okay me with a Shylock, Morty?" one of these suppliants will ask. "You know I'm an honest man." "In what way?" Morty demands cynically if he does not know the man well. If the fellow says, "In every way," Morty refuses to okay him, because he is obviously a crook.

The prizefight managers who hang in the Jollity Building are, as one might expect, of an inferior order. The boys they handle provide what sports writers like to call the "stiff opposition" against which incubating stars compile "sterling records." "When the Garden brings in some fellow that you never heard of from Cleveland or Baltimore or one of them other Western states, and it says in the paper he has had stiff opposition," says a Jollity Building manager known as Acid Test Ike, "that means the opposition has been stiffs. In other words, the class of boys I got." It is Acid Test who manages Jack in all of his comebacks. For each comeback, Ike and Jack go to some place like Lancaster, Pennsylvania, or Wheeling, West Virginia, where there happens to be a novice heavyweight, and Ike tells the sports editor of the local newspaper, "My man will give this kid the acid test." Then Jack gets knocked out. Naturally, Ike also has to manage smaller fighters who will get knocked out by middleweights and lightweights. "A fellow could make a pleasant dollar with a stable of bums," he sometimes says, "only the competition is so terrific. There is an element getting into the game that is willing to be knocked out very cheap." Acid Test Ike always wears a bottle-green suit, a brick-red topcoat, and an oyster-white hat. "It don't take brains to make money with a good fighter," he says rather bitterly when he feels an attack of the miss-meal cramps coming on. "Running into a thing like that is just luck."

Performers, when they arrive at the Jollity Building looking for work, usually take an elevator straight to the floor on which the agent who most often books them is located. After leaving this agent, they make a tour of the other agents' offices to see if anyone else has a job for them. Only when rendered desperate by hunger do they stray down to the third floor, where the people Morty calls the heels hold forth in furnished offices each about the size of a bathroom. Since the heels constitute the lowest category of tenant in the building, no proprietor of a first-class chop-suey joint or roadhouse would call on them for talent. "The best you can get there," performers say, "is a chance to work Saturday night at a ruptured saloon for *bubkis*." "*Bubkis*" is a Yiddish word which means "large beans."

One of the most substantial agents in the building is Jerry Rex, a swarthy, discouraged man who used to be a ventriloquist. He has an unusually large one-room office, which was once the studio of a teacher of Cuban dancing. The walls are painted in orange-and-black stripes, and there are several full-length wall mirrors, in which the pupils used to watch themselves dance. Mr. Rex sits at a desk at the end of the office opposite the door, and performers waiting to speak to him sit on narrow benches along the walls. Rex has an assistant named Dave, who sits on a couch in one corner of the room. Rex always professes to be waiting for a call from a theater owner in, for example, Worcester, Massachusetts, who will want four or five acts and a line of eight girls. He urges all the entertainers who drop in at his place to sit down and wait with him. "Also, a fellow who owns the biggest night club in Scranton is going to pop up here any minute," he tells the performers confidentially. "You better wait around." The man from Worcester never calls up, but the performers don't mind killing a half-hour with Jerry. "It rests your feet," one woman singer has said, "and also you meet a lot of people you know." Jerry leaves Dave in charge of the office when he goes out. "If Georgie Hale pops up here looking for me," Jerry always says in a loud voice as he is leaving, "tell him that Billy Rose pulled me over to Lindy's for a bite." Then he goes downstairs to the lunch counter, where he may try to talk Barney, the proprietor, into letting him charge a cup of coffee. Rex, when he is not attempting to impress performers or rival agents, is a profoundly gloomy man. "You got only three classes of performers today," he sometimes says. "Class A, which means, for example, like Al Jolson and Eddie Cantor; Class B, like the Hartmans, for instance, or Henny Youngman, that can yet get a very nice dollar, and Class Z, which is all the little people. Small-time vaudeville is definitely out. All you got is floor shows, fraternal entertainments, and in the summer the borsch circuit. An entertainer who can average thirty dollars a week all year is Class Z tops. There ain't no such entertainer. A husband-and-wife team *might* make it."

Jerry does not consider his large office an extravagance, because he lives in it twenty-four hours a day, which is a violation of the building laws, and saves the price of a hotel room. He sleeps on the couch, while Dave, a blue-chinned young man with the mores of a tomcat, sleeps on one of the wall benches. Jerry occasionally buys a bottle of beer for the porter who cleans the offices. The grateful porter always does Jerry's first, so the agent can get a good night's rest. Every morning, Jerry washes and shaves in the men's room on his floor. Dave often contents himself with smearing face powder over his beard. Dave is of a happier temperament than his employer. He likes to think of himself as a heartbreaker and is full of stories about the girls who wander through the Jollity Building halls. He calls them heads and boskos. *Bosko* has a definitely roguish connotation. One may safely say to a friend, "That was a beautiful head I seen you with," even if one does not know who the head was. But if one says "bosko," and the woman turns out to be the friend's wife, one has committed a social error. Dave has a tried technique for forming acquaintanceships in the Jollity Building. "I know this head is a performer, or she would not be in the building," he says. "So I go up to her and say, 'What do you do?' If she says, 'I dance,' I say, 'Too bad, I was looking for a singer.' If she says 'sing,' I say, 'Too bad, I was looking for a dancer.' In that way we get acquainted, and if she looks promising, I pull her down to Barney's for a celery tonic."

Women performers have a better chance of getting cabaret jobs than men, because they mix with the customers. Jerry, who grew up in the sheltered respectability of vaudeville, resents this. "I booked a man with a trained dog into one trap in Astoria," he recently said, "and after one night they canceled him out because the dog couldn't mix. There never was such a tough market for talent. I book an acrobatic act in which, as a finish, one guy walks offstage playing a mandolin and balancing the other guy upside down on his head. The understander only plays a couple of bars, you see, for the effect. I booked them for an Elks' smoker in Jersey, and the chairman of the entertainment committee didn't want to pay me because he said the members don't like musical acts. To stand this business, you got to have a heart of steel." Most agents in the Jollity Building, when they supply talent for a whole show, book themselves as masters of ceremonies and collect an extra ten dollars for announcing the acts. Jerry has given up this practice.

"When I get out on the stage and think of what a small buck the performers are going to get, I feel like crying," he says, "so I send Dave instead."

A fair number of the performers who look for jobs in the Jollity Building have other occupations as well. Many of the women work as receptionists or stenographers in the daytime and make their rounds of agents' offices after five o'clock. Hockticket Charlie, an agent who is one of Jerry Rex's neighbors on the fourth floor, has a side line of his own. Hockticket Charlie is a tall, cross-eyed man with a clarion voice and a solemn manner. By arrangement with a number of pawnbrokers of his acquaintance, he sells pawn tickets. The chief reason anyone purchases a pawn ticket is that he holds the common belief that a watch accepted in pawn for ten dollars, for example, must in reality be worth around forty dollars. The fellow who buys a ticket for five dollars is therefore theoretically able to obtain a forty-dollar watch for a total outlay of fifteen dollars. Hockticket Charlie's pawnbroker friends, aware of this popular superstition, make out a lot of tickets to fictitious persons. Charlie sells the tickets for a few dollars each to performers in the Jollity Building. Each ticket entitles the purchaser to redeem a piece of secondhand jewelry—for not more than three times its value—which the broker has bought at an auction sale. Hockticket nearly always pays off colored performers with pawn tickets which will theoretically permit them to purchase diamonds at a large reduction. By paying ten dollars to a broker, the holder of one of these tickets can often acquire a ring easily worth three dollars. Sometimes Hockticket engages a number of performers to play a date in what he calls "a town near here," and tells them to meet him at the Jollity Building, so that they can all ride out to the date together. He loads them into a rickety bus which he has chartered for ten dollars, and the "town near here" turns out to be Philadelphia. If the acts traveled there singly, they would collect railroad fares for the round trip. Instead, Charlie collects all the railroad fares from the Philadelphia house manager who has booked the show. He often succeeds in paying the bus owner with hock tickets. Morty Ormont has a sincere admiration for Hockticket Charlie.

Another agent on the fourth floor, and the most sedate one in the building, is a woman named Maida Van Schuyler, who books stag shows for conventions and for the banquets large corporations give in honor of newly elected vice-presidents or retiring department heads. Mrs. Van Schuyler, a tall, flat-chested woman with fluffy white hair, was at one time a singer of arch numbers like "I Just Can't Make My Eyes Behave" and "Two Little Love Bees Buzzing in a Bower." As such, she recalls, she lent a touch of class to New England and Ohio vaudeville around 1912. The walls in an anteroom of her office are hung with numerous framed mottoes, such as "What Is More Precious Than a Friend?" and "Seek for Truth and Love Will Seek for You." A plain young woman sits in the anteroom and takes the names of visitors in to Mrs. Van Schuyler. When Mrs. Van Schuyler does not wish to see them, she sends out word that she is terribly sorry but one of her best-beloved friends has just passed away and she is too broken up about it to talk. If the visitor waits around a minute, he may hear a loud, strangling sob. Mrs. Van Schuyler, who is very much interested in spiritualism, often says that she would like to retire from the stag-show business and become a medium. "There isn't a dime left in this lousy business," she remarks. "The moving pictures have spoiled it, just like they did with vaudeville."

Every now and then, one of Mrs. Van Schuyler's shows is raided but the detectives give her advance notice because she provides the entertainments for a number of police banquets. "We have to make a pinch, Mrs. Van Schuyler," they say apologetically, "because the shooflies are working in our territory and we can't let a big brawl like this run without getting turned in." Shooflies, as all the world knows, are policemen in mufti assigned to make a secret check on the activities of other policemen. Within a week or two after the raid, which never results in a conviction, the friendly detectives return and say, "It's all right, Mrs. Van Schuyler, we got the shooflies taking now." With this assurance, Mrs. Van Schuyler can go ahead with her business. She seldom employs the ordinary entertainers who wander around the Jollity Building, but relies on specialists whom she lists in a large card file. "It is a highly specialized field of entertainment, darling," she tells gentlemen who are negotiating with her for their organizations. "Our girls must have poise, discretion, and savoy faire." To old friends like Morty Ormont, she sometimes says less elegantly, after an all-night party with a convention of textbook publishers or refrigerator salesmen, "You ought to seen those apes try to paw the girls."

Performers on their way to see one of the agents on the fourth floor are sometimes frightened by wild fanfares from an office occupied by an Italian who repairs trumpets. A musician who brings a trumpet to the Italian always blows a few hot licks to demonstrate that the instrument is out of true. When he calls for the trumpet, he blows a few more to see whether it is all right again. Once a swing dilettante stood in the hall for half an hour listening to the noises and then walked in and said that it was the best band he had ever heard and he wanted it to play at a rent party he was giving for some other cognoscenti.

Not all the transients in the Jollity Building halls are entertainers making the rounds of the agents. There is a fellow known as Paddy the Booster, who sells neckties he steals from haberdashers, and another known as Mac the Phony Booster, who sells neckties which he pretends to have stolen but are really shoddy ties he has bought very cheaply. Naturally, Paddy looks down on Mac, whom he considers a racketeer. "It takes all kinds of people to make up a great city," Jack McGuire sometimes tells Paddy, trying to soothe him. Also, every floor of the building has at least one bookmaker, who hangs in the hall. "In winter, the bookmakers complain because we don't heat the halls better," the beleaguered Morty Ormont says. A dollar is the standard Jollity Building wager. The accepted method of assembling it is to drop in on an acquaintance and say, "I got a tip on a horse, but I'm short a quarter." One repeats this operation until one has accumulated four quarters. It sometimes takes a long time, but there is always an oversupply of that. This system reduces

the risk of betting to a minimum. On the infrequent occasions
when some momentarily prosperous tenant bets important money
on a race—say, five dollars—two or three of the hall bookmakers
get together and divide up the hazard.

A stranger would be puzzled by some of the greetings exchanged by performers wandering between agents' offices. "Why,
Zasu Pitts!" a gaunt young man wearing suede shoes and an overcoat of mattress filling will shout at a girl younger, twenty pounds
heavier, and obviously poorer than Miss Pitts, whom she doesn't
even faintly resemble. "Clark Gable!" the girl will shout, throwing
her arms around him. "I haven't seen you since I thumbed a ride
from that crumb in Anniston, Alabama!" The man and woman are
not talking this way for a gag; they are survivors of a Hollywood-
double troupe, a form of theatrical enterprise that has replaced the
Uncle Tom show in out-of-the-way areas of the United States. In a
double troupe, which usually travels in a large, overcrowded old automobile, all the members are supposed to be able to imitate Hollywood stars. They play in moving-picture theaters or Grange halls,
usually for a percentage of the receipts. Members of these companies seldom know each other's real names, even when they have
heard them. In recounting their wanderings, they are likely to say,
"Mae West was driving, see, and she goes to sleep. And only Ray
Bolger seen the truck coming and grabbed the wheel, we would of
all landed in some broken-down hospital in Henderson, North
Carolina." The Hollywood doubles earn less and eat worse than the
barnstormers of fifty years ago, but they have the pleasure of identifying themselves with the extremely wealthy. Some players are able
to impersonate two or even three Hollywood stars to the complete
satisfaction of an audience in Carbondale, Illinois. Sleeping on
dressing tables, the doubles dream that they are lolling at Palm
Springs, like in the *Daily Mirror*. A boy who impersonates Ned
Sparks and Jimmy Durante once told Jerry Rex that he was down-
hearted only once in his mimetic career. That was at a county fair in
Pennsylvania where some doubles were performing on an open-air
stage under a hot sun. "I give them everything I had," the boy said,
"and them apple-knockers just sat there from sorrow. They never

even heard of Jimmy Durante or Ned Sparks. They broke my heart."

Summer, which used to be the dead season for entertainers, is now the period during which they eat most frequently. There are several rehearsal rooms in the Jollity Building, and throughout June they are full of uproar as the performers prepare for their migration to the Catskill Mountains resorts. "Up there the kids work for pot cheese," Jerry Rex says. "Here they don't even make themselves a chive." In the Catskills, a personable young man who can act as master of ceremonies, tell funny stories, give lessons in the conga, perform card tricks, direct amateur theatricals, do a screamingly funny eccentric dance, and impersonate stars of screen and radio can earn twenty-five dollars a week and room and board for ten consecutive weeks, provided he has a sensational singing voice. Performers at various hotels add to their incomes by uniting for occasional benefit shows, the beneficiary always being the entertainer at the hotel where the show is staged. "If a guy does not shoot crap with the guests," Jerry Rex says, "he has a chance to save himself a buck." Returning from the mountains after Labor Day, bloated with pot cheese, the actor sometimes survives until October, Jerry says, before developing doughnut tumors, a gastric condition attributed by him to living on crullers and coffee and which is usually a forerunner of the miss-meal cramps. By November, the performer no longer feels the cramps, because he is accustomed to being from hunger and not having what to eat. Then he starts talking about a job that has been promised to him in Miami if he can get there, and he tries, unsuccessfully, to promote somebody for railroad fare. Meanwhile, he plays any date he can get. Sometimes he doesn't work for a week and then has a chance to play a couple of dates in a night, perhaps a smoker in the west Bronx and a church party in Brooklyn, the first of which will net him $4.50 and the second $2.70, after the deduction of Jerry Rex's commissions.

The Jollity Building has at least a dozen tenants who teach voice, dancing, and dramatic art, and a few who specialize in Latin-American dance routines and acrobatics. The financial condition of the professors, which is solvent in comparison to that of the per-

formers, musicians, and theatrical agents in the building, is a perpetual source of amusement to Morty Ormont. "The singers are
from hunger," he says; "the performers are from hunger, and every
day we get saps in the building who pay for lessons so they can be
from hunger, too." Parents who believe their children are talented
are the staple prey of the professional teachers. Seldom does a Jollity Building elevator make a trip without at least one bosomy and
belligerent suburban woman, holding fast to the hand of a little girl
whose hair is frizzled into a semblance of Shirley Temple's. Often
several of the Shirleys and their mothers find themselves in a car together. The mothers' upper lips curl as they survey the other mothers' patently moronic young. The Shirleys gaze at each other with
vacuous hostility and wonder whether their mothers will slap them
if they ask to go to the bathroom again. All the Shirleys have bony
little knees and bitter mouths and, in Morty's opinion, will un-
doubtedly grow up to be ax murderesses.

3. A SOFT DOLLAR

Barney, who owns the lunch counter in the basement of the so-
called Jollity Building, never turns his head away from his customers for a second while working. Even when he is drawing coffee
from the urn, he keeps looking over his shoulder, and this, in the
course of his eighteen years in business, has given him a nervous
neck twitch. "I know their nature," Barney says in explanation of
this mannerism. "If I'll turn my head, they'll run away without paying." With all his vigilance, Barney cannot foresee when a client will
eat two pastrami sandwiches and then say, after fumbling in a vest
pocket, "Gee, Barney, I thought I had a quarter in my pocket, but it
turned out to be an old Willkie button." Barney is a short, gray-
faced man in his fifties who looks at his customers through thick,
shell-rimmed spectacles that are usually clouded with steam from
the coffee urn or with dabs of corned-beef grease. The customers
see Barney against a background of cans of beans, arranged in pyramids. The cans, stacked on a shelf behind his counter, constitute a

decorative scheme he never changes, except when he lays a fat, shiny stick of bologna across the can forming the apex of one of the pyramids.

Once, recently, Barney startled Hy Sky, the Jollity Building sign painter, and Morty Ormont, the renting agent, by announcing the return of prosperity. This was an event that neither of his listeners, confined for the most part in their associations to theatrical people, had suspected. "The taxi drivers who come in here are asking for sandwiches on thin bread, so they can taste the meat, and they are eating two sandwiches for lunch, usually," Barney said. "From 1929 until very lately, everybody was asking for sandwiches on thick bread, one sandwich should fill them up." The lunch counter is at one end of the Jollity Building's poolroom, and most of Barney's customers are either people who work in the building or pool players. The taximen are his only customers from the daylight world.

"The bookmakers in the building are also eating regular," Barney said, continuing his survey of business conditions, "and even a couple of prizefight managers recently came in and paid cash. With musicians, of course, is still the Depression. Also with performers." Barney takes it for granted that anyone connected with the stage is broke, and if he can detect a speck of theatrical make-up under a woman's chin or behind an ear, he will refuse to give her credit. He even declines to believe that any performers receive regular remuneration in Hollywood. "It is all publicity," he says. "George Raft still owes me thirty-five cents from when he used to hang here." Musicians, although imperceptibly less broke, on the average, than actors or dancers, are almost as irritating to Barney. They sit at his counter for hours, each with one cup of coffee, and discuss large sums of money. Since most of the year musicians wear big, shaggy coats made of a material resembling the mats under rugs, they fill twice as much space as bookmakers or taxi drivers. Their coats overflow onto adjoining stools. "Three hours is average for a musician to drink a cup of coffee," Barney says, "and then sometimes he says he hasn't got the nickel, he'll see me tomorrow. Tomorrow is never."

Regulars who hang at Barney's counter may be identified by the manner in which, before sitting down, they run their hands under the counter. They are reaching for a communal dope sheet, a ten-cent racing paper giving the entries at all tracks. The regulars at Barney's chip in and buy one copy every day. This economy permits each of them to lose to bookmakers every week several dimes that would otherwise have been spent at newsstands. Barney has little contact with the pool players, although he does a good deal of business with them. A number of mulatto girls who rack up the balls on the pool tables also act as waitresses for the players. The girls pay Barney cash for all the cups of coffee they carry away. Presumably they collect from the players. "It is a pleasure they can have," says Barney.

One of the more conspicuous fellows who eat at the lunch counter and spend a good deal of time there between meals drinking coffee is called Marty the Clutch. Marty gets his name from his humorous custom of mangling people's fingers when he shakes hands with them. Strangers to whom he is introduced usually sink to their knees screaming before he releases their right hand. Casual acquaintances consider Marty a big, overgrown boy brimming with animal spirits. Only old friends really appreciate him. They know that when Marty has numbed a stranger's hand, he can often get a ring off the fellow's finger unnoticed. "It is very cute when you think of it," says Acid Test Ike, who is a manager of punch-drunk prizefighters. "I once seen the Clutch get a rock off a ticket broker big enough to use for a doorstop. By the time the scalper noticed the ring was gone, he thought a bosko he knew had clipped him for it, so he busted her nose." The Clutch is a big, square-shouldered man with a forehead barely sufficient to keep his hair from meeting his eyebrows. He used to be a prizefighter, but, he says, he worked with a gang of hijackers several nights a week and this interfered with his training, because he was always getting shot. Acid Test Ike considers this an amiable prevarication. "The Clutch never was a hijacker," he says. "He just gives that as a social reference. Really, the Clutch is a gozzler." This term means a fellow who gozzles people—chokes them in order to rob them. The gozzling business cannot be very good, because Marty is customarily as broke as most other patrons of the lunch counter. Every time Barney looks at Marty the Clutch, he rubs his throat nervously.

To Barney, the most interesting people in the Jollity Building are the promoters, the fellows who are always trying to earn, in the local idiom, a soft dollar. This is a curiosity he shares with Hy Sky and Morty Ormont, and sometimes the three of them get together at the lunch counter and discuss, with happy chuckles, the outrageous swindles perpetrated by fellows they know. One mental giant of whom all three speak with awe is a chap known as Lotsandlots, or Lots for short, who is in the land-development business. Lots's stock in trade is a tract of real estate in the Jersey marshes and a large supply of stationery bearing the letterheads of nonexistent land companies and the Jollity Building's address. Prospects are carefully selected; generally they are close-fisted men with a few thousand dollars saved up. Each receives a letter informing him that he has won a lot in a raffle conducted by one of the land companies to publicize a new development. The winner, according to the letter, is now the owner, free and clear, of one building lot in some out-of-the-way district. With the lot goes an option to buy the lots on either side of it for a couple of hundred dollars apiece. The man receiving such a letter is distrustful. He knows that one house lot is not much use, and he suspects that the whole thing is just a dodge to sell him more land, so he doesn't even go out to look at his prize. In a week or so, Lotsandlots calls on the skeptic and says he hears that the man is the lucky owner of three lots in a certain undeveloped neighborhood. Lotsandlots says he represents a company that is assembling a site for a large industrial plant. He offers to buy the man's three lots for a good price, but begs him to keep the offer confidential, as publicity would interfere with his firm's efforts to pick up land. The lucky man of property always lets Lotsandlots think that he owns all three plots outright. He says that Lotsandlots should give him time to think the matter over and come back in a couple of days. Then, as soon as Lotsandlots leaves, the fellow hurries down to the land company's office in the Jollity Building to exercise his option on the two adjoining lots, which he expects to sell at a whacking profit. He pays four hundred dollars or five hundred dollars to the "office manager," an assistant promoter in Lotsandlots' employ. The manager gives him clear deed and title to two lots in a salt marsh. The man goes away happily, and then waits the rest of his life for Lotsandlots to reappear and conclude the deal.

"The art in it," Hy Sky says admiringly, "is the sap never knows Lots is running the land company. A good boy, Lots." Lots is a humorist, too. When anyone asks him if he does much business, he says, "Lots and lots," which is how he got his name. When he says it, he rolls his eyes so knowingly that Hy Sky, if he is around, suffers an attack of laughter resembling whooping cough.

Another respected promoter is Judge Horumph, a bucolic figure of a man who wears a stand-up collar, a heavy gilt-iron watch chain with a seal ring on it, and high, laceless shoes with elastic sides. The Judge's face is tomato red marked by fine streaks of eggplant purple. Barney and his customers are disposed to believe Judge Horumph's story that he was once a justice of the peace in a Republican village upstate, a region in which about one man in every three enjoys that distinction. The Judge, when he is working, sits at a telephone all day, calling various business houses that like to keep on the good side of the law—particularly firms with large fleets of trucks, because such firms are constantly dealing with traffic and parking summonses, and they don't want to offend anybody. He says, "This is Judge H-r-r-umph." The name is indistinguishable, but no layman knows the names of a tenth of the judges in New York, and it would be impolite to ask a judge to repeat. "I am giving some of my time to a little charitable organization called Free Malted Milk for Unmarried Mothers," the Judge says. "I know that ordinarily it would be an imposition to bother you people, but the cause is so worthy . . ." Rather often, the owner or manager of the firm tells the Judge he will send five or ten dollars. "Oh, don't say 'send,'" Judge Horumph booms jovially. "I know how prone we all are to forget these little things. I'll send a telegraph boy right over to get your contribution." The Judge is a man of real culture, Morty Ormont says, but he has one failing, and that is strong drink. Judge Horumph's one serious run-in with the law resulted from his throwing a whiskey bottle at a Jollity Building wag who offered to buy him a malted milk.

The hero of the best stories that Barney and Hy Sky and Morty Ormont sit around telling one another is a promoter named Maxwell C. Bimberg, who used to be known in the Jollity Building as the Count de Pennies because he wore a pointed, waxed, blond mustache just like a count and because he was rather stingy except about gambling and women. The Count was a tiny, fragile man with large, melting eyes and a retreating chin. "He was a little wizened man that didn't look like nothing at all," Hy says, "but Maxwell C. Bimberg had a brilliant mind."

Hy recalls how he helped the Count de Pennies conduct a crusade against pari-mutuel betting in New York State in which the Count fleeced a prominent bookmaker who felt that his business was menaced by the movement to legalize the betting machines. The Count induced the bookie to finance a campaign of street advertising against the proposition, which was to be voted on at the polls. The Count was to have twenty signs painted, large enough to cover the side of a wagon. The signs were to say, "Mayor La Guardia says vote 'No'!" Then the Count was to hire ten wagons, put the signs on them, and have them driven around the center of town the day before the referendum. The bookie peeled several hundred-dollar bills off his bank roll to pay for the operation. The promoter went to Hy Sky and ordered just two signs, allowing the painter a generous profit on them. He had the signs placed on a wagon that he hired for one hour. The wagon then drove a couple of times through the Duffy Square region, where the bookmaker hung, and returned to the stable. There the signs were shifted to another wagon, which made the same circuit, and so on. The bookie saw several wagons during the day and was happy. Count de Pennies saved the price of eighteen signs and reduced wagon hire by 90 percent. "Maxwell C. Bimberg had a brilliant mind!" Hy Sky repeats when he tells of this successful promotion.

Morty Ormont's reminiscences about the Count are not all tender. "He was always borrowing a nickel for a telephone call, but one day he asked me for a loan of three dollars so he could get his teeth out of hock to con a sucker," Morty says. "I loaned it to him, and the next day I saw him looking very happy, with his teeth in. As soon as he spotted me he started with a small mouth. 'I am sorry, Morty,' he says, 'but the sucker didn't show, so I haven't got the three bucks.' So I turned him upside down—you know how little he was—and six hundred dollars fell out of his left breech."

The Count's admirers in the Jollity Building generally speak of him in the past tense, although it is improbable that he is dead. Some detectives employed by a railroad are looking for the wizened man as a result of one of his promotions, and consequently he has not been seen for some time around the Jollity Building. The project which irritated the railroad was known as the Dixie Melody Tours. The Count sold bargain-rate tour tickets to Florida which included train fare, hotel rooms, and meals. At the end of every month, the Count settled with the railroad and the hotels for the accommodations the tourists had bought through him. The tours were actually bringing the Count a fair income when, at the end of the third or fourth month, he decided to pay the railroad with a bad check. "It must have been a terrible temptation to him to stay honest," Morty says, "but he resisted it." "He always thought very big," Barney recalls affectionately. "I said to him lots of times, 'Be careful, Count. Nobody can promote a railroad.' He would say, 'What do you mean? This is strictly legitimate.' But I could see in his eyes he was thinking of larceny. 'Already I promoted some of the smartest people on Broadway,' he was thinking. 'Why not a railroad?' He always thought too big."

The Count made his first appearance in the Jollity Building a dozen years ago, when he was the manager of the widow of a famous gunman. He rented a furnished office, about six feet square, on the third floor and pasted on the outer side of the door a card saying, "Maxwell C. Bimberg, Presentation of Publicized Personalities." He booked the gunman's widow as an added attraction in burlesque theaters, and since that seemed to work out pretty well, he tried to sign up several acquitted female defendants in recent and prominent murder cases. The women were eager to sign contracts, but the Count found it difficult to make money with them. One reason, he said, was that "it is hard to write a routine for an acquitted murderess. If she reenacts the crime, then the public gets the impression that she should not have been acquitted."

One Wisconsin woman who had been acquitted of killing her husband with ground glass came to New York and rented an apartment to live in during her stage career under his management. She used to invite the Count to dinner every evening, and he had a hard time thinking of excuses which would not offend her. "Every time she says 'Home cooking,' " the Count would tell Barney, "I feel like I bit into a broken bottle." At last the life of the gunman's widow was violently terminated by one of her husband's business associates. An astute detective sat down next to the telephone in the murdered woman's flat and waited for the murderer to call up, which to a layman would have seemed an unlikely eventuality. The first person to call was the Count. He was phoning to inform his star that he had booked her for a week's engagement at a theater in Union City, New Jersey. The detective had the call traced. A couple of other detectives arrested the Count in the Jollity Building and pulled out his mustache one hair at a time to make him tell why he had killed his meal ticket. This experience cured the Count of his desire to make other people's crimes pay. After his mustache grew again, he decided to marry an elderly Brooklyn woman whom he had met through an advertisement in a matrimonial journal. The bride was to settle three thousand dollars on him, but the match fell through when she declined to give the Count the money in advance. "If you have so little confidence in me, darling," he said, "we would never be happy." "And also," he told Morty Ormont subsequently, "I didn't want to lay myself open for a bigamy rap."

The Count next organized a troupe of girl boxers, whom he proposed to offer as an added attraction to the dance marathons then popular. "It was not that the idea was any good," Morty Ormont says when he tells about the Count, "but it was the way he milked it. After all, what is there smart about selling a guy a piece of something that might make money? Smart is to sell a guy for a good price a piece of a sure loser. The Count went out and promoted Johnny Attorney, one of the toughest guys on Broadway, for a grand to pay the girls' training expenses and buy them boxing trunks and bathrobes. The Count trembled every time Johnny looked at him, but with him, larceny was stronger than fear. So he gives all the girls bus fare to Spring Valley, New York, and tells them he will meet them there and show them the training camp he has engaged. Then he takes the rest of the grand and goes to Florida." When Morty reaches this point in the story, Hy Sky can seldom restrain himself from saying, reverentially, "Maxwell C. Bimberg had a brilliant mind!"

"By the time the Count came back from Florida," Morty says, "Johnny Attorney was running a night club on Fifty-second Street. The Count walks into Johnny's joint as if nothing had happened, and in fifteen minutes he cons Johnny into making him a banquet manager. He booked a couple of nice banquets into there, but when Johnny would send the bill to the chairman of whatever club it was that held the banquet, the chairman would write back and say, 'I see no mention on your bill of the deposit I paid your Mr. Bimberg.' The Count had glommed the deposits. So after that he had to play the duck for Johnny for a couple of years. Whenever Johnny would get shoved in the can for assault or manslaughter, the Count would come back to town. That gave him quite a lot of time in town, at that."

Morty and Hy agree that the Count had a rare gift of making women feel sorry for him because he looked so small and fragile. "He made many a beautiful head," Morty concedes with envy. "If I had met a refined, educated girl like you when I was still young, my whole life would have been different," the Count would tell a head who might be a minor burlesque stripper. He would invite her to his tiny office in the Jollity Building to plan her Hollywood career. This office, he would assure her, was just a hide-out where he could get away from the crowds of people who besieged him for bookings at his regular place of business. The Count always made a point of stopping at the switchboard which then served the furnished-office tenants, collectively known to Morty Ormont as the heels. "Did that girl from the Paradise Restaurant call me this afternoon?" he would ask the operator. "You know, the one I got a job for last week? And by the way, if Monte Proser calls up in the next half-hour, tell him I'm out. I'm going to be busy." The mainsprings of feminine character, the Count used to tell his friends, were avarice and mother love. He would make extravagant promises of contracts in shows or moving pictures which he would tell every girl he was on the point of closing for her. Then he would say sadly, "Your success is assured, but I will never be happy. I am a Broadway roué, and no decent girl would look at me." "Oh, don't say that, Mr. Bimberg," a girl might beg, remembering she had not yet signed the contract. (The Count used to say, "You would be surprised how sorry a girl can feel for a man that is going to make a lot of money for her.") "Oh yes, I cannot fool myself," the Count would sob to the girl, and tears would flow from his large, protruding eyes as he grabbed for his protégée's hand. If the girl put an arm around his narrow shoulders to steady him, he would work into a clinch. If she pulled away from the lead, the Count would sometimes fall to his knees and sniffle. "Why should I live another day?" he would wail. "Tomorrow your contract is coming through. If I lived through tonight, I could collect my ten percent commission, which would amount to perhaps a couple of thousand bucks. Is that a reason to live?" Usually the girl would think it was a pretty good reason. The Count did not always succeed. "When a bosko wouldn't have nothing to do with him," Hy Sky says, "Maxwell C. Bimberg became very emotional." He once offered a female boxer forty dollars to let him hold her hand. The boxer declined, saying, "I would rather wake up in a hole with a snake than in a room with Count de Pennies." The Count was very discouraged by her remark and hated to hear it quoted.

An enterprise which the Count's admirers remember with considerable pleasure was the Public Ballyhoo Corporation, Ltd. To launch this concern, the Count spent a couple of weeks promoting a bookmaker known as Boatrace Harry. The Count kept on telling Boatrace Harry about the great incomes that he said were earned by publicity men like Steve Hannagan, Benjamin Sonnenberg, and Richard Maney. Then he allowed Harry to invest a couple of thousand dollars in Public Ballyhoo, Ltd. He had letterheads printed saying that Public Ballyhoo, Ltd., would supply "anything from an actress to an alligator" for publicity stunts. The Count became so interested in his idea that he forgot to duck with Boatrace Harry's money. The manager of a theater showing the first run of a picture called *Eskimo* asked the Count to secure a genuine Eskimo to pose on top of the marquee with a team of huskies. The Count made a good try. He found in the telephone directory some kind of society for the preservation of the American Indian and obtained from it the addresses of two alleged Eskimos. One turned out to be a Jewish tailor in Greenpoint; this was obviously a wrong listing. The other, who lived in Bay Ridge, was a real Eskimo who had a job in a foundry. He turned down the job, however, and begged the Count not to give his secret away, because his girl would make fun of him.

The Count had a number of other disappointments. He saw a classified advertisement inserted in a newspaper by a man who said he wanted to buy cockroaches in quantity. The Count knew where he could buy some large tropical roaches which had been a feature of a recently raided speakeasy called La Cucaracha, where the customers could race roaches along the bar, instead of rolling dice, to see who would pay for their drinks. In his enthusiasm, the Count bought five hundred *cucarachas*, at a nickel apiece, from the Prohibition agents who had raided the place. The Count knew some newspaper reporters from the days when he had exploited murderesses and boxing girls, so he called several of them up and told them of the big deal he had on the fire. They thought it was funny, and the story was published in the early editions of a couple of afternoon papers. The advertiser, however, did not want racing cockroaches. He wanted to feed the roaches to tropical birds, and the Count's acquisitions could have eaten the birds. Ordinary household roaches, obtainable from small boys in tenement neighborhoods at low cost, were better for the aviarist's purpose. The Count was stuck with five hundred hungry bugs. He turned them loose on the third floor of the Jollity Building and left for Florida with what remained of Boatrace Harry's money. Barney attributes the unusual size of the bugs in the Jollity Building today to the thoroughbred outcross.

Morty was naturally quite angry with the Count at first, but after a few weeks began to miss him. "You have to hand it to him. He had a good idea all the same," Morty says now. "The story about the roaches was in all the papers, and with that kind of publicity he could have gone far. A week after he left, a guy called up and asked for Mr. Bimberg. I asked him what did he want, and he said he had read about Public Ballyhoo, Ltd., and he was in the market for some moths. So I told him, 'I haven't any moths, but if you'll come up here, I'll cut holes in your pants for nothing.' "

The Count de Pennies must have convinced himself that he was a publicity man. When he reappeared in the Jollity Building after he had lost Boatrace Harry's money at Tropical Park, he got a job with a new night club as press agent. The place had one of those stages which roll out from under the bandstand before the floor show starts. The Count decided he could get a story in the newspapers by sending for the police emergency squad on the pretext that one of the show girls had been caught under the sliding stage. The policemen arrived, axes in hand, and refused to be deterred by the Count's statement that there was no longer any need of them because he had personally rescued the girl. "You know very well that poor little girl is still under there!" the sergeant in charge roared reproachfully, and the coppers hilariously chopped the stage to bits. The Count lost his job.

What was perhaps the zenith of the Count's prosperity was reached during the brief life of the Lithaqua Mineral Water Company. Lithaqua was formed to exploit a spring on the land of a Lithuanian tobacco farmer in Connecticut. The water of the spring had a ghastly taste, and this induced the farmer to think it had therapeutic qualities. A druggist who was related to a murderess the Count had formerly managed organized a company to market the water. He gave the Count 10 percent of the common stock to act as director of publicity. The Count "sent out the wire," as fellows in the Jollity Building sometimes say when they mean that a promoter has had a third party act as go-between, to Johnny Attorney and Boatrace Harry. "Why be thick all your life?" he had his intermediary ask Johnny. "The Count has something big this time. If you will

call it square for the few hundred he owes you, he will sell you
ten percent of the mineral-water company for exactly one grand."
The Count had the same offer made to Boatrace Harry, and he sold
his 10 percent of the stock to each of them for one thousand dollars.
He sold his share in the enterprise to five other men, too, and was
just beginning to think he had better go to Florida again when a
chemist for a consumers' research group discovered that seepage
from the vats of a near-by dye works accounted for the bilious
flavor of the tobacco farmer's water. This got the Count out of a
difficult situation. Even Johnny and Boatrace could understand that
10 percent of a worthless business was not worth quarreling about.

During this period of affluence, the Count lived in a hotel on
West Forty-eighth Street. "There was even a private shower," inti-
mates recall solemnly when they evoke the glories of that era. The
Count took to wearing cinnamon-colored suits with pointed lapels
that flared from his waistline to an inch above his shoulders and
trousers that began just below his breastbone. Every day he bet on
every race at every track in the United States and Canada, and he invariably lost. Almost four weeks elapsed, Morty Ormont recalls
with astonishment now, before the Count again had to borrow
nickels to make telephone calls.

The Dixie Melody Tours followed several promotions of an increasingly prosaic nature. "The tours was too legitimate for his
character," Hy Sky says sadly. "There was nobody left for him to
promote, only the railroad. So he went ahead and promoted it.
Maxwell C. Bimberg was too brilliant!" Morty Ormont is more realistic. "In every class of business there has got to be a champion,"
he says. "The Count de Pennies was never no good to nobody, but
he was the champion heel of the Jollity Building."

(1938)

from The Honest Rainmaker

The Life and Times of Colonel John R. Stingo

THE LEGEND

There was once a sheik, the richest and most puissant in all Arabia, and he owned thousands of swift dromedaries, the best in all Arabia, and thousands of thoroughbred Arabian steeds, the fastest in all Arabia, and his years were four score and nineteen, and his sons long since had reconciled themselves to his demise. So when, one eve, as the sun sank sad on the west side of the Euphrates, the old sheik summoned his eldest son to the side of his couch, the son sensed that it was the finish, although the word official *had not yet flashed on the odds board.*

"Draw near, my son," the old man croaked, "for my voice is feeble with years, and I would have you hear me."

The son, who was himself a green three score and ten, inclined obediently above his sire, and placed his right ear near the old sheik's mouth.

"You know, my son, that I own thousands of swift dromedaries," the old man said, "the best in all Arabia."

"Yes, Father," the eldest son said, "I know."

"And you know I own thousands of fat-tailed sheep, the fattest in all Arabia."

"Yes, Father," the eldest son said, "I know."

"And you know I own thousands of thoroughbred Arabian horses, the fastest in all Arabia."

"Yes, Father," said the eldest son, "I know."

"Well, Son," the old sheik said, "I bet on those horses.

"And now the First National Bank of Mecca holds a mortgage on the thousands of swift dromedaries, the best in all Arabia.

"And the First National Bank of Medina holds a mortgage on the thousands of fat-tailed sheep, the fattest in all Arabia.

"And the First National Bank of Trans-Jordan has foreclosed on the horses, and they are to be sold at auction in the paddock at Babylon to-morrow.

"So I have no material goods to leave to you."

The eldest son's heart was heavy within his breast, but he was a dead-game sport.

"It is well, Father," he said.

Then the old man, with a last mighty effort, sat up straight on his couch of gazelle skins and said:

"But I have something more precious to bequeath to you, my counsel."

"Yes, Father," the eldest son said, "I hear."

"My son," the old man said. "Never work a day. And NEVER, NEVER, take an honest dollar."

—Favorite barroom recitation of
Colonel John R. Stingo

I. THE PLUG IN THE DOOR

When *The New York Times* published the news a while back that 169 towns and individuals upstate had filed damage claims against New York City for $2,138,510 and no odd cents, Colonel John R. Stingo was politely amused. The claims rested upon the city's efforts to produce rain from clouds over its Catskill Mountain reservoirs during a water shortage in 1950. These involved seeding clouds with dry ice, and were carried out by a meteorologist named Dr. Wallace E. Howell, who had a contract from February 1950 until February 1951 to help it rain. The upstaters accused Dr. Howell of drowning them out, even charging him with the tornado which swept the whole Atlantic coast on November 25. It seemed to be up to the city to prove Dr. Howell's experiments hadn't worked, although at the time they were made it had intimated they were at least partially successful.

Colonel Stingo sometimes refers to himself as the Honest Rainmaker, as in the phrase, "the Honest Rainmaker, who is among those with the Prattle of a Babe and the soul of Jimmy Hope the Bank Robber." When he read the story in the *Times* he said, "I'm astonished that these modern professionals, men of authenticated science, wind up with damage suits and hard feelings. When my rain-inductive colleagues and I concluded a campaign, we were invariably the guests of the benefited community at a banquet where *sec* and *brut* flowed like the showers in the dressing room of the St. Louis Cardinals after a sixteen-inning game on a day of record heat. We would all get stiff as boards and they would invite us to come back next season."

Colonel Stingo is a nom de plume, but hardly anybody calls the Colonel anything else, and not many of his casual acquaintances know he has another name. He has been a newspaperman, off and on, for sixty-five years by his own count, and is now, for that matter, but he has never seen a future in it. The Colonel has always believed that fortune swims, not with the main stream of letters, but in the shallows where the suckers moon. In pursuance of this theory, he has acquired a varied experience, which he willingly shares with his friends.

Colonel Stingo's real name is James A. Macdonald, and half a century ago, when he was writing about horse races for the New York *Evening Journal*, he used to sign it J. S. A. Macdonald, which led critical colleagues to call him Alphabet. The *S* stood for Stuart, a name he has since discarded, because, he says, it made him seem a Young Pretender. In that dawn age of Hearst journalism in New York he was a favorite of Arthur Brisbane, who saw in his damascened style the making of a Hearst editorial writer. "But I stuck to the turf," Colonel Stingo says. "I knew the money was in the side lines." Reminded that Brisbane died with around twenty million dollars, the Colonel comes up with a correction. "Thirty-nine million," he says. "But it was a fluke." The Colonel himself lives in what he terms a "one-room suite" in a hotel built over a bus terminal.

During the Hearst days a competitor, outraged by the Colonel's exclusive report of a projected hundred-thousand-dollar match race between Irish Lad and a kangaroo backed by a millionaire Australian, wrote: "Alphabet Macdonald never permits facts to interfere with the exercise of his imagination." The Colonel rightly considered this a tribute to his mastery of his material.

"The sculptor," he says, "imposes his design on the Parian marble." But in most of his tales there is an element of truth which passes through the finest filter, so it is impossible to class them as fiction.

It is a matter of taxonomy, and immaterial.

The Colonel is a small, lively man with a back as straight as the wide part precisely in the middle of his hair, which becomes wider but no less precise with the passage of the years. His straightness, his neatness, and a certain old-fashioned formality of diction befit an old military man, and there are a good many impressionable bartenders on Broadway who believe he is. He wears bow ties, clothes that have an archaic dash, even when they are a trifle worn, and pointed shoes that show off his elegantly diminutive feet.

"When I was young," he sometimes says, harking back to what he calls "the days of halcyon, before Charles Evans Hughes leveled a deathblow at gracious living in America—I wore shiny patent-leather shoes with sharp points, and if I didn't like you I'd kick you and you'd bleed to death." This is by some of his acquaintance considered an allegorical allusion to the power of the press. But the Colonel has not elucidated it.

Hughes, while Governor of New York, signed a bill abolishing betting on race tracks here. A few years later the bookmakers found a way around it which tided them over until track bets were again legalized in 1934. But the Colonel still thinks of the late Chief Justice of the United States Supreme Court as the man who ushered in the Dark Ages of Hypocrisy. "Prohibition was an inevitable sequela," he says, "and so was the sordid pari-mutuel." Hughes was also indirectly responsible for the Colonel's withdrawal from the New York scene. When the unplucked statesman was elected Governor in 1906 he was already pledged to stop racing. There didn't seem to be any future for a racing writer in New York, and so the Colonel snapped at a chance to go out to Los Angeles as sporting editor of Hearst's *Examiner*, in that then distinctly minor-league city. He didn't get back for twenty-three years, and it is in this period of *wanderung* that he places many of his most picturesque and least checkable anecdotes.

There is usually a white carnation in the Colonel's buttonhole, and almost invariably, when he is seen in public, a beer glass in his right hand. For a period before lunch, which is customarily his first meal of the day, he devotes himself to gold gin fizzes, which are made with the yolk of the egg. During this process of remedial imbibition he is morose and does not appreciate company. "I met a villain last night," he will say in explanation of his mood, "and he led me down the path of dalliance Gambrinian." If the bartender in setting down the shaker bangs it against the wood, the jangled Colonel will say, "Doctor, don't cut too deep! I have been riding the magic carpet." But he eats his lunch with good appetite. He often says he is a "good doer." On surveying the menu he says, "The entry list seems to have filled well," and then he goes down the line with few scratches. After lunch he makes what he calls "the Great Transition," switching from hard liquor to beer, which he continues to drink from then until he goes to bed, unless he meets a villain who induces him to deviate.

In periods when Colonel Stingo is what he describes as "nonholding," or financially straitened, he spends a large part of his time in the reading room of the New York Public Library, seeding the clouds of printed erudition above his already overflowing reservoir of odd information. Such knowledge he refers to verbally as "esatoric," although he can spell the word all right. When he ceases to be non-holding, and has an adequate amount of what he refers to as "Tease," he makes his *rentrée*, usually telling his favorite bartenders in detail about conditions in some place he has been reading up on in the Public Library. "Glad to get back," he says. "There's no place like New York."

He doesn't like to be in bars when he can't buy his share of the drinks or undergo an occasional small bite. "I am a man of money," he likes to say when he has any at all. "The next round is on me."

Since the Kefauver committee began its revival of the Hughes Inquisition, the Colonel has had time to do a record amount of reading. His job, writing a column for a newspaper called the New

York *Enquirer*, is irreproachably legitimate, but carries no salary. His income has been derived from its perquisites, which are commissions on the ads he attracts to the paper's sports pages. Nearly all of these are from turf analysts, which means tipsters. Their profession too is irreproachably legitimate, since freedom of opinion is guaranteed by the Bill of Rights. But nobody is going to pay for a tip when he can't find a bookmaker to play it with. The harder things get for the bookies, the more nearly impossible they become for the purveyors of purported information. As the latter drop their ads, the Colonel's absences from his Gambrinian haunts become longer and more frequent, until at one time they threatened to merge in one long continuous hiatus, like that induced by the Hughes Law. Some of his friends, making an erroneous inference from his age and the protraction of his nonappearance, began to refer to him in the past tense.

At the moment of his remark about the decline of good feeling in the rainmaking business, I knew by a sure sign he was nonholding: he asked me how he could earn some money. I have known Colonel Stingo for five years, during which I had occasionally heard him allude to his career as a rainmaker, but I had never heard him tell the full story. I therefore suggested that he set it forth.

"If you write it," I told him, "you might be able to sell it."

"It's a strange idea, Joe," he said, "but I'll try it."

Before he would begin, though, he insisted that I promise to stand by to help.

We took rendezvous for that day at Gough's, a bar on West Forty-third Street where there is a life-size oil portrait of John L. Sullivan wearing a frock coat. The Colonel was to bring with him a rough draft of at least a substantial part of the story of the Honest Rainmaker.

"While I am about it," he said, "I might as well write my autobiography, of which this is only one of the episodia minora. I shall call it *The Plug in the Door*."

"It is an ominous title, Colonel," I said.

"It is indeed," he said. "A phrase fraught with fear for hundreds of thousands of habitual hotel inhabiters. What mockery lies in the word *guest* as employed by the average flinthearted hotelier! His so-called hospitality is limited by the visible extent of the inmate's liquid assets. He has a memory as short as a man who borrows five dollars; the months of faithful acquitment of obligations by the patron avail him nothing—the hotel man's recollection extends back only as far as the last presentation of the bill. The sealed keyhole," he said, in his emotion mixing metaphors as smoothly as a bartender blends gin and vermouth, "is the sword of Damocles suspended by an economic hair over a large proportion of the American people.

"And yet," he added, a gentler light suffusing his rugged countenance, for the Colonel is a man of everchanging mood, "I have known the plug in the door once to save a friend of mine from trancelike despair. It was a snowy night in January, and he had just descended from an office where he had been trying for hours to write a story that seemed to him of less moment every time he looked at it. Ultimately he had thrown it into the wastebasket. He had bet on fourteen consecutive losers at Hialeah, his wife had left him to run off with an advertising man, and from a vertiginous pounding in his ears he felt himself due for a coronary occlusion. Proceeding but a few yards, he found himself at the corner of Forty-fourth Street and Times Square, the southeast one. He had had some idea of seeking out a place to eat, but he had no appetite and he could not decide where to go. Then it began to seem to him that it wasn't worth the trouble to go anywhere. The snow continued to fall, and he began to assume the aspect of a well-powdered Christmas tree.

"The discordant laughter of a party of revelers, outward bound from some dispensatorium of cheer, recalled him to a sense of his situation. He cringed at the thought of being accosted by a copper solicitous of his compos mentis, and the hilarity suggested to him a possible source of assuagement. So he entered the bar of the old Hotel Cadillac, which at that time still stood at Forty-third Street.

"The Cadillac was a hotel harboring a most Bohemian motley, particularly in the last phase of its existence; it was the last stand of many old show people fallen from high estate, and also of elements more riffraffian. My friend entered the bar. A mere partition set it off from the lobby. It was thronged with raucousness; the atmosphere was most convivial. He wedged his way between two blondes to attain contact with the mahogany; they evinced no indignation, although he ignored them. He drank one, two short Scotches before he even began to look about him. By the seventh he was on terms of pleasant familiarity with his neighbors adjacent; he took them out to dinner and had a hell of an evening, winding up by inviting them to visit his apartment, solitary since his wife's defection. When he awoke next morning they were both still there. They had returned to their room at the Cadillac on the previous evening only to find their door plugged, they explained, and had adjourned to the bar, the habitat of wisdom and inspiration, to reflect upon their situation, when they made the happy encounter. Had the management not locked them out, my friend might have succumbed to despair and self-destruction, which would have been a pity because his wife left the advertising man and came back to him three days later. They lived happily ever after, until she ran away with the night manager of an automat."

We shook hands and parted.

2. THE PASHA STRIKES OUT

Gough's is a saloon which has been on Forty-third Street for only five or six years, but the portrait of Sullivan gives it an air of maturity. One item of décor like that can make a place. I remember when a man I know opened a speakeasy in 1925 and put a suit of armor in it. As soon as you saw the armor you knew the proprietor had confidence he would last, investing in such superfluous elegance. And it couldn't be a clip joint, or they would never have anything around that a drunk who got rolled could come back and identify. The armor established the place. A lot of saloons are open for years without getting established.

A life-size portrait of Sullivan is of necessity a big thing. He was six feet tall and the artist naturally had to leave something for him to stand on and something over the head so you can see he isn't wearing a hat. This is a very dark portrait, so it is hard to see in places whether the black is frock coat or background. The picture looks as if it had been painted in the nineties, after Sullivan had lost the title and gone on the wagon. His face is fat, he is wearing a fine mustache, and his right hand is on his belly, as if he is going to begin a temperance lecture. There is a light at the top of the frame and a little sign at the lower right-hand corner of the picture which says, "John Lawrence Sullivan, Heavyweight Champion of the United States, Born, Boston, Mass., 1858—Died, 1918."

The sign was put there a couple of months ago, after a stranger had come in and looked at the portrait for a while and then burst out laughing. The stranger had walked over to the bar and said to the bartender: "I know who that is, it's John L. Sullivan."

"Who else would it be?" the bartender had asked.

"Well, I'm from Naval Intelligence," the stranger had said, and he had a card to prove it, "and some fool reserve officer was in here and reported to us that there was a bar on Forty-third Street with a life-size portrait of Stalin and a votive light over it."

The sign went on next day.

The portrait is signed by somebody named Daunton, but the Colonel, who has a scheme to sell it to a millionaire Texan with an Irish name for a quarter of a million, believes that this is a case of wrong attribution.

"Daunton may have been some dauber engaged to clean the picture," he once told me. "I never heard of him. I believe the painter to be Copley. Much better price." When I reminded him that Copley had lived in the eighteenth century, he said, "I meant Copley the grandson." He has an answer for everything.

The Colonel, by his own account, was born in 1874 in New Orleans, and there is no reason to quibble over the date. He has no trace of Southern accent, and this has led certain friends to the assertion that his true birthplace was considerably north of Louisiana, in Montreal or Brooklyn, and that his present version of his origin was suggested by the name of the hotel where he now lives, the Dixie. But if his cradle was not bowered by magnolias, it should have been. He is a true romantic.

Personally, I believe the New Orleans story, even though one of the Montreal-theory men who knew the Colonel fifty years ago insists that from the day of his arrival here the Colonel was a good ice skater. "There were no artificial rinks in the nineteenth century," he says. The way I figure it, what the man really remembers is that the Colonel *told* him he was a good ice skater, which is not the same thing.

The Colonel himself has spoken to me of his regret at losing his Louisianian accent, by a process he describes as slow attrition. "It got rubbed off, Joe, like pollen off the bee, by contact with a thousand charming flowers," he said. "In the speech of each I left some trace of my native music. From each I received in return some nasal diphthong or harsh consonant. It was a heavy price." In a more practical vein he added, "The accent would have been of great assistance if I had wished to set up on my own as a turf adviser. A Southern accent is an invaluable asset to a tout.

"Also," he said, "it would have aided me in religious work. The great Dr. Orlando Edgar Miller, an evangelist who took in more money at Carnegie Hall than Paderewski, used to say to me, 'Jim, if you were a taller man and you hadn't lost your Southern twang, you'd be a hell of a revivalist.' " Religion has played a large part in the Colonel's life. I once heard him say, "It's the strongest thing man ever invented, with the possible exception of the Standard Oil Company."

As in journalism, Colonel Stingo believes, the real money is in the side lines. "The immediate collection is of little import," he says. "The Rev. Dr. Hall, with whom I was once associated, had a self-exegetic Bible, which he sold for a hundred dollars a copy, but only on the written agreement of the subscriber that it would remain in his personal possession until transmitted to his heir. It was a masterwork superb. I wrote a chapter myself. To be eligible to buy a copy you had to be a graduate of the salon classes for ladies, six lessons for fifty dollars; or of the esatoric course for men, twelve sessions for two hundred and fifty. We sold four hundred and twelve Bibles in the first month of one race meeting at Seattle. The bookmakers made us a proposition to leave town because we were getting all the Tease. That was before the Reverend Doctor began betting on the horses. After that they offered to pay the rent on a hall if we would stay."

The Colonel's habitual expression is that of a stud-poker player with one ace showing who wants to give the impression that he has another in the hole. He looks as if he knew something amusing that he didn't have the right to say. In poker this may be either a bluff or fake bluff, designed to induce other players to get into the two aces. In the Colonel's case, however, the expression means only that he finds the world a funny place.

When he showed at Gough's with the first section of his manuscript, he made me think he was a veritable Georges Simenon or Edgar Wallace, or that in the manner of the elder Dumas or Henry Luce he had placed himself at the head of a literary factory, for he produced from the diagonal slash pockets of his nubbly blue jacket two long manila envelopes bulging with manuscript.

"I suggest that you have a look at the autobiography first," he said, handing one of the envelopes across the table to me.

On the first sheet, under a neat row of asterisks, he had typed the title:

PLUG IN THE DOOR

and then, after four blank lines:

    Projected Story in Book Form of Everyday
People in Everyday Life.

On the next page it said:

    Characters in the Story Play
      The Duchess
      The Millionaire Kid
      Dynamite Jack Thornby
      "Wild Bill" Lyons
      Harry the Coupon King
      Mike The Bite

```
Senator Casey
Mary The Martyr
The Singing Kid
Madame Alda
   &
Colonel John Adams Howard,
   Circle C Ranch
      Cheyenne, Wyoming
```

On the third page, a memorandum on procedure, it said:

```
      Establish Personal Basis.
  Developing Story to Bring in Alluring Events
  Over the Chronological Sequence.
```

The fourth page said just:

```
            Chapterial Outline
```

and led to twelve pages each headed by a chapter subject but otherwise bare. On the page following the Colonel had taken a fresh start.

```
            Plug In The Door
```

This one said:

```
        A Story of a Life Variegated
```

Finally, on about the twentieth page, the Colonel had apparently taken his spring.

```
    The Stories and Rhymes heard at Mother's
  knee in the prattling days of childhood
  persist and live to the end of the recipient's
  tenure here below.
```

```
    The inclining influence there exerted upon
the delicate tendril of babydays shapes and
directs the Fate and Destiny of all men, of
all women, no matter who or what they may be;
as illustrious as a Caesar, as squalid as the
Thief of Bagdad.
    But, strange as it may be, it is of my
Grandmother and my Great Grandmother that,
perforce, I must talk in getting along with
the Story of A Life, my life, we've, you
and I, thought up under the aforementioned
titleage of Plug In The Door, a circumstance
and a terror uncounted multitudes of ordinary
mortals know so well.
```

All the remaining pages were blank.

"I couldn't go on after that," the Colonel said. "I was over-come by emotion. But the lead is the main thing, Joe. Everything will follow along nicely after I once barge into the episodia."

I was, quite truthfully, not much disappointed. What I had wanted him to write was a story about rainmaking. To set down his life from its beginning, I felt, might be a valuable spiritual exercise for my friend, but the years stretching from his great-grandmother's knee to early manhood could have only a limited popular appeal. They wouldn't help much to keep the plug out of his door at the Dixie.

"It reads very well, what there is of it, Colonel," I said. "But how about *The Honest Rainmaker*?"

The Colonel smiled and handed over the second well-stuffed envelope. The pages in this one were covered with typescript. The first began:

Rain—its abundance, its paucity—meant Life and Death to the Ancients, for from the lands and the flocks, the herds, the fish of the sea, the birds of the air, the deer, and the mountain goat they found sustenance and energized being. All the ele-

ments depended upon the Fall of Rain, ample but not in ruinous overplus, for very existence.

Through all human history the plenitude of Rain or its
lack constituted the difference between Life and Death, the
Joy of Rain or existence and misery.

"That's the first part of a speech I used to deliver to chapters of
the Farmers' Guild in California when I was clinching deals for Professor Joseph Canfield Hatfield," the Colonel explained, gesturing
to the waitress to bring him a second bottle of delight Gambrinian.
"The next ten pages are on the same high level, but I would not
suggest they are of the highest interest to our potential readers.
Anyway, it will give you an idea of what I can do when the Ark of
the Covenant falls upon me.

"Rain has always made the difference between plenty of Tease
and non-holding for those farmers in the California valleys, a circumstance of which I was made much aware in July 1908, when I
was one of three hundred guests of a rich man named Captain
James McKittrick on his stupendous estate, the Rancho del McKittrick, twenty miles from Bakersfield, at a party to celebrate the advent of Sudi Witte Pasha, a rainmaker the Captain had imported at
vast expense from the Sudan. The episode begins on page ten."

I found the place and read:

This enormous Rancho comprised 212,000 acres, an area so
large that it required a Cowhand, with many pinto relays,
two days and two nights to cross it, West to East or North to
South.

But the world's prime essential, golden Wheat, remained
the prime crop. With rain precipitation at the very right
moment the year for Rancho del McKittrick, with its
62,000 acres to Wheat, would be beneficently happy. Otherwise, no Rain no joy in Mudville, mighty Casey, he struck
out. So the expansive Capt. McKittrick had brought on Sudi
Witte Pasha, the World's Heavyweight Champion Rainmaker, to see what he could do about the anguishing situa-

tion in the Lower San Joaquin Valley—no rain and ruin around the corner.

The old Pasha had twenty-two Professors and Holy Men in his Mob and a whole mobile Library of Books with imploring Cantors, bewhiskered Priests, Bell Ringers, Soothsayers, and Pricemakers—all quartered in the lap of luxury in the Santa Clara Villa, an adjunct of the Manor House, with a retinue of Chefs, Servitors, and Body Guardsmen at command. We all understood that the Captain agreed to pay Pasha and his lads the sum of $150,000 and all expenses, to and from Cairo, Egypt, for a three months' service and demonstration of his magic Bag O'Tricks.

In the middle of July 1908, with two million dollars' worth of Wheat just beginning to ripen off in the field, the Egyptian Rainmaker went to work to bring on the aqueous dispensation. His chatty Camp Followers first greeted the Morning Sun and took a dip in the cold waters of Cherry Creek before going into the big Two-Day Fast, touched off by a little body lashing, and a sort of an ear piercing Indian War Dance, much like those you see done by the Indians in Arizona.

The real Kick-Off came the third day with a series of Incantations and the throwing about of quite a deal of reddish colored powder and sweet smelling myrrh. The pretty Samia never swung such belly convulsions in her Royal Court Dance at Hotel Mecca, beneath the Pyramids, as did little Miss Matti, the Pasha's apple of eye, towards the end of the Exhortation to the Spirits of Rain. We were told by Interpreters what the dance meant.

The fourth day was given over to the throwing upon the Runways surrounding the miles of Wheat Fields a brownish sort of little nut, known as the Kofu Bean from the Eufrates Country in ancient Persia—all ground up fine. It was done en masse, the Pasha in command, and with his impressed Rancho help of about two hundred cowboys, cowgirls, and field workers going down the furrows ladling

out the seeds, right and left, one might recall the Ancients
sowing their fields in biblical times out of shoulder bags with
a blessing and hope of a fruitful harvest in the months to
follow.

That night in the Great Hall of the Manor House was
staged a feast of Food, Fun, and Frivol, the likes of which I
had never seen before or since. It was for about three hundred persons, and lasted until sundown the following day.
Chefs down from San Francisco "curried" everything within
sight—even Sherry's ice cream, rushed through by special
train from New York. Choice vintage of Paul Masson, one of
California's choicest, flowed like water. The Feast of Belshaz-
zar was pikish compared to this Orgy in Imploration for
Rain; yet dire was the choleric ranchero's reaction when
nothing happened.

After fifty-six hours we were to see results, affirmed the
Pasha; meantime, to engage in supplication and reverent
prayer. Well, we waited and waited for exactly nine days
but not a sign of rain; then came the Blow Off. The jolly
Captain—the Show had cost him an additional forty
thousand dollars—came to a sudden and drastic decision;
"Enough is enough," he said while forthwithedly ordering
prepared at once his two special railroad cars, the "Erma" and
the "Sally Jane," lying in the Southern Pacific Railroad siding,
a mile down Cherry Creek, for an immediate emergency itin-
erary—to take the whole caboodle of Oriental scientists and
rainmakers to the nearest station on the Sunset Route, the
Old Santa Fe town of Barstow, where arrangements had
been made to attach the cars to the outgrowing Pelican Express for Phoenix, Fort Worth, and New Orleans; with a stop
over for a resumption of egress by Cromwell Line steamer
from the Crescent City through the Straits of Gibraltar to the
palm-waving beaches of dear old Cairo and the verandah at
Shepherd's Hotel.

So it ended. I went back and reread that one tremendous climactic sentence, in which the irate millionaire sweeps the whole ca-

boodle from the shores of the Pacific to the palm-waving beaches of old Cairo, with glimpses in transit of Barstow, Phoenix, Fort Worth, New Orleans, and the Straits of Gibraltar. Eight thousand miles or so in a few seconds. It made me visualize the soothsayers, price makers, and dancing girls picking themselves up off their rumps on the beaches and waving *their* palms in astonishment, as if they had been dropped by a Djinn, or Genius. The genius in this case is the Colonel's.

"It must have been quite a party," I said. Colonel Stingo gave the barmaid a sign of the hand to bring on another round for both of us, and when he had seen this signal honored, he acknowledged that I was right. "It was a stupendous quaffery," he said. "Of course, my interest in the proceedings was purely cultural and Belshazzarian. I was engaged in the promotion of race tracks, and our mutual interest in the turf, rather than agriculture, had brought me into contact with Captain McKittrick, a grand fellow. But I could see the strength of the Pasha's racket immediately. If the Fates had been kind enough to vouchsafe a normal rainfall, he could have parlayed it into an empire like Pizarro's. Where there is a need, someone will arise to fill it. I didn't think his presentation was particularly adapted to the American market, though. The exotic inspires distrust. A display of cold science, with impressive paraphernalia, is more effective, especially if combined with a spiritual note."

The Colonel had by now emptied a third bottle of the Gambrinian amber. "The subsidization of the Pasha was not the first attempt to influence the rain gods in California," he said. "For years wheat growers had been bringing in bands of Apaches from a reservation at Douglas, Arizona, to do rain dances. It didn't cost much and they figured it couldn't do any harm. That's why I was intrigued by this clipping"—and he handed me a paragraph that looked as if it had been cut from a Sunday magazine section:

OLD ORDER CHANGETH: Navajo Indians near Gallup, N.M., have become skeptical of—or just plain bored with—their ancient rain-making rites. During a recent drought, they hired professional rainmakers to seed the clouds over their reservation. Result: one-and-a-half inches of rain.

3. TOAD IN SPRING

"My own entry into the rainmaking arena did not immediately follow my perception of its potentialities," the Colonel said. "I followed after false gods. I started a race track at Salt Lake City in 1909; had to do business with the elders of the Mormon Church to get the green light. Our track was out at a place called Lagoon. After we got our track going nicely an outraged husband, an old-time Mormon, shot our track manager for the usual reason. The Mormons, although sub-roseately polygamous, were monopolistic in their conjugal views. This caused a scandal, and the elders shut down our track and opened one of their own. Afterward I got a heavyweight prizefighter named Tommy Burns, who is now a faith healer in Coalinga, California. We are still dear friends and correspond incessantly."

As if in evidence, the Colonel displayed a calling card which read:

Compliments of
TOMMY BURNS
FORMER WORLD'S HEAVYWEIGHT BOXING CHAMPION
A demonstrator of Universal Love

PHONE 442   BOX 566
Coalinga, California, U.S.A.

Scrawled over the print was a line in handwriting: *God is Life & God is Love & not a human being up in the sky.* On the back of the card was a printed message, headed: THINKING KINDLY MAKES PERFECTION.

"He's a dear old Tommy," the Colonel said. "We severed our professional connection in Reno, Nevada, the day after the fight between Jim Jeffries and Jack Johnson on July 4, 1910. Jeffries never hit Johnson a punch. Burns and I had previously agreed he should retire, but Tex Rickard, the promoter of the Jeffries-Johnson fight, offered us twenty-five thousand dollars to fight Stanley Ketchel, the Michigan Assassin. I put it up to Tommy. 'You fight him,' he said. 'I'm going fishing.' "

The Colonel sighed. "We could have beaten Ketchel, too," he said. "After that I engaged in a variety of promotional ventures too multifarious to recount now. I would see an enterprise that needed the services of a good public relations man, and I would talk myself in, always for a piece. It was in that manner I encountered Professor Joseph Canfield Hatfield, in about 1912. I was in a town called Modesto, California, where the chief attraction of the particular evening was a cocking main, to be held in the auditorium of the Salvation Army Temple following a meeting of the Modesto local of the Farmers' Guild.

"Cockfighting is not my idea of the sport supreme, but having nothing better to do I attended, and for the same reason I got there early. Here this tall angular individual, Professor Joseph Canfield Hatfield—a squinty-eyed old fellow around fifty or so—was up on the platform lecturing about 'the induction of rainfall by vibratory detonation.' He had already been around for perhaps fifteen years with his theory, but had never yet made a major score.

"The first wheat growers in California had been the owners of huge ranches, but after the introduction of Turkey Red wheat to California between 1875 and '90, a variety that could grow on poor and semiarid lands, there got to be more and more 'small' wheat growers with ranches of about twenty-five hundred acres. These made up the membership of the Farmers' Guild."

This was a field on which the Colonel had me completely at his mercy, since it was impossible to check his statements by reference to the American Racing Manual or Nat Fleischer's Ring Record Book, my usual editorial resources.

I ordered up a replenishment of the Gambrinian, and Colonel Stingo continued.

"Always the dread of the wheat grower in California in the valleys of the San Joaquin and the Sacramento River and further north in the terrain of the Columbia River and the tortuous Fraser River is lack of rain precipitation. But the Professor didn't quite know how to transmute their apprehension into auriferous deposit."

I cite, from his manuscript:

In all sincerity this old Prof. Hatfield believed that Cannon Detonation at certain times under certain conditions would induce Rainfall; he said he had been successful in South Africa, round about Pretoria and Ladysmith and along the Tugela River bottoms in creating Rain Precipitation at the very precise time when the downpour saved the Boers vast crops of grain and fodder. He claimed credit for prolonging the Boer War a whole year.

This incongruous Hatfield, a highly religious man, continuously bespoke the Deities in his exhortations as though his Gatling Gun would more surely serve scientific expectations through the kindly office of the Occult. He availed fasting and a wing and buck salute to the Morning Sun as a means to further favorable propituary. At the same time, I would remark at this juncture, recollection suggests the Professor knew the practical difference between the Net and the Gross and the possibilities thereof.

Marco Polo returned from Cathay with an explosive yellow powder to the Savants Salon in Venice with the story of the first known attempts at Rain Precipitation through chemical action or physical impact according to Prof. Hatfield.

Before not fewer than four thousand curious long-haired gentry in Angelus Temple, Los Angeles, Calif., in his first days in the Golden State the mystic Prof. Hatfield, put to it by a Platform Barnyard Committee on Science, stated that it was his understanding that the Ancients exploded the powder by centralizing the sun's actinic rays but that he, "the master," used a more effective modern device—"the awful Gatling Gun with its discharge of pure dynamite: the gun which had won the Battle of San Juan Hill in the Spanish-American War and elected a Rough Rider to the appalling office of President of the United States of America."

The yokelic audience evocated in unison "Amen, crack again."

I did the spade work and brought the situation to a near climax by assembling two representatives from each of the eighty Locals of the Guild with power to sign up on the Professor's neatly contrived contract of service and payment. We signed the contract at Tulare.

The proposition was for each Local to guarantee Prof. Hatfield just one thousand dollars, to be deposited at the Title Guarantee Trust Company in Tulare in advance. On the part of the Hatfield Rain Precipitation Corporation, through device and services of our scientific Detonationary Method, we were to assume all expenses and full direction. The official Gauges, Containers, and Measuring Paddles were approved and the centrifical point of test and calculation to be the Roof of the Court House at Visalia, Calif., in the heart of the Drought Wheat Lands with crops, in case of Rain, worth at least two million dollars in jeopardy.

We, the Rainmakers, the Party of the First Part, always Innocents Abroad and Unsuspecting, had thirty-two days and nights in which to deliver 4.10 (four decimal ten) inches' depth of rain water. Rainmakers were to receive $10,000 an inch for every inch from 3 inches and below, up to 4.10 inches. If 'the can' ever showed as much as 4 inches we, the Rainmakers, were to receive the sum of $20,000 an inch for the whole amount of precipitation. We could win $80,000 and the Professor's expenses for the thirty days' Preliminary Campaign had been just $6,120: we got $1,200 of this back from the Sunny Jim Breakfast Food Co.'s advertising campaign — so that our Nut was about $5,000.

There was not one of the Delegates, and not a Wheat Grower in the Valley, but wished heartily for the Rainmakers' success; they did not begrudge the money and wished us well. The women prayed in the churches for our success and a score or more Barn Dances and Picnics were given in our behalf, for the Professor was a natural friend maker and great alround wonderful old thief and grand good fellow. I wore off the O'Sullivan rubber heels from French, Shriner & Urner twenty-dollar shoes that month of July dancing with the buxom farm girls. And what hoedowns they were — from sunset to sunrise. Their homemade whiskey and kitchen beer would cure cancer first time at bat.

They say all first-class Boob Traps must contain a real smart Ace-In-The-Hole. The Rainmakers on this occasion, as well as on all other similar occasions, possessed that desideratum to a high degree.

It was just the Meteorological Tables and Rain Precipitations for Central California issued by the Weather Bureau of the United States and the Analytical Charts and Study Averages issued by the Department of Agriculture, Washington, D.C. Then there were the Tables on Rain Precipitation from Sacramento and the Merchants

Exchange, San Francisco. Many the long-hour midnight vigil I spent over those masses of demonical figures and equations in collaboration with Mr. "Kid" Bloggs, a mighty man with Horse Figures, who was, and is, a smart Handicapper of the Gees at home and abroad.

Without going into a labyrinth of meaningless Figures to the layman it may suffice to state the Rundown showed that for the Thirty-two-Day Period it was 55 percent in the Rainmakers favor, viz., that 4 inches of Rain would fall regardless of Prof. Hatfield and his Gatling Guns and stores of "pure" dynamite.

Before an immense gathering on the North Slope of Mount Meadows, a sort of junior mountain, foregathered State, Civic, and Departmental officials and the Locals turned out to a man—about five thousand persons on a hot dry afternoon beneath a burning Mid-California "desert" sun. After the speeches and the Band had droned its last brassy blare Prof. Hatfield announced his retirement with Staff and ascent, not to heaven, but to the mountain's apex and bade the crowds retire to safe distance on the lower slopes. The double Battery of Gatlings went off like the Clap of Doom with a repeat, every five hours under Director of Ordnance Dr. G.A.I.M. Sykes.

Just about midnight a perfect deluge suddenly engulfed the countryside causing Prof. Hatfield to swell his chest and bleat his salutations like a toad in springtime. The old boy thought in his inner soul that he had something on the ball but was not thoroughly convinced the Occult Powers had not framed up on him by staging a Show for his benefit and especial delight; perhaps he deserved the indulgence of the Fates, he thought. The Precipitation was 1⅛ inches, which is a lot of rain in anybody's country. Next day all the newspapers were full of the story and the Professor became slightly deified; the whole Valley stood enraptured and the fields and the ripening grain bloomed forth in gentle freshness wonderful to behold. The farmers were so happy, and even the banks began to loan money.

Three times more during the thirty-odd days and nights we had real heavy downpours. We made a Gross Total of 3⅜ inches;—just under the full 4 inches. The overjoyed Locals held a Special Meeting and voted us the full $80,000 and invited Prof. Hatfield to return next season. The crop came in most beautifully. It was a bumper. That winter many a California wheat grower spent Christmas at New York and the childhood home in New England.

We were paid all O.K. My cut was about $22,000. On the strength of our success the Hatfield Outfit was invited by the Farmers of the Columbia River in Oregon to a conference the following year in Salem. Meanwhile the puffed up Prof. Hatfield had received overtures from interests in the Sudan in Egypt and accepted the offers but he left us all behind.

It was a great opportunity for Dr. Sykes and myself to go ahead on our own hook. Overnight the Doctor became the Miracle Man and I the Chief Salesman. We kept on our Staff of nine people and a Battery of Cannon used in the Civil War. Same old deal and once again we are hoping for good luck with the lay of the cards all in our favor or comparatively so based on the Rain Precipitation Figures covering the Oregon Territory. To make a long long story short we win again and the world is ours. My take is $9,200. Paid off the Boys and Girls and disband for further orders.

But we never did come together again for the reason that the Guildsmen found out they could do just as well themselves provided they had the right sort of Cannon.

While shooting off their Cannon one Guildsman lost his leg and several Farmers were chewed up a bit. The rain fell just the same and the jig was up. The idea cooled off to a whisper and a story of the yesteryear.

The rain, the cold November rain, beat down on Forty-third Street as I finished reading the Colonel's story.

"In this climate," I said, forgetting 1950, "they ought to pay somebody to prevent rain."

"I was in that business too," Colonel Stingo said.

4. THE THIRD PALACE

The Palace Bar and Grill, on Forty-fifth Street off Longacre Square, has not, like Gough's, the air of a shrine. It is a salon. Sophie Braun, who presides over it, suggests a collaboration between Vigée-Lebrun and Rubens, with soft white hair, pink skin, and substantial proportions. She is a woman whose quiet courtesy inspires courteous quiet in a potentially obstreperous clientele, and it was this power of Mrs. Braun's that first attracted Colonel Stingo to the place.

Joe Braun, her consort, has an equally restful personality. A sallow, stocky man of fixed habits, he goes to the races on each of the 198 afternoons of the New York season and bets five dollars on every horse Ted Atkinson rides. This is in addition to his otherwise-motivated betting—a sort of left-hand bass to his play on the other side of the piano. He also places much faith in the advice of a friend who sells pari-mutuel tickets at a hundred-dollar window. It is impossible to tell from Joe's expression at the moment of encounter, however, whether Atkinson is on a winning or a losing streak, or whether the hundred-dollar bettors are doing any better than the herd. He smokes cigars and removes them from his mouth for only brief lapses into speech. Once an unfortunate fellow player, who had borrowed a considerable sum from Joe, paid him off with a number of plots in a Jewish cemetery. "I thought I might as well take them before he bet them on some pig," Joe said.

This left Mr. Braun with several surplus resting places, as he and Sophie had no children. So he presented one to Colonel Stingo, who accepted. "I couldn't be in better company," the Colonel declared, with feeling.

It was at the Palace that I awaited the arrival of the Colonel with the second installment of his story.

He arrived, smiling as he showed off an envelope as rounded on the sides as a rye loaf.

"Joe," he said, "if I say so myself this is a *pisseur*." The Colonel frequently lends elegance to an old-fashioned turn of speech by Frenchifying it. Thus he will sometimes refer to a figurator, or man who sells ratings on horses, as a *rateur*. "A touch of French here and there challenges the reader," he says. He often speaks of a rich man as a member of the *bourgeoisie*, pronouncing the *s* as a second *g*. "A rich man, a powerful man, plain as an old shoe, and as sweet a fellow as you would ever want to meet," he will say describing some prestigious figure of his youth. "A member of the *bourgeoigie*, and a great old thief." *Pisseur* is reserved for objects of his highest approval, like P. T. Barnum's Jumbo or the swindler George Graham Rice.

We took possession of one of the Palace booths, and the Colonel said, "I would suggest, if I might, a libation to the Goddess Pluviosa, synonymous, in the life of the Honest Rainmaker, with Fortune. In the summer of 1930, having transferred my pursuit of the Golden Fleece back to the eastern theater of operations, I was decidedly non-holding. Old Dr. Orlando Edgar Miller, my principal in a campaign of religious education, had been laid by the heels in California. He was in durance vile, as a result of persecution by the American Medical Association, which contended he could not prolong people's lives by swinging them in a hammock, thus extending their vertebrae. An ice-skating rink which I promoted in San Francisco had been eclipsed by the subsequent erection of a larger rival, and it was too late to arrange a comeback for Tommy Burns, even had he been willing, because he was by now on the half-century mark. A storm cloud lowered over the American economy, and the moment seemed inauspicious for any kind of a score.

"Hearing of my lack of immediate projects, an old California friend of mine who had himself scored handily in New York had written to me, urging me to challenge the big city once again. I recalled a phrase I had once heard from the lips of Elbert Hubbard, also about New York. 'It's a hard place to live, Little Mac, but the money's there.' I had a house near Golden Gate Park, in San Francisco, staffed by a Chinese couple, man and wife, whose stipendia were somewhat in arrears. I presented them with the house and came on like the Argonauts, by a slow ship through the Panama Canal. But venture capital had apparently taken refuge. The Depression of October 1929 refused to rescind itself, and the old town had changed. I had a room at the old Hotel Imperial and office space in the Knickerbocker Building at Forty-second and Broadway, but I was beginning to worry about the plug in the door.

"When without specific objective, I have often found it rewarding to go to the race track. I have made it a lifelong rule, since the age of fifteen, never to bet on horses. Freed of this vulgar preoccupation, a man at the track can sometimes see opportunity beckon."

"Didn't you ever bet a horse?" I asked, incredulous.

"At an early age I learned the futility of the practice," the Colonel said, reminding me, as he spoke, of another friend, Izzy Yereshevsky, the proprietor of the I & Y Cigar Store, which remains open twenty-four hours a day except on Yom Kippur at Forty-ninth Street and Seventh Avenue. There is a cigar box on the counter which also remains open twenty-four hours a day, into which customers drop contributions toward the burial expenses of old horse players. "Don't any of the boys win?" I once asked Izzy, who is, like the Colonel, a nonplayer.

"How did you think them horses gets feeded?" Mr. Yereshevsky asked me.

"I have just finished a section of my autobiography," the Colonel said, "which will shed light on what you seem to regard as an eccentricity." Before I could steer him back onto the story of the Honest Rainmaker, he had planted in front of me a chapter of *The Plug in the Door*, and since he then turned all his attention to a *delice Gambrinienne*, I had nothing to do but read.

5. BAPTISM OF FIRE

"It was 1888. Back home in New Orleans my destiny became the live subject of commentation at all family gatherings. What to do with him? In those times Springfield Lodge, my ancestral home, filled me with delight always. It cost my Grandfather a great deal of money and was regarded as one of the most typical and palatial in the whole South.

"My dear Mother finally announced that she had achieved the brave heights by securing 'James Aloysius'—that's me—a job with a weekly Irish Catholic newspaper. A fine kindly gentleman was Father John Quinn, the Editor of the New Orleans *Catholic Register*. I'm assigned the task of securing Data and writing pieces about the 'dear departed' of St. Jerome's Parish and collecting sales returns from the news stands based upon the prior week's sales. I would have been much more at home keeping score of the Southern League games at Heinneman Park for the Pelicans.

"After writing a few dandy pieces about prominent decedents of the Parish, and after aggrandizing twenty dollars or so from the downtown news stands and top carriers, a comforting discovery came to me—I learned, much to my surprise and delight, that a perfectly adorable spot to rest the body and cool the fetid brow from much deep-sea thinking and unremitting pave-pounding, was 'Sitting Bull' Bush's barnlike Poolroom, where business was done on five different Fields of Horses in five different cities. Also, the newly established Young Men's Gymnastic Club's tremendous Training Quarters for Pugilists, Wrestlers & Chicken Fighters provided elegant and restful surcease for a young and aspiring journalist who, after all, liked the finer and higher things of life.

"But one day Fate stepped in. On this occasion a prominent Parishioner had gone on to his paradisical reward. He was big, he was top news. To acquire the facts and picture necessitated a trudge away out Canal Street and here I was some sixty-dollar winner on the horses in Mr. Bush's cool-off Poolroom. All based on the 'monetary leverage' for I was utilizing the News Stands Collections to sustain my speculative moves. To tear myself away from such idyllic environment and engaging occupation would be unthinkable to most mortals, and it certainly appealed to me in that direction. I figurated there was justifiable cause.

"So a way out popped from the box.* I consulted the Town Oracle, who stood at my right side where he could get a clearer view of the chalked-up prices on the First Three of the last heat at Lato-

---

* The Colonel is fond of figures of speech taken from the game of faro (originally *pharaon*, another example of his Gallic predilection). He will bet this game or bank it whenever he gets a chance. "The percentage is almost nil," he says, "unlike the pari-mutuels with their fearful sixteen percent bite. The complexity of the game and its equality, however, militate against its survival. Gambling houses, even in Nevada, are full of slot machines now. It is an age debased and mechanical."

nia. 'Why Mr. John Sidney White, the guy you say has kicked off, I knew him well. I can and will tell you all you wish to know about him.' This was comforting and everything I might hope for in realization. Said I, hastily getting Pad and Pencil together, 'That is fine. You have saved my neck. Please let me have it in gobs.' And the considerate Horse Player just did that little thing. 'The late Mr. White,' said he, 'was cut down in the very prime of life. He was one of the most athletic and herculean types of men our city had ever known. He could beat ten flat in the hundred and put the sixteen-pound shot at Yale in his Sophomore Year no fewer than fifty-nine feet. And how those women in the Rotunda of the French Opera went for White, a walking Adonis. And you say it was Heart Disease. Well, well I so regret to hear the sad intelligence.'

"After close of the Poolroom operations, and, by the way, I may say my speculation turned out to be a stalemate—quit even—I repaired to McConkey's marble-tabled short-order Bazaar in Commercial Alley and transposed the above facts as related by the Town Oracle into a right nice piece for the *Catholic Register*, wherein it duly appeared the next Sunday. Recently, the dear Father had complimented me by suggesting I should take the Junior Class at Sunday School next week. Looked like I am standing high in his estimation.

"Rather early on the succeeding Monday the Reverend Father sends for me.

"So I look into the eye of Father Quinn wonderingly. What wrong had I done anyway? You could see he intended to be stern. So here goes. Here is what he said to me. 'Mr. Macdonald, you have been doing very nicely on our *Register*,' said the Editor, 'but in reference to that glowing symposium on the late Mr. White's physical perfection, I recall you said he was the modern Adonis, I must call to your attention that Mr. White had lost his left leg at the siege of Port Hudson and the absence of his nose was due to the ravage of malignant cancer. Now, Mr. Macdonald, we who have the destiny of the *Register* in hand do not claim to rank in journalistic brilliance with "Marse" Henry Watterson, Horace Greeley, or Charles A. Dana, but we are sticklers for authenticity. We're very aggrieved, Mr. Macdonald.'

"Some time went on and I'm a regular at Bush's Poolroom. Somehow I'm never much loser, never much winner. But one Saturday night when the Deadline for News Stands Collections is at hand I'm short eighteen dollars, current exchange, and no fussing around. Like a brave bull in the afternoon, I walk into Father Quinn's study with the salutation: 'Father Quinn, may I ask an indulgence please, sir. I find myself incommoded in the sum of twenty dollars which I extracted from Collections this very day. Shall come in with it next Monday noon. Is that all O.K., Father?' This kindly man and fine Editor looked at me with his two saucer-shaped blue eyes, rejoining: 'My boy, worry no further. Mr. Bush sent for it and I've paid him the eighteen dollars. I'm busy, I'll be seeing you later.'

"But one day this very human and monumental spirit of goodness said, 'My boy, don't you know this is no paper for you to be working on. I've gotten a new position for you this coming Monday on Mr. O'Malley's very sedate New Orleans daily *Item*. I'm sorry to see you go but destiny for you beckons to other and larger fields of newspaper endeavor.'

"And, so it was that I reported to the *Item* front boss and was assigned a desk and utensils. No sooner had I gotten well set in my work than two belligerent Editors began shooting at the visiting Chief of Police, the slugs skimming over my head but some of them bouncing merrily off 'n a steel pictorial cut extended in front of me for final check up and O.K.

"And that was my beginning in a chosen field of Destiny, the newspaper business, a story of a Lifetime in the pursuit of the Fourth Estate."

6. A DAY WITH DOMINICK O'MALLEY

"You see what race-track betting brought me to," the Colonel said when he perceived I had finished. "Do you blame me for refraining in the intervening years?"

"On the contrary, I admire you," I said. "But what brought you into the line of fire?"

"Mr. O'Malley had abandoned his desk at the usual hour of twelve and betaken himself for prandial relaxation first to the bar of the St. Charles Hotel, where he had a three-bagger of Sazeracs, then to Hymen's bar on Common Street, where he increased his aperitif by four silver gin fizzes, and after that over to Farbacher's saloon on Royal, where he had a schooner or two of Boston Club punch. O'Malley was not of that *sang-pur* elegance which would have got him past the portal of the august Boston Club, the most revered in New Orleans, but he had bribed a fancy girl to wheedle the formula from the Boston Club bartender. It consisted of twelve bottles of champagne, eight bottles of white wine, one and one half bottles raspberry syrup, one half bottle brandy, one half bottle kirschwasser, one quarter bottle Jamaica rum, one quarter bottle Curaçao, two pineapples, two dozen oranges, two and one half pounds sugar, seltzer, and ice. This was enough to serve several persons.

"When he had finished his preparations bacchanalic he strolled over to Antoine's, where he had four dozen freshly shucked oysters without any muck on them, a red snapper flambée in absinthe, a salmi of three woodcock and four snipe, a chateaubriand, *bleu*, six bottles of Bass's ale, and a magnum of La Mission Haut Brion of the comet year. After that he smoked a made-to-measure cigar, as long as his arm from the inside of the elbow to the tip of the middle finger, and drank a dipper of Calvados from a cask that had been brought to Louisiana from Normandy with the first cargo of sparkle-eyed Cyprians in 1721. Not more than one quart had been drawn from the cask in any one year since, and it had been carefully replenished each time. Having effectuated the *trou normand*, O'Malley consumed an *omelette au kirsch* and a small baked alaska, followed by a *caffé espresso* for which he sent the maître d'hôtel to a dive operated by the Mafia. 'The hardest thing to get in New Orleans,' he always said, 'is a decent cup of coffee.' He then started to walk back toward the office, which was on Camp Street, with some vague notion of pausing on the way to drape a beautiful octoroon's ivory throat with pearls, and would have arrived at his usual hour, after half-past four, had he not met with an unforeseen vicissitude."

The Colonel paused and looked about him with an expression that approximated distaste. When he is in such moods his current Gambrinian haunts seem to him to lack éclat.

"I'll settle for another beer," he said, and when it had been brought continued.

"I, a mere kid, had been entranced from the moment of Mr. O'Malley's exit by the notion of seating myself in his swivel chair and cocking my feet on his desk," he said. "Expecting momentarily his return, for I had heard that secular newspapermen ate, so to speak, *sur le pouce*, I refrained for the first four hours and fifteen minutes. Then, deciding that he might not be back at all, I yielded. I made my way furtively to his desk, sat down, swung my legs up, and encouraged by the smiles of the older men, even took the boss's green eyeshade off the blotter and placed it on my towish potato. I then raised a steel line cut from the desk and, pretending to inspect it, held it in front of my face, thus veiling my identity. I did not know it was the habit of Mr. David Hennessy, the Chief of Police of New Orleans, to arrive at the *Item* office each afternoon at four-thirty-five to shoot at Mr. O'Malley. The fellows in the composing room set their watches by it and sent the second edition to press.

"It was a tryst. O'Malley would arrive at four-thirty, hang up his frock coat, lay out his revolvers on the desk in front of him, and start to write a leader taking the skin off Hennessy. He would indite daily a virulent editorial charging the Chief with official dereliction by permitting the poolrooms, policy bazaars, brothels and bagnios, the stews and knocking shops, to run wide open every day including Sunday, a day of extreme reverence south of the Tennessee River. Mr. O'Malley was in political control of the city and figured that any madame who wanted a Sunday turn at bat should apply to him personally. At four-thirty-five the Chief, who had been steaming up on Creole coffee laced with contraband Cuban rum at Mc-Conkey's in Commercial Alley, would proceed across Camp Street and ascend to the first landing in the *Item* building. He gave Mr. O'Malley five minutes to get set. With little knowledge of trigonometry, but with natural copperial intuition, Mr. Hennessy would select a likely angle of trajectory through the wooden partition screening the city room and the corner where Mr. O'Malley sat in pontifical augustity.

"These first shots were a long price to wing Mr. O'Malley but a good bet to drive him under his desk in search of cover, a position from which he could not efficiently retaliate. Advancing behind the barrage, Mr. Hennessy would reach a spot from which he could survey the city room. But there he would be caught in a cross fire between the sports editor and the editor of the religious page, and after emptying both revolvers would be impelled to retreat. It was a lesson in logistics which I have never forgotten.

"But do not think that Mr. O'Malley had not his troops in elegant élan and precise readiness for these maneuvers. At the first muffled roar and crackling sound of timber rendered, all hands except the enfilading pair—from the city editor to the meekest copy boy—would secure shotguns conveniently placed for the purpose and rush to the front windows looking out on the street below, knowing full well that the miscreant Hennessy must, perforce, make egress and present briefly a target. After I had survived my first payday I was initiated into the routine. But on this first day of employment I was completely unprepared when a bullet from a Smith & Wesson whammed into the steel plate I held in front of me, knocking it from my hands and me *derrière dessus* behind Mr. O'Malley's desk. I learned afterward that it was the most accurate opening shot Mr. Hennessy had ever fired. 'A perfect carom,' the religious editor said. 'He played it off that new machine, the typewriter. I always said they had no place in a newspaper office.'

"After Mr. Hennessy had retreated, shrinking up close to the front of the *Item* building so as not to give the boys with the fowling pieces a clean shot, all my seniors apologized profusely for not having tipped me off. They hadn't thought I was in any real danger, they explained, and had just wanted to see some of the cockiness taken out of me when the first missile whistled overhead. 'It is ceasing to be fun,' the sports editor said. 'Also, I suspect the Chief of wearing the cover of a wash boiler inside the seat of his pants. The man in the slot had what looked like a clean hit on him day before yesterday and the only result was a loud clang. What worries me, though, is what has happened to the boss? He is either in the clink or some panelworker has stolen his trousers again.' "

The Colonel's wide, generous nose is slightly retroussé, and when he looks up at me his nostrils form a deeply indented *M*. They have a look of unshakable sincerity.

"The first surmise was correct," he said. "Mr. O'Malley, returning to the office from his last mysterious port of call, had been hurrying through Commercial Alley, a narrow lane between St. Charles and Camp Streets, in order to arrive at the rendezvous before Mr. Hennessy. Had Hennessy got there first, Mr. O'Malley would have found himself cut off from his base. But in making his way through the alley, the editor, a man of generous girth, came into abrupt collision, like a crack flyer of the Southern Railroad meeting a freight train of the Louisville & Nashville, with the editor of a rival newspaper, the New Orleans *States*, headed in the opposite direction. The two had exchanged acrimonious ink about a suggestion, publicized by Mr. O'Malley, that a bank of which his fellow editor was a director was on the point of failure. Mr. O'Malley had been refused a loan. The bank was the Hibernia National, known in New Orleans of the epoch as the Irish Rock.

"The editor of the *States*, whose name, as I recollect it, was Ewing, invariably carried an umbrella with a sharp ferrule, vouchsafing it served him as a sunshade in the summer. He thrust it immediately at Mr. O'Malley's left eye, being resigned to an exchange of shots and thinking that by this preliminary he might impair Mr. O'Malley's aim. He missed the eyeball, however, although he put a nice hole in Mr. O'Malley's brow, and forthwith the fusillade began. Of course down there in those days there was so much shooting the general public knew just what to do. The patrolmen on St. Charles and Camp detoured all traffic headed past the ends of the alley, and a number of shopkeepers on Commercial reached out from their doorways and grabbed the right hands of the contestants, an efficacious method of terminating hostilities. Sometimes they made a mistake; one of the duelists was left-handed. The effect of the error could prove lethal. Both Mr. O'Malley and Mr. Ewing, however, were conventionally orientated, and there were no casualties beyond the effusion of gore from Mr. O'Malley's punctured pumpkin.

"The police escorted both men before a magistrate, and from the clutches of these Dogberries O'Malley would soon have talked himself free, had not Ewing, himself a political power, sworn out a warrant against him for impairing the credit of the Hibernia National and causing a run on the Irish Rock. The judge happened to own stock in that institution. O'Malley was therefore immured, soon to be joined by a Mr. Kiernan, who published the New Orleans *News*, and who had joined in his campaign of retribution against the Hibernia. A swift messenger informed us at the *Item* office of their predicament."

"What happened to Ewing?" I asked. "He started the fight, didn't he?"

"He was released," the Colonel said. "In those days a mere felonious assault was considered of no moment."

I found this easier to believe because of a conversation I once had with a leading member of the Bar in Nevada, where the law still has a decent respect for human combustibility. We were talking about a friend of ours in Reno who had got shot in an argument about something or other a couple of years previously. "Harry got it in the liver," the jurist said. "They were laying five to one against recovery in the morning line at the Nevada Turf Club. But there happened to be an ace surgeon in town who still had a couple of days to wait for his decree, and he got the slug out without hurting him."

"What happened to the other fellow?" I had asked then, and the legal light had answered:

"He's fine, just fine. Saw him down at the Golden Hotel bar last week."

"Did they arrest him?" I asked.

Eminent counsel looked at me with some astonishment. "Why, no," he said. "If Harry had *died* we would have arrested him, though."

"A high bail had been set," the Colonel said, unaware how far west my thoughts had strayed, "and while the senior members of the staff sought bond for the captives, I was dispatched to the

St. Charles Parish Prison, where they were incarcerated, in a hired hack with a case of vintage Irroy *brut*, and Mr. O'Malley's English bulldog, Mike, whom he had left tied to the umbrella stand when he went out to lunch. I found the prisoners in good spirits and left them in better after they had emptied the first three bottles, kindly inviting me and the turnkey to have a glass with them. I went out thinking I had landed in the pearl of professions. And so it was, in those days of halcyon, the very cap and zenith of American journalism."

The Colonel appeared to ruminate for a while, and I thought I could visualize the procession of eminent zenithians, like Marse Henry Watterson and the youthful William Randolph Hearst, that must be passing behind his eyelids. But he was thinking of something else.

"I have never ceased to regret, Joe," he said, "that on my first day at the *Item* I was the indirect though innocent cause of Chief Hennessy's death. The bullet that struck the plate in my hand ricocheted through the flimsy ceiling and hit an old-style Southern gentleman in the business office in the calf of the leg. His name, as I remember it, was Mr. Troup Sessams, and he had withheld his fire previously because he considered the shooting downstairs a strictly editorial matter. When the bullet arrived, Mr. Sessams said, 'This is no damn joke.'

"He closed up his roll-top desk, hung his alpaca office coat on a hook, put on his long-tailed frock coat and a hat with a five-inch brim, and withdrew from the lower drawer of the desk a rosewood case containing two long-barreled dueling pistols with which he had eliminated all antebellum rivals for the hand of his wife, at that time heiress to a plantation Faulknerian, but since, like so many of us, non-holding. He loaded the pistols and placed one inside each breast of his frock coat, in the long pockets provided for that purpose by antebellum tailors. He then walked downstairs, limping a little—the shot had only grazed him—and followed Hennessy out into the night. It was the end of the Chief. His perforated body was discovered next morning. The year was 1889; the precise date eludes me."

"But wasn't Hennessy the New Orleans police chief who was killed by the Mafia?" I exclaimed, beginning to think I remembered something I had once read.

"That was the common theory, Joe," the Colonel said, "and the citizens of New Orleans acted upon it to the extent of shooting eleven Italians and then hanging them to trees. But those foreigners were desperate characters anyway, and doubtless deserved their fate."

In the course of a recent visit to New Orleans, I sought corroboration of Colonel Stingo's recollections. My research there seems to indicate that while the years may have blurred his memory in regard to some of the facts and caused it to embellish, if not invent, others, there is a certain hard core of veracity in what he remembers and no doubt at all that at least some of his cast of characters did exist in roles more or less akin to those he ascribes to them. There is the matter of Mr. O'Malley's embonpoint, for instance; I learned of one editorial fracas in which it served him ill and rather more gravely so than in the one recounted by Colonel Stingo. This was a duel between Mr. O'Malley and Colonel Harrison Parker, editor of the *Picayune*. Mr. O'Malley had published in the *Item* a cartoon representing Colonel Parker as a dog led on a string by the Governor of Louisiana, whom Mr. O'Malley disliked. The newspaper offices were on opposite sides of Camp Street. One day, both editors emerged into the street at the same time, bound for lunch—apparently the lunch hour was reserved for shootings in that miraculous city. "O'Malley fired first and winged Colonel Parker, crippling his accustomed pistol arm," a local historian who described the incident to me said. "Colonel Parker took his pistol in his left hand, but knowing he could not shoot accurately with it, walked across the street to get close to O'Malley before pulling the trigger. Colonel Parker had commanded a regiment in the Confederate Army, and the pistol was a Tranter fifty-two, a monstrous weapon throwing a slug as big as a heavy machine gun. Mr. O'Malley, not caring to confront his fire, tried to scrounge himself up behind a telegraph pole, of which we then had many in the downtown section. But he was so big and fat his belly protruded beyond the defilade furnished by that improvised position of defense, and Colonel Parker, advancing to the opposite side of the telephone pole, leaving a trail of sanguinary testimony to his courage as he walked, took careful aim and shot his man right through the protuberance, the bullet entering under one end of his watch chain and emerging from under the other. Both men were seriously discommoded."

As for Mr. O'Malley's connection with the *Item*, it appears that he did not become proprietor of that newspaper until 1894 or '95, half a dozen years after Chief Hennessy's death. A police reporter emeritus, almost as old as the Colonel, told me that there was a New Orleans Chief of Police who sometimes used to shoot O'Malley (although you couldn't set your watch by it), but his name was Ed Whitaker, and he didn't become chief until 1906, when Stingo was thirty-two years old. However, Whitaker was a recorder, or police magistrate, during the nineties, and he may have started shooting O'Malley then. Hennessy and O'Malley were deadly enemies during the Mafia days, but at that time O'Malley was a private detective, not yet an editor. It is suspected that O'Malley bribed a juror during a trial of the eleven Italians for Hennessy's murder, and so secured a hung jury and a mistrial. The lynching followed. O'Malley's fee is said to have provided the capital with which, when things had quieted down, he bought the *Item* and set up as a reforming editor. O'Malley lisped. He had an old iron safe in his editorial office which he used to say contained dossiers on every outwardly respectable citizen of New Orleans, accumulated during his days as a private detective. "You see that safe?" he used to say to callers when he was premeditating a front-page attack on some particularly saintly target. "It's full of that sonofabits."

It would seem that the Colonel has intertwined elements of the Hennessy-O'Malley cycle with others of the O'Malley-Whitaker cycle, to produce a result artistically superior to either. The Tristan legend underwent an analogous development. The roles, and even the identities, of the two Iseuts are inextricably confused, like those of Hennessy and Whitaker. Only the hero, O'Malley-Tristan, remains a constant.

7. REUNION AT BELMONT

"This has been a labyrinthian digression," Colonel Stingo said, with a handkerchief dabbing the Gambrinian foam from beneath his nostrils, and signaling his readiness for a refill. "But here I am, this fine though overcast early afternoon in September 1930, if memory serves, the Wednesday following the opening on Monday, Labor Day, when the Fall Highweight Handicap had been won by that marvelous sprinter, Balko, under a hundred and thirty-six pounds. The second day's racing had been marred by a torrential downpour beginning after the second race, and the question of weather for the rest of the short meeting, only twelve more days, but including the Grande Semaine of American racing, was naturally a subject of managerial preoccupation. The Westchester Racing Association was offering a generous stake list—the purses had been announced at a period when the country looked financially impregnable—but for the first time since the end of the First World War attendances at all sporting events had fallen off, a circumstance imputable to the quasi-disappearance of Tease from public circulation. The pari-mutuels were not yet grinding out their vast gist of vulgar gelt for the New York tracks, though they were in operation in other regions, and not even bookmaking had been formally legalized, as it was in a few years to be. The hand of Charles Evans Hughes still lay heavy on the state that had gifted him with its highest office.

"The tolerated bookies, who discreetly received bets on the track, presumably only from members of their acquaintance, bought their operating franchises from the Association by paying a high rent, nominally for boxes in the grandstand. But the income from this source was limited. So the gate money was vital if Belmont was to meet the nut, and the directors of the Association, although all millionaires, had not got that way by losing money, an ordeal to which they were still painfully unaccustomed although in many cases recently initiated. The president, Mr. Joseph E. Widener of Philadelphia, was even less accustomed than the lesser millionaires who surrounded him. He was a Prince of Good Fellows, attired in atelier-like clothes, and possessed of the divine inflatus for money-getting. I knew him from the happy days preceding the advent of Charles Evans Hughes, when I had frequently chronicled the triumph of his racing colors, the red and white stripes.

"From here on, Joe, you may as well read my account of the sequelae." And the Colonel, leafing through his manuscript, found a jump-off spot for me, passed the bundle across the table, and signaled to Louie, the lunch-counter man who doubles as waiter, to bring him another Gambrinian libation.

"Upon arrival at the Park," I read, "I made my way to Mike the Bite's lucky Shoe Shine Stand just in off the Betting Ring, the scourge of the Pari-Mutuels not having descended upon the tranquil scene of the Oralist, as yet, in 1930, in fact, it was not to be for ten years later. The proprietor, a slightly colored man, perhaps an octoroon, was of true name William Beeson, but styled Mike the Bite because he was such an easy fellow to promote for a loan. This was because of native generosity, not lack of business acumen, for Willie had built up for himself a considerable fortune by his occult activities. The stand provided but a small portion of his revenues. He paid three hundred dollars a month rental for the two-seated stand and charged twenty-five cents for a slap-dash polish with quick brush-off. But he also sold, to customers both male and female, a daily rabbit's foot for two dollars and an agreement to bet two dollars for him on his third-race selection. He must have been quite a figurator, or else quite a salesman, because he put out around fifty rabbits' feet per diem. Not all the rabbits' feet customers took shines.

"On two long hanger racks in the rear the Bite undertook to care safely for your overcoat or umbrella; his way of assuring himself the customer's return and, above all, payoff. If the Bite's selection came down in front in the third, it requires no great computation to see he was a sure thing to become rich.

"The second dodge of the Bite was quite classic. Early in life his back was broken during a Tornado at his place of nativity down South, notoriously the home of high winds, viz., Gainesville, Georgia. Nobody ever had such a magnificently large Hunch as the Bite believe me.

"And be assured the Bite made the Hunchback Business pay

him better than it had Lon Chaney, who played Quasimodo in the silent films. He made a play for the lady Horse Players only. He bought two suits a year, one for the summer and one for the chilly days of autumn, generally at thirty-five dollars each. But he paid five dollars extra for a very special alteration. Where the coat rested plumb atop the Hunch this mastermind contrived a large Patch Pocket that opened and closed on a shiny zipper about six inches long.

"For years, the Bite held to the psychic fixation, in effect, experience had shown him, that only women could enjoy good luck in playing the horses by the laying on of the hands upon the prodigious Hump. He would say oftentimes that under no circumstance would he sell 'a tough,' as he termed the merchandise, to a man, only to a woman, and never less than ten dollars.

"As the years went by the Bite built up a large and steady patronage among the women turf speculators. They would come sidling up quietly to the Shoe Shine Stand and back in the rear of the hanger racks. The Bite would follow, tip toeish like, and in a flash a tug on the zipper would bring exposure of the Hump. By a quick and dexterous move the lady Horse Player reached down a 'pinky' and 'the touch' became achieved.

"I climbed up on Mike's stand not because I was a candidate for the eleemosynary department, still less to get a horse in the third, but because it provided a perch from which I might survey briefly the hurrying throng, all panting with greed, intent on the accumulation of unearned increment. Also I liked to exchange a greeting with the Bite, who had a particular esteem for me because I always addressed him as Willie, his real given name. And from my perch I perceived a friend of olden times, the tall, gaunt, Professor George Ambrosius Immanuel Morrison Sykes, D.D. (Zoroastrian), whom I had known first as assistant to Dr. Joseph Canfield Hatfield, the father of artificially induced precipitation, and later as my own partner in the Honest Rainmaking business.

"He was hurrying with long strides, but not in the direction of the Betting Ring, from which I judged he was on some tryst intent. Since he was not given to extra-conjugal romance I took it that his appointment was with a solvent boob. I followed with my eyes his progress across the Clubhouse lawn, and to my astonishment recognized the resplendent form encountering his as that of Mr. Widener, who was accompanied by the Racing Secretary of the meeting, a Mr. Schaumberg, since, like his boss, gone under the wire.

"The incongruous three joined in colloquy and shortly moved away to a tree surrounded by benches, where they seated themselves. I, having by now felt the tug at my trouser-leg which was the Bite's signalization of the completion of his onceover, descended from the chair and followed them. It was a cinch, I had already estimated, that Mr. Widener would not wish Dr. Sykes to bring on *more* rain, so I wondered if the Good Doctor had found a method of keeping it away.

"The gentlemen had selected for the talk the Joyner Oak, set within a richly verdured parkway enclosed by four brightly striped benches of heavy hickory wood and spiked in the supporting headpieces by wooden stanchions, instead of modern steel clavers.

"The benches had been presented to the Westchester club by the late Pierre Lorillard, the Master of Rancocas Farms, Jobstown, N.J., as an ornament to Belmont Park when it was first opened.*

"Across the Lawn stood the entrance to the private elevator which would take Mr. Widener to his offices in the upper reaches in the Club Preserves within the huge grandstand, and quite apart from the expensive Turf and Field Club in the ancient Manice Mansion further along and across the green swarded Paddock with its celebrated group of Old English Trees and Rose Bushes in hedge formation. Suddenly, the knot of earnestly conferring men became restive, and Mr. Widener made his adieu with a gentle move towards the elevator entrance. Messrs. Sykes and Schaumberg would be obliged to cross my path if they directed their way to the Racing Secretary's Office.

"Sure enough, that was the direction they took. Almost abreast

---

* This is the kind of thing on which I never know how far the Colonel is spoofing, if at all.

of me, Dr. Sykes suddenly saw and recognized me. An effusive greeting followed.

"Suddenly, from here, there, and everywhere, occurred a rush of persons from beneath the Paddock trees, from underneath the grandstand and out of the recesses of the Racing Administrative Building, all towards the trackside rail, all in answer to the thrilling alarum, 'They're off.' Like a red coon dog catching high scent, the Secretary broke into a run and was gone.

"That was the cue for me to isolate Dr. Sykes from the mass of possible interference round about; I edged him away to Mike the Bite's stand and maneuvered him back behind the hanger racks, where we could talk unobserved. He came quickly to the point; he had been doing business in late years as the Weather Control Bureau, of Burbank, Calif. Out there, he said, he had received a letter from a lady in New York with a name fragrant of millions, asking whether he could prevent as well as cause rainfall. If so, she said, she would be willing to defray the expense of a conference here in New York. On arrival here he was to report to the offices of the Westchester Racing Association, when a meeting would be arranged between him and Mr. Widener. The Good Doctor had come on speedily.

" 'My latest apparatus has proved as efficacious in driving away rain as in inducing it,' he said with a perfectly straight face. 'But I would appreciate your assistance with the meteorological data. It's a good thing to know what you have to contend against.' He had reported on arrival, and Mr. Schaumberg had made the appointment for him with Mr. Widener.

" 'Funny thing about him, though,' the Doctor said. 'He said he couldn't make up his mind on the deal until we'd both talked it over with the lady. Said he had great confidence in her intuition. So we made another appointment for tomorrow, same time, but out at the Widener barn, where the lady's car will be parked. These rich Easterners are very suspicious. He seemed to doubt my good faith.'

" 'That's because he has never done business with an Honest Rainmaker,' I said, and we both laughed. 'I have known Mr.

Widener for many years,' I added, 'and I am prepared to corrobo-
rate whatever assertions you may make, within reason, about your
past accomplishments. Also, as you may recollect, I have an adroit-
ness in handling the feminine component, a way with the ladies,
and I suspect that Mrs. Harriman'—that was the fair one's name—
'will have the determining voice.' So I was in like Flynn, for 45 percent of the whole deal, which like a promising but untried mining
claim we did not yet know the full value of, yet it bore a Bonanza
aspect. The old Doc stipulated 10 percent for Mrs. Sykes, who he
said had accompanied him to New York, and 45 percent for himself.
I contributed my office facilities, desk space, and mail service at the
Knickerbocker Building, so that the Weather Control Bureau could
offer a New York address, always a denotation of substantiality. I
was to be the outside man, or talker, and old Doc was to profess the
zealot, unapproachable and hard to understand.

   " 'Now,' I said, 'I would suggest that Mr. Widener, who has in
his life drag-netted a vast accumulation of profits, is more attracted
by the possibility of making money than of guaranteeing against
loss. I would therefore suggest that we offer him a forfeit for non-
fulfillment of our promise—something like double his money back
if it rains.' I had in the back of my mind that it rains less than once a
week on the average in early September, a hot, sultry time in the
vicinity of New York usually, but I was going to check it before
I made the price.

   "So the Good Doctor and myself left Mike the Bite with his
Lares & Snares; making headway to the Doctor's brand new Buick
we soon found ourselves speeding along the Boulevard en route
to New York; we felt no desire to see the rest of the races, having
matters more emergent on our minds. I for one had to see what
Weather reports for the Long Island district in past years were available at the New York Public Library, my source of avail in an endless variety of situations. The appearance of the Doctor's vehicle did
not deceive me; I was acquainted with the liberal credit arrangements available in a time of increasing automotive merchandising
difficulty.

   " 'Are you holding, Doctor?' I asked him. He shook his head.

'Just enough to live nice for a couple of weeks,' he said. My resources were similarly limited. I thought that some small capital might be necessary to launch the enterprise. But I had already fixed in my mind a potential source for such collateral. '*Semper Paratus*' is the motto of the Long Riders."

"The Long Riders" is a term the Colonel likes to apply to himself and all his associates, past and present, in allusion to the train robbers who used to ride out of the Indian Territory of Oklahoma with Al Jennings, a character Colonel Stingo claims as a boyhood friend. The analogy is purely poetic, however. The only gun point at which the Colonel has ever taken money is the muzzle of Professor Hatfield's cannon.

"Doctor and Mrs. Sykes had taken a month's lease on an old brownstone house in the West Eighties," the manuscript went on. "There I joined them in the late evening, after a long afternoon profitably spent in meteorological figuration. We could afford to lay Mr. Widener 2 to 1 and still have a percentage of .7499 in our favor, I had discovered, while the greediest bookmakers content themselves with .15 and .20, and the remorseless Pari-Mutuel as at present constituted but .16. But by a subtlety in the wording of our wager I could bring the real odds down still further for the Grande Semaine, beginning with Saturday, Sept. 6, the date of the Lawrence Realization and Champagne Stakes, and running through Saturday the 13, Futurity Day, on which the best two-year-olds in the country were to vie for the championship and a prize of more than $100,000. It turned out to be $121,670. We had an edge in our favor beyond the dreams of avarice.

"But this old joker Sykes maintained the pretext that his manipulations were in fact capable of affecting the result, and that my calculation of probabilities was only supplemental. 'A lot of things have developed in our profession since your time, Little Mac,' he told me, 'including radio.'

"That night we dined with fine gusto, and remained at table for hours at Café Conte on Astor Place recalling old times and old friends. Mrs. Sykes was a big woman with a blarney and a swagger that would have been useful in a sideshow of Adam Forepaugh's

Three-Ring Circus of ancient time. In the Rainmakers' Campaigns in the Far West it had been her specialty to attend gatherings of the women of the Farmers in their churches and Meeting Houses where she would lead the exercises and the prayers. This time, she said, she would exercise another talent. She could mix drinks as expertly and diabolically as any leering Night Club Bartender I ever knew. 'It should help with public relations,' she said.

"With a freshening shower and spanking breakfast, I was in fine fettle as Dr. Sykes and myself stepped into his car for the long ride to Belmont Park next morning.

"And now the Bugle Call for the opening race of this drizzling murky day here at Belmont Park clarioned through the Paddock and across the vast stretches of the Queen of All Racing Courses in the New World.

"We knew that within ten minutes we would be at Mrs. Harriman's side, along with Messrs. Widener and Schaumberg."

8. "LONG, LISSOME, LUCREFEROUS"

"Precisely on the dot, we kept our appointment with Mrs. Harriman at the Turf & Field Club. A very gracious lady and one of the real beautiful women of her day and time, she chose to receive us upon the Driveway leading up to the Clubhouse verandah while seated in a handsome custom built, eight-cylinder, imported Hispano-Suiza.

"I afterwards learned this motor car cost, laid down in New York from Toledo, Spain, the surprising sum of $22,000, one of the most luxurious and expensive jobs in the United States in 1930. On the direction of Madame, the tonneau's side door swung ajar, revealing a vista of rich and ravishing splendor—upon her Golden Barge in the simmering moonlight of a sheening night on the Nile, I am sure Cleopatra never looked more completely devastating than does dear Mrs. Harriman as she reclines her elongated figure lissomely strewn, lengthwise upon the satin-cushioned coach seat while smoking a costly heaven-scented Carolina Perfecto, à la

Panatela, with the poise of a Winston Churchill tweezing a Wheeling stogie.

"In quiet souciance, a quick glance measured Dr. Sykes and myself for her Ladyship, and we were evidently satisfactory for she said, 'Now boys what may be your first name—yes you, blue eyes—yours?' Timidly abashed, I squeaked up—'Jim.' Dr. Sykes merely suggested, 'Just call me Doc.' Then came the first imperial command from the Royal Divan's purpled folds to a Club attendant—'Please, immediately, chairs for the gentlemen from the Clubhouse.'

"Now, all of us are nicely grouped about Mrs. Harriman and her Throne Room in commodious club chairs awaiting the opening phases of the impending Grand Symposium.

"Tall, slim, and elongated she was, and her wide wondering eyes were in shade the color of sea shells along the Caribbean beachway at sunrise; her honey-tone-colored hair, bunched in braids after the affectation of Elizabeth Barrett Browning, generally matched up with a single California pink rose in long tendril, while her every physical movement bespoke the Della Sarte motif in its fullest synchronization—albeit she appeared languorously and coquettishly lazy."

I paused in my reading to congratulate the Colonel on his descriptive powers.

"It reads like Dr. Faustus casing Helen," I said. "Mrs. Harriman must have been a remarkable woman."

"She had a weakness, however, Joe," he answered—"an inquiring mind. She was curious of the occult, and had landed on the mailing list of every peddler of the esatoric, from Father Divine to the Omnipotent Oom and the Rosicrucians. It was through one of her yogi cronies, no doubt, if not through a Bahai, that she had learned of Dr. Sykes's prowess, for the old boy ranked high in the mystic confraternity. She was therefore predisposed in our favor."

The Colonel is a strong rooter for the opposite sex, whom he considers it impossible to buck.

"Since you cannot defeat them," he sometimes says, "it is necessary to win them over to your side. There is not a man, however intelligent, who is one half as smart as any woman."

The Colonel's ideal of feminine beauty remains constant.

In this he resembles an old wartime friend of mine named Count Prziswieski, a minor figure in the exiled Polish Government.

"All my life I have been faithful to one woman," the Count once said to me—"a fragile blonde with a morbid expression."

He found this woman in every country, and she never aged, although the Count did. The fragile blonde with a morbid expression, wherever she turned up, was in her twenties.

My knowledge of the Count's predilection saved us both embarrassment one week end when I was away from my London hotel and returned to find he had been a guest there during my absence.

"Do you know the Count Ginwiski?" the night porter, an inquisitive sort, asked me. "Said 'e knew you. Rum cove."

"I certainly do know him," I said. "One of the county families of Poland."

"And do you know the Countess?" the porter asked artfully.

"Very well," I answered. "Thin blonde woman, much younger than he is, speaks English perfectly."

"Good night, sir," the porter said in a disappointed tone.

The Colonel's ideal is a dashing woman, tall, lissome, understanding, and, above all, loaded down with Tease. He represents her in a prototype called the Duchess, who appears throughout his writings columnistic and his reminiscences, but who is not permanently identified with any individual. Like the fragile blonde, she stays the same age, but the Colonel's ideal is thirty-five rather than twenty, for at thirty-five a woman has at once more dash and more understanding. The Colonel's affair with the Duchess began, he says, when he was getting out a weekly paper called the *Referee* in San Francisco, in the period following the retirement of his pugilistic meal ticket. The *Referee* dealt largely with night life—"which was in those days variegated," the Colonel says. It was his sharp, shiny-shoe period. He wrote a column of night-spot notes under the signature of the Duchess, "a woman of the world, well heeled and a hell of a good fellow, who visited the resorts both advertising and non-advertising and commentated on the personalities she encountered there. There soon ceased almost totally to be non-advertisers." He has revived the

Duchess many times—she was the only woman present at the Gans-Nelson fight in 1906, according to one of his columns for example, and also the most beautiful spectator of the finish of Middleground's Kentucky Derby in 1950, not a grayed-eyelash older.

His description of Mrs. Harriman conforms to this type, and possibly Mrs. Harriman did. I have not looked her up in a picture morgue.

The *Referee*, with many enterprises of vaster commercial import, was submerged, the Colonel says, in a reform wave which swamped San Francisco just previous to the Panama-Pacific exposition. There was a conflict of maelstrom proportions before the reformers won out, he says, with a slight shudder at the recollection, but in the end they shut the town tighter'n a drum.

"And what was the editorial policy of the *Referee* during this struggle for righteousness?" I once asked him.

" 'Let Paris be gay!' " he answered.

But this is what the Colonel himself would call a labyrinthian digression.

9. "THE DETONATORY COMPOUND"

I returned to the manuscript. Mrs. Harriman was speaking.

" 'Here at Belmont Park this season we're confronted by a severe Depression and a continued period of rain would ruin us,' explained Mrs. Harriman, 'and I thought you California experts might be able to prevent it. What may be your reaction?'

"The nudge that Dr. Sykes trained into my ribs was quite unnecessary for I realized my time at bat had come to hand. Slowly from my brief case emerged the Syllabus which I had prepared the night before on Rain Prevention and what we could do for the panicky top people at Belmont Park.

" 'The new and most modern method of meteorological control and precipitation engenderment will be utilized, the Silver Iodine Spray based on Canalized Wave Vibration,' I intoned. 'The cost of installation for the term of ten racing days or less will not exceed five thousand dollars and it is our firm belief, after many years in the ancient and honorable profession of the Rainmaker, you will not have more than two days with a perceptible rainfall.'

"Syllabus explained that our Proposition is based solely upon an ability to prevent rain. It is *not* a bet, like rain insurance as offered by Lloyd's of London, but a measure designed to insure good racing conditions as well as protect the sportsmen backing the meet from loss. However, as a guarantee of our seriousness, we included an indemnity provision.

"Then came the all-important Denouement: 'the terms.' They embraced simply this: 'We, the U.S. Weather Control Bureau, hereinafter to be styled party of the first part, agree to induct, maintain, and operate the Iodine Silvery-Spray and Gamma-Ray-Radio system, the cost to us not to exceed $5,000, cost of buildings and labor to be defrayed by the Westchester Racing Association. The party of the second part agrees to pay party of the first part $2,500 on Saturdays, Sept. 6 and Sept. 13, and $1,000 on each intervening weekday for its services in preventing rain. Party of the first part agrees to pay to party of the second part $2,000 on any day on which United States Weather Bureau reports rain, even a trace, within purlieus of Belmont Park between 11:00 A.M. and 5:30 P.M. Payment to be made each day at 6:00 P.M. at the Office of the Westchester Racing Association, Belmont Park.'

"This looked like a two-to-one bet but it wasn't. It was even money on weekdays and we couldn't lose if we tried on Saturdays.

"When I read off, 'cost of buildings and labor to be defrayed by the party of the second part,' the Good Doctor Sykes shifted nervously while his face assumed the ghastly aspect of an Egyptian mummy. If we had had to get up that Tease we would have been in trouble. But Mr. Widener acceded. He said though that he thought we should get up a certified check for two thousand dollars, the amount of our forfeit in case we failed on the first Saturday, as earnest of our corporate responsibility. It was up to me to find the two grand, as I was handling the business side of the enterprise.

"Mr. Widener still hesitated, as one who feared a trap. The sum involved could to him be of no consequence, a fleabite, but he fancied himself a sharp guy.

"Sharply sudden came a lull in the negotiative colloquy with all eyes and attention veered upon Mrs. Harriman; her brow bore a knitted texture just for a fleeting second or two, then came a far-away look evidently penetrating the distant realm of occult portent, for with beatific transition she suddenly exclaimed: 'Joe, my boy, it comes to me as clear as crystal, the augury is for you and fine success. Close the Deal with the gentlemen.'

"That was a lucky trance for us Rainmakers I may assure you. Without further ado, Mr. Widener accepted terms, extended a handshake to me along the diameter of the friendly little circle. The deal was a bet and was on as sure as you live. On Mrs. Harriman's suggestion we adjourned to the Turf & Field Club for a snack and a service of illicit but authentic Irroy *brut*.

"With laughter and banter the gathering broke up, Mrs. Harriman, womanlike, having the last word. She expressed the thought to Dr. Sykes—said she, 'Well, Doc, your partner, Jim, is quite a lawyer fellow, isn't he?' The Good Doctor said I was not a man of the law.

" 'What has he ever done?' the lady inquired.

"Replying, Dr. Sykes rejoined—'Well, up in the Lehigh Valley once he talked a mocking bird out of a tree.'

"With an all around expression of good luck and high hope for keeping that rain away from the door we all went our various ways. We the Rainmakers stood to make ten thousand dollars if every day was clear, or lose four thousand dollars if it rained every day.

"But where would I get that two thousand dollars in those Hooverized days of tight money? Why, sure enough, there he was—dear old Mike the Bite, a real natural. 'Fade my four for the Lord's sake,' as Dr. Orlando Edgar Miller would say on occasion.

"Making my way from the haunts of the Haute Bourgeoisie in the Turf & Field to the moiling fringe of the Betting Ring, I braced him.

"I found him in good spirits; his tip for the third race, Baba Kenny, had won, although paying only even money. That had meant fifty-three-times-two-dollars profit to him, however, as well as satisfaction, and he had bet it back on a filly named Chalice in the fifth, which was just coming up. Our conversation and the jollification in the Clubhouse had consumed considerable time. 'I got it right from Ollie Thomas, the clocker,' he said to me, 'and she is 25 to 1 in the ring.' That was one occasion on which my adherence to nonspeculation proved costly, for the filly came down in front, a gray by Stefan the Great, she took the lead from the first jump and increased it with every stride, a *pisseuse*.

"Availing of the auspicious moment, I said, 'Willie, I have an opportunity to make a good score, but I need the use of two grand until Futurity Day.' And I explained to him as much of the project as I thought necessary.

" 'When I see you two buzzing Mr. Widener and Mr. Schaumberg yesterday out there on the lawn I wondered what you could be up to now,' he said.

"I averred abiding faith in Dr. Sykes's powers, but Willie was a man of occult intuition himself. 'It looks like the Racing Association made a dutch book,' he said. 'You got a good bet there.'

" 'I will pay you $2,200 next Saturday,' I promised him. 'If you wish, I will give you a note.'

" 'No need of that,' the Bite said. And he got his checkbook out of the drawer of the oldfashioned cash register and wrote out a check, telling me I could have it certified at his bank next morning, but it wasn't necessary—Mr. Widener knew him. I heard tell afterwards that when Mike the Bite died, in 1946, he was worth $600,000 in securities and property.

"And that was our last major obstacle overcome. We were turning into the stretch, with a clear field in front of us and in a contending position. Such loans could be negotiated only on the Race Track, where there was to be found a breed of men and a business method, together with an instinct, found nowhere else. But the noisome breath of the mechanical maw of the mutuels has changed all that, and the Old Breed is dying out.

"I carried the check back to the Racing Secretary's Office. Mr. Schaumberg smiled when he saw the signature. 'You couldn't have a better man on your side,' he said.

"Now we were set to go, but we had only about thirty-six hours left to install all our apparatus, for the Good Doctor declaimed he needed a start of a few hours to dispel rain clouds that might converge upon the track Saturday noon. 'It is not an instantaneous process,' he said. 'There are some types of clouds I can dispel with one punch, but others require a couple of hours of softening up before I shoot it to them.'

"My role changed. Instead of a silver-tongued advocate I now became a construction superintendent."

At this point in my reading I became a trifle boorish. "Colonel," I said to my old friend, "do you mean to say this really happened?"

A pained expression contracted the Colonel's nostrils, but he recovered quickly.

"I expected you'd ask that sooner or later, Joe," he said. "Anybody would. And so I brought along a few old clippings from New York newspapers of that period that I happen to have preserved at the Dixie. There are more in the newspaper collection of the New York Public Library."

I had not attended any race meetings in the summer of 1930 myself—I had been working out of town—and I had assumed as I read along that the Colonel was writing about a scheme that had abutted in fiasco. I was waiting for the point in the manuscript at which the plan of the Rainmakers would go sour.

"Allow me to introduce my exhibits at the proper place in the narration," the Colonel said. "The points at which they are appropriate are marked in the manuscript."

So I read on.

"It was agreed we, the Rain Preventers, were to have at disposal every possible facility available at trackside, including the fine old disused Clubhouse at the head of the stretch, abandoned when the finish line was moved in 1926, and a constricted area of about one half acre at the head of the Widener Course, the straightaway down which the celebrated Futurity is run off annually. Sweeping down past the long grandstand, on the afternoon of Friday, Sept. 5, 1930, the observer arriving by the old Clubhouse would have seen piles of our paraphernalia and materials with workmen and installators standing about awaiting our instructions.

"Inside the old Clubhouse on the top floor, busy as the proverbial bees, Dr. Sykes and his Mrs. were directing workmen in the setting up of the two heavy Vibrator Units and the Chemicalized Repository; I am not adept in machinery so I cannot describe their aspect more technically than to say they looked ominous. The lady, noisy as a steam tea kettle, had just issued orders that no person might enter 'the laboratory' from this moment on except by presentation of a Permit Card.

"The weird-looking Detonatory Compound at the head of the Widener Course had been completed during the morning and its equipment completely installed. Under the experienced eye of the Doctor and my urgings, vehement rather than initiate, all matters had progressed as per schedule and we would open on the morrow.

"There was little architectural ingenuity employed in the design of the Compound thus established out in deep right field; it was a one-room structure made of plain lumber, a pentagon 16 feet high in height and 12 feet on a side, with an earth floor and no doors and no windows, an important point counter-espionage-wise. A veritable packing box. Entrance was made through a tunnel of 9½ feet from an entrance immediately to the north of the layout—you had to bend down to get in.

"Sprouting from the Roof were two Vibratory Rods of shiny steel and within an evil looking contraption best described as suggesting an abandoned oldtime Refrigerator with an electric charged battery, quite concealed, and a washtub full of the most noxious-smelling chemicals outside a slaughter house."

The Colonel had next pasted up a clipping from Audax Minor's department in *The New Yorker* of that September 13, 1930.

"The rain control machine is very hush-hush. Both the negative and positive actions, which are interchangeable, are under guard. The five-sided shack in the hollow near the training track interested us most. There is something cabalistic about it, with planks and two-by-fours laid out in curious designs around it, and the five scantlings nailed to the sides of the shed that shelters the remote radio control with a spider web of wires. Then, too, there's the big five-pointed star strung with radio aerial wire and festooned with ornaments from discarded brass beds and springs from box mattresses. The star always faces the way the wind blows. I'm quite sure Dr. Sykes has read *Rootabaga Stories* and how, 'on a high stool, in a high tower, on a high hill, sits the Head Spotter of the Weather Makers,' for he has a platform like a starter's box, several feet higher than the shed, from which he may direct the magnetic impulses — or he may be practicing to be a starter."

The Colonel's manuscript continued:

"Audax was never in a position to describe the interior. Mr. Widener himself was admitted only once to the Holy of Holies, and in negotiating the low tunnel suffered the sacrification of a $250 imported English suit draped by Carabis of 3 Creechurch Lane, London, and the wreckage of a solid gold wrist watch presented to him by Lord Derby, another racetrack promoter. Once in he looked around in amazement but received a convincer when the Good Doctor coyly edged him into contact with the rusty steel shell of the Detonatory Giant; old man John Franzel, the Lord High Executioner in the Death House at Sing Sing, never was more facile in the feathering of a switch than Dr. Sykes, for the tall Mr. Widener received an electric shock that left no further doubt in his mind but that the occult forces of nature and the Detonatory Pulsations of Higher Physics were at work in the Grand Cosmic Order.

"As a survivor, he afterwards expressed to the panting Newspapermen, a week later, that he felt lucky to escape the lair and snare of Dr. Faustus with his life. Yes sir, it's true; it's facts and history.

"The only Scribe to make the tunneled passage and live to tell the tale was Mr. Ned Brown, then the Sporting Editor, New York *World*, and he became teetotally bald within five days and has remained denuded ever since, complete and totally, yea verily.*

---

* This is a house joke. Ned Brown, an old friend of the Colonel's, who is at present editor of the sterling publication *Official Wrestling*, was bald before he ever heard of Dr. Sykes, and denies that he ever penetrated into the Paracelsian Dungeon. He was in 1930 not sporting editor, but boxing columnist of the *World* (his column was called "Pardon My Glove") and spent most of his summer afternoons at the race

"Between the Compound and the Laboratory, a distance of a good Yorkshire Mile, ran the Ethereal Conduit upon which traveled with the speed of Light augmented thirty-thousand-fold the initiatory Pulsations to the Vibrator, and thence, via the antennae, to the natural Air Waves and channeled Coaxial Appendixtum.

"Without the permission of Consolidated Edison, the devious Sykes pair diverted from the blue ambient some 32,400 kilowatts of electric energy daily to the Ethereal Conduit, thereby greatly annoying, and in some remote instances, totally frustrating, the good House Wives of Hempstead Plains busy with their can openers and electric stoves in the preparation of the evening meal for the lowly husbandman plodding his weary way homeward at day's end. From that day to this, Edison has not even filed a bill let alone received compensation for service rendered.*

"But, ah, back to the good old Clubhouse. The scene suggested the gauze and tinsel of the Bazaar of Bagdad, for here in long rows stood bright-colored glass jars, containing the various elemental chemicals used in explosive composition which in turn discharged upon the Air Currents the silver-crested Eidems which dispelled aqueous concentrations on contact, thus lessening the incidence of rain precipitation. From the top of the Vibrator, similar in grotesque appearance to the one set up at the Compound, ran an insulative tubing to the Ethereal Conduit jutting out from the building's rooftop to the skies above."

"What was really in those jars?" I asked the Colonel.

"I think it was colored water," he said, "but the Good Doctor never told me." I returned to my reading:

---

track, since, as he explains, he did not have to go to work until evening and he always had a badge. As a spectator he remembers full well the Colonel's surface activities at the racecourse in behalf of the Weather Control Bureau, he says, but he did not enter into the subterranean.

"When I was a cub reporter," says Mr. Brown, recalling an era virtually Triassic, "Jimmy Macdonald was already a top turf writer. So when I ran across him at Belmont, we used to chew over the rainmaking business, in which he was then engaged."

* I hope this passage does not bring down upon the Colonel a posse of collectors from the Edison Company. He is still non-holding.

"Hours after the running of the last race the General Staff of the Rain Preventers and a numerous detail of workmen remained at the Laboratory and the Compound. Every last item had been perfected in readiness for the great scientific enterprise of the morrow.

"Lights twinkled in the Clubhouse and away across midfield under the rising Harvest Moon the eerie structure of the Compound loomed in ghostly outline; across on the backstretch the Recreation Center, where foregather nightly the Trainers, Grooms, Swipes, and Gallop Boys, stood out in full glow, and a bonfire at the entrance to the main track which nightly incinerates the trashy odds and ends engendered during the busy daytime hours shone its red fire while its illuminant rays disclosed a circle of men and boys busily engaged in what appeared to the trained eye of the old Frontiersman, peering through the lenses of Mrs. Sykes's imported French Lemaire binoculars, a roaring oldtime Crap Game in full locomotion.

"The yawning grandstand stood out against the night skies like a hulking Naval Aircraft Carrier, stranded, silent, and menacing, against the background of sentient silence, a fearsome suggestion of what might happen should it rain ten hours hence; here and there over the vast expanse the searching lights of the night patrol of Pinkertons in protectory guard of the giant plant twinkled their assurance of an undeviating maintenance of their faithful Watch. Gallant Fox and Questionnaire, entered to contend in the Lawrence Realization Stakes, worth fifty thousand dollars to the winner, next day at one mile and five furlongs, were wound up no tighter than we."

10. "LA GRANDE SEMAINE"

"This is the day of days. At eight o'clock in the morning a cold gray mist came in off Jamaica Bay and overcast the whole backstretch area but only for a brief moment, for as the last batch of horses working out with their Trainers and Swipes had departed the quarter-stretch, the mists disappeared with them, and a golden sweep of sunshine overspread the scene, bringing much joy and hope to the inwardly sweating coterie of Rain Preventers.

"All that happened was it cleared up, but naturally we took full credit for it. We had engaged a publicity man, at two hundred dollars for the week, and he invited all interested Newspapermen to drop in at the Sykes's town house, any time after hours, and sample Mrs. Sykes's Pisco Punch, a drink whereof she professed to have the ancient Peruvian formula, delivered to her by a medium who had wheedled it from the ghost of the Inca High Priest during a séance in Riverview, California. Naturally the press was not unfavorably disposed towards us, and we were away running.

"The funny thing about it is that a lot of the other people around the track began to believe there was something in it as soon as they read it in the newspapers. Racetrack habitués are in any case given to superstition, as the Bite daily demonstrated, and I sometimes encounter oldtime turfites even today who will asseverate with conviction that Professor Sykes must have had something.

"The day was a success extraordinaire. Twenty-five thousand persons paid admission, an excellent attendance for those depressed days, and William Woodward's mighty three-year-old colt, Gallant Fox, prevailed by a mere nose over James Butler's Questionnaire, his keenest rival. Gallant Fox had been beaten only once in his career—in the Travers at Saratoga, on a muddy track. We of the Weather Control Bureau could flatter ourselves that we had preserved him from a second such disaster. We received, however, no token of recognition from Mr. Woodward, which saddened us, for his horse had won $29,160, no meager increment. I shall always remember a sentence written by George Daley, of the *World*, recounting Gallant Fox's victory:

" 'One hundred yards from the wire the Fox appeared to hang and looked beaten, but just when a sob went up from the throats of many, he again settled to his bitter, grinding task and he prevailed.' In the secondary feature, the Champagne Stakes for two-year-olds, Mate, a horse destined to win the Preakness Stakes the following spring, defeated the immortal Equipoise by a head.

"But the most pleasing feature of the day for us, the Rain Preventers, occurred at 6:00 P.M. when, without demurrer and amid general acclaim, we collected our first check for $2,500. 'Weather Clear; track fast,' the chart said.

"After cooling out we decided to pay Willie Beeson, the Bite, his two thousand dollars forthwith, and the two hundred dollars interest on the following Saturday as promised. So, after the proper endorsement by Dr. Sykes as President and myself as Treasurer of the Weather Control Bureau I scampered over to the stand where the Bite was making all secure for the night.

"The Bite seemed as tickled as I was at our success. He said, 'You boys just forget that two hundred dollars. Getting the big chunk back is good enough for me.'

"The next five racing days were like a dream. Weather clear; track fast. We collected one thousand dollars every night. The newspaper men and women were our chief trouble. We wanted to avoid too detailed disclosure, because the Good Doctor and I felt that if we went through this one undefeated, we might get more racing contracts. In the middle of the week the feature editor of the *Telegram*—it hadn't become the *World-Telegram* yet—had a brainstorm. Home radios, as the mind of man runneth not to the contrary, had not achieved perfection in 1930. People were wont to exchange remedies for static, as for horse lumbago in days of bucolic old. Dr. Sykes, unfortunately, had let it be bruited about that we had one of the most powerful radio installations in the Western Hemisphere, and the editor sent a reporter out to ask the Good Doctor if that might not be responsible for the radio interference now so prevalent in Queens and Nassau counties on both sides of Belmont Park, where the *Telegram* was trying to build circulation. The Doctor, although denying him ingress to the sanctum sanctorum, oracled that it might. The *Telegram* published the story, with one of those playful leads about how 'householders who have been wondering why their pet radio programs sound like jabberwocky can blame it all on Dr. G.A.I.M. Sykes.'

"In a couple of days two inspectors from the Federal Communications Commission appeared at Belmont and insisted on examining our installation. After looking it over they exonerated us, naturally. But some revengeful Hildy Johnson who had over-indulged in our Pisco Punch, a skull-popper, got wind of their visit and interviewed them. The result was a first-page story in the *World* saying that the inspectors had minimized the efficacy of our equipment, maintaining its radiaction was imperceptible.

"We chose to ignore it as a canard, standing upon results for the authentification of our claims. The beautiful Indian summer weather brought on a track lightning-fast with a dusty cushion flying at all times. Belief in the efficacy of our manipulations even caused us some embarrassment when an associate of Dutch Schultz propositioned the Good Doctor to bring on a heavy rain overnight because the boys had a good spot for a mudder in the fifth race on the morrow. 'Mud brings this mule up thirty pounds,' the emissary enlightened us. 'We been running him on the fastest tracks we could find and he hasn't finished better than next to last since Christmas. He'll go away at 40 to 1.' They offered us ten thousand down and a bet of another ten going for us. The Good Doctor wanted to take him up. It was then I began to look askance at the old boy, wondering if perchance he had begun to believe he was genuine. I talked him out of it, saying that if we failed to produce good weather for the Association we would forfeit only two thousand dollars, but if we failed to produce a deluge for the mob we would die the death horrible. 'And there is always a chance of a slipup, Doc,' I told him. So we told the hood we would do our best, but could promise nothing. When the next day dawned clear, as usual, they scratched the horse, and I breathed as with a sense of calamity averted.

"The situation was complicated by the intervention presently of another mugg, who represented himself as a friend of Al Capone, requesting assurance of a fast track for the sixth on the same day his competitor had asked mud for the fifth. They had a speed horse going and would bet a couple of thousand for us. 'We will do our best,' I said, 'but promise nothing.' The horse come in at 4 to 1 but the hoods would give us only four thousand dollars, pretexting they had been unable to get down all the money they had intended to bet. We professed indignation but pocketed the four thousand.

'You will pay us the balance the next time you come here to get any weather,' I told the plenipotentiary, 'or no dice. The Honest Rainmaker hath spoken.'

"Coming up to Saturday, Futurity Day, the last inning, it begins to look like Dr. Sykes, with good support from the Rainmakers' infield, is on the way to a No Hitter victory over the elements, and the Rainmakers could afford to sit back and enjoy the hubbub their advent had engendered on the Race Track, in Society, and within the Mystic Circles of the Town. We had banked six checks in succession, one for $2,500 and five for a grand each and were $7,500 in hand and in front at the Night & Day Bank at Broadway and Fortieth, Manhattan, beside the $4,000 bonus legitimately acquired from the Speedhorse Boys. I will note here that of the first five days of the meeting, without the intervention of the Ethereal Conduit and the Giant Detonator, on only one had there been rain. Skeptics continued to suggest we were riding with the season.

"Certainly the old Ford Model T engine in the Vibrator at the Laboratory had been servicing us just dandy, while the Galaxy of Varicolored Bottles and their chemical content had played a role in noble inspiration. There were sixteen of these Bottles of all manner of shade and tint suggesting the oldtime Drug Store with its window display of tiger fat, snake serum, and good luck potion in huge glass demijohns. The ancient Cigar Store highbred wooden Indian, could he come to life, might have had a good snicker at the spectacle.

"We could win $2,500 on the last day, if the weather remained fair, enabling us to pocket our fee intact, or take only $500 if it rained and we had to cough up our $2,000 forfeit. In any case the campaign averred itself a glorious victory, and Mrs. Sykes decided to throw herself around socially and hospitably by giving a soiree at the Red Room of the Hotel Imperial, Herald Square, Manhattan, the night after the Futurity, and 330 invitations were sent out, saying bring your friends.

"On the last day there was a precipitation no more substantial than that from an atomizer, but we accepted our responsibilities, however we might have felt, inwardly, about the Bourgeoisie exacting its Pound of Flesh on such a technicality. The races drew 25,000 paid admissions, as they had the previous Saturday, and the great Jamestown, owned by George D. Widener, the President's brother, won the Futurity by a nose from the great Equipoise, with Mate third. The total stakes were $121,760, of which the victor's share was $99,600. The Grande Semaine thus ended pleasantly for all concerned: the Westchester Racing Association, which had maintained its attendance; the Widener family; and even the general public, which had heavily backed Jamestown, a favorite at odds of 11 to 5.

"But most especially was it a victory for the United States Weather Control Bureau, which showed a net profit of eight thousand dollars in eight days including a nonprofitable Sunday, not bad on an investment of zero capital, and in addition to the unofficial supplementary income of four grand from the Mob.

"Mr. Widener, in handing over the final five-hundred-dollar check, thanked us for our satisfactory services, and said he hoped to see us back again the following season. I understand that to the end of his days he deprecated derision of Dr. Sykes and his theories. He maintained that the United States Weather Bureau, whose meteorologist ridiculed the Good Doctor, had little cause to carp, when its own predictions for the New York area were notoriously inaccurate."

I looked up from the last page of the story of the Honest Rainmaker.

"Did you ever work the dodge again?" I asked.

The Colonel shook his head. "The newspapers killed it," he said. "But poor old Dr. Sykes assisted them. He walked right into a haymaker. I should have kept him incommunicado with his arcane impedimenta. It seems that right at the top of his success some Park Row wag had accused him of ineffectuality and taking a free ride. The old boy, incensed, had said that he would show he *could* control weather, by producing rain as soon as his contract was finished. Monday, September 15, the next racing day after the Futurity, was set for the test. The old boy, who was really pretty weatherwise, the result of long speculative observation, may have believed that with the approach of the September equinox the weather was in fact due to change. The clouds on Futurity Day bore out in a general way this prognostication. But he overweened himself.

"He promised these reporters that he would produce torrents of

rain on the track between two-thirty and four-thirty on Monday afternoon. The next day's papers chronicled the event. I was not even
out at the track myself, for the Doctor had purposely neglected to
inform me of his foolhardy undertaking. If he had pulled it off it
would have been a great publicity stunt. But when you are sitting
pretty you should refrain from endangering your position; it is like
breaking up a full house to draw for four of a kind.

"The day dawned bright and sunshiny, the papers reported. The
mockers assembled just before post time for the first race, when the
Good Doctor strode out to his cavern and interred himself. Almost
immediately clouds began to gather. At three he emerged from the
depths and informed observers that there would be a whale of a
storm at four. He explained that he needed the intervening time to
assemble more clouds. It was cloudy and threatening all afternoon,
but the deadline came and passed without an obedient drop, and
the old Doc looked mighty chapfallen.

"Colonel Matt Winn, who had made us a tentative offer to prevent rain at the Churchill Downs meeting in Kentucky, dropped the
proposition like an option on a horse that proves unsound, and the
deluge of derision breaking upon our heads deterred Mr. Widener
himself from extending another contract. So, as once before in California, the rainmaker's art died the death, not to be revived for a
score of years. You have to have an airplane now to practice it, and
I am too old to qualify for a pilot's license."

"And what happened to old Doc Sykes?" I asked.

"I don't know," the Colonel said. "I haven't heard from or of
him in many a year, and if he's still alive he must be near ninety."
(Dr. Sykes still is alive, or was as late as September 1952, I learned
subsequently. And he is, or was, only about as old as the Colonel.
But they had apparently lost contact during the biographical inter-
stice.)

He appeared to find insufficient solace in his beer. Then a recollection cheered him.

"Joe," he said, "you should have had a snort of Mrs. Sykes's
Pisco Punch. It was a grand party. Sherry did the catering and the
Philharmonic Chamber Music Quartet entertained the guests play-

ing everything from *Wozzeck* to 'Turkey in the Straw.' The Banjo-Eyed Kid, Coon-Can Artie, and Commodore Dutch lent their arms to the season's debutantes preferred for the grand march. But the Pisco Punch constituted the standout.

"It was said New York had not before ever seen or heard of the insidious concoction which in its time had caused the unseating of South American governments and women to set world's records in various and interesting fields of activity. In early San Francisco, where the punch first made its North American appearance in 1856, the police allowed but one drink per person in twenty-four hours, it's that propulsive. But Mrs. Sykes served them up like *pain, à discrétion*, as the signs used to say in front of the little restaurants in Paris, meaning you could have all the bread you wanted. As a consequence, discretion vanished.

"Two hours after the salon had gotten under way even the oldest gals were still hunting the bartenders. Many of the old-time veteran Cellini, who hadn't scaled a garden wall in forty years, made a double score for themselves that evening, a memorable amoristic occasion. It was a famous victory, said little Peterkin. What I tell you about it now will be little noted and soon forgotten, but what those women did will be long remembered."

Daylight died in Forty-fifth Street outside the Palace Bar and Grill, and the Honest Rainmaker, who seldom feels in form before electric-light-time, continued to perk up.

"Joe," Colonel Stingo said, "last summer a tout introduced me to an Argentine trainer who knows a lot of people who own cattle ranches down there. Anyplace there are ranches they must need rain. If I had the courage of my convictions I'd go out and buy myself a Spanish grammar."

II. THE LIFE SPIRITUAL

When I first worked upon Colonel Stingo to set down his memoirs, he said, "You don't know what you're getting into, Joe. I am not the fine man you take me to be."

My effort to set him right on that score resulted in an estrangement, but we became friends again.

At another time he appeared to believe I was giving him too much of the worst of it, for he said:

"It is only a boob that conducts an enterprise in such a manner that it leads to embroilment with the law. I myself have never collided with it head on. But I have had many associates less wise or fortunate. One was Dr. Orlando Edgar Miller, a Doctor of Philosophy of the University of the Everglades, Rushton, Florida. Dr. Miller, when I first met him, was of appearance preeminent. Sixty years old, straight as an arrow, with snow-white hair and black eyelashes. He affected a Panama hat, Palm Beach suit, and white buckskin shoes even in the dead of a New York winter. He presented an undeviating outward semblance of sanctity, but he was a deviator, a dear old fellow. Having drawn the multitude toward him, first thing you know he had his hands in all their pockets.

"During the course of the revivals he conducted, frequently lasting for weeks if the supply of boobs held out, he professed a diet of one orange a day, but he was a practiced voluptuary. He did not like oranges, but he ingested plenty other comestibles. 'We eat too much and no mentality can be alert when the body is overfed,' he used to proclaim in Carnegie Hall, where he lectured to throngs, and then he would take a taxi to a speakeasy called the Pennwick and eat a steak with a coverture of mushrooms like the blanket of roses they put on the winner of the Kentucky Derby.

"After that he would plunge his fine features in eight or nine seidels of needled beer, about forty proof, a beverage worthy of revival, for it combined the pleasant Gambrinian taste with an alcoholic inducement to continue beyond the point of assuagement. Or he would decimate a black bottle of Sandy Macdonald Scotch landed at Rockaway Point and conveyed fresh to the table by courtesy of Big Bill Dwyer. Scotch, like the lobster, tastes best when fresh from the ocean, a truth which we have forgotten since repeal.

"But let him, in the lobby of Carnegie Hall after one of his meetings, be introduced to a man with upwards of fifty thousand dollars and he would ostentatiously gnaw an orange peel. It was my duty to keep him informed of the financial status of the potentially regenerate, a task for which I was well-qualified by my experience as credit man for Tex Rickard's old Northern gambling house at Goldfield, Nevada, and in a similar capacity for Canary Cottage at Del Monte, California, and the late Colonel Edward Riley Bradley at his Casino, Palm Beach, Florida. Many a man rife with money makes no outward flaunt. His habiliments, even, may be poor. But, Joe, when it comes to rich men, I am equipped with a kind of radar. The houses I worked for collected on ninety-five percent of markers, an unchallenged record.

" 'Not the mythical bacilli but improper breathing causes tuberculosis,' this old Dr. Miller would hold forth in public. 'Among the ancient races who understood proper breathing there was no such disease.' The cure he espoused was by the laying on of hands, calisthenics, and giving the right heart, and the women flocked to be laid hands on, even the most buxom averring a fear of dormant maladies. In his pulpit appearances he stressed spiritual values—Biblical exegesis, personality, and love. He advised women to pull their husbands' hair to prevent baldness. He was a regular cure-all.

"He was accompanied on his forays by the Countess Bonizello, a lady born in Davenport, Iowa, but who had married, she recounted, an impoverished member of the Italian nobility, since deceased. She had at any rate been long enough on the Continent to acquire that little froufrou, and spoke a certain patois—French and English. She gave evidence of having been in early life a beauty, and she was full of guile and could handle men and was a real good fellow. When they hit a town she would take a suite at the best hotel and he would assume a simple lodging in accord with his ascetic pose. She would play the role of a wealthy devotee who had followed him from Europe, platonically, of course, and she would organize the social side of the revival.

"She had in fact met him in England, so they said. There, in 1914 just before the First World War, he had conducted revivals in the Albert Hall. He induced the Duke of Manchester to put the okay on a line of credit for him, and was going to build a sanatorium for the cure of tuberculosis by his methods when unfortunately a woman died under his ministrations, and the British Medical Association, 'captious without a point of criticism,' the old Doctor used to say, had him hauled before a Court. 'As if other practitioners never lost patients,' he said. 'Why, an Austrian prince named Hohenlohe paid me a thousand quid, when the pound was worth $4.86 and several mils, because he was so pleased with the way I treated him. That was what inflamed Harley Street against me.' The Court let him off with a reprimand, but the publicity queered his act in England, and he came home. Here he emphasized the spiritual shots in his bag, preaching that right living is the road to health, but the American Medical Association suspected he was laying hands in private, and he had to put up with persecution which seldom affected his monetary success."

A look of reminiscent admiration suffused the old Colonel's countenance.

"Of my adventures with Dr. Miller I could speak endlessly," he said, "but my purpose is only to illustrate the fine line between *fas* and *nefas*. There was no need for him to transgress that line. He was a man of great animal magnetism, reminding me of the appellation by Max Lerner of General Dwight D. Eisenhower—'the charismatic leader,' which Mr. Lerner says means one you follow because he seems to have a kind of halo around him. Dr. Miller once said he was good for $250,000 a year on a purely spiritual plane. He drew Tease from the repentant like soda through a straw.

"But eventually the day came when the old Doctor overweened himself. Some Hollywood sharks sold him the idea of becoming a movie star. The old ham could fancy himself and the Countess bedazzling unseen multitudes. There seemed to him nothing ludicrous in the proposition. Essentially he was a boob too. The idea was to form an independent producing company and sell stock to people who came to his revivals. The way of separating the sheep from the goats, to wit the holding from the non-holding, at these meetings was to distribute envelopes among the multitude, specifying that only contributions of a dollar or more were to be enclosed, and the donors were to write their addresses on the envelope if they wished free literature.

"The Doctor was not interested in the addresses of people with less than a buck. Such were requested to drop their coins in the velvet-lined collection box, where they wouldn't jingle. The jingle has a bad effect on suggestible people who might otherwise give folding money.

"We had a follow-up system on the names. Paid workers followed up each prospect. If, as occasionally occurred, they encountered a scoffer who had invested a buck just to see what would happen, the name was scratched from the mailing list. Incidentally they were pretty good estimators of a chump's net wealth. I went to one of a series of meetings an exegizer held at Carnegie Hall this winter, and the old operating procedure is still standard. We left no room for improvement.

"When we swapped towns with another big preacher, like Dr. Hall the hundred-dollar-Bible man, we sometimes swapped mailing lists. But we would always keep out a few selected prospects, and so, I suspect, would the other prophet. The ready-made list helped in the beginning, but the one you could trust was the one you made yourself. The purpose of this labyrinthian digression is to indicate that after ten years of listmaking, old Dr. Miller had a mighty lever to place in the hands of a stock salesman.

"I was assigned to write the scenario and it was unique, indisputably. It was the only one I had ever written. It was called the *Bowery Bishop* and was based on what I remembered reading about Jerry McCauley's Bowery Mission. Dr. Miller, of course, was to play the saintly missionary, and there were two young lovers. It had been intended that the Countess should play half the love interest, though her bloom was no longer of the first blush pristine, but at the last minute she backed out. She said there were reasons why she did not want her photograph too widely distributed. This was of good augury for the enterprise, the promoters said, as the film would be surer to click if the Doctor had the support of some well-known movie names.

"We engaged two great stars of the silent films to play the young lovers. With a scenario, stars, and a sucker list, the promoters were all set to go. The stock salesmen were getting twenty-five percent commission. The nature of the promotion literature was such, however, that I felt sure trouble impended. Purchasers were not only assured of a large profit, but guaranteed against loss. I declined office in the company. I went out to Honolulu to arrange a great Miller revival there, which was to begin simultaneously with the release of the picture, and when I returned to California, the inevitable had ensued.

"Stock had been sold to the amount of $320,000, of which $240,000 had been turned in to the treasury. With part of the $240,000 a picture had been made. But only a handful of theaters were available to show the film, which was, as one might expect, a turkey. The old Doctor, seized by foreboding, had hit the booze and played away the rest of the money on horses and the stock market, deluding himself that he might thus recoup solvency. I advised him to lam before the inauguration of the uproar, and he sought sanctuary in Australia, where I commended him to the good offices of some friends I had in the fight game there. The Countess Bonizello left by the same boat. I had one or two letters from him after he got out to Sydney saying he was making plenty Tease. The revival business in the Antipodes had been in a crude stage before he arrived, he wrote. The surpliced choir with which he embellished his performances and the social éclat imparted by the Countess had remedied all that.

"But such peripheral triumphs did not content him. In 1926 or so I had a letter from him dated Calgary, Alberta, and so I knew he had ventured back to the outskirts of the battlefield, and he was contemplating a new campaign. The next tidings were bad. He was under arrest, and California authorities were trying to extradite him. They did, and he got six.

"We disappeared from the surfaces of each other's conscious lives, like two submarines, interrupted in a mission of destruction, which submerge without the formalities of parting.

"Now," Colonel Stingo said, "we do a fade-out and pick up the thread of our narrative again in the winter of 1936. The place is New York and my condition is distinctly non-holding. I am inhabiting a rendezvous of the discomfited known ironically as the Little Ritz, on West Forty-seventh Street, in New York, and in the period subsequent to Dr. Miller's misfortune I have known many ups and downs, but now I am for the nonce down. I have the price of a meal, though not in a restaurant such as the Voisin, the Colony, or Shine's, and I am heading for the Automat. But before eating I decide to take a walk to increase my appetite, for I may not be able to raise the price of another repast that day. Chicken today, feathers tomorrow, and dear old Dr. Miller is far from my mind.

"It is snowing, and I cannot help regretting the climate of California, and perhaps conceding the foolhardiness of my renewed challenge to the metropolis. But as I pass the Union Church on West Forty-eighth Street I see a message of hope: the Rev. Orlando Edgar Miller is conducting a service there. I enter and there he is in the pulpit, as straight as ever. The ten years, including six with time off for good conduct, have touched him but lightly. I tried to make my advent unobtrusive, secreting myself in a side pew, but the dear old rascal made me immediately.

" 'I see among us a dear good friend, Mr. James Macdonald of California,' " he said. 'I am sure he has a Message for us. Will you come forward, Jim?' So I walked down the center aisle.

"Were you abashed?" I asked the Colonel. "Or were you prepared to speak after such a long spiritual layoff?"

"I have an invaluable precept for public speech," the Colonel said. "It is to think of five topics, one for each finger of the hand. On this occasion, I remember, I thought of the Christmas season, which it was, the miracle of the loaves and fishes, the Poor Little Match Girl, Oliver Twist, and Tiny Tim. I began by saying that as I gazed upon the countenance of my reverend friend, Dr. Miller, the Ark of the Covenant of the Lord had fallen upon me, and that I was moved beyond expression to find here, at this Christmas season, when so many were in want, a living reminder of the miracle of the loaves and fishes, whereby the Lord had provided for many although the supply of comestibles looked limited. My prospects for spiritual nourishment had looked bleak as I wandered down the cold street, I said, and then I saw the name of Orlando Edgar Miller and knew my hunger would be satisfied. These were the times when multitudes, like the Poor Little Match Girl, were expiring of hunger, spiritual hunger, and cold, not knowing that just around the corner was a man who might warm them and stoke them to Divine Grace. He was not angry when, like Oliver Twist in the story, they turned to him again and asked for More, evermore—and like Tiny Tim—

" 'We shall have to let Tiny Tim go until some other time,' that dear old rascal Doctor said, 'for we have so many other beautiful features of our services to complete before six o'clock, when we must vacate the premises according to the terms of our lease. This church is not ours alone, though I would willingly remain far into the night to hear the conclusion of Brother Macdonald's beautiful train of thought.'

"I could tell from his dear old face that he had a hard time restraining hilarity, knowing full well the purport of my parablism. He motioned me to a seat on the front bench until the end of the service. The collection, I was glad to see, was of comfortable proportions, including many envelopes. When he came down from the platform I went up and shook hands with him and he gave me the address in the West Seventies where he was living and told me to go on ahead up there and he would come along as soon as he had finished his routine of benevolent adieus. 'I must clinch my sales for God,' he said.

"I went on along up to the address, which was an old brownstone house that he had taken over in toto. The Countess was not in evidence but three hatchet-faced old secretaries, well past the mid-century, were. It was a ménage most circumspect, and I could sense that the field of the old scalawag's deviations had narrowed with the infirmities of age. The Florabels regarded me with some suspicion, as of an outwardly unsanctified appearance, but when the old boy arrived, he led me directly into his study.* There, having locked the door, he went to an old-fashioned wall safe and drew out of it a black bottle of unclerical demeanor and we went to it and had a fine time.

"We rode upon the flying carpet of reminiscence: for example

---

* A Florabel, in the Colonel's idiom, is the antithesis of a Lissome, his highest term of aesthetic praise for a female. It had its origin in his reaction to the newspaper photograph of a woman so named.

how we had prevailed upon one of the leading oyster growers of the Pacific coast, a Scandinavian gentleman, to endow a two-week revival featuring hymns with special lyrics composed in his honor, as: 'Thank you, Mr. Snorensen,' to the tune of 'Onward Christian Soldiers.' The lyrics were thrown upon a screen, as those of popular songs were in movie theaters of that era. I had first used this device to publicize a fight between Burns and an Australian heavyweight named Bill Squires, at Colma, California, in 1906. After the revival proper Mr. Snorensen treated all the executives of his company and their wives to an esatoric course with graduation ceremonies in white robes and white mortarboard hats and presented them all with fountain pens. We beat that squarehead for forty grand, and he had starved hundreds of oyster shuckers to death.

" 'Those were wonderful days, wonderful,' the dear old Doctor said. 'And by the way, Jim, we parted so hastily that I never did pay you the last week's salary you had earned.' This was a bow to convention, simply the old man's way of offering aid without embarrassment to me, for he knew full well that I had held out an ample share of the Hawaiian contributions to the revival he had never held there. So he slipped me a hundred, which in those Depression days was riches.

"When we had fortified ourselves enough to face those Gorgonic old spinsters we sallied forth and took them all out to a vegetarian restaurant where they stuffed themselves with nuttose and date pudding, and then the old Doctor put them in a taxi and said he and I would walk home together, since he had not completed his daily pedestrian exercise of fifteen miles. We went to Al Muller's bar north of Madison Square Garden and got stiff as boards, and finally the Ark of the Covenant of the Lord fell upon the old Doctor, and he spake.

" 'Jim, there is just one thing I have never been able to understand,' he said.

" 'Why did they leave you outside when they put me in?' "

(1952)

Boxiana

Sugar Ray and the Milling Cove

Part of the pleasure of going to a fight is reading the newspapers next morning to see what the sports writers think happened. This pleasure is prolonged, in the case of a big bout, by the fight films. You can go to them to see what *did* happen. What you eventually think you remember about the fight will be an amalgam of what you thought you saw there, what you read in the papers you saw, and what you saw in the films.

The films are especially insidious. During the last twenty seconds or so of the fight between Sugar Ray Robinson and Randy Turpin, for example, it seemed to me from where I sat, in the lower stand at the Polo Grounds, that Robinson hit the failing Turpin with every blow he threw—a succession of smashing hits such as I had never before seen a fighter take without going down. The films show that Robinson missed quite a few of them, and that Turpin, although not able to hit back, was putting up some defensive action until the last second—swaying low, with his gloves shielding his sad face, gray-white in the films. It was the face of a schoolboy who has long trained himself not to cry under punishment and who has had endless chances to practice, like an inmate of Dotheboys Hall. That's the way I now catch myself remembering Turpin's face in the last seconds, although I couldn't see it at the Polo Grounds because Robinson was between us and both were a good distance from me anyway. The face isn't gray-white in real life, but a kind of dun.

The films of the first nine rounds of the fight upset my original impressions in the same way. Those rounds seem exciting now, because I look for hints of what is to come in the tenth, which contained all the fight's excitement. I forget that when they were being fought I saw them only as nine very bad rounds, almost a hoax on the 61,370 spectators, who, in the consecrated formula, had paid $767,630 for the privilege of watching them. All they seemed likely to lead to was six more bad rounds and a decision that would be sure to provoke an argument, since the boxers were going nowhere at the same pace. In the third, or maybe the fourth, round, the fans in the general-admission seats began to clap in unison, as they do at small clubs when two preliminary boys either can't or won't fight. I wondered if either Robinson or Turpin had ever before been treated so disrespectfully. Their styles seemed just made to reduce each other to absurdity. But years from now, when I reminisce about the fight, I'll probably say it was tense all the way, and I'll believe it.

I still think the referee, Ruby Goldstein, was right to stop the fight; no referee should take it upon himself to gamble on a man's recuperative powers. One more punch like the ones Robinson was throwing might have ended the boxing days of any fighter—even Turpin, who is what *Boxiana* would have called "a prime glutton." *Boxiana* is one of my favorite books, and, because of the international nature of the fight, I had a refresher glance at it before going up to the Polo Grounds.

On the night of the fight I started out early, in the true Egan tradition. In his time, the migration to a fight would begin days in advance, when the foot-toddlers (fellows who couldn't afford horse-drawn transportation) would set out on the road for the rumored meeting place. Rumors were all they had to go on because in England at that time prizefighting, although patronized by the Prince Regent, was illegal. A day or so later, the milling coves and the flash coves (fighters and knowing boys) would set out in wagons or hackneys, with plenty of Cyprians and blue ruin (sporting girls and gin) to keep them happy on their way. The Cyprians counted on making new and more profitable connections later. Last of all, the Corinthians (amateurs of the fancy and patrons of pugilists) would take the road in their fast traps and catch up with the others in time to get their bets down before the fight. But blue ruin stopped many a wagon before it got there; milling coves and flash coves both were lushing coves.

Attendance at an old-time British fight was preceded, for all classes, by a visit to the pubs of the contending heros, to wish them success. In accordance with this tradition, at six o'clock on the evening of the Robinson-Turpin fight I made my way to Sugar Ray's, which is Robinson's pub, on the west side of Seventh Avenue between 123rd and 124th Streets. Improvements in transportation have made it unnecessary to start for a fight days in advance, unless one is to foot-toddle. I approached the pub by taxi, the equivalent of a hackney, but sans Cyprian, and disembarked on the northeast corner of Seventh Avenue and 124th Street, in front of the Citadel of Hope Mission, which was not getting much of a play. I got out there because if I'd got out on the Robinson side of the street I'd have had to step on somebody's feet. With the time to go to the fight drawing near, the sidewalk in front of his bar-and-grill had vanished. The sidewalk in front of the Hotel Theresa, which extends from 124th to 125th Street on the west side of Seventh Avenue, was similarly jammed with Harlemites, and the narrow traffic island in the middle of the avenue was also filled with Negroes, who were gazing up at the hotel.

A small colored boy, presumably from the Citadel of Hope, handed me a throwaway preaching class war. "There are two classes of people in the world—the righteous and the wicked," it read. "You belong to one of these two classes. Which?"

"Let me ask you a question," I said to the boy. "Who is up in that hotel?"

"Randy," the boy answered. "He's resting until the fight."

I looked about me and imagined the trade consequences of a Turpin victory. I could visualize the thousands of shoulders draped in British tweed, and the equal number of feet, now impacted one on another, encased in shoes by Maxwell of Dover Street. In Harlem, fashion follows the brave. It seemed to me I could already detect a slight premonitory change, in the accent of the first man who spoke to me, but he may have been a West Indian. "Randy is superior," he said. "He's overconfi*dence*. I mean he feel no fear."

I crossed the street and worked my way into the lobby of the

Theresa, which is the largest hotel under Negro management in America and about the busiest hotel anywhere—a contrast to its moribund last twenty years in white hands. Joe Louis was standing, almost unnoticed, with a group of friends near the door. He's still a favorite, but no novelty. Everybody was waiting for a look at Randy.

Coming out of the Theresa, I stood on the inner edge of the sidewalk and allowed myself to be propelled slowly half a block downtown, being carried past the Golden Glovers' Barbershop and the store-front office of Ray Robinson Enterprises. (Robinson is in almost as many businesses in Harlem as Father Divine was before that divinity moved to Philadelphia.) I detached myself from the current just in time to duck into Sugar Ray's, which is a narrow but deep saloon with walls of blue glass chips tastefully picked out with gold. The bar was as crowded as the street outside, but at the back of the place, where the bar ends, Sugar Ray's widens out enough to permit three parallel rows of tables, one row against each side wall and the third between them, and there were a few empty seats. Since I could find no place to stand up, I sat down at a table.

This rear section of Sugar Ray's is decorated with four huge photomontages, two on each side wall. Two show him making a fool of Kid Gavilan, the Cuban fighter, who is a competitor of his for local fame. Another shows Robinson bringing an expression of intensely comic pain to the face of the French middleweight Robert Villemain, a muscle-bound, pyknic type with a square head. The fourth shows him standing above Georgie Abrams, a skillful pugilist who is so hairy that when knocked down he looks like a rug. Abrams got up after his knockdown, but from the picture it doesn't seem as if he ever would.

I asked a man at the table next to mine, who looked like an old colored milling cove, whether the boss was around, and he said he wasn't. "He left about an hour ago," he said. "He's taking this one serious. He was carrying his bag, and I told him, 'Now, don't you stop on the way to do any training?'" Some women at the cove's table laughed, and so did I. I dined on bourbon and the largest, pinkest pork chops I have ever seen, priced at $1.65. "They're mighty good," I said to the cove, who seemed to be regarding me with interest. "They ought to be," he said. "I once fought a man eight rounds for not much more than that."

I approved of Robinson's decision to leave early. Drinking with customers just before a battle was a practice deprecated by Egan. There was, to give you an example from *Boxiana*, Dan Donnelly, an Irish heavyweight, who was never beaten but who fell dead in his own bar after drinking forty-seven whiskey punches with well-wishers. His epitaph read:

O'ERTHROWN BY PUNCH,
UNHARMED BY FIST,
HE DIED UNBEATEN PUGILIST!

A slim, earnest black man with a briar pipe in his right hand walked down between the tables, saying in a peremptory voice, "A hundred to seventy-five. A hundred to seventy-five." "*What* you betting?" another man asked him. "I bet Robinson," the man with the pipe said. "Everybody here betting him," the second man said. "That ain't no odds." The man with the pipe walked away, and I asked the second man, "Who do you think will win?" "Ray," he said. "Ray, sure. He always win when the chips are down." I did not tell him about the statement of Colonel Stingo, whom I had encountered the day before and who had seen the films of the London bout in which Turpin defeated Robinson for the middleweight championship. The Colonel said Turpin appeared to be a very strong boxer, and had kept crowding Robinson from the beginning of the bout. "Ray has never looked too good against a crowding fighter," the Colonel said, "and now he's getting old. He's got to make a different kind of a fight to win this one." He added that he had just been talking to Jack Kearns, the former manager of Jack Dempsey. Kearns had been out to Pompton Lakes to watch Sugar Ray train, and had said that he was "dry"—not sweating well—which is considered an indication of poor condition. "It'll take him a year to get back in shape," Kearns had told the Colonel. "Paris licked him."

When I arrived at the Polo Grounds, a short time before the first preliminary bout, the place was only half full, but the people running the show had already effected an almost complete strangulation of movement as far as the customers were concerned. By setting up wire gates between various sections of the stand, probably to prevent ticket holders from "creeping" forward to better seats than they had paid for, they had made long detours necessary for anyone trying to get anywhere. Since even the ushers, of whom there were few, didn't know where the temporary barriers were, they couldn't tell people how to avoid them. A lane so narrow that it could be threaded only in single file had been left between the lower-stand boxes and the first row of lower-stand seats, and customers coming in through runways at the ends of this lane had to struggle against each other to reach the aisles leading up into the stands. Once I had made it to my own seat, in the first row of the lower stand, the struggle provided a sort of preliminary to the preliminaries.

The "ringside" seats, which covered the baseball diamond and reached well into the outfield, were for the most part empty at that stage of the evening. They filled slowly; many of the people who buy them do not much like boxing but go to big fights so that they can talk about them afterward, and they seldom arrive before the main bout. But I knew they would be along; this was something you had to see, like *Guys and Dolls* or a van Gogh show at the Metropolitan. Midway through the preliminaries, hundreds of young hoodlums in Hawaiian shirts, all of whom had clearly come in on general admission—unless they had scaled the fence—dashed down the aisles of the stands in back of third base, vaulted the wire barriers with admirable ease, and hurtled onto the field, racing to occupy empty ringside seats. It was a concerted break, and there weren't nearly enough special cops to stop them. Once in a seat, each of these fellows would try to avoid attention until the rightful ticket holder arrived, upon which, after a conversational delaying action, the interloper would move to another empty seat, continuing to move until the lights went out for the main bout. Then, if evicted again, he would squat in an aisle. The specials were flushing them all through the show, in a succession of comedy chases. The rush, because it was so concerted, did not amuse me; in a previous decade and in other circumstances, the louts might have been wearing black or brown shirts, I thought, and a time might come when they would be again. The night was sweating hot.

I could identify one ticket holder who was already in his seat. He was a man who looks like Ethel Waters, especially when he has his mouth open, and who calls himself Prince Monolulu. He says he is an Ethiopian prince, and wears a bright-red jacket embroidered with the Star of David and the signs of the zodiac, as well as a headdress of ostrich plumes and a set of flowing skirts. These make him fairly easy to recognize if you have seen him once, and I had seen him several times in England—once at Epsom, plying his regular trade as a race-track tout, and on endless Sundays at Hyde Park Corner, where he preaches Zionism. I had read in the morning paper that he'd come over on a chartered plane with fifty other Turpin supporters. When working, Prince Monolulu shouts, at unpleasantly frequent intervals, "I got a 'orse!" and then, to those who gather around in response to his shouts, he tells about the dialogue between the camiknickers and the nightgown, winding up by selling his horse, on a folded slip of paper, for a modest half crown. I bought Black Tarquin from him at Epsom, and it beat twenty-four other horses, finishing eighth. At the Polo Grounds, I noticed, he was silent. He may have been molting.

In the very first preliminary, one boy knocked the other down for a count of nine in the first round, and the referee stopped the fight. This apparently exaggerated solicitude, I felt sure, could be attributed to the death of a preliminary fighter named Georgie Flores, who had been fatally injured when knocked out in Madison Square Garden a couple of weeks earlier.

In another preliminary Jackie Turpin, an older brother of the champion's and a featherweight, defeated a boy named Wamsley in six rounds. Jackie is a light tan, like his bigger brother, but on the night of this fight the resemblance ended there. I thought he boxed a bit like Jackie (Kid) Berg, an English lightweight of the thirties, getting inside fast and throwing dozens of punches, most of which landed but none of which seemed solid. Still, the other boy went down for short counts twice, and Turpin earned the decision. I knew that somewhere in the stands there were five hundred members of the *Queen Elizabeth*'s crew, and the cheering for the featherweight Turpin showed where they were sitting—behind the third-base line.

The semifinal was between two big Negro heavyweights, one of whom, apparently beaten, knocked the other out in the last thirty seconds. "How do you like that?" one of two Garment Center Corinthians on my right asked his companion. "Just before he landed the winning punch, he was supremely out."

Then the ring was full of fighters, the majority of them colored, being introduced to the crowd, and the belated ringside-seat holders were pouring in, a number of pretty women with them. Jersey Joe Walcott, then the heavyweight champion; Ezzard Charles, his predecessor; and Joe Louis entered the ring together and were introduced, one at a time; Louis got an ovation, although he was then just the champion-before-last. (When he walked out on the field to his seat before the semifinal, he was given a bigger hand than General MacArthur, who preceded him.) Louis looks like a champion and carries himself like a champion, and people will continue to call him champion as long as he lives.

The two seats at my left, which had been vacant all evening, were now occupied by a couple. The girl, a smashing blonde in a backless black evening dress, must have expected that she was going to sit out in ringside, where people could see her. A woman somewhere behind her said, but not to her, "I call that a vulgar way to dress." It seemed to cheer the blonde, but the man with her looked uncomfortable.

Everybody stood up for a long recorded version of "God Save the King," with a vocal chorus. It reminded me of the time they played the "Marseillaise" for Marcel Cerdan before he knocked out Tony Zale in Jersey City, and the machine wouldn't stop. "God Save the King" received polite applause. The applause for "The Star-Spangled Banner," which followed it, was tumultuous.

The principals came into the ring. Robinson, the challenger, was first—tall, slender, and dark brown, wearing a blue-and-white robe. He discarded the robe, revealing white trunks with a blue stripe, and jigged furiously up and down to limber his leg muscles. Turpin followed, in a yellow bathrobe over black trunks with a white stripe, sat down in his corner, and remained seated, even during the introduction, while Robinson stood and waved to the crowd. Robinson acted like a young, nervous fighter; Turpin, eight years his junior and fighting for the first time in this country, was calm as a Colchester oyster. When the bell rang, it was the same way. Robinson was making the play. Turpin wasn't crowding this time; he was taking it easy, as if sure Robinson would slow down. Jimmy Cannon, of the *New York Post*, wrote afterward that Turpin "moved with a clumsy spryness and appeared to be serenely anticipating Robinson's collapse." The trouble with this policy was that it gave the much older Robinson a chance to make his own pace, fighting in spurts and then resting. He was still about the fastest thing in the world for thirty seconds or so, as Turpin was to find out.

Turpin stood more like some of the illustrations of boxers in *Boxiana* than a modern fighter. He had his left knee far forward, the leg almost straight out, and all the weight of his body back. It made him hard to get at, but it also made it hard for him to get at Robinson. (I had often wondered, looking at those illustrations, how men could hit from that position. Now I understand why *Boxiana* lists so many fifty- and sixty-round fights.) When Turpin did hit— with marvelous speed, most of which was wasted in coming such a long way around—it was always at some curious angle. One punch for the body looked like a man releasing a bowling ball; another, a right for the head, was like a granny boxing a boy's ears. His jab was like a man starting his run for the pole vault. If he hit conventionally, from the shoulder, he would be less disconcerting, but he might also be one of the hardest hitters in history. For he is the strongest middleweight I have ever seen—built like a heavyweight, and tall, too. I haven't figured yet how he can be so big all around and still make 160 pounds.

Turpin was so strong that his unconventional blows shook Robinson when they landed, although Robinson knew that, according to the book, they shouldn't. When the warning whistle blew ten seconds before the beginning of the second round, Robinson stood up. I thought it a rash gesture, because it meant that now he would have to spend an extra ten seconds on his feet at every interval. If he stayed down, it would be a public confession that he was tired. Turpin sat the full minute.

"The kid's got nothin', nothin', absolutely nothin', " one of the fellows next to me began saying during the fifth or sixth round, meaning Turpin, and he continued to repeat it, like an incantation: "Nothin', nothin'. " He must have had a good bet on Robinson, because he sounded worried.

"If Turpin hasn't got anything, what's Robinson got?" I finally asked him. "It's even, isn't it?"

"Even?" He looked at me as if I were mad. "Turpin ain't took a round," he said.

The referee's card had four rounds for each fighter and one even, up to the tenth round.

A stout colored man in back of me was wearing a bright-green suit, a Tattersall waistcoat with a green stripe, a yellow tie, and a maroon silk shirt with two-inch white polka dots. If he had taken off jacket, waistcoat, and about forty pounds, he would have been dressed to ride for the Woolford Farm Stable, of Kansas City, Missouri. Every time Sugar Ray started a punch, this man would grunt like a bullfrog and then softly moan, as if enduring the agony of a shattered Turpin, even when the punch didn't land.

I was beginning to resent my neighbors bitterly by the time the tenth round came and Robinson, with his eye cut, either by a butt or by a blow, put together the really amazing attack that finished poor Turpin off—or didn't quite, according, next day, to Turpin's manager and to some of the British boxing writers, who hadn't been hit. When the referee stepped between the fighters and grabbed Turpin in his arms, I thought I had never seen a man so game or so beaten as the mulatto from Leamington Spa. Within a minute, the ring was full of policemen, who lined the ropes; I don't exactly know why, since there appeared to be no danger of a riot. There seemed to be nothing to argue about.

On the way down the ramp to the exit, I saw a sight that struck the proper note—a tall, grave, fair-haired man, with a pipe in his mouth, walking silently beside an equally grave blond boy of around fifteen, who was carrying a furled Union Jack. By contrast, as I got out onto Eighth Avenue, under the "El," I nearly bumped into three men who turned out to be sailors from the *Elizabeth*, and though they were wearing Turpin buttons in the lapels of their land-going clothes, they were all laughing. "I feel like 'iding my fice," one of them was saying. "What a 'iding 'e took!" "What I'm laughing at," said another, "was old Bill, 'ere. 'Go right in, Randy,' 'e says. 'What are you afraid of?' " They were, I felt, devoid of proper patriotic sentiment.

Since there were no taxis to be had and the subway entrances, choked with struggling human bodies, looked slightly less inviting in that heat than gas chambers, I started to foot-toddle down Eighth Avenue, hoping to encounter a cab along the way. After I'd gone a block or so, I was stopped by another British seaman, a square-faced bloke who looked as if he might once have boxed a bit himself. He wanted to know the way to the entrance to the Eighth Avenue subway I had just passed up. I told him, and added consolingly, "I never saw a gamer man than your fellow." "Oh, 'im," the seaman said. " 'E's a good lad, sir, but no experience. No defense. No class, sir. Forget about 'im." This, too, seemed hardly right.

Eighth Avenue, from the Polo Grounds south, is Harlem, but it's poor Harlem, unrelieved by bright lights or jive. I walked past store fronts fetid with the smell of old vegetables, and dismal houses that never were much and now are less, where ill-dressed Negroes sat on the doorsills. Other people walking from the fight, or perhaps a radio bulletin, had carried the news ahead of me. (The fight itself, of course, hadn't been broadcast or televised—for New York audiences, at any rate.) All along the way, the people in the doorways knew that Sugar Ray had won, but they didn't seem excited. Perhaps it was the heat.

I stopped in at a bar at 145th Street for a drink—it was not festive there, either—and then switched over to Seventh Avenue, still looking for a taxi. At 143rd and Seventh, two men in their twenties were bullying a boy of about eighteen. They had him backed up against an automobile, and whenever he turned on one, the other would kick him. A crowd of women had gathered around, at a safe distance. The men had been drinking and looked rough. "You let him alone!" a woman cried. "He's only a young boy!" In a nearby saloon, there was another row going on. Just then, I sighted a cab headed uptown empty, and I stopped it and got aboard. "Drive me downtown, past Sugar Ray's," I said.

As we approached the Theresa, the avenue was so jammed up with traffic that we could barely move. People were packed around the safety islands and overflowed onto the street. Somebody was beating an oilcan like a tomtom, and a tall, limber man was dancing in the street. Any idea I may have had of stopping at Sugar Ray's for a nightcap left me when I saw the crowd in front of the door.

My maid walked by Sugar Ray's a couple of days after the fight, and she said there were twenty-five Cadillacs parked in front of the place. "Any that weren't 1951 had to double-park," she said. "His is a big pink one. He was standing outside, with just a small patch over his eye, and everybody that came by shook hands with him."

I went up to Sugar Ray's myself on the following Sunday, but it was very quiet, with only a girl about five feet tall behind the bar, and a monumental cash register and a sign that read, "Try Sugar Ray's Bolo, 55 cents." The bolo, which is named after one of Robinson's favorite punches, is made of rum. There were enough customers to keep the girl busy, but they all looked tired, as if they had been celebrating for several nights in a row and had just come in for pick-me-ups.

(1951)

Ahab and Nemesis

Back in 1922, the late Heywood Broun, who is not remembered primarily as a boxing writer, wrote a durable account of a combat between the late Benny Leonard and the late Rocky Kansas for the lightweight championship of the world. Leonard was the greatest practitioner of the era, Kansas just a rough, optimistic fellow. In the early rounds Kansas messed Leonard about, and Broun was profoundly disturbed. A radical in politics, he was a conservative in the arts, and Kansas made him think of Gertrude Stein, *les Six*, and nonrepresentational painting, all novelties that irritated him.

"With the opening gong, Rocky Kansas tore into Leonard," he wrote. "He was gauche and inaccurate, but terribly persistent." The classic verities prevailed, however. After a few rounds, during which Broun continued to yearn for a return to a culture with fixed values, he was enabled to record: "The young child of nature who was challenging for the championship dropped his guard, and Leonard hooked a powerful and entirely orthodox blow to the conventional point of the jaw. Down went Rocky Kansas. His past life flashed before him during the nine seconds in which he remained on the floor, and he wished that he had been more faithful as a child in heeding the advice of his boxing teacher. After all, the old masters did know something. There is still a kick in style, and tradition carries a nasty wallop."

I have often thought of Broun's words in the years since Rocky Marciano, the reigning heavyweight champion, scaled the fistic summits, as they say in *Journal-Americanese*, by beating Jersey Joe

Walcott. The current Rocky is gauche and inaccurate, but besides being persistent he is a dreadfully severe hitter with either hand. The predominative nature of this asset has been well stated by Pierce Egan, the Edward Gibbon and Sir Thomas Malory of the old London prize ring, who was less preoccupied than Broun with ultimate implications. Writing in 1821 of a milling cove named Bill Neat, the Bristol Butcher, Egan said, "He possesses a requisite above all the art that *teaching* can achieve for any boxer; namely, *one hit* from his right hand, given in proper distance, can gain a victory; but three of them are positively enough to dispose of a giant." This is true not only of Marciano's right hand but of his left hand, too— provided he doesn't miss the giant entirely. Egan doubted the advisability of changing Neat's style, and he would have approved of Marciano's. The champion has an apparently unlimited absorptive capacity for percussion (Egan would have called him an "insatiable glutton") and inexhaustible energy ("a prime bottom fighter"). "Shifting," or moving back to the side, and "milling in retreat," or moving back, are innovations of the late eighteenth century that Rocky's advisers have carefully kept from his knowledge, lest they spoil his natural prehistoric style. Egan excused these tactics only in boxers of feeble constitution.

Archie Moore, the light-heavyweight champion of the world, who hibernates in San Diego, California, and estivates in Toledo, Ohio, is a Brounian rather than an Eganite in his thinking about style, but he naturally has to do more than think about it. Since the rise of Marciano, Moore, a cerebral and hyper-experienced light-colored pugilist who has been active since 1936, has suffered the pangs of a supreme exponent of bel canto who sees himself crowded out of the opera house by a guy who can only shout. As a sequel to a favorable review I wrote of one of his infrequent New York appearances, when his fee was restricted to a measly five figures, I received a sad little note signed "The most unappreciated fighter in the world, Archie Moore." A fellow who has as much style as Moore tends to overestimate the intellect—he develops the kind of Faustian mind that will throw itself against the problem of perpetual motion, or of how to pick horses first, second, third, *and* fourth in every race. Archie's note made it plain to me that he was honing his harpoon for the White Whale.

When I read newspaper items about Moore's decisioning a large, playful porpoise of a Cuban heavyweight named Nino Valdes and scoop-netting a minnow like Bobo Olson, the middleweight champion, for practice, I thought of him as a lonely Ahab, rehearsing to buck Herman Melville, Pierce Egan, and the betting odds. I did not think that he could bring it off, but I wanted to be there when he tried. What would *Moby-Dick* be if Ahab had succeeded? Just another fish story. The thing that is eternally diverting is the struggle of man against history—or what Albert Camus, who used to be an amateur middleweight, has called the Myth of Sisyphus. (Camus would have been a great man to cover the fight, but none of the syndicates thought of it.) When I heard that the boys had been made for September 20, 1955, at the Yankee Stadium, I shortened my stay abroad in order not to miss the Encounter of the Two Heroes, as Egan would have styled the rendezvous.

In London on the night of September 13, a week before the date set for the Encounter, I tried to get my eye in for fight-watching by attending a bout at the White City greyhound track between Valdes, who had been imported for the occasion, and the British Empire heavyweight champion, Don Cockell, a fat man whose gift for public suffering has enlisted the sympathy of a sentimental people. Since Valdes had gone fifteen rounds with Moore in Las Vegas the previous May, and Cockell had excruciated for nine rounds before being knocked out by Marciano in San Francisco in the same month, the bout offered a dim opportunity for establishing what racing people call a "line" between Moore and Marciano. I didn't get much of an optical workout, because Valdes disposed of Cockell in three rounds. It was evident that Moore and Marciano had not been fighting the same class of people this season.

This was the only fight I ever attended in a steady rainstorm. It had begun in the middle of the afternoon, and, while there was a canopy over the ring, the spectators were as wet as speckled trout. "The weather, it is well known, has no terrors to the admirers of Pugilism of Life," Egan once wrote, and on his old stamping ground this still holds true. As I took my seat in a rock pool that had collected in the hollow of my chair, a South African giant named Ewart Potgieter, whose weight had been announced as twenty-two stone ten, was ignoring the doctrine of Apartheid by leaning on a Jamaican colored man who weighed a mere sixteen stone, and by the time I had transposed these statistics to 318 pounds and 224 pounds, respectively, the exhausted Jamaican had acquiesced in resegregation and retired. The giant had not struck a blow, properly speaking, but had shoved downward a number of times, like a man trying to close an overfilled trunk.

The main bout proved an even less grueling contest. Valdes, eager to get out of the chill, struck Cockell more vindictively than is his wont, and after a few gestures invocative of commiseration the fat man settled in one corner of the ring as heavily as suet pudding upon the unaccustomed gastric system. He had received what Egan would have called a "ribber" and a "nobber," and when he arose it was seen that the latter had raised a cut on his forehead. At the end of the third round, his manager withdrew him from competition. It was not an inspiring occasion, but after the armistice eight or nine shivering Cubans appeared in the runway behind the press section and jumped up and down to register emotion and restore circulation. "*Ahora Marciano!*" they yelled. "Now for Marciano!" Instead of being grateful for the distraction, the other spectators took a poor view of it. "Sit down, you chaps!" one of them cried. "We want to see the next do!" They were still parked out there in the rain when I tottered into the Shepherd's Bush underground station and collapsed, sneezing, on a train that eventually disgorged me at Oxford Circus, with just enough time left to buy a revivifying draft before eleven o'clock, when the pubs closed. How the mugs I left behind cured themselves I never knew. They had to do it on Bovril.

Because I had engagements that kept me in England until a few days before the Encounter, I had no opportunity to visit the training camps of the rival American Heroes. I knew all the members of both factions, however, and I could imagine what they were thinking. In the plane on the way home, I tried to envision the rival patterns of ratiocination. I could be sure that Marciano, a kind, quiet, imperturbable fellow, would plan to go after Moore and make him fight continuously until he tired enough to become an accessible target. After that he would expect concussion to accentuate exhaustion and exhaustion to facilitate concussion, until Moore came away from his consciousness, like everybody else Rocky had ever fought. He would try to remember to minimize damage to himself in the beginning, while there was still snap in Moore's arms, because Moore is a sharp puncher. (Like Bill Neat of old, Marciano hits at his opponent's arms when he cannot hit past them. "In one instance, the arm of Oliver [a Neat adversary] received so paralyzing a shock in stopping the blow that it appeared almost useless," Egan once wrote.) Charlie Goldman would have instructed Marciano in some rudimentary maneuver to throw Moore's first shots off, I felt sure, but after a few minutes Rocky would forget it, or Archie would figure it out. But there would always be Freddie Brown, the "cut man," in the champion's corner to repair superficial damage. One reason Goldman is a great teacher is that he doesn't try to teach a boxer more than he can learn. What he had taught Rocky in the four years since I had first seen him fight was to shorten the arc of most of his blows without losing power thereby, and always to follow one hard blow with another—"for insurance"—delivered with the other hand, instead of recoiling to watch the victim fall. The champion had also gained confidence and presence of mind; he has a good fighting head, which is not the same thing as being a good mechanical practitioner. "A *boxer* requires a *nob* as well as a *statesman* does a HEAD, coolness and calculation being essential to *second* his efforts," Egan wrote, and the old historiographer was never more correct. Rocky was thirty-one, not in the first flush of youth for a boxer, but Moore was only a few days short of thirty-nine, so age promised to be in the champion's favor if he kept pressing.

Moore's strategic problem, I reflected on the plane, offered more choices and, as a corollary, infinitely more chances for error. It was possible, but not probable, that jabbing and defensive skill would carry him through fifteen rounds, even on those old legs, but I knew that the mere notion of such a *gambade* would revolt Moore. He is not what Egan would have called a shy fighter. Besides, would Ahab have been content merely to go the distance with the White Whale? I felt sure that Archie planned to knock the champion out, so that he could sign his next batch of letters "The most appreciated and deeply opulent fighter in the world." I surmised that this project would prove a mistake, like Mr. Churchill's attempt to take Gallipoli in 1915, but it would be the kind of mistake that would look good in his memoirs. The basis of what I rightly anticipated would prove a miscalculation went back to Archie's academic background. As a young fighter of conventional tutelage, he must have heard his preceptors say hundreds of times, "They will all go if you hit them right." If a fighter did not believe that, he would be in the position of a Euclidian without faith in the 180-degree triangle. Moore's strategy, therefore, would be based on working Marciano into a position where he could hit him right. He would not go in and slug with him, because that would be wasteful, distasteful, and injudicious, but he might try to cut him up, in an effort to slow him down so he could hit him right, or else try to hit him right and then cut him up. The puzzle he reserved for me—and Marciano—was the tactic by which he would attempt to attain his strategic objective. In the formation of his views, I believed, Moore would be handicapped, rather than aided, by his active, skeptical mind. One of the odd things about Marciano is that he isn't terribly big. It is hard for a man like Moore, just under six feet tall and weighing about 180 pounds, to imagine that a man approximately the same size can be immeasurably stronger than he is. This is particularly true when, like the light-heavyweight champion, he has spent his whole professional life contending with boxers—some of them considerably bigger—whose strength has proved so near his own that he could move their arms and bodies by cunning pressures. The old classicist would consequently refuse to believe what he was up against.

———

The light-heavyweight limit is 175 pounds, and Moore can get down to that when he must, in order to defend his title, but in a heavyweight match each Hero is allowed to weigh whatever he pleases. I was back in time to attend the weighing-in ceremonies, held in the lobby of Madison Square Garden at noon on the day set for the Encounter, and learned that Moore weighed 188 and Marciano 188¼—a lack of disparity that figured to encourage the rationalist's illusions. I also learned that, in contrast to Jack Solomons, the London promoter who held the Valdes-Cockell match in the rain, the I.B.C., which was promoting the Encounter, had decided to postpone it for twenty-four hours, although the weather was clear. The decision was based on apprehension of Hurricane Ione, which, although apparently veering away from New York, might come around again like a lazy left hook and drop in on the point of the Stadium's jaw late in the evening. Nothing like that happened, but the postponement brought the town's theaters and bars another evening of good business from the out-of-town fight trade, such as they always get on the eve of a memorable Encounter. ("Not a bed could be had at any of the villages at an early hour on the preceding evening; and Uxbridge was crowded beyond all former precedent," Egan wrote of the night before Neat beat Oliver.) There was no doubt that the fight had caught the public imagination, ever sensitive to a meeting between Hubris and Nemesis, as the boys on the quarterlies would say, and the bookies were laying 18–5 on Nemesis, according to the boys on the dailies, who always seem to hear. (A friend of mine up from Maryland with a whim and a five-dollar bill couldn't get ten against it in ordinary barroom money anywhere, although he wanted Ahab.)

The enormous—by recent precedent—advance sale of tickets had so elated the I.B.C. that it had decided to replace the usual card of bad preliminary fights with some not worth watching at all, so there was less distraction than usual as we awaited the appearance of the Heroes on the fateful evening. The press seats had been so closely juxtaposed that I could fit in only sidewise between two colleagues—the extra compression having been caused by the injection of a prewar number of movie stars and politicos. The tight quarters were an advantage, in a way, since they facilitated my conversation with Peter Wilson, an English prize-ring correspondent, who happened to be in the row behind me. I had last seen Mr. Wilson at White City the week before, at a time when the water level had already reached his shredded-Latakia mustache. I had feared that he had drowned at ringside, but when I saw him at the Stadium, he assured me that by buttoning the collar of his mackintosh tightly over his nostrils he had been able to make the garment serve as a diving lung, and so survive. Like all British fight writers when they are relieved of the duty of watching British fighters, he was in a holiday mood, and we chatted happily. There is something about the approach of a good fight that renders the spirit insensitive to annoyance; it is only when the amateur of the Sweet Science has some doubts as to how good the main bout will turn out to be that he is avid for the satisfaction to be had from the preliminaries. This is because after the evening is over, he may have only a good supporting fight to remember. There were no such doubts—even in the minds of the mugs who had paid for their seats—on the evening of September 21.

At about ten-thirty the champion and his faction entered the ring. It is not customary for the champion to come in first, but Marciano has never been a stickler for protocol. He is a humble, kindly fellow, who even now will approach an acquaintance on the street and say bashfully, "Remember me? I'm Rocky Marciano." The champion doesn't mind waiting five or ten minutes to give anybody a punch in the nose. In any case, once launched from his dressing room under the grandstand, he could not have arrested his progress to the ring, because he had about forty policemen pushing behind him, and three more clearing a path in front of him. Marciano, tucked in behind the third cop like a football ball-carrier behind his interference, had to run or be trampled to death. Wrapped in a heavy blue bathrobe and with a blue monk's cowl pulled over his head, he climbed the steps to the ring with the cumbrous agility of a medieval executioner ascending the scaffold. Under the hood he seemed to be trying to look serious. He has an intellectual appreciation of the anxieties of a champion, but he has a hard time forgetting how strong he is; while he remembers that, he can't worry as much as he knows a champion should. His attendants—quick, battered little Goldman; Al Weill, the stout, excitable manager, always stricken just before the bell with the suspicion that he may have made a bad match; Al Columbo—are all as familiar to the crowd as he is.

Ahab's party arrived in the ring a minute or so later, and Charlie Johnston, his manager—a calm sparrow hawk of a man, as old and wise in the game as Weill—went over to watch Goldman put on the champion's gloves. Freddie Brown went to Moore's corner to watch *his* gloves being put on. Moore wore a splendid black silk robe with a gold lamé collar and belt. He sports a full mustache above an imperial, and his hair, sleeked down under pomade when he opens operations, invariably rises during the contest, as it gets water sloshed on it between rounds and the lacquer washes off, until it is standing up like the top of a shaving brush. Seated in his corner in the shadow of his personal trainer, a brown man called Cheerful Norman, who weighs 235 pounds, Moore looked like an old Japanese print I have of a "Shogun Engaged in Strategic Contemplation in the Midst of War." The third member of his group was Bertie Briscoe, a rough, chipper little trainer, whose more usual charge is Sandy Saddler, the featherweight champion—also a Johnston fighter. Mr. Moore's features in repose rather resemble those of Orson Welles, and he was reposing with intensity.

The procession of other fighters and former fighters to be introduced was longer than usual. The full galaxy was on hand, including Jack Dempsey, Gene Tunney, and Joe Louis, the *têtes de cuvée* of former-champion society; ordinary former heavyweight champions, like Max Baer and Jim Braddock, slipped through the ropes practically unnoticed. After all the celebrities had been in and out of the ring, an odd dwarf, advertising something or other—possibly himself—was lifted into the ring by an accomplice and ran across it before he could be shooed out. The referee, a large, craggy, oldish man named Harry Kessler, who, unlike some of his better-known colleagues, is not an ex-fighter, called the men to the center of the ring. This was his moment; he had the microphone. "Now Archie and Rocky, I want a nice, clean fight," he said, and I heard a peal of silvery laughter behind me from Mr. Wilson, who had seen both of them fight before. "Protect yourself at all times," Mr. Kessler cautioned them unnecessarily. When the principals shook hands, I could see Mr. Moore's eyebrows rising like storm clouds over the Sea of Azov. His whiskers bristled and his eyes glowed like dark coals as he scrunched his eyebrows down again and enveloped the Whale with the Look, which was intended to dominate his will power. Mr. Wilson and I were sitting behind Marciano's corner, and as the champion came back to it I observed his expression, to determine what effect the Look had had upon him. More than ever, he resembled a Great Dane who has heard the word *bone*.

A moment later the bell rang and the Heroes came out for the first round. Marciano, training in the sun for weeks, had tanned to a slightly deeper tint than Moore's old ivory, and Moore, at 188, looked, if anything, bigger and more muscular than Marciano; much of the champion's weight is in his legs, and his shoulders slope. Marciano advanced, but Moore didn't go far away. As usual, he stood up nicely, his arms close to his body and his feet not too far apart, ready to go anywhere but not without a reason—the picture of a powerful, decisive intellect unfettered by preconceptions. Marciano, pulling his left arm back from the shoulder, flung a left hook. He missed, but not by enough to discourage him, and then walked in and hooked again. All through the round he threw those hooks, and some of them grazed Moore's whiskers; one even hit him on the side of the head. Moore didn't try much offensively; he held a couple of times when Marciano worked in close.

Marciano came back to his corner as he always does, unimpassioned. He hadn't expected to catch Moore with those left hooks anyway, I imagine; all he had wanted was to move him around. Moore went to his corner inscrutable. They came out for the second, and Marciano went after him in brisker fashion. In the first round he had been throwing the left hook, missing with it, and then throwing a right and missing with that, too. In the second he tried a variation—throwing a right and then pulling a shoulder back to throw the left. It appeared for a moment to have Moore confused, as a matador might be confused by a bull who walked in on his hind legs. Marciano landed a couple of those awkward hooks, but not squarely. He backed Moore over toward the side of the ring farthest from me, and then Moore knocked him down.

Some of the reporters, describing the blow in the morning papers, called it a "sneak punch," which is journalese for one the reporter didn't see but technically means a lead thrown before the other man has warmed up or while he is musing about the gate receipts. This had been no lead, and although I certainly hadn't seen Moore throw the punch, I knew that it had landed inside the arc of Marciano's left hook. ("Marciano missed with the right, then the left, and Moore stepped inside it," my private eye, Whitey Bimstein, said next day, confirming my diagnosis, and the film of the fight bore both of us out.) So Ahab had his harpoon in the Whale. He had hit him right if ever I saw a boxer hit right, with a classic brevity and conciseness. Marciano stayed down for two seconds. I do not know what took place in Mr. Moore's breast when he saw him get up. He may have felt, for the moment, like Don Giovanni when the Commendatore's statue grabbed at him—startled because he thought he had killed the guy already—or like Ahab when he saw the Whale take down Fedallah, harpoons and all. Anyway, he hesitated a couple of seconds, and that was reasonable. A man who took nine to come up after a punch like that would be doing well, and the correct tactic would be to go straight in and finish him. But a fellow who came up on two was so strong he would bear investigation.

After that, Moore did go in, but not in a crazy way. He hit Marciano some good, hard, classic shots, and inevitably Marciano, a trader, hit him a few devastating swipes, which slowed him. When the round ended, the edge of Moore's speed was gone, and he knew that he would have to set a new and completely different trap, with diminished resources. After being knocked down, Marciano had stopped throwing that patterned right-and-left combination; he has a good nob. "He never trun it again in the fight," Whitey said next day, but I differ. He threw it in the fifth, and again Moore hit him a peach of a right inside it, but the steam was gone; this time Ahab couldn't even stagger him. Anyway, there was Moore at the end of the second, dragging his shattered faith in the unities and humanities back to his corner. He had hit a guy right, and the guy hadn't gone. But there is no geezer in Moore, any more than there was in the master of the *Pequod*.

Both came out for the third very gay, as Egan would have said. Marciano had been hit and cut, so he felt acclimated, and Moore was so mad at himself for not having knocked Marciano out that he almost displayed animosity toward him. He may have thought that perhaps he had not hit Marciano *just* right; the true artist is always prone to self-reproach. He would try again. A minute's attention from his squires had raised his spirits and slicked down his hair. At this point, Marciano set about him. He waddled in, hurling his fists with a sublime disregard of probabilities, content to hit an elbow, a biceps, a shoulder, the top of a head—the last supposed to be the least profitable target in the business, since, as every beginner learns, "the head is the hardest part of the human body," and a boxer will only break his hands on it. Many boxers make the systematic presentation of the cranium part of their defensive scheme. The crowd, basically anti-intellectual, screamed encouragement. There was Moore, riding punches, picking them off, slipping them, rolling with them, ducking them, coming gracefully out of his defensive efforts with sharp, patterned blows—and just about holding this parody even on points. His face, emerging at instants from under the storm of arms—his own and Rocky's—looked like that of a swimming walrus. When the round ended, I could see that he was thinking deeply. Marciano came back to his corner at a kind of suppressed dogtrot. He didn't have a worry in the world.

It was in the fourth, though, that I think Sisyphus began to get the idea he couldn't roll back the Rock. Marciano pushed him against the ropes and swung at him for what seemed a full minute without ever landing a punch that a boxer with Moore's background would consider a credit to his workmanship. He kept them coming so fast, though, that Moore tired just getting out of their way. One newspaper account I saw said that at this point Moore "swayed uncertainly," but his motions were about as uncertain as

Margot Fonteyn's, or Arthur Rubinstein's. He is the most premeditated and best-synchronized swayer in his profession. After the bell rang for the end of the round, the champion hit him a right for good measure—he usually manages to have something on the way all the time—and then pulled back to disclaim any uncouth intention. Moore, no man to be conned, hit him a corker of a punch in return, when he wasn't expecting it. It was a gesture of moral reprobation and also a punch that would give any normal man something to think about between rounds. It was a good thing Moore couldn't see Marciano's face as he came back to his corner, though, because the champion was laughing.

The fifth was a successful round for Moore, and I had him ahead on points that far in the fight. But it took no expert to know where the strength lay. There was even a moment in the round when Moore set himself against the ropes and encouraged Marciano to swing at him, in the hope the champion would swing himself tired. It was a confession that he himself was too tired to do much hitting.

In the sixth Marciano knocked Moore down twice—once, early in the round, for four seconds, and once, late in the round, for eight seconds, with Moore getting up just before the bell rang. In the seventh, after that near approach to obliteration, the embattled intellect put up its finest stand. Marciano piled out of his corner to finish Moore, and the stylist made him miss so often that it looked, for a fleeting moment, as if the champion were indeed punching himself arm-weary. In fact, Moore began to beat him to the punch. It was Moore's round, certainly, but an old-timer I talked to later averred that one of the body blows Marciano landed in that round was the hardest of the fight.

It was the eighth that ended the competitive phase of the fight. They fought all the way, and in the last third of the round the champion simply overflowed Archie. He knocked him down with a right six seconds before the bell, and I don't think Moore could have got up by ten if the round had lasted that long. The fight by then reminded me of something that Sam Langford, one of the most profound thinkers—and, according to all accounts, one of the greatest doers—of the prize ring, once said to me: "Whatever that other man wants to do, don't let him do it." Merely by moving in all the time and punching continually, Marciano achieves the same strategic effect that Langford gained by finesse. It is impossible to think, or to impose your thought, if you have to keep on avoiding punches.

Moore's "game," as old Egan would have called his courage, was beyond reproach. He came out proudly for the ninth, and stood and fought back with all he had, but Marciano slugged him down, and he was counted out with his left arm hooked over the middle rope as he tried to rise. It was a crushing defeat for the higher faculties and a lesson in intellectual humility, but he had made a hell of a fight.

The fight was no sooner over than hundreds of unsavory young yokels with New England accents began a kind of mountain-goat immigration from the bleachers to ringside. They leaped from chair to chair and, after they reached the press section, from typewriter shelf to typewriter shelf and, I hope, from movie star to movie star. "Rocky!" they yelled. "Brockton!" Two of them, as dismal a pair of civic ambassadors as I have seen since I worked on the Providence *Journal & Evening Bulletin*, stood on Wilson's typewriter and yelled "Providence!" After the fighters and the hick delinquents had gone away, I made my way out to Jerome Avenue, where the crowd milled, impenetrable, under the "El" structure.

If you are not in a great hurry to get home (and why should you be at eleven-thirty or twelve on a fight night?), the best plan is to walk up to the station north of the stadium and have a beer in a saloon, or a cup of tea in the 167th Street Cafeteria, and wait until the whole mess clears away. By that time you may even get a taxi. After this particular fight I chose the cafeteria, being in a contemplative rather than a convivial mood. The place is of a genre you would expect to find nearer Carnegie Hall, with blond woodwork and modern functional furniture imported from Italy—an appropriate background for the evaluation of an aesthetic experience. I got my tea and a smoked-salmon sandwich on a soft onion roll at the counter and made my way to a table, where I found myself between two young policemen who were talking about why Walt Disney has never attempted a screen version of Kafka's "Metamorphosis." As I did not feel qualified to join in that one, I got out my copy of the official program of the fights and began to read the high-class feature articles as I munched my sandwich.

One reminded me that I had seen the first boxing show ever held in Yankee Stadium—on May 12, 1923. I had forgotten that it *was* the first show, and even that 1923 was the year the Stadium opened. In my true youth the Yankees used to share the Polo Grounds with the Giants, and I had forgotten that, too, because I never cared much about baseball, although, come to think of it, I used to see the Yankees play occasionally in the nineteen 'teens, and should have remembered. I remembered the boxing show itself very well, though. It happened during the spring of my second suspension from college, and I paid five dollars for a high-grandstand seat. The program merely said that it had been "an all-star heavyweight bill promoted by Tex Rickard for the Hearst Milk Fund," but I found that I could still remember every man and every bout on the card. One of the main events was between old Jess Willard, the former heavyweight champion of the world, who had lost the title to Jack Dempsey in 1919, and a young heavyweight named Floyd Johnson. Willard had been coaxed from retirement to make a comeback because there was such a dearth of heavyweight material that Rickard thought he could still get by, but as I remember the old fellow, he couldn't fight a lick. He had a fair left jab and a right uppercut that a fellow had to walk into to get hurt by, and he was big and soft. Johnson was a mauler worse than Rex Layne, and the old man knocked him out. The other main event, *ex aequo*, had Luis Angel Firpo opposing a fellow named Jack McAuliffe II, from Detroit, who had had only fifteen fights and had never beaten anybody, and had a glass jaw. The two winners, of whose identity there was infinitesimal preliminary doubt, were to fight each other for the right to meet the great Jack Dempsey. Firpo was so crude that Marciano would be a Fancy Dan in comparison. He could hit with only one hand—his right—he hadn't the faintest idea of what to do in close, and he never cared much for the business anyway. He knocked McAuliffe out, of course, and then, in a later "elimination" bout, stopped poor old Willard. He subsequently became a legend by going one and a half sensational rounds with Dempsey, in a time that is now represented to us as the golden age of American pugilism.

I reflected with satisfaction that old Ahab Moore could have whipped all four principals on that card within fifteen rounds, and that while Dempsey may have been a great champion, he had less to beat than Marciano. I felt the satisfaction because it proved that the world isn't going backward, if you can just stay young enough to remember what it was really like when you were really young.

(1955)

The University of Eighth Avenue

In every great city certain quarters take on the color of an industry. Fifty-second Street between Sixth and Fifth Avenues in New York, for example, is given over to strip-tease palaces. In addition to electric signs and posters advertising the Boppa La Zoppas and Ocelot Women inside, it can be identified in the evening by the thin line of non-holding males along the curb who stand on tiptoes or bend double and twist their necks into periscopes in what must surely be an unrewarding effort to see through the chinks in the draperies. This is known as the old college try, since it is practiced largely by undergraduates.

Forty-seventh Street between Sixth and Fifth, for another example, is devoted to polishing and trading diamonds. It is lined with jewelers' exchanges, like North African souks with fluorescent lighting, inside which hordes of narrow men rent jumping-up-and-sitting-down space with a linear foot of showcase immediately in front of it. The traders who don't want to sink their funds in overhead stand out on the sidewalk. There is a social distinction even among them: between two-handkerchief men, who use one exclusively for diamond storage, and one-handkerchief men, who knot their diamonds in a corner of their all-purpose *mouchoirs*.

The block on the west side of Eighth Avenue between Fifty-fourth and Fifty-fifth Streets is given over to the polishing of prizefighters. It has a quiet academic charm, like West 116th Street when you leave the supermarkets and neighborhood movie houses of upper Broadway and find yourself on the Columbia campus with its ivy-hallowed memories of Sid Luckman and Dwight D. Eisenhower. It is a sleepy block whose modest shops are given over to the needs of the student body—a couple of hock shops, a pet store, and a drugstore which sells bandages and gauze for taping fighters' hands. A careful etiquette reigns in this student quarter, as it is impossible to know if you can lick even the smallest man looking into the pet shop next door to No. 919 Eighth Avenue, which is the Old Dartmouth, or Nassau Hall, of the University of Eighth Avenue.

Old Stillman, as this building is named in honor of the founder, is three stories high, covered with soot instead of ivy and probably older than most midwestern campuses at that. It is a fine example of a postcolonial structure of indefinable original purpose and looks as if it had been knocked down in the Draft Riots of 1863 and left for dead. It hides its academic light behind a sign which says "Stillman's Gym," against a background resembling an oilcloth tablecloth from some historic speakeasy specializing in the indelible red wine of the age of F. Scott Fitzgerald and Warren Gamaliel Harding. Maybe that is where the artist got the canvas; it is an economical neighborhood. The sign also says "Training Here Daily," and in smaller letters "Boxing Instruction—See Jack Curley." This is the university's nearest approach to a printed catalog. Doctor Lou Stillman, the president, knew when he put out his sign in 1921 that an elaborate plant does not make a great educational institution. In the great schools of the Middle Ages, scholars came to sharpen their wits by mutual disputation. Prizefighters do likewise.

The narrow window of the pet shop is divided by a partition, and the show is always the same. Monkeys on top—which is Stillmanese for "in the feature attraction"—and a tolerant cat playing with puppies underneath, which is Stillmanese for the subordinate portion of the entertainment, as for example a semifinal. Dangling all over the window are parakeets and dog collars. The window draws very good, to stay with the scholastic jargon, before noon, when the fighters are waiting for Old Stillman to open, and around three, when the seminars are breaking up. A boy wins a fourrounder, he buys a parakeet and dreams of the day he will fight on top and own a monkey. There was a time when a boxer's status was reflected by the flash on his finger, now it is by his pet. Floyd Patterson, a brilliant star on the light-heavyweight horizon, owns a cinnamon ringtail.

Whitey Bimstein, the famous trainer, had one of the pet-shop monkeys hooking off a jab pretty good for a while. Whitey, a small bald man with sidehair the color of an Easter chick, would stand in front of the window darting his left straight toward the monk's face and then throwing it in toward the body, and the monk would imitate him—"better than some of them kids they send me from out of town," Whitey says. Then one day he noticed a cop walking up and down the other side of the street and regarding him in a peculiar manner. "I figure he thinks I'm going nuts," Whitey says. "So I drop the monk's education."

"You probably couldn't of got him a license anyway," Izzy Blank, another educator, said consolingly.

The affinity between prizefighters and monkeys is old; the late Jack McAuliffe, who retired as undefeated lightweight champion of the world in 1896, once had one that rode his neck when he did roadwork. Twenty miles was customary in those days—they trained for finish fights—so the monkey and McAuliffe saw a lot of territory together. "The monk would hold on with his legs around my neck, and if I stopped too fast he would grab my ears to keep from falling off," the old hero told me when I had the good fortune to talk to him. McAuliffe was a great nature-lover and political thinker. When he told me about the monkey he was sixty-nine years old and running in a Democratic primary for assemblyman to annoy his son-in-law, who would give him no more money to lose at the races.

"I went into this contest," he said, "because the taxes are too high, the wages of the little fellow are being cut, and nobody has ever went right down to the basis. There are men in our Legislature today who remind me of Paddy the Pig, who would steal your eye for a breastpin." Not drawing a counter in the political department, he told me about the monkey.

McAuliffe in his glory had been a great friend of John L. Sullivan and of a bantamweight named Jack Skelly from Yonkers. The three were engaged to perform in a Salzburg festival of the Sweet Science promoted by the Olympic Club of New Orleans in September 1892. On September 5 McAuliffe was to defend his lightweight title against Billy Myer, the Streator (Ill.) Cyclone. On the sixth, Skelly would try to win the featherweight championship from the incumbent George Dixon, the great Little Chocolate. And on the third, climactic night, the great John L. would annihilate an upstart from San Francisco named Jim Corbett.

"I thought the monk would bring us all luck," the old man said. "He started good. When I knocked Billy out in the fifteenth the monk was up on the top rope as the referee said 'Ten!' and hop, off onto my shoulder before the man got my hand up. I took him and threw him into the air and caught him again, I was so happy.

" 'Oh, you jool of a monkey!' I said, and when I was on the table after the fight he played in the hair on my chest like I was his brother.

"Then Skelly fought Dixon, and when Dixon knocked him out I thought I noticed a very peculiar look on the monkey's face, like he was glad to see Skelly get it. I said to myself, 'I wonder who you are.' I gave him the benefit of the doubt, but when Corbett stopped Sullivan, I grabbed the monkey by the neck and wrung it like he was a chicken. I've often felt bad about it since. God help me, I had a very bad temper."

I cite this only to prove the ring is a continuum with fixed values and built-in cultural patterns like Philadelphia or the world of Henry James.

Monkeys can fight like hell when properly trained, incidentally, and Jacco Maccacco, the Fighting Monkey, weighing twelve pounds, had a standing challenge to kill any twenty-pound dog in Jane Austen's England. He had a considerably greater public reputation than Wordsworth.

On the second floor of a taxpayer at the northwest corner of Fifty-fourth and Eighth, the International Boxing Guild maintains a brand-registry office for the purpose of preventing managers from stealing other managers' fighters and renaming them. They do not nick the kids' ears or cut their dewlaps, but they keep complete files, so if a rustler lures a boxer under contract to a Guild member from, say, Spokane to Toronto, both out-of-town points, word of the theft goes out. Then no Guild manager will fight him. That is to say, of course, no Guild manager will let his chattels fight him. It is a simpler process than going to law, because the rustler may have an edge in his home town and you cannot carry your own judge with you. It is a handy location, because if anybody smuggled anybody else's fighter into town, Stillman's is where he would be most likely to show up, like a stolen diamond on Forty-seventh Street. It is harder to ring a fighter than a horse, because in order to disguise him you have to change his style, which is more trouble than developing a new fighter.

The whole block is handy to the building called Madison Square Garden, at Fiftieth Street and Eighth, where the International Boxing Club maintains offices and promotes boxing matches on Friday nights when the house hasn't been rented out to Ringling Brothers' Circus or Sonja Henie or the Rodeo. This is of considerable economic advantage to members of the academic community, since they can drop down to the Garden and talk their way into some complimentary tickets without spending an extra subway fare. It is doubly convenient for managers who are discontented with Billy Brown, the I.B.C. matchmaker, a sentiment they usually communicate by sitting around his office and making faces. By walking down from Stillman's, bumming comps, and making a face, they effect a double saving. This advantage is purely fortuitous because when Stillman opened his place in 1921 the Madison Square Garden stood at Madison Square. Not even Stillman contends they tore it down and built the present one just to get near him.

The modest entrance to Old Stillman is the kind of hallway you would duck into if you wanted to buy marijuana in a strange neighborhood. There are posters for the coming week's metropolitan fight shows—rarely more than one or two nowadays since television has knocked out the nontelevised neighborhood clubs. There is a wide wooden staircase leading up to the gym. Although Dr. Stillman locks a steel grille across the doorway promptly at three, keeps it locked until five-thirty, when working scholars come in for the poor man's session, and then locks it again religiously at seven, the joint always smells wrong. Dr. Stillman, like so many college presidents nowadays, is not himself a teacher but rather an administrator, and the smell in the hall makes him feel there are limits to academic freedom. He is a gaunt man with a beak that describes an arc like an overhand right, bushy eyebrows, a ruff of hair like a frowsy cockatoo, and a decisive, heavily impish manner. He has the reputation of never having taken any lip off anybody, which is plausible, because he seldom gives the other fellow a chance to say anything. In earlier stages of his academic career he used to speak exclusively in shouts, but now that he is in his latter sixties, his voice has mellowed to a confident rasp. The great educator has never, so far as is known, himself put on the gloves; it might prove a psychological mistake. Stillman excels in insulting matriculants so casually that they don't know whether to get sore or not. By the sixth time Stillman has insulted a prizefighter the fighter feels it would be inconsistent to take offense at such a late stage in their personal interrelationship. When that happens, Stillman has acquired the edge.

Dr. Stillman has not been so styled since birth. His original surname was Ingber, but he got into the gymnasium business by working for a philanthropist named Alpheus Geer who ran a kind of Alcoholics Anonymous for burglars trying to go straight. Geer called his crusade the Marshall Stillman movement, and he thought the best kind of occupational therapy was boxing, so he opened a gym, which young Ingber managed. The burglars got to calling Lou Ingber, Lou Stillman, and after they stole all the boxing gloves and Mr. Geer quit in disgust, Ingber opened a gymnasium of his own, farther uptown than this Old Stillman, and legally adopted his present name.

Occasionally Dr. Stillman has a problem student who does not know when he is being insulted, and then he has to think up some more subtle psychological stratagem. Tommy (Hurricane) Jackson, a heavyweight who has to be driven out of the gymnasium at the end of every session because he wants to punch the bag some more, has been a recent disciplinary challenge. Jackson, who is six feet two inches tall and of inverse intellectual stature, would occupy a box-ing ring all the time if Stillman let him. He would like to box fifteen or thirty rounds a day, but this would be of no value to his fellow-students, even those who worked with him, because Jackson is a purely imitative boxer. He waits to see what the other fellow will do and then does it right back at him until the guy drops from exhaus-tion. Against a jabber he will jab and against a mauler he will maul; it is the exact opposite of Sam Langford's counsel: "Whatever that other man want to do, don't let him do it. Box a fighter and fight a boxer." Jackson will box a boxer, after a fashion, and fight a fighter, in a way, but he can never decide for himself. Knowing this, most boxers who work with him step in with a right to the jaw, planning to knock him out before he can begin his systematic plagiarism. But he has a hard jaw. Whitey and Freddy Brown, his trainers, who are partners, attribute his lack of originality to an emotional conflict, but it has not yielded to any kind of permissive therapy like buying him a .22 rifle to shoot rats, or letting him drink soda pop on fight nights. "He is not too smart of a fellow," Freddy Brown has con-cluded.

Jackson, when not exercising, likes to walk around Stillman's with a shiny harmonica at his mouth, pretending to blow in it. A small, white camp follower trails in his wake, completely concealed from anybody in front of Jackson, and plays a real tune on another harmonica. It is Jackson's pose, when detected, that this is an elabo-rate joke because he could play a tune too, if he wanted to. Dr. Still-man once invited him to play a tune into the microphone with which the president of the University of Eighth Avenue announces the names of students defending theses in the rings. "Give us all a chance to hear you," he snarled invitingly. Tommy backed off, and Stillman grabbed a moral ascendancy. Whenever Jackson is ob-streperous now, the good Doctor points to the microphone, and the Hurricane effaces himself.

To gain access to the hall of academe you must pass a turnstile guarded by Professor Jack Curley, the assistant to the president who the sign says is the fellow to see about boxing instructions. The only person who ever did was a follower of Father Divine named Saint

Thomas. Curley signed him up as a heavyweight contender before letting him through the gate where the managers could see him. Saint Thomas was a hell of a natural fighter if you believe Curley, but they split on theological grounds such as he wanted Father Divine, in absentia, to okay his opponents by emanation. Later he backslid and stabbed a guy, and is now in a place where he has very little opportunity for roadwork. The sign is as sensible as one would be on the door of Yale saying "Instruction in reading and writing, see Professor Doakes." Old Stillman is no elementary school.

There are two ways of getting by Professor Curley. The more popular is to invoke the name of some manager or trainer you know is inside, claiming an urgent business mission. Professor Curley will deny he is there, but if you ask some ingoing fighter to relay the message, the fellow will come out and okay you. Curley will then assume the expression of a baffled witch in a London Christmas pantomime, but he will let you in without payment. The second method is to give him fifty cents, the official price of admission, which he doesn't expect from anybody who looks familiar. Through decades of practice he has trained his facial muscles not to express recognition, but he is violently disconcerted when the other fellow does not demand to be recognized. After you give him the fifty cents he has another problem—whether to say hello. This would be a confession he had known you all along. He compromises by giving you what is known on campus as "a cheap hello," looking over his shoulder as if he might be talking to somebody else.

On the main floor of Old Stillman there are two boxing rings set close together. The space in front of the rings is for spectators, and the relatively narrow strip behind them for boxers and trainers. To get from one zone to the other, the latter must pass directly in front of Dr. Stillman, who stands behind an iron rail leaving a passageway perhaps two feet wide. This is a big help in the collection department, because a boxer who is in arrears can't get into the ring to spar unless the president, who doubles as bursar, gives him an extension. When granted, this is usually on the grounds that the delinquent has a fight coming up.

Boxers pay six dollars a month for a locker and eleven dollars a month for a dressing room, which means a stall just wide enough for a rubbing table. The deluxe dressing rooms have hooks on the plywood partitions. Stillman has a microphone in back of his stand and in the back of his head a rough list of the order in which fighters will go into the rings. Some fighters he knows by sight; trainers have to prompt him with the names of others. Most of the present crop, the Doctor says, he would like to forget as rapidly as possible. When he says the names into the mike they come out equally unintelligible, so it doesn't matter. Most of the spectators know who the guys are anyway, despite the increasingly elaborate headgears which make them look like Tlingit witch doctors.

In the days when 375 boxers trained at Stillman's and the majority actually had bouts in sight, there was considerable acrimony about the scheduling. Trainers were afraid that some of their boys who needed sparring would be crowded out. Now that fewer fellows use the place and are in less of a hurry, everybody gets a chance. The enrollment at Old Stillman is less than a hundred, which is not bad when you reflect that there are only 241 licensed professional boxers in the whole of New York State and this number includes out-of-state fighters who have had to take out a license for a New York appearance.

The main operating theater at Stillman's is two stories high. There is a gallery which, in the halcyon days before television, used to accommodate spectators, but which now serves as a supplementary gym. The light and heavy bags are up there, and so is most of the space for skipping rope. In pre-television times Stillman's had an extensive bargain clientele of fans who couldn't afford the price of admission to regular boxing shows, but now these non-holders see their fights free.

Only knowing coves come to Stillman's these days—fellows who have more than a casual interest in boxing or are out to make a buck, like the diamond traders. Few managers today have offices of their own—there are only a half-dozen such grandees—and the rest transact their business walking around Stillman's or leaning against the radiators. There are seats for ordinary spectators, but managers consider it unprofessional to sit down. Even managers who have offices use them chiefly to play klabiash or run up telephone bills; they think better on their feet, in the mingled aura of rubbing alcohol, sweat, and hot-pastrami-on-the-lunch-counter which distinguishes Old Stillman from a gym run by Helena Rubinstein or Elizabeth Arden.

The prevailing topic of conversation at Stillman's nowadays is the vanishing buck. Boxers are in the same predicament as the hand-loom weavers of Britain when Dr. Edmund Cartwright introduced the power loom. Two boxers on a national hookup with fifty major-city outlets can fill the place of a hundred boxers on top ten years ago, and for every two eliminated from on top, at least ten lose their work underneath. The boxer who gets the television assignment, though, is in the same spot as the hand-loom weaver who found work driving a power loom—he gets even less money than before. This is because while wads of the sponsors' tease go to networks for time and camera fees, to advertising agencies in commissions based on the purchased time, to producers for creating the drivel between rounds, and even to the promoters who provide the boxers, the boxers themselves get no more than they would have drawn in an off night in Scranton in 1929. Naturally, this is a discouraging technological circumstance, but the desire to punch other boys in the nose will survive in our culture. The spirit of self-preservation will induce some boys to excel. Those who find they excel will try to turn a modest buck by it. It is an art of the people, like making love, and is likely to survive any electronic gadget that peddles razor blades.

Meanwhile the contraction of the field has led to a concentration of talent at Old Stillman. These days good feature-bout fighters, who were sure of ten thousand dollars a year not long ago, are glad to sell their tutorial services as sparring partners for five or ten dollars a session. This is particularly true of the colored boys who are not quite champions. Trainers who in the flush times accepted only stars or near-stars as students will now take on any kid with a solvent sponsor. The top trainers, whose charges appear frequently on televised shows, still make out pretty well.

Trainers, like the teachers in medieval universities, are paid by their pupils or their pupils' sponsors. A couple of trainers working as partners may have fifteen fighters, all pretty good, if they are good trainers. If they cannot teach, they get no pupils and go emeritus without salary. There are two televised boxing cards originating in New York clubs every week—the St. Nick's on Monday evening and the International Boxing Club show from the Garden on Friday. When the Garden is occupied by other events, the I.B.C. runs its show from out of town, which is a blank margin around New York City, extending for several thousand miles in every direction but east. A team of trainers like Whitey Bimstein and Freddy Brown, or Nick and Dan Florio, or Chickie Ferrera and Johnny Sullo, figures to have at least one man in one of the three features every week, and a couple underneath. The trainer customarily gets 10 percent of his fighter's end of the purse. Because of their skill as seconds they are also sure to get calls to work in the corners of men they don't train. Noted Old Stillman trainers are called out of town for consultations almost as often as before television, because while there are many less fights, the out-of-town trainer as a species has for that very reason nearly vanished. In most places it is a part-time avocation.

Their reputation is international—last year, for example, Whitey Bimstein was retained to cram a Canadian giant named James J. Parker for a bout for the Canadian heavyweight championship at Toronto. Parker is not considered much of a fighter here—a good banger, but slow of intellection. In Canada, however, he is big stuff—he weighs over 210 pounds. The Canadian champion (now retired), whom Parker was to oppose, was Earl Walls, also a pretty good banger but a slow study.

Whitey took Parker up to Greenwood Lake, N.Y., where his troubles started when the Canadian insisted on doing his roadwork on the frozen surface of the lake. "He might fall through and roon the advance sale," Whitey said. Not wishing to increase the weight on the ice, Whitey declined to accompany him. He would watch him from a window of the inn where they were staying, prepared to cut loose with a shotgun if Parker slowed to a walk. Trainers blanch when they tell of the terrible things fighters will do to get out of roadwork. Nick Masuras, one of Whitey's friends, once had a fighter up at the Hotel Peter Stuyvesant, across the street from Central Park at Eighty-sixth, and every morning he would send him out to run a couple of times around the Central Park Reservoir, which is right there practically. Masuras would then go back to sleep. By and by the fellow would come in panting and soaking wet, and it wasn't until three days before the fight that Nick learned he had just been sitting on park benches talking to nursemaids, after which he would come in and stand under a warm shower with his clothes on. After that Nick moved to a room on the eighth floor, with a park view. But it was too late. The guy's legs went back on him and he lost the fight. "He done it to himself, no one else," Nick says, mournfully, as he polishes beer glasses in his saloon, the Neutral Corner, which is the Deux Magots or Mermaid Tavern of the fighters' quarter. Instead of training fighters, Nick has taken to feeding them.

Parker, on the other hand, didn't skimp his training. He heeded everything Whitey told him. As a consequence, Whitey says, "He give this Walls a hell of a belting and in the sixth round cut his left eye open so bad that if you were a doctor you had to stop it." The Canadian doctor, however, didn't stop it. "He was pertecting Walls," Whitey says. "The guy could of lost his eyesight." Walls had in his corner another ambassador of culture from Stillman's, Nick Florio. Florio patched the eye up so well that Walls went the distance, twelve rounds. Whitey felt like calling Florio a carpetbagger. The announcer then collected the slips of the two judges and the referee, read them, and proclaimed James J. Parker, Whitey's candidate, "Winner and new champion"—of Canada, naturally. "But," Whitey says, "they take it very serious." Whitey posed for victory pictures, allowing Parker to get into the background, and then led him away to his dressing room. There, five minutes later, another man came in and said the announcer had made a mistake—it was really a draw, so Walls was still champion. "It was a outrage," Whitey says. "They pertected him." He came back from Canada with a bale of Toronto newspapers, which said Walls's cut eye had required sixteen stitches. "They were those wide Canadian stitches,"

Whitey said. "Here they took them kind of stitches to make him look better." The fight, which was not televised, drew thirty thousand dollars and the fighters whacked up eighteen thousand dollars. This was much better than they would have done at the Garden, where each would have received four thousand dollars from television and a purely nominal sum from the almost nonexistent gate.

For most fighters, however, pickings are lean between infrequent television appearances—so lean that they are beginning to recall the stories old-timers tell about the minuscular purses in the nineties. One of the best lightweights in the world, for example, went up to Holyoke, Mass., from the campus on Eighth Avenue not too long ago and fought on top of the gate against a tough local boy whom he knocked out in five rounds. He had signed for a percentage of the gate which turned out to be $115. After he had deducted railroad fare, the price of a Massachusetts boxer's license, and a few dollars for a local helper in his corner, he wound up with $74. Freddy Brown, the trainer, wouldn't accept a fee, and the fighter's manager wouldn't cut the fighter because the guy was broke and he would have had to lend him the money back anyway. He had been out for several months with a broken rib sustained in another fight.

The club in Holyoke, one of the few stubborn survivors, functions Tuesday nights because of television boxing Monday, Wednesday, and Friday.

All the great minds of the university have gone a few rounds with this problem, but none has come up with a thesis that his colleagues at the lunch counter couldn't flatten in the course of a couple of cups of tea. One school of savants holds that if the television companies are going to monopolize boxing they should set up a system of farm clubs to develop new talent. Another believes the situation will cure itself, but painfully. "Without the little clubs, nobody new will come up," a leader of this group argues. "The television fans will get tired of the same bums, the Hooper will drop, the sponsors will drop boxing, and then we can start all over again." Meanwhile a lot of fighters have had to go to work, a situation the horror of which was impressed upon me long ago by the great Sam

Langford, in describing a period of his young manhood when he had licked everybody who would fight him. "I was *so* broke," he said, "that I didn't have *no* money. I had to go to work with my hands." Manual labor didn't break his spirit. He got a fight with Joe Gans, the great lightweight champion of the world, and whipped him in fifteen rounds in 1903, when Sam says he was seventeen years old. The record books make him twenty-three. (They were both over the weight, though, so he didn't get the title.) After the fight he was lying on the rubbing table in his dressing room feeling proud and a busted-down colored middleweight named George Byers walked in. "How did I look?" Langford asked him. "You strong," Byers said, "but you don't know nothing."

Langford wasn't offended. He had the humility of the great artist. He said, "How much you charge to teach me?" Byers said, "Ten dollars." Langford gave him ten dollars. It was a sizable share of the purse he had earned for beating Gans.

"And then what happened?" I asked Sam. He said, "He taught me. He was right. I didn't know nothing. I used to just chase and punch, hurt my hands on hard heads. After George taught me I made them come to me. I made them lead."

"How?" I asked.

"If they didn't lead I'd run them out of the ring. When they led I'd hit them in the body. Then on the point of the chin. Not the jaw, the point of the chin. That's why I got such pretty hands to-day." Sam by that time was nearly blind, he weighed 230 pounds, and he couldn't always be sure that when he spat tobacco juice at the empty chitterling can in his hall room he would hit.

But he looked affectionately at his knees, where he knew those big hands rested. There wasn't a lump on a knuckle. "I'd belt them oat," he said. "Oh, I'd belt them oat."

When I told this story to Whitey he sucked in his breath reverently, like a lama informed of one of the transactions of Buddha.

"What a difference from the kids today," the schoolman said. "I have a kid in a bout last night and he can't even count. Every time he hook the guy is open for a right, and I tell him: 'Go twicet, go twicet!' But he would go oncet and lose the guy. I don't know what they teach them in school."

After Sam tutored with Professor Byers he grew as well as improved, but he improved a lot faster than he grew. He beat Gans, at approximately even weights, but when he fought Jack Johnson, one of the best heavyweights who ever lived, he spotted him 27 pounds. Langford weighed 158, Johnson 185. Sam was twenty-six, according to Nat Fleischer, or twenty-five, according to Sam, and Johnson twenty-eight. Sam knocked Johnson down for an eight count, Johnson never rocked Sam, and there has been argument ever since over the decision for Johnson at the end of the fifteen rounds. Sam's effort was a succès d'estime for the scholastic approach to boxing, but Johnson, an anti-intellectual, would never give him another fight.

Johnson, by then older and slower, did fight another middleweight in 1909—Stanley Ketchel, the Michigan Assassin. Ketchel's biographers, for the most part exponents of the raw-nature, or blinded-with-blood-he-swung-again school of fight writing, turn literary handsprings when they tell how Ketchel, too, knocked Johnson down. But Johnson got up and took him with one punch. There was a direct line of comparison between Langford and Ketchel as middleweights. They boxed a six-round no-decision bout in Philadelphia which was followed by a newspaper scandal; the critics accused Langford of carrying Ketchel. Nobody accused Ketchel of carrying Langford. I asked Sam once if he *had* carried Ketchel, and he said, "He was a good man. I couldn't knock him out in six rounds."

Their artistic statures have been transposed in retrospect. The late, blessed Philadelphia Jack O'Brien fought both of them. He considered Ketchel "a bum distinguished only by the tumultuous but ill-directed ferocity of his assault." (That is the way Jack liked to talk.) Ketchel did knock Mr. O'Brien non compos his remarkable mentis in the last nine seconds of a ten-round bout (there was no decision, and O'Brien always contended he won on points). Jack attributed his belated mishap to negligence induced by contempt. He said Langford, though, had a "mystic quality."

"When he appeared upon the scene of combat you knew you were cooked," Jack said.

Mr. O'Brien was, in five.

11

One thing about the Sweet Science upon which all initiates are in agreement is that it used to be better. The exact period at which it was better, however, varies in direct ratio with the age of the fellow telling about it; if he was a fighter, it always turns out to be the time when he was fighting, and if a fight writer, the years before he began to get bored with what he was doing. Fight writers, since they last longer than boxers, are the most persistent howlers after antiquity; but Dr. Jack Kearns, the doyen of active fight managers who are doing all right, turned on them in 1952, when they were being particularly derisive of his current meal ticket, Joey Maxim, a light heavyweight who, Kearns said, was as good as Dempsey except he couldn't hit. Since Dempsey could do little else, this was a combination of big talk and veracity illustrative of the Doctor's genius. Back in 1919 and the subsequent years of universal inflation, Kearns had Dempsey, and the older fight writers of the time used to ask what good man he ever licked. "They said Corbett would of killed him," Dr. Kearns recalled.

The reason Kearns has more perspective than most old-timers is that he is still eating in expensive restaurants. "What right have the writers got to beef?" the good Doctor wanted to know. "In the old days they used to have good *fight writers*. That Damon Runyon, before he went on the wagon, could lay on the floor and write better than most of these guys."

Writers were always nostalgic. William E. Harding, the sporting editor of the *Police Gazette*, who was the undisputed leader of critical thought in the eighties, when that publication was the tables of the law for the American milling world, held that Jem Mace, the English Gypsy, was "the most scientific pugilist that ever stood in a ring." Mace had retired in 1871. Harding, whose woodcut portrait shows a figure of superb dignity in a wing collar, stock, and frock coat, with two feet of watch chain cascading down his stomach and his elbow on an Empire desk, rendered the opinion in 1881, when he reported the Sweet Science in a state of galloping decline. The heavyweight champion (bare knuckles) was Paddy Ryan, and the challenger a young fellow named John L. Sullivan, who, Harding said, was a mere boxer, a glove-fighter. Mace, according to Harding, would have confuted the two of them in a simultaneous disputation.

Yet 1851, when Mace was launching his career by knocking out Jack Pratt of Norwich in eight rounds that lasted a mere fifty-nine minutes—a round under London Prize Ring rules ended only with a knockdown—was a year made noteworthy in English literature by the publication of *Lavengro*, in which George Borrow lamented the downfall of the ring. Borrow said there hadn't been a true good bit of stuff since Tom Spring, who retired as champion in 1824, when Borrow was twenty-one. Tom Spring takes us back to the glorious days of Pierce Egan—the fighting son of Clio, the Muse of history—who covered the combats of heroes for some thirty years and published them in magazines of his own editing for nearly that long. Egan, a better fight writer than Runyon or Harding or William Hazlitt—who was a dilettante—was not a pitched-battle man himself. He believed in the division of labor. Egan recognized, as he wrote after the demolition of Dandy Williams, a highly touted gentleman boxer, by Josh Hudson, the "True Blue Bulldog" British pugilist, in 1820, that "drummers and boxers, to acquire excellence, must begin young. There is a peculiar *nimbleness* of the *wrist* and exercise of the shoulder required that is only obtained from growth and practice."

From about 1800 on to the 1820s, the fighters, trainers, seconds, betting men, the idly curious, and the swells who backed fighters for heavy sums—a fighter was small-time until he found a patron— used to assemble daily at the Fives Court, a covered handball court in St. Martin's Street, near what is now Leicester Square, to spar and watch the sparring. It was the place where fighters learned from other fighters, where they could show their stuff, where they did part of their conditioning, and where a lot of matches were made. The Fives Court was in short the Stillman's Gym of Lord Byron's England, and Byron would hang out there between cantos when his mistresses' husbands were all in town at the same time. He liked to spar, but not in public. John Jackson, a retired champion of England, would come to his lordship's rooms in the Albany and spar with him, sometimes for an hour at a time. Jackson conned his lordship into thinking he had a hell of a right hand; he advised him never to let it go at a husband or he might kill him and have to marry the widow. There are no swell backers around Stillman's now, but there is some Garment Center money, and some of the boys are hoping to interest Robert R. Young and a couple of Texas oilmen. Admission to the Fives Court was three shillings, or seventy-five cents at the old rate of exchange; Stillman's gets only fifty cents now, but there is no added attraction like Byron.

"Some are of the opinion that *Sparring* is of no great use," Egan wrote, "and that it takes from the natural powers of manhood, while it only teaches finesses, that cannot prove hurtful to a courageous adversary. This, however, is merely reviving an opinion maintained by the pupils of the Old School, in which strength generally prevailed over skill."

Whitey Bimstein, Freddy Brown, and other lights of the faculty at the University of Eighth Avenue get a number of young fighters who have Old School opinions on this subject, but they generally iron them out by putting them in with some six-round kid who proves how hurtful a little finesse can be. Irving Cohen, the mildest-mannered of fight managers, a plump, fair little man with a wide baby-blue stare, says: "Fighting is like education. The four-round fights are elementary school. Six-rounders is high school. Feature bouts is college, but nowadays without the small clubs we got too many boys in college without sufficient preparation."

Ten years or so ago Cohen as manager and Bimstein as trainer had a boy who would have worn the Old School tie if he had ever worn a tie at all. He was a fellow named Rocky Graziano, who, like Jack Scroggins, one of Egan's heroes, relied purely on *"downright ferocity."* "Nobody never learned him nothing," Professor Bimstein concedes. Graziano had, however, a precious asset in addition to a punch, which latter is not as rare as you might think. "If he hurt you, he wouldn't lose you," Professor Bimstein's associate, Professor Brown, descanted in one of a recent series of lectures on Mr. Graziano. "He would never let you go. If he had to he would grab you by the throat and knock your brains out and apologize after the fight." Fighters who do not warm up until stung are a dime a dozen, but the colleagues have a high esteem for a fighter who warms up when he stings the other guy. Graziano's scholastic deficiencies became apparent when he stopped fighting men lighter than he was. He met two good middleweights (he was a middleweight) in his life, Tony Zale and Ray Robinson, and they knocked him out three times in a total of twelve rounds. Against Robinson, Graziano was like Scroggins when the latter met the scientific Ned Turner, who could box *and* hit, at Sawbridgeworth in Hertfordshire, in 1817. "He was at sea without a rudder—no sight of land appeared in view." In between the Zale knockouts, though, Graziano knocked Zale out once, which remains as his only solid accomplishment in the record books. But as a drawing card he was, like Scroggins long ago, immense. "In point of attraction, what Kean has been to the boards of Drury Lane theatre, Scroggins has proved to the prize ring," Egan wrote in 1818.

Within an easy jaunt of the Fives Court there were numerous pubs that welcomed the trade of the milling coves and their knowing friends. The Castle, Holborn, which was kept in turn by three famous heroes—Bob Gregson, Tom Belcher, and finally Tom Spring himself—was perhaps the best known. Gregson was a vast lump of a heavyweight who never quite won the championship, although he made several desperate bids for it. Tom Belcher—he had an even more famous older brother—was a cutie and a gentleman. In the Castle the critics would dissect the latest battles. The fighters would try to provoke turnups with more illustrious colleagues which might lead to official battles later on. The fighter who made a good showing in a rough-and-tumble in a well-frequented pub might attract a patron who would back him in a regular battle. If the fighter won, the patron took down the stakes, but he might give some to the fighter. When Tom Cribb beat Tom Molineaux in 1811, for example, Captain Barclay, a famous sport of the day, won ten thousand pounds over the match. Cribb got four hundred pounds—and all Boxiana thought it generous of the captain. Cribb had to fight only eleven rounds to win Barclay's bet, anyway—a breeze.

The fighters joined their admirers in lushing Blue Ruin, which was just another name for Daffy, or gin, and Heavy Wet, which was ale. There was a belief that a pint of Wet, taken after every gill of Daffy, would keep the drinker sober longer; the present notion is that a beer chaser, or boilermaker's helper, accelerates intoxication. So does medical theory swing full circle with the ages. The Blue Ruin was calculated to put the fighters in a proper mood for ad lib assaults upon their friends. The Wet was recommended to build up their constitutions. Water was considered debilitating. Some care had to be exercised, however, even in the use of nourishing intoxicants. An 1821 treatise on training is explicit: "Our man may avoid taking the beer of two different breweries in the same day; for the variety of proportions and kinds of ingredients used, (if nought worse), will kick up a combustion in his guts."

Dutch Sam, the greatest little man of his age—he weighed 131 pounds and beat good men of 160—trained on Blue Ruin, but his practice was not endorsed by the Bimsteins of his time. In fact when, in 1814, at the age of thirty-nine, Sam succumbed in only thirty-eight rounds to Bill Nosworthy, the Baker, they all said that if he had stuck to Heavy Wet he would not have had such a premature downfall.

The Neutral Corner, at Eighth Avenue and Fifty-fifth Street, is to Stillman's what the Castle Tavern was to the Fives Court. Managers and trainers adjourn there after Dr. Lou Stillman, the president of the University of Eighth Avenue, locks the iron grille across the portals of his Ivy-League sweatbox at three in the afternoon. The managers receive telephone calls at the Neutral, and the trainers exchange gripes, often about a hostile region known as out-of-town, which in their stories is the equivalent of west of the Missouri in the works of A. B. Guthrie. Referees and judges out-of-town are notoriously treacherous, and the boxing commission physicians there are even worse. They will stop a fight if the New York boxer has an eyelash brushed back into his eye, but they will let the out-of-town fellow continue even if he looks like he had been hit by a Cadillac. Out-of-town it has gotten so you cannot even rely on an opponent. An opponent is supposed to offer a credible degree of opposition. That is why he is called an opponent. But a trainer who hangs out in the Corner came back from Washington, in the state of D.C., a week or two ago, spluttering with rage because the promoter had provided a cut-price opponent. "The opponent comes out in the first round and goes down three times without we had hit him yet," the trainer raved. The commission had accordingly declared the bout no contest, and held up the purse of the fighter the opponent had not waited to be hit by. "Can you imagine?" the trainer said. "A bum like that has the nerve to call himself an opponent."

Nick Masuras, behind the bar, said: "Out-of-town you're dead."

Nick, a restaurant man who used to be an armory middleweight, is one of the three proprietors of the Neutral. He thought of the name and founded the place, later taking in as partners Chickie Bogad, a former matchmaker, and Frankie Jacobs, better known as Frankie Jay, a former manager. That gives them quite a diversity of points of view on the Sweet Science, and a visit to the Neutral Corner has a didactic value for undergraduates of the University of Eighth Avenue, who go there to play shuffleboard, put slugs in the cigarette machine, and listen to their elders if that is indispensable in persuading Nick to let their tabs run another week on account the six in Danbury fell through. Trainers do not mind their clean-cut American youths being in a saloon where they can watch them. Many features of the Neutral are qualified to instruct, for example the hundreds of photographs of old-time worthwhile fighters, men who have become classics, like the portraits of John Marshall and Coke and Blackstone in a law school.

Nick is a big man nowadays; he was a tall, rangy middleweight who broadened with the years. As senior proprietor he works the day shift, and as he knows all the day customers he can tell them where to get off. "Don't be miserable," he will call out to an ex-pug who wants service when Nick wants to talk baseball at the other end of the bar, or "What makes you so miserable?" to a manager who wants change for a quarter so he can put in a call for out-of-town and ask if they will accept the charges. If Nick is looking up some important fact in Nat Fleischer's *Ring Record Book and Boxing*

Encyclopedia, which is kept in the drawer of the cash register to set-tle bets, he will let the manager wait a long time. When Nick, who is forty-eight, was fighting, Whitey, who is fifty-nine, was already a trainer. (When Whitey was fighting, he would never train, but he does not emphasize that in his lectures.) Sometimes, when under-graduates are within earshot—they would have to go out the front door and run a block to get out of it—Nick tells about a time he was fighting a guy in the 102d Medical Regiment Armory and he was so arm-weary that he said to Whitey, between rounds, "Be care-ful with that sponge, Whitey, you're getting water on my gloves. It makes them heavy.

"And Whitey looks up at me," Nick says, "and he says, 'You little bum, if you done your roadwork right you wouldn't feel this way. I hope he kills you.'"

At this point an irreverent undergrad sometimes asks: "How many miles you run every morning in them days, Nick? A hunnerd, or a hunnerten?"

Nick goes on without honoring the interruption. "And the guy I was fighting was a bum," he says. "A nothing fighter. I done it to myself."

All the Neutral Corner wits consider it a misfortune that the period of technological unemployment in the Sweet Science caused by television should coincide with a time when the cost of feeding fighters has reached an unprecedented peak. It is an old, convention-ridden art, and none of the trainers has yet tried to feed Cheeri-wobbles, Pipsqueaks, or any other form of succedaneum for nourishment advertised by the sponsors of competing television programs, which might reduce feeding costs. Nick, who is a good restaurant man and has a good cook, Jimmy the Chef, says it costs at least $3.50 a day to feed a fighter three meals, "and that's only giv-ing him a steak every other night. If he has a fight coming up he's got to have a steak every day." Maybe he doesn't, but everybody connected with the Sweet Science believes he does, and there is a morale factor involved. A tear still wells to each eye when I remem-ber a story by Jack London I read when I was twelve about a fighter in Australia, a has-been, whose family butcher refuses him credit for a bit of steak before his last stand. It is a real Jack London fight, like Marlon Brando versus Burt Lancaster on a carpet of eyeballs, and the veteran needs the strength for just one more appallingly terrific punch to pull it out—but he hasn't had the steak. His arm falls as limp as a vegetable dinner, and the sirloin-stuffed betting choice knocks him out. It would make a great brochure for the American Meat Institute. The managers, who usually okay the bills for fighters *en pension* at the Neutral, are lucky at that that they aren't living in the days of John L. Sullivan, who ate beefsteaks or mutton chops three times a day when he trained.

"Sullivan rises at seven A.M. and washes, brushes his teeth and rinses his mouth, and takes a swallow of pure spring water," it says in *The History of the Prize Ring* (1881), with lives of Paddy Ryan and John L. Sullivan, a work long wrongly attributed to William Dean Howells,

> then removes his night clothes and is sponged with sea water [so his skin wouldn't cut], rubbed perfectly dry with coarse towels, dresses himself and takes a walk of a mile. It is then about eight A.M., at which time he breakfasts on beefsteak or mutton chops cooked to suit the taste, coarse bread, with butter, and a cup of weak tea. His appetite is always good, and there is no occasion for an appetizer. Half an hour after breakfast (he is dressed so as to be comfortable for the purpose) he takes a brisk walk of from eight to ten miles, the last two of which are with an increase of speed to bring on a good perspiration. Going direct to his room he is stripped and rubbed down with the coarse towels. When perfectly cool he is sponged with sea water and given another good rubbing. Then he dresses and remains quiet until dinner, which is at one o'clock P.M., and consists of beef or mutton, roasted or boiled, plenty of stale bread, with butter and one or two potatoes. [Being a heavyweight, he naturally wasn't worried about poundage.] He remains quiet after dinner for an hour, when he commences exercise in hitting a football suspended from the ceiling, or using dumbbells or club

swinging, or short splint [*sic*] races, such as suits his fancy. He takes supper at six P.M., of cold roast beef or mutton or mutton chops, stale bread with butter, plain apple sauce and weak tea, and once or twice a week Irish or Scotch oatmeal, well cooked, with milk. After supper he takes a moderate walk of half an hour and retires at nine P.M., sleeping in none of the clothes worn during the day. He has sufficient cover on his bed to be comfortable and no more, as he says he never perspires excepting when exercising.

Sullivan, although it is scarcely likely that he had read Egan, held with the Old School of nonsparrers. He had a chopping left and a swinging right, and believed in bottling up his energy until he saw the other fellow in front of him, when he would simply rush. Anybody who read his daily menu could have predicted that he would outlast Ryan, who breakfasted on "mutton chops or beefsteak, medium cooked, with just enough salt upon it to make it palatable," dined on "roast beef and sometimes a leg of mutton," with a bottle of Bass or Scotch ale, but then weakened and took for supper "a couple of boiled eggs, some toast and a cup of tea." He obviously lacked stamina. Ryan had won his claim to the world championship by beating a man named Joe Goss in eighty-seven rounds, but Sullivan did him in in nine.

One of the results of high maintenance costs is that a good many kids go to work. This is a test of dedication. Ernie Roberts and Earl Dennis, two fine colored welterweights I know, do their roadwork in the streets at five o'clock in the morning, shower, change into business clothes, go into the center of Manhattan and work an eight-hour day, do their sparring after hours, and then go home to their respective wives and families. The menace in this situation, from a cultural point of view, is that the fighter may get to like his job. Roberts is already betraying an alarming interest in the hardware business. Dennis appears to have a more definite vocation. "I have fighting all through me," he told me once. "Before I turned professional I used to walk down the street and hope somebody would give me a hard look. But then I decided if I get my head beat in I want to get it for money." Dennis won a voice contest at the Apollo Theatre in Harlem, however, and now every time he sings a cadenza in the shower, a shadow crosses his manager's face.

A visitor who brightens the Neutral Corner whenever he shows up is Charlie Goldman, Rocky Marciano's trainer, leading claimant of the American derby-hat-and-double-breasted-suit championship since the death of James Joy Johnston, the great manager known into his seventies as the Boy Bandit. The championship fell into Johnston's handkerchief pocket when Jimmy Walker skipped the herring pond in 1931, and when the Boy Bandit died, Goldman was left in a class by himself. Mr. Goldman, who is on sabbatical leave from the University of Eighth Avenue during Marciano's professional life expectancy, is a jockey-sized man with a mashed, intelligent face, who had four hundred fights as a bantamweight, sixty with the same adversary, a contemporary named Georgie Kitson. They were as well known in their field as Van and Schenck, or Duffy and Sweeney. In the late thirties Goldman used to train a large stable of fighters for Al Weill, for whom he trains Marciano now. Weill kept the whole herd in a brownstone house on West Ninety-first Street, near the Central Park Reservoir, and Goldman had the front parlor bedroom so he could check on them. "In those days," Goldman said, joining one of the conversations on commissary problems, "Al would give each fighter a five-dollar meal ticket good for five dollars and fifty cents in trade at the coffee pot on the corner of Columbus, and most of the kids made the week on one ticket. We were feeding four and a half fighters for what one costs today, and they were all feature fighters." It is a dismal statistic that a four-round fighter eats as much as a star.

Mr. Goldman, however, does not blame the present low level of artistic competence upon either television or the high cost of living. "It is compulsory education," he says. "You take a kid has to stay in school until he is sixteen, he is under a disadvantage. All the things he should have learned to do when he was young he has to start at the beginning. How to move his feet, slip a punch, throw a hook— like finger exercises on the piano. [Here was Egan's old analogy with the drummer, proving that the Sweet Science is indeed a perpetuum, like the Manipuri dance or "My Darling Clementine." The tune of Clementine was old in sixteenth-century Spain.] A fighter shouldn't have to think about those things, he should think about how to use them. A kid learns them before he begins to think about girls, they are the most important thing in the world to him. Sixteen is too old, especially the way kids are today."

Professor Goldman himself, who is a modish sixty-seven if you accept the birth date in the record books, began to box professionally when he was nine years old, having been a mere street fighter before that. Goldman lived near Terrible Terry McGovern in South Brooklyn then—McGovern was a veteran still in his teens, with a string of knockouts as long as your arm. McGovern had a kid brother about Goldman's age, and Sam Harris, McGovern's manager, used to set them to fighting. Harris was George M. Cohan's partner in the theater. He bought the boys boxing gloves and tights—real fighters wore tights that covered their legs then, a vestigial relic of the bare-knuckle days. Combining his flair for the ring and theater, Harris used to present the boys in three-round bouts at smokers. Terry would work his kid brother's corner and another Brooklyn fighter named George Munroe would second Charlie. "We learned a lot that way," the savant says. "They always had a bet going, so we had to take it serious." By the time he was fourteen he was traveling around the country, arranging his own fights and collecting his purses when possible; and when he was sixteen he could place women in their proper perspective. "I never married," the Professor says. "I always live à la carte." Women are probably the most delicate pedagogical obstacle a trainer has to temporize with. "You can sweat oat beer," the great aphorist Sam Langford once said, "and you can sweat oat whiskey. But you can't sweat oat women." There is a theory among less profound exponents of the Science, though, that love, once legitimized, is no longer vitiating, and athletes with proper religious feelings who have been wary, moderate sinners sometimes become self-destructively uxorious after the church has solemnized the union. Professor Goldman sometimes has to function as a marriage counselor despite his inexperience, but he finds it a handicap. "One guy said to me his wife told him, 'What does Goldman know about it? He's never been married,' " the Professor says.

Marciano is the partial exception to all Goldman's rules. The heavyweight champion started late, but take him all in all, his preceptor says, he is a hell of a fighter. He always takes Charlie's advice. Also he is the hardest-working heavyweight who ever lived, training as if he purposed to make up all the lessons he missed before the age of twenty-three. (He is thirty-one now.) His great assets are stamina and leverage, but the Professor has taught him a lot about how to use them. "I don't like to be away from him long," Professor Goldman said. "He forgets. It isn't like he learned them things when he should. We got to have half an hour every day for review." Mr. Goldman was in the Corner not long ago when a resonant old gentleman—wiry, straight, and white-haired—walked into the saloon and invited the proprietors to his ninetieth birthday party, in another saloon naturally. The shortly-to-be nonagenarian wore no glasses, his hands were shapely, his forearms hard, and every hair looked as if, in the cold waterfront metaphor, it had been drove in with a tenpenny nail. On the card of invitation he laid on the bar was printed:

BILLY RAY
LAST SURVIVING BARE KNUCKLE FIGHTER

and he wouldn't let anybody in the joint buy a drink. His purse-bearer, a large subservient Irishman who looked like a retired cop, put the money on the bar for him; the protocol recalled the days when every fighter had his retinue, with a first, second, and third accredited toady.

I asked Mr. Ray how many fights he had had, and he said: "A hundert forty. The last one was with gloves. I thought the game was getting soft, so I retired." A minute later he was telling an affectionate but indelicate story about his seventh wife, now of course dead, and shortly after that complaining of the high cost of living for a male these days, citing with regret the consumer price index on Water Street, near the East River, in 1885. "Four bits then was as good as eight dollars and fifteen cents today," he said.

He said he had fought George Dixon, the immortal Little Chocolate whose yellowed photograph hangs among the immortals over
the Neutral Corner bar, and I felt as if he had said that he once
wrestled Abe Lincoln. "But the best I ever fought was Ike Weir, the
Belfast Spider," he said. "He was the cleverest man ever lived, only
his hands were so broke up he wouldn't hit you a hard one on the
jaw. Jabs and body blows is how he done it." Weir fought between
1885 and 1894, Dixon from 1886 to 1906; my own father saw him
lose the featherweight championship to the much younger Terry
McGovern in 1900, and he held Dixon was the cleverest man ever
lived. He had never seen Weir. The older you are, the further back
your candidate is likely to be. Ray said he had fought Dixon before
the latter won his first world's title as a bantam in 1890. They were
thoroughly illegal fights, for trifling sidebets in the back rooms of
saloons, and they do not appear in the record books, nor do hundreds of other fights the old-timers had.

Ray grew up in the gracious old Brooklyn of Henry Ward
Beecher, in which prizefighting was as much against the law as
cocking mains or dogfights, but less frowned upon, since there
were no Humane Societies needling the police to stop the fist
fighters. Left to their own devices the police were lenient. "A fellow
named Hughie Bart ran a great place around 1882," Mr. Ray said. "It
was right across the street from Calvary Cemetery and there would
be dogfights in the basement, rooster fights on an upper floor, and
we would be fighting on the ground floor, all at the same time.
Mourners would stop in on their way back, to take their mind off
their loss. The gravediggers were old tads with beards. They'd sit in
Hughie's drinking between jobs, and when they were watching a
fight you dassn't quit, because they would split your skull with
a spade." Sometimes Mr. Ray and other Brooklyn fighters, like the
original Jack Dempsey, the Nonpareil—"He was the *real* gentleman fighter," Mr. Ray said—would invade Henry James's New York
and show at Owney Geoghegan's or Harry Hill's or the Bucket
of Blood, all sporting establishments that ran variety shows and
pickup fights. "You would fight on a stage against a house heavyweight," the old gentleman said. "And the idea was to go fifteen

minutes without being knocked out. I weighed around one twenty. If you stayed you got three dollars. If you looked like making it, the game was to back you up against the stage curtain and a fellow would hit you on the back of the head with a hammer. If you knew it, though, you would try to work the house fighter up against the curtain. Then he had to come straight at you, so you could measure him for a counter. It was a nice easy touch, not like a finish fight. It took the place of sparring, and you got paid good for it."

Mr. Ray and his purse-bearer walked out to spread more invitations; Billy waltzed out as brisk as if he heard the gong for his ninety-first year. Mr. Goldman laughed happily. "It makes me feel young when an old guy like that comes in that was around when I just started boxing," he said. "I remember him when I was with McGovern, and he was already saying: 'You should have seen the Belfast Spider.' "

One thing you have to grant the Sweet Science, it is joined onto the past like a man's arm to his shoulder.

(1955)

Poet and Pedagogue

When Floyd Patterson regained the world heavyweight championship by knocking out Ingemar Johansson in June 1960, he so excited a teen-ager named Cassius Marcellus Clay, in Louisville, Kentucky, that Clay, who was a good amateur light heavyweight, made up a ballad in honor of the victory. (The tradition of pugilistic poetry is old; according to Pierce Egan, the Polybius of the London Prize Ring, Bob Gregson, the Lancashire Giant, used "to recount the deeds of his Brethren of the Fist in heroic verse, like the Bards of Old." A sample Gregson couplet was "The British lads that's here/Quite strangers are to fear." He was not a very good fighter, either.) At the time, Clay was too busy training for the Olympic boxing tournament in Rome that summer to set his ode down on paper, but he memorized it, as Homer and Gregson must have done with their things, and then polished it up in his head. "It took me about three days to think it up," Clay told me a week or so ago, while he was training in the Department of Parks gymnasium on West Twenty-eighth Street, for his New York debut as a professional, against a heavyweight from Detroit named Sonny Banks. In between his composition of the poem and his appearance on Twenty-eighth Street, Clay had been to Rome and cleaned up his Olympic opposition with aplomb, which is his strongest characteristic. The other finalist had been a Pole with a name that it takes two rounds to pronounce, but Cassius had not tried. A book that I own called *Olympic Games: 1960*, translated from the German, says, "Clay fixes the Pole's punch-hand with an almost hypnotic stare and by nimble dodging renders his attacks quite harmless." He thus risked being disqualified for holding and hitting, but he got away with it. He had then turned professional under social and financial auspices sufficient to launch a bank, and had won ten tryout bouts on the road. Now he told me that Banks, whom he had never seen, would be no problem.

I had watched Clay's performance in Rome and had considered it attractive but not probative. Amateur boxing compares with professional boxing as college theatricals compare with stealing scenes from Margaret Rutherford. Clay had a skittering style, like a pebble scaled over water. He was good to watch, but he seemed to make only glancing contact. It is true that the Pole finished the three-round bout helpless and out on his feet, but I thought he had just run out of puff chasing Clay, who had then cut him to pieces. ("Pietrzykowski is done for," the Olympic book says. "He gazes helplessly into his corner of the ring; his legs grow heavier and he cannot escape his rival.") A boxer who uses his legs as much as Clay used his in Rome risks deceleration in a longer bout. I had been more impressed by Patterson when *he* was an Olympian, in 1952; he had knocked out his man in a round.

At the gym that day, Cassius was on a mat doing situps when Mr. Angelo Dundee, his trainer, brought up the subject of the ballad. "He is smart," Dundee said. "He made up a poem." Clay had his hands locked behind his neck, elbows straight out, as he bobbed up and down. He is a golden-brown young man, big-chested and long-legged, whose limbs have the smooth, rounded look that Joe Louis's used to have, and that frequently denotes fast muscles. He is twenty years old and six feet two inches tall, and he weighs 195 pounds.

"I'll say it for you," the poet announced, without waiting to be wheedled or breaking cadence. He began on a rise:

"You may talk about Sweden [down and up again],
You may talk about Rome [down and up again],
But Rockville Centre is Floyd Patterson's home [down]."

He is probably the only poet in America who can recite this way. I would like to see T. S. Eliot try.

Clay went on, continuing his ventriflexions:

"A lot of people say that Floyd couldn't fight,
But you should have seen him on that comeback night."

There were some lines that I fumbled; the tempo of situps and poetry grew concurrently faster as the bardic fury took hold. But I caught the climax as the poet's voice rose:

"He cut up his eyes and mussed up his face,
And that last left hook *knocked his head out of place*!"

Cassius smiled and said no more for several situps, as if waiting for Johansson to be carried to his corner. He resumed when the Swede's seconds had had time to slosh water in his pants and bring him around. The fight was done; the press took over:

"A reporter asked: 'Ingo, will a rematch be put on?'
Johansson said: 'Don't know. It might be postponed.' "

The poet did a few more silent strophes, and then said:

"If he would have stayed in Sweden,
He wouldn't have took that beatin'. "

Here, overcome by admiration, he lay back and laughed. After a minute or two, he said, "That rhymes. I like it."

There are trainers I know who, if they had a fighter who was a poet, would give up on him, no matter how good he looked, but Mr. Dundee is of the permissive school. Dundee has been a leading Italian name in the prizefighting business in this country ever since about 1910, when a manager named Scotty Monteith had a boy named Giuseppe Carrora, whom he rechristened Johnny Dundee. Johnny became the hottest lightweight around; in 1923, in the twilight of his career, he boiled down and won the featherweight championship of the world. Clay's trainer is a brother of Chris Dundee, a promoter in Miami Beach, but they are not related to Johnny, who is still around, or to Joe and Vince Dundee, brothers out of Baltimore, who were welterweight and middleweight champions, respectively, in the late twenties and early thirties, and who are not related to Johnny, either.

"He is very talented," Dundee said while Clay was dressing. It was bitter cold outside, but he did not make Clay take a cold shower before putting his clothes on. "He likes his shower better at the hotel," he told me. It smacked of progressive education. Elaborating on Clay's talent, Dundee said, "He will jab you five or six times going away. Busy hands. And he has a left uppercut." He added that Clay, as a business enterprise, was owned and operated by a syndicate of ten leading citizens of Louisville, mostly distillers. They had given the boy a bonus of ten thousand dollars for signing up, and paid him a monthly allowance and his training expenses whether he fought or not—a research fellowship. In return, they took half his earnings when he had any. These had been inconsiderable until his most recent fight, when he made eight thousand dollars. His manager of record (since somebody has to sign contracts) was a member of this junta—Mr. William Faversham, a son of the old matinee idol. Dundee, the tutor in attendance, was a salaried employee. "The idea was he shouldn't be rushed," Dundee said. "Before they hired me, we had a conference about his future like he was a serious subject."

It sounded like flying in the face of the old rule that hungry fighters make the best fighters. I know an old-style manager named Al Weill, who at the beginning of the week used to give each of his fighters a five-dollar meal ticket that was good for five dollars and fifty cents in trade at a coffeepot on Columbus Avenue. A guy had to win a fight to get a second ticket before the following Monday. "It's good for them," Weill used to say. "Keeps their mind on their work."

That day in the gym, Clay's boxing had consisted of three rounds with an amateur light heavyweight, who had been unable to keep away from the busy hands. When the sparring partner covered his head with his arms, the poet didn't bother to punch to the body. "I'm a head-hunter," he said to a watcher who called his attention to this omission. "Keep punching at a man's head, and it mixes his mind." After that, he had skipped rope without a rope. His flippancy would have horrified Colonel John R. Stingo, an ancient connoisseur, who says, "Body-punching is capital investment," or the late Sam Langford, who, when asked why he punched so much for the body, said, "The head got eyes."

Now Cassius reappeared, a glass of fashion in a snuff-colored suit and one of those lace-front shirts, which I had never before known anybody with nerve enough to wear, although I had seen them in shirt-shop windows on Broadway. His tie was like two shoestring ends laid across each other, and his smile was white and optimistic. He did not appear to know how badly he was being brought up.

Just when the Sweet Science appears to lie like a painted ship upon a painted ocean, a new Hero, as Pierce Egan would term him, comes along like a Moran tug to pull it out of the doldrums. It was because Clay had some of the Heroic aura about him that I went uptown the next day to see Banks, the *morceau* chosen for the prodigy to perform in his big-time debut. The exhibition piece is usually a fighter who was once almost illustrious and is now beyond ambition, but Banks was only twenty-one. He had knocked out nine men in twelve professional fights, had won another fight on a decision, and had lost two, being knocked out once. But he had come back against the man who stopped him and had knocked *him* out in two rounds. That showed determination as well as punching power. I had already met Banks, briefly, at a press conference that the Madison Square Garden corporation gave for the two incipient Heroes, and he seemed the antithesis of the Kentucky bard—a grave, quiet young Deep Southerner. He was as introverted as Clay was extro. Banks, a lighter shade than Clay, had migrated to the automobile factories from Tupelo, Mississippi, and boxed as a professional from the start, to earn money. He said at the press conference that he felt he had "done excellently" in the ring, and that the man who had knocked him out, and whom he had subsequently knocked out, was "an excellent boxer." He had a long, rather pointed head, a long chin, and the kind of inverted-triangle torso that pro-proletarian artists like to put on their steelworkers. His shoulders were so wide that his neat ready-made suit floated around his waist, and he had long, thick arms.

Banks was scheduled to train at two o'clock in the afternoon at Harry Wiley's Gymnasium, at 137th Street and Broadway. I felt back at home in the fight world as soon as I climbed up from the subway and saw the place—a line of plate-glass windows above a Latin-American bar, grill, and barbecue. The windows were flecked with legends giving the hours when the gym was open (it wasn't), the names of fighters training there (they weren't, and half of them had been retired for years), and plugs for physical fitness and boxing instruction. The door of the gym—"Harry Wiley's *Clean* Gym," the sign on it said—was locked, so I went into the Latin-American place and had a beer while I waited. I had had only half the bottle when a taxi drew up at the curb outside the window and five colored men—one little and four big—got out, carrying bags of gear. They had the key for the gym. I finished my beer and followed them.

By the time I got up the stairs, the three fellows who were going to spar were already in the locker room changing their clothes, and the only ones in sight were a big, solid man in a red jersey, who was laying out the gloves and bandages on a rubbing table, and a wispy little chap in an olive-green sweater, who was smoking a long rattail cigar. His thin black hair was carefully marcelled along the top of his narrow skull, a long gold watch chain dangled from his fob pocket, and he exuded an air of elegance, precision, and authority, like a withered but still peppery mahout in charge of a string of not quite bright elephants. Both men appeared occupied with their thoughts, so I made a tour of the room before intruding, reading a series of didactic signs that the proprietor had put up among the photographs of prizefighters and pinup girls. "Road Work Builds Your Legs," one sign said, and another, "Train Every Day—Great Fighters Are Made That Way." A third admonished, "The Gentleman Boxer Has the Most Friends." "Ladies Are Fine—At the Right Time," another said. When I had absorbed them all, I got around to the big man.

"Clay looks mighty fast," I said to him by way of an opening.

He said, "He may not be if a big fellow go after him. That amateur stuff don't mean too much." He himself was Johnny Summerlin, he told me, and he had fought a lot of good heavyweights in his day. "Our boy don't move so fast, but he got fast hands," he said. "He don't discourage easy, either. If we win this one, we'll be all set." I could see that they would be, because Clay has been getting a lot of publicity, and a boxer's fame, like a knight's armor, becomes the property of the fellow who licks him.

Banks now came out in ring togs, and, after greeting me, held out his hands to Summerlin to be bandaged. He looked even more formidable without his street clothes. The two other fighters, who wore their names on their dressing robes, were Cody Jones, a heavyweight as big as Banks, and Sammy Poe, nearly as big. Poe, although a Negro, had a shamrock on the back of his robe—a sign that he was a wag. They were both Banks stablemates from Detroit, Summerlin said, and they had come along to spar with him. Jones had had ten fights and had won eight, six of them by knockouts. This was rougher opposition than any amateur light heavyweight. Banks, when he sparred with Jones, did not scuffle around but practiced purposefully a pattern of coming in low, feinting with head and body to draw a lead, and then hammering in hooks to body and head, following the combination with a right cross. His footwork was neat and geometrical but not flashy—he slid his soles along the mat, always set to hit hard. Jones, using his right hand often, provided rough competition but no substitute for Clay's blinding speed. Poe, the clown, followed Jones. He grunted and howled "Whoo-huh-huh!" every time he threw a punch, and Banks howled back; it sounded like feeding time at a zoo. This was a lively workout.

After the sparring, the little man, discarding his cigar, got into the ring alone with Banks. He wore huge sixteen- or eighteen-ounce sparring gloves, which he held, palm open, toward the giant, leading him in what looked like a fan dance. The little man, covering his meager chest with one glove, would hold up the other, and Banks would hit it. The punch coming into the glove sounded like a fast ball striking a catcher's mitt. By his motions the trainer indicated a scenario, and Banks, from his crouch, dropped Clay ten or fifteen times this way, theoretically. Then the slender man called a halt and sent Banks to punch the bag. "Remember," he said, "you got to keep on top of him—keep the pressure on."

As the little man climbed out of the ring, I walked around to him and introduced myself. He said that his name was Theodore McWhorter, and that Banks was his baby, his creation—he had taught him everything. For twenty years, McWhorter said, he had run a gymnasium for boxers in Detroit—the Big D. (I supposed it must be pretty much like Wiley's, where we were talking.) He had trained hundreds of neighborhood boys to fight, and had had some good fighters in his time, like Johnny Summerlin, but never a champion. Something always went wrong.

There are fellows like this in almost every big town. Cus D'Amato, who brought Patterson through the amateurs and still has him, used to be one of them, with a one-room gym on Fourteenth Street, but he is among the few who ever hit the mother lode. I could see that McWhorter was a good teacher—such men often are. They are never former champions or notable boxers. The old star is impatient with beginners. He secretly hopes that they won't be as good as he was, and this is a self-defeating quirk in an instructor. The man with the little gym wants to prove himself vicariously. Every promising pupil, consequently, is himself, and he gets knocked out with every one of them, even if he lives to be eighty. McWhorter, typically, said he had been an amateur bantamweight in the thirties but had never turned pro, because times were so hard then that you could pick up more money boxing amateur. Instead of medals, you would get certificates redeemable for cash—two, three, five dollars, sometimes even ten. Once you were a pro, you might not get two fights a year. Whatever his real reason, he had not gone on.

"My boy never got nothing easy," he said. "He don't expect it.

Nobody give him nothing. And a boy like that, when he got a chance to be something, he's dangerous."

"You think he's really got a chance?" I asked.

"If we didn't think so, we wouldn't have took the match," Mr. McWhorter said. "You can trap a man," he added mysteriously. "Flashy boxing is like running. You got a long lead, you can run freely. The other kid's way behind, you can sit down and play, get up fresh, and run away from him again. But you got a man running after you with a knife or a gun, pressing it in your back, you feel the pressure. You can't run so free. I'm fighting Clay my way." The substitution of the first for the third person in conversation is managerial usage. I knew that McWhorter would resubstitute Banks for himself in the actual fight.

We walked over to the heavy bag, where Banks was working. There was one other downtown spectator in the gym, and he came over and joined us. He was one of those anonymous experts, looking like all his kind, whom I have been seeing around gyms and fight camps for thirty years. "You can tell a Detroit fighter every time," he said. "They're well-trained. They got the fundamentals. They can hit. Like from Philadelphia the fighters got feneese."

McWhorter acknowledged the compliment. "We have some fine *trainers* in Detroit," he said.

Banks, no longer gentle, crouched and swayed before the bag, crashing his left hand into it until the thing jigged and clanked its chains.

"Hit him in the belly like that and you got him," the expert said. "He can't take it there."

Banks stopped punching the bag and said, "Thank you, thank you," just as if the expert had said something novel.

"He's a good boy," McWhorter said as the man walked away. "A *polite* boy."

When I left to go downtown, I felt like the possessor of a possibly valuable secret. I toyed with the notion of warning the butterfly Cassius, my fellow-litterateur, of his peril, but decided that I must remain neutral and silent. In a dream the night before the fight, I heard Mr. McWhorter saying ominously, "You can trap a man." He had grown as big as Summerlin, and his cigar had turned into an elephant goad.

The temperature outside the Garden was around fifteen degrees on the night of the fight, and the crowd that had assembled to see Clay's debut was so thin that it could more properly be denominated a quorum. Only fans who like sociability ordinarily turn up for a fight that they can watch for nothing on television, and that night the cold had kept even the most gregarious at home. (The boxers, however, were sure of four thousand dollars apiece from television.) Only the sports writers, the gamblers, and the fight mob were there—nonpayers all—and the Garden management, solicitous about how the ringside would look to the television audience, had to coax relative strangers into the working-press section. This shortage of spectators was too bad, because there was at least one redhot preliminary, which merited a better audience. It was a six-rounder between a lad infelicitously named Ducky Dietz—a hooker and body puncher—and a light heavy from western Pennsylvania named Tommy Gerarde, who preferred a longer range but punched more sharply. Dietz, who shouldn't have, got the decision, and the row that followed warmed our little social group and set the right mood for the main event.

The poet came into the ring first, escorted by Dundee; Nick Florio, the brother of Patterson's trainer, Dan Florio; and a fellow named Gil Clancy, a physical-education supervisor for the Department of Parks, who himself manages a good welterweight named Emile Griffith. (Griffith, unlike Clay, is a worrier. "He is always afraid of being devalued," Clancy says.) As a corner, it was the equivalent of being represented by Sullivan & Cromwell. Clay, who I imagine regretted parting with his lace shirt, had replaced it with a white robe that had a close-fitting red collar and red cuffs. He wore white buckskin bootees that came high on his calves, and, taking hold of the ropes in his corner, he stretched and bounced like a ballet dancer at the bar. In doing so, he turned his back to the other, or hungry, corner before Banks and his faction arrived.

Banks looked determined but slightly uncertain. Maybe he was trying to remember all the things McWhorter had told him to do. He was accompanied by McWhorter, Summerlin, and Harry Wiley, a plump, courtly colored man, who runs the clean gym. McWhorter's parchment brow was wrinkled with concentration, and his mouth was set. He looked like a producer who thinks he may have a hit and doesn't want to jinx it. Summerlin was stolid; he may have been remembering the nights when he had not quite made it. Wiley was comforting and solicitous. The weights were announced: Clay, 194½; Banks, 191¼. It was a difference too slight to count between heavyweights. Banks, wide-shouldered, narrow-waisted, looked as if he would be the better man at slinging a sledge or lifting weights; Clay, more cylindrically formed—arms, legs, and torso—moved more smoothly.

When the bell rang, Banks dropped into the crouch I had seen him rehearse, and began the stalk after Clay that was to put the pressure on him. I felt a species of complicity. The poet, still wrapped in certitude, jabbed, moved, teased, looking the *Konzertstück* over before he banged the ivories. By nimble dodging, as in Rome, he rendered the hungry fighter's attack quite harmless, but this time without keeping his hypnotic stare fixed steadily enough on the punch-hand. They circled around for a minute or so, and then Clay was hit, but not hard, by a left hand. He moved to his own left, across Banks's field of vision, and Banks, turning with him, hit him again, but this time full, with the rising left hook he had worked on so faithfully. The poet went down, and the three men crouching below Banks's corner must have felt, as they listened to the count, like a Reno tourist who hears the silver-dollar jackpot come rolling down. It had been a solid shot—no fluke—and where one shot succeeds, there is no reason to think that another won't. The poet rose at the count of two, but the referee, Ruby Goldstein, as the rules in New York require, stepped between the boxers until the count reached eight, when he let them resume. Now that Banks knew he could hit Clay, he was full of confidence, and the gamblers, who had made Clay a 5–1 favorite, must have had a bad moment. None of them had seen Clay fight, and no doubt they wished they hadn't been so credulous. Clay, I knew, had not been knocked down since his amateur days, but he was cool. He neither rushed after Banks, like an angry kid, nor backed away from him. Standing straight up, he boxed and moved—cuff, slap, jab, and stick, the busy hands stinging like bees. As for Banks, success made him forget his whole plan. Instead of keeping the pressure on—moving in and throwing punches to force an opening—he forgot his right hand and began winging left hooks without trying to set Clay up for them. At the end of the round, the poet was in good shape again, and Banks, the more winded of the two, was spitting a handsome quantity of blood from the jabs that Clay had landed going away. Nothing tires a man more than swinging uselessly. Nevertheless, the knockdown had given Banks the round. The hungry fighter who had listened to his pedagogue was in front, and if he listened again, he might very well stay there.

It didn't happen. In the second round, talent asserted itself. Honest effort and sterling character backed by solid instruction will carry a man a good way, but unearned natural ability has a lot to be said for it. Young Cassius, who will never have to be lean, jabbed the good boy until he had spread his already wide nose over his face. Banks, I could see, was already having difficulty breathing, and the intellectual pace was just too fast. He kept throwing that left hook whenever he could get set, but he was like a man trying to fight off wasps with a shovel. One disadvantage of having had a respected teacher is that whenever the pupil gets in a jam he tries to remember what the professor told him, and there just isn't time. Like the Pole's in the Olympics, Banks's legs grew heavier, and he could not escape his rival. He did not, however, gaze helplessly into his corner of the ring; he kept on trying. Now Cassius, having mixed the mind, began to dig in. He would come in with a flurry of busy hands, jabbing and slapping his man off balance, and then, in close, drive a short, hard right to the head or a looping left to the slim waist. Two thirds of the way through the round, he staggered Banks, who dropped forward to his glove tips, though his knees did not touch canvas. A moment later, Clay knocked him down fairly with a right hand, but McWhorter's pupil was not done.

The third round was even less competitive; it was now evident that Banks could not win, but he was still trying. He landed the last,

and just about the hardest, punch of the round—a good left hook
to the side of the poet's face. Clay looked surprised. Between the
third and fourth rounds, the Boxing Commission physician, Dr.
Schiff, trotted up the steps and looked into Banks's eyes. The Detroit lad came out gamely for the round, but the one-minute rest
had not refreshed him. After the first flurry of punches, he staggered, helpless, and Goldstein stopped the match. An old fighter,
brilliant but cursed with a weak jaw, Goldstein could sympathize.

When it was over, I felt that my first social duty was to the
stricken. Clay, I estimated, was the kind of Hero likely to be around
for a long while, and if he felt depressed by the knockdown, he
had the contents of ten distilleries to draw upon for stimulation. I
therefore headed for the loser's dressing room to condole with
McWhorter, who had experienced another almost. When I arrived,
Banks, sitting up on the edge of a rubbing table, was shaking his
head, angry at himself, like a kid outfielder who has let the deciding
run drop through his fingers. Summerlin was telling him what he
had done wrong: "You can't hit anybody throwing just one punch
all the time. You had him, but you lost him. You forgot to keep
crowding." Then the unquenchable pedagogue said, "You're a better fighter than he is, but you lost your head. If you can only get
him again . . ." But poor Banks looked only half convinced. What he
felt, I imagine, was that he *had* had Clay, and that it might be a long
time before he caught him again. If he had followed through, he
would have been in line for dazzling matches—the kind that bring
you five figures even if you lose. I asked him what punch had
started him on the downgrade, but he just shook his head. Wiley,
the gym proprietor, said there hadn't been any one turning point.
"Things just went sour gradually all at once," he declared. "You got
to respect a boxer. He'll pick you and peck you, peck you and pick
you, until you don't know where you are."

(1962)

The Press

The World of Sport

(NOVEMBER 6, 1947)

A police reporter sees more than he can set down; a feature writer sets down more than he possibly can have seen. I was eager to get a job as a police reporter after I took my degree. As a maraschino cherry on the sundae of academic absurdity, the degree was entitled Bachelor of Literature, although what literature had to do with rewriting the *Times* paragraphs I never found out. I went swimming on commencement day.

There were no police jobs going; in fact for a while there seemed to be no jobs going at all for beginners. The assistant city editor—I seldom got as far as the city editor himself—would ask me if I had had experience in Denver or Texas. They seemed to think it cheeky for a New Yorker to ask for a job. Translating the Italian book for Max and Denison, I had read a lot about the immigrant custom of getting a job in a firm and then bringing on all one's *paesani*, peasants from the same village in Apulia or Lucania. It seemed to be an old custom in New York newspaper offices too, except that the *paesani* came from places like Binghamton and East St. Louis.

I have always thought that a dozen young men fresh out of the top third of the senior class in the liberal-arts course at Columbia, N.Y.U., C.C.N.Y., or Brooklyn College would make a more valuable reinforcement for a newspaper staff than the same number of men freshly arrived from the bush with ten years' small-city experience apiece. The New York boys would be more mature emotionally and more literate. They would have a local news background acquired from reading New York newspapers all their lives. Also

they would romanticize themselves less. I have known out-of-
towners on newspapers whose primary urge toward journalism had
been a consuming desire to escape from Iowa.

I know this is a controversial subject, and I seem to be the only
one on my side of the controversy, due to the continuous rumble of
logs being rolled for one another by the staunch Hoosier-Sooners
and Razor-backed Rocky Mountain Boys, but I am sure I've got
something.

I looked about for a job for portions of six weeks. It was summer, and the beach at Far Rockaway diverted me from job hunting
pretty often. Then a copyreader named Laurence J. Spiker in the
sports department of the *Times* called Professor Cooper one day
and asked the old boy if he had an ex-student with the makings of a
copyreader. By this, I presume, he meant a broad bottom and a captious disposition. Coop recommended me, and I went unromanti-
cally to work sitting down. In the back of my mind was the thought
that after a tour of sedentary duty I might convince some editor I
had experience enough to use my legs. This was a faulty line of
thought, for trained copyreaders are usually harder to find than reporters, and few editors will turn an experienced copyreader into
an inexperienced outside man. It often, but not always, works the
other way—when a fellow's legs give out he comes inside, providing he can read and write.

In addition to the frustrated reporters who know exactly how a
story should be covered because they have never covered one, and
the superannuated reporters who are just resting their feet, there are
in every newspaper office the congenital, aboriginal, intramurals.
They are to be distinguished from the frustrates because they have
never even wanted to see the world outside. They come to newspapers like monks to cloisters or worms to apples. They are the dedicated. All of them are fated to be editors except the ones that get
killed off by the lunches they eat at their desks until even the most
drastic purgatives lose all effect upon them. The survivors of gastric
disorders rise to minor executive jobs and then major ones, and the
reign of these nonwriters makes our newspapers read like the food
in *The New York Times* cafeteria tastes. It is as if, in football, only bad

players were allowed to become coaches. Indifference to language thus becomes hierarchized. The proprietor wouldn't know decent writing if he saw it; the managing editor wouldn't know
decent writing if he saw it. No one who even aspires to be a managing editor will admit knowing anything about writing if he
knows what is good for him.

At any rate, I went to work. It was arranged that I was to receive
eight dollars a day, six days a week. My pay was on a daily basis so
that, if the *Times* found my work inadequate, it would not feel
obliged to give me a week's notice. It was a paper with sensibilities.
After I had worked there five months I was raised to fifty dollars a
week. My parents moved back to Manhattan from Long Island in
the fall of 1925, and since they insisted that I live rent-free with them
in an apartment hotel near Central Park, I found my salary more
than adequate. This gave me a less than realistic first impression of
the economic aspect of newspaper work.

I spent eight months on the *Times*, and they gave me my first
and, I am thankful, only sample of what must be the common experience of the great majority of workers—a clean, painless job
without any intrinsic interest. Sports copyreading is as easy to learn
as how to play a fair game of anagrams. You check on scores: for example, you make sure, in basketball, that the field goals and foul
goals do not add up to more or less than the final score. If they
don't check, you give some player a couple of extra points, or
maybe deprive him of one or two. This goes for baseball, football,
and any other game you can think of. We never did have a copyreader who could fathom a cricket score, so that copy always went
to type just as it was brought in, handwritten, by a long-haired
British gentleman who attended the matches, most of which, I
think, were held on Staten Island. Reader interest was nil, but Major Thomson, the sports editor, thought cricket high class. The
cricket correspondent also covered chess matches. There was a
copyreader, John Drebinger, who understood what the chess reports were about, and he would sometimes protest at the small size
of the headline he was ordered to put over a chess story. "That's a
hot match!" he would complain. "Lasker held to a draw in sixty-

three moves!" We called him Bogglejobble, after the Russian chess-master, Bogoljubow, one of his favorites.

Drebinger, incidentally, is one of the few confirmed copyreaders ever to escape into the outside world. A few years later he became the *Times* correspondent with the New York Giants. I think Drebinger effected his release by pretending to be a bourgeois type, extremely contented with his life on the copy desk. This so irritated the higher powers, used to copyreaders' continual complaints, that they decided to make Drebinger unhappy too, and kicked him into exactly the place he wanted to get.

Having verified, or at least rectified, the statistical matter which forms the real meat of the story, and "cleared it"—that is, sent it up to the composing room to be set in agate type—the sports copyreader takes a cursory look at the sports writer's text. He quickly learns not to try to improve it, as sports writers are a temperamental lot and like to get maximum mileage out of the used adjectives they lease from the Merriam-Webster Dictionary Company at the beginning of every season. The copyreader is, however, allowed to sneer.

"Old Dick Vidmer has moved the slough of despond over to Pittsburgh," he may whisper roguishly to the colleague sitting at his right. "Yesterday he had the Dodgers in the slough of despond in Cincinnati and last Friday they were in it in Chicago. Must be part of their traveling equipment, like a bat bag." All sports copyreaders feel that sports writers are overpaid and overrated windbags who spend their time sleeping off drunks in the open air while the copy-readers have to sleep off their drunks at home and in the daytime, which is a great hardship.

Once the text has been cleared, the sports copyreader has a chance for his nearest approach to creative effort: the composition of a headline. This is a form of art, like the Japanese nō poem or writing on the head of a pin, which must be exercised within extremely exiguous limits. One form of head I remember called for two lines of 16½ spaces maximum (16 was preferable) with a dozen words falling away under them in an inverted pyramid called a bank. A space is a unit used in headline writing, roughly equivalent to the space a letter takes up. However, *M* and *W* count 1½ spaces, and *I* counts only ½. The interval between two words is counted a ½ space. So a fellow can write "Giants Beat (or defeat, stop, topple, batter) Reds," but just "Giants Trip Pirates," because *Pirates* is 2½ spaces longer than *Reds*. "Giants Trip Pirates" would not look quite so crowded. In the second line you can elaborate "2–1 as Ott Homers," perhaps. Of course not many ballplayers have names as easy to fit in a headline as Ott. You'd be surprised how quickly an evening passes amid big intellectual problems like that.

To *top* is probably the most useful headline synonym for to *beat*, *defeat*. It occupies only *three* spaces instead of four. The trouble with it is that sometimes all the copyreaders on a desk start to use it simultaneously and every baseball headline has somebody "topping" somebody else. Then the man in the slot gets stuffy and accuses his subordinates, the men on the rim, of a certain lack of originality.

On the *Times* I used to come to work at seven in the evening, six o'clock on Saturdays, which was the busy day, and get through at about one-thirty in the morning. There was no lunch period, but at about midnight a boy brought us a cup of bad tepid coffee at the desk, or else we went up in couples to the cafeteria in the Times Building, to drink the equally bad but warmer coffee available there. After one-thirty the gayer elements of the group—"of whom I was," to borrow a phrase from a Russian colonel I once knew— went out to have a few glasses of beer needled with alcohol in the speakeasies around Times Square before going home. We slept late.

It must be like that in a lot of industries. When you come to work all you think of is what you are going to do when it is over. It was no use trying to throw yourself heart and soul into making *Giants* fit into 4½ spaces, because you couldn't anyway. And there are a lot of other jobs in the world with limitations just as rigid.

There was, however, for a man of twenty-one, as I was, a fascinating sense of being a dashing chap just because one was in the newspaper game. A fellow named John Muldowney, who had been the youngest copyreader until my advent, was my most frequent companion on the speakeasy circuit, but other copyreaders often came along. And once we got our flat feet on the brass rail and the twenty-five-cent needle beer in front of us, we felt the social and professional equals of Frank Ward O'Malley or any other son-ofabitch we wanted to tell lies about.

There was, in truth, more of interest outside the *Times* sports department than inside it, so that no man in his right senses could have made the work his main preoccupation. Social intercourse among newspapermen, and for that matter among all kinds of people then, was not restricted by any difference of ideologies. The touchstone of liberalism was opposition to the liquor laws and we were all liberals. Anybody you met in a speakeasy had to be a liberal too, or he wouldn't be there. Our idea of a great liberal statesman was Al Smith, because he came right out and told the farmers, knowing in advance that they weren't going to vote for him anyway, exactly where he stood. He stood on the same side of the bar we did. This bond of liberal faith predisposed us favorably toward anybody we encountered in a saloon and made for quick friendships. We felt there had to be some good about anybody that resisted tyranny.

It made us feel a responsibility for drunks that I happily feel no longer. I remember one bleak January night Muldowney and I found a young fellow lying in the snow on Forty-fifth Street between Sixth and Seventh and we decided it would be wrong to let him freeze to death. We barked lightheartedly, doubtless a matter of allusion to St. Bernard dogs, and picked him up. He was rigid, more probably with liquor than cold, but he felt as if he weighed not more than fifteen pounds. Either he was a levitationist or it was good alcohol they put in the beer at Canavan's. "Where do you live?" Mul asked the impersonation of a corpse, and it murmured, "United States." With an intuition born of liquor we understood that he meant the Hotel America, on Forty-seventh Street, so we carried him up there.

"What's your name?" Mul asked him when we arrived at the hotel, and the corpse said, "Johnny." "Johnny what?" "Ask m'brother." "Ah," I said, "he has a brother in the hotel." So we entered and carried him through the lobby to the elevator. "Where does this man's brother room?" I asked the night elevator man (it was the kind of hotel where the night elevator man sometimes had to distribute people to their rooms). He gave us the number and we carried Johnny to the door and knocked. "Who the hell is it?" somebody shouted gratefully, and we said: "It's your brother." The door swung open, although no light went on, and the same voice shouted: "Throw the bastard in!" Mul and I threw him in and the door slammed shut. We went on our way knowing we had done a good action. If I saw a man lying in the snow like that now, I would just jump over him and leave him for dead.

There were eight or nine sports copyreaders, besides two or three reporters who joined us Saturday nights, when there was a big sports section, to earn an extra eight dollars reading copy. Prices were not low in 1925, and my senior colleagues were not affluent, but the whole scale of pay was much higher than it was in the shacks at Police Headquarters. In 1934, when the *World-Telegram* unit of the American Newspaper Guild won a minimum wage of thirty-five dollars for experienced reporters, an old-time police reporter whom I knew down there said that the contract would bring him *a higher wage than he had ever had in his life*. This man, in 1925, must have been getting around twenty-five dollars.

The rewards of office in the sports department did not seem to me particularly brilliant, but they were sufficient to motivate a tangle of political intrigue. Once I had learned to compose headlines I became bored with the whole business. It wasn't that I disliked sports; the fact was that I had never in my life, since the age of six years, had so little contact with sports. Nineteen twenty-five was the first football season since 1917 when I didn't see a single college game. I had to be in the office early Saturdays. I saw no boxing because I worked evenings, and no horse racing or baseball because it seemed a shame to pay admission when I worked in a sports department, even though I was so junior that I never got any of the office passes. I used to go down to Police Headquarters sometime in the afternoons just to make sure that the world was still going on. On these occasions I was pleased to note that I was accepted by my former overlords as a real newspaperman because I was making fifty dollars a week.

Winter was a quieter season for sporting news then than it is now. Professional ice hockey had just come to New York, and had not yet been built up into something almost as much publicized as baseball. Basketball was still played only in college and school gymnasiums, and winter horse racing didn't amount to much. So we used to fiddle around a lot with such picayune matters as scholastic basketball, pocket-billiard matches—the head of the sports copy desk did publicity for a manufacturer of billiard equipment—and Class B chess tournaments. At about half-past ten dozens of schoolboys with changing voices would begin to call up to tell how St. Ambrosius had defeated Sodom Academy, or the High School of Sales Management had won an uphill battle with the Letchworth Village School for Feebleminded Children. Major Thomson had an idea that we ought to get the names of all the dashing adolescents and how many baskets they had scored. He had heard that the more names you got into a paper the more people would read it. This accounts for the high reader interest of the telephone directory. Also he was in a race with the *Herald Tribune* to see who could publish more schoolboy scores. This competition in inclusiveness had started during the football season, centering first, however, on college football scores. After we had compiled our list of College Games each Saturday we would wait until the copy boy brought in the first copies of the *Herald Tribune* and eagerly count to see whether they had any we didn't. It was by keeping this list of results (a chore that always devolved upon the newest copyreader) that I acquired a repertory of names of American colleges unmatched except by textbook salesmen. If the *Tribune* had the score of the Muskingum–Baldwin-Wallace game and we didn't, Major Thomson was inconsolable, even though we might have scooped them on two other games, Upsala–Rider College of Trenton, N.J., and Cornell (Ia.)–Columbia (Ia.) perhaps. Sometimes he even suspected the *Tribune* of ringing in a couple of colleges that didn't exist.

Early in November the struggle seemed fated to end in a deadlock. A conviction began to dawn that both papers were publishing the scores of every game on earth. Then we got a new correspondent in a Southern state who sent us the scores of dozens of games the *Tribune* didn't carry, games played by teams with names like Lincoln and Virginia State. It wasn't until the following week that Thomson learned that all these teams were colored. The question then was whether he should keep them all out of the next issue, since the *Tribune* apparently disdained them, or strike a simultaneous blow for liberalism and the prestige of the *Times* sports section by keeping them in, so we would have the longest list of college football results in the city. Thomson was tempted by the second alternative, but it was too radical for him. He threw the colored colleges out and finished in a dead heat with the opposition.

This Thomson was an extraordinary sort for a sports editor. He was a Canadian of the type that plays British, and had been a captain in the First World War, but he seemed more like an old trouper than an old trooper. He was a tall man with a purplish face and black hair parted in the middle. He liked to wear colored silk shirts, white flannel pants, and white buckskin shoes in summer. He walked with long, determined strides, as if he were continually on his way to do something important (but what?), and he acknowledged a profound dislike for sports of all kinds. Frederick P. Birchall, the managing editor of the *Times*, was British and choleric and walked the same way. I am not in a position to say that the sports editor patterned his manner on Birchall's, since I had known neither before their conjuncture on the *Times*, but I have noticed a mimetic tendency among executives on other papers. It is a constant of the newspaper business.

The very existence of the *Times* sports section marked a concession to frivolity on the part of Adolph Ochs, the great merchandiser of stodginess, but the old man had determined that if he had to have a sports page at all, it would be as uninteresting as possible. Thomson was an ideal choice to keep it that way.

One night some boy with pimples in his voice called up from Brooklyn to tell the *Times* about a particularly unfascinating contest between two Catholic-school fives. I took the call and noted down all the drear details until I got to who was the referee. "Who was he?" I asked. "I don't know," the kid said, "and anyway I ain't got any more nickels." So he hung up. We couldn't use a basketball score in the *Times* without the name of the referee. So I wrote in "Ignoto," which means "unknown" in Italian. Nobody caught on, and after a while I had Ignoto refereeing a lot of basketball games, all around town. Then I began bragging about it, and after a short while my feeble jest came to the ears of Thomson.

"God knows what you will do next, young man," he told me after the first edition had gone to press on a bitter night in March. "You are irresponsible. Not a *Times* type. Go."

So I lost my first newspaper job.

My Name in Big Letters

(NOVEMBER 6, 1947)

In September 1930, when I left the Providence *Journal*, it was apparent that Mr. Hoover had laid his egg. But I had a plan to get a job. I had thought of it so often that I didn't see how it could fail. . . .

As soon as we got to New York, I looked in the classified telephone directory for a sign painter. I found one with a shop fairly near the Grand Central Station and ordered a sign to be carried by a sandwich man. The sign was to say, front and rear, "Hire Joe Liebling." The sign painter, a Hungarian who liked to use bright colors, advised an orange job with blue lettering. It cost eleven dollars, fully rigged. I gave him a five-dollar deposit. He promised he would have it ready next day.

I then went down to Battery Park, where there always were sandwich men advertising passport photographers. The passport bureau was at the Custom House then; there was none at Radio City because Radio City hadn't been built. I addressed myself to a man who was carrying a sign that said 6 PHOTOS FOR 75 CENTS, and asked him if he knew any sandwich men at liberty who would consider an engagement for a couple of days. He said sure, there were lots of colleagues laying off, because the volume of display advertising had fallen off drastically. He lived in a rooming house on Greenwich Street, under the elevated railway, that was largely patronized by sandwich men. He promised to find a good reliable practitioner for me. The regular tariff, he said, was two dollars a day. I said I would want the man only from early noon to sundown.

Jim Barrett, the city editor of the *World*, was the man I wanted to see the sign, and Barrett wasn't at the office mornings. I guess I wasn't interested in a job on the *Evening World*. I gave my sandwich man friend the sign painter's address and told him to have his candidate meet me there at noon next day.

The man who reported to me on the morrow was a superannuated Norwegian seaman named, with startling originality, Larsen. He wore a full beard. I considered this an extra attention-getter which made him a bargain at the two-dollar rate. I gave him his sign and his instructions. He was to walk up and down Park Row in front of the entrance to the Pulitzer Building, and not talk to anybody unless they asked him what the sign meant. If that happened he was to say he didn't know. But he would report to me at six each evening in front of a cafeteria on the west side of City Hall Park, to describe the people who had asked him questions. We then rode downtown together on the subway and I told him to go to work.

I watched him for a while from a bench in City Hall Park. Seeing my name on the sign made me feel self-conscious and furtive, as if the people around me knew who I was. Larsen was a good, experienced sandwich man. I could tell from the way he slid his feet over the sidewalk. It must be extremely difficult to walk that slow without standing still. After a time I got tired of seeing my name in big letters and went away for a walk of my own without getting paid for it.

At six I kept my rendezvous with Larsen and bought him a dinner at the cafeteria. As we ate I asked him about his day. Nobody had spoken to him whose description at all resembled Barrett's. It had been my hope, of course, that Barrett would see him. It would hit Barrett right on the funny bone and he would see what a resourceful young fellow I was. When I walked in, perfectly deadpan, and sent in my name to him, he would start laughing again and ask me to come in and choose a job. I arranged with the boss of the cafeteria to leave the sign in his basement overnight so Larsen could get it next afternoon.

Again I went to the park to watch him, and again I met him at the cafeteria at six. People by now had accepted his presence, it seemed, and weren't asking questions. Maybe they thought Joe Liebling was another passport photographer. After the third day I figured Barrett must have at least heard of the gag, so I paid Larsen off for the last time and stowed the sign away in a friend's apartment, where for all I know it still is.

On the fourth afternoon I went to see Barrett. He greeted me cordially but without any unusual emotion. "I hadn't any idea you were in town," he said. "Thought you were still up in Providence."

I didn't know whether or not he was kidding me, but I weakened. "Haven't you seen my sign?" I asked pitifully.

He said no, he hadn't. When I told him about it, he said that he always used the rear entrance to the building, on William Street, so that it was no wonder that he hadn't seen a sandwich man walking on Park Row. He thought it was a funny story, but it hadn't proved to him that I was very resourceful. I should have either learned Barrett's route in advance or made the old sailorman circumnavigate the building instead of just working one door. Barrett said the *World* wasn't hiring—nobody was. The panic was on.

I eventually recovered the capital I had invested in the sandwich-man deal.

I sold the story of the misadventure to the Sunday *World* metropolitan section, at space rates, for $12.50, late that year, and in January sold it again to *Editor & Publisher*, the newspaper trade magazine, for $7.50. As I had paid out only $11.00 for the sign and $6.00 in wages, this left me with a net profit of $3.00, if you don't count my time or the meals I bought for Larsen.

Obits

The authors of newspaper obituaries, or obits, are a frustrated and usually anonymous tribe. The biographical notices of public characters which they prepare in advance of their subjects' departures are filed away in the papers' libraries marked, for example, "Hold until wanted—bring up to date 1947," and can be released only by the deaths of the protagonists. This is naturally a source of anxiety to the obit writer who has embalmed a subject with phrases in which he feels he can take some pride. Sometimes the obituarist conceives a deep grudge against an elder notable who, by stubbornly refusing to expire, delays public recognition of a superior rewrite job. The late John D. Rockefeller, Sr., outwore the patience and contributed to the alcoholism of three newspaper generations. Much of the decline in editorial esteem of the late David Lloyd George, and perhaps also of George Bernard Shaw, may be ascribed to irritation of a like origin.

Theodore Dreiser, who died on December 28 in his seventy-fifth year, probably suffered somewhat from this professional reaction. By contrast, General George S. Patton, Jr., who predeceased Dreiser by a week, was sixty years old and at the very peak of his obituary value. Patton had been in the news more prominently since 1942 than ever before in his life, and since there was always a possibility during the war that even a very superior officer might decease abruptly, his obits had been kept up to date by highly rated members of the New York newspaper rewrite batteries. It is probable, also, that during the strike last summer of the newspaper delivery men, high-priority obits in all offices received a good refurbishing. Dreiser's, to judge from internal evidence, had on most papers been confided to young reporters who had returned early from dinner assignments where the guest of honor failed to show up. There was therefore a piquant discrepancy between the newspaper treatments of the two decedents. Only *PM* (a day or two late, as usual) gave Dreiser a more considerable sendoff than Patton. Max Lerner, of that paper, wrote a full-page editorial on the novelist, while Ralph Ingersoll polished the General off in five paragraphs and a line.

A member of the *Daily News* staff named Kermit Jaediker set the tone for the Patton pieces when he retrospectively chronicled the General's birth as the most prodigious since that of Pantagruel. "This laconic young man with the pink complexion, the sandy hair, the steel-blue eyes, and the stuff of legend woven into his six feet of bone and muscle was born Nov. 11, 1885, on his father's ranch in San Gabriel, California," Jaediker wrote. Born six feet high and with all his hair, Patton never stopped growing in the minds of rewrite men and their editors, and after his death one or another of the New York papers gave him credit for every achievement of Allied arms in the European Theater of Operations except the Battle of Stalingrad. This is a convention of the Only Free Press in the World, like a preacher's eulogy at a funeral. When you write a man's obituary, you become his advocate.

It is probably this tradition which explains why the *Sun* said, "The troops under him, revivified by his leadership, swept up Gafsa on the long drive to El Guettar, Mateur, Bizerte, and triumph in North Africa." The "long drive" south from Gafsa to El Guettar is perhaps nine miles, and that is as far as the troops got under Patton. Mateur and Bizerte are in the opposite direction, about 150 miles to the north. The Americans won their great North African victory there—under the command of General Omar N. Bradley. The *Times* leaned even farther from the perpendicular when it related that at El Guettar Patton won "the first major American victory over Nazi arms." Major General Terry Allen commanded the First Division when, without assistance from Corps, it won the wholly unpremeditated battle of El Guettar, repulsing a surprise attack by the German Tenth Armored Division. The First was technically under Patton's command, of course, just as he was under the British General Alexander's and Alexander was under General Eisenhower's. But Allen won the battle.

Mr. Jaediker pursued the motif with the not unpicturesque statement "The legend burgeoned in the African campaign when the rasping, swearing tankman, two pearl-handled six-shooters dangling on his hips, led our forces in the conquest of Tunisia." If Patton rasped for Jaediker, he went "swashbuckling his way across the sands of North Africa" for a writer named George Adams, of the rival *Mirror*. "Swashbuckling," I take it, is a sort of third gait, between a walk and a run. The *Herald Tribune* said he had more flair than any other general since Custer, though what poor Custer had a flair for I wouldn't know—certainly not Indians. There are limits, however, even to the convention of the funeral whoop-it-up-and-holler, and I thought that Donald Mackenzie, another *Daily News* writer, transcended them when he wrote of "the brilliant breakthrough by his [Patton's] Third U.S. Army at St. Lô and Avranches." The Third Army was not activated until after the breakthrough near St. Lô, which was managed by four infantry and two armored divisions of the First Army, under the command, for the operation, of General J. Lawton Collins, of the VII Corps. St. Lô itself had been taken several days earlier, by the 29th Division, also of the First Army. Avranches was not reached until after the breakthrough, and as a consequence of it, on July 28. Patton's army began its existence on August 1.

Future Plutarchs, if they use the files, will have the same difficulty in selecting anecdotes to season their narratives as they will in determining General Patton's share in operations. There were plenty of stories, and the obituarists told them differently. The *Herald Tribune*, for example, said that Patton waded across the Sure River on a submerged footbridge, while the *Daily News* said that he swam across it twice (with the corroborative detail that it was flooded "in the depth of winter"). The *Times*, probably referring to the same river, called it the Sauer and said that he had denied swimming in it.

Then there is the matter of narrow escapes. Several of the papers were in accord that he had had three during the European campaign. One was when a large dud shell hit eight feet from his motor vehicle, which is close. Another occurred when a shell hit his headquarters while he wasn't there, which seems to me a rather commonplace type of escape, like that of the people who don't take trains for Miami that get wrecked. On the third escape, however, there was disagreement. The *Herald Tribune* said it happened when flak hit his private plane. The *Times* said it was when a German fighter dived at the plane and Patton's pilot had to touch down quickly. The *Herald Tribune* didn't mention the fighter. The *Times* didn't mention the flak. Could there have been two separate episodes, or did the flak hit the fighter? Mackenzie, the *Daily News* man, added to the standard three/four escapes one that nobody else recorded. He said he had seen a bridge at Chartres blow up "right in Patton's face," covering him with mortar dust but not causing him to turn a hair. Mackenzie could not have been sure of that if the General was wearing a hat. The Plutarchs will learn from practically all the obits that when Patton was a young lieutenant, posted to a new regiment, he asked his commanding officer if there was stabling for his mounts and, when assured that there was, appeared with a whole string of polo ponies. But whereas the *Herald Tribune* said there were a dozen ponies, the *Sun* said twenty-six. And one of the papers even said that only one of his sidearms was a pearl-handled six-shooter. The other, it stated, was a .45 automatic, which he never completely trusted.

The General's temperamental difficulties were conscientiously minimized. The *Mirror*'s Mr. Adams said, "Frequently criticized at home, his impetuousness won nothing but admiration from the embattled English and the liberated French." Adams added that Patton got quick results: "When his Third Army slowed at the approaches to the formidable fortress of Metz for lack of gasoline, he acted without hesitation. Officers were sent to the rear with authority to halt all supply vehicles, dump their loads, and send them back for gas. . . . Patton got his fuel." The fact is that in real life Patton got nothing, and his army was stalled for want of gas—though it was not his fault—for two months. "The thing that we [Third Army correspondents] loved him most for," Mackenzie said, "was that he never took one cent of his pay. He sent it all back to soldiers' charities. Patton was a millionaire and didn't have to fight for money." Even a Third Army correspondent, it seems to me, should have understood that being a millionaire made it easier for Patton to give his pay away. What interested me was the implication that all soldiers not millionaires did fight for money.

The most important thing that any of the obit authors set down about Patton, I think, was buried in the body of a story by Robert Richards of the United Press which I read in the *Mirror*. "Despite his reckless reputation in battle, he seldom wasted lives," Richards wrote. "He took big chances only when the stakes were worth it." As Ingersoll said the next day, "He saved many lives. . . . He won battles with thousands of men that might have taken other generals tens of thousands to win."

Patton labored under continual anxiety. Cautious, hardworking, and terribly ambitious, he was the kind of competitor who, in the old Greek phrase, always smelled of the oil of the gymnasium rubbing room. At West Point he never missed football practice but could never make the team. At polo he developed slowly, by dint of enormous concentration and heavy expenditure for mounts. His highest handicap, 4, was attained in 1932, when he was forty-seven years old. He built up his professional skills in the same way, by internal sweat, but he had them ready by the time of the war. The clownish, swashbuckling façade was as spontaneous as the lobby display at Radio City Music Hall.

I can think of several officers other than Patton who might have commanded the Third Army, but nobody but Theodore Dreiser could have written *Sister Carrie*. Only the *Times* and the *Journal-American*, however, thought Dreiser's death worthy of a place on Page 1. He made Page 8 in the *Sun*, 11 in the *World-Telegram*, and 12 in the *Herald Tribune*, which in 1944 devoted a two-column spread on the front page to the end of William Allen White. The hands that performed the latest revisions of the Dreiser obituaries evidently belonged to men for whom he was already a figure of the past.

Literary historians will have as many conflicts to resolve if they take the Dreiser obits seriously as the military boys will be up against reading the Patton pieces. The *Times* and the *World-Telegram*, for example, said flatly that Dreiser, when he died, was a member of the Communist Party, but the *Sun* said, "He was never accepted as a member of the party," and the *Herald Tribune* said only, "On his sixty-fourth birthday he told interviewers he was through with Communism."

The *Journal-American* obit writer said of *Sister Carrie*, "That novel, which, by today's standards, is comparatively harmless, deals simply with the sorrowful life of a village maiden in a big city." The *Herald Tribune* said, more accurately, that the great protest against *Carrie* in 1900, when the book appeared, was based on the circumstances that the heroine was not a maiden and that the story nevertheless had a reasonably happy ending. The *Journal-American* also said that "Dreiser's struggle against the school of Dean [*sic*] Howells and Louisa May Alcott, his fight against the prettyfying of the basic facts of living, opened the door to an era that gave the world such writers as Sinclair Lewis and William Faulkner." These pairings seemed to me a bit mysterious, but at least the sentiment was right.

The *World-Telegram* held Dreiser down to six paragraphs, including the statement about his party affiliation; the *Post* said pontifically that he was "oversentimental from his earliest days in Terre Haute, Ind.," and the *Sun* was sober and factual (except about the party matter). But the *Herald Tribune*'s story, I thought, was the daisy of the lot. Nastily patronizing, it began with the premise that Dreiser did not know how to write. "In 1921 the New York *Tribune* wrote of him," the *Herald Tribune* said in 1945, " 'he is probably the worst writer who ever wrote a good novel in the history of all literature.' " Since the measure of writing is its total aesthetic effect, this makes as little sense as a reference to a bad cook who produces excellent food. Some good books are better written than others, some bad books are worse written than others. *Herald Tribune* '45 contained no hint of who the *Tribune* '21 critic was, or what he has written since, or whom among his contemporaries he considered "good writers."

Having put old Dreiser in his place, the *Tribune* obit man must have reached for another batch of envelopes, which turned out to be full of clippings about the time, in 1931, the deceased had slapped Sinclair Lewis's face. The *Herald Tribune* treated this significant episode at considerably greater length than the story of how Patton slapped the soldier. Mr. Lewis, the obit noted, had (before the slapping, of course) told reporters that if the 1930 Nobel Prize had not gone to him, it should have gone to Dreiser. The obit writer seemed to feel that Dreiser should have been grateful.

The obit went on to quote "one critic" who said of Mr. Dreiser that "he was himself an American Tragedy," and to recite his participation in "various liberal movements that caught his fancy," as a result of which "he raised his voice again and again" as his "liberalism gained momentum." It also talked a lot about a dispute Dreiser had with Paramount Pictures and three times referred to his novel *Jennie Gerhardt* as *Jennie Gebhardt*. There was nothing in it to indicate that Dreisers outrank four-star generals.

The Man Who Changed the Rules

(SEPTEMBER 8, 1951)

The New York daily newspapers' treatment of William Randolph Hearst's death, at the age of eighty-eight, reflected a considerable difference of opinion not only about Mr. Hearst but about how much space he was worth. In the columns of the *Journal-American* and *Mirror*, both Hearst papers, the funeral ululations are still reverberating as I write, nearly two weeks after the *Journal-American*'s eight-column black banner head in 172-point type reading, W. R. HEARST DEAD, apprised the public of the news on the afternoon of Tuesday, August 14. The *Journal-American* ran a full-page editorial, tricked out with all the mortuary embellishments of the printing trade. It started off:

> The world has lost a colossus. William Randolph Hearst has passed into history.
>
> He was the last of the dauntless pioneers, the last of the indomitable individualists. . . .
>
> Such a man as he, who became a legend within his lifetime, we shall not see again.
>
> Only he withstood a regimentation and socialization which overwhelmed and obliterated so many of his able and powerful contemporaries, until he remained the sole surviving giant tree where once had been a forest of titanic men.

There was also a biography, running to about fifteen standard columns, which began:

Out of the incredible vigor of his mind and body William Randolph Hearst wrought, in more than a half century of sustained effort, the mightiest publishing venture the world has known. . . .

The greatest inheritance Mr. Hearst received from his mining-statesman father and his beloved mother was not measured in gold [his inheritance was, in fact, estimated at only about thirty million dollars] but in the bequest of an ineradicable faith in America.

Soon the eulogy of the departed turned to a reassurance of the solidity of the mighty publishing venture he had left behind:

For Mr. Hearst so contrived his enterprises, and so caused them to be buttressed against all contingencies, that no man's passing—not even his own—could shake their strength or swerve them from their course, which is the service of the American people. . . .

His chain of newspapers stretch along the Atlantic and Pacific seaboards and thrive in the great industrial centers of the Middle West.

His magazines, representing the cream of fiction, fashion, articles, and specialized information, blanket the nation and even extend into Great Britain, as separate publishing enterprises there.

In addition there are the worldwide network of news wires, the tremendous feature service, radio stations, land and mine holdings, a separate philanthropic organization, and a priceless art collection.

These activities may be grouped under the general title of the Hearst Organization.

The obituary, which for a column or so at this point read more like a stock prospectus, then enumerated the newspapers (sixteen daily, two Sunday only), the services (one news and one photo), and the magazines (nine). After that, it got back to Mr. Hearst.

The *Mirror*, a sister unit in the "mightiest publishing venture the world has known," used the same biography on Wednesday. James Padgitt, of the International News Service, which is a part of the mightiest publishing venture, wrote the lead news story in the *Mirror*, in which he recorded a phenomenon unreported by other correspondents in Beverly Hills, California, where Mr. Hearst died. "The people stood in stunned silence in realization of their loss," Mr. Padgitt stated.

The *Times, Herald Tribune, News, World-Telegram & Sun,* and *Post* took the event more calmly. The difference in tone was exemplified the following Sunday by the *Herald Tribune*'s treatment of a statement by William Randolph Hearst, Jr., second of the publisher's five sons, speaking for himself and his brothers. The statement had originally appeared in both the *Journal* and the *Mirror* and read, in part, "Will you please convey to the readers of the Hearst newspapers our pledge to continue to operate our father's publications as he guided us, and our determination to carry on in the tradition of his life which was dedicated to the service of America and the best interests of the American people." The *Tribune* man, Ralph Chapman, reviewing the week's news, translated this to read, "Continuance of the sensational journalistic practices established by their father was pledged by the sons of William Randolph Hearst."

The *World-Telegram*, which ranks second to the *Journal-American* in afternoon circulation, and the *News*, whose only competition in the morning tabloid field comes from the *Mirror*, showed a tendency, I thought, to underplay Mr. Hearst. The motivations of publishers in dealing with other publishers in such circumstances are ambivalent: a desire to respect a competitor's sorrow coincides with a wish to give it the minimum of publicity. The *World-Telegram*, which is part of another mighty journalistic venture, the Scripps-Howard newspapers, confirmed the *Journal-American*'s identification of Mr. Hearst as a colossus—"Men both blessed and cursed the towering colossus of journalism," one of its writers declared in a sketch of Mr. Hearst's career. "A man praised and execrated, in equal measure, to a greater extent, perhaps, than any other notable figure of his times," the piece went on. "Equal measure," it seemed to me, was giving the defunct an edge in the scoring.

The *World-Telegram* held Mr. Hearst down to a couple of columns on the afternoon of his death. On the following day, it printed a message to the bereaved family from Roy W. Howard, president of Scripps-Howard, who is the *Telegram*'s own small colossus. "No man in history has had a greater impact on American journalism or contributed more to its sturdiness or devoted himself more unceasingly to making it the nerve center of American patriotism," Mr. Howard wrote. An editorial in the same issue said, "William Randolph Hearst was one of the most controversial figures of our times, and he left a vast imprint on journalism and American life." There was no attempt to define the imprint.

The *News* didn't use the word *colossus* once, and wound up its obituary with a quote from Allan Nevins, a historian at Columbia, that I thought underrated Mr. Hearst: "His importance has lain in the huge scale of his operations, and though he hardly ranks as a great innovator—his sensationalism imitated Pulitzer's, while E. W. Scripps preceded him in forming a newspaper chain—the Hearst methods have profoundly influenced American journalism." His innovation, as I intend to point out later, was one of means rather than method, and far transcended Pulitzer's. On the same page as the obit appeared a reminder of why the *News* didn't consider Mr. Hearst quite in the colossus class. This was a message from Colonel Robert R. McCormick, editor and publisher of the *Chicago Tribune* and overlord of the *News*, to William Randolph Hearst, Jr. Around the *News*, obit writers don't have to be told who is a colossus. "My sincere sympathy to you in the loss of your father, news of whose death reached me over the radio," Colonel McCormick had wired. "His life up to the moment of his passing was devoted to the interests of his country and humanity." It was well for Colonel McCormick's disposition, I thought, that he had learned the news from the radio and not from the editorial page of a Hearst paper. Colonel McCormick knows who is the last of the dauntless pioneers, the sole surviving giant tree, and so does every man jack who works for him.

The three colossi have been as one politically, even while they scrabbled against each other like Algerian shoeshine boys for circulation coppers. In the case of the *Herald Tribune* and the *Post*, however, neither political affinity nor the considerations of circulation was a matter of concern, and yet their stories were disappointing. The *Tribune*'s obit treated the late publisher simply as a whacking success, even if a bit of an oddity. "An extraordinary newspaper talent combined with a consuming ambition for power were the principal factors in shaping the career of William Randolph Hearst," the biography began. ". . . Mr. Hearst never permitted anyone to call him by his first name. To his employees he was known simply as 'The Chief.' He wielded an iron hand over all of them, treating them with utter cynicism, if not contempt." (The fellows who wrote about him in the Hearst papers invariably remembered him as a lovable character.) Editorially, the *Tribune* said, "The strange, erratic, and powerful genius of William Randolph Hearst has colored the American political journalistic scene for so many decades that it is difficult now to realize that it has been extinguished at last. About the genius there has never been any doubt. About the uses to which he put it there has been constant and usually impassioned controversy throughout the more than half a century in which he held a place on the national stage."

The *Post*, describing Hearst as "fabulous," showed its fearlessness by recalling that he had left Harvard by request in his senior year "after he had sent chamber pots, unsuitably inscribed, to his instructors." (The *Telegram* referred to this incident as a "campus prank," while the ruggeder *News* called it a "ribald joke.") The *Post* also alluded to a report that he had once asked his wife for a divorce so that he could marry Marion Davies, in whose residence the old man died. (All the newspapers persisted in referring to it as his house, but there was an understandable confusion. It was Miss Davies's house originally, but she deeded it to him, and then he deeded it back to her.)

Where all the papers I have quoted from so far fell down, I thought, was in the way they treated the story of Hearst as a closed episode, and an unqualified success story, at that. Moreover, they failed to bring out what seems almost certain to be, in the light of history, the most significant aspect of his career. It occurs to me that what is really important about Hearst is not whether or not he was a great newspaperman, or a talented and cynical amateur, or a great humanitarian, or a genius, or a liberal, or a reactionary; he could have been any of these, but I believe that as the years pass he will be remembered primarily as the man who introduced the use of big money into the newspaper business. It was only in the *Times* that I found what seemed to me to be adequate coverage of Mr. Hearst's prodigal, and not always successful, use of money to buy his way to the top. In fact, the *Times*, in its various departments, carried off all the honors of the campaign. For one thing, its lead story, by one of its own correspondents, Gladwin Hill, was naturally better than the press-association leads in other papers. Press-association stories are written for a theoretical average subscribing newspaper in a small city and consequently have to explain a story before they tell it. Hill stuck close to the Beverly Hills angle of the story: the publisher's apparent degree of control of the editorial policy of his mighty venture up to his death (more than you might think, according to Mr. Hill), the reported presence of Miss Davies as well as of the Hearst sons at the bedside, the seeming confusion in the Hearst organization in the hours following his death. The confusion must have been considerably augmented, later, by the report from Beverly Hills that the colossus and Miss Davies had drawn up an agreement vesting control of the Hearst Corporation in Miss Davies. The administrators of the Hearst estate, in the *Journal-American* of August 27, stated, however, "This so-called agreement dated Nov. 5, 1950, was never executed and for this and many other reasons has no more effect than if it never existed." The question is, presumably, to be left to the courts. The *Times*'s long, unsigned biography of Hearst, measured and occasionally wry, led off, "At the height of his career, William Randolph Hearst was one of the world's wealthiest and most powerful newspaper owners. . . . At the peak of his influence he engendered the heat of controversy more than any other American." Here it was at least implied that the height and the peak were past. There had not, in fact, been much controversy about Hearst for the last thirty years—nothing, that is, to compare with the controversy over Franklin D. Roosevelt or Harry S. Truman. And even at the height of his career he was never able to demonstrate the power he claimed. "Actually, few persons ever succeeded in picking the lock of his character to discover the demarcation line between self-interest and public interest," the *Times* obituarist continued. "He often expressed the belief that his mind was the same as the collective mind of the American people, a belief that the American people did not always share."

The *Times*'s three best stories on the subject were deep inside the paper—one, on the financial history of Hearst's corporations, by Burton Crane; another, on Hearst's adventures in New York City real estate, by Lee E. Cooper; and a third, unsigned, on his self-invited misfortunes as an art collector. Crane's piece, particularly, seemed to me to get near the nub of the Hearst story. All the other newspaper approaches to Hearst, friendly or objective, assumed that he was, materially, a tremendous and continuing success, however "controversial" his character and policies may have been. (Most comments on these "controversial" aspects were astonishingly guarded, by the way, far more so than they would have been seven, or twenty, or thirty years ago. Hearst's chauvinism had by the time of his death made him a kind of sacred symbol, like Senator McCarthy.) There were, it is true, in some of the papers other than the *Times*, respectful allusions to Hearst's financial difficulties, owing to the Depression, a circumstance beyond even colossal control—difficulties from which the publisher had somehow escaped. "It was World War II, ironically, which put many of Mr. Hearst's tottering enterprises back on their feet," the *Tribune* said. "By mid-1945 every unit in the Hearst empire was making money again." There was left an implication that every unit still was.

Crane's financial history, based on facts easily accessible to every newspaper, cast considerable doubt upon this implication. Crane made it obvious that while no lay mind could be expected to comprehend the intricacies of Hearst's financial operations, there is plenty of evidence—watered stock, reorganizations, forced sales of property, and the like—that the business structure the publisher set up was and is not exactly in the same class as, say, General Motors or A.T.&T. "The story of the newspaper empire of William Randolph Hearst," Crane began, "is the story of a man who started with an inherited gold-mining fortune and accumulated more newspapers, radio stations, news services, and real estate than probably any other man had ever owned. But he never wanted to let anything go. It is also the story of a man who, for the last fourteen years of his life, seldom enjoyed more than nominal control of the dominion that bore his name." By 1924, long before the Depression, Hearst "was pressed for ready cash," Crane went on. "His properties were costing him more than they were bringing in." (But there was the inherited thirty million dollars, largely in mines that were throwing off money steadily. What would have happened to the mightiest publishing venture without this steady support from the Hearst underground is problematical.) So a magazine holding company, known as Hearst Magazines, was formed in 1927 and a newspaper holding company, known as Hearst Consolidated Publications, in 1930. Hearst Consolidated Publications gave Mr. Hearst, through a third holding company, a note for fifty million dollars and all the common stock, and then paid off the note with the receipts from preferred stock, "sold at $25 a share with the aid of a great stock-selling campaign in Hearst papers," to quote Mr. Crane. "They inveighed strongly against spurious stock deals," he added.

Crane noted that in 1935, after Hearst had pocketed the $50,000,000, *Fortune* appraised the publisher's gross assets at $220,000,000 and his net worth at $142,000,000. "In view of what happened in the years immediately following, this appears to have been something of an overstatement," Crane remarked. He then listed the principal Hearst "holdings" (so tenuously, yet so ostentatiously, held) in 1935, and described the legal apparatus whereby they were manipulated. "But apparently all was not so rosy as it seemed," Crane wrote.

In 1935 American Newspapers, Inc. [Hearst's principal holding company], sold its newspapers in Baltimore, Atlanta, and San Antonio to Consolidated [in which the public held the

$50,000,000 of preferred] for $8,000,000 . . . despite the fact that the three papers had lost $550,000 in 1934. This transaction was later questioned in a stockholders' suit. There was considerable water in the Hearst structure. . . . When a registration statement was filed by Consolidated in 1936, the company revealed that, between 1924 and 1930, it had written up the value of tangible assets by $4,490,863 and of intangibles by $58,261,820. . . . The attempt to hold on to everything for the sake of mere size proved unsuccessful. . . . Mr. Hearst held more than 2,000,000 acres of real estate and most of it yielded nothing.

So a corporate dictator, Clarence John Shearn, was named by a group of Hearst's creditors in 1937 and, as Crane put it, "set to work to clean up some of the mess. He immediately withdrew . . . some projected financing, because the Securities and Exchange Commission demanded additional information that the Hearst interests would have been embarrassed to reveal." Shearn, according to Crane, jettisoned five newspapers, a news service, and seven radio stations. But troubles continued to pile up. Hearst-Brisbane Properties, Inc., a New York real-estate corporation, ducked under the ropes, taking advantage of a mortgage moratorium. Hearst Magazines passed to the control of the Chase National Bank. Hearst's salary from Consolidated was cut from $500,000 to $100,000 a year. The dividends of the fifty thousand holders of preferred stock were cut from $1.75 a share to nothing at all. Harry Chandler, publisher of the *Los Angeles Times*, who held a mortgage of $600,000 on Hearst's San Simeon estate, "goodnaturedly agreed not to foreclose." (A point of intercolossal courtesy, perhaps.) The fifty thousand shareholders came near taking over the best newspaper properties. They would have had the right to do so if a fourth consecutive dividend had been passed, on March 15, 1939. But somehow Mr. Shearn got up the scratch, and the Hearst organizations flopped into the healing shadow of the war.

"By 1945," Crane wrote, "the Hearst papers were making money again. Mr. Hearst was back in San Simeon—but 165,000 acres had

been sold off to get $2,000,000 and only 75,000 acres were left."
(Return to a bobtailed farm like that must have seemed a humiliation.) Shearn, Crane continued, was succeeded by a triumvirate,
dominated by John W. Hanes, a former Under-Secretary of the
United States Treasury, who found that ninety-four Hearst organizations owed a total of $126,000,000 even after the war-stimulated
improvement in the publisher's affairs. "In 1945, although Gimbels
department store was still unloading Hearst art treasures, there
seemed reason for hope," Crane wrote.

> No Hearst paper had been sold since 1939. All the New York
> real estate had been sold, including the Ritz Tower, where
> Mr. Hearst lived when here, and all the hundreds of thou-
> sands of unprofitable acres. . . . But by the spring of this
> year the financial affairs of at least one Hearst corporation—
> Consolidated, which controls the biggest newspapers—were
> beginning to take another form. . . . Their operating revenue
> had slipped to $90,321,000. They voted to defer the dividend
> to the 1,198,848 shares of Class A stock. It is now $8.75 a share
> in arrears.

The *Times*'s story on the Hearst art collection made a fitting pen-
dant to Mr. Crane's. "In cost and total value [cost, $40,000,000;
value, estimated in 1937, $15,000,000] Mr. Hearst's collection
ranked with the great collections of his time," this account stated.
"But the publisher, unlike his contemporaries, seemed to have
bought everything, from Egyptian mummies to a Spanish abbey of
the medieval period. . . . It cost Mr. Hearst about $400,000 to
bring the abbey here. . . . Marked down from $50,000, it was sold
for $19,000 to an anonymous buyer in 1942." In the Gimbels sales
of Hearst art, the *Times*'s story recalled, Egyptian statuettes sold for
thirty-five, sixty, and ninety-five cents.

Lee Cooper's piece on the real estate filled in a bit of New York
City history. Buildings, for a city man, acquire personal, as well as
visual, associations, and their origins and ownership are as interesting as those of cattle to a farmer or ships to a Norwegian. The Ritz

Tower (which never had a Ritzian quality), the Warwick (which has a good bar), and the Ziegfeld Theatre are more than abstract things, and they deserved a story to themselves in the New York newspapers. I sometimes think the reason editors forget about such matters is that most of them used to be small-town boys and are now suburban residents. "It was in cooperation with the late Arthur Brisbane, and largely under Mr. Brisbane's tutelage and influence" that Mr. Hearst invested, Cooper wrote. (Brisbane died worth twenty million dollars.) "Mr. Brisbane, at one time, had felt certain a railroad bridge would be constructed across the Hudson River in the neighborhood of Fifty-seventh Street, and had made his major investments in the Fifties." Cooper didn't mention the innumerable editorials that Brisbane used to turn out for the Hearst papers extolling the future of the district in which he and the boss had invested. The other newspapers painted Brisbane only as an assistant colossus of fabulous genius. I found the real-estate relationship between the two men more diverting.

Thus the *Times*'s stories made clear that, whatever Hearst's talents as a newspaperman and an operator of newspapers, his principal contribution to American journalism—a contribution that changed the whole nature of the profession—was to demonstrate that a man without previous newspaper experience could, by using money like a heavy club, do what he wanted in the newspaper world except where comparable wealth opposed him. It was a concept as simple as a very big bank roll in a very small crap game. There were one or two fortunes of a few million dollars apiece in the newspaper field when Hearst, at the age of twenty-three, decided to go into it, but they had been made in newspapers, by men who started with little. It had not occurred to any other mining millionaire that a man without experience but with money had a vast advantage over any editor who ever lived. Hearst went into the business as an acknowledged imitator of Joseph Pulitzer, but with enough money to hire any man he wanted. Some of the time he wasn't even selective: he hired help in platoons—the whole Sunday staff of the New York *World* at one swoop, for example. He brought $7,500,000 of his mother's money to New York with him when he came here in 1895 to buy and build up the *Journal*, and he could, quite naturally, hire more comic artists, more blood-and-thunder editorialists, more sports writers, and more fakers of crime stories than anybody else in town. He lost money on his newspapers until they acquired vast circulation, but he put on such a show that in the end people had to buy them. It is a method open to few. The same scheme would probably have been just as successful, at the time, in the field of the conservative press. If Hearst had wanted to work that side of the street, he could have hired away from the *Herald* the foreign staff built up by James Gordon Bennett and then tripled it, beating out the *Herald*, or he could have provided such complete financial coverage that the *Times*, just beginning its climb, could not possibly have competed. But he had a predilection for the side of the street he chose.

After building his circulations, Hearst profited by practices new in journalism but old in big business: he got a rebate of five dollars a ton on newsprint, for instance, because he bought so much. But when he hit a city like Chicago, where the *Tribune* was entrenched behind an even denser concentration of wealth (built up by the newspaper itself, however, over a stretch of fifty years), he took a fearful beating. Hearst wrangled rebates, but the *Tribune* owned paper mills. When he offered five hundred dollars a day in free handouts to readers—a form of lottery—the *Tribune* offered seventeen thousand dollars a day. His paper never made a dent in the *Tribune*, and he quit trying after thirty-seven years of losses. When he reached the point, in the twenties, where the store-bought empire had to support itself from its own earnings, his long retreat began.

"The question was asked on one occasion what the losses had been, first to last, in Atlanta," a man named Jim Brown wrote in the August 18 issue of *Editor & Publisher*, which was practically a Hearst memorial. "The reply was—$21,000,000." (The Hearst organization has had no paper in Atlanta since 1939.) The prerequisite for losing $21,000,000 is not genius; it is to have $21,000,000.

It was said in some of the obituaries that Hearst had a flair for hiring good writers, but one must read page after page of his papers to find a trace of it. He certainly employed some talented men, but there has never been a time within my memory when they were not flanked by others who were hilariously inept, and the bad writers often enjoyed more esteem within the Hearst organization, and better pay, than the good. The truth seems to be that he bought talent the way he bought art—indiscriminately.

Hearst's two New York papers, in the first few days after his death, afforded a sample of what he had wound up with, as byliner after byliner approached the edge of the grave in print and threw a ceremonial fit. On Wednesday, August 15, in the *Journal*, Cholly Knickerbocker led his column with a paragraph that read, "America's Irreplaceable Loss—William Randolph Hearst has passed on but his greatness will survive eternally. No leader, president or king, has ever given so much of himself to the guidance and uplifting of his people as had The Chief. The underdog's corner was his corner, and right was his might." In the next paragraph, Cholly was back at his regular job. "Beautiful Mary Sinclair, the actress, is in Reno to divorce producer George Abbott, and, her friends say, she has her next husband already picked out," he wrote inconsolably. Dorothy Kilgallen awarded the departed full credit for promoting her career. "William Randolph Hearst gave me the space and the assignments," she wrote, "and everything I have done in other fields since then has stemmed from his long-distance faith in a very young girl, and his paper remains my first love." E. V. Durling, who writes a column called "Life with Salt on the Side," wrote, "William Randolph Hearst was the finest, most considerate, kindliest and generous man I ever worked for. . . . Come to think of it, Mr. Hearst was probably the best friend all newspapermen ever had in the newspaper business. It was he who raised their standards of employment to a point comparable to their talents." (If he had, a number of Hearst columnists would have starved to death.) Artists were not excused from the funeral detail. Burris Jenkins, Jr., provided a dramatic drawing of the Statue of Liberty with a mourning band around her arm, marked "William Randolph Hearst." On Thursday morning, August 16, in the *Mirror*, Nick Kenny, the radio editor, produced a poem entitled "The Chief Passes," of which I shall quote only the first stanza, although the others are even more beautiful:

> The Chief is gone, the man we all called Boss . . .
> Colossus of an age that changed the world.
> The galleons of his genius knew their course,
> His fingertips around the cosmos curled.

Kenny was one of The Chief's favorite writers, and Hearst quoted the poet several times in his own occasional column, called "In the News."

That same morning, Dan Parker, the *Mirror*'s sports editor, contributed a bluff, regular-guy double column about Mr. Hearst in sports, from which I remember particularly the sentence "When racketeers invaded boxing, Mr. Hearst wouldn't let his newspapers be used to exploit the public." I suppose this referred to the time when a number of Hearst boxing writers resigned after it was disclosed that they had been receiving salaries as sub-rosa executives of Mike Jacobs's Twentieth Century Sporting Club to puff its attractions. "To say that Mr. Hearst was a great American is, to me, like saying that Ty Cobb was a great baseball player," Bill Corum wrote in the *Journal* on the afternoon of August 16, making a hook slide to get to the headstone in a tie with his colleague.

Great or not, Hearst was the man who changed the rules of American journalism. He made it so expensive to compete that no mere working newspaperman has been able to found an important paper in this century.

Death on the One Hand

(MARCH 28, 1953)

Inconsiderate to the last, Josef Stalin, a man who never had to meet a deadline, had the bad taste to die in installments. This posed a problem for newspaper editors, who had to decide whether to use their prepared obituary notices and shoot the works generally on Wednesday, March 4, the day Tass, the Russian news agency, announced that the Premier had suffered a brain hemorrhage, which even to the most casual reader looked like the end, or to wait until he officially expired, by which time the story might have lost the charm of novelty. What made it even stickier for the editors was the paucity of news that could be expected out of Moscow, where there were but six correspondents for the whole American press; the three major news agencies were represented, and *The New York Times* had its own man, Harrison E. Salisbury. The number has declined steadily since late 1946, when the Russians began refusing visas to new correspondents. Because of the visa situation, there was no way of sending reinforcements to cover the big event, and because each of the correspondents had to file a lead story for his own employer, their efforts were bound to parallel each other. The wire-service reporters—Henry Shapiro, for the United Press; Eddie Gilmore, for the Associated Press; and an International News Service man who for some reason got no byline in the Hearst papers—and Salisbury did an excellent job qualitatively, but quantitatively their aggregate efforts were necessarily skimpy.

According to newspaper canon, however, a big story calls for a lot of copy. The New York papers rose to the occasion by resorting

to a procedure known, variously, as constructive journalism, interpretive reporting, and the crystal ball, but for which I now prefer a
term I owe to James Reston of *The New York Times*, one of its recent, and probably reluctant, practitioners. Mr. Reston, in the *Times*
of March 5, a day when Stalin lay moribund and so did real news,
recounted a conversation he had had with a Democratic senator
who had lunched at the White House on the previous day. He
asked the senator what the President seemed to think about the situation. The senator told him that the President had discussed the
Stalin illness "about the way everybody else discussed it all day, saying 'on the one hand this and on the other hand that.'" This is a
perfect description of what the newspapers filled up with, and they
ended by completely submerging the news story, which was simple
enough: a formidable old man had died and nobody knew what to
expect as a consequence.

The annoying hiatus that the old Bolshevik permitted to intervene between his syncope and his demise put a strain on even the
ruggedest professional seers, who had to start explaining the
significance of his death before he had actually died and then keep
on inventing exegeses until he was in his tomb. Altogether, their ordeal lasted a full week, but they stood it better than their readers.

It was the United Press that furnished the lead story for
the *News*, the *Mirror*, and the *Herald Tribune* on the morning of
March 4, when the news broke—a sober, factual bulletin beginning
"Premier Josef Stalin is seriously ill, it was announced today," and
including the essential clinical details. It was accompanied by the
official text of the medical bulletin signed by Stalin's physicians.
Caught that way, the papers had no chance to do anything constructive about the story. The *News* gave the story the headline
STROKE FELLS STALIN and barely found opportunity for a couple
of parenthetical inserts in the U.P. text:

(There was evidence of the morbid suspicion with which
Russians traditionally view each other. A government announcement said the eight physicians' treatment of Stalin is
"conducted under the constant supervision of the Central
Committee . . . and the Soviet Government.")

and

> (Diplomatic circles in London began speculating immediately on possible repercussions in Soviet satellite states of Stalin's illness—or possible death. All Eastern Europe was considered facing eruptive consequences.)

It also appended a paragraph to the story that appeared in none of the other papers:

> Among those whose names have been frequently mentioned to succeed the dictator are Vyacheslav M. Molotov, the former foreign minister; Andrei Andreyev, the vice prime minister; and Georgi Malenkov, member of the Communist Central Committee and a longtime protege of Stalin.

This, incidentally was the only call Andreyev got during the newspaper straw vote for Despot of All the Russias.*

The *News*, obeying the precept to strike first with the maximum force, also committed to the press the obit it had been long preserving against the day of Stalin's death. It began, "For more than a quarter of a century Stalin, 'The Man of Steel,' has lived up to his pseudonym as the ruthless dictator of 180,000,000 Russians and the most inscrutable of all statesmen in a world continuously on tenterhooks." After that, the story ran on for three tabloid columns—pretty dry.

The four-star final edition of the *Mirror* I saw had just the United Press story from Moscow, with an add, probably tacked on in the U.P. office here, quoting from Winston Churchill's Iron Curtain speech in Fulton, Missouri, in 1946. The *Mirror*'s headline on the story read: STALIN NEAR DEATH!

The *Herald Tribune*'s eight-column front-page streamer read: STALIN HAS STROKE; HEART AND BRAIN AFFECTED.

---

* As the attentive reader will note, nobody mentioned a man named Khrushchev to take all. This is not a reflection on the expertise of experts, but on the futility of flapdoodle.

All the *Tribune* had on the story was the U.P. piece, including the Churchill quote, and some biographical matter. It held on to its own prepared Stalin obituary, taking no chances on a treacherous recovery. I felt sorry for the Alsop brothers, Joseph and Stewart, who can turn in as good a job of constructive interpretation as anybody in the business, because their column, "Matter of Fact," had evidently gone into print before they had a chance to tell the *Tribune* readers what the Premier's indisposition foreboded. They had been caught flat-footed with a piece about the perpetual crisis in Iran; they said that it was entering one of its incandescent phases, in which the need was certainly dire and the picture somber (in an incandescent way, I suppose), and that steps had to be taken or the Middle East was likely to burst into flames.

The *Times*, as was to be expected, carried the wariest headline: STALIN GRAVELY ILL AFTER A STROKE; PARTLY PARALYZED AND UNCONSCIOUS; MOSCOW DISCLOSES CONCERN FOR HIM. This was only four columns wide, and topped a bulletin from Salisbury, to which was appended the same United Press dispatch that had appeared in the other papers. The *Times* was first off the mark in the department of speculation, however, with a story by James Reston, under a Washington dateline, that bore the three-column head WASHINGTON JOLTED BY NEWS, FEARS RISE OF RED EXTREMISTS. "The speculation in well-informed quarters here was that if the Soviet Premier died he would probably be replaced by one of three high aides: Georgi M. Malenkov, Lavrenti P. Beria, or V. M. Molotov," Mr. Reston wrote, and then, going into on-the-one-hand-this, added, "Though Mr. Stalin was a symbol of all the anguish of the 'cold war' period that followed World War II, the paradox of the situation here this morning was that his death or incapacitation might signify an even more tense period in the relations between the Communist world and the free world. . . . It was for this reason that the news of his illness produced some apprehension when it was first received in Washington." Switching to on-the-other-hand-that, he continued, "There was, however, another reaction, no less prominent. This was that the death of the Soviet Premier or his prolonged incapacitation might lead to an intense struggle within the Politburo for control of the Soviet dictatorship." Here Mr. Reston quoted Winston Churchill on how the Mongol hordes had turned back from the conquest of Europe to choose a successor to their Great Khan, and had never recovered their impetus. The story ran about a column and a half. The *Times* carried a box noting that Stalin's stroke was similar to the one that killed Lenin. The *News* said it was like the one that killed Franklin D. Roosevelt.

It was with the afternoon papers that constructive journalism came into its own. STALIN'S LIFE FADING; HENCHMEN TAKE HELM, the *World-Telegram & Sun*'s headline read, but the main news story, by Shapiro, saying that Stalin's condition had not improved, interested me less than the interpretive pieces the newspapermen had evolved. For example:

WILL KOREA REDS' MORALE TAKE DIP?

WASHINGTON, March 4—Gen. James A. Van Fleet replied "I don't know" when asked today whether the death of Russia's ailing Premier Stalin might lead to a weakening of Communist morale in Korea.

And:

ROY HOWARD SEES NO ATTACK ON WEST

MANILA, March 4—Roy W. Howard, the first foreign correspondent to interview Premier Josef Stalin, said tonight there probably would be no violent anti-western reaction from Russia as a result of Stalin's critical illness. Mr. Howard, president and editor of the New York *World-Telegram & Sun*, is on an extended tour of the Orient.

Reassured by Mr. Howard, I turned to the first page of the second section, and there found:

STALIN ILLNESS MAY
HOLD PERIL OF WAR

BY PHIL NEWSOM
UNITED PRESS FOREIGN NEWS EDITOR

Taking sharp issue with the president and editor of the paper, Mr. Newsom began, "Josef Stalin near death is more dangerous than Stalin alive and in good health." Together, the two pieces constituted a clear case of on-the-one-hand-this and on-the-other-hand-that.

W. A. Ryser, billed as a United Press staff writer, contributed a much longer piece, headed

IF STALIN GOES, THEN WHAT?

EXPERT SAYS WAR DANGER
WOULD DECREASE AT FIRST

Mr. Ryser was writing under a London dateline. The *World-Telegram*, recommending him to its readers, said, "He has excellent news sources among persons who have lived in Russia and know political affairs there well." Mr. Ryser promised "answers to some of the questions raised by Josef Stalin's illness," and led off: "Q. Will the death of Stalin increase or decrease the chances of World War III? A. It probably will decrease them, at least temporarily." Mr. Ryser touted Malenkov, Molotov, and Beria, in that order, for the succession, and answered Q's about all of them. The *World-Telegram* also went in for a bit of long-range medical diagnosis, under the byline of Delos Smith, United Press Science Editor. "Josef Stalin is on his deathbed, two American physicians concluded today from studying the medical bulletin of his nine attending physicians," this story began. "Even 90 physicians could not save him, they said." This approach must have made quite a hit with the U.P.'s clients, because the Providence *Evening Bulletin*, which I chanced to see the same day, not only ran it but checked with a Rhode Island neurologist to make sure the U.P. doctors weren't pulling its leg. This provided a local angle.

The *Post* devoted its tabloid-sized front page to a picture of the patient in Moscow and the simple legend in type three and a quarter inches high, HE'S DYING. It ran the same United Press lead story as the *World-Telegram* and the same medical story (without credit to Mr. Smith or the United Press, in the edition I saw). In the on-the-one-hand-this department, the *Post*, as I had anticipated, yielded to no competitor. STALIN STROKE MAY PRODUCE WORLD CRISIS was the head over a story by Joseph P. Lash. The illness had plunged "the world into perilous seas," he announced, going on to say that diplomats feared the question of war or peace would become "inextricably entangled with the struggle for Stalin's mantle." I had not yet seen any story that admitted the possibility there might *not* be a struggle; I repressed the fantastic thought.

"Who Will Grasp Power?" the *Post* asked, over a layout of pictures of Molotov, Malenkov, and Beria, reading from top to bottom. The layout man could have got the answer by turning to Max Lerner's column, on Page 40: "It doesn't take much predicting to predict Malenkov will be the next dictator of the Soviet Union," Lerner said. ". . . What have we of the free world to gain or lose by Stalin's death? This is not as easy as some commentators who shoot from the hip have in the past assumed. . . . But there can be little doubt that Stalin's death will prove a great unsettling force both in Russian internal politics and in the world situation. Does this mean that we can soon expect a popular revolt inside the Soviet Union? I will go out on a limb and say No."

The *Journal-American* had a story by Kingsbury Smith, out of Paris, commencing: "Some West European diplomats believed today that Soviet Premier Stalin might already be dead. . . . Their other immediate reaction to the electrifying news that he was paralyzed and in grave condition was that this lessened the danger of any East-West war in the immediate future."

That made the stargazer count three (Newsom, Lash, and Lerner) for increased probability of war; three (Howard, Ryser, and Kingsbury Smith) for decreased probability of war; and one (Reston) for a draw. It was a split decision, inextricably entangled with the tenterhooks of eruptive consequence.

When I opened my copy of the *Times* next morning, I could see that the editors, with twenty-four hours to turn around in, had been able to lay on a somberly incandescent display of tangential coverage. The four-column headline and one-column drop said:

STALIN'S CONDITION BECOMES WORSE
HIS ASSOCIATES DIRECT GOVERNMENT;
EISENHOWER AND EDEN MEET HASTILY

PREMIER IS FAILING

DOCTORS REPORT DECLINE
AS ARTERIO-SCLEROSIS
COMPLICATES CASE

SECOND BULLETIN GLOOMY

OLD COMRADES OF SOVIET CHIEF
TAKE CONTROL OF REGIME—
CHURCHES JOIN IN PRAYER

This had the disadvantage, from an artistic point of view, of telling practically the whole available story. It was followed by an Associated Press lead, which expanded it somewhat, and the A.P. story, in turn, was followed by one from the *Times*'s own Mr. Salisbury, which said that the doctors were doing their best, that Russia "and most of the civilized world" awaited news, and that since the previous Sunday night—forty-eight hours before the announcement of the stroke—the Government had been directed by a group including Malenkov, Beria, Marshal Bulganin, Marshal Voroshilov, and Molotov. "An Associated Press dispatch that passed Moscow's censorship said it would be extremely foolish to speculate on any change in Russian policy at this time," the *Times* interpolated here. Never was a warning less heeded. All in all, the copy out of Moscow ran to about two columns; to the total bulk of reading matter served up, however, those two columns bore the same relation that the male angler fish bears to the female: a small, scarcely perceptible bump, serving only to fertilize her. The copy that I would class under the heading of on-the-one-hand-this-and-on-the-other-hand-that ran to eighteen columns, or nine times the linage of straight news.

A first-page Washington story by Mr. Reston, headed SUDDEN WHITE HOUSE PARLEY BELIEVED TO CONCERN SOVIET, reported that President Eisenhower had talked with the Secretary of State, the British Foreign Secretary, and the head of the Central Intelligence Agency but that nobody knew what they had said. The *Times* correspondent added, "Dependable information on the situation within the Soviet high command was so scarce that speculation on the dictator's successor could not be solidly grounded." He then quoted about a column and a half of unsolidly grounded speculation on all phases of the situation, winding up with the quotation from the Democratic senator, for which I remain eternally in his debt.

Another first-page story, by a *Times* man named Harry Schwartz, who specializes in constructive interpretation of Soviet subjects, began, "Most available evidence points to Georgi M. Malenkov as the man most likely ultimately to inherit Josef Stalin's power [on-the-one-hand-this] but that result is not yet a foregone conclusion [on-the-other-hand-that]." Mr. Schwartz went a couple of columns, handily. In addition, the *Times* covered the story from Tel Aviv (Israeli analysis of the situation), the United Nations Building (delegates shocked, express apprehension), Berlin (rumors flew there), Tokyo (the news received calmly), Bonn (where Drew Middleton discovered a new terror; i.e., that the Kremlin was expected to relax pressure on West, and thus de-frighten Europeans, retarding formation of European Army), Kansas City (where Harry S. Truman said he was "sorry to hear of his trouble—I'm never happy over anybody's physical breakdown"), Rome (where an "unofficial source" had little that was encouraging to say about Stalin's prospects in the hereafter), the *Daily Worker* office ("deepest grief"), Belgrade (convinced hell is busting loose in Moscow already), Hong Kong ("swift speculation here on what effect"), and Taipei (where I can't remember what). It also carried interviews with four former United States Ambassadors to Russia; of whom Averell Harriman predicted a reign of terror, Admiral William H. Standley predicted a revolt, General Walter Bedell Smith predicted a rule by a triumvirate (Malenkov, Molotov, Beria), and William C. Bullitt predicted that if there were a triumvirate it would "tread softly" in international affairs. A brain specialist at the Columbia–Presbyterian Medical Center and a neurologist at the New York University–Bellevue Medical Center assured the *Times* that Stalin's recovery appeared unlikely. (The *Times* insists on its own, nonsyndicated doctors.) From London, C. L. Sulzberger, the *Times*'s chief foreign correspondent, wrote, without straining the bounds of plausibility, "The apparently approaching death of Premier Stalin will almost certainly precipitate a period of great uneasiness in world affairs." I had an ungenerous feeling, while paddling through all this virtually identical speculation, that I was watching a small boy pull a cud of chewing gum out to the longest possible string before it broke.

The *Herald Tribune*, which usually does the same kind of thing as the *Times* but less of it, ran only eleven columns of creative interpretation in its news sections, along with the essential two columns of news. But it supplemented its reportorial crystal-gazers with a couple of professional on-the-one-handers: David Lawrence and Walter Lippmann. Mr. Lawrence was monitory: ". . . the tendency will be to exaggerate the significance of the occurrence," he warned, "and to assume that the removal of one evil man suddenly makes the other twelve in the Kremlin virtuous. It will take a little while for the disillusionment to come—but it will come." As for Mr. Lippmann, perhaps the greatest on-the-one-hand-this writer in the world today, he appeared to be suffering from buck fever when confronted with so magnificent an opportunity for indecision. "The kind of power that Stalin has exercised cannot be transferred intact," he wrote, for his on-the-one-hand-this. "It is a kind of power that has to be grasped by the new pretender and made his own by his own actions. . . . It is hard to believe that this can happen easily or quickly." Then, switching to on-the-other-hand-that, he added, "If it does, it will be the greatest surprise, and the most disconcerting, that has yet come out of Soviet Russia."

As for the morning tabloids, the *News*'s forthright editorialist went on the on-the-one-hand-this circuit with the gruff declaration "As we see coming Russian events, the only certainty is that there are going to be changes, and that those switches are bound to affect the world, for better or worse." From the tone of the *Mirror*'s editorial ("There is reason for cautious optimism in the condition of a dying despot whose end may have been hastened by his own realization that the game was up—and his plan of world conquest a bloody failure"), I gained the impression that the writer had personally induced the Russian Premier's condition by punching him on the chin. Hard as nails.

By afternoon, the *World-Telegram* had its crystal ball shining like the Scripps-Howard lighthouse in the upper corner of its front page. Ludwell Denny, the Scripps-Howard foreign editor, filed a story from Bonn that appeared on Page 7, headed HEIR TO STALIN MAY NEED WAR TO HOLD POWER. The head over another exercise in omniscience, by Isaac Don Levine, who was given a buildup as "an acknowledged authority on Soviet Russia," proclaimed, on Page 8: KREMLIN'S NEW RULERS NEED PEACE TO SOLVE PROBLEMS.

In the *Post*, Mr. Lash, who had plunged the world into perilous seas on the previous day and got it inextricably entangled in a struggle for Stalin's mantle, now thought that "no immediate open struggle for power nor violent shift in Soviet foreign policy" need be expected. Another *Post* writer, Murray Kempton, wrote a real artistic piece. "Oh, sun, oh, summer sunshine, oh, Josef Djugashvili, oh, Josef Stalin, oh, Koba or all the other dozen names a professional revolutionary had occasion to call himself; what do the survivors know of you?" Mr. Kempton apostrophized the invalid of the day. It reminded me of a song written by Chris Smith, an old colored man I knew long ago:

> Down in Louisiana, among the sugar cane—
> Oh! Oh! Oh!

The plot of Kempton's story was that Stalin was dying and that no one remembered what a dirty dog he had been because he had killed all the witnesses. "Alone among the old Bolsheviks he would lie in a marked and honored tomb. He had destroyed them all, and now he too would go to join the revolution in the grave." His secret would have been safe if he had remembered to destroy Kempton.

One of the points Kempton made about Stalin was that Trotsky once described him as "the most eminent mediocrity in the party." The *Post* editorialist said the same thing about the dying man: "He was our century's most successful bore. Stalin was the Babbitt of Bolshevism." The *Telegram* editorialist said, "He spread hate and evil throughout the world, and that evil will live on after Stalin is in his grave."

Meanwhile, the *Journal-American*, a trifle slow in getting under way the first day, had picked a long shot to succeed the dying marshal. (Joseph Newman, the *Herald Tribune*'s figurator, had, by the way, touted Molotov.) STALIN'S SON SEEN AS "DARK HORSE," a head on the *Journal*'s Thursday first page announced. There was a picture of young Stalin in uniform, wearing earphones, and a caption reading, "Anything can happen. . . . Heavy-drinking Vassily Stalin (above) is a 'dark horse' possibility to seize power when his father dies, according to the observation today of Arkadi Svobodin, whose series, 'I was Stalin's Nurse,' appeared in the *American Weekly*." Mr. Svobodin himself had been a dark horse to me until that moment, but I like a handicapper who will pick something at a price. Next to the picture was an editorial by William Randolph Hearst, Jr., the *Journal-American*'s publisher. "Apart from the hypocritical, that is to say, diplomatic, words of regret from various heads of state concerning Premier Josef Stalin," it said, "it seems to us there has never been a more appropriate time for the expression, 'I hope it's nothing trivial.'"

The official news of the death, and of Malenkov's subsequent elevation, came as an anticlimax, I thought. When you fill your news columns with stuff that is only 10 percent news, I suppose you create in the reader's mind a doubt that any of it is news. Anyway, I have formed a definite impression on the one hand that Malenkov is not a man at all but a large articulate dummy, with Leon Trotsky inside him. (That explains the small intelligent eyes peering out from behind the cruel mask.) And on the other hand, when you stop to think of it, Stalin may still be alive.

Harold Ross—The Impresario

(APRIL 13, 1959)

It is hard for a writer to call an editor great, because it is natural for him to think of the editor as a writer manqué. It is like asking a thief to approve a fence, or a fighter to speak highly of a manager. "Fighters are sincere," a fellow with the old pug's syndrome said to me at a bar once as his head wobbled and the hand that held his shot glass shook. "Managers are pimps, they sell our blood." In the newspaper trade, confirmed reporters think confirmed editors are mediocrities who took the easy way out. These attitudes mark an excess of vanity coupled with a lack of imagination; it never occurs to a writer that anybody could have wanted to be anything else.

I say, despite occupational bias, Ross, the first editor of *The New Yorker*, was as great as anybody I ever knew, in his way. He was as great as Sam Langford, who could make any opponent lead and then belt him out, or Beatrice Lillie, who can always make me laugh, or Raymond Weeks, who taught romance philology at Columbia and lured me into the Middle Ages, or Max Fischel, who covered New York Police Headquarters for the *Evening World*, and was the best head-and-legman I ever saw. The head helps the legs when it knows its way around.

Given the address of a tenement homicide, Max would go over the roofs and down while the younger men raced down to the street and then around the block and up. They would arrive to find him listening sympathetically to the widow if the police had not already locked her up, or to a neighbor if they had. People in jams liked to talk to him because he never talked at them.

Ross was as great as Max, or as a man named Flageollet, who kept a hotel with eight rooms at Feriana in Tunisia and was one of the best cooks I have known, or another named Bouillon, who had a small restaurant on the Rue Sainte-Anne in Paris. (It is odd that I should have known two great cooks with comestible names.) He was as great as Eddie Arcaro, the rider, or General George Patton or Bobby Clark and Paul McCullough, or a number of women I have known who had other talents. Ross would not have resented any of these comparisons, and the ones with Max and Patton would have flattered him particularly, because he was a newspaper and Army buff. One thing that made him a great editor was his interest in the variety of forms greatness assumes. He saw it in the entertainers he hired, as cheaply as possible so that they would work harder, to appear in his Litterographic Congress of Strange (Great) People of the World. The Greatest One-Gag Cartoonist, the Greatest Two-Gag Cartoonist, the Greatest Cartoonists Waiting for a Gag; the Greatest One-Note Male Short-Story Writer, the Greatest Half-Note In-Between Short-Story Writer, the Greatest Demi-Semi-Quaver Lady Short-Story Writer Ending in a Muted Gulp; The Greatest Woman Who Ever Married an Egyptian, the Greatest Woman Who Ever Married a Patagonian, the Greatest Woman Who Ever Married a Dravidian Pterodactyl. These latters' stories always began: "My mother-in-law could never get used to my wearing shoes," and still do, although sales territory is becoming rapidly exhausted; the only franchises still available to marry into are the Andaman Islands and Washington Heights. Ross cherished half-bad Great talents too; he knew there will never be enough good ones to go around.

E. B. White once said to me that the relation between Ross and him was like that of two railroad cars—they met only at one point. White was with Ross from the beginning of the magazine in 1925, but he admits he knew only one Ross personally and a couple of dozen others by intuition, hearsay, brag, or reputation. Ross had some raffish friends I envied him and some stuffed-shirt friends I wouldn't be seen dead with. He was equally proud and I think equally fond of all of them. He liked anybody who had a lot of money or a good story to tell, and since these are minerals seldom found in conjunction, he prospected around. *The New Yorker* he made reflected this idiosyncrasy, but not what the kids now call dichotomy. There was no conflict; he just had more interests than most people. I think that a number of men who knew Ross underrated him because, coming up on him always from one direction, they found him sometimes preoccupied with what was going on in another ring.

It was as if a wire-walker expected a ringmaster to be as exclusively interested in high-wire acts as he was. Of course Ross couldn't write as well as Thurber or Joe Mitchell, or draw as well as Steinberg. He didn't know as much as Edmund Wilson is supposed to, and there were at any given period of *The New Yorker*'s existence eighty-four people around who knew more about France or the East Side or where to buy a baby bottle with an aquamarine nipple for Christmas. But he had his own greatness—he put the show together. Why he wanted to I don't know. What made Arcaro a jockey?

Early in December 1951, when Ross had been ill since the previous April, I said to Bill Shawn, who was doing his work and has since succeeded him, "If I knew he was going to die, I'd put my arm around his shoulder and say I'd always liked him. But if he recovered, he'd never forgive me."

That was at a time when the doctors had not admitted his condition was critical, but when the length of the illness had made us all suspicious. He died about a week later, but I think he knew that I liked him, in a way, and I know he liked me, in a way, and that's about as close as I ever got to him in an acquaintance of eighteen years, sixteen of them on *The New Yorker*.

The only letter of his I have chanced to preserve is one I got in Reno, Nevada, in the summer of 1949. He felt there was a great story in Reno, but did not know just what it was. He wrote, "But of course you are a better reporter than I am. (The hell you are!)" He couldn't give a compliment without taking it back in the next sentence—afraid you'd get a swelled head, I suppose. I disappointed him with a slight report on Reno I wrote then, but I took east the seed of a much better story, which germinated until I went out to Nevada again in the fall of 1953 and reported and wrote it. He never saw it, of course.

He was a great hunch man, which is part of being a great editor. Many aspects of life entranced him imprecisely, and he knew that where there was entrancement there was a story, if he could just bring the right kind of man into its vicinity. Like a marriage broker, he could bring together a couple, writer and subject, who ought to hit it off. But sometimes not even Ross could make them go to bed together.

He was also good at sensing a mismatch. Immediately after the end of the war I told him that I would like to travel in the un-known—to me—interior of this country and write about the Mid-west as I would of any other strange land.

"You wouldn't like it, Liebling," he said. "You wouldn't like it."

I spent the winter of 1949–50 in Chicago, and he was dead right.

Later in my Nevada summer he came to Reno with some of his Hollywood pals—Chasen and Capra and Nunnally Johnson—on a holiday. He was very happy, happier than I have seen him in any other setting. He liked the West (as distinguished from Mid-) and pretending to be a Westerner. (He had left the West when a kid, and by the time I knew him was an indefinitely urban type, though never a New Yorker.) He got me to sit in with him at the open poker game in the Bank Club, together with the old sheepherders and railroad pensioners. There are always at least three one-armed men in that game—brakemen who fell under trains. I played a half-hour, lost twenty dollars, and got out. He stayed an hour and said he won sixty. Later he went back, played until five in the morning, and returning to the Riverside Hotel, cashed a check for five hun-dred. I heard about it at breakfast from the night manager of the game room, who was just going off duty. At lunch Ross told me he had cleaned up, but I knew better.

When he was young, vaudeville was the chief national entertain-ment industry, and I often thought he would have made a first-class booker for variety shows. This is no faint compliment, for I adored vaudeville, which lasted well on into my own youth. So must Ross have done; he had a great affection for old comics like Joe Cook and Chasen. He put on a weekly variety bill of the printed word and the graphic gag—always well-balanced and sufficiently entertaining to bring the audience back next week. He booked the best acts he could, but he knew that you couldn't get the best specialists in every spot every week. When he had no headline comic, he built the show around a dancer or even a juggler. One week he might have a cartoon that people would remember with pleasure for years. The next it might be a good profile, and the week after that the Fratellini of prose, Sullivan and Perelman, or a tear-jerking fiction turn by Dorothy Parker or O'Hara. Vaudeville, too, had its sacred moments; next to a good laugh there is nothing so nice as a sniffle.

Ross tried to polish old acts or develop new ones, but he never let his notion of what he wanted get in the way of his clear apprehension of what was to be had. In the late thirties, when all his new writers came from newspaper staffs where they had sweated through the Depression, he said to me, "Liebling, I wish I could find some young conservative writers who could write, but there aren't any."

He was by inclination a kind of H. L. Mencken conservative himself, but he wouldn't book a dancer who couldn't dance just because he liked the shape of her derriere. This is a higher integrity than either right-wing or left-wing editors possessed in those days. The writing in the *New Masses* was as bad, in a different way, as the writing in *Time*. (The transition, as Whittaker Chambers found out, was easy.) Ross's loyalty was to his readers. He treasured Alva Johnston, an earlier convert from the newspaper fold than we were, who wrote excellent profiles and at the same time held that stupid Presidents were best, because they let big businessmen run the country, and businessmen had brains.

Alva's only objection to Herbert Hoover was that he was too bright. He was a hard man to satisfy; it is a pity he did not live to see Eisenhower. Ross relished Johnston's concurrent political opinions as lagniappe; he wouldn't have given a hoot about them if he hadn't esteemed Alva's technique of defining character by a series of anecdotes on an ascending scale of extravagance, so that the reader of the sixth installment wolfed yarns that he would have rejected in the first.

Nor did Ross insist on playing types of acts that had lost their vogue. During the late twenties and very early thirties *The New Yorker* frequently ran a type of profile of rich and successful men that was only superficially distinguishable from the Success Stories in the late *American Magazine*. (The difference was that the *New Yorker* writer might attribute to the protagonist some supposedly charming foible like wearing crimson ties although he had attended Princeton.) The hallmark of this kind of profile was a sentence on the order of "Although Jeremy P. Goldrush is as rich as rich, you would never think from his plain old two-hundred-dollar suits that he was more than an ordinary weekend polo player."

After a couple of these heroes had landed in state prisons, Ross became receptive to portraits in a less reverent style. Although Ross loved the smell of success, he was emotionally irreverent and always enjoyed learning that a fellow he had accepted as a monument to society was in fact a sepulchre with a runny coat of whitewash.

He made the same good adjustment to World War II as to the Depression. He would have preferred not to have it, but he didn't deny it was on. That got me a break. He sent me to France in October 1939. I attracted the assignment by telling McKelway how well I could talk French. McKelway could not judge. Besides, I was a reasonable age for the job: thirty-five.

Ross was forty-seven then, and in the newspaper world where we came out in different decades, twelve years is a great gap. When we talked I called him "Mr. Ross." I was never an intimate of his—just an act he booked and learned to appreciate, though never highly enough in my opinion. I think that all the reporters of my *New Yorker* generation—Mitchell and Jack Alexander and Dick Boyer and Meyer Berger and I—had the same classical ambivalent son-to-father feeling about him. We were eager to please him and cherished his praise, but we publicly and profanely discounted his criticism. Especially we resented his familiarity with the old-timers—the Companions of the Prophet—and his indulgence for them. Our admiration for their work was not unqualified or universal. (I still think *The New Yorker*'s reporting before we got on it was pretty shoddy.)

I find it hard to admit how jealous I was one day in 1946 when Wolcott Gibbs, who was very ill, called up while Ross and I were working over proofs. Ross told him to take care of himself and said, "Don't worry about money." That was white of him, I thought, but he had never said that to me. It was a true sibling emotion. In fact, Ross thought that a healthy writer wouldn't write unless he had had to emit at least two rubber checks and was going to be evicted after the week end. It was an unselfish conviction, a carry-over from his newspaper days. He reminded me of a showman I knew named Clifford G. Fischer—the impresarial analogy pops up constantly when I think of Ross. Fischer spoke to actors only in a loud scream, and when I asked him why, replied, in a low conversational voice he used on nonactors, "Because they are abnormal people. To abnormal people you got to talk in an abnormal voice."

Ross liked writers, but he would no more have thought of offering a writer money than of offering a horse an ice-cream soda. "Bad for them, Liebling," he would have said. But you could promote a small advance if you were in a bad jam. What continually amazed me about Ross, and convinced me of his greatness, was that he took the whole show seriously—from the fiction, which I seldom can read, to the fashion notes that I never try to. He knew no more of horse racing than a hog of heaven, but he knew how to find and keep Audax Minor, G. F. T. Ryall, whose tone is precisely right for *The New Yorker*. Here again he had the instinct of a showman, who wants the whole bill to be good, while I have that of an educated seal, who thinks that when he plays "Oh, say can you see" on the automobile horn, it is the high spot of the evening. After that the crowd can go home.

A lot has been written about Ross as an editor of manuscript, as distinguished from Ross the editor-impresario. There should be different words for the two functions in English as there are in French—*directeur* for the boss and *rédacteur* for the fellow who works on the copy. Ross did both, but he impressed me less as *rédacteur* than as *directeur*. His great demand was clarity. This is a fine and necessary quality, but you can go just so far with it. You cannot make subtlety or complexity clear to an extraordinarily dull reader, but Ross in editing would make himself *advocatus asinorum*. He would ask scores of marginal questions, including many to which he full well knew the answers, on the off chance that unless all were pre-explained in the text some particularly stupid woman might pick up a *New Yorker* in a dentist's waiting room and be puzzled. Out of the swarm of questions there were always a few that improved the piece—on an average, I should say, about 2¾ percent, and none that did any harm, because you could ignore the silliest and leave Shawn to talk him out of the rest.

I never thought this quest for clarity naïve. It was part of a method he had thought out for putting his "book" across in the early days. If the silliest *New Yorker* readers could go through a piece on a "sophisticated" subject and understand every word, they would think themselves extremely intelligent and renew their subscriptions. But there are subjects not susceptible of such reduction; the only way of making clear pea soup is by omitting the peas. Ross continued his queries compulsively long after the time when *The New Yorker* had to recruit readers. A point had been reached when the silly ones would pretend to understand even if they didn't. This vestigial reminder of the "book's" early hard times was exasperating, but not serious. The writer got his way in the end. Just because he was a great editor, Ross knew when to back down.

I have heard that he made a fetish of Fowler's *Modern English Usage*, a book I have never looked into. (It would be like Escoffier consulting Mrs. Beeton.) He never suggested the book to me, nor told me how to write that mythical thing, the "*New Yorker* style." What is affected as a "*New Yorker* style" by undergraduate and British contributors is, to judge from specimens I have seen, a mixture of White's style, Gibbs's, and S. J. Perelman's, but as none of these three is like either of the others, the result is like a "Romance language" made up by jumbling French, Portuguese, and Romanian. It is not a satisfactory medium of communication. I don't know anybody who has written a good story for *The New Yorker* in "*New Yorker* style."

Personally, I had a tough first year on *The New Yorker*, from the summer of 1935 to the summer of 1936, because I brought to it a successful newspaper short-feature method that was not directly transferable to a magazine, especially in long pieces. It would have been like running a mile in a series of hundred-yard dashes. I rescued myself by my reporting on a profile of Father Divine. I found out more of the inner inwardness and outward outerness of that old god in a machine than anybody else had. The machine was a $150 Rolls-Royce acquired during the Depression when nobody else wanted a car that burned that much gas. The old newspaperman in Ross came to the top; he stopped my salary of $65 a week and gave me a drawing account of $90. I have never been out of debt to *The New Yorker* since.

And still, that isn't the whole story. It is hard to be entirely kind to Ross, and he found it hard to be entirely kind to others, as I recalled earlier on. But through five years of war I liked to know that he was behind me, unashamedly interested in what I was doing and seeing, like a kid watching a high-wire act, and that my copy would run as I wrote it. He never usurped the right to tell me what I saw, or to turn my report into a reflection of an editorial conference in Rockefeller Plaza strained through a recollection of Plattsburg in the First World War. That used to happen constantly to the collective journalists who worked for Henry R. Luce. Ross appreciated a good story, too. He seldom gave unqualified praise to a person—and who deserves it?—but he once cheered me with a note about the "unbelievably high quality" of a piece. He was a ham and understood them.

I wish I had told him once how much I liked him.

The Earl of Louisiana

"Joe Sims, Where the Hell?"

Southern political personalities, like sweet corn, travel badly. They lose flavor with every hundred yards away from the patch. By the time they reach New York, they are like Golden Bantam that has been trucked up from Texas—stale and unprofitable. The consumer forgets that the corn tastes different where it grows. That, I suppose, is why for twenty-five years I underrated Huey Pierce Long. During the early thirties, as a feature writer for a New York evening paper, I interviewed him twice—once at the brand-new Waldorf and once at the brand-new Hotel New Yorker. The city desk showed what it thought of him by sending me instead of a regular political reporter; the idea was that he might say something funny but certainly nothing important. He said neither. Both times he received me in his pajamas, lying on top of his bed and scratching himself. It was a routine he had made nationally famous in 1930, when, as Governor of Louisiana, he so received the official call of the commander of a German cruiser visiting New Orleans, causing the Weimar Republic to make diplomatic representations. New York reporters couldn't figure out how he expected to get space with the same gag every time he came to town, but now I think I understand. He was from a country that had not yet entered the era of mass communications. In Louisiana, a stump speaker still tells the same joke at every stop on a five-speech afternoon. He has a different audience each time, like an old vaudeville comic, and Huey just hadn't realized that when a gag gets national circulation it's spoiled.

It was the same with his few remarks intended to be serious. He would boast of free schoolbooks, which we had had in New York since before he was born, and good roads, which ditto. Then, talking in the shadow of the new Empire State Building, he would brag about the thirty-four-story Capitol he had built in Baton Rouge. As for the eight bodyguards he brought with him, they seemed in New York an absurd affectation: didn't he know we had cops? And who would bother to shoot him anyway? It is hard to put yourself across as a buffoon and a potential martyr at the same time, and Huey did not convince us in either role. A chubby man, he had ginger hair and tight skin that was the color of a sunburn coming on. It was an uneasy color combination, like an orange tie on a pink shirt. His face faintly suggested mumps, and he once tipped the theater-ticket girl in the lobby of the Hotel New Yorker three cents for getting him four tickets to a show that was sold out for a month in advance.

Late in July 1959 I was in Baton Rouge, and I took a taxi out to the Capitol, where he is buried. Standing by Huey's grave, I had him in a different perspective. A heroic, photographically literal statue of him stands on a high pedestal above his grave in the Capitol grounds. The face, impudent, porcine, and juvenile, is turned toward the building he put up—all thirty-four stories of it—in slightly more than a year, mostly with Federal money. The bronze double-breasted jacket, tight over the plump belly, has already attained the dignity of a period costume, like Lincoln's frock coat. In bronze, Huey looks like all the waggish fellows from Asheville and Nashville, South Bend and Topeka, who used to fill our costlier speakeasies in the late twenties and early thirties. He looks like a golf-score-and-dirty-joke man, anxious for the good opinion of everybody he encounters. Seeing him there made me feel sad and old. A marble Pegasus carved in bas-relief below his feet bears a scroll that says, "Share Our Wealth." That was one of Huey's slogans; another was "Every Man a King."

I walked along well-tended paths between melancholy Southern trees to the entrance of the Capitol, which is reached by forty-eight granite steps, each bearing the name of a state, in order of admission to the Union; to include Alaska and Hawaii, Louisiana will have to raise the Capitol. My taxi driver, a tall prognathous type who was a small boy when Huey was killed, had parked his cab somewhere and now sociably rejoined me. "The newspapers gave old Huey hell when he built that for five mil-li-on," he said, waving toward the skyscraper. "You couldn't build it now for a hundred mil-li-on." He talked of Huey as a contemporary, the way some people in Springfield, Illinois, talk of Lincoln.

Inside the Capitol, which is air-cooled, I paused, breathless with gratitude. Outside, the heat was pushing a hundred. The interior of the building is faced with agate, porphyry, basalt, alabaster, and such—more than thirty kinds of stone, the *Louisiana Guide* says. It is the richest thing in its line since they moved the barbershop in the Grand Central Station upstairs. The rotunda, as slick as mortuary slabs on end, reminded me pleasurably of Grant's and Napoleon's tombs, the shrines that early fixed my architectural tastes forever. Marble, high ceilings, and a reverential hush are the things I like inside a public building—they spell class. In addition to all this, and air-conditioning, the Capitol has its legend, and perhaps its ghost, hurrying along the corridor at the rear of the first floor. Looking around, I thought of what the Chief Justice of the Supreme Court of Louisiana had told me a day earlier about how Huey was shot in this monument he had erected to himself.

At sixty-four the Chief Justice, the Honorable John Baptiste Fournet, is still a formidable figure of a man—tall and powerful and presenting what might be considered in another state the outward appearance of a highly successful bookmaker. The suit he had on when I saw him, of rich, snuff-colored silk, was cut with the virtuosity that only subtropical tailors expend on hot-weather clothing. Summer clothes in the North are makeshifts, like seasonal slipcovers on furniture, and look it. The Chief Justice wore a diamond the size of a Colossal ripe olive on the ring finger of his left hand and a triangle of flat diamonds as big as a trowel in his tie. His manner was imbued with a gracious warmth not commonly associated with the judiciary, and his voice reflected at a distance of three centuries the France from which his ancestors had migrated, although he pronounces his name "Fournett." (The pronunciation of French proper names in Louisiana would make a good monograph. There was, for example, a state senator named DeBlieux who was called simply "W.") I had gone to the Chief Justice to talk politics, but somehow he had got around to telling me instead about the night of September 8, 1935, which has the same significance among Long-ites that St. Bartholomew's Day has for French Protestants.

Huey had come down from Washington, where he was serving as United States Senator, to run a special session of the Louisiana Legislature, Justice Fournet said. He controlled the state from Washington through a caretaker Governor named O. K. Allen, but whenever there was a bit of political hocus-pocus to be brought off that he thought was beyond Allen's limited competence, he would come home to put the legislators through their hoops himself. When Huey was in Baton Rouge, everybody called him Governor. Since he feared assassination, he had a flat furnished for him on the thirty-fourth floor of the Capitol, and theoretically he would retire to it at the end of each legislative day, but, Fournet said, "He was the kind of man who was always running around so they couldn't keep him in that apartment. He was a hard man to guard." Fournet himself had served as Speaker of the House—it was he who ad-journed the Legislature when Huey's enemies were about to im-peach him—and, after that, as Lieutenant Governor under Allen. Huey had later looked after his old friend by pushing his election as an Associate Justice of the State Supreme Court. The Court was in the front line of conflict, because, as the Chief Justice explained to me, "There was hardly a piece of legislation that Huey introduced that the other side didn't carry to litigation. Huey had what he called a 'deduct' system—ten percent of the salary of every state em-ployee for his political fund. It sounds raw, but he had to take the money where he could; the other side had all the money of Stan-dard Oil to pay its attorneys. I was elected for a term of fourteen years, and on the day I took the oath of office I had to start think-ing about my campaign for reelection." On September 8, 1935, the Chief Justice said, he had to see Huey personally about some friends who needed political help, so he drove up to Baton Rouge from New Orleans, where the Supreme Court sits, and arrived at the Capitol just before nine at night, when the Legislature was to recess. Here he offered a slight digression. "People from out of state sometimes ask me why the Supreme Court sits in New Orleans when the capital is Baton Rouge, only eighty miles away," he said. "I tell them the truth—that there wasn't a road you could count on until Huey got in office, so the busy lawyers of New Orleans would have spent half their lives traveling back and forth. Now you can make it in an hour and a half, thanks to Huey, but the Court has stayed in New Orleans, mostly from habit."

When Fournet reached the Capitol, Huey was in the House chamber, on the main floor, coordinating the efforts of his legislators, and Fournet walked in and took a seat. He had the Senator under his eye, but when the session broke, there were a number of people between them, and Huey started out the door so fast that Fournet couldn't get to him. "That man never walked," he told me. Huey headed toward the corridor in the rear of the building that led to Governor Allen's office, and Fournet followed, content to catch Huey when he came out after leaving a few instructions with the titular Governor of Louisiana. There were bodyguards in platoon strength in front of the Senator and behind him as he trotted. Entering the corridor, Fournet saw a couple of rich dilettante politicians who were always good for a campaign contribution. He stopped to talk to them and then went on. Huey had disappeared into Allen's office. Fournet, as he followed him, passed two or three men standing in a recess in the wall, talking. He paid them no heed, assuming that they had just emerged from the House chamber, as he had. Then Huey came out of Allen's door, turning, with the knob still in his hand, to shout an inquiry back into the room. Fournet heard the answer: "All of them have been notified, Governor." He started toward Huey, and as he did a young man came up on his right side and passed him, walking fast. What attracted the Justice's attention was that he had a stubby black pistol in his right hand. "It was a hot night—before air-conditioning—and I perspire exceptionally," Justice Fournet said. "So I was holding my Panama hat in my right hand while I wiped my head with a handkerchief in my left. Without thinking, I hit at the man with my hat, backhand. But he reached Huey and fired, and Murphy Roden, a bodyguard, grabbed his gun hand and got a finger inside the trigger guard, else he would have killed Murphy. Huey spun around, made one whoop, and ran down the hall like a hit deer. Murphy and the young man went to the floor, both holding that gun and Murphy trying to reach his own gun with his other hand. I was leaning over them, thinking to grab hold, and Elliott Coleman, another guard, leaned, too, and fired two bullets that passed, by the mercy of God, between Murphy and me and killed the fellow. He let go his gun and lay there. He had black hair, combed down a little slick, as I remember it, and black-rimmed eyeglasses. Huey ran clear to the end of the hall and down a flight of stairs. Then the other guards pulled the body over to the wall and emptied their guns into it. It sounded like machine guns."

When Huey got to the lower hall, a couple of fellows he knew stopped him. One said, "Are you hit?" and he said, "Yes." The other said, "Are you hurt bad?" and Huey said, "I don't know." They put him in their car and took him to the Our Lady of the Lake Hospital. There, the examining surgeon found that the bullet had perforated Huey's colon and part of one kidney. "I couldn't ride with Huey, because it was a two-seated car," the Chief Justice said, "so I went to get mine, parked not far away, and by the time I saw him again he was on the examining table at the hospital. He felt strong and didn't think he was going to die. 'I want you to be more charitable toward Wade Martin and Ellender,' he said." (Martin was the chairman of the Public Service Commission, and Allen Ellender is now the senior United States Senator from Louisiana.) "He knew that all three of us wanted to be Governor, but he wanted us to get along together." It reminded me of how an old friend of mine, Whitey Bimstein, described the death of Frankie Jerome, a boxer he was seconding in the Madison Square Garden ring. "He died in my arms, slipping punches," Whitey said. Huey, mortally shot, talked politics.

———

Alone, except for the taxi driver, in the rotunda of the Capitol, I thought I heard Huey make his one whoop, but the sound may have been a mere hallucination. In any case, I felt different about Huey when I walked out into the heat. By that time I had been in Louisiana about ten days, and I had also changed my mind about Earl Long, then Governor of the state. Earl was Huey's brother, his junior by two years and his survivor by a quarter of a century, and although Fournet had said that Earl "wouldn't make a patch on Huey's pants," it seemed to me that he was filling a pretty fair pair of country britches.

For one thing, the expression of conventional indignation is not so customary in Louisiana as farther north. The Louisianians, like Levantines, think it naïve. A pillar of the Baton Rouge economy, whom I shall here call Cousin Horace, had given me an illustration, from his own youth, of why this is so.

"When I was a young man, fresh out of Tulane," he said, "I was full of civic consciousness. I joined with a number of like-minded reformers to raise a fund to bribe the Legislature to impeach Huey. To insure that the movement had a broad popular base, subscriptions were limited to one thousand dollars. When I went to my father, who was rich as cream, to collect his ante, I couldn't get but five hundred from him—he said he felt kind of skeptical. So I put up a thousand for me and the other five hundred for him. I wouldn't pass up a chance to give the maximum for such a good cause.

"A vote of two-thirds of each house was needed to impeach, and there were then thirty-nine state senators. But before our chairman could see enough of them, Huey induced fifteen—a third plus two—to sign a round robin stating they would not impeach no matter *what* the evidence was. Earl says now that he thought of that scheme. We were licked, so I went around to the eminent reform attorney who was treasurer of our enterprise and asked for my money back.

" 'Son,' he said, 'I am keeping *all* the subscriptions as my fee.'

"I was mad as hell, and told Dad, and he said, 'Son, it shows I did right to hold out my other five hundred—I gave it to Huey as part of the contribution he levied on me to pay the fellows on *his* side.' "

Cousin Horace, who looks like Warren Gamaliel Harding, the handsomest of Presidents, imbibed deeply of a Ramos gin fizz.

"Right then," he said, after the interval, "I made up my mind that it didn't make any difference which side was in in Louisiana, and I have stuck to business ever since."

It was Cousin Horace who told me that the disparity between the two Longs was not one of shrewdness but of scope. "Earl is just as smart a politician inside the state as Huey was," he said, "but Huey saw things big.

"I'll give you an example. One evening during Prohibition, Huey came around to my dad's house and said, 'Telemon, I need a drink.' My father went down to his cellar—he prided himself on it—and brought up a bottle of pre–World War One Jack Daniel's. When he started to open it Huey said, 'Don't open that bottle for me, Telemon; it's too good. I'll take it.'

"So he put it in his pocket and left. Earl would have given Dad a drink out of the bottle."

I had left New York thinking of Earl as a Peckerwood Caligula. Dispatches in the New York papers had left small doubt that he had gone off his rocker during the May session of the Legislature, and I wanted to see what happens to a state when its chief executive is in that sort of fix. The papers reported that he had cursed and hollered at the legislators, saying things that so embarrassed his wife, Miz Blanche, and his relatives that they had packed him off to Texas in a National Guard plane to get his brains repaired in an asylum.

By late July, when I arrived in Louisiana, he had heaved himself back into power by arguing his way out of the Texas sanitarium, touching base at a New Orleans private hospital, and legalizing his way out of the Southeast Louisiana State Hospital, at Mandeville. Then he had departed on a long tour of recuperation at out-of-state Western race tracks that most of the lay public had never heard of before he hit them. Just after I disembarked from my plane in New Orleans I read in the local *Times-Picayune* that the "ailing Governor" had got as far back toward home as Hot Springs, Arkansas, a resort famous for reconditioning old prizefighters and race horses. He had promised to be back in the state on August 1, in time to begin stumping for renomination as Governor in the Democratic primary elections, four months away.

"You know, I think ol' Earl will just about do it again," the taxi driver said as we descended the Capitol's forty-eight states. The place had started him thinking about the Longs. "It don't set good how they done him like they done, y'unnerstand. Those doctors. And his wife. Saying he was crazy. It'll be like the last time he run, in 'fifty-six. Two days before the primary, you couldn't find nobody to say he was going to vote for him. Then they all voted for him. And two days later you couldn't find nobody would admit to have voted that way."

With the Governor unavailable, I sat down in New Orleans to await his return and meanwhile try to build up a frame of reference, as the boys in the quarterly magazines would say. Politics is to the conversation of Louisiana what horse racing is to England's. In London, anybody from the Queen to a dustman will talk horses; in Louisiana, anyone from a society woman to a bellhop will talk politics. Louisiana politics is of an intensity and complexity that are matched, in my experience, only in the republic of Lebanon. The balance between the Catholics in southern Louisiana and the Protestants in northern Louisiana is as delicate as that between the Moslems and the Christians in Lebanon and is respected by the same convention of balanced tickets. In Louisiana there is a substantial Negro vote—about 150,000—that no candidate can afford to discourage privately or to solicit publicly. In the sister Arab republic, Moslem and Christian candidates alike need the Druse vote, although whoever gets it is suspected of revolutionary designs.

The grand gimmick of Louisiana politics, however, providing it with a central mechanism as fascinating as a roulette wheel, is the double-primary system for gubernatorial nominations. The first primary is open to anyone who can get up the registration fee of $210. This brings out as many entries as the Preakness or the Kentucky Derby. If any candidate has more than 50 percent of the total votes, he wins the nomination, which means that he will automatically be elected, since Democratic nomination is a ticket to the Governor's Mansion. If no one has a clear majority, the two top men have a runoff in a second primary, held about a month later.

It is unusual for a candidate to win first time around, and if one does he arouses a certain amount of resentment as a spoilsport. After the first primary, each beaten candidate and his backers trade off their support to one of the two men who are still alive, in exchange for what he will bind himself to do for them in the way of legislation, patronage, or simple commercial advantage. Naturally, the runoff candidate who looks more likely to win can buy support at lower political prices than the other fellow, but by trying to drive too hard a bargain he may send the business to the underdog. Many a man has beaten himself that way. A Louisiana politician can't afford to let his animosities carry him away, and still less his principles, although there is seldom difficulty in that department.

In the campaigning days before the first primary, topics of conversation are delightfully unlimited; the talkers guess at not only how many votes a candidate will get in the first primary but what he will trade them off for, and to whom, if he fails to make the second. It is like planning carom shots or four-horse parlays.

In 1959, the date for the first Louisiana primary was December 5, and in July conversation was already intense. The talk centered on Long and whether he would be able to get to the post. I found few people, even among Long's worst friends, who believed that he was "crazy," although there were some who said he had been at the time of his deportation. (This second position, however, was hard to defend in public discussion. "Crazy" and "not crazy," like "guilty" and "not guilty," are terms that, in popular usage, admit of no shading in between; being crazy or being not crazy is considered a permanent condition, like having one leg.) In New York, the stories of his conduct on his Western tour of convalescence may have seemed clear evidence that the old boy was mad—the phrenetic betting on horse races, the oddly assorted roadside purchases (forty-four cases of cantaloupes, seven hundred dollars' worth of cowboy boots, and such), the endless nocturnal telephone calls, the quarrels with his friends and guards—but seen from New Orleans they indicated a return to normal. Earl had always been like that, fellows who knew him said. A summary of his physical condition had been released to the press by the physicians who examined him after his discharge from the State Hospital at Mandeville on June 26. The doctors' workup on the Governor looked dreadful to a layman—bum ticker, series of cerebral accidents, hardening of the arteries, and a not otherwise described condition called bronchiectasis. But there were lay experts who said that it was all a fake—that no doctor had been able to lay a hand on Earl to examine him.

A Louisiana political tipster never expresses a reservation, and when politics extends over into the field of pathology the positiveness extends with it. "I know a fella that Earl carries with him all the time, hear? and he says Earl just playing mousy, y'unnerstand?" summed up one extreme position. The opposing view could be summarized as "I know a fella told me they gave him adrenaline right in his heart, hear? and that means the old alligator is in extremis, y'unnerstand?" On my first evening in New Orleans, I received forty-two other prognoses in between.

Nor was there any agreement on the efficacy of the device whereby Earl, in entering the primaries, was challenging the Louisiana constitution, which provides that a Governor may not succeed himself directly. Earl, bowing to this law, had dropped out after his 1948–52 term, and then had returned in 1956. Now, however, he was raising the point that if he resigned before election —the formal, post-primary, election, that is—his Lieutenant Governor would become Governor, and so he, coming in to begin a new term, would be succeeding not himself but the fellow who had succeeded him. Even Huey had not thought of that one.

What I heard from Long men was that it was the way the law read that counted, hear? and not what the framers had wanted it to signify. From the other side I heard that there wasn't a court in the country but would hold against a little fine-print loophole, and yeah, you resigned, but, yeah, you can't get away with that. Another point of dispute was how near the Governor stood to Federal prison.

The income-tax people were reportedly on his trail, and apparently they were not being as hermetically secretive as they are supposed to be, or else the Natty Bumppos stalking Earl had stepped on a couple of dry twigs. The range of the opinion on this point lay between "They got it on him this time, hear?" and "Uncle Earl is just too smart to get caught so easy. Whatever he got, he'll say it was campaign contributions, same as Nixon in 'fifty-two. That's why he's got to keep on campaigning, y'unnerstand?" (There is no statutory limit on campaign contributions in the state of Louisiana, and Earl Long often said, like Brother Huey before him, that he was campaigning all the time.)

Arranged in capsule form, all the areas of disagreement about the Governor, peacefully soaking his hide in the Arkansas vats, came to this: The perfect sour-on-Long man held that he was likely to die before the primaries, sure to get licked if he survived, certain to be thrown out by the State Supreme Court if nominated, and bound to be in jail before he could be inaugurated. The perfect Long man expressed faith that the Governor was as full of fight as a man twenty years younger, that he would probably win the first primary with 70 percent of the vote, that he had the Louisiana Supreme Court in his pocket, and that if campaign contributions weren't income for a Republican like Nixon, they weren't income for a Democrat like Uncle Earl.

On my first night in town, before I had finished my third Sazerac at the little bar in Arnaud's Restaurant while waiting for a table, I was not only indoctrinated but willing to bet. An outsider, I had no feedbox information and less idea of the form, but I had an analogy, and nothing can seem more impressive to a man drinking on an empty stomach.

"When Pat McCarran was seventy-one," I said to the pair of home experts with me, "he had a heart attack so bad that they were laying eight to one against him in the Nevada Turf Club, but he recovered and lived seven years to ruin every politician who hopped off him when he was sick. He was mean. How old is Uncle Earl?"

"Sixty-three," said one expert.

"Is he mean?"

"Mean as hell," said the other.

"You see?" I said. "It's a lock." It was an insight that wouldn't have come to me if Arnaud's had not been doing such a good business, but we got a table just in time to prevent my laying money.

When we had ordered moderately—crabmeat Arnaud, filet mignon *marchand de vin*, and a bottle of Smith-Haut-Lafitte '47— we got back to politics. One of my convives, a lawyer, said that the Governor had deep pockets lined with fishhooks: "When you're with him and he picks up a newspaper, you lay down the nickel." The other man, a newspaperman and former Nieman Fellow at Harvard named Tom Sancton, whom I had known for some time, maintained that old Earl wasn't so bad. "He gives money to every kid he meets," he said. " 'A quarter to whites and a nickel to niggers' is the way you hear it around here."

The "nickel to niggers" is a key to the Long family's position on the Southern issue. "They do not favor the Negro," a Negro educator once told me, "but they are less inflexibly antagonistic than the others."

"Earl is like Huey on Negroes," Tom said. "When the new Charity Hospital was built here, some Negro politicians came to Huey and said it was a shame there were no Negro nurses, when more than half the patients were colored. Huey said he'd fix it for them, but they wouldn't like his method. He went around to visit the hospital and pretended to be surprised when he found white nurses waiting on colored men. He blew high as a buzzard can fly, saying it wasn't fit for white women to be so humiliated. It was the most racist talk you ever heard, but the result was he got the white nurses out and the colored nurses in, and they've had the jobs ever since."

A Negro minister in Baton Rouge said to me, later: "Earl is a politician—and a human being." The combination, he evidently felt, was rare.

Since the Governor was not available in the flesh, my friends took me after dinner to see and hear him on film. In the projection room of television station WDSU, which is off a handsome Creole courtyard in the French Quarter, they had arranged for a showing of a documentary composed of various television-newsreel shots, and from this encounter I date my acquaintance with Uncle Earl.

The cameramen had covered all the great moments of that fulminating May session of the Legislature, which began with the Governor riding high and ended, for him, when he was led from the floor, tired and incoherent, by Margaret Dixon, the managing editor of the Baton Rouge *Advocate*.

A day later he was under heavy sedation and on his way to Texas, where he arrived, he subsequently said, with "not enough clothes on me to cover a red bug, and a week later I was enjoying the same wardrobe." But within a fortnight he had talked a Texas judge into letting him return to Louisiana on his promise to matriculate at a private hospital in New Orleans. After signing himself in and out of the New Orleans hospital, the Governor had started for Baton Rouge to assume power, only to be stopped by sheriff's deputies at the behest of his wife, Miz Blanche, who had then committed him to the State Hospital at Mandeville. Thence he had been rescued by a faithful retainer, the lawyer Joe Arthur Sims, who sought a writ of habeas corpus. Once the Governor had regained temporary liberty, he completed the job by firing the director of the Department of Hospitals and the superintendent of the hospital, who, in the normal course of events, might have appeared against him to contend that he was insane.

In the opening newsreel shots Long appeared a full-faced, portly, peppery, white-haired man, as full of hubris as a dog of ticks in spring, sallying out on the floor of the Legislature to wrest the microphone from the hands of opposition speakers. "Let him talk, Governor, let him talk," a man in the foreground of the picture—perhaps the Speaker—kept saying during these episodes, but the Governor never would. He would shake his finger in his subjects' faces, or grab the lectern with both hands and wag his bottom from side to side. He interrupted one astonished fellow to ask, "What's your name?"

"John Waggoner, from Plain Dealing." (This is the name of a town.)

"Well, well, you look like a fine man. Don't let nothing run over you."

Some of the newsreel clips were of the Governor's press conferences, and in one, when a reporter asked him whether he thought he could manage his legislators, he said, "You know, the Bible says that before the end of time billy goats, tigers, rabbits, and house cats are all going to sleep together. My gang looks like the Biblical proposition is here." This was the first good sample of his prose I had had a chance to evaluate, and I immediately put him on a level with my idol Colonel John R. Stingo, the Honest Rainmaker, who, at the age of eighty-five, is selling lots at Massena, New York, a community he predicts will be the Pittsburgh of the future.

In another remark to a reporter I thought I detected a clue to what was to set him off. The Governor said he had reduced 29 pounds, from 203 to 174, in a few months at his doctor's behest. To do this he must have been hopped up with thyroid and Dexedrine, and his already notorious temper, continually sharpened by ungratified appetite, had snapped like a rubber band pulled too hard.

Khrushchev, too, looks like the kind of man his physicians must continually try to diet, and historians will some day correlate these sporadic deprivations, to which he submits "for his own good," with his public tantrums. If there is to be a world cataclysm, it will probably be set off by skim milk, Melba toast, and mineral oil on the salad.

The newsreel also included a sequence in which the Governor sounded off on Mayor deLesseps S. Morrison of New Orleans, who for years had been his rival in Democratic primaries. "I hate to say this—I hate to boost old Dellasoups—but he'll be second again." (Long beat Morrison badly in the 1956 race for Governor. He always referred to him as "Dellasoups" and represented him as a city slicker.) "I'd rather beat Morrison than eat any blackberry, huckleberry pie my mama ever made. Oh, how I'm praying for that stump-wormer to get in there. I want him to roll up them cuffs, and get out that little old tuppy, and pull down them shades, and make himself up. He's the easiest man to make a nut out of I've ever seen in my life." The "tuppy," for "toupee," was a slur on Morrison's hair, which is thinning, though only Long has ever accused him of wearing a wig. As for the make-up, Morrison occasionally used it for television. Earl's Morrison bit was a standard feature of his repertoire, and I could see from the mobile old face how he enjoyed it. Morrison took the "dude" attacks so to heart that in his last campaign he performed dressed like Marlon Brando in dishabille.

And, as if to illustrate the old Long vote-getting method, which had worked in Louisiana ever since Huey took the stump in 1924, the newsreel anthologist had included part of a speech of the Governor's, evidently favoring a higher license fee for heavy (rich men's) vehicles. "Don't you think the people that use the roads ought to pay for building them? Take a man out in the country, on an old-age pension. He don't own an automobile, can't even drive one— do you think he should pay for highways for overloaded trucks that tear up the highways faster than you can build them? We got a coffee-ground formation in south Louisiana—it cost three times more to build a road in south Louisiana than it does in west Texas—but still the *Picayune* says they don't know, they can't understand. Well, there's a hell of a lot that they don't understand—that they *do* understand but they don't want *you* to understand. And you can say this, as long as I've got the breath and the life and the health, I've got the fortitude and the backbone to tell 'em, and dammit they know I'll tell 'em, and that's why they're against me. You can only judge the future by the past."

Almost all the elements of the Long appeal are there, starting with the pensions, which Huey conceived and sponsored, and on which a high proportion of the elderly people in Louisiana live— seventy-two dollars a month now, a fine sum in a low-income state. "But still the *Picayune* says they don't know, they can't understand" refers to the good roads whose high price the *Times-Picayune* constantly carps at, because, the Longs always imply, the *Picayune*, organ of the czarists, secretly wants *bad* roads. "They know I'll tell them, and that's why they're against me" means that the press—a monopoly press in New Orleans now—has always been against the Longs, the champions of the poor; when all the press consistently opposes one skillful man, he can turn its opposition into a back-handed testimony to his unique virtue.

"You can only judge the future by the past" is a reminder that the past in Louisiana, before Huey, was painful for the small farmers in the northern hills and along the southern bayous. It is not hard to select such an all-inclusive passage from a Long speech; they recur constantly, the mixture as before.

Then followed clips showing the crucial scrimmages on the floor of the Legislature. In the beginning, I could see, the Governor was as confident as Oedipus Tyrannus before he got the bad news. He felt a giant among pygmies, a pike among crappies, as he stood there among the legislators, most of whom owed him for favors—special bills passed for their law clients, state jobs for constituents, "contributions" for their personal campaign funds, and so on. But that day the Governor was rushing in where the dinner-party liberals who represent one or two Southern states in Washington have steadily refused to tread. Old Earl was out to liberalize the registration law, passed in Reconstruction times, that gives parish (i.e., county) registrars the power to disqualify voters arbitrarily on "educational" grounds. Except in a few rural parishes, the effect of this law has been on the decline for decades, but now a white-supremacy group in the Legislature had moved for its strict enforcement—against colored voters, of course. It took me a minute or two to realize that the old "demagogue" was actually making a civil-rights speech.

"Now, this registration you're talking about," he said. "That was put through in carpetbag days, when colored people and scalawags were running rampant in our country. You got to interpret the Constitution. There ain't ten people looking at me, including myself, who, if properly approached or attacked, could properly qualify to vote. They say this a nigger bill—ain't no such." (The old law, if enforced impartially, would also have disqualified a number—large but hard to estimate—of older white men and women who had been on the rolls since they were twenty-one but were not Ph.D.'s. Needless to say, the bill's proponents did not expect enforcement to be impartial.)

At this point, the camera focused on a young man with slick black hair and a long upper lip who was wearing a broad necktie emblazoned with a Confederate flag and who addressed a microphone with gestures appropriate to mass meetings. "It's Willie Rainach, the Citizens' Council boy," one of my mentors told me. Rainach, who is a state senator from Summerfield, in Claiborne Parish, pleaded with his colleagues not to let Long "sell Louisiana down the river." (I felt another concept crumbling; I had always thought it was Negroes who got sold down rivers.)

Long, grabbing for a microphone—probably he had no legal right to be in the argument at all—remonstrated, "I think there's such a thing as being overeducated. Scientists tell me there's enough wrinkles up there"—tapping his head—"to take care of all kinds of stuff. Maybe I'm getting old—I'm losing some of mine. I hope that don't happen to Rainach. After all this is over, he'll probably go up there to Summerfield, get up on his front porch, take off his shoes, wash his feet, look at the moon, and get close to God." This was gross comedy, a piece of miming that recalled Jimmy Savo impersonating the Mississippi River. Then the old man, changing pace, shouted in Rainach's direction, "And when you *do*, you got to *re*cognize that *niggers* is human beings!"

It was at this point that the legislators must have decided he'd gone off his crumpet. Old Earl, a Southern politician, was taking the Fourteenth Amendment's position that "no State shall make or enforce any law which shall abridge the privileges or immunities of citizens of the United States . . . nor deny to any person within its jurisdiction the equal protection of the laws." So sporadic was my interest in Southern matters then that I did not know the Federal Department of Justice had already taken action against Washington Parish, over near the Mississippi line, because the exponents of the law that Earl didn't like had scratched the names of 1,377 Negro voters, out of a total of 1,510, from the rolls. (When, in January 1960, six months later, United States District Judge J. Skelly Wright, a Louisianian, ordered the Negroes' names put back on the rolls, no dispatch clapped old Earl on the back for having championed them. Nor, in February, when Louisiana appealed Judge Wright's decision and the Supreme Court sustained it, did anybody give the old battler credit for having battled. The main feature of the civil-rights bill passed by Congress was, in fact, an affirmation of the Earl Long argument that led to his sojourn in Texas, but nobody recalled the trouble that his fight for civil rights had cost him.)

"There's no longer *slavery!*" Long shouted at Rainach. "There wasn't but two people in Winn Parish that was able to own slaves— one was my grandpa, the other was my uncle—and when they were freed, they stayed on" (here his voice went tenor and sentimental, then dropped again) "and two of those fine old colored women more or less died in my Christian mother's arms—Black Alice and Aunt Rose." He sounded like a blend of David Warfield and Morton Downey. "To keep fine, honorable gray-headed men and women off the registration rolls, some of whom have been voting as much as sixty or sixty-five years—I plead with you in all candor. I'm a candidate for Governor. If it hurts me, it will just have to hurt."

He didn't believe it would hurt, but it did. In any case, he was taking a chance, which put him in a class by himself among Southern public men.

This was the high point of the Governor's performance, an Elizabethan juxtaposition of comedy and pathos; weeks after witnessing it, I could still visualize Senator Rainach up on his porch in Summerfield, looking at the moon, foot in hand, and feeling integrated with his Creator. As the session continued, the old man, blundering into opposition he hadn't expected, became bitter and hardly coherent.

The theme of one long passage was that many legislators had Negro or at least part-Negro relatives in the bar sinister category, to whom they now wanted to deny the vote. He told a story about his own uncle who, climbing into bed with a Negro woman, had given umbrage to her husband, then present.

Here the Governor's voice was sad, like the voice of a man recounting the death of Agamemnon: "He shot my poor uncle"—a one-beat pause—"and he died." If white men had let Negro women alone, he said, there wouldn't be any trouble.

The squabble continued, Uncle Earl growing progressively less effective, but with flashes of humor: of some fellow on his own side, he said once, "Why does the *Picayune* hate him—is why I like him. When he makes the *Picayune* scratch and wiggle, he is putting anointed oil on my head."

The others snarled him down, and Mrs. Dixon led him from the floor.

The light in the projection room went on, as if at the end of a first act, and there was a pause while the operator loaded a new reel. When the show went on again, I saw a shocking change. The Governor, between his exit from the screen and his reappearance, had made the tortuous journey to Texas and back. Extended on a pallet in a dusty little hotel at Covington, where he lay after winning his way to freedom by firing the hospital officials, he recalled old newsreel shots of Mahatma Gandhi. His pale, emaciated arms and chest showed over the top of a sheet that covered the rest of his body, and he addressed the reporters in a hoarse whisper that was hard to understand because he had mislaid his dentures. It was the beginning of the second chapter of the legend of Long-family martyrdom: following the assassination of Huey, the crucifixion of Earl.

"I'm very happy to be relieved from hijacking, kidnapping, punctures, needles, and everything they could use," he said, "and one of the first things I'm going to do is see that no person, colored or white or what, has to go through the same humiliation, the same intimidation, the same hurts and bruises that I did. I think it was politics—I think some of my enemies thought that this was a way to get rid of old Uncle Earl.

"In my opinion, instead of hurting me politically, I think this is going to make me," the old boy moaned happily, transmuting his hurts into votes even as he ached, "I b'lieve our state and nation needs a few senior statesmen to hold the younger ones down—when you get to be sixty you realize what it's all about."

Here he closed his eyes, as if in mystic prayer, and one of the Faithful around him, a woman with a big chin, hauled off and recited W. E. Henley's "Invictus," the Long family anthem since Huey's day—it was the only poem Huey ever liked.

His appearance and weakness at this interview had set many re-

porters to predicting that his death was imminent. But his perfor-
mances within the next month had stimulated a counter-rumor that
the whole episode was from beginning to end a fake, put on to
build up a defense against income-tax prosecution. The second report credited its hero with a yogi's gift of physical retraction—he
had lost another thirty pounds between the Baton Rouge and Covington scenes.

Now, in a motel near Covington, a day later, he was on the subject of his wife, talking with a touch more vigor as he picked up
strength: "There hasn't been a woman employed by me that she
didn't worry about—any decent, nice-looking woman. How can an
old man like me take care of three or four of them when I'd do well
to take care of one and know I'm doing a bum job at that—that's
why she tried to get rid of me—I don't blame her."

The next sequence was pastoral—on the veranda of Earl's old-
fashioned farm at Winnfield, in his home parish, where it is politically inadvisable to paint the house too often. The horrors of Texas
and Mandeville were beginning to recede. "Now I'm at my little ol'
peapatch farm in Winnfield, where I raise some billy goats, shoats,
cows, got two or three old plug horses, but they suit me," he said.
"I knew I was a little run down in the Legislature. Only two weeks
to go, and I knew there was lots of important things that would fall
if I wasn't there. When they kidnapped me, I lost the loan-shark
bill." This was a bill to regulate rates of interest charged by small-
loan companies, and the Governor's tone made me tremble for
the small debtors of Louisiana, left naked to the exactions of the
Shylocks.

The respite at Winnfield was brief, however—just a couple of
days, while he prepared for a few nonpolitical, precampaign stump
speeches. The screen showed one of these stump appearances, too.
The Governor was weak and had to be helped up some wooden
steps set against the side of the flat-bodied truck from which he
spoke. The sun, to judge from the sweaty faces of the crowd, must
have been killing. He didn't say much; the main purpose of his appearances was to show the voters that Lazarus was in business at the
old stand. Joe Arthur Sims, his disciple-at-law, made the principal

speech. Mr. Sims is a big young man, about six feet four, with a big face windowed in tortoise shell, a big chin, and a big voice.

His delivery is based on increasing volume, like the noise of an approaching subway train; when he reaches his climaxes, you feel almost irresistibly impelled to throw yourself flat between the rails and let the cars pass over you. "When our beloved friend, the *fine* Governor of the Gret Stet of Loosiana, sent for me in his need at Mandeville," Mr. Sims said, "his condition had been *so* MISREPRE-SENTED"—here he took the train around a loop and up to Seventy-second Street before he started down again—"that people I knew said to me, 'Don't you go up there, Joe Sims. That man is a *hyena*. He'll BITE YOU IN THE LAIG.' But I went. I went to Mandeville, and before I could reach my friend, *the armed guard had to open ten locked doors*, and lock each one of 'em again after us. And theah, *theah*, I found the FINE Governor, of the GRET Stet of Loosiana"—and here his shocked voice backed up way beyond Columbus Circle—"without SHOES, without a stitch of CLOTHES to put awn him, without a friend to counsel with. And he was just as rational as he has ever been in his life, or as you see him here today. He said, 'JOE SIMS, WHERE THE HELL YOU BEEN?' "

(1960)

Nothing but a Little Pissant

The entry of a hero on the public scene goes unnoticed, but his *rentrée* always has an eager press. Napoleon coming back from Elba, Robert Bruce from rustication among the spiders, and Jim Jeffries from retirement in 1910, all drew a heavy coverage; so, no doubt, did Odysseus after he announced his arrival at Ithaca. The betting public, sentimental only to a point, wants to know whether the hero's legs are sound, his spirits good, whether he has shed the lard of sloth, and if so, whether he has weakened himself taking off weight.

Such was the mood of Louisiana when, on the afternoon of August 2, Tom and I started from New Orleans in his battered station wagon to go to the midstate city of Alexandria, where Earl was to make the first major stump speech of his campaign for renomination on the Democratic ticket.

Opinion, all biased, was split on how the Governor would shape up. The *Times-Picayune*, like the Royalist journals in 1815, held that the man from Elba was a burned-out shadow of a hollow shell. But Jim Comiskey, boss of the Old Regulars, had assured me "Oil is on da steady improve and champing on da bit to go." Mr. Comiskey was, for the moment, a red-hot Long man.

Tom was about as neutral as a Louisianian can be during a primary fight, which is to say about as calm as a cat can stay with catnip under its nose. He erred, however, in overweighting medical testimony. This is a mistake journalists have made increasingly since 1955, when, after President Eisenhower's heart attack, the statements of physicians in attendance became more newsworthy than good triangle murders. Abruptly, any utterance of an M.D. rated as much space as the award of an honorary degree to the publisher of the paper, and editors, not content with the daily bulletins from Denver, Washington, and Harvard, sent reporters out to ask local cardiologists everywhere for inside comments on the Chief Executive's viscera. These covered everything from the effect of fried mush to how many times a day a middle-aged man ought to lose his temper. Reporters, always confused between what is news and what makes sense, began to take the doctors seriously. After that the cholesterol was in the fire.

Tom was impressed because half the doctors in the South and Southwest had tabbed Uncle Earl as infected with all known diseases, from paranoid schizophrenia to warts and bronchiectasis, which means difficulty in clearing the throat. Even his own experts, who denied he was demented, said in explanation of his antislavery views that he was beset by arteriosclerosis, several small strokes, oscillatory blood pressure, and an irreverent gleam in his left eye. The collective diagnosis recalled the doctor described in the great book *The Flush Times in Alabama and Mississippi*, who would "fire at random a box of his pills into your bowels, with a vague chance of hitting some disease unknown to him." It was Tom who, years before, had first called my attention to the *Flush Times*, by Joseph G. Baldwin, a happy 1853 antidote to the mystic-memories-of-magnolia school of Southern writing.

"There is an expert at Tulane they call 'Dr. Schizophrenia,'" Tom said to me. "He says Earl hasn't got it. But what he says he has is progressive deterioration of the memory caused by an occluded ventricle. Once they got that, they're gone."

I myself inclined to the theory that if a man knows enough to go to the races, he needs no doctor. A good tout is the best physician for a confirmed horseplayer, and any prescription he writes that pays 5 to 1 or better tonifies the blood, synchronizes the pulse, regularizes the functions, and lets bygones be bygones.

The distance from New Orleans to Alexandria is about 190 miles. The first 90 miles, from New Orleans to Baton Rouge, are on a throughway, a straight, fast road on the east side of the Mississippi, far enough back from the bank to avoid meanders, and high enough over the marshes to obviate bridges. There is nothing worth a long look. The bayous parallel the road on either side like stagnant, weed-strangled ditches, but their life is discreetly subsurface—snapping turtles, garfish, water moccasins, and alligators. The mammals are water rats and muskrats and nutria, a third kind of rat. The nutria, particularly ferocious, is expropriating the other rats. Bird life, on the day we drove through, was a patrol of turkey buzzards looking down for rat cadavers. There pressed down on the landscape a smell like water that householders have inadvertently left flowers in while they went off for a summer holiday. It was an ideal setting for talk about politics.

The old station wagon slammed along like an old selling plater that knows a course by heart.

"It's the most complex state in the South," my companion said. "In just about every one of the others you have the same battle between the poor-to-middling farmers on the poor lands—generally in the hills—that didn't justify an investment in slaves before the war, and the descendants of the rich planters on the rich lands, who held slaves by the dozen to the gross. Slaves were a mighty expensive form of agricultural machinery, with a high rate of depreciation. You could only use them to advantage on land that produced a cash crop. We had that same basic conflict, and it lasted longer than anywhere else, for reasons I'm going to give, but in addition, we have a lot that are all our own. In the other states it was just between poor Anglo-Saxon Protestant whites and rich Anglo-Saxon Protestant whites. But here we got poor French Catholic whites and poor Anglo-Saxon whites and rich French Catholic whites and rich Anglo-Saxon Protestant whites. Sometimes the Catholic French get together against the Anglo-Saxon Protestants and sometimes the rich of both faiths get together against the poor, or the poor against the rich.

"And there's always been another problem in Louisiana that no other Southern state has. There are other large collections of people living close together in the South, but they are not big cities, just overgrown country towns like Atlanta. They may have corruption, but not sophistication. They lack the urban psychology, like ancient Athens, that is different, hostile, and superior, and that the country-man resents and distrusts. So you get a split along another line—you got not only poor rural French Catholic, rich rural white Protestant, rich rural French Catholic, and poor rural white Pro-testant, but poor urban Catholic, not exclusively French, rich urban Catholic, poor urban Protestant (mainly Negro), and rich urban Protestant. Making out a ticket is tricky.

"Alick, in Rapides Parish, is the political navel of the state, right in the middle." (Alick is Alexandria.) "Southern, bilingual, French Catholic Louisiana, the land of the bougalees, shades into northern monolingual, Anglo-Saxon Protestant Louisiana, the land of the rednecks. But in Rapides itself and the parishes across the center of the state you get both kinds. So there's always a lot of politicking and name-calling in Alick, and when Earl picked it to stump in he showed he was ready to fight."

He sounded as complacent as a man I remembered on the road to Baalbek, telling me of the Ten Varieties soup of politico-religious divisions within Lebanon.

The old car banged along. Its speedometer was not working, but it had a clock in its head, like an old horse that an old trainer, set in his ways, has worked a mile in 1.47 every Wednesday morning since it was three years old.

"Orleans Parish—that's the city of New Orleans—and Jefferson, across the river, which is its dormitory country—have about a quar-ter of a million voters between them," my instructor said. "That's between twenty-five and thirty percent of the state vote. All the parishes north of a line through Rapides have maybe twenty per-cent and all the parishes south of it and west of the Mississippi maybe twenty to twenty-five. The central chunk, on an axis from Al-ick to Baton Rouge and on east, has the balance of strength. To get a majority of votes on the first primary, a candidate got to win big in one of the four regions and make it close in the others, or win big in three and lose big in one. They're so different and so opposed historically that it's hard to imagine a candidate running evenly in all four. Old Earl was so strong in 1956 that he ran *almost* even in the metropolis. For an upstate candidate that's great. He won easy everyplace else.

"If Earl is too sick to run, a Catholic from New Orleans like Morrison might win big in New Orleans and south Louisiana, but he would be snowed under in the north, and he would have to run like hell in Alick and Baton Rouge to make it. So probably there would be no winner the first time around, and then, in the runoff between the two high men, anything could happen. Generally all the losers gang up against the top guy. Hard to name a favorite in the betting until the day before the second runoff, and then often you're wrong anyway."

"Then how did Huey Long put all the bits and pieces together?" I asked.

"Huey got all the poor people over on one side," my friend said. "And there were a lot more of them. He made the poor redneck and the poor Frenchman and the poor Negro see that what they had in common was more important for voting purposes than the differences. The differences couldn't be changed by ballots. The Depression helped, of course.

"When people are living good again they can afford to fight over unessentials. The regime that ran Louisiana right on from the Purchase discouraged the idea that a man had the right to live decently. It was new stuff down here when Huey put it out: 'Share Our Wealth'; 'Every Man a King'; and remember, he got to be Governor four years before Franklin D. Roosevelt was elected President. Huey got after the out-state oil companies and the in-state oil companies, and the old-family bench and bar that held with the out-state money, and anybody that gave him an argument for any reason he blackened with being a hireling of Standard Oil. I don't know how much money he made out of it, but certainly less than a lot of politicians make taking the easy money side.

"And whether he did it all because he loved the sense of power is moot—you could say the same thing against any leader you didn't like. I think up North you got the idea that the man who killed him became a popular hero, like William Tell or Charlotte Corday. Incidentally, Charlotte Corday wouldn't have won any Gallup polls in

Paris in her day. There were editorials that said, 'Louisiana heaved a sigh of relief and raised her tear-stained head from the dust.'

"But, in fact, Dick Leche and Earl Long, who ran for Governor and Lieutenant Governor on the Long ticket in 1936, got sixty-seven and a tenth percent of the popular vote, even though there was a fight among the Long people themselves and Leche was next to unknown then. That was a better percentage than even Roosevelt got against Landon that year. The vote came straight from the tear-stained head."

We got hungry and stopped at a glass-and-Monel-metal hangar that advertised "Shrimp, BarBQue, PoBoy" (this last the Louisiana term for what we call Italian hero sandwiches). The BarBQue was out, the shrimps stiff with inedible batter, the coffee desperate. Southern cooking, outside New Orleans, is just about where Frederick Law Olmsted left it when he wrote *The Cotton Kingdom*. A PoBoy at Mumfrey's in New Orleans is a portable banquet. In the South proper, it is a crippling blow to the intestine.

"We're hitting a new culture belt," I said. "This is the kind of cooking that goes right on up the center of the United States with the Mississippi until it hits the Great Lakes. It's nearer akin to what we'd get in a roadside diner in La Grange, Illinois, than to the poorest oyster bar in New Orleans, sixty miles behind us."

Tom, New Orleans born, of parents born there, said, "You're right on that. We're Mediterranean. I've never been to Greece or Italy, but I'm sure I'd be at home there as soon as I landed."

He would, too, I thought. New Orleans resembles Genoa or Marseilles, or Beirut or the Egyptian Alexandria more than it does New York, although all seaports resemble one another more than they can resemble any place in the interior. Like Havana and Port-au-Prince, New Orleans is within the orbit of a Hellenistic world that never touched the North Atlantic. The Mediterranean, Caribbean, and Gulf of Mexico form a homogeneous, though interrupted, sea. New York and Cherbourg and Bergen are in a separate thalassic system.

Hellenism followed the Mediterranean littoral; it spread to the shores of the Caribbean and Gulf. The Hellenistic world stopped short of the Atlantic edge of Europe, but its Roman conquerors got there with a version in *Reader's Digest* form, like Irish missionaries of a Jewish religion. Culture on both shores of the North Atlantic is therefore a paraphrase, as if Choctaws had learned English from Cherokees.

The Mediterraneans who settled the shores of the interrupted sea scurried across the gap between the Azores and Puerto Rico like a woman crossing a drafty hall in a sheer nightgown to get to a warm bed with a man in it. Old, they carried with them a culture that had ripened properly, on the tree. Being sensible people, they never went far inland. All, or almost all, the interior of North America was therefore filled in from the North Atlantic Coast, by the weakest element in that incompletely civilized population— those who would move away from salt water.

The middle of Louisiana is where the culture of one great thalassic littoral impinges on the other, and a fellow running for Governor has got to straddle the line between them.

When Tom and I were sufficiently disgusted with the coffee of the inland-dwellers, we resumed our ride, bypassing the center of Baton Rouge to cross the Mississippi by the Baton Rouge bridge, and after that leaving the monotony of the throughway for the state roads with their complete lack of variety. By now I had begun to sneak compulsive glances at my watch. We had left New Orleans at four, and Earl was slated to speak at eight. The owner of the old station wagon had said he could make it to Alick in four hours easy. It began to look not all that easy.

I tried to estimate the station wagon's speed by clocking it between signposts. From "Bunkie, 27 Mi." to "Bunkie, 20 Mi.," I caught it in a consoling seven minutes, but the next post, a good bit farther on, said, "Bunkie, 23." Bunkie is the leading bourgade between Baton Rouge and Alick—it has a population of 4,666—but there were other one-street-of-storefronts towns that the road ran through. By now it was dusk and the stores were lighted, so that, coming out of the dark, we galloped episodically between plywood maple-finished bedroom suites in the windows on one side of the street and mannequins with $7.98 dresses on the other, scaring from our course gaunt hounds that looked like Kabyle dogs.

The entrance to Alick was little more impressive than these others, except for two electric signs. One was a straw-hatted spook flapping great wings over the Hocus-Pocus Liquor Store and the other a symbolic giraffe and dachshund over a used-car lot. They disappeared at every other flash in favor of a legend: "High Quality, Low Prices."

Hurrying through otherwise undistinguished streets, we passed between cars parked thick along the approaches to the courthouse square and heard the loud-speaker blaring long before we got there. Somebody was on the platform in front of the courthouse steps, standing too close to the microphone and blasting. The crowd, massed immediately around the speaker's stand, thinned out toward the sidewalks.

My companion let me out and drove on to find a parking space, and I ran onto the lawn for my first look at the Imam in the flesh. As I crossed over to the forum, a boy handed me a pink throwaway, which I examined when I got within range of the light diffused from the floodlamps over the platform:

GOVERNOR LONG SPEAKS

Governor Long Opens Campaign for Re-Election

Come Out and Bring All your friends to hear the truth.
Come out and see Governor Long in person. Nothing will
be said to offend or hurt anyone.

The Governor, on the platform, was saying to somebody I could not see over in the other wing of the audience:

"If you don't shut up your claptrap, I'm going to have you forcibly removed. You just nothing but a common hoodlum and a heckler."

"Amen," an old man in front of me yelled. "Give it to him, Earl."

Whoever it was that Earl was talking to in the crowd had no microphone, so we couldn't hear him, but he must have answered in tones audible to the Governor, because the latter shouted into the mike:

"I knew your daddy, Camille Gravel, and he was a fine man. But you trying to make yourself a big man, and you nothing but a little pissant."

"Amen, Earl," the old man yelled. "Give it to him."

The fellow in the crowd, now identified for me as a lawyer from Alick who was the Democratic National Committeeman from Louisiana, must have spoken again, for the Governor thundered:

"Mr. Gravel, I got nothing against you personally. Now you keep quiet and I won't mention your name. If you don't I'll have you removed as a common damn nuisance." He paused for the answer we couldn't hear and then bellowed:

"If *you* so popular, why don't *you* run for Governor?"

It sounded like a dialogue between a man with the horrors and his hallucinations. But the National Committeeman, Earl's interlocutor, was there in the flesh. He had brought his ten children, and they were all mad at the Governor.

The night was like a heavy blanket pressed down on the lawn. Men stood in their sleeveless, collarless shirts, and sweat caked the talcum powder on the backs of the women's necks. Anti-Long newspapers the next day conceded the crowd was between three and four thousand, so there may well have been more. Plenty of Negroes, always in little groups, were scattered among the whites, an example, I suppose, of Harry Golden's "vertical integration," because in public gatherings where there are seats, the two colors are always separated into blocs.

"That's the way I like to see it," the Governor said, from the stand. "Not all our colored friends in one spot and white friends in another. I'm the best friend the poor white man, and the middle-class white man, and the rich white man—so long as he behave himself—and the poor colored man, ever had in the State of Loosiana. And if the NAACP and that little pea-headed nut Willie Rainach will just leave us alone, then *sen*sible people, not cranks, can get along in a *reas*onable way. That Rainach wants to fight the Civil War all over again."

There were two colored couples, middle-aged, in front of me, next to the old white man who didn't like Gravel, and now one of the colored men shouted "Amen!" The old white man gave him a reproving look, but he couldn't bawl him out for agreeing with a Long. Nobody can object to *reas*onable and *sen*sible, but Long hadn't said what he thought *reas*onable and *sen*sible were, and it occurred to me that he probably never would.

I had been looking at him with an amateur clinical eye since I got there, and his physical condition seemed to me to have improved several hundred percent since his stump appearance with Joe Sims on the Fourth of July. Late hours and a diet of salted watermelon, buttermilk, and Vienna sausages cut up in chicken broth had put a dozen pounds back on his bones. Walking between grandstands and paddocks had legged him up, and he pranced under the floodlights that must have raised the temperature to a hundred and ten or so. I remembered when I had seen first the referee Ruby Goldstein and then the great Sugar Ray Robinson himself collapse under the heat of similar lights in a ring on a less oppressive night in New York.

Uncle Earl wore a jacket, shirt, and tie, a pattern of statesmanlike conventionality on a night when everybody off the platform was coatless and tieless. The tie itself was a quiet pattern of inkblots against an olive-and-pearl background, perhaps a souvenir Rorschach test from Galveston. The suit, a black job that dated from the days when he was fat and sassy, hung loosely about him as once it had upon a peg in the supermarket where the Governor liked to buy his clothes.

He left the dude role to Morrison. And in fact, before the evening was over, he said:

"I see Dellasoups has been elected one of the ten best-dressed men in America. He has fifty-dollar neckties and four-hundred-dollar suits. A four-hundred-dollar suit on old Uncle Earl would look like socks on a rooster."

It is difficult to report a speech by Uncle Earl chronologically, listing the thoughts in order of appearance. They chased one another on and off the stage like characters in a Shakespearean battle scene, full of alarums and sorties. But Morrison, good roads, and old-age pensions popped in quite often.

Of Dodd, the State Auditor, a quondam ally and now a declared rival for the Governorship, he said, "I hear Big Bad Bill Dodd has been talking about inefficiency and waste in this administration. Ohyeah. Ohyeah. Well let me tell you, Big Bad Bill has at least six streamlined deadheads on his payroll that couldn't even find Bill's office if they had to. But they can find that *Post Office* every month to get their salary check—Ohyeah."

It was after the "*reas*onable and *sen*sible" bit that he went into his general declaration of tolerance. "I'm not against anybody for reasons of race, creed, or any ism he might believe in except nuttism, skingameism, or communism," he said.

"I'm glad to see so many of my fine Catholic friends here—they been so kind to me I sometimes say I consider myself forty percent Catholic and sixty percent Baptist" (this is a fairly accurate reflection of the composition of the electorate). "But I'm in favor of *every* religion with the possible exception of snake-chunking. Anybody that so presumes on how he stands with Providence that he will let a snake bite him, I say he deserves what he's got coming to him." The snake-chunkers, a small, fanatic cult, do not believe in voting.

"Amen, Earl," the old man said.

The expressions on the Governor's face changed with the poetry of his thought, now benign, now mischievous, now indignant. Only the moist hazel eyes remained the same, fixed on a spot above and to the rear of the audience as if expecting momentarily the arrival of a posse.

"I don't *need* this job," he said. "I don't *need* money." He stopped and winked. "I don't miss it except when I run out."

There were shouts of laughter, the effect he courted.

"Amen, Earl. You tell 'em, Earl."

His face turned serious, as if he had not expected to be so cruelly misunderstood.

"I'm serious about that," he said. You know I'm no goody-goody. But if I have ever misappropriated one cent, by abuse of my office, and anyone can prove it, I'll resign.

"I know lots of ways to make a living. I know how to be a lawyer, and a danged good one. I know how to be a traveling salesman. I know how to pick cotton, and have many times, although I've seen the days when to get my hundred pounds I had to put a watermelon in the bag."

There were gales of tolerant laughter now, even from farmers who would shoot any of their own help they found cheating on weight.

"All I ask," he said, with the honesty throbbing in his voice like a musical saw, "is a chance once again to help the fine people of the Great State of Loosiana, and to continue to serve them as their Governor."

Even a group of great louts in T-shirts, perhaps high-school football players, were silent and by now impressed; earlier in the address they had made a few feeble attempts at heckling, like yelling, "Hey, Earl, what's in the glass?" when the Governor paused for a drink of water. These boys might be from well-to-do anti-Long families, but they had the endemic Southern (and Arabic) taste for oratory, and they knew a master when they heard him.

Mr. Gravel, down near the platform, must have again attracted the Governor's attention, but now Uncle Earl, the creature of his own voice, was in a benign mood from offering his own body to the Great State of Loosiana.

"Mr. Gravel," he said, "you got ten beautiful children there, I wish you would lend five of them to me to bring up." It was one of Earl's well-publicized sorrows that he, like the Shah of Iran then, had no legitimate heir, and he handed peppermint candies or small change to all children he saw, even in years when there was no election. "He bought those candies by grosses of dozens," an ex-associate told me.

Mr. Gravel, still inaudible except to Earl, must have declined this overture, because the Governor shouted to the crowd: "He used to be a nice fellow, but now he just a God-damn hoodlum!"

"Leave him alone, Earl, we come to hear *you* talk!" the old man near me shouted back.

"I was in Minneannapolis once, talking to the Governor of Minnesota, a great expert on insanity," Uncle Earl said, "and he told me an astonishing fact—there are ten times as many crazy people in

Minnesota as Louisiana. I suppose that is on account of the cold climate. They cannot go around in their shirt sleeves all year around, go huntin' and fishin' in all seasons, as we do. We got a wonderful climate," he said, and paused to wipe the sweat from his face with a handkerchief soaked in Coca-Cola, which he poured from a bottle out of a bucket of ice handed him by one of the lesser candidates on his ticket. The bugs soaring up at the edge of the lighted area and converging on the floodlights formed a haze as thick as a beaded curtain.

"On account we got so few crazy people, we can afford to let Camille Gravel run around."

"Leave him up, Earl," the old man yelled. "You got him licked."

"Some sapsuckers talk about cutting down taxes," the Governor said, apropos of nothing he had been talking about. "Where are they going to start cutting expenses? On the *spastic* school?" (When any opponent suggests a cut in welfare expenditures, Earl accuses him of wanting to take it out on the spastics. This is the equivalent of charging the fellow would sell his mother for glue.) "They want to cut down on the *spastics*? On the little children, enjoying the school lunches? Or on those fine old people, white-haired against the sunset of life"—and he bowed his own white head for a split second—"who enjoy the most generous state pensions in the United States?

"We got the finest roads, finest schools, finest hospitals in the country—yet there are rich men who complain. They are so tight you can hear 'em squeak when they walk. They wouldn't give a nickel to see a earthquake. They sit there swallowin' hundred-dollar bills like a bullfrog swallows minners—if you chunked them as many as they want they'd bust."

"Amen, Earl," the old man said. "God have mercy on the poor people."

"Of course, I know many *fine* rich people," the Governor said, perhaps thinking of his campaign contributors. "But the most of them are like a rich old feller I knew down in Plaquemines Parish, who died one night and never done nobody no good in his life, and yet, when the Devil come to get him, he took an appeal to St. Peter.

" 'I done some good things on earth,' he said. 'Once, on a cold day in about 1913, I gave a blind man a nickel.' St. Peter looked all through the records, and at last, on page four hundred and seventy-one, he found the entry. 'That ain't enough to make up for a misspent life,' he said. 'But wait,' the rich man says. 'Now I remember, in 1922 I give five cents to a poor widow woman that had no carfare.' St. Peter's clerk checked the book again, and on page thirteen hundred and seventy-one, after pages and pages of how this old stump-wormer loan-sharked the poor, he found the record of that nickel.

" 'That ain't neither enough,' St. Peter said. But the mean old thing yelled, '*Don't* sentence me yet. In about 1931 I give a nickel to the Red Cross.' The clerk found that entry, too. So he said to St. Peter, 'Your Honor, what are we going to do with him?' "

The crowd hung on Uncle Earl's lips the way the bugs hovered in the light.

"You know what St. Peter said?" the Governor, the only one in the courthouse square who knew the answer, asked. There was, naturally, no reply.

"He said: 'Give him back his fifteen cents and tell him to go to Hell.' "

He had the crowd with him now, and he dropped it.

"Folks," he said, "I know you didn't come here just to hear me talk. If this big mouth of mine ever shut up I'd be in a devil of a fix. I want to introduce to you some of the fine *sin*cere candidates that are running with me on my ticket. My ticket and the independent candidates I have endorsed are trained, skilled, and have the wisdom and experience to make you honest, loyal, and *sin*cere public servants."

He turned to the triple row of men and women who sat behind him on undertaker's chairs, the men swabbing, the women dabbing, at their faces with handkerchiefs, while the Governor talked like an intrepid trainer who turns his back on his troupe of performing animals.

A reporter who had his watch on the Governor said that his talk had lasted fifty-seven minutes, and he was not even blowing.

"And first," he said, "I want to introduce to you the man I have selected to serve under me as Lieutenant Governor during my next term of office—a fine Frenchmun, a fine Catholic, the father of twenty-three children, Mr. Oscar Guidry."

The number of children was politically significant, since it indicated that Mr. Guidry was a practicing, not a soi-disant, Catholic. The candidate for Lieutenant Governor had to be a Frenchman and a Catholic, because Uncle Earl was neither.

Mr. Guidry, a short, stocky man who reminded me of a muscular owl, arose from his chair like a Mr. Bones called to front center by Mr. Interlocutor. He appeared embarrassed, and he whispered rapidly to Uncle Earl.

"Oscar says he has only fourteen children," the Governor announced. "But that's a good beginnin'. "

Mr. Guidry whispered again, agitated, and Earl said, "But he is a member of a family of twenty-three brothers and sisters." He turned away, as if washing his hands of the whole affair, and sat down.

Mr. Guidry, throwing back his head and clasping his hands in front of him, as if about to intone the "Marseillaise," began with a rush, sounding all his aitches:

"I am *honored* to be associated with the Gret Governeur of the Gret Stet on his tiquette. Those who have conspired against him, fearing to shoot him with a pistol-ball . . ." and he was off, but Earl, seated directly behind him, was mugging and catching flies, monopolizing attention like an old vaudeville star cast in a play with a gang of Method actors.

Pulling his chair slightly out of line, he crossed his legs and turned his profile to the audience, first plucking at his sleeves, which came down about as far as his thumbnails, then, when he had disengaged his hands, picking his nose while he looked over at Alick's leading hotel, the Bentley, across the street, described by the Louisiana State Guide as "a six-story building of brick and stone, with a columned façade and a richly decorated interior." He stared at it as if it contained some absorbing riddle.

When he had finished with his nose, he began to bathe his face, his temples, and the back of his neck with Coca-Cola from the cold bottle, sloshing it on like iced cologne.

"Cool yourself off, Earl," a voice piped up from the crowd, and the Governor shouted back, "I'm a red-hot poppa."

When he had wet himself down sufficiently, he drank the heel-tap and set the bottle down. Then he lit a cigarette and smoked, dramatically, with the butt held between his thumb and middle finger and the other fingers raised, in the manner of a ventriloquist. While he smoked right-handed he pulled out his handkerchief and blotted his wet face with his left.

He sat unheeding of the rumpus raised by his adherents, like a player in a jazz band who has finished his solo, or a flashy halfback who poses on the bench while the defensive team is in. The candidates ranted and bellowed, putting across a few telling although familiar points.

"In the great state of Texas, biggest and richest in the United States, there is an old-age pension of thirty-one dollars a month. Here in Loosiana we got seventy-two."

But the bored crowd stood fast, knowing that a whistle would blow and the star would throw off his blanket and come onto the field again to run rings around the forces of Mammon. Sure enough, after what seemed to me an endless session of subordinate rant, the Governor threw away the last of a chain of cigarettes and shook his head like a man waking up on a park bench and remembering where he is. He got up and walked to the microphone so fast that the man using it had barely time to say "I thank you" before the Governor took it away from him.

"You shall know the truth, and the truth shall set you free," the Governor said, "but you will never get to know the truth by reading the Alexandria *Town Talk*. You all read in that paper that I am crazy. Ohyeah. Do I look any crazier than I ever did? I been accused of saying the fella that owns that paper is a kept man. Maybe he ain't, but I'd like to be kep' as good as he is. He married a rich woman. That's about the best way I know to save yourself about ninety-eight years' hard work."

"Amen, Earl, it's the truth," the old man in front of me cried, and the Negroes laughed at what was apparently a well-established local joke.

"Maybe some of you are here because you've never seen a man out of a nuthouse before," the Governor said tolerantly. "Maybe you want to see a man who has been stuck thirty-eight times with needles. Oh, the first man stuck me, stuck me right through the britches. He didn't get me in the fat part, either, and oh, how it hurt! Maybe I lost a little weight, but you would have, too. Occasionally I say hell or damn, but if it had happened to you all, you'd say worse than that. Christ on the Cross himself never suffered worse than poor old Earl!

"Oh, not that I'm fit to walk in Christ's shoes!" he bellowed to preclude any confusion. "I'm not good enough, when a fellow slugs me on one cheek, to turn the other side of my scheming head. I'm going to slug him back."

"Amen, Earl. You tell him, Earl. Who you goin' to hit first, Earl?"

"Down there in that court in Texas in Galveston before that Texas judge, I felt like Christ between the two thieves. He reared back his head and he said, 'Father, forgive them, for they know not what they do!' "

At this point he was interrupted by wild handclapping from a group of elderly ladies wearing print dresses, white gloves, straw hats, and Spaceman eyeglasses, who had been seated quietly on the platform through the earlier proceedings. They were under the impression that it was an original line.

I next remember the Governor in his seat again, head down, exhausted, having given his all to the electorate, in a pose like Bannister after running the first four-minute mile. It occurred to me that he was like old blind Pete Herman fighting on heart alone, by a trained reflex. Pete is a friend of the Governor's.

As Earl sat there, one of the assisting speakers, a fellow with a strong voice, grabbed the microphone and declaimed the family battle ode, "Invictus."

When the man came to the part where it says:

> Under the bludgeonings of fate
> Ma haid is bloody, but *unbowed*

Earl flung up his head like a wild horse and got up like a fighter about to go into a dance to prove he hasn't been hurt. He called for a show of hands by everybody who was going to vote for him, and I waved both of mine.

I left him surrounded by children to whom he was passing out coins, "a quarter to the white kids and a nickel to the niggers."

My companion had rejoined me after parking the car, and we walked together through the breaking crowd.

"How could his wife have done him like she done?" a woman was asking another, and a man was saying, "Got to give da ol' dawg what's coming to him."

My friend saw Gravel, a handsome, tanned man in a white sports shirt and black slacks, standing where the lawn ended at the pavement, and walked over to him. Two or three reporters were already there, asking Gravel what he had said when Earl said what.

The National Committeeman said he had come to hear the speech because two or three men close to Earl had called him up and warned him that Earl was going to blacken his name.

"I wanted to be there to nail the lie," he said. He said Earl started the argument.

Six or eight of the ten Gravel children played hide-and-seek around their father's legs, and as he talked, another boy, about eleven years old, ran up and said to a slightly younger girl, his sister, "The Governor wanted to give me a quarter, but I wouldn't take it."

"Why not?" the girl asked, and I decided she had a bigger political future than her brother.

Gravel said he had to go home because there was a wedding reception there, and the rest of us walked back toward the Bentley, where all the rocking chairs on the porch were already occupied. The row of glowing cigar ends swaying in unison reminded me of the Tiller Girls in a glow-worm number.

(1960)

Blam-Blam-Blam

There had been so many people in the room, and for so long, that they had taken the snap out of the air-conditioning. The men staying on for dinner—about fifteen of us—took off their coats and laid them down on chairs and sofas.

One of the women guests, a Northerner, inadvertently sat on a jacket a political gent had laid aside. It was a silvery Dacron-Acrilan-nylon-airpox miracle weave nubbled in Danish-blue asterisks. She made one whoop and rose vertically, like a helicopter. She had sat on his gun, an article of apparel that in Louisiana is considered as essential as a zipper. Eyebrows rose about as rapidly as she did, and by the time she came down she decided that comment would be considered an affectation.

A colored man brought a glass wrapped in a napkin to the Governor—"Something for my throat," the latter explained—and the members of his inner council gathered at his flanks and knees for the powwow on catfish bait. One of the bills Earl had in mind would give individual members of the Legislature scholarship funds to allot personally to young people in their districts. Another would raise the salaries of assistant attorney generals, whose friends in the Legislature might be expected to respond. There were various local baits, funds for construction. The compounders kept their voices low and mysterious, as if saying "One-half pint of fish oil, one ounce of tincture of asafetida, one ounce of oil of rhodium—that will fetch them," or "Mix equal parts of soft Limburger cheese and wallpaper cleaner—never fails." Sometimes a conspirator would be unable to suppress a laugh.

A Mr. Siegelin, a political catfisherman arriving late, brought with him two children, a girl of about ten and a boy of five.

"Give them Cokes," the Governor said, and while a state cop hurried off to fill the order, he said to the little girl, "I hope you ain't going steady yet."

The little girl shook her head, and Uncle Earl said, "That's right. I went with more than a hundred before I made up *my* mind."

Made it up too soon at that, he probably thought, as he wondered about Miz Blanche and the mortgage money.

The children took their Cokes and settled down on facing identical love seats to drink them, while their father, a fair man in shirt sleeves, sat down to join in the bait suggestions, with his equivalent of "Cut smoked herring into bits. Soak in condensed milk several days." The group was still in the midst of bait-mixing when a plug-ugly, either a state trooper or a bodyguard from civilian life, came to the top of the steps leading to the dining room and shouted, "It's ready!" By his tone I judged him ravenously hungry.

The catfishermen remained engrossed in their concoctive deliberations, and the plug-ugly shouted at Mrs. Dixon, whom he judged less engaged, "C'mawn, *Maggie!*"

Mrs. Dixon rose, and the catfishermen, Southern gentlemen after all, perforce rose too and rushed toward the dining room in her wake, the Governor dragging the two children.

The ballroom smacked of Bachelors' Hall, lacking the touch of a woman's fastidious hand, but the dining end of the Mansion, I was happy to see, was well kept up. The long table under the great chandelier was covered with a mountain range of napkins folded into dunce caps, with streams of table silver in the valleys between them, and the iced tea, Sargassified with mint and topped with cherry, was pretty near *Ladies' Home Journal* color-ad perfection. Negro waiters and waitresses swarmed about, smiling to welcome Odysseus home. None of them, either, seemed to miss Penelope. The wanderer, his heart expanding in this happy atmosphere, propelled me to a seat at the head of the table.

He took his place at my left, with the Northern lady across the table from him. Around the long board crouched plug-uglies in sports shirts, alternating with the guests: Tom, Mrs. Dixon, Senator Fredericks, Siegelin, the two Siegelin children clutching Coca-Cola bottles, and half a dozen politicians I hadn't met. The colossal figure of Mr. Joe Arthur Sims, the Governor's personal counsel, dominated the other end of the table. Mr. Sims had his right arm in a plaster cast that kept his hand above his head, as if perpetually voting Aye. He had sustained an odd sort of fracture on July 4, he explained. It had followed hard on his stump speech for the Governor, a great oratorical effort, but he denied that he had thrown the arm out of joint. He said he was in an auto crash.

The Governor said, "We don't serve hard liquor here. Da church people wouldn't like it. But I'll get you some beer. Bob," he called to one of the somber seneschals, "get da man some beer." Quickly, the waiter fetched a can, two holes newly punched in the top, ready for drinking, and set it down on the table.

The beer bore an unfamiliar label, and the Governor said, "Dat looks like some of dat ten-cent beer from Schwegmann's." (He had probably bought it himself, on one of his raids for bargains.) "Dat looks like some of da stuff dat when da brewers got an overstock, dey sell it to da supermarkets. Get da man some *good* beer. And bring a glass—hear?"

He looked so healthy now that I ventured a compliment.

"You fooled those doctors, all right," I said. "You're like that Swede Johansson—you have your own way of training."

"You see dat fight?" the Governor asked, suspending his attack on the salad, which he was tossing between his dentures with the steady motion of a hay-forker. I said I had.

"I didn't see it, but I would have if I thought da fellow had a chance to lick Patterson," the Governor said. "Patterson's pretty good." (If he looked at the return fight, he was let down again.)

"I hear they've got a law here in Louisiana that a white boy can't even box on the same card with colored boys," I said.

"Yeah," said the Governor, "but dat kind of stuff is foolish. If dere's enough money in it, dey're bound to get together."

I recognized the theory of an economic resolution of the race conflict.

He sat there like a feudal lord, and his *maisnie*, the men of his household, leaned toward him like Indians around a fire. The trenchers went around, great platters of country ham and fried steak, in the hands of the black serving men, and sable damsels toted the grits and gravy. There was no court musician, possibly because he would have reminded the Earl of Jimmie Davis, but there was a court jester, and now the master called for a jape.

"Laura, Laura," he called out to one of the waitresses, "set your tray down—dere, hand it to Bob. Tell us what your husband does for a living."

"Prizefighter, sir," the girl said.

"Show us how he does when he goes in da ring," the Governor ordered.

The girl, long, thin, and whippy, was instantly a-grin. This was evidently a standard turn, and she loved the spotlight. She got rid of the tray and showed how her husband climbed through the ropes, lifting her right knee high to get over the imaginary strand, and holding the hem of her short skirt against the knee as a boxer sometimes holds his robe to keep it from getting in his way. Once inside, she danced about the ring, waving her clasped hands at friends in the imaginary crowd. Then she retired to a corner and crouched on an imaginary stool until the Governor hit the rim of a glass with a gravy spoon.

The girl came out, sparring fast, dancing around the ring and mugging for friends at ringside, with an occasional wink. The opposition didn't amount to much, I could see. Laura's husband, impersonated by Laura, was jabbing him silly. Then her expression changed; the other man was beginning to hit her husband where he didn't like it. Her head waggled. She began to stagger. Even the bodyguards, who must have seen the act often, were howling.

"Show us how your husband does when he gets tagged," the Governor ordered, and Laura fell forward, her arms hanging over the invisible ropes, her head outside the ring, her eyes bulged and senseless.

The feudal faces were red with mirth. I applauded as hard as I could. Laura stood up and curtsied.

"You gonna let him keep on fightin'?" the Governor asked.

"I don't want him to," Laura said, "don't want him get hurt. But I don't know if he'll quit."

"Is he easier to live with when he loses?" a state senator asked.

"Yes, sir, he is," the jester said, and took her tray back from the colleague who had been holding it.

The meal went on.

"Dat's da way some a dese stump-wormers going to be when dis primary is over," Uncle Earl said. "Hanging on da ropes. If it's a pretty day for the primary, I'll win it all. I'll denude dem all, da *Times-Picayune* included."

Outside the air-conditioned keep the enemy might howl, but inside, the old vavasor held his court without worrying.

"Da voting machines won't hold me up," he said. "If I have da raight commissioners, I can make dem machines play 'Home Sweet Home.' " He laughed confidingly. "Da goody-goodies brought in dose machines to put a crimp in da Longs," he said. "Da first time dey was used, in 1956, I won on da first primary. Not even my brother Huey ever did dat.

"Da machines is less important dan who's allowed to vote," he said. "I appointed a man State Custodian of Voting Machines here dat run up a bill of a hundred and sixty-three thousand dollars for airplane hire in one year, just flying around da state, inspecting da machines. Good man, Southern gentleman—da *Times-Picayune* recommended him and I thought I'd satisfy dem for once. Den he got an appropriation from da Legislature to keep da machines in repair, but it said in da contract with da voting-machine company dat da company had to keep dem in repair for one year for free. So he split da money wit da company—dey sent him six thousand dollars, and den another six thousand, but I grabbed half of da second six thousand for my campaign fund. Should have took it all."

The cellarer he had sent for the name-brand beer returned with a report that none except the supermarket kind was cold.

"Dey keeping da good beer for demself," the Governor said indulgently. "You drink dis." It tasted fine.

The Northern woman, who had listened with awe to the career of the voting-machine man, asked, "What happened to him?"

"I denuded him," the Governor said. "It's an elective office now."

"And where is he now?" the woman asked, expecting, perhaps, to hear that he was confined in a *cachot* beneath the Mansion.

"He's hypnotizing people and telling fortunes and locating oil wells," the Governor said, "and he got himself a fine blonde and built her a big house and quit home."

Outside of the *Lives of the Troubadours*, which was compiled in the thirteenth century, I had never known a better-compressed biography. I felt that I knew the denuded hypnotist well. I remembered the comparable beauty of the Governor's account of the last day of a beloved uncle in Winnfield: "He got drunk and pulled a man out of bed and got into bed with the man's wife, and the man got mad and shot my poor uncle, and he died."

I asked him what he thought of Governor Faubus of north-neighboring Arkansas, who had won a third term by closing the schools, and he said Faubus was a fine man, but nobody had told him about the Civil War.

"Fellas like Faubus and Rainach and Leander Perez and da rest of da White Citizens and Southern Gentlemen in dis state want to go back behind Lincoln," he said. "And between us, gentlemen, as we sit here among ourselves," he said, arresting a chunk of fried steak in midair and leaning forward to give his statement more impetus, "we got to admit dat Lincoln was a fine man and dat he was right."

Then, as he turned back to the steak, skewering it against a piece of ham before swallowing both, he caught my look of astonishment and cried, too late, "But don't quote me on dat!"

Since he has won his last primary, I disregard his instructions. It was a brave thing for a Governor of Louisiana to say and would have made a lethal headline in his enemies' hands: "Long Endorses Lincoln; Hints War Between States Ended."

We had us another can of beer, and the Governor and I shared it with a sense of double complicity.

"Laura, Laura," the Governor called to his jester, "get rid of dat tray."

"Yes, sir, Mister Governor," and the star turn passed the grits to a co-worker.

"Now, Laura," the Governor said, "can you make a speech like Mr. McLemore?" (McLemore had been the White Citizens' candidate in '56.)

This was plainly another well-used bit of repertory. The Prize-fighter and Mr. McLemore may be Laura's *Cavalleria* and *Pagliacci*, always done as a double bill. But I'd love to hear her sing Jimmie Davis.

She took a stance, feet wide apart and body stick-straight, looking as foolish as she could.

"Ladies and gentlemen," she said, "do not vote for Mr. Earl Long, because he has permitted da Supreme Court of da United States to make a decision by which, by which, Little White Johnny will have to attend da same school with Little Black Mary. If you wish to prevent dis, vote for, vote for"—and she hesitated, like a man fumbling in his mind for his own name. Then, running her hands over her body, she located, after some trouble, a white card in her breast pocket. The card, a planted prop, showed she had expected to perform. She took the card, peered at it, turned it around, and finally read, "McLemore. Dat's it. Vote for McLemore."

The Earl howled, and so did all his guests and men-at-arms. I do not imagine that Penelope would have found it all that funny. She probably cramped his style.

The meal ended with a great volume of ice cream. The Governor, in high humor and perhaps still thinking of the frustrated voting machines, said to the lady across from him, "Would you mind if I told you a semi-bad story?"

She said she would not mind, and the Governor began: "There was an important man once who had a portable mechanical-brain thinking machine that he carried everywhere with him. Da machine was about as big as a small model of one of dose fruit machines dey have in a Elks clubhouse. When he wanted a answer: How many square feet in a room by so and so much? or, Has dat blonde a husband and is he home? he submitted his question and da machine answered it correctly. He would write out da question on a piece of paper and put it in a slot, da machine would read it, and pretty soon it would go blam, blam, blam—blam, blam, blam—dat was da brain working, and it would give him a printed slip with da correct answer. Well, finally da man got jealous of dis machine, it was such a Jim-cracker, and he thought he take it down a little for its own good.

"So he wrote out a message: 'Where is my dear father at this minute, and what is he doing?' He put it in da slot, and da machine says, 'Blam, blam, blam,' very calm, like he had asked it something easy, and it write out da answer, 'Your dear father is in a pool hall in Philadelphia, *Penn*sylvania, at dis moment, shooting a game of one hundred points against a man named Phil Brown. Your dear father is setting down watching, and Phil Brown has da cue stick and is about to break.'"

"Philadelphia, *Penn*sylvania," had the romantic sound in the Governor's mouth of Coromandel in Sinbad's.

The Governor's manner changed, and his voice became indignant. " 'Why,' da man says, 'dat's da most unmitigated libelous slander I ever heard of. My dear father is sleeping in da Baptist cemetery on da side of da hill in *Pitts*burgh, Pennsylvania, and has been for da last five years. I am sure of da dates because my dear mother who is still living reminded me of da anniversary of his death and I telegraphed ten dollars' worth of flowers to place on his grave. I demand a *re*-investigation and an *apology*.'

"And he writes it out and puts it in da slot. 'Dis time I got you,' he says. 'You ain't nothing but a machine anyway.'

"Da machine reads da message and gets all excited. It says, 'Blam, *Blam*' and 'Blam, *blam*,' like it was scratching its head, and den 'Blam, blam, blam, blam . . . blam, blam, blam, blam,' like it was running its thoughts through again, and den 'BLAM!' like it was mad, and out comes da message."

All eyes were on the Governor now, as if the ladies and men-at-arms half expected him to materialize the ticker tape.

"Da message said, 'REPEAT,' " the Governor said. "It said 'RE-PEAT' and den, 'RE-REPEAT. Your dear father is in a pool hall at Philadelphia, *Penn*sylvania, playing a game with a man named Phil Brown. YOUR MOTHER'S LEGALLY WEDDED HUSBAND is in the Baptist cemetery on the side of the hill in *Pitts*burgh, *Penn*sylvania, and has been there these last five years, you BASTARD. The only change in the situation is that Phil Brown has run fourteen and missed, and your old man now has the cue stick. I predict he will win by a few points.' "

It broke everybody up, and soon the Governor said to the outsiders politely, "Y'all go home. We got a lot to do tonight." But he said he might be able to see me at nine next morning.

I arose at that hour and got over there, but there were already so many cars on the driveway that if it hadn't been morning I would have guessed there was a cockfight in the basement. Inside the Mansion, the nearly bookless library on the right of the door that serves as a waiting room was full of politicians, all wearing nubbly suits and buckskin shoes, and each sporting the regulation enlargement of the left breast beneath the handkerchief pocket. (This group included no left-handed pistol shot.) The length of the queue demonstrated that the public reaction to the speeches had been favorable, and that the sheiks who had raided the herds in Earl's absence were there to restore the stolen camels.

A Negro in a white jacket came in and asked the ritual "Y'all have coffee?" Since I had no deal to offer, I just had coffee and went.

Odysseus ruled in Ithaca again.

(1960)

Epilogue
Paysage de Crépuscule

From the window at which I write, I can look west between two walls of high buildings to the North River. A warehouse stands at the end of the street, and the Palisades, on the other shore, appear suspended above it; the interposed river is invisible. Beyond the Palisades, a taller range, which I take to be the Orange Mountains, forms a horizon. The skyscrapers that make up the two walls date from the twenties, the period of the hollow ziggurat. The signature skyscraper of our own age is the upended glass coffin. When I look at the set-back shoulders of the old ones, I visualize them at the date of the crash, with suiciding holders of mortgage bonds cascading from level to level, like spent fish coming down a salmon ladder. It was a brilliant epoch.

The highest peak on the uptown side of this brief canyon on Forty-third Street is the Paramount Theatre Building; the downtown side is dominated by the Hotel Dixie, a hundred yards to the west. Each blots out the lesser heights behind it. I tell time by the clock on the Paramount, but the Dixie is my moral beacon. Colonel John R. Stingo, my favorite writer, lives there, as snug as a Mexican jumping bug in a bean. I work best at night, when the Dixie is easy to identify by the red electric sign on the roof which reads DIXIE HOTEL, and by the vertical one:

H
O
T
E
L

D
I
X
I
E

Whenever I look over there, I think of how the Colonel is cheered by the sight of hundreds of lights in office buildings at night. "It reminds me of Ricecakes," he says. "Ricecakes" is his *petit nom* for George Graham Rice, a departed Wolf of Wall Street. " 'Just think,' Ricecakes would say. 'Behind each of those windows, a man is awake, scheming to take somebody else's money.' It gave him a group feeling, and I was never mean enough to advert him that they in most instances signalized the nocturnal labors of honest charwomen. He would have detested the thought."

I, in turn, am cheered when I think of the Colonel up in his room, which faces the Flea Circus, on the Forty-second Street side of the hotel. He is better company, even two blocks away, than a bust of Pallas sitting up above my chamber door, and of more solace than a good conscience, for he indicates that the future is long. When I first knew the Colonel, in 1946, I congratulated him on his *bonne mine*. He was then, by his own count, seventy-two. "I have three rules for keeping in condition," he said. "I will not let guileful women move in on me. I decline all responsibility. And, above all, I avoid all heckling work. Also, I shun exactious luxuries, lest I become their slave."

Along the approaches to the Dixie I can see foothills, one of them a narrow hotel called the Strand, just west of Seventh Avenue. There, once, in the early 1930s, when I was a reporter for the *World-Telegram*, I interviewed a man with an electric shirt front, a dickey filigreed with the name of a brand of cigars. He wore an electric bulb, worked by a battery that was fastened to his chest behind this display space, and he could turn the light off and on from a switch in his left pants pocket. With his right hand, he would move a cigar in and out of his face. He would stroll along Broadway of nights, an ambulatory rival of the spectaculars on costly rented space. He

wore a high silk hat, a white vest, and tails. This self-propelled illu-
mination was of a most impressive appearance—six feet plus, with a
cherry-pop complexion and a gray mustache and goatee. He told
me that his ambition was to manage a heavyweight champion of
the world, and that the excess of his income over his needs during
the Depression permitted him to subsidize a succession of towering
louts. All of them deserted at their first chance to obtain employment. They lacked what Colonel Stingo calls the Divine Inflatus.
The electric man, for revenge, beat them up when he could catch
them. He was an arrogant man, and bibulous. I remember that
on the morning when I talked to him he had a hang-over, and the
high hat and the rest of the glad rags, strewn about his small room,
made it look as if he had been out celebrating New Year's Eve in
about 1898. The room was darkened by the shadow of an electric
sign just outside. Years later, the wartime dimout extinguished his
profession, since the Civilian Defense authorities deemed him an
air-raid risk, and I do not know what then became of him.

On my own side of the canyon, the top third of the old Hotel
Woodstock intervenes between me and the lower stories of the
Paramount. I have no intimate memories of the Woodstock, which
is perhaps evidence of its respectability, but I know a fellow who
lives there when he is not at sea as a physiotherapist on the *America*,
of the United States Lines. He is an astrologo-nutritionist, yogist,
and poet, and is even more distinguished in my book by being the
only prizefighter I've ever known who was ruined by orange juice.
Jack Willis, to give him his public name, or William Hamby, as he
signs ships' articles, changed his name when he was young, so that
his father wouldn't find out what he was doing. He came out of
Texas in 1924 carrying a bag that contained a spare shirt, a tube of
Vaseline for his hair, boxing trunks, a pair of ring shoes, and a roll
of bicycle tape. Wrapping the tape around his hands before each
fight, he left a wake of concussions from Baton Rouge, Louisiana,
to Portland, Maine, having successively established himself in each
place as a local boy with a job in the lumberyard. He reached his
peak in California. But during the second half of the twenties, when
he was a prominent middleweight, he began to notice that fellows

like Mickey Walker were getting up off the floor after he knocked them down. As he usually broke a hand with the first knockdown, he lost several fights. "It wasn't until I began to study nutrition, years afterward, that I understood what had happened," Willis told me. "I used to drink orange juice by the bucket, under the impression it was good for me, and it leached all the calcium out of my fists, leaving them brittle. I might as well have been hitting those guys with a china cup. Unconsciously, I began to pull, and then they didn't even go down the first time. If I had stuck to whiskey in moderation, I would have been all right. Of course, it might have made some difference that the California Boxing Commission made me quit using the bicycle tape. But the orange juice is what did the business."

Willis became convinced of the power of yoga during a scheduled twenty-round bout with a light heavyweight his manager had erroneously selected for him as a soft touch on July 4, 1930, in Reno, Nevada. He had a broken rib from the previous soft touch when he went into the ring—his manager was an optimist—and the Reno soft touch, twenty-five pounds heavier than Willis, was killing him when my friend suddenly achieved perfect concentration and flattened the bum with a punch. His hands were already going then, though. It was too late to start a new career on a Vedantic basis. Astrology, yoga, and poetry are the troika of humanities that most interest him now, and he has driven them in harness ever since the failure of an attempt to hitch astrology with horseplaying. The horseplaying fiasco is still a sore subject with Mrs. Willis-Hamby, who is an astrologist, too, but does not think that the science should be milked for safe long shots. The Willis-Hambys say that when they met, at a party in London while the *America* was turning around, they knew at once that they were predestined mates, and their true selves have never quarreled since. Each has *two* selves, however, and the short-tempered doppelgänger sometimes tangle over things like betting. Willis is a big, impressive man, a heavyweight now, who walks with his face tilted upward, as if he were looking for a star working three furlongs. (It is a shipboard habit, he says; nights at sea, he can stargaze full time without fear of being run over.)

Willis's verse, in which he shows a frequent preoccupation with the transmigration of souls, is published every now and then in the magazine *American Astrology*. A pretty fairly typical stanza from one poem goes:

> I was king, and a god in India,
>   You were Sita, my heavenly queen.
> I was both Rama and Indra,
>   Lord of the storms, supreme.

After a recent retrospective discussion of horseplaying, though, he sent me the original manuscript of a poem that he had just dedicated to his wife:

TO YOU WHO SPOIL THE PRESENT BY ALWAYS TALKING ABOUT THE PAST

> When the past is gone forever,
>   Lost in an avalanche of time,
> Why bring it back to the present
>   By your concentration of mind?
>
> Why destroy the present moment
>   By dragging back a painful past?
> Perhaps it could be forgotten,
>   If this attempt could be your last.
>
> All the money in the world
>   Can't buy your happiness today,
> So enjoy these precious moments,
>   Don't you know they're slipping away?

I said that it showed he still had a smooth shift, and he said that Mrs. Willis had not referred to gambling since she read the lyric, which showed she got the message.

———

The Paramount Theatre Building itself is haunted for me by the memory of a romance in which I didn't get out of the starting gate. It was there, to a dressing room above the backstage, that I went in about 1931 to garner, for my newspaper, the words of Pola Negri, a femme fatale I had first glimpsed in the German-made silent film *Passion*, which was the *La Dolce Vita* of my adolescence. I had seen it at the Nugget Theatre in Hanover, New Hampshire, while I was a junior at Dartmouth, shortly to be expelled for overcutting chapel. That preliminary ogle had made me Negri's slave forever. I had acquired a carapace of savoir-faire in the intervening eight years, but it melted to the texture of cold jellied turtle soup in her sensed proximity, and when I knocked at her starred door I felt like a pitcher from a prison team starting for the first time in the Yankee Stadium.

Miss Negri was making a personal appearance at the Paramount which was designed to prove she had a voice for the new talkies. Previous to my call, I had caught her act from out front. She floated upon a swing and growled a refrain that went, "And when I *hold* your hand, mm-mm-mm-mm, mm-mm-mm-mm . . ." She was a kind of basso-contralto. When, at the door, I heard "*Komm*," with a couple of added "mm-mm"s that I read in, my legs started to fold under me, but I braced myself on the doorknob and managed to stay upright as I entered. Miss Negri, who used dead-white makeup and had jet-black hair, lay in a white peignoir along a white chaise longue—like a passion-crumpled gardenia petal, as I jotted down on my folded copy paper as soon as I could control my trembling fingers. *Her* fingers trailed limply from her arm, as if dabbling in a stream—"like Cleopatra in the simmering moonlight of a sheening night on the Nile" is how Colonel Stingo once described a lady in a similar pose. The Colonel is a much better writer than I am, and I call him from the bullpen when I cannot get the simile across the plate. By Miss Negri's water-lily-white digits stood a champagne cooler filled with ice. An unopened bottle nestled in its core.

I settled in a straight-backed chair, as if at Camille's bedside. A retainer who looked like the electric-shirt-front man entered and twirled the bottle, but he did not open it.

"*Merci*, Baron," Miss Negri murmured, and he withdrew.

Miss Negri smiled faintly. Her performance had evidently been a great strain upon her. The air was heavy with a scent of tuberoses.

"You have a lovely perfume," I began. "What is it?"

"It is not a pairfume," Miss Negri said, sounding wounded. "It is me. It is my naturahl o-door."

Cursing my clumsiness, I recoiled to think of another overture.

Upon her dressing table stood a photograph of Rudolph Valentino. It was in a silver frame about two feet by eighteen inches and weighing, I estimated, four or five pounds. She had, I remembered from the newspapers, flung herself upon his bier, in what must now seem to her, I imagined, a lifetime of agonies ago.

"Can you bear to speak of him?" I asked, tilting my head in the direction of this Comstock Lode.

"Why not?" Miss Negri asked bravely, like one long accustomed to having thorns stuck in her heart. "He was the only man I evair lawved. But I am fated always to be unhappy in lawv."

The retainer reentered and twirled the bottle again. This time, I hoped, he would open it, and she would pour out her confidences with the wine. Then I might have the courage to console her. But the henchman left the bottle in the bucket.

"*Merci*, Baron," Miss Negri said, and he withdrew, enveloping her in a glance of unrequited passion.

"He is so loyal, so faithful, the Baron," Miss Negri said. "But he is not for me. Always I am disappointed."

Shocked, I cried, "But surely you, you with all your beauty . . ." I was pleading for another chance for a sex that had failed in its mission.

"No!" she groaned. "No!" And then, apologetic but resigned, she said, "You see, I EXPECT SO MAWCH!"

I fled, and in the corridor I passed the reporter from the *Journal*, who had been waiting his turn. Behind his shoulder, the Baron awaited his cue to twirl the bottle.

I cite these associations because I do not wish readers to think Manhattan has no soul. Every corner is fraught with memory. In the

Dixie, the Colonel is poised midway between the raffish penny arcades of Forty-second Street and the ecclesiastical atmosphere with which the *Times* invests the block on Forty-third. "The *Times* is the modern Herodotus," the Colonel often observes. "It soothes as it informs. What a marvelous institution!"

The Colonel's geriatric rules have worked well, because today, at what I calculate to be eighty-nine, he is, in his own terms, running easy on the last turn. He has even, it seems to me, begun to step up the pace a little, because he avers himself ninety-one, and has thus run his last nineteen years in seventeen flat. He is leveling on the century, and, like a good jockey, taking the short way home. My encounters with the Colonel have become less frequent in these latter years, however, because he makes a practice of not answering the telephone. He says it is almost always somebody who wants to know how he is getting along, and this makes him nervous. The protocolary way to arrange a meeting is to call him up several days in advance and leave a message for him to call you, but this does not always work, for he sometimes lets messages accumulate in his box until he finds it quite hopeless to try to cope with them retroactively, and so throws all of them away.

The Colonel has been fated to turn out most of his own stylistic exercises for publications less sedate than the *Times*. He was the racing editor of the old *Evening Journal* in the early 1900s, before the antibetting law promulgated by Charles Evans Hughes as governor blighted New York State. He wrote then under his civilian name, J.S.A. Macdonald. (The *S.*, which he has since dropped, stood for Stuart, he says, adding as explanation, "The Young Pretender.") To his colleagues, in this period, he was known as Alphabet Macdonald. It was while he was running a small periodical called the *Wasp* in San Francisco during the horse hiatus, he says, that he became smitten with pseudonymity and commissioned himself a colonel. As Colonel John R. Stingo, for thirty years he wrote a column called "Yea Verily" for a Sundays-only paper called the New York *Enquirer* and its successor, the *National Enquirer*, which bills itself as "The World's Liveliest Newspaper," in order, no doubt, to avoid confusion with the *Chicago Tribune*, which is the World's

Greatest Newspaper. He received no direct emolument for what he wrote, although he is in my opinion the best curve-ball writer since Anatomy Burton and Sir Thomas Browne, making the prose of his contemporaries look shabby and unfurnished. His sentences soar like laminated boomerangs, luring the reader's eye until they swoop in and dart across the mind like bright-eyed hummingbirds, for a clean strike every time. A column was principally useful as leverage, the Colonel said. In his, he treated frequently of people who won large sums of money by following the advice of turf consultants, analysts, and figurators. The touts, by coincidence, advertised in the *Enquirer*, and the Colonel received a fixed percentage of the advertising revenue accruing to the newspaper. The column, however, was no mere congeries of puffs. It was the best reading in the paper—or, for that matter, any other paper—and the profitable allusions were no more conspicuous than birdshot in quail. His income was subject to no editorial whim but was like a permanent Guggenheim or Ford Foundation grant. It left him a free man.

A couple of years ago, I was walking up Sixth Avenue on a sunny October day when I saw a familiar figure, small, erect, and infused with a military jauntiness, well ahead of me. (The Colonel took over, with his rank, the other attributes of a retired officer of the *Seaforth* or the *Coldstream*.) I caught up with the Colonel, not without difficulty, and hailed him; then we dropped into a worthy saloon, which has since been displaced by a new claptrap hotel. I proposed a cup of coffee, but the Colonel remonstrated that his physician had enjoined a moderate amount of alcohol for the benefit of his ticker, and that he had not yet had his daily dosage. "May I be so bold as to suggest a Jack Daniel's Sourmash Perfecto?" he said. He had three before our conversation ended. The Colonel told me he had retired—or, as he phrased it, "assumed the emeritus" —owing directly to trouble with his left typewriter hand. He was not the kind of author who dictates, being convinced that style is a visual as well as an aural matter. "As a consequence, I am just learning the benefits of fresh air," he said. "I was on the way to Central Park, where it abounds." The Colonel appeared as cheerful as a cricket, or a wasp, and averred himself to be "holding"—an expression by which he denotes a state of solvency, with no threat of the Plug in the Door, the Damoclean sword that hangs over all habitual hotel guests, preventing their use of their key until they adjust their bill. Racing was experiencing a period of unparalleled prosperity, he explained, and with investors extant in redundancy the turf analysts were prosperous. They advertised, and the management of the *Enquirer* held itself honor-bound to continue payment of the Colonel's commission. "It bears out what I have often told you, Joe," the Colonel said. "Shun commodity. Avoid it like the plague. The tangible is perishable, but a concept bears fruit perpetually. Had I invested in dill pickles or steel rails, I might not be able to sell them, but Si and Smudgie, the Kentucky Colonel, Flying Horse, the Masked Jockey, and my other benefactors will continue their pursuit of the turf investor's dollar, and I will sit snug."

This particular meeting with the Colonel took place during the season when Governor Rockefeller was calling for an air-raid shelter in every back yard and the public press was full of a debate as to whether the antlike *prévoyant* who built his family a proper shelter would, in the event of atomic war, be justified in shotgunning to death his grasshopper-directed neighbor who tried to get into it with him. The paroxysms of anxiety are, like the worst moments of toothaches, hard to remember. I forget why during the early autumn of 1961 the country was so shelter-minded, but it was. (It would seem equally rational or irrational to be so today, but the country isn't.) "Man," the Colonel abruptly began, as if addressing an audience, "can build no structure that will withstand the Blight of Atomic Might." This reminded me of the opening of the speech with which, he used to tell me, he was accustomed, as an associate, to introducing Hatfield the Rainmaker in the drought areas of California in 1912: "Rain—its abundance, its paucity—meant Life and Death to the Ancients, for from the lands and the flocks, the herds, the fish of the sea, the birds of the air, the deer and the mountain goat they found sustenance and energized being. All the elements depended upon the Fall of Rain, ample but not in ruinous overplus, for very existence. Through all human history, the plenitude of Rain or its lack constituted the difference between Life and Death." This time, the Colonel did not fill out his speech to the old orotundity but proceeded summarily—a mere sketch. "Only the Divinity has been able to fabricate the Perfect Answer to the Menace His short-sighted children were to produce," the Colonel intoned. "A Mountain!" And he looked up at me from under his heavy lids and smiled happily. As I did not at once catch his drift, he repeated, chiding me for being so slow, "A Mountain!" and went on, "Joe, if I were only seventy again, I would by now have every mountain in New York State under a ninety-nine-year lease. All I would need to get the thing started is five thousand dollars. I would give that to a smart lawyer who knew all about leases, and then I would go to those boob legislators and lease every mountain in the state parks, without saying why, except to the occasional thief who could penetrate my purpose. Naturally, I would declare such, when inevitable, in. I would then deposit conspicuously several old bulldozers and steam shovels on the slopes of a couple of the mountains and let it be known that I was going to install vaults, living quarters, swimming pools, and air-conditioned handball courts in their recesses. I would put on an advertising campaign, by radio, television, and the good old press, addressing myself to the three hundred and ninety-eight people who enjoyed incomes of a million dollars or more last year, but promising to consider applications from those of lowlier, though amply holding, status. The Survival of the Fittest, I would imply subtly, was a Law of Nature, and who Fitter to Survive than a man with the price of a Mountain? My text would be based, roughly, on a story a racing friend of mine once told me about some trainers who went on a fishing expedition in Louisiana with a horse owner, an oilman of transcendent wealth. A great storm arose, and the trainers, though apprehensive, pretended to make little of it. But the owner, impatient, said, 'Boys, this may be all right for you, but I've got a hell of a lot of money.' All I lack now," the Colonel said, in regretful conclusion, "is the energy."

I took the Colonel home to the Dixie in a taxi. The lobby of that hotel is as far from New York as you can get. It is like a tropical-fish tank, insulated from the streets on either side, and windowless. It is accessible from the Forty-second Street side only by a long arcade—

like the snout of a steamer clam buried beneath the surface—and from the Forty-third Street side by a staircase. Within the tank, the accents of all regions of the United States except New York are pervasively to be heard, and the transient occupants of the lobby chairs appear to be inhabitants of Little Rock, Arkansas, and Moline, Illinois, who have carried their environment with them in the form of a vast plastic bubble. In the Plantation Bar, which has a décor like that of the lobby of the Capitol Theatre in 1926, a virtuoso at a mammoth console organ plays afternoon and evening, on a podium with a tilted back mirror of glass that exposits his technique to the audience, which crouches back among the luxuriant shadows; I sometimes wonder that the waiters do not carry flashlights, like movie ushers, in order to find their way. It seems a perfect environment for a confidence man, although, as I shall explain, it isn't. I myself, always on the lookout for a hideaway after my contemplated perfect crime, encountered the Dixie through my acquaintance with the Colonel, and adopted it as the address to which I would move with my booty rather than head for Brazil. I was sure that nobody I knew would ever turn up there, and I was sure that it was a haven for minor-league hoods, the womanless men I saw lurking in the corners of the barroom with the lids of their hats pulled down over their eyes. Nothing could be further from the truth, I learned after years of lulling myself with my illusion. It was fortunate that I had not yet committed my crime or taken refuge in that inviting trap. The men in the hats are for the most part G-men, Internal Revenue fellows, and narcotics inspectors, who frequent the Dixie because of the paucity of the government per diem allowance for federal employees on missions in New York. Mr. Hyman B. Cantor, the proprietor of the Dixie, himself explained this to me one day, in discussing his business policies. "I know those guys haven't got money to throw away, so I let them stay five in a room, for three dollars apiece," he said. "That way, we get fifteen dollars for a key, and they are happy, too; they get a clean bed and a bathroom." If Mr. Cantor, who is a high type, noticed that I blenched, he could not have understood that it was because I recognized the gap that had been yawning at my feet. "It insures a nice class of customers, too," Mr. Cantor said. "Like having a cat in the house. The mice stay away."

In the middle of the lobby stands a glass case containing a scale model of a ninety-thousand-ton, 260,000-horsepower ship, Mr. Cantor's pet project. It is one of two ships that, when his plans work out, will ply the Atlantic in four-day shuttles, carrying six thousand passengers at a minimum fare, applicable to one fifth of the berths, of fifty dollars, not including food, which the passengers will buy, if they feel like it, in the ships' cafeterias. The seasick passenger will have the consolation of saving money. It is a sensible proposition, as Mr. Cantor, a vast, towheaded man in his early sixties, explains it, and it gives the Colonel a sensation he loves—that of living in the midst of a giant promotion. Pictures of the ships, and brochures on the projects of what Mr. Cantor calls the Sea Coach Transatlantic Lines, are handed out regularly throughout the hotel, and you have the feeling while you are there that they actually exist. Compared to the Sea Coach Transatlantic Lines, a scooped-out mountain seems as simple as a baked potato.

High above the lobby and Mr. Cantor, the Colonel lives in a room-with-bath that effectually preserves him from the danger of enslavement by exactious luxuries. He moved into the hotel in 1940, when the Dixie was relatively new and, like other hotels in New York, was making a determined effort to keep full by offering special terms to residents over long periods. When war came, these people attained the rent-protected status of tenants in apartment houses, and the Colonel's economic position, consequently, has been privileged. For a decade or so, the management demanded an almost inhuman punctuality in the rendition of rent. This inspired his haunting fear of the Plug in the Door. Afterward, finding him immovable, the hotel management first acquiesced and then gloried in his tenancy, and he is now the Dixie's senior resident. Age, too, has helped stabilize his finances, by diminishing sudden demands upon them.

"Some Friday nights, I sit up there in my room at the Dixie, working away on my column," he once said to me, in those days that were only the afterglow of his middle age but now seem like the white heat of youth. "I finish, and it is perhaps one o'clock. If I were sagacious, I would put on my hat and go to bed. I always keep an old felt hat by my bedside, because I like to sleep with my windows wide open and bedclothes make no provision for the protection of the thinly veiled cranium. The brain, like Rhenish wine, should be chilled, not iced, to be at its best. Women, however, are best at room temperature. Up there in my retreat, I feel the city calling to me. It winks at me with its myriad eyes, and I go out and get stiff as a board. I seek out companionship, and if I do not find friends, I make them. A wonderful, grand old Babylon."

Times have changed. "Now," the Colonel said to me a while ago, by telephone, "when I hear the city calling, I just turn over on the other ear and go to sleep again. It's ten o'clock to bed every night."

But when I am in my office at night, looking over at the Dixie, it pleases me mightily to know that the Colonel is still there.

(1964)